Reflections on the Work of C.A.R. Hoare

Cliff B. Jones • A.W. Roscoe • Kenneth R. Wood
Editors

Reflections on the Work of C.A.R. Hoare

Editors
Cliff B. Jones
School of Computing Science
Newcastle University
Newcastle NE1 7RU
United Kingdom
Cliff.Jones@ncl.ac.uk

Kenneth R. Wood
Microsoft Research Ltd.
7 JJ Thomson Avenue
Cambridge CB3 0FB
United Kingdom
Ken.Wood@microsoft.com

A.W. Roscoe
Oxford University Computing
Laboratory
Wolfson Building
Parks Road
Oxford OX1 3QD
United Kingdom
Bill.Roscoe@comlab.ox.ac.uk

ISBN 978-1-4471-6152-3 ISBN 978-1-84882-912-1 (eBook)
DOI 10.1007/978-1-84882-912-1
Springer London Dordrecht Heidelberg New York

British Library Cataloguing in Publication Data
A catalogue record for this book is available from the British Library

Cover design: SPi Publisher Services

Printed on acid-free paper

Springer is part of Springer Science+Business Media (www.springer.com)

Endorsements

"There is much to celebrate in Tony Hoare's ideas and personal influence in the theory of programming, which has benefitted several generations of computer scientists. This volume collects papers from a network of collaborators, rivals and disciples on contemporary topics to which Hoare has provided insight and direction."

Swansea University, UK *John Tucker*

Sir Tony and Lady Jill Hoare

Preface

This volume has its origins in a meeting held at Microsoft Research, Cambridge, in April 2009 to celebrate Tony Hoare's 75th Birthday (actually 11 Jan 2009). All the technical papers except for those written by Abramsky, Jackson, Jones and Meyer are based – sometimes closely, sometimes not – on presentations given at that meeting. The idea for the meeting arose in conversations between ourselves and Andrew Herbert of Microsoft, who hosted a truly memorable and happy event.

The meeting was organised by ourselves and Ken Wood, with the financial support of Microsoft Research and Formal Systems (Europe) Ltd, and held over two days. We would like to record particular thanks to Angela Still of Microsoft for making all the local arrangements at Cambridge and much more: the meeting would not have happened without her.

While the majority of the papers in this volume are technical, we asked authors to reflect on the influence of Hoare's work on their own fields and to make appropriate remarks on it. All the technical papers were refereed.

Discussions with Wayne Wheeler of Springer inspired the two of us to write the scientific biography of Hoare that is the first paper in this volume. Though we have both known Tony well for many years, we were amazed at how many discoveries about him we made during the process of writing this article.

We would like thank Wayne and his assistant Simon Rees for their help in preparing this volume as well as their patience. Much of the work in gathering the papers, ensuring consistency of LaTeX styles, etc., was done by Lucy Li of Oxford University Computing Laboratory and we thank her warmly.

Tragically, Ken Wood's wife Lisa died after a long illness in September 2009. We dedicate this volume to her memory.

January 2010

Cliff Jones
Bill Roscoe

Contents

Chapter 1
Insight, Inspiration and Collaboration

C.B. Jones and A.W. Roscoe

Abstract Tony Hoare's many contributions to computing science are marked by insight that was grounded in practical programming. Many of his papers have had a profound impact on the evolution of our field; they have moreover provided a source of inspiration to several generations of researchers. We examine the development of his work through a review of the development of some of his most influential pieces of work such as Hoare logic, CSP and Unifying Theories.

1.1 Introduction

To many who know Tony Hoare only through his publications, they must often look like polished gems that come from a mind that rarely makes false steps, nor even perhaps has to work at their creation. As so often, this impression is a further compliment to someone who actually adds to very hard work and many discarded attempts the final polish that makes complex ideas relatively easy for the reader to comprehend. As indicated on page xi of [HJ89], his ideas typically go through many revisions.

The two authors of the current paper each had the honour of Tony Hoare supervising their doctoral studies in Oxford. They know at first hand his kind and generous style and will count it as an achievement if this paper can convey something of the working methods of someone big enough to eschew competition and point scoring. Indeed it will be apparent from the following sections how often, having started some new way of thinking or exciting ideas, he happily leaves their exploration and development to others. We have both benefited personally from this.

C.B. Jones (✉)
School of Computing Science, Newcastle University, UK
e-mail: cliff.jones@ncl.ac.uk

A.W. Roscoe
Oxford University Computing Laboratory, UK
e-mail: Bill.Roscoe@comlab.ox.ac.uk

C.B. Jones et al. (eds.), *Reflections on the Work of C.A.R. Hoare*,
DOI 10.1007/978-1-84882-912-1_1, © Springer-Verlag London Limited 2010

Tony retired from Oxford in 1999 and has had, as we write this, 10 extremely active years at Microsoft, improving that company's software development techniques, engaging enthusiastically in the debates of the computer science and software engineering world, promoting Grand Challenges such as the Verifying Compiler, and taking renewed interests in programming logic thanks to topics such as Separation Logic. We, however, have restricted ourselves to studying his work up to 1999 on the grounds that 10 years is already too short a time to understand the impact of academic work.

In writing about the various phases and topics of Tony's career we have tried to analyse the influences and developing themes that have run through it.

1.2 Education and Early Career

Charles Antony Richard Hoare, the eldest of five children (he has two brothers and two sisters), was born of British parents on 11 January 1934 in Colombo in what was then called Ceylon (now Sri Lanka). Ceylon was at that time part of the British Empire. His father and maternal grandfather were both Englishmen engaged in the business of Empire, and from somewhat upper-class backgrounds.[1]

After his family returned to England at the end of World War II, Tony attended the Dragon School, Oxford and King's School, Canterbury before going to Oxford University to study Greats (formally known as *Literae Humaniores*) at Merton College between 1952 and 1956. Greats is Oxford's classics course, in which students study Latin and Greek for the first two years, and concentrate on philosophy, literature and ancient history for the final two. Tony specialised in modern philosophy, being taught by John Lucas, an expert on logic and Gödel in particular, who was then a Junior Research Fellow[2] at Merton. By the time the authors studied at Oxford from the mid-1970s to early 1980s, Greats had gained the reputation of being one of the best courses to do at Oxford if you wanted to become a computer programmer. So perhaps the training Greats offered in systematic thinking, particularly given Lucas' influence, was in fact the ideal education for an early computer scientist. There was no undergraduate course in computer science at Oxford until about a decade after Hoare returned as a professor.

In 1956 Tony was called up into the Royal Navy to do his "National Service", two years' military service that was compulsory for young men in the UK until the early 1960s. Perhaps thanks to his linguistic background, he went on a course on the Russian language while in the Navy.

Tony returned for a further year at Oxford after completing his National Service, studying Statistics. During that year he took a course in programming

[1] See `thepeerage.com`, for example.

[2] This is a a type of position given by Oxford Colleges to allow leading young academics to pursue their research.

(Mercury Autocode) from Leslie Fox, the founding Director of Oxford University Computing Laboratory, about two years after the Laboratory was founded. Fox, one of the great figures of Numerical Analysis, remained Director until he retired in 1983, at which point Hoare took over this role.

In 1959, Tony went to Moscow State University as a graduate student and studied Machine Translation, along with probability in the school of the great Russian Mathematician Andrey Kolmogorov. Tony states that it was there, in the context of dictionary processing, that he invented Quicksort while unaware of any sorting algorithms other than bubblesort, which he had rediscovered and decided was too slow. At the same time he began translating Russian literature on computer science into English.

On his return to England in 1960 he joined the small British computer company Elliott Brothers, by whom he had been recruited while still in Moscow. One of the first tasks he was given there was to implement Shellsort in Elliott 803 Autocode. He remarks in [Hoa81b] that he then bet his manager that he had an algorithm that would usually run faster. He remarks how difficult Quicksort was to explain in the language of the time; but he won his sixpenny (£0.025) bet. He famously led the team that wrote one of the first ALGOL 60 compilers, for the Elliott 503 (the curiously numbered successor to the 803), a computer with 8K of 39-bit words and which was advertised as being able to run "as many as 200 programs per day".[3] By the time this compiler was released in 1963 Tony had married (in 1962) Jill Pym, a member of his team. The ALGOL compiler was "one pass": in other words it only required a single pass through the source code tree of the object program.

There is no doubt that Tony's work on ALGOL helped to define his understanding of the nature of programming. Indeed, in [Hoa81b], he writes "It was there [an ALGOL 60 course in Brighton by Naur, Dijkstra and Landin which inspired him to choose this language for Elliott] that I first learned about recursive procedures and saw how to program the sorting method which I had earlier found such difficulty in explaining."

In [Hoa81b] Tony goes on to explain how his understanding of programming and the need for clear semantics of programming languages developed as the result of the failure to deliver an operating system for the Elliott 503 Mark II, and how this, in particular, inspired his work on concurrency:

> I did not see why the design and implementation of an operating system should be so much more difficult than that of a compiler. This is the reason why I have devoted my later research to problems of parallel programming and language constructs which would assist in clear structuring of operating systems–constructs such as monitors and communicating processes.

Tony reached the position of Chief Engineer at Elliott Brothers, but decided to leave because of the effects of the company being taken over in 1968. His academic career therefore began after he saw an advertisement for the position of Professor at

---

[3] According to [27] when the compiler was run on the much slower 803 a typical half-page ALGOL program would take half an hour to compile and execute.

the Queen's University, Belfast. By this time his position in the developing subject of computer science was secure thanks not only to Quicksort but, perhaps more importantly, to the collaborations and contacts he obtained through his ALGOL work and the work he was doing on the ALGOL Working Group (IFIP WG2.1). By the time Tony was recruited to Oxford in 1977 no application was necessary: he was simply contacted and told that he had been elected to the job.

1.3 Programming Languages

Hoare's most explicit set of positive rules for designers of programming languages was titled "Hints on Programming Language Design". This was originally written for the first (ACM SIGPLAN) POPL conference held in Boston in October 1973. Sadly, the paper did not appear in the proceedings but has been reprinted several times in slightly different forms – probably the most accessible electronic version is [Hoa73a]. Rather than repeat the points in this important paper, can we encourage our readers to study it? This plea is most strongly addressed to anyone who is thinking of designing a new language.

The importance that Tony Hoare attaches to programming languages is made abundantly clear in his acceptance speech for the ACM Turing Award.[4] This 1980 speech is published as [Hoa81b]. As mentioned in Section 1.2, he remarks there how he could only express Quicksort elegantly after he had seen ALGOL.

Hoare also makes clear that he sees it "as the highest goal of programming language design to enable good ideas to be elegantly expressed". Later in the same paper he observes the importance of "programming notations so as to maximise the number of errors which cannot be made, or if made, can be reliably detected at compile time."

ALGOL 60 had been devised by a committee; but a committee of the highest calibre. Hoare was invited to join IFIP WG 2.1 in August 1962. One of the proposals on which he looked back with pride is the "switch" concept.

His work with Niklaus Wirth to clean up ALGOL 60 led to the elegant ALGOL W proposal in [WH66] which in turn paved the way for Pascal.[5] Sadly, WG 2.1 saw fit to go another way and invent ALGOL 68 [Hoa68]: a language which gives rise in [Hoa81b] to one of Tony's most biting aphorisms

> There are two ways of constructing a software design: one way is to make it so simple that there are *obviously* no deficiencies and the other way is to make it so complicated that there are no *obvious* deficiencies.

---

[4] The Turing Award is often referred to as the "Nobel Prize for computing". It is not clear that the Kyoto Prize committee would concede this – but Tony Hoare has been awarded both.

[5] Probably because of his respect for this language, Hoare outlined its defects in [WSH77].

He recounts the final denouement at which a subset of the members of WG 2.1 submitted a minority report containing the comment "as a tool for *reliable creation* of sophisticated programs, the language was a failure."

The over-ambitiousness of the PL/I project is also described in [Hoa81b] from the standpoint of the ECMA committee of which Tony was initially a member and which he ultimately chaired. After listing an (extremely sobering) litany of failures, Tony writes "I knew that it would be impossible to write a wholly reliable compiler for a language of this complexity and impossible to write a wholly reliable program …". Again, he ends his observations on this language with the withering observation "The price of reliability is the utmost simplicity. It is the price that the very rich find most hard to pay."

The obvious and then topical reason for selecting the theme of programming language design for his Turing Award lecture was the evolution of the language which became known as Ada. As he observes, Tony had offered advice and judgement that largely went unheeded.

What he did instead was to lead by example. Mastering concurrency is still a major challenge for designers of programming languages. Tony's early work in this area is described in Section 1.6.1, but once he saw the depth of the questions surrounding communication, he took the radical step of studying it as "Communicating Sequential Processes": CSP is explored in Sections 1.6.2 and 1.6.3. This in turn led to his work on occam (see Section 1.7), a language named after an earlier Oxford philosopher whose famous principle *Occam's Razor* was in harmony with Tony's views on programming languages: *entia non sunt multiplicanda praeter necessitatem*, in other words "entities must not be multiplied more than necessary".

1.4 Reasoning About Sequential Programs

Hoare's "Axiomatic basis" paper [Hoa69] is one of the most influential in the computing literature. It marks a transition from simply adding assertions to programs towards a position that increasingly emphasised reasoning in entirely non-operational terms about the claim that programs match their specifications.

To understand its contribution, it is essential to outline where most researchers in the field stood in the 1960s. There are hints of the need to reason about programs in [12] and Turing's proposal in [35] for an approach that uses a clear notion of assertions being added to a flow chart of a program. The latter paper went unnoticed for decades and had no influence on the development of ideas. Furthermore, as the only mention traced in his writing, one can only guess at the scope of what Turing had in mind. Turing's assertions appear to be limited to relational expressions between (values of) variables of the program. Far more influential than either of these contributions from the 1940s was Bob Floyd's paper [10]. Floyd again places his assertions on a flow chart but the language in which the assertions are written here is (first-order) predicate calculus. This means that Floyd could be, and was, much more precise than Turing was about the validity of assertions; the fact that he was using a higher-level programming language than his predecessor also helped.

Somewhat before 1969 – in 1964 to be precise – there was an important meeting in Baden-bei-Wien (Austria) organised by Heinz Zemanek of the IBM Vienna Laboratory. This was, in fact, the first of many highly influential IFIP working Conferences and led to the creation of IFIP Working Group 2.2. The proceedings took some time to be published but [33] is invaluable in understanding scientific opinion of the time and, specifically, in charting the development of Hoare's thinking. From the conference proceedings, it is clear that considerable attention was given to the need for, and challenges of, formally defining the semantics of programming languages. McCarthy's clarion call of [21] to define semantics formally is backed up in [22] by an operational semantics of "Micro-ALGOL". Both Strachey and Landin discuss the connections between programming languages and Church's Lambda Calculus. On the other hand, Jan Garwick's paper opens with the provocative sentence: "No programming language for a given computer can be better defined than by its compiler."

Hoare did not present a formal contribution, but one of the helpfully recorded discussion items [33, pp. 142–143] indicates his perception of "the need to leave [aspects of] languages undefined". At the following meeting of IFIP WG 2.1, Hoare gave the example of fixing the meaning of functions like *mod* (modulus) by stating their required properties.

The IBM Vienna group borrowed concepts from McCarthy, Landin and Cal Elgot as the basis for the first version of the huge operational semantics for the language PL/I. This approach was to be named "Vienna Definition Language" (VDL) – see [20]. In 1965, Hoare attended a course in Vienna on VDL. The Vienna Lab at that time tended to do things in style and the ECMA TC10 guests were booked into the Hotel Imperial (where the British Queen stayed on her visit a few years later). On paper of that imperious hotel, Tony Hoare wrote a sketch of his first attempt at an axiomatic treatment of languages. Of the two-part draft dated December 1967, the first axiomatised execution traces as a partial order on states. It is probably fair to say that the objectives are clearer in the 1967 draft than the outcome. Hoare sent these notes to (at least) Peter Lucas of the Vienna group.

Tony recalled years after the event that, on his arrival to take up his chair in Belfast in October 1968, he "stumbled upon" the mimeographed draft (dated 20 May 1966) of Floyd's paper [10]. Peter Lucas had sent this partly as a response to Hoare's 1967 draft. Floyd's ideas on predicate calculus assertions had a major impact on Hoare's thinking and the debt is clearly acknowledged in [Hoa69]. Hoare produced in December 1968 a further two-part draft that strongly resembles the final Communications of the ACM paper. The first part addresses the thorny issue that numbers stored in computers are not quite the same as those of mathematics – in this Hoare was following van Wijngaarden's lead in [36], which is again gratefully acknowledged in the CACM paper. The second part of the 1968 draft contains the core of what is today called "Hoare axioms".

In this draft, Hoare followed Floyd's original "forwards" assignment axiom, which requires an existential quantifier in the postcondition of any assignment statement. The now common "backwards" rule that only needs substitution was first published in Jim King's thesis [17], where he attributes it to his supervisor Bob Floyd. Hoare uses this in the published version of "axiomatic basis" [Hoa69];

he was made aware of the idea by David Cooper who gave a seminar at Belfast on his return from a sabbatical in Pittsburgh. Hoare's decision to use this version possibly sparked the later development of "weakest precondition" thinking.

Hoare's paper was quickly accepted by CACM and was far more approachable than Floyd's earlier paper. Where Floyd had bundled together many ideas including early hints of what would later become known as "healthiness conditions" for proof rules, Hoare limited what he covered even to the point of not handling termination.[6]

Much the most important step was the move away from Floyd's flow charts to a view of program texts decorated with axioms as part of a unified formal system. It was this point that changed the way whole generations of researchers have been persuaded to approach programming. Hoare's decision to use postconditions of the final state alone led to concise axioms, but it is fair to say that later he conceded the value of using relational postconditions that link to the initial state as well.

As soon as a decade after the first appearance of the "axiomatic basis" paper, Krzysztof Apt published a summary of its already significant impact in [2].[7] Hoare's language had only sequential composition, conditional and a "while" repetitive construct; attention soon turned to tackling other features commonly found in high-level programming languages and relevant papers include [Hoa71a, Hoa72a, ACH76]. An attempt at the whole of Pascal [HW73] was however incomplete but this is indicative of the fact that formalism makes its largest contribution if used during – rather than after – design. In fact, the only language with a complete Hoare axiom system is probably "Turing" [13].

Given the unbridled enthusiasm of researchers to propose new languages, a far more productive avenue was probably that of showing where clean axiomatisations were consistent with subsets of languages. Peter Lauer did part of his PhD under Tony Hoare in Belfast and Lauer's thesis [18] is clearly summarised in their joint paper [HL74]. A fuller discussion of the history and impact of research on reasoning about programs can be found in [15].

1.5 Formal Program Development

Hoare's axioms in [Hoa69] possessed a crucial property that was not exploited within that paper: the given axioms are "compositional" in a sense that made it possible to employ them to reason about combinations of yet-to-be-developed code (e.g. one can prove that a while construct satisfies a specification even where its body is so far only a specification). Technically, each axiom is monotonic in the satisfaction ordering; practically, this opens the door to their use in a stepwise development. Hoare first wrote his "Proof of a Program: *Find*" as a *post facto* proof of correctness

[6] In terminology that some find unfortunate – but that has become ubiquitous – he limited himself to "partial correctness" whereas Floyd treated "total correctness".

[7] The slightly enigmatic "Part I" sub-title indicates Apt's strong interest in non-determinism which he covered in [3].

but revised it before publication as [Hoa71b] to describe a stepwise development. The omission in not revising the title is surprising from a writer who takes such care with the prose of each revision.

The final text in [Hoa71b] is far more readable than the first version and, more importantly, it is also much more convincing. Recall that there were almost no programs available in the early 1970s to check (let alone help construct) such predicate calculus proofs, so the move to a top-down development of *Find* decomposed the proof into more manageable steps. Given the comments in Section 1.4, it will come as no surprise that the termination proof (that Tony conceded "was more than usually complex") had to be handled separately from that for correctness (see [Hoa71b, §4]). Furthermore, the decision to use postconditions of only the final state left the need for a section entitled "Reservation" ([Hoa71b, §5]) that concedes "one very important aspect of correctness has not been treated, namely that the algorithm merely rearranges the elements of array *A* without changing any of their values"; postconditions of two states would have allowed the "permutation" property to have been handled within the main proof.

One extremely important and far sighted point was the recognition of the way that programs can be designed via their loop invariants.

Having developed the method, it was possible in fairly short order to apply it to a range of problems:

- [FH71] returns to the *Quicksort* algorithm discussed in Section 1.2 and presents its stepwise development.
- [Hoa72c] tackles finding primes using the "sieve of Eratosthenes" (a problem which is used to illustrate the development of concurrent implementations in [Hoa75] and by other subsequent authors).
- [Hoa73b] nicely links to Hoare's work on operating systems by tackling a structured paging system.

1.5.1 "Structured Programming"

Many who know the literature on "Structured Programming" might be surprised that the important book [Hoa72b] has not yet been mentioned. The book is widely cited and the topic of its title has had major impact on software design. Like many successful ideas, however, the term was abused to cover a range of things from a narrow message of "avoiding goto statements" through to systematic, justified design processes. Hoare's solo chapter [DDH72][8] starts with the ringing

> In the development of our understanding of complex phenomena, the most powerful tool available to the human intellect is abstraction.

and goes on to provide a masterly description of concepts of data structuring for programming languages.

---

[8] The material had been presented in his Marktoberdorf lectures of 1970.

1.5.2 Data Refinement

Another important contribution to the formal, stepwise, development of programs was the recognition of the importance of using, in specifications, objects that are abstract in the sense that they match the problem being described. Development by data refinement can then bring in representations on which efficient programs can be based as part of the design process. Hoare's paper [Hoa72d] is widely cited as one that recognised this aspect of formal program development. In common with other authors, Hoare recognised later that the neat homomorphism rule does not cover all situations and was a coauthor of [HHS86] which presents a more general rule.

An interesting success of Tony's ability to inspire other scientific activity was the way he brought Jean-Raymond Abrial and the first author together in Oxford. In 1979, Abrial was working on ideas that were eventually developed into the "Z" specification language. Jones had been a key member of the Vienna work on denotational semantics which had been published in [4, 5] and had developed his earlier ideas on program development to provide the other part of VDM: [14] was printed in the famous "red and white" Prentice-Hall series edited by Hoare.

Tony thought it would be interesting for both Abrial and Jones to share an office when they both arrived in Oxford in 1979 – at that time the "Programming Research Group" (PRG) had rather cramped quarters in 45 Banbury Road. This was certainly an inspired and inspiring idea. Often a discussion would result in a blackboard containing a mixture of notations but the fact that the basic ideas of abstraction were shared meant that the focus was on the underlying issues.[9]

The language known as "Z" continued to develop after Abrial and Jones left Oxford and has become a widely used specification language with tool support. Its use on IBM's "CICS" system led to a Queen's Award for Technological Achievement to the Oxford PRG group in 1992.

1.6 Concurrency

As shown by the quotation in Section 1.2, Hoare's work on concurrency was inspired by the problems of operating system design. This influence is still very much apparent in the text and examples in his 1985 book on CSP (Chapter 6, for example).

The driving theme in his work is the need to keep separate threads from interfering with each other in ways that are undesired or hard to understand. We can see this in the evolution from work based on shared memory to CSP, in which all interaction is via explicit communication over channels.

[9] The development of Abrial's ideas through to "B" [1] (and beyond) deserves separate discussion elsewhere.

1.6.1 Concurrency with Shared Variables

Before turning, as we do in the next section, to Tony's most radical and influential suggestion of communication-based concurrency, it is important to understand his earlier attempts to tame its shared-variable cousin. It is easy to decry the use of variables that can be changed by more than one thread, but at the machine interface there is little else. There were various suggestions for programming constructs to make this troublesome fact tolerable: the hope to extend the axiomatic approach to concurrency was already there in [Hoa69]; in [Hoa72e], Hoare had tackled the sort of disjoint parallelism that could be controlled by conditional critical sections. In [Hoa75] he moves on to more general concurrency governed by his "monitor" proposal [Hoa74].

In "Parallel Programming: An Axiomatic Approach", Hoare carefully distinguishes:

- Disjoint processes: [Hoa75, §3] essentially reproduces the earlier "symmetric parallel rule", but the rule is still limited to partial correctness. In view of the way parallelism is often used, this is perhaps more reasonable here.
- Competition ([Hoa75, §4]) clearly establishes the notion of ownership.[10]
- Cooperation ([Hoa75, §5]) recognises the importance of a commutativity requirement between operations in the cooperating processes. It is here that Hoare returns to the "sieve of Eratosthenes" from [Hoa72c]: he also concedes that "when a variable is a large data structure ... the apparently atomic operations upon it may in practice require many actual atomic machine instructions". The atomicity issue is extremely important and has been pursued by other researchers (e.g. [16]).
- The section on communication gives an insight into the way Hoare develops ideas: Hoare ([Hoa75, §6]) recognises that communication does not fit the commutativity property above; he introduces a notion of "semi-commutativity" that clearly only handles uni-directional communication. One can see here the seeds of CSP (see Section 1.6.2) whose realisation took several years of further hard struggle, before it could be published.

1.6.2 Imperative CSP

Tony published two works entitled "Communicating Sequential Processes", the CACM paper from 1978 and the 1985 book. The languages in these publications are very different from each other. In this section and the next we discuss the development of the two versions, and try to understand why they are as they are. The first

[10] At the April 2009 event to celebrate Tony's 75th birthday, Peter O'Hearn linked this to his own research on Separation Logic.

version of the language is essentially Dijkstra's language of guarded commands [8] (a simple imperative language) with point-to-point communication added, so we have termed it *Imperative* CSP.

Hoare states[11] that the move from studying concurrency via shared variables and monitors to explicit communication over channels was inspired by the advent of the microprocessor and the thought (later realised in the transputer) of these "communicating with other microprocessors of a similar nature along wires".

An Imperative CSP program is a parallel composition of named sequential processes: the only parallelism is at the highest level. Thus this language fits the name *Communicating Sequential Processes* much better than Algebraic CSP, where the parallel operator would be on a par with all others, or even occam where the same is true.

Hoare was clearly inspired by examples such as the sieve of Erastothenes, where it was natural to create an array of processes with closely related structure, and included explicit notation for addressing members of an indexed array of processes in the language.

He specifies that communication between processes is *synchronised* (only taking place when both outputter and inputter are ready) but gives little explanation of this decision, which was to prove so important in the structure of the many languages and theories that would be inspired by CSP. This clearly fits well with the intuition of communication being direct from one process to another along a piece of wire, and Hoare implies that where buffering is wanted it can be introduced explicitly via buffer processes.

It is natural in contemplating communications between two processes to think of one as outputting and one as inputting, and in this first version of CSP Hoare makes this an important distinction. For example, as would later be the case in occam, only the input end of a communication may appear with alternatives. He does, however, discuss allowing outputs in guarded alternatives, and in doing so raises the possibility of proving the parallel program $[X!2 \parallel Y!3]$ equivalent to a sequential one, while commenting that this is not achieved by the program

$$[\mathit{true} \rightarrow X!2;\ Y!3 \ \Box\ \mathit{true} \rightarrow Y!3;\ X!2]$$

in which the implementation is permitted to resolve the choice, thereby flagging the importance of non-determinism in reasoning about CSP. This problem would be solved by using outputs directly in the guards:

$$[X!2 \rightarrow Y!3 \ \Box\ Y!3 \rightarrow X!2]$$

This is one example and the motivation behind it is a powerful indication of an inevitable move towards an algebra of communication, concurrency and non-determinism.

---

[11] In the interview with Bowen cited in Sources.

1.6.3 Algebraic CSP

The language in the 1985 book started to develop even before the 1978 paper was published. Indeed, by the time the second author joined Tony as a research student in October 1978 the *process algebra* CSP (i.e. the one in the 1985 book) was almost completely formed as a notation and Tony was working on his traces model.

The most obvious difference between the old and new CSPs is that the former is a conventional programming language with point-to-point communication added in a natural way, whereas the new one looks like some sort of abstract algebra, hence our name *Algebraic CSP*. Indeed it is one of the first two developed examples (the other being CCS) of what rapidly became known as a *process algebra*: a notation for creating algebraic terms representing the interacting behaviour of a number of distinct *processes*. These processes are themselves patterns of communication: it would be wrong to call them *threads* since there is no guarantee that the processes are sequential. Indeed, in both CSP and CCS and most subsequent process algebras, there is no semantic distinction between sequential and parallel processes, and every parallel process is equivalent to a sequential one.

From this discussion alone the reader will appreciate that the creation of these first process algebras represented a huge intellectual step: that from a programming language to calculi that attempt to attribute meaning to patterns of communication.

The need for such a meaning was clear from the fact that concurrent programs behave so differently from sequential ones, with phenomena such as deadlock and livelock to worry about, as well as the non-determinism caused by resource contention (common in operating systems) and similar situations that are intrinsic to concurrency. This led both Hoare and Milner down remarkably similar paths: discarding almost all the things that programs do between communications, and developing notations that allowed them to concentrate purely on the synchronised communications between processes and the way in which patterns of these arise.

Whether CSP and CCS seem similar to a reader will depend on his or her viewpoint, but certainly they are very similar when viewed from the standpoint of Imperative CSP. Both Hoare and Milner were working on this convergent course before either had a clear idea of what the other was doing. Milner, indeed, had been looking at the semantics of interaction since the early 1970s. He had started off [23] working on the semantics of shared-variable "transducers" and by 1977 was working on "flow graphs", a partly graphical notation of parallel composition that was not specific about the protocol used on channels. They only got a clear vision of each other's work at a meeting in Aarhus in June 1977, by which time Hoare had already put considerable efforts into understanding the algebra of CSP. Hoare's paper at that workshop (which we have unfortunately been unable to locate) was entitled "A relational trace-oriented semantics for Communicating Sequential Processes". W.P. de Roever worked with Hoare in Belfast in 1977 on the semantics of CSP, the results of which were reported in [FHLdR79]. Both this work and Milner's initial thoughts on concurrent semantics centred on domain theory. This was very natural in the context of the times, given the success of Strachey, Scott and others in developing and applying domain theory to the semantics of a wide range of programming language constructs in the preceding years. The main challenge to domain theory inherent in giving semantics to communicating processes was the need to handle an interleaving sequence of external choices and non-deterministic choice. External choices could be handled with function spaces, which work extremely elegantly in domain theory. But non-deterministic choice seemed to require *powerdomains* [26], in other words a domain-theoretic analogue of the powerset operator.

There are two major problems with powerdomains. The first is that it proves very difficult to combine the natural set theoretic order structure with the order of the underlying domain in a satisfactory way, and none of the available orders (including the strong Egli-Milner order of the Plotkin powerdomain and the angelic order of the Hoare powerdomain[12]) produce equivalences between processes at a persuasive level of abstraction. The second is that the powerdomains are in themselves difficult to understand, meaning that any semantics based on them is unlikely to be useful in explaining concurrency beyond a select group of researchers.

Of course the reason for needing domain theory for other "interesting" languages is the quality of self-referentiality they have, in particular programs that accept other programs as functional arguments, as exemplified by the λ-calculus. A program in Dijkstra's guarded command language, without such constructs, can easily be given a semantics as a relation on $S \times (S \cup \{\bot\})$, where S is the set of states and $\bot$ represents non-termination or *divergence*. So while concurrency is itself certainly "interesting", there is nothing in Imperative CSP that implies the need for domain theory. And both Milner and Hoare, in turn, reacted against powerdomains. Indeed Willem-Paul de Roever tells us this was evident during his 1977 visit: the powerdomain models were "not to Tony's taste", and Tony would regularly propose models that were converging on the traces model.

Milner chose an operationally based theory in which equivalences are developed between processes described as labelled transition systems. Hoare has stated that his approach to process equivalence, based on algebraic laws relating processes and behaviourally based models, was a reaction against Milner's operational approach. Both their philosophies, quite clearly, have been extremely successful. Of course they have long since reconciled, for example by the development of operational semantics for CSP and the testing equivalences for CCS. It was these constrasting decisions, of course, which led to the different choice operators of CCS [25] and CSP: the CCS "+" being the obvious operational version.

There are two other interesting contrasts between CCS and (Algebraic) CSP. The first is that CSP contains a great many more operators than CCS, such as sequential composition, very general renaming and interrupt. Here, Hoare seems to have been driven by the types of system he wished to model, for example ones previously described in Imperative CSP (with sequential composition, of course) whose variables are now modelled as parallel processes, and operating systems where processes are interrupted and checkpointed.

[12] The powerdomain of downward-closed sets was not developed by Hoare, but named after him by Plotkin, because of its close relationship to Tony's important work on partial correctness.

The second is the very different factorisation of the "natural" parallel construct in which multiple processes communicate point-to-point over channels with these communications internalised, or hidden. Here Hoare seems to have been inspired by the algebra of synchronisation, interleaving and hiding, which required process *alphabets* to determine which events are synchronised. Milner, on the other hand, has stated that he decided to avoid using alphabets, and he was able to do so by devising an extremely clever device whereby (1) events synchronise not with themselves but with duals, (2) dual events in parallel processes can either synchronise to become τ or happen independently, and (3) such "free radical" events are restricted outside the syntactic level where synchronisation can occur. This approach is already evident in his flow-graph work, for example [24]. Milner's trick makes multi-way synchronisation unnatural (because of the duality), and in any case requires events to be hidden once synchronised. So CSP ended up with much more flexible parallel and hiding operators, at the expense of the need to declare (in one way or another) the interfaces that parallel processes use to communicate with each other.

It is hard to overstate the importance of algebraic laws in guiding Hoare's intuition about what were the "right" models of CSP. In particular, his belief in the laws of distribution over non-deterministic choice corresponds almost exactly, theoretically, to the decision to model processes as sets of *linearly observable* behaviours. This means that each behaviour may be observed as time progresses forward on a single execution of the process: in particular no branching behaviour is recorded.

The following few paragraphs describe the development, during 1979, of the failures model. It was clear that the traces model was too weak: a model was required that distinguished non-deterministic from external choice, and which captured the phenomena of deadlock and livelock accurately.

The failures model started its life as the *acceptances* model, in which a process was modelled as the set of pairs (s, A) where s is a trace and A is a set of events from which the process accepts. The meaning of this phrase is deliberately vague, since HBR (Hoare, Brookes and Roscoe) spent some time experimenting with it. After a few weeks working on this, they came to the conclusion that a good way to interpret this was "the process can choose to restrict its next actions to being within A". In other words, P *actually* offers some subset of A. HBR realised the interesting fact that this interpretation fails to distinguish between the processes[13]

$$STOP \sqcap (?x : \{a, b\} \rightarrow STOP) \quad \text{and}$$
$$STOP \sqcap (a \rightarrow STOP) \sqcap (?x : \{a, b\} \rightarrow STOP)$$

even though the first (unlike the second) has no state from which it *actually* accepts $\{a\}$. Nevertheless, the interpretation in which these two are equated was found to be a congruence which, if one interprets livelock as the most non-deterministic process

[13] $P \sqcap Q$ is a *non-deterministic* process which is itself allowed to decide which of P and Q to run. Thus the second of these two processes can opt to offer just the event a, while the first has to offer nothing at all ($STOP$) or $\{a, b\}$.

CHAOS, seemed to satisfy the better set of algebraic laws than did what is now known as the *acceptances*, or *ready sets* congruence, which distinguishes these two processes. In the latter, the algebraic law $P = P \Box P$ does not hold, for example.[14] That congruence was later developed by Hoare and Olderog [HO83].

Quickly after this, HBR decided to turn their somewhat convoluted acceptance sets into refusal sets by the simple device of complementation: where A was an acceptance set, $\Sigma \setminus A$ (Σ being the set of all visible events) was a *refusal set*, which could be understood as being a set of events that the process might not accept a member from, even if offered it for ever. Since HBR's acceptance sets were upward closed (if a process can accept from A, it can also accept from $A' \supseteq A$), refusal sets became downward closed, but somehow this seemed much more natural.

The result, a pair (s, X) where s is a trace and X is one of these refusal sets, was called a *failure* because it represents an experiment to which the process fails to respond. The model of [HBR81, BHR84] is, of course, excellent at representing non-determinism, and makes it very clear that $P \sqsubseteq Q$ (refinement modelled by reverse containment) corresponds to P being more non-deterministic than Q. It is worth noting that the healthiness conditions of this model were in effect a statement of what a process *should* look like, rather than being derived from an operational semantics, since none of these then existed and LTSs were not considered!

It was immediately apparent that the refinement maximal elements of this model were in natural 1–1 correspondence with the traces model and were exactly the deterministic processes, judged extensionally. Its refinement-minimum element was *CHAOS*, the most non-deterministic process which contained every failure imaginable.

The obvious choice for a least fixed point based semantics for recursion was therefore based on the refinement order, but this was in any case appealing since it meant iteration that corresponded to reduction of non-determinism and identified the undefined recursion $\mu\, p.p$ with the sort of divergence produced by hiding $(\mu\, p.a \to p) \setminus \{a\}$.

Unsurprisingly, given the heritage we have described, the second author discovered the fatal flaw in the original failures model by observing that a self-evident law failed, namely

$$(P \parallel Q) \setminus A = (P \setminus A) \parallel (Q \setminus A) \quad \text{if } A \cap \alpha P \cap \alpha Q = \emptyset$$

This is the principle that, provided no synchronised events are hidden, one can distribute hiding over parallel. The fatal flaw is that the identification of divergence with *CHAOS* is not robust enough to survive some of the operator definitions in CSP, so the expression on the right above might have some of the behaviours introduced

[14] $P \Box Q$ means that the environment has the choice of the initial events offered by P and Q. The counter-intuitive failure of this law comes about because in $P \Box P$ the two copies of P might, because they resolve non-determinism differently, choose to offer different sets, which the operator combines into a single offer that P alone cannot make. This distinction is made in the acceptances or ready-sets congruence, but not using the upwards-closed version of acceptances.

from divergence removed by the parallel composition. This flaw was also discovered by De Nicola and Hennessy [9]. Their work was communicated to Brookes, who had recently moved to Pittsburgh with Dana Scott. The fix to this flaw, the *failures-divergences* model in which the failure set was augmented, was thus discovered separately by Brookes and the second author, appearing in [6, 7, 28]. This model, consistently with the intuition about divergence in [BHR84], has explicitly *strict* divergence: no attempt is made to see what goes on after a process might have diverged.[15]

This brought the theory of CSP to the level that was presented in the 1985 book, and since Hoare's involvement in the development of its core theory since then has been relatively small we will leave it here.[16]

This book was developed by Tony over a period of several years, parts of it having appeared as a technical report in 1983, together with a separate set of exercises. Tony was able to try it on numerous groups of students, for example those studying the MSc in Computation which Tony had helped set up in Oxford in 1979.

In the early 1980s, Hoare developed techniques [Hoa81a, Hoa85a] both for specifying and giving semantics to CSP processes in the predicate calculus: a program or specification is described as a predicate calculus formula over formal variables representing a typical trace, a typical refusal set coupled with that trace, a divergence, etc. By describing not the whole process, but a typical individual behaviour, in this way, the resulting semantics – albeit just a recoding of the set-theory based ones discussed above – gained much in elegance. For example, the specification that a process P whose alphabet is $in.T \cup out.T$ is a buffer in terms of traces is just written P **sat** $tr \downarrow out \leq tr \downarrow in$, with the quantification of tr over all traces of P being implicit. This work was not restricted to CSP, as shown by the paper "Programs are Predicates" [Hoa85b], which clearly links it with the earlier work on Hoare logic.

As part of this project he developed some new logical notations, such as $x \,\triangleleft b \triangleright\, y$, the infix version of *if b then x else y*. The point of the operator $\triangleleft b \triangleright$, of course, is that it puts conditional choice at the same linguistic level as the other choice operators $\sqcap$ and $\Box$, allowing it to be compared with these and reasoned about with similar laws.

By incorporating ideas such as these he made the 1985 book a masterpiece of presentation: it succeeded in making material which in truth is really quite difficult seem accessible, natural and elegant.

[15] The intuition that divergence should be disastrous, derived from the first failures model, was very strong at that time. It is interesting that neither Brookes nor the second author then discovered the "stable failures model", in which divergence is not recorded, so (as in the traces model) the simply divergent process is top of the refinement order. The existence of that model was conjectured by Albert Meyer and Lalita Jagadeesan in the late 1980s, and developed by the second author following a conversation with them.

[16] The second author's paper elsewhere in this volume illustrates how well CSP has stood the test of time. His 1997 book [31] and forthcoming book [32] both give extensive updates on CSP, its theory, tools and applications.

1.7 Occam and the Transputer

In 1978 the UK government sponsored the creation of a company called inmos, led by Iann Barron, part of whose vision was to create components for parallel processing systems. This would be a microchip company to rival the foreign giants, it was hoped. Its design operations were based in Bristol and it had a fabrication plant in Newport, South Wales. Barron's vision of a network of components interacting via serial links emerged from his work for the Science Research Council on its Distributed Computing Program. This brought him into contact with the ideas of Hoare and Milner, and the more practically based work of David May at Warwick on the design and implementation of distributed systems and languages to program them.

inmos's early products were memory chips, but it was always anticipated by Barron that its flagship product would be the *transputer*, a single chip that contained a processor, cache memory and communications hardware. Barron hired Hoare and May as consultants in 1978, and the latter joined inmos as full-time "Chief Technologist" in mid-1979. This team refined the concept of a transputer.

May, with input from Hoare, designed the *occam* programming language, which is a low-level imperative language based on CSP, inheriting features both of Imperative CSP and Algebraic CSP (the latter including the idea of parallel as a first-class language construct). May has told us various respects, such as having the `ALT` construct analogous to external choice $\Box$ rather than explicit channel polling, in which occam moved closer to CSP during its design process. This particular change – lobbied for by Hoare – was doubtless in pursuit of the stated goal of giving occam the cleanest possible semantics. The fact that occam was so cleanly defined and so close to CSP meant that it had clean *formal* semantics. The second author and Hoare each played a large role in defining these through papers such as [29] (denotational semantics), [HR84] (logical semantics in the sense discussed above) and [RH86] (algebraic semantics).

It was, of course, extremely bold (and some might put it stronger than that) of inmos to base itself on such a novel product and a completely novel language. The transputer's primary market was intended, from a fairly early stage, to be in embedded applications, but naturally it was the prospect of large parallel systems composed of many transputers that caught the imagination. The first (16-bit) transputers were delivered in 1985, with 32-bit ones following soon afterwards.

May and Hoare had extraordinary vision when it came to the use of occam, and the language quickly became the main medium by which hardware was specified within inmos. They realised that the clean semantics of occam made this an excellent vehicle for formal verification work. The first major exercise in this did not involve occam's parallel capabilities at all, but solely involved reasoning about sequential occam programs: the microcoded instructions for the FPU of the T800 transputer. This project, which was conceived by Hoare and May, involved translating the IEEE 754 floating-point number standard into Z, developing correct occam programs from that for its various operations, and proving these equivalent to highly stylised occam programs representing the microcode programs designed for a special data path. The translation of the specification was done by Geoff Barrett, as was the derivation of the top level programs from these. The proofs of equivalence were performed by David Shepherd using the *occam transformation system* [11], a tool that implemented the algebraic semantics for occam developed by Hoare and the second author in [RH86].

The error-free FPU was developed at a considerable saving to what would have been achieved with a traditional testing regime.[17]

The use of occam in hardware design at inmos was taken to entirely new levels in the design of the T9000: a pipelined processor, executing RISC-style instructions that were automatically grouped into compound instructions, and with far more advanced communications hardware. Associated formal methods work was successful [30], but no longer involved Hoare closely.

Unfortunately it became apparent that a company of the size of inmos (by 1990 a branch SGS Thomson Microelectronics) could no longer compete with the investment put in by the giants in leading-edge microprocessors, so the transputer concept and with it its implementation of CSP ceased to be developed in the early 1990s.

It is of course interesting that the lesson of how valuable formal methods are to microprocessors was not learned by these giants until one of them had a problem with a floating point unit some years after the successful Oxford/inmos collaboration. These companies are now by far the biggest users of formal verification.

1.8 Unifying Theories of Programming

He Jifeng first came to work in Oxford in 1984, and he remained there, either full or part time, until 1998: one year before Tony's retirement. For most of this time, he and Tony were a close working partnership. As Tony's ideas stretched beyond CSP to the idea of correctness in a completely general setting, Jifeng provided him with mathematical support in a similar sense that Brookes and the second author had done on CSP and occam.

One early project was "The laws of programming" [HHH$^+$87], a project that drew on earlier work on algebra for the more complex language occam [19] and set out a programme for using algebraic laws for language definition and formal methods. Part of this programme was the use of *weakest prespecifications*, as defined in [HH86], the paper which began the serious Hoare/He effort to understand programming and specification via the relational calculus.

They used the relational calculus to discover much about the nature of specification and implementation, using such tools as Galois connections to relate programming and specification constructs. One important idea that emerged from this work was that of an operational semantics defined in terms of algebraic transformation towards normal form: see [HHS93], for example.

[17] This work led to Oxford and inmos receiving the Queen's Award for Technological Achievement in 1990.

Hoare and He took on the extremely ambitious project of creating a framework in which one could give semantics, make specifications, reason about and relate a wide range of programming languages such as imperative, logical and concurrent languages. This led to the book *Unifying Theories of Programming* [HH98], and, though the book makes few explicit references to the relational calculus, it is there throughout as the mathematical foundation upon which this work is built.

In the book, we can see direct influences from all the previous joint work of Hoare and He that we have discussed in this section as well as Hoare's earlier work on algebraic laws, coding semantics in predicate calculus, and logical notation. Certainly it is easy to see the roots of it in Hoare's intuitions about CSP and its presentation in the late 1970s and early 1980s. In this respect we are thinking not only of the importance of algebraic laws and of the logical representation of observable behaviour, but also about the problem of how to construct denotational semantics without domain theory.

1.8.1 Sources

The main source we used on Tony's research is, of course, his published work of which we give a bibliography below. He has also written several articles containing reminiscences, most notably [Hoa81b], and there are several published interviews with him, of which we have used the following:

```
www.simple-talk.com/opinion/geek-of-the-week/
sir-tony-hoare-geek-of-the-week

archive.computerhistory.org/resources/text/
Oral_History/Hoare_Sir_Antony/102658017.05.01.pdf
```

This paper has two bibliographies. The first lists all of Hoare's papers that we have either cited above or which do not appear in the bibliography of his papers to 1987 that appeared in *Essays in computing science* [HJ89], a book that arose from discussions between the first author and Tony in Austin Texas. The second bibliography consists of all those papers we have referred to that do not have Tony as an author. To help the reader distinguish between the two, citations in the Hoare bibliography (which is sorted into date order) are given thus [Hoa81b] while those in the second (sorted alphabetically) are numerically labelled [7].

Acknowledgements The authors are grateful to Tony Hoare and Robin Milner for their recollections about the development of process algebra, to David May, Gordon Plotkin, Brian Randell, Willem-Paul de Roever and others for their memories and comments, and to many of Tony's academic descendants for contributing to the family tree below.

We are extremely grateful to Lucy Li of Oxford University Computing Laboratory who undertook the monumental task of assembling the family tree as well as helping us to put together the extended bibliography.

The first author's research is supported by the EPSRC Platform Grant on "Trustworthy Ambient Systems" and EU FP7 "DEPLOY project". The second author's is supported by the EPSRC Grant "CSP Model Checking: New Technologies and Techniques" and by grants from the US ONR.

Bibliography 1: Papers by Hoare

[Hoa68] Hoare, C.A.R.: Critique of ALGOL 68. *ALGOL Bullet.* **29**, 27–29 (November 1968).

[Hoa69] Hoare, C.A.R.: An axiomatic basis for computer programming. Commun. ACM **12**(10), 576–580, 583 (October 1969).

[FH71] Foley, M., Hoare, C.A.R.: Proof of a recursive program: Quicksort. BCS Comput. J. **14**(4), 391–395 (November 1971).

[Hoa71a] Hoare, C.A.R.: Procedures and parameters: An axiomatic approach. In: Engeler, E. (ed.), Symposium on Semantics of Algorithmic Languages – Lecture Notes in Mathematics 188, pp. 102–116. Springer (1971).

[Hoa71b] Hoare, C.A.R.: Proof of a program: Find. Commun. ACM **14**(1), 39–45. Springer Berlin/Heidelberg (January 1971).

[DDH72] Dahl, O.-J., Dijkstra, E.W., Hoare, C.A.R. (eds.), Structured Programming. Academic (1972). London; San Diego: Academic Press, 1990, ©1972.

[Hoa72a] Hoare, C.A.R.: A note on the FOR statement. BIT **12**(3), 334–341 (1972).

[Hoa72b] Hoare, C.A.R.: Notes on data structuring. In Dahl, O.-J., Dijkstra, E.W., Hoare, C.A.R. (eds.), Structured Programming, pp. 83–174. Academic (1972). London; San Diego: Academic Press, 1990, ©1972.

[Hoa72c] Hoare, C.A.R.: Proof of a structured program: 'The Sieve of Eratosthenes'. BCS, Computer J. **15**(4), 321–325 (November 1972).

[Hoa72d] Hoare, C.A.R.: Proof of correctness of data representations. Acta Informatica **1**(4), 271–281 (1972).

[Hoa72e] Hoare, C.A.R.: Towards a theory of parallel programming. In: Operating System Techniques pp. 61–71. Academic (1972).

[Hoa73a] Hoare, C.A.R.: Hints on programming language design. Technical Report STAN-CS-73-403, Stanford (October 1973).

[Hoa73b] Hoare, C.A.R.: A structured paging system. BCS Comput. J. **16**(3), 209–215 (August 1973).

[HW73] Hoare, C.A.R., Wirth, N.: An axiomatic definition of the programming language PASCAL. Acta Informatica **2**(4), 335–355 (1973).

[HL74] Hoare, C.A.R., Lauer, P.E.: Consistent and complementary formal theories of the semantics of programming languages. Acta Informatica **3**(2), 135–153 (1974).

[Hoa74] Hoare, C.A.R.: Monitors: An operating system structuring concept. Commun. ACM **17**(10), 549–557 (October 1974).

[Hoa75] Hoare, C.A.R.: Parallel programming: An axiomatic approach. Comput. Languages **1**(2), 151–160 (June 1975).

[ACH76] Ashcroft, E.A., Clint, M., Hoare, C.A.R.: Remarks on "program proving: Jumps and functions". Acta Informatica **6**(3), 317–318 (1976).

[WSH77] Welsh, J., Sneeringer, W.J., Hoare, C.A.R.: Ambiguities and insecurities in PASCAL. Software Practice Experience **7**(6), 685–96 (November–December 1977).

[FHLdR79] Francez, N., Hoare, C.A.R., Lehmann, D.J., de Roever, W.P.: Semantics of nondeterminism, concurrency and communication. J. Comput. System Sci. **19**(3), 290–308 (December 1979).

[HBR81] Hoare, C.A.R., Brookes, S.D., Roscoe, A.W.: A theory of communicating sequential processes. Technical Report PRG 16, Oxford University Computing Laboratory, Programming Research Group (1981).

[Hoa81a] Hoare, C.A.R.: A calculus of total correctness for communicating processes. The Sci. Computer Programming **1**(1–2), 49–72 (October 1981).

[Hoa81b] Hoare, C.A.R.: The emperor's old clothes. Commun. ACM **24**(2), 75–83 (February 1981).

[HO83] Hoare, C.A.R., Olderog, E.R.: Specification-oriented semantics for communicating processes. In: Automata Languages and Programming 10th Colloquium, vol. 154 of Lecture Notes in Computer Science, pp. 561–572. Springer (1983). ISBN 3-540-12317-2.

[BHR84] Brookes, S.D., Hoare, C.A.R., Roscoe, A.W.: A theory of communicating sequential processes. J. ACM **31**(3), 560–599 (July 1984).

[HR84] Hoare, C.A.R., Roscoe, A.W.: Programs as executable predicates. In: Proceedings of the International Conference on Fifth Generation Computer Systems, November 6–9 1984, Tokyo, Japan, pp. 220–228. ICOT (1984).

[Hoa85a] Hoare, C.A.R.: Communicating Sequential Processes. Prentice-Hall (1985). 256 pp., ISBN 0-13-153271-5. Prentice Hall International, Hemel Hempstead, Herts, England.

[Hoa85b] Hoare, C.A.R.: Programs are predicates. In: Hoare, C.A.R. Shepherdson, J.C. (eds.), Mathematical Logic and Programming Languages, pp. 141–154. Prentice-Hall (1985). Prentice Hall International, Hemel Hempstead, Herts, England.

[HH86] Hoare, C.A.R., He, J.: The weakest prespecification I. Fundamenta Informaticae **9**(1), 51–84 (March 1986).

[HHS86] He, J., Hoare, C.A.R., Sanders, J.W.: Data refinement refined. In Robinet, B., Wilhelm, R. (eds.), ESOP '86: Proceedings of the European Symposium on Programming, vol. 213 of Lecture Notes in Computer Science. Springer (1986).

[RH86] Roscoe, A.W., Hoare, C.A.R.: Laws of occam programming. Monograph PRG-53, Oxford University Computing Laboratory, Programming Research Group (February 1986).

[HHH+87] Hoare, C.A.R., Hayes, I.J., He, J., Morgan, C.C., Roscoe, A.W., Sanders, J.W., Sørensen, I.H., Spivey, J.M., Sufrin, B.A.: The laws of programming. Commun. of the ACM **30**(8), 672–687 (August 1987). see Corrigenda in Commun. ACM **30**(9), 770.

* *

The following is a list of all Hoare's papers since 1988, complementing the list published in [HJ89].

[HG88] Hoare, C.A.R., Gordon, M.J.C.: Partial correctness of CMOS switching circuits: An exercise in applied logic. In: LICS, pp. 28–36 (1988).

[RH88] Roscoe, A.W., Hoare, C.A.R.: The laws of occam programming. Theoret. Comput. Sci. **60**, 177–229 (1988).

[HH89] He, J., Hoare, C.A.R.: Categorical semantics for programming languages. In: Mathematical Foundations of Programming Semantics, pp. 402–417 (1989).

[HJ89] Hoare, C.A.R., Jones, C.B.: Essays in Computing Science. Prentice Hall International, 1989.

[Hoa89] Hoare, C.A.R.: The varieties of programming language. In: TAPSOFT, Vol.1, pages 1–18, 1989.

[BHL90] Bjørner, D., Hoare, C.A.R., Langmaack, H.: VDM '90, VDM and Z – Formal Methods in Software Development, Third International Symposium of VDM Europe, Kiel, FRG, April 17–21, 1990, Proceedings, vol. 428 of Lecture Notes in Computer Science. Springer (1990).

[Hoa90a] Hoare, C.A.R.: Fixed points of increasing functions. Inf. Process. Lett. **34**(3), 111–112 (1990).

[Hoa90b] Hoare, C.A.R.: Let's make models (abstract). In: CONCUR, p. 32 (1990).

[Hoa90c] Hoare, C.A.R.: A theory of conjunction and concurrency. In: PARBASE / Architectures, pp. 18–30 (1990).

[Hoa91a] Hoare, C.A.R.: A theory for the derivation of combinational CMOS circuit designs. Theoret. Comput. Sci. **90**(1), 235–251 (1991).

[Hoa91b] Hoare, C.A.R.: The transputer and occam: A personal story. Concurrency Practice Exp., **3**(4), 249–264 (1991).

[MHH91] Martin, C.E., Hoare, C.A.R., He, J.: Pre-adjunctions in order enriched categories. Mathematical Struct. Comput. Sci. **1**(2), 141–158 (1991).

[ZHR91] Zhou, C.C., Hoare, C.A.R., Ravn, A.P.: A calculus of durations. Inf. Process. Lett. **40**(5), 269–276 (1991).

[HG] Hoare, C.A.R., Gordon, M.J.C. (eds.), Mechanised Reasoning and Hardware Design. Prentice Hall International Series in Computer Science. ISBN 0-13-572405-8 (1992).

[Hoa92] Hoare, C.A.R.: Programs are predicates. In: FGCS, pp. 211–218 (1992).

[ZH92] Zhou, C., Hoare, C.A.R.: A model for synchronous switching circuits and its theory of correctness. Formal Methods System Design **1**(1), 7–28 (1992).

[HH93] He, J., Hoare, C.A.R.: From algebra to operational semantics. Inf. Process. Lett. **45**(2), 75–80 (1993).

[HHS93] Hoare, C.A.R., He, J., Sampaio, A.: Normal form approach to compiler design. Acta informatica **30**(8), 701–739 (1993).

[Hoa93] Hoare, C.A.R.: Algebra and models. In: SIGSOFT FSE, pp. 1–8 (1993).

[HHF+94] He, J., Hoare, C.A.R., Fränzle, M., Müller-Olm, M., Olderog, E.-R., Schenke, M., Hansen, M.R., Ravn, A.P., Rischel, H.: Provably correct systems. In: FTRTFT, pp. 288–335 (1994).

[Hoa94] Hoare, C.A.R.: Editorial. J. Log. Comput. **4**(3), 215–216 (1994).

[HP94] Hoare, C.A.R., Page, I.: Hardware and software: The closing gap. In: Programming Languages and System Architectures, pp. 49–68 (1994).

[Hoa95] Hoare, C.A.R.: Unification of theories: A challenge for computing science. In: COMPASS/ADT, pp. 49–57 (1995).

[vKH95] van Karger, B., Hoare, C.A.R.: Sequential calculus. Inf. Process. Lett **53**(3), 123–130 (1995).

[Hoa96a] Hoare, C.A.R.: How did software get so reliable without proof? In: FME, pp. 1–17 (1996).

[Hoa96b] Hoare, C.A.R.: The logic of engineering design. Microprocess. Microprogramm. **41**(8-9), 525–539 (1996).

[Hoa96c] Hoare, C.A.R.: Mathematical models for computing science. In: NATO ASI DPD, pp. 115–164 (1996).

[Hoa96d] Hoare, C.A.R.: The role of formal techniques: Past, current and future or how did software get so reliable without proof? (extended abstract). In: ICSE, pp. 233–234, (1996).

[Hoa96e] Hoare, C.A.R.: Unifying theories: A personal statement. ACM Comput. Surv. **28**(4es) 46 (1996).

[WH66] Wirth, N., Hoare, C.A.R.: A contribution to the development of ALGOL. Communi. of the ACM **9**(6) 413–432 (June 1966).

[HH97] Hoare, C.A.R., He, J.: Unifying theories for parallel programming. In: Euro-Par, pp. 15–30 (1997).

[HH98] Hoare, C.A.R., He, J.: Unifying Theories of Programming. Prentice Hall (1998).

[HH99a] He, J., Hoare, C.A.R.: Linking theories in probabilistic programming. Inf. Sci. **119**, (3-4) 205–218 (1999).

[HH99b] Hoare, C.A.R., He, J.: A trace model for pointers and objects. In: ECOOP, pp. 1–17 (1999).

[Hoa99a] Hoare, C.A.R.: Theories of programming: Top-down and bottom-up and meeting in the middle. In: Correct System Design, pp. 3–28 (1999).

[Hoa99b] Hoare, C.A.R.: Theories of programming: Top-down and bottom-up and meeting in the middle. In: World Congress on Formal Methods, pp. 1–27 (1999).

[JRH+99] Peyton Jones, S.L., Reid, A., Henderson, F., Hoare, C.A.R., Marlow, S.: A semantics for imprecise exceptions. In: PLDI, pp. 25–36 (1999).

[SSH99] Seres, S., Spivey, M.J., Hoare, C.A.R.: Algebra of logic programming. In: ICLP, pp. 184–199 (1999).

[HH00] He, J., Hoare, C.A.R.: Unifying theories of healthiness condition. In: APSEC, pp. 70–, 2000.

[HHS00] Hoare, C.A.R., He, J., Sampaio, A.: Algebraic derivation of an operational semantics. In: Proof, Language, and Interaction, pp. 77–98 (2000).

[Hoa00a] Hoare, C.A.R.: Assertions. In: IFM, pp. 1–2 (2000).

[Hoa00b] Hoare, C.A.R.: A hard act to follow. Higher-Order and Symbolic Comput **13**(1/2), 71–72 (2000).
[Hoa00c] Hoare, C.A.R.: Legacy code. In: ICFEM, p. 75 (2000).
[Hoa01a] Hoare, C.A.R.: Growing use of assertions. In: TOOLS (38), p. 3 (2001).
[Hoa01b] Hoare, C.A.R.: Legacy. Inf. Process. Lett., 77(2-4):123–129, 2001.
[BFG+02] Boyer, R.S., Feijen, W.H.J., Gries, D., Hoare, C.A.R., Misra, J., Moore, J., Richards, H.: In: memoriam: Edsger w. Dijkstra 1930–2002. Commun. ACM 45(10):21–22 (2002).
[Hoa02a] Hoare, C.A.R.: Assertions in modern software engineering practice. In: COMPSAC, pp. 459–462 (2002).
[Hoa02b] Hoare, C.A.R.: Assertions in programming: From scientific theory to engineering practice. In: Soft-Ware, pp. 350–351 (2002).
[Hoa02c] Hoare, C.A.R.: Towards the verifying compiler. In: 10th Anniversary Colloquium of UNU/IIST, pp. 151–160 (2002).
[Hoa03a] Hoare, C.A.R.: Assertions: A personal perspective. IEEE Ann. History Comput. **25**(2), 14–25 (2003).
[Hoa03f] Hoare, C.A.R.: The verifying compiler: A grand challenge for computing research. J. ACM **50**(1), 63–69 (2003). (This paper also appeared in a number of other publications).
[BHF04] Butler, M.J., Hoare, C.A.R., Ferreira, C.: A trace semantics for long-running transactions. In: 25 Years Communicating Sequential Processes, pp. 133–150 (2004).
[FHRR04] Fournet, C., Hoare, C.A.R., Rajamani, S.K., Rehof, J.: Stuck-free conformance. In: CAV, pp. 242–254 (2004).
[Hoa04a] Hoare, C.A.R.: Process algebra: A unifying approach. In: 25 Years Communicating Sequential Processes, pp. 36–60 (2004).
[Hoa04b] Hoare, C.A.R.: Towards the verifying compiler. In: Essays in Memory of Ole-Johan Dahl, pp. 124–136 (2004).
[BBF+05] Bruni, R., Butler, M.J., Ferreira, C., Hoare, C.A.R., Melgratti, H.C., Montanari, U.: Comparing two approaches to compensable flow composition. In CONCUR, pp. 383–397 (2005).
[HH05] He, J., Hoare, C.A.R.: Linking theories of concurrency. In: ICTAC, pp. 303–317 (2005).
[HM05a] Hoare, C.A.R., Milner, R.: Grand challenges for computing research. Comput. J. **48**(1), 49–52 (2005).
[HM05b] Hoare, C.A.R., Misra, J.: Verified software: Theories, tools, experiments vision of a grand challenge project. In: VSTTE, pp. 1–18 (2005).
[BHH+06] Beckert, B., Hoare, C.A.R., Hähnle, R., Smith, D.R., Green, C., Ranise, S., Tinelli, C., Ball, T., Rajamani, S.K.: Intelligent systems and formal methods in software engineering. IEEE Intelligent Systems **21**(6), 71–81 (2006).
[BHW06] Bicarregui, J., Hoare, C.A.R., Woodcock, J.C.P.: The verified software repository: A step towards the verifying compiler. Formal Asp. Comput. **18**(2), 143–151(2006).
[HH06] He, J., Hoare, C.A.R.: CSP is a retract of CCS. In: UTP, pp. 38–62 (2006) TCS 411 (issue 11–13), pp. 1311–1337, 2010 doi:10.1016/j.tcs.2009.12.012.
[Hoa06b] Hoare, C.A.R.: The ideal of verified software. In: CAV pp. 5–16 (2006).
[Hoa06c] Hoare, C.A.R.: Why ever CSP? Electr. Notes Theoret. Comput. Sci. **162**, 209–215 (2006).
[VHHS06] Vafeiadis, V., Herlihy, M., Hoare, C.A.R., Shapiro, M.: Proving correctness of highly.concurrent linearisable objects. In: PPOPP, pp. 129–136 (2006).
[Hoa07a] Hoare, C.A.R.: Fine-grain concurrency. In: CPA, pp. 1–19 (2007).
[Hoa07b] Hoare, C.A.R.: The ideal of program correctness: Third Computer Journal lecture. Comput. J. **50**(3), 254–260 (2007).
[Hoa07c] Hoare, C.A.R.: Science and engineering: A collusion of cultures. In: DSN, pp. 2–9 (2007).
[HO08] Hoare, C.A.R., O'Hearn, P.W.: Separation logic semantics for communicating processes. Electr. Notes Theoret. Comput. Sci. **212**:3–25 (2008).

[Hoa08a] Hoare, C.A.R.: Keynote: A vision for the science of computing. In: BCS Int. Acad. Conf., pp. 1–29 (2008).
[Hoa08b] Hoare, C.A.R.: Verification of fine-grain concurrent programs. Electr. Notes Theoret. Comput. Sci. **209**, 165–171 (2008).
[Hoa08c] Hoare, C.A.R.: Verified software: Theories, tools, experiments. In: ICECCS, p. 3 (2008).
[HM09] Hoare, C.A.R., Misra, J.: Preface to special issue on software verification. ACM Comput. Surv. **41**(4) (2009).
[HMLS09] Hoare, C.A.R., Misra, J., Leavens, G.T., Shankar, N.: The verified software initiative: A manifesto. ACM Comput. Surv. **41**(4), (2009).
[HMSW09a] Hoare, C.A.R., Möller, B., Struth, G., Wehrman, I.: Concurrent Kleene algebra. In: CONCUR, pp. 399–414 (2009).
[HMSW09b] Hoare, C.A.R., Möller, B., Struth, G., Wehrman, I.: Foundations of concurrent Kleene algebra. In: RelMiCS, pp. 166–186 (2009).
[Hoa09] Hoare, C.A.R.: Viewpoint – retrospective: an axiomatic basis for computer programming. *Commun. ACM* **52**(10), 30–32 (2009).
[WHO09] Wehrman, I., Hoare, C.A.R., O'Hearn, P.W.: Graphical models of separation logic. Inf. Process. Lett. **109**(17), 1001–1004 (2009).

Bibliography 2: Papers by Other Authors

1. Abrial, J.-R.: The B-Book: Assigning Programs to Meanings. Cambridge University Press, Melbourne, Australia (1996).
2. Apt, K.R.: Ten years of Hoare's logic: A survey – part I. ACM Trans. Programm. Languages Systems **3**, 431–483 (1981).
3. Apt, K.R.: Ten years of Hoare's logic: A survey – part II: Nondeterminism. Theoret. Comput. Sci., **28**, 83–109 (1984).
4. Bekič, H., Bjørner, D., Henhapl, W., Jones, C.B., Lucas, P.: A formal definition of a PL/I subset. Technical Report 25.139, IBM Laboratory Vienna (December 1974).
5. Bjørner, D., Jones, C.B. (eds.), The Vienna Development Method: The Meta-Language, vol. 61 of Lecture Notes in Computer Science. Springer (1978) ISBN 3-540-08766-4.
6. Brookes, S.D., Roscoe, A.W.: An improved failures model for communicating processes (1985), Proceedings of Pittsburgh Seminar on Concurrency, Springer LNCS 197, 1984, Berlin/Heidelberg.
7. Brookes, S.D.: A mathematical theory of communicating processes. PhD thesis, University of Oxford (1983).
8. Dijkstra, E.W.: A Discipline of Programming. Prentice-Hall (1976).
9. De Nicola, R., Hennessy, M.C.B.: Testing equivalences for processes (1983).
10. Floyd, R.W.: Assigning meanings to programs. In: Proc. Symp. in Applied Mathematics, Vol.19: Mathematical Aspects of Computer Science, pp. 19–32. American Mathematical Society (1967).
11. Goldsmith, M.H., Roscoe, A.W.: Transformation of occam programs. In: Design and Application of Parallel Digital Processors, 1988, pp. 180–188 (1988).
12. Goldstine, H.H., von Neumann, J.: Planning and coding of problems for an electronic computing instrument, 1947. Part II, Vol. 1 of a Report prepared for U.S. Army Ord. Dept.; republished as pp. 80–151 of [34].
13. Holt, R.C., Matthews, P.A., Rosselet, J.A., Cordy, J.R.: The Turing Programming Language: Design and Defintion. Prentice Hall International, Hemel Hempstead, Herts, England (1988).
14. Jones, C.B.: Software Development: A Rigorous Approach. Prentice Hall International, Hemel Hempstead, Herts, England (1980).
15. Jones, C.B.: The early search for tractable ways of reasoning about programs. IEEE, Annals of the History of Comput. **25**(2), 26–49 (2003).

16. Jones, C.B.: Splitting atoms safely. Theoret. Comput. Sci. **357**, 109–119 (2007).
17. King, J.C.: A Program Verifier. PhD thesis, Department of Computer Science, Carnegie-Mellon University (1969).
18. Lauer, P.E.: Consistent Formal Theories of the Semantics of Programming Languages. PhD thesis, Queen's University of Belfast, 1971. Printed as TR 25.121, IBM Lab. Vienna.
19. INMOS Ltd. Occam Programming Manual. Prentice Hall International, Hemel Hempstead, Herts, England (1984).
20. Lucas, P., Walk, K.: On the Formal Description of PL/I, vol. 6, Part 3 of Annual Review in Automatic Programming. Pergamon Press, New York (1969).
21. McCarthy, J.: A basis for a mathematical theory for computation. In: Braffort, P., Hirschberg, D. (eds.) Computer Programming and Formal Systems, pp. 33–70. North-Holland (1963). (A slightly extended and corrected version of a talk given at the May 1961 Western Joint Computer Conference).
22. McCarthy, J.: A formal description of a subset of ALGOL. In: [33], pp. 1–12 (1966).
23. Milner, R.: Processes: a mathematical model of computing agents. In: Logic Colloquium.73. North Holland (1973).
24. Milner. R.: Flowgraphs and flow algebras. J. ACM **26**(4), 794–818 (1979).
25. Milner, R.: A Calculus of Communicating Systems. Springer, New York, Inc. Secaucus, NJ, USA (1982).
26. Plotkin, G.D.: A powerdomain construction. SIAM. Comput. **5**, 452 (1976).
27. Reilly, E.D.: Milestones in Computer Science and Information Technology. Greenwood Pub Group (2003).
28. Roscoe, A.W.: A mathematical theory of communicating processes. PhD thesis, University of Oxford (1982).
29. Roscoe, A.W.: Denotational Semantics for occam (1985) Proceedings of Pittsburgh Seminar on Concurrency, Springer LNCS 197, 1984, Berlin/Heidelberg.
30. Roscoe, A.W.: Occam in the specification and verification of microprocessors. Philosophical Transactions: Physical Sciences and Engineering, pp. 137–151 (1992).
31. Roscoe, A.W.: The Theory and Practice of Concurrency. Prentice Hall International, Hemel Hempstead, Herts, England (1997).
32. Roscoe, A.W.: Understanding Concurrent Systems. Springer, London (2010).
33. Steel, T.B.: Formal Language Description Languages for Computer Programming. North-Holland (1966).
34. Taub, A.H. (ed.), John von Neumann: Collected Works, vol. V: Design of Computers, Theory of Automata and Numerical Analysis. Pergamon Press (1963).
35. Turing. A.M.: Checking a large routine. In: Report of a Conference on High Speed Automatic Calculating Machines, pp. 67–69. University Mathematical Laboratory, Cambridge (June 1949).
36. van Wijngaarden, A.: Numerical analysis as an independent science. BIT **6**:66–81 (1966). (Text of 1964 talk).

The Academic Family Tree of C.A.R. Hoare

We began this article with some remarks about Tony's family background. We conclude it with as much as we have been able to piece together about his *academic* family, of which we are both proud members, namely his doctoral students, their doctoral students and so on. To become a member of the family below we asked that a student had successfully completed his/her doctorate by the time this article was finalised. This family is not entirely without incest, in that some students were jointly supervised by two other members of the tree (sometimes including Tony himself). We have organised the tree below so that each student is given as short a route to Tony as possible. Entries in *italics* (e.g. Roscoe's supervision of Kong) indicate that the student's main entry is elsewhere. A joint supervisor (JS) in *italics* is elsewhere in the tree.

In most cases, for brevity, we give here the *topic* or *area* of the thesis, rather than its title.

We intend to supply our information, including titles where we have them, to the Mathematics Genealogy Project[18], from where, in turn, some of this information was gathered. Therefore if you have any corrections or additions to this tree, we encourage you to upload the details there.

C.A.R. Hoare

1 Peter Lauer, Belfast 1971, *Axiomatic semantics*

- 1.1 Eike Best[19], Newcastle[20] 1981, *Concurrency* (JS Brian Randell)
  - 1.1.1 Lucia Pomello, Milano and Torino 1988, *Petri nets* (JS Giorgio De Michelis and Mariangiola Dezani-Ciancaglini)
    - 1.1.1.1 Stefania Rombolà, Milano-Bicocca 2009, *Concurrency theory* (JS Luca Bernardinello)
  - 1.1.2 Javier Esparza, Hildesheim 1993, *Model checking*
    - 1.1.2.1 Richard Mayr, Munich 1998, *Infinite state systems*
      - 1.1.2.1.1 Noomene Ben Henda, Uppsala 2008, *Infinite-state systems*
    - 1.1.2.2 Stephan Melzer, Munich 1998, *Verifying distributed systems*
    - 1.1.2.3 Stefan Römer, Munich 2000, *Verification using unfoldings*
    - 1.1.2.4 Christine Röckl, Munich 2001, *Validation of reactive and mobile systems* (JS Davide Sangiorgi)
    - 1.1.2.5 Leonor Prensa-Nieto, Munich 2002, *Verification of parallel programs in Isabelle/HOL* (JS *Nipkow*)
    - 1.1.2.6 Stefan Schwoon, Munich 2002, *Checking pushdown systems*
    - 1.1.2.7 Barbara König, Stuttgart 2004, *Analysing dynamic systems*
    - 1.1.2.8 Alin Stefanescu, Stuttgart 2006, *Distributed systems*
    - 1.1.2.9 Claus Schröter, Stuttgart 2006, *Partial-order verification*
    - 1.1.2.10 Dejvuth Suwimonteerabuth, Munich 2009, *Pushdown systems*
    - 1.1.2.11 Stefan Kiefer, Munich 2009, *Positive polynomial equations*

[18] http://genealogy.math.ndsu.nodak.edu/

[19] Esparza, Lavrov and Wimmel were Habilitation rather than doctoral students of Best.

[20] University of Newcastle upon Tyne.

1.1.3 Hans-Günther Linde-Göers, Hildesheim 1994, *Partial order semantics*
1.1.4 Hanna Klaudel, Paris 1995, *Algebraic Petri net models* (JS Elisabeth Pelz)
1.1.4.1 *Robert-Christoph Riemann*, (see 1.1.6)
1.1.4.2 Franck Pommereau, Paris 2002, *Petri nets & real-time* (JS Pelz)
1.1.4.3 Cécile Bui-Thanh, Paris 2004, *OO concurrent programs*
1.1.4.4 Cédric Siléo, Evry 2007, *Adaptive systems* (JS Hutzler)
1.1.4.5 Benoît Calvez, Evry 2007, *Agent-based Simulations* (JS Hutzler)
1.1.4.6 Anastassia Yartseva, Evry 2007, *Modelling of biological networks* (JS Franois Képès and Raymond Devillers)
1.1.5 Jon Hall, Newcastle 1996, *An Algebra of high-level Petri nets* (JS Maciej Koutny and Richard Hopkins)
1.1.5.1 Adrian Hilton, OU[21] 2004, *Hardware–software co-design*
1.1.5.2 Zhi Li, OU 2007, *Deriving specifications* (JS Lucia Rapanotti)
1.1.5.3 Derek Mannering, OU 2009, *Systems engineering* (JS Rapanotti)
1.1.5.4 Robert Logie, OU 2009 *Nested agent interactions* (JS Waugh)
1.1.6 Robert-Christoph Riemann, Hildesheim/Paris 1999, *Petri net refinement* (JS *Klaudel* and Pelz)
1.1.7 Bernd Grahlmann, Hildesheim 1999, *Parallel programs*
1.1.8 Thomas Thielke, Oldenburg 1999, *Coloured Petri nets*
1.1.9 Alexander Lavrov, Kiev 2000, *Combined semantic methods*
1.1.10 Andreea Barbu, Oldenburg/Paris 2005, *Mobile agents* (JS Pelz)
1.1.11 Harro Wimmel, Oldenburg 2007, *Decidability in Petri nets*
1.2 Yiannis Cotronis, Newcastle 1982, *Asynchronous systems*
1.2.1 Zacharias Tsiatsoulis, Athens 2005, *Distributed systems*

2 William Stewart, Belfast 1974, *Markov chains in operating systems*

2.1 Steven Dodd, NCSU 1982, *Shape preserving splines*
2.2 John Koury, NCSU 1983, *Near-complete-decomposable systems*
2.3 Patricia Snyder, NCSU 1985, *Non-product form queues*
2.4 Munkee Choi, NCSU 1989, *Multiclass queueing networks*
2.5 Halim Kafeety, NCSU 1991, *Aggregation/Disaggregation methods*
2.6 Tugrul Dayar, NCSU 1994, *Stability and conditioning*
2.6.1 Oleg Gusak, Blikent 2001, *Analysis of Markov chains*
2.7 Walter Barge, NCSU 2002, *Autonomous solution methods*
2.8 Amy Langville, NCSU 2002, *Preconditioning techniques*

[21] Open University.

- 2.9 Bin Peng, NCSU 2004, *Convergence, rank reduction*
- 2.10 Ning Liu, NCSU 2009, *Spectral clustering*

3 Masud Malik, Belfast 1975, *Data representation*
4 John Elder, Belfast 1975, *Data representation*
5 Jim (Wolfgang) Kaubisch, Belfast 1976, *Discrete event simulation*
6 Richard Kennaway, Oxford 1981, *Concurrency and nondeterminism*

- 6.1 Sugwoo Byun, East Anglia 1994, *Term rewriting*
- 6.2 Alex Peck, East Anglia 2006, *Procedural animation*

7 Cliff Jones, Oxford 1981, *Software Development*

- 7.1 Kevin Jones, Manchester 1984, *Formal development*
- 7.2 Ann Welsh, Manchester 1984, *Database programming*
- 7.3 Lynn Marshall, Manchester 1986, *User interface description*
- 7.4 Tobias Nipkow, Manchester 1987, *Nondeterministic data types*
  - 7.4.1 Franz Regensburger, TUM[22] 1994, *HOL*
  - 7.4.2 Christian Prehofer, TUM 1995, *Higher-order equations*
  - 7.4.3 Dieter Nazareth, TUM 1995, *Polymorphism in specification*
  - 7.4.4 Olaf Müller, TUM 1998, *Verification of I/O-automata*
  - 7.4.5 Konrad Slind, TUM 1999, *Recursion in HOL*
  - 7.4.6 David von Oheimb, TUM 2001, *Analyzing Java*
  - 7.4.7 Leonor Prensa Nieto, TUM 2002, *Parallel program verification*
  - 7.4.8 Markus Wenzel, TUM 2002, *Human-readable formal proofs*
  - 7.4.9 Gerwin Klein, TUM 2003, *Verifying a bytecode verifier*
    - 7.4.9.1 Harvey Tuch, UNSW 2008, *Formal memory models*
  - 7.4.10 Stefan Berghofer, TUM 2003, *Executable specifications*
  - 7.4.11 Gertrud Bauer, TUM 2006, *Plane graph theory*
  - 7.4.12 Norbert Schirmer, TUM 2006, *Verifying sequential code*
  - 7.4.13 Martin Wildmoser, TUM 2006, *Proof carrying code*
  - 7.4.14 Amine Chaieb, TUM 2008, *Automated formal proofs*
  - 7.4.15 Tjark Weber, TUM 2008, *SAT-based finite model generation*
  - 7.4.16 Steven Obua, TUM 2008, *Flyspeck II: The basic linear programs*
  - 7.4.17 Alexander Krauss, TUM 2009, *Recursion in higher-order logic*
  - 7.4.18 Florian Haftmann, TUM 2009, *Code generation*
- 7.5 Mario Wolczko, Manchester 1988, *Semantics of OO languages*
- 7.6 Ralf Kneuper, Manchester 1989, *Symbolic execution*
- 7.7 Jean Alain Ah-Kee, Manchester 1989, *Operation decomposition*
- 7.8 Ketil Stølen, Manchester 1990, *Parallel programs*
  - 7.8.1 Ida Hogganvik, Oslo 2007, *Security risk analysis*
  - 7.8.2 Ragnhild Kobro Rund, Oslo 2007, *UML interaction diagrams*
  - 7.8.3 Mass Soldal Lund, Oslo 2008, *Sequence diagram specifications*
  - 7.8.4 Atle Refsdal, Oslo 2008, *Probabilistic sequence diagrams*
  - 7.8.5 Bjørnar Solhaug, Bergen 2009, *Sequence diagrams*

---

[22] Technical University of Munich.

7.9 John Fitzgerald, Manchester 1991, *Formal specification*
  7.9.1 Andrej Pietschker, Newcastle 2001, *Automated Test Generation*
  7.9.2 Daniel Owen, Newcastle 2005, *Real-time networks*
  7.9.3 *Neil Henderson, Newcastle 2006, Asynch. communications* (see 7.14)
7.10 Alan Wills, Manchester 1993, *Formal methods in OO*
7.11 Carlos de Figueiredo, Manchester 1994, *Object-based languages*
  7.11.1 Elaine Pimentel, UFMG[23] 2001, *Sequent calculus* (JS Dale Miller)
  7.11.2 Cristiano Vasconcellos, UFMG 2004, *Type inference*
7.12 Juan Bicarregui, Manchester 1995, *Model-oriented specification*
7.13 Steve Hodges, Manchester 1996, *Development of object-based programs*
7.14 Neil Henderson, Newcastle 2006, *Asynch. communications* (JS *Fitzgerald*)
7.15 Tony Lawrie, Newcastle 2006, *System dependability*
7.16 Martin Ellis, Newcastle 2008, *Compiler-generated function units*
7.17 Joseph Coleman, Newcastle 2008, *Operational semantics*
7.18 David Greathead, Newcastle 2008, *Code comprehension* (JS George Erdos and Joan Harvey)
7.19 Ken Pierce, Newcastle 2009, *Atomicity in refinement*

8 Bill Roscoe, Oxford 1982, *Concurrency*

8.1 *Tat Yung Kong, Oxford 1986, Digital topology* (see 14)
8.2 Andrew Boucher, Oxford 1986, *Real-time semantics for occam*
8.3 Mike Reed[24], Oxford 1988, *Timed CSP*
  8.3.1 Steve Schneider, Oxford 1989, *Timed CSP*
    8.3.1.1 Carl Adekunle, RHUL 2000, *Feature interaction*
    8.3.1.2 Helen Treharne, RHUL 2000, *Controlling specifications*
      8.3.1.2.1 Damien Karkinsky, Surrey 2007, *Mobile B*
      8.3.1.2.2 Chris Culnane, Surrey 2009, *Digital watermarking*
    8.3.1.3 James Heather, RHUL 2000, *Security protocols*
      8.3.1.3.1 Kun Wei, Surrey 2006, *Automated proofs and CSP*
      8.3.1.3.2 James Salter, Surrey 2007, *P2P networks* (JS Antonopoulos)
      8.3.1.3.3 *Zhe Xia, Surrey 2009, Electronic voting* (see 8.3.1.8)
    8.3.1.4 Neil Evans, RHUL 2003, *Security*
    8.3.1.5 Roberto Delicata, Surrey 2006, *Security*
    8.3.1.6 Wilson Ifill, Surrey 2008, *CSPB*
    8.3.1.7 Siraj Shaikh, University of Gloucestershire 2008, *Security*
    8.3.1.8 Zhe Xia, Surrey 2009, *Electronic voting* (JS *Heather*)

---

[23] Federal University of Minas Gerais, Brazil.

[24] Mike Reed has two doctorates, one from Auburn in 1970 under Ben Fitzpatrick on Set-theoretic Topology, and the one listed above. In addition to Reed's Computer Science students listed above, he has had a number in topology, but we have decided not to list those here.

8.3.2 David Jackson, Oxford 1992, *Verification of timed CSP*
8.3.3 Abida Mukkaram, Oxford 1993, *Refusal testing in CSP*
8.3.4 Joel Ouaknine, Oxford 2001, *Timed CSP*
8.4 Naiem Dathi, Oxford 1989, *Deadlock avoidance*
8.5 Martin Ward, Oxford 1989, *Program transformation*
8.5.1 Matthias Ladkau, De Montfort 2008, *Program transformation*
8.5.2 Shaoyun Li, De Montfort 2008, *Program transformation*
8.5.3 Stefan Natelberg, De Montfort 2009, *Prog. transf.* (JS Zedan)
8.6 Geoff Barrett, Oxford 1989, *Operational semantics of the transputer*
8.7 Alan Jeffrey, Oxford 1989, *Timed concurrency*
8.7.1 Ralf Schweimeier, Sussex 2000, *Categorical models*
8.8 Gavin Lowe, Oxford 1993, *Priority and probability in timed CSP*
8.8.1 Mei Lin Hui, Leicester 2001, *Security protocols*
8.8.2 Gordon Rohrmair, Oxford 2005, *Security*
8.8.3 Chris Dilloway, Oxford 2008, *Security protocols*
8.8.4 Allaa Kamil, Oxford 2009, *Security protocols*
8.9 Brian Scott, Oxford 1995, *Semantics of occam II*
8.10 Lars Wulf, Oxford 1996, *Noninterference security*
8.11 Bryan Scattergood, Oxford 1998, *Tools for CSP*
8.12 Ranko Lazić, Oxford 1999, *Data independence*
8.12.1 *Tom Newcomb, Oxford 2003, Data independence* (see 8.16)
8.12.2 Aleksandar Dimovski, Warwick 2007, *Game semantics*
8.13 Richard Forster, Oxford 1999, *Non-interference*
8.14 Sadie Creese, Oxford 2001, *Inductive proofs of networks*
8.15 Philippa Broadfoot, Oxford 2002, *Cryptographic protocols*
8.16 Tom Newcomb, Oxford 2003 *Data independence* (JS *Lazić*)
8.17 Richard Tolcher, Oxford 2006, *Ethnomethodology*
8.18 Lee Momtahan, Oxford 2007, *Data independence*
8.19 Eldar Kleiner, Oxford 2008, *Security protocols*
8.20 Long Nguyen, Oxford 2009, *Pervasive computing security*

9 Geraint Jones, Oxford 1983, *Timed concurrency*
10 Stephen Brookes, Oxford 1983, *Concurrency*

10.1 Michel Schellekens, CMU 1995, *Semantics and complexity*
10.1.1 David Hickey, UCC[25] 2008, *Static analysis*
10.1.2 Maria O'Keeffe, UCC 2008, *Analysis of algorithms*
10.2 Shai Geva, CMU 1996, *Higher-order sequential computation*
10.3 Susan Older, CMU 1996, *Fair communicating processes*
10.3.1 Dan Zhou, Syracuse 1999, *Secure email*
10.3.2 Jang Dae Kim, Syracuse 2002, *Instruction-set calculus*
10.3.3 Byoung Woo Min, Syracuse 2005, *Instruction-set calculus*
10.3.4 Polar Humenn, Syracuse 2008, *The authorisation calculus*
10.4 Denis Dancanet, CMU 1998, *Intensional investigations*

[25] University College Cork.

- 10.5 Jüergen Dingel, CMU 1999, *Parallel programs*
  - 10.5.1 Jeremy Bradbury, Queen's University[26] 2007, *Mutation testing* (JS JimCordy)
  - 10.5.2 Michelle Crane, Queen's University 2008, *UML modeling*
  - 10.5.3 Hongzhi Liang, Queen's University 2009, *Sequence diagrams*
- 10.6 Kathryn Van Stone, CMU 2003, *Denotational complexity*

11 Andrew Black, Oxford 1984, *Exception handling*

- 11.1 Leif Nielsen, UW[27] 1986, *Concurrent program development*
- 11.2 Norman Hutchinson, UW 1987, *Distributed systems* (JS Hank Levy)
  - 11.2.1 Clair Bowman, Arizona 1990, *Descriptive naming*
  - 11.2.2 Michael Coffin, Arizona 1990, *Parallel programming*
  - 11.2.3 Sean O'Malley, Arizona 1990, *Programming with protocols*
  - 11.2.4 Siu Ling Lo, UBC[28] 1995, *Real-Time tasking*
  - 11.2.5 Peter Smith, UBC 1998, *Process migration*
  - 11.2.6 Alistair Veitch, UBC 1998, *Operating systems*
  - 11.2.7 Dwight Makaroff, UBC 1998, *Media file-servers*
  - 11.2.8 Dima Brodsky, UBC 2005, *Policy driven replication*
  - 11.2.9 Chamath Keppitiyagama, UBC 2005, *Multiparty communication*
  - 11.2.10 Lechang Cheng, UBC 2009, *Distributed systems*
- 11.3 Eric Jul, UW 1988, *Object mobility* (JS Hank Levy)
  - 11.3.1 Charlotte Lunau, Copenhagen 1989, *OO programing*
  - 11.3.2 Birger Andersen, Copenhagen 1991, *OO parallelism*
  - 11.3.3 Niels Juul, Copenhagen 1993, *Concurrent garbage collection*
  - 11.3.4 Povl Koch, Copenhagen 1996, *Distributed systems*
  - 11.3.5 Jørgen Hansen[29], Copenhagen 2000, *Distributed systems*
  - 11.3.6 Czeslaw Kazimierczak, Copenhagen 2001, *Distributed systems*
- 11.4 Emerson Murphy-Hill, Portland State 2009, *Refactoring tools*

12 Christopher Dollin, Oxford 1984, *Language definition*

13 Alex Teruel,[30] Oxford 1985, *Formal specification*

[26] Queen's University, Kingston, Ontario.

[27] University of Washington.

[28] University of British Columbia.

[29] Hansen supervised a number of students in Health-related topics at Groningen before undertaking his doctoral studies with Jul.

[30] Alex Teruel set up the Parallel and Distributed Research Group at Simon Bolivar University, Venezuela. He supervised numerous MSc students there but advised them to do their PhDs abroad. He is happy to report that since a number of these people did this successfully and now have completed PhD students of their own, the fruits of Tony's advisorship are thriving in Venezuela.

14 Tat Yung Kong, Oxford 1986, *Digital topology* (JS *Roscoe*)

14.1 Cherng-Min Ma, CUNY[31] 1994, *Digital topology*
14.2 Chyi-Jou Gau, CUNY 2005, *Digital topology*

15 Bryan Todd, Oxford 1988, *Formally based diagnostics*
16 Stephen Page, Oxford 1988, *Music information retrieval*
17 Jeremy Jacob, Oxford 1989, *Shared systems*

17.1 Phillip Brooke, York 1999, *Timed semantics for DORIS*
17.1.1 Shukor Razak, Plymouth 2007, *Intrusion detection*
17.1.2 Paul Hunton, Teesside 2007, *Performance management*
17.1.3 Graham Evans, Teesside 2009, *Technology enabled change*
17.2 John Clark, York 2001, *Metaheuristic search in cryptology*
17.2.1 Thitima Srivatanakul, York 2005, *Security analysis*
17.2.2 Howard Chivers, York 2006, *Security analysis*
17.2.3 Yuan Zhan, York 2006, *Test-set generation*
17.2.4 Paul Massey, York 2007, *Quantum Software*
17.2.5 *Hao Chen, York 2007, Security protocol synthesis* (see 17.5)
17.3 Sun Woo Kim, York 2001, *OO mutation testing*
17.4 Nathalie L Foster, York 2003, *Security protocol development*
17.5 Hao Chen, York 2007, *Security protocol synthesis* (JS *Clark)*

18 Clare Martin, Oxford 1991, *Predicate transformers*
19 Ken Wood, Oxford 1992, *Parallel logic simulation*
20 Augusto Sampaio, Oxford 1993, *Compiling using normal forms*

20.1 Leila de Almeida e Silva, UFPe[32] 2000, *HW/SW partitioning*
20.2 Alexandre Cabral, Mota UFPe 2001, *Model checking CSPZ*
20.2.1 Adalberto Cajueiro de Farias, UFPe 2009, *Abstraction in CSPZ*
20.3 Roberta Lopes, UFPe 2003, *Formal methods for genetic algorithms*
20.4 Adolfo de Almeida Duran, UFPe2005, *Algebraic design of compilers*
20.5 Adnan El Sherif, UFPe 2006, *Formal methods in timed systems*

21 Stephen Brien, Oxford 1995, *Generically typed set theory*
22 Paul Rudin, Oxford 2001, *Diagrammatic reasoning*

[31] City University of New York.
[32] Federal University of Pernambuco, Brazil.

Chapter 2
From CSP to Game Semantics

Samson Abramsky

Abstract In this short essay, we describe in informal terms how game semantics can be seen to arise as a perturbation of process calculi such as CSP, by making an explicit distinction between the rôles of the System and the Environment. Drawing out the consequences of this distinction uncovers a wealth of mathematical structure, with Game intuitions entering in a natural and compelling fashion. This leads ultimately to the elaboration of mathematically well-structured and behaviourally expressive semantic universes for computation. These provide a basis for fully abstract models of a wide range of programming languages, and lead on to algorithmic methods, with applications to compositional model-checking and program analysis.

2.1 Introduction

Tony Hoare has been a major influence on me, as on so many of my generation of computer scientists. Moreover, he has always shown a keen interest in the work on game semantics by myself and others, and his remarks have often forced me to sharpen my thinking. In this short note, a mini-essay rather than a paper, I will try to present and motivate some key features of game semantics from the point of view of CSP and other process calculi. I will try to convey how we can see game semantics as arising from a small — but significant! — perturbation of the CSP paradigm. We add one, apparently minor, piece of additional structure, and from this much else follows.

2.2 Polarity

We shall assume some background in CSP [18, 32], or other process calculi such as CCS [27]. We know that these calculi are designed to express **communication**, or more generally **interaction**, between concurrent processes. This is achieved in each

S. Abramsky (✉)
Oxford University Computing Laboratory, Wolfson Building, Parks Road, Oxford OX1 3QD, UK
e-mail: samson@comlab.ox.ac.uk

C.B. Jones et al. (eds.), *Reflections on the Work of C.A.R. Hoare*,
DOI 10.1007/978-1-84882-912-1_2,

case by some form of synchronized communication which is built into the semantics of the parallel composition operation.

Although CSP allows for value-passing idioms, at a more fundamental level, these are "flattened out" or "compiled away" into pure atomic actions. Similar comments can be made for CCS. In the case of CCS, a basic distinction is made between actions and coactions (α and $\bar{\alpha}$), but this is purely formal, and its purpose is to support the particular form of binary "synchronization algebra" of CCS.[1]

In principle, then, all actions in process calculus are at the same level; each action could, a priori, be performed by any process. In the language of logic, actions do not have (positive or negative) **polarities**; in the language of category theory, they do not have (co- or contra-) **variance**.

A basic starting point for game semantics is the recognition that introducing an explicit notion of **polarity of actions** provides a modest-looking fulcrum which we can use to lever up a great deal of structure. Moreover, this notion arises in a very direct fashion from basic intuitions about interactive systems.

The basic idea flows naturally from the observation that our universe of study in the arena of concurrent, distributed, mobile and pervasive processes is that of **open systems**. That is, we study systems which must be seen as embedded in some larger, and as yet not completely specified, system. (Just think of the Internet.) This means that a key part of identifying and delimiting any system we study is that we have a **boundary** between the system being considered, and the larger system which contains it. We call the system under consideration simply the System; and everything outside the boundary is the Environment. Actions can then be classified as performed by the System (under its control) or by the Environment (not under its control). The essence of the behaviour of the System is **how it interacts** with its Environment across this boundary.

To specify a System in these terms is to specify how it will react in the presence of an (unknown) Environment. Thus we must specify what the System will (or would) do given any possible behaviour by the Environment. This assumes a natural **nested conditional** or **hypothetical** form:

If the Environment initially does e_1,
then the System responds with s_1;

[1] The input–output distinction does occur in a more fundamental way in the π-calculus [28–30]. However, even here there are symmetric variants such as the fusion calculus [31], and the π-calculus does not seem to force a fundamental modification of the distinction we are making here.

If the Environment then does e_2,
then the System responds with s_2;
⋮

This apparently minor manoeuvre, of expressing the System/Environment dichotomy directly in our classification of actions, releases much additional mathematical structure, as we shall now see.

2.3 Games

With the introduction of polarized moves, the **games** metaphor becomes natural, and indeed compelling. We think of the System and the Environment as the players in a two-person game. The hypothetical specification of the actions of a System in response to those of its Environment then exactly fits the game-theoretic notion of **strategy**; so we have a natural reading of processes in this polarized framework as strategies.

In this way, we start to use the basic notions of game theory to structure our semantic universe, and we are well on the road to game semantics. But this is only the first step.

One immediate consequence of adopting the game perspective is that we have a natural "dynamic" take on **negation** and **duality**: as interchange of polarity (reversal of rôles in the game) rather than interchange of truth-values.

Referring back to our intuitive reading, this corresponds to the fact that our choice of point of view across the System–Environment boundary is conventional; we could as well take the Environment as the System under consideration, and vice versa. This ability to interchange between different points of view on the same interaction is characteristic of game-theoretic reasoning.

2.4 Determinism

We now proceed to elaborate further structural consequences of our basic move to polarization. We start in a low key, with a humble yet profoundly useful notion: that of **deterministic computation**. The intuitive notion of a deterministic program or computation is rather clear: **at each step, what the program does next is uniquely determined by the previous history of the computation**. The lack of an explicit distinction between the actions of the process and those of its environment means that the notion of deterministic computation in this sense in the standard setting of process calculi is a very limited one.[2]

[2] These calculi do have notions of "deterministic" and "confluent" process as part of their theory [27, 32], but these notions refer to the absence of **non-observable branching** in the system.

By contrast, in the polarized setting, the obvious notion of deterministic strategy – one for which the System actions are uniquely determined by the preceding Environment actions – easily and naturally cover the full sweep of deterministic computation. Because of polarization, one can distinguish between the Environment actions, which a strategy for System cannot control, and hence must be allowed to branch arbitrarily; and the System actions, which in the case of a deterministic strategy must be uniquely determined by what has gone before. In this way, a large portion of what would usually be encoded as non-determinism in the process calculus setting is simply referred to the Environment, while the strategy remains perfectly deterministic.

2.5 Interaction

As we have already mentioned, each process algebra has its own hand-crafted primitives and semantics for communication and synchronization. There are many plausible variations, and different styles suggest different models and process equivalences. This profusion of choices is something of an embarrassment – an instance of the "next 700" syndrome [4, 20].

By contrast, the polarization structure of games entails an **intrinsic notion of interaction**: namely the basic notion in extensive game theory of playing a strategy (for System) off against a counter-strategy (for the Environment) (or "evaluating a strategy profile"). The specification of a strategy for System, as we have already seen, allows for arbitrary branching at Environment moves, while specifying what the System then does in response. A counter-strategy works dually. Thus the strategy and counter-strategy "fit" together, just by the logic of polarization, without need of any synchronization algebra. Note in particular that in the case that the strategy and the counter-strategy are both deterministic, the result of this interaction is a **uniquely determined computation trace**.

This idea really becomes powerful when we combine it with **types**, to which we now turn.

2.6 Types

Process calculus is fundamentally untyped, although sometimes a rudimentary sorting by action alphabet is used. More elaborate type systems for process calculi have been proposed and studied, but they are a kind of super-structure, motivated more by specification and verification issues than by articulating the structure of the universe of processes.

They do not directly correspond to the sense in which the computation of a standard functional or imperative program is deterministic.

Once again the game metaphor shows its ability to reveal significant additional mathematical structure. We have already been led to a view of processes as strategies, but for which games? If we constrain the moves which can be made by a player (System or Environment) at each stage where it may perform an action, we are led to the usual notion of a game tree (game in extensive form), and we can see that games play the role of **types** in a very natural and intuitive fashion.

The real power of this step comes when we consider the possibility of building **compound types** expressing the behaviour of systems built hierarchically from sub-systems. These compound types will be interpreted as constructions on games, which build more complex games, e.g. by combining "game boards". Indeed, it is by virtue of this step to compound games that we can see why it is plausible to restrict ourselves to two-person games. System and Environment may each actually comprehend a "team" of players; the important point is that we are drawing a boundary between the teams, and distinguishing the actions of one team from the other. A useful analogy is with the theory of functions. By using type constructions such as cartesian product, it suffices to develop a theory of one-place functions, rather than having to treat n-place functions as primitive for each n. Indeed, note that functions can be seen as special cases of (deterministic) strategies; where the System allows the Environment to branch on the input, and then produces the corresponding output.

As a direct consequence of this idea of using structured types to build specifications of complex systems, we shall show how the primitive form of interaction intrinsically supported by games leads on to the fundamental notions of **composition** and **identity**.

2.7 Identity and Composition

2.7.1 Copy-Cat Strategies

Consider the following little fable, illustrated by Fig. 2.1. The idea is to rely on logic, rather than on any talent at Chess. We arrange to play two games of Chess with the grandmaster, say Gary Kasparov, once as White and once as Black. Moreover, we so arrange matters that we start with the game in which we play as Black. Kasparov makes his opening move; we respond by playing the **same** move in the **other** game – this makes sense, since we are playing as White there. Now Kasparov responds (as Black) to our move in that game; and we copy that response back in the first game. We simply proceed in this fashion, copying the moves that our opponent makes in one board to the other board. The net effect is that **we play the same game twice – once as White, and once as Black**. (We have essentially made Kasparov play against himself.) Thus, whoever wins that game, we can claim a win in one of our games against Kasparov! (Even if the game results in a stalemate, we have done as well as Kasparov over the two games – surely still a good result!) Of course, this idea has nothing particularly to do with Chess. It can be applied to any two-person

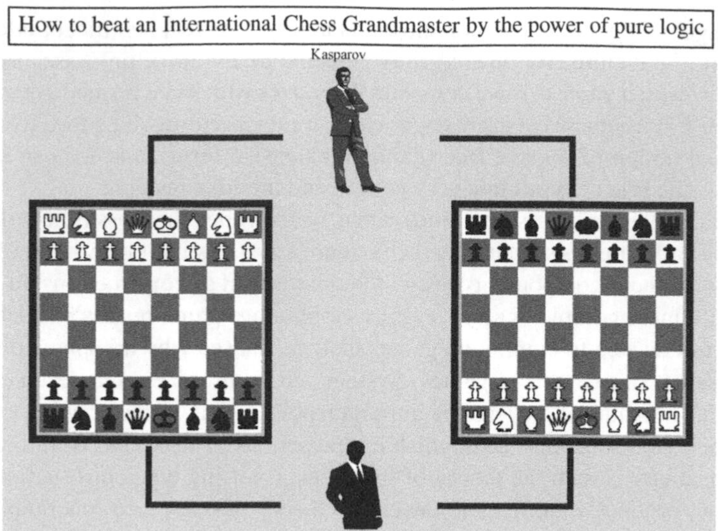

The copy-cat strategy

Fig. 2.1 How to beat a Grandmaster

game of a very general form. The use of Chess-boards to illustrate the discussion will continue, but this underlying generality should be kept in mind.

What are the salient features which can be extracted from this example?

A Dynamic Tautology There is a sense (which will shortly be made more precise) in which the copy-cat strategy can be seen as a **dynamic version** of the tautology $A \vee \neg A$. Note, indeed, that an essential condition for being able to play the copy-cat is that the roles of the two players are inter-changed on one board as compared to the other. Note also the disjunctive quality of the argument that we must win in one or other of the two games. But the copy-cat strategy is a **dynamic process**: a two-way channel which maintains the correlation between the plays in the two games.

Conservation of Information Flow The copy-cat strategy does not **create** any information; it reacts to the environment in such a way that information is conserved. It ensures that exactly the same information flows out to the environment as flows in from it. Thus one gets a sense of logic appearing in the form of **conservation laws for information dynamics**.

The Power of Copying Another theme which appears here, and of which more will be seen later, concerns the surprising power of simple processes of copying information from one place to another. Indeed, as shall eventually be seen, such processes are **computationally universal**.

The Geometry of Information Flow From a dynamical point of view, the copy-cat strategy realizes a channel between the two game boards, by performing the **actions** of copying moves. But there is also some implicit **geometry** here. Indeed, the very idea of two boards laid out side by side appeals to some basic underlying spatial structure. In these terms, the copy-cat channel can also be understood geometrically, as creating a graphical link between these two spatial locations. These two points of view are complementary, and link the logical perspective to powerful ideas arising in modern geometry and mathematical physics.

Further evidence that the copy-cat strategy embodies more substantial ideas than might at first be apparent, can be obtained by varying the scenario. Consider now the case where we play against Kasparov on **three boards**; one as Black, two as White.

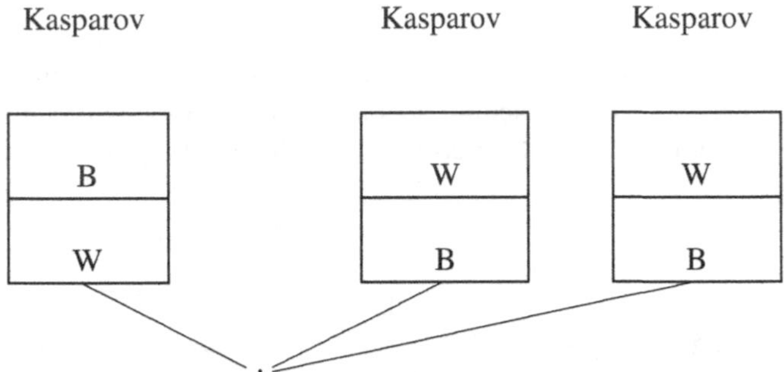

Does the copy-cat strategy still work here? In fact, it can easily be seen that it does **not**. Suppose Kasparov makes an opening move m_1 in the left-hand board where he plays as White; we copy it to the board where we play as White; he responds with m_2; and we copy m_2 back to the board where Kasparov opened. So far, all has proceeded as in our original scenario. But now Kasparov has the option of playing a **different** opening move, m_3 say, in the rightmost board. We have no idea how to respond to this move; nor can we copy it anywhere, since the board where we play as White is already "in use". This shows that these simple ideas already lead us naturally to the setting of a **resource-sensitive** logic, in which in particular the Contraction Rule, which can be expressed as $A \to A \wedge A$ (or equivalently as $\neg A \vee (A \wedge A)$) cannot be assumed to be valid.

What about the other obvious variation, where we play on two boards as White, and one as Black?

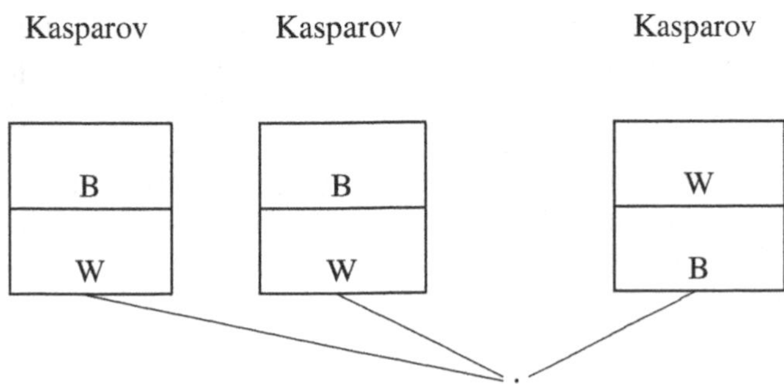

It seems that the copy-cat strategy **does** still work here, since we can simply ignore one of the boards where we play as White. However, a geometrical property of the original copy-cat strategy has been lost, namely a **connectedness** property, that information flows to every part of the system. This at least calls the corresponding logical principle of Weakening, which can be expressed as $A \wedge A \rightarrow A$, into question.

These remarks indicate that we are close to the realm of Linear Logic and its variants, and, mathematically, to the world of monoidal (rather than cartesian) categories.

2.7.2 *Composition as Interaction*

We also show how interaction can be explained in the same terms: Constructors create "potentials" for interaction; the operation of plugging modules together so that they can communicate with each other **releases** this potential into **actual computation**.

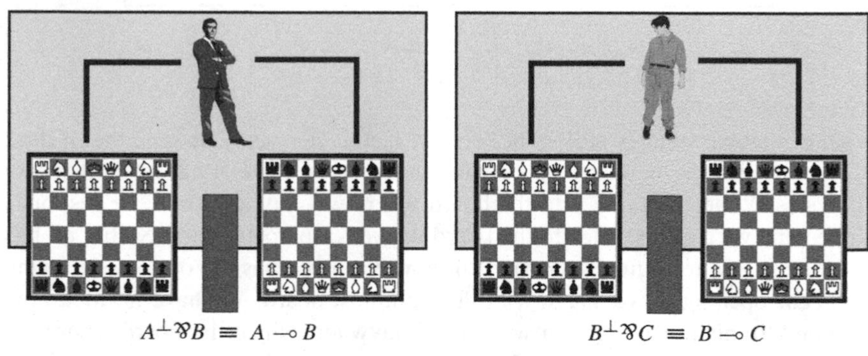

Here we see two separate sub-systems, each with a compound structure, expressed by the **logical types of their interfaces**. What these types tell us is that these systems are **composable**; in particular, the **output type** of the first system, namely B, matches the input type of the second system. Note that this "logical plug-compatibility" makes essential use of the duality, just as the copy-cat strategy did. What makes Gary (the player for the first system) a fit partner for interaction with Nigel (the player for the second system) is that they have **complementary views** of their locus of interaction, namely B. Gary will play in this type "positively", as Player (he sees it as B), while Nigel will play "negatively", as Opponent (he sees it as $B^{\perp}$). Thus each will become part of the environment of the other – part of the potential environment of each will be realized by the other, and hence part of the **potential** behaviour of each will become **actual** interaction.

This leads to a dynamical interpretation of the fundamental operation of **composition**, in mathematical terms:

$$\frac{A \xrightarrow{\text{Gary}} B \xrightarrow{\text{Nigel}} C}{A \xrightarrow{\text{Gary; Nigel}} C}$$

or of the **Cut rule**, in logical terms:

$$\text{Cut:} \quad \frac{\vdash \Gamma, A \quad \vdash A^{\perp}, \Delta}{\Gamma, \Delta}$$

P
Q
A
$A^{\perp}$
...
...
Γ
Δ

Composition as Interaction

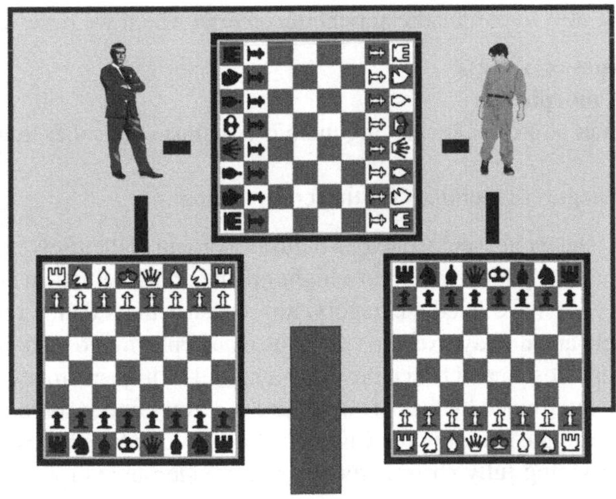

The picture here shows the new system formed by plugging together the two sub-systems. The "external interface" to the environment now shows just the left-hand board A as input, and the right-hand board C as output. The Cut formula B is hidden from the environment, and becomes the locus of interaction inside the black box of the system. Suppose that the Environment makes some move m in C.

This is visible only to Nigel, who as a strategy for $B \multimap C$ has a response. Suppose this response m_1 is in B. This is a move by Nigel as Player in $B^{\perp}$, hence appears to Gary as a move by Opponent in B. Gary as a strategy for $A \multimap B$ has a response m_2 to this move. If this response is again in B, Nigel sees it as a response by the environment to his move, and will have a response again; and so on. Thus there is a sequence of moves $m_1, \ldots, m_k$ in B, ping-ponging back and forth between Nigel and Gary. If, eventually, Nigel responds to Gary's last move by playing in C, or Gary responds to Nigel's last move by playing in A, then this provides the response of the **composed strategy** Gary; Nigel to the original move m. Indeed, all that is visible to the Environment is that it played m, and eventually some response appeared, in A or C.[3]

Summarizing, the two strategies are played off against each other in the shared part of their interfaces (where one plays as White and the other as Black – corresponding to matching of logical polarities), leaving a residual interface to the environment. Note the "duality" between this operation and the copy-cat (Identity and Cut): the copy-cat strategy makes **the same thing happen in two different places**, while composition makes **two different things (with opposite polarities, hence non-conflicting) happen in the same place**.

2.8 Categories: the "Objective Structure" of Interaction

Putting together the various ingredients we have developed from the basic idea of polarization, we now have a mathematical universe in which we have:

- Games as **types** or **objects**
- Strategies as **morphisms**
- Composition of strategies by playing them off against each other in the common subgame
- Copy-cat strategies as identities for this composition

This means that the games and strategies naturally organize themselves into a **category**. This immediately moves us onto a higher plane of mathematical organization. Recall that once we have fixed a category, any constructions defined by universal properties therein are already fixed up to unique isomorphism. For example, if a category is cartesian closed, and hence provides a model of higher-order computation, this is uniquely determined by the bare structure of arrows under composition in the category. This example is highly relevant, since the successful application of game semantics to providing fully abstract models for a wide range of λ-calculus based

[3] It is also easy to show that if Nigel and Gary are both playing **winning strategies**, meaning that they always have a response to the Environment's actions, and that the infinite plays which may arise from following these strategies satisfy some given **liveness specifications**, then the composed strategy will again be a winning strategy, with respect to a liveness specification defined compositionally in a natural fashion from the given ones. See [1] for details and a proof of this.

programming languages rests upon the construction of suitable cartesian closed categories of games and strategies. The mathematical structure present in a category is objectively **there**, it is not a matter of one of "700 choices".

In fact, categories of games and strategies have fascinating mathematical structure. They give rise to:

- Constructions of **free categories with structure** of various kinds.
- **Full completeness** results characterizing the "space of proofs" for various logical systems.
- There are even connections with **geometry**, e.g. Temperley-Lieb and other diagram algebras [5].

2.9 Developments: The Game Semantics Landscape

Over the past 15 years, there has been an extensive development of Game Semantics in Computer Science.[4] One major area of application has been to the semantics of programming languages, where it has led to major progress in the construction of **fully abstract models** for programming languages embodying a wide range of computational effects, and starting with the first semantic construction of a fully abstract model for PCF, thus addressing a famous open problem in the field. It has been possible to give crisp characterizations of the "shapes" of computations carried out within certain **programming disciplines**: including purely functional programming [2, 19], stateful programming [9], general references [7, 33], programming with non-local jumps and exceptions [21, 22], non-determinism [16], probability [11], concurrency [15], names [6], and more. In many cases, game semantics have yielded the first, and often still the only, semantic construction of a fully abstract model for the language in question.

There has also been a parallel line of development of giving **full completeness** results for a range of logics and type theories, characterizing the "space of proofs" for a logic in terms of informatic or geometric constraints which pick out those processes which are proofs for that logic [8, 10, 12, 13, 25]. This enables a new look at such issues as the boundaries between classical and constructive logic, or the fine structure of polymorphism and second-order quantification.

More recently, there has been an algorithmic turn, and some striking applications to verification and program analysis [3, 6, 14, 24].

[4] A key quality of this form of game semantics, as compared to earlier work in the logical literature, such as the Game-Theoretical Semantics of Hintikka [17] and the Dialogical game semantics of Lorenzen and his school [26], is its **syntax-independence and compositionality**. Here compositionality refers, crucially, to the level of **strategies** as well as merely to the games.

2.10 Concluding Remarks

It should be emphasized that game semantics cannot be said to **subsume** CSP or other process calculi. Indeed, by imposing more structure, it makes it harder to achieve the same breadth of expressive power. Game semantics has been extended to concurrent languages with some success [15, 23], but the treatment to date is far from comprehensive. Moreover, in the course of modelling concurrent programming languages, some of the familiar issues of a proliferation of models and equivalences tend to recur, albeit in a considerably reduced form, as the setting is much more constrained.

Nevertheless, it seems fair to say that game semantics has found a fruitful path, combining the mathematical structure of denotational semantics with much of the behavioural expressiveness of process calculi. We hope to have conveyed something of how this trend in semantics arises naturally as a refinement of the CSP and process calculus point of view. It is a tribute to Tony Hoare's vision that many of his insights persist in this new guise, and combine gracefully with other structures, seemingly of quite a different character.

Acknowledgements My thanks to Bill Roscoe and Paul Levy for their comments on an earlier version of this paper, which led to several clarifications. The remaining obscurities and inaccuracies are entirely my responsibility.

References

1. Abramsky, S.: Semantics of interaction: an introduction to game semantics. In: Dybjer, P., Pitts, A. (eds.), Proceedings of the 1996 CLiCS Summer School, Isaac Newton Institute, pp. 1–31. Cambridge University Press, Cambridge (1997).
2. Abramsky, S., Jagadeesan, R., Malacaria, P.: Full abstraction for PCF. Inform. Comput. **163**, 409–470 (2000).
3. Abramsky, S.: Algorithmic game semantics: a tutorial introduction. In: Proof System-Reliability, pp. 21–47. Kluwer (2002).
4. Abramsky, S.: What are the fundamental structures of concurrency?: We still don't know! Electr. Notes Theor. Comput. Sci. (ENTCS) **162**, 37–41 (2006).
5. Abramsky, S.: Temperley-Lieb algebra: from knot theory to logic and computation via quantum mechanics. In: Chen, G., Kauffman, L., Lomonaco, S., (eds.), Mathematics of Quantum Computation and Quantum Technology, pp. 415–458. Taylor & Francis, New York (2007).
6. Abramsky, S., Ghica, D.R., Murawski, A.S., Stark, I.D.B., Ong. C.-H.L.: Nominal games and full abstraction for the nu-calculus. In: Proceedings LICS 150–159 (2004).
7. Abramsky, S., Honda, K., McCusker, G.: A fully abstract game semantics for general references. In: Proceedings LiCS 334–344 (1998).
8. Abramsky, S., Jagadeesan, R.: Games and full completeness for multiplicative linear logic. J. Symbolic Logic **59**, 543–574 (1994).
9. Abramsky, S., McCusker, G.: Linearity, sharing and state. In: O'Hearn, P., Tennent, R.D. (eds.) Algol-Like Languages, pp. 317–348. Birkhauser, Basel (1997).
10. Abramsky, S., Mellies, P.-A.: Concurrent games and full completeness. In: Proceedings LiCS 431–442 (1999).
11. Danos, V., Harmer, R.: Probabilistic game semantics. ACM Trans. Comput. Log. **3**(3), 359–382 (2002).

12. Blute, R., Hamano, M., Scott, P.J.: Softness of hypercoherences and MALL full completeness. Ann. Pure Appl. Logic **131**(1–3), 1–63 (2005).
13. Devarajan, H., Hughes, D., Plotkin, G., Pratt, V.: Full completeness of the multiplicative linear logic of Chu spaces. In: Proceedings LiCS 234–242 (1999).
14. Ghica, D.R., McCusker, G.: Reasoning about idealized algol using regular languages. In: Proccedings ICALP'00, pp. 103–116 (2000). LNCS 1853.
15. Ghica, D.R., Murawski, A.S.: Angelic semantics of fine-grained concurrency. In: Proccedings FOSSACS'04, pp. 211–225 (2004). LNCS 2987.
16. Harmer, R., McCusker, G.: A fully abstract game semantics for finite nondeterminism. In: Proceedings LiCS (1999).
17. Hintikka, J., Sandu, G.: Game-theoretical semantics, in van Benthem and ter Meulen. Handbook of Logic and Language. Elsevier, Amsterdam (1996).
18. Hoare, C.A.R.: Communicating Sequential Processes. Prentice Hall, New Jersey (1985).
19. Hyland, J.M.E., Ong, C.-H.L.: On full abstraction for PCF. Inform. Comput. **163**, 285–408, (2000).
20. Landin, P.J.: The next 700 programming languages. Commun. ACM (CACM) **9**(3), 157–166 (1966).
21. Laird, J.: Full abstraction for functional languages with control. Extended abstract. In: Proceedings LICS (1997).
22. Laird, J.: A fully abstract games semantics of local exceptions. Extended abstract. In: Proceedings LICS (2001).
23. Laird, J.: Game semantics for higher-order concurrency. In: Proceedings FSTTCS 2006, Springer LNCS Vol. 4337 pp. 417–428 (2006).
24. Legay, A., Murawski, A.S., Ouaknine, J., Worrell, J.: On automated verification of probabilistic programs. TACAS 173–187 (2008).
25. Loader, R.: Models of lambda calculi and linear logic. D.Phil. thesis, Oxford University (1994).
26. Lorenzen, P.: Ein dialogisches Konstruktivitätskriterium. In: Infinitistic Methods, 193–200 (1961).
27. Milner, R.: Communication and Concurrency. Prentice Hall, New Jersey (1989).
28. Milner, R., Parrow, J., Walker, D.: A calculus of mobile processes, I Inf. Comput. **100**(1), 1–40 (1992).
29. Milner, R., Parrow, J., Walker, D.: A calculus of mobile processes, II Inf. Comput. **100**(1), 41–77 (1992).
30. Milner, R.: Communicating and Mobile Systems: The Pi Calculus. Cambridge University Press, Cambridge (1999).
31. Parrow, J., Victor, B.: The Fusion Calculus: Expressiveness and Symmetry in Mobile Processes LICS 1998: 176–185.
32. Roscoe, A.W.: The Theory and Practice of Concurrency. Prentice Hall (1997).
33. Tzevelekos, N.: Full abstraction for nominal general references. In: Proceedings LICS pp. 399–410 (2007).

Chapter 3
On Mereologies in Computing Science

Dines Bjørner

Abstract In this paper we solve the following problems:

- We give a formal model of a large class of mereologies, with simple entities modelled as parts and their relations by connectors.
- We show that class applies to a wide variety of societal infrastructure component domains.
- We show that there is a class of `CSP` channel and process structures that correspond to the class of mereologies where mereology parts become `CSP` processes and connectors become channels; and where simple entity attributes become process states.

We have yet to prove to what extent the models satisfy the axiom systems for mereologies of, for example, [12] and a calculus of individuals [13]. Mereology is the study, knowledge and practice of part-hood relations: of the relations of part to whole and the relations of part to part within a whole. By parts we shall here understand simple entities – of the kind illustrated in this paper.

Manifest simple entities of domains are either continuous (fluid, gaseous) or discrete (solid, fixed), and if the latter, then either atomic or composite. It is how the sub-entities of a composite entity are "put together" that "makes up" a mereology of that composite entity – at least such as we shall study the mereology concept. In this paper, we shall study some ways of modelling the mereology of composite entities. One way of modelling mereologies is using sorts, observer functions and axioms (McCarthy style), another is using CSP.

IFIP WG2.3: A Laudatio and a Memory

This paper is in honour of Sir Tony Hoare. And the paper is in memory of Douglas Taylor Ross (1929–2007). The latter speculated quite a lot about mereologies at many IFIP WG2.3 meetings; not quite all members and

---

D. Bjørner (✉)
Fredsvej 11, DK-2840 Holte, Denmark
e-mail: bjorner@gmail.com, URL: www.imm.dtu.dk/~db

C.B. Jones et al. (eds.), *Reflections on the Work of C.A.R. Hoare*,
DOI 10.1007/978-1-84882-912-1_3, © Springer-Verlag London Limited 2010

observers understood everything; certainly not I. But I somehow knew it was a relevant issue. I think I now understand what Doug was saying. Here then, in this paper, is my interpretation of Doug's discourses. The former, today's celebrant, has given us many deep, yet simple, hence elegant, concepts. CSP is one of them. Therefore CSP will be applied, at the end of the paper, to express mereologies. IFIP WG 2.3 meetings in my days certainly weren't boring. I think that today I present a simple explanation of what then appeared as a not so simple concept. And I think that I can relate it to CSP.

3.1 Introduction

3.1.1 Physics and Societal Infrastructures

Physicists study that of nature which can be measured within us, around us and between "within" and "around"! To make mathematical models of physics phenomena, physics has helped develop and uses mathematics, notably calculus and statistics.

Domain engineers primarily studies societal infrastructure components which can be reasoned about, built and manipulated by humans. To make domain models of infrastructure components, domain engineering makes use of formal specification languages, their reasoning systems: formal testing, model checking and verification, and their tools.

Physicists turns to algebra in order to handle structures in nature. Algebra appears to be useful in a number of applications, to wit: the abstract modelling of chemical compounds. But there seem to be many structures in nature that cannot be captured in a satisfactory way by mathematics, including algebra and when captured in discrete mathematical disciplines such as sets, graph theory and combinatorics the "integration" of these mathematically represented structures with calculus (etc.) becomes awkward; it seems so much so that I know of no successful attempts.

Domain engineers turn to discrete mathematics – as embodied in formal specification languages and as "implementable" in programming languages – in order to handle structures in societal infrastructure components. These languages allow (a) the expression of arbitrarily complicated structures, (b) the evaluation of properties over such structures, (c) the "building & demolition" of such structures, and (d) the reasoning over such structures. They also allow the expression of dynamically varying structures – something mathematics is "not so good at" ! But the specification languages have two problems: (1) they do not easily, if at all, hhhhhandle continuity, that is, they do not embody calculus, or, for example, statistical concepts, etc., and (2) they handle actual structures of societal infrastructure components and attributes of atomic and composite entities of these – usually by identical techniques thereby blurring what we think is an important distinction.

3.1.2 From Simple Entities to Processes

We shall first consider the structural components of societal infrastructures as **simple entities**, without considering any operations on these entities. In fact, in this paper, we shall not consider operations on entities at all. This is possible, we claim, and in a sense in clear defiance of algebraic approaches – say as embodied in OO-methodologies – since, as we are claiming, that "world" of societal infrastructure components can be understood to quite some depth without considering their operations.

We shall then "map" parts and wholes into **processes** ! By an "ontological trick" we re-interpret simple entities as processes and their connections, i.e., how they are put together, as channels between processes.

It is all very simple, or, at least, we need to first make it simple before we complicate things. In this paper, we will only present the easy picture.

3.1.3 Structure of This Paper

The rest of the paper is organised as follows. In Sect. 3.2 we give a first main, a meta-example, of syntactic aspects of a class of mereologies. It narrates and formalises an abstraction of what is here called "parts": "assemblies" and "units". That is, structures of units with connectors that may be used to provide connections between parts. So an assembly has a mereology represented by units and sub-assemblies and their actual connections.

In Sect. 3.3 we informally show that the assembly/unit structures of Sect. 3.2 indeed model structures of a variety of infrastructure components.

Then, in Sect. 3.4, we discuss concepts of atomic and composite simple entities. With atomic simple entities we associate attributes, and these may exhibit conceptual structures, and with composite simple entities we associate attributes, any number of simple sub-entities and their mereology. We discuss notational and semantic means of expressing attributes and their possible structures, and sub-entities, and their mereologies. And we relate our presentation to the wider concept of mereology.

Section 3.5 "performs" the ontological trick of mapping the assembly and unit entities and their connections exemplified in Sect. 3.2 into CSP processes and channels, respectively – the second and last main – meta-example and now of semantic aspects of a class of mereologies.

The paper does not discuss relations between what is presented here and other approaches. As such we have renounced on the paper being a proper attempt at a proper scientific paper. We apologise.

3.2 A Syntactic Model of a Class of Mereologies

3.2.1 Systems, Assemblies, Units

We speak of systems as assemblies. From an assembly we can immediately observe a set of parts. Parts are either assemblies or units. We do not further define what assemblies and units are.

```
type
    S = A, A, U, P = A | U
value
    obs_Ps: (S|A) → P-set
```

Parts observed from an assembly are said to be immediately embedded in, i.e., within, that assembly. Two or more different parts of an assembly are said to be immediately adjacent to one another.

A system includes its environment. And we do not worry, so far, about the semiotics of all this !

Embeddedness and adjacency generalise to transitive relations.

Given obs_Ps we can define a function, xtr_Ps, which applies to an assembly a and which extracts all parts embedded in a and including a. The functions obs_Ps and xtr_Ps define the meaning of embeddedness.

```
value
    xtr_Ps: (S|A) → P-set
    xtr_Ps(a) ≡
        let ps = {a} ∪ obs_Ps(a) in ps ∪ union{xtr_Ps(a′)|a′:A•a′ ∈ ps} end
```

union is the distributed union operator. Parts have unique identifiers. All parts observable from a system are distinct.

```
type
    AUI
value
    obs_AUI: P → AUI
axiom
    ∀ a:A •
        let ps = obs_Ps(a) in
        ∀ p′,p″:P • {p′,p″}⊆ps ∧ p′≠p″ ⇒ obs_AUI(p′)≠obs_AUI(p″) ∧
        ∀ a′,a″:A • {a′,a″}⊆ps ∧ a′≠a″ ⇒ xtr_Ps(a′)∩ xtr_Ps(a″)={} end
```

3.2.2 "Adjacency" and "Within" Relations

Two parts, p,p′, are said to be *immediately next to*, i.e., i_next_to(p,p′)(a), one another in an assembly a if there exists an assembly, a', equal to or embedded in a such that p and p′ are observable in that assembly a′.

value

$\text{i\_next\_to}: P \times P \rightarrow A \xrightarrow{\sim} \textbf{Bool}, \textbf{pre}\ \text{i\_next\_to}(p,p')(a): p \neq p'$
$\text{i\_next\_to}(p,p')(a) \equiv \exists\, a':A \bullet a'=a \vee a' \in \text{xtr\_Ps}(a) \bullet \{p,p'\} \subseteq \text{obs\_Ps}(a')$

One part, p, is said to be *immediately within* another part, p′, in an assembly a if there exists an assembly, a′, equal to or embedded in a such that p is observable in a′.

value

$\text{i\_within}: P \times P \rightarrow A \xrightarrow{\sim} \textbf{Bool}$
$\text{i\_within}(p,p')(a) \equiv$
$\quad \exists\, a':A \bullet\ (a=a' \vee a' \in \text{xtr\_Ps}(a)) \bullet p'=a' \wedge p \in \text{obs\_Ps}(a')$

We can generalise the immediate "within" property. A part, p, is (transitively) within a part p′, within(p,p′)(a), of an assembly, a, either if p is immediately within p′ of that assembly, a, or if there exists a (proper) part p″ of p′ such that within(p″,p)(a).

value

$\text{within}: P \times P \rightarrow A \xrightarrow{\sim} \textbf{Bool}$
$\text{within}(p,p')(a) \equiv$
$\quad \text{i\_within}(p,p')(a) \vee \exists\, p'':P \bullet p'' \in \text{obs\_Ps}(p) \wedge \text{within}(p'',p')(a)$

The function within can be defined, alternatively, using xtr_Ps and i_within instead of obs_Ps and within:

value

$\text{within}': P \times P \rightarrow A \xrightarrow{\sim} \textbf{Bool}$
$\text{within}'(p,p')(a) \equiv$
$\quad \text{i\_within}(p,p')(a) \vee \exists\, p'':P \bullet p'' \in \text{xtr\_Ps}(p) \wedge \text{i\_within}(p'',p')(a)$

lemma: $\text{within} \equiv \text{within}'$

We can generalise the immediate "next to" property. Two parts p, p′ of an assembly, a, are adjacent if they are either "next to" one another or if there are two parts p_o, p'_o such that p, p′ are embedded in respectively p_o and p'_o and such that p_o, p'_o are immediately next to one another.

value

$\text{adjacent}: P \times P \rightarrow A \xrightarrow{\sim} \textbf{Bool}$
$\text{adjacent}(p,p')(a) \equiv$
$\quad \text{i\_next\_to}(p,p')(a) \vee$
$\quad \exists\, p'',p''':P \bullet \{p'',p'''\} \subseteq \text{xtr\_Ps}(a) \wedge \text{i\_next\_to}(p'',p''')(a) \wedge$
$\qquad ((p=p'') \vee \text{within}(p,p'')(a)) \wedge ((p'=p''') \vee \text{within}(p',p''')(a))$

3.2.3 Mereology, Part I

So far we have built a *ground mereology* model, $\mathcal{M}_{ground}$. Let $\sqsubseteq$ denote *parthood, x is part of y, $x \sqsubseteq y$.*

$$\forall x(x \sqsubseteq x)^1 \tag{3.1}$$

$$\forall x, y(x \sqsubseteq y) \wedge (y \sqsubseteq x) \Rightarrow (x = y) \tag{3.2}$$

$$\forall x, y, z(x \sqsubseteq y) \wedge (y \sqsubseteq z) \Rightarrow (x \sqsubseteq z) \tag{3.3}$$

Let $\sqsubset$ denote *proper parthood, x is part of y, $x \sqsubset y$.* Formula 3.4 defines $x \sqsubset y$. Equivalence 3.5 can be proven to hold:

$$\forall x \sqsubset y =_{\text{def}} x(x \sqsubseteq y) \wedge \neg(x = y) \tag{3.4}$$

$$\forall \forall x, y(x \sqsubseteq y) \quad \Leftrightarrow \quad (x \sqsubset y) \vee (x = y) \tag{3.5}$$

The *proper part* $(x \sqsubset y)$ relation is a strict partial ordering:

$$\forall x \neg(x \sqsubset x) \tag{3.6}$$

$$\forall x, y(x \sqsubset y) \Rightarrow \neg(y \sqsubset x) \tag{3.7}$$

$$\forall x, y, z(x \sqsubset y) \wedge (y \sqsubset z) \Rightarrow (x \sqsubset z) \tag{3.8}$$

Overlap, $\bullet$, is also a relation of parts: Two individuals overlap if they have parts in common:

$$x \bullet y =_{\text{def}} \exists z(z \sqsubset x) \wedge (z \sqsubset y) \tag{3.9}$$

$$\forall x(x \bullet x) \tag{3.10}$$

$$\forall x, y(x \bullet y) \Rightarrow (y \bullet x) \tag{3.11}$$

Proper overlap, $\circ$, can be defined:

$$x \circ y =_{\text{def}} (x \bullet x) \wedge \neg(x \sqsubseteq y) \wedge \neg(y \sqsubseteq x) \tag{3.12}$$

Whereas Formulas 3.1–3.11 hold of the model of mereology we have shown so far, Formula 3.12 does not. In the next section we shall repair that situation.

The *proper part* relation, $\sqsubset$, reflects the *within* relation. The *disjoint* relation, $\not\!\phi$, reflects the *adjacency* relation

$$x \not\!\phi\, y =_{\text{def}} \neg(x \bullet y) \tag{3.13}$$

Disjointness is symmetric:

$$\forall x, y(x \not\!\phi\, y) \Rightarrow (y \not\!\phi\, x) \tag{3.14}$$

[1] Our notation now is not RSL but some conventional first-order predicate logic notation.

The *weak supplementation* relation, Formula 3.15, expresses that if y is a proper part of x then there exists a part z such that z is a proper part of x and z and y are disjoint That is, whenever an individual has one proper part, then it has more than one.

$$\forall x, y(y \sqsubset x) \Rightarrow \exists z(z \sqsubset x) \wedge (z \not\oint y) \tag{3.15}$$

Formulas 3.1–3.3 and 3.15 together determine the *minimal mereology*, $\mathcal{M}_{\mathcal{M}\text{inimal}}$. Formula 3.15 does not hold of the model of mereology we have shown so far. We shall comment on this in Sect. 3.4.2.

3.2.4 Connectors

So far we have only covered notions of parts being next to other parts or within one another. We shall now add to this a rather general notion of parts being otherwise related. That notion is one of connectors.

Connectors provide for connections between parts. A connector is an ability to be connected. A connection is the actual fulfillment of that ability. Connections are relations between pairs of parts. Connections "cut across" the "classical" *parts being part of the (or a) whole* and *parts being related by embeddedness or adjacency*.

For now, we do not "ask" for the meaning of connectors !

Figure 3.2 on the facing page "adds" connectors to Fig. 3.1. The idea is that connectors allow an assembly to be connected to any embedded part, and allow two adjacent parts to be connected.

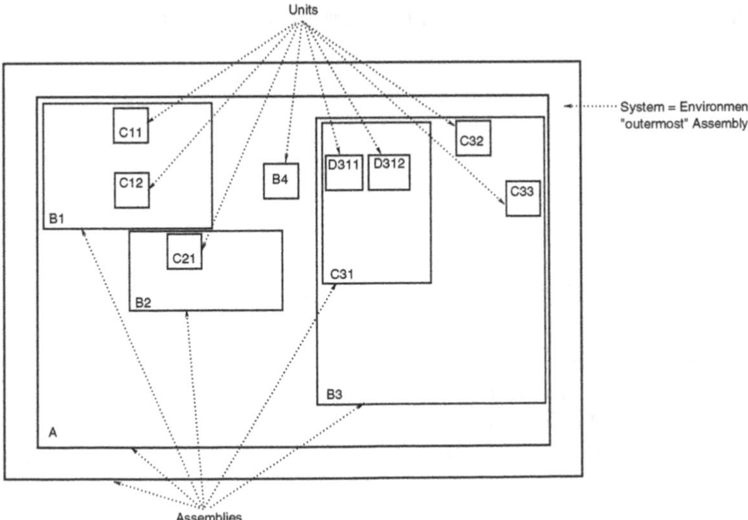

Fig. 3.1 Assemblies and units "embedded" in an Environment

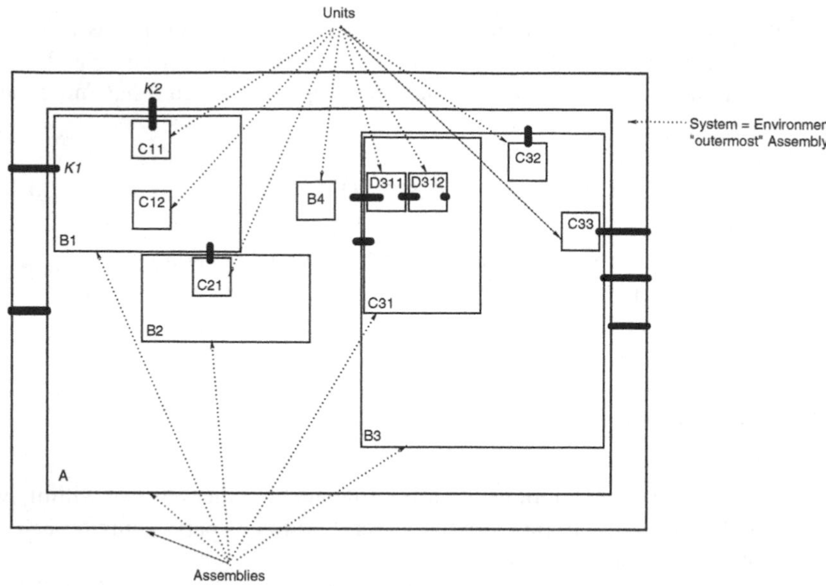

Fig. 3.2 Assembly and unit connectors: internal and external

In Fig. 3.2 the environment is connected, by *K2* (without, as we shall later see, interfering with assemblies A and B1), to part C11; the "external world" is connected, by K1, to B1; etc. Later we shall discuss more general forms of connectors.

From a system we can observe all its connectors. From a connector we can observe its unique connector identifier and the set of part identifiers of the parts that the connector connects. All part identifiers of system connectors identify parts of the system. All observable connector identifiers of parts identify connectors of the system.

type
  K
value
  obs_Ks: S → K-**set**
  obs_KI: K → KI
  obs_Is: K → AUI-**set**
  obs_KIs: P → KI-**set**
axiom
  ∀ k:K • **card** obs_Is(k)=2,
  ∀ s:S,k:K • k ∈ obs_Ks(s) ⇒
    ∃ p:P • p ∈ xtr_Ps(s) ⇒ obs_AUI(p) ∈ obs_Is(k),
  ∀ s:S,p:P • ∀ ki:KI • ki ∈ obs_KIs(p) ⇒
    ∃! k:K • k ∈ obs_Ks(s) ∧ ki=obs_KI(k)

This model allows for a rather "free-wheeling" notion of connectors: one that allows internal connectors to "cut across" embedded and adjacent parts; and one that allows external connectors to "penetrate" from an outside to any embedded part.

We need to define an auxiliary function. xtr∀KIs(p) applies to a system and yields all its connector identifiers.

```
value
    xtr∀KIs: S → KI-set
    xtr∀Ks(s) ≡ {obs_KI(k)|k:K•k ∈ obs_Ks(s)}
```

3.2.5 *Mereology, Part II*

We shall interpret connections as follows: A connection between parts p_i and p_j that enjoy a p_i adjacent to p_j relationship means $p_i \circ p_j$, i.e., although parts p_i and p_j are adjacent they do *share* "something", i.e., have something *in common*. What that "something" is we shall comment on in Sect. 3.5.4. A connection between parts p_i and p_j that enjoy a p_i within p_j relationship, does not add other meaning than commented upon in Sect. 3.5.4.

With the above interpretation we may arrive at the following, perhaps somewhat "awkward-looking" case: a connection connects two adjacent parts p_i and p_j where part p_i is within part p_{i_o} and part p_j is within part p_{j_o} where parts p_{i_o} and p_{j_o} are adjacent but not otherwise connected. How are we to explain that ! Since we have not otherwise interpreted the meaning of parts, we can just postulate that "so it is" ! We shall, in Sect. 3.5.4, more satisfactory explanation.

In Sect. 3.2.3 we introduced the following operators: $\sqsubseteq, \sqsubset, \bullet, \circ$, and $\not\!\!\!\phi$. In some of the mereology literature [12–14] these operators are symbolised with caligraphic letters: $\sqsubseteq$: $\mathcal{P}$: part, $\sqsubset$: $\mathcal{PP}$: proper part, $\bullet$: $\mathcal{O}$: overlap and $\not\!\!\!\phi$: $\mathcal{U}$: underlap.

3.2.6 *Discussion*

3.2.6.1 Summary

This ends our first model of a concept of mereology. The parts are those of assemblies and units. The relations between parts and the whole are, on one hand, those of embeddedness, i.e., within, and adjacency, i.e., adjacent, and on the other hand, those expressed by connectors: relations between arbitrary parts and between arbitrary parts and the exterior.

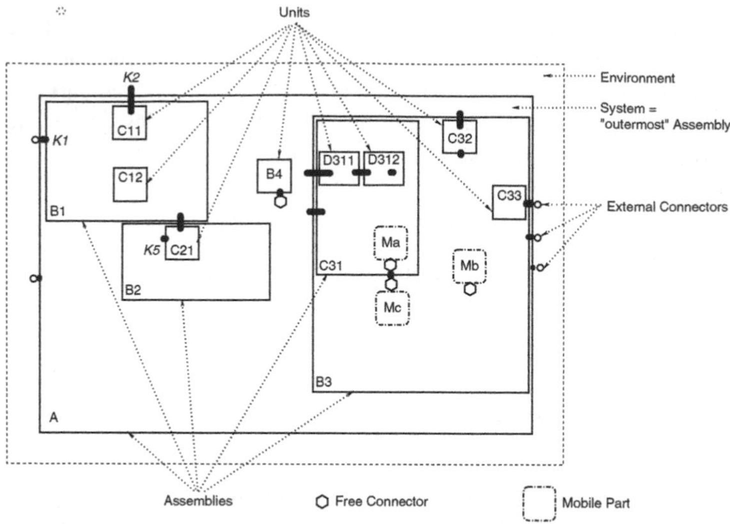

Fig. 3.3 Mobile parts and free connectors

3.2.6.2 Extensions

A number of extensions are possible: one can add "mobile" parts and "free" connectors, and one can further add operations that allow such mobile parts to move from one assembly to another along routes of connectors. Free connectors and mobility assumes static versus dynamic parts and connectors: a free connector is one which allows a mobile part to be connected to another part, fixed or mobile; and the potentiality of a move of a mobile part introduces a further dimension of dynamics of 3.2.6.3 comments a mereology.

We shall leave the modelling of free connectors and mobile parts to another time. Suffice it now to indicate that the mereology model given so far is relevant: that it applies to a somewhat wide range of application domain structures, and that it thus affords a uniform treatment of proper formal models of these application domain structures.

3.3 Discussion & Interpretation

Before a semantic treatment of the concept of mereology let us review what we have done and let us interpret our abstraction (i.e., relate it to actual societal infrastructure components).

3.3.1 What We Have Done So Far ?

We have presented a model that is claimed to abstract essential mereological properties of machine assemblies, railway nets, the oil industry, oil pipelines, buildings and their with installations, hospitals, etc.

3.3.2 Six Interpretations

Let us substantiate the claims made in the previous paragraph. We will do so, albeit informally, in the next many paragraphs. Our substantiation is a form of diagrammatic reasoning. Subsets of diagrams will be claimed to represent parts, while other subsets will be claimed to represent connectors. The reasoning is incomplete.

3.3.2.1 Air Traffic

Figure 3.4 shows nine (9) boxes and eighteen (18) lines. Together they form an assembly. Individually boxes and lines represent units. The rounded corner boxes denote buildings. The sharp corner box denotes an aircraft. Lines denote radio telecommunication. Only where lines touch boxes do we have connections. These are shown as red horizontal or vertical boxes at both ends of the double-headed arrows, overlapping both the arrows and the boxes. The index ranges shown attached to, i.e., labelling each unit, shall indicate that there are a multiple of the "single" (thus representative) unit shown. Notice that the "box" units are fixed installations and that the double-headed arrows designate the ether where radio waves

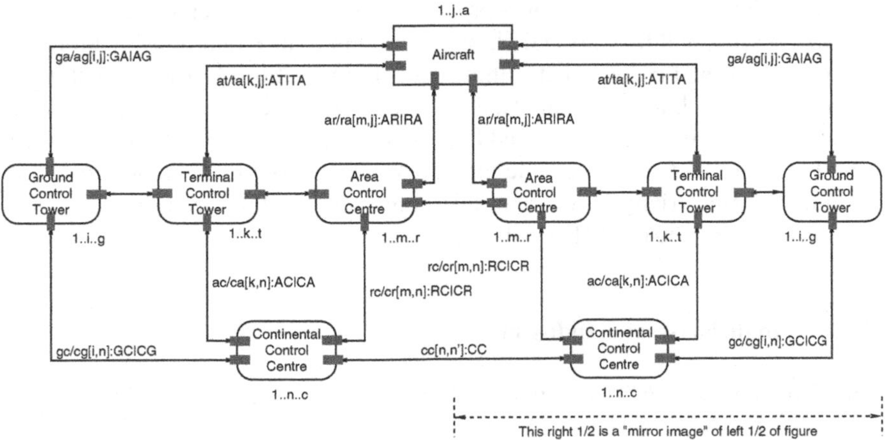

Fig. 3.4 An air traffic system. *Black boxes* and *lines* are units; *red boxes* are connections

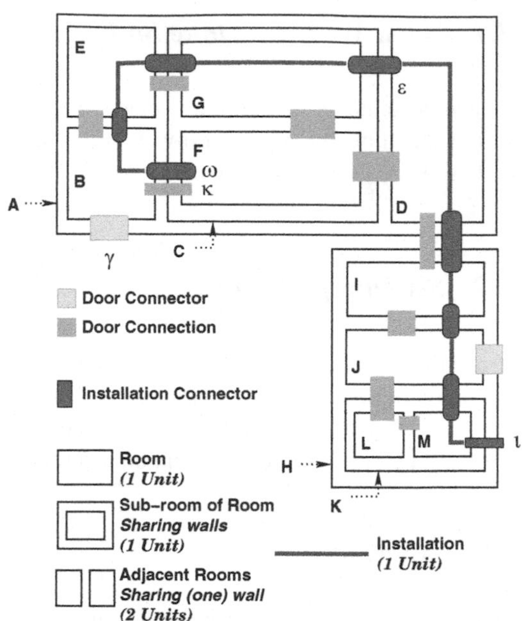

Fig. 3.5 A building plan with installation

may propagate. We could, for example, assume that each such line is characterised by a combination of location and (possibly encrypted) radio communication frequency. That would allow us to consider all line for not overlapping. And if they were overlapping, then that must have been a decision of the air traffic system.

3.3.2.2 Buildings

Figure 3.5 shows a building plan – as an assembly of two neighbouring, common wall-sharing buildings, A and H, probably built at different times; with room sections B, C, D and E contained within A, and room sections I, J and K within H; with room sections L and M within K; and F and G within C. Connector γ provides means of a connection between A and B. Connection κ provides "access" between B and F. Connectors ι and ω enable input, respectively, output adaptors (receptor, resp. outlet) for electricity (or water, or oil), connection ϵ allow electricity (or water, or oil) to be conducted through a wall, etc.

3.3.2.3 Financial Service Industry

Figure 3.6 shows seven (7) larger boxes (six of which are shown by dashed lines) and twelve (12) double-arrowed lines. Where double-arrowed lines touch upon (dashed) boxes we have connections (also to inner boxes). Six (6) of the boxes, the dashed line boxes, are assemblies, five (5) of them consisting of a variable number of units;

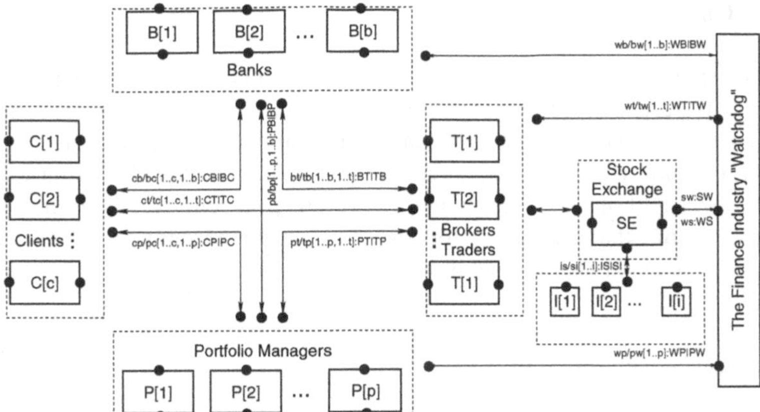

Fig. 3.6 A financial service industry

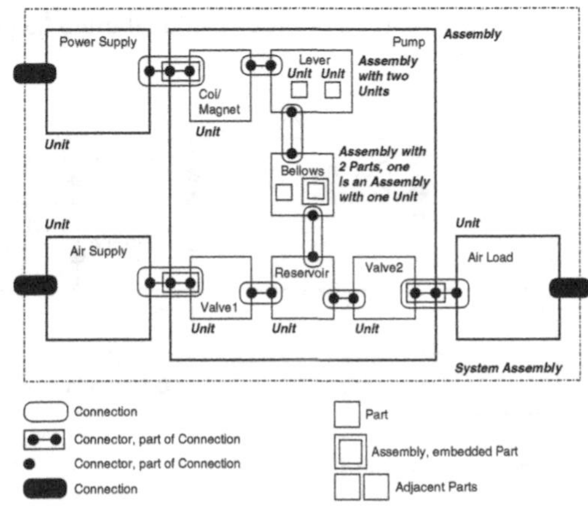

Fig. 3.7 An air pump, i.e., a physical mechanical system

five (5) are here shown as having three units each with bullets "between" them to designate "variability". People, not shown, access the outermost (and hence the "innermost" boxes, but the latter is not shown) through connectors, shown by bullets, •.

3.3.2.4 Machine Assemblies

Figure 3.7 shows a machine assembly. Square boxes show assemblies or units. Bullets, •, show connectors. Strands of two or three bullets on a thin line, encircled by a rounded box, show connections. The full, i.e., the level 0, assembly consists of four parts and three internal and three external connections. The pump unit is an assembly of six (6) parts, five (5) internal connections and three (3) external connectors, etc. One connector and some connections afford "transmission" of electrical power. Other connections convey torque. Two connectors convey input air, respectively, output air.

3.3.2.5 Oil Industry

Figure 3.8 shows an assembly consisting of fourteen (14) assemblies, left-to-right: one oil field, a crude oil pipeline system, two refineries and one, say, gasoline distribution network, two seaports, an ocean (with oil and ethanol tankers and their sea lanes), three (more) seaports, and three, say gasoline and ethanol distribution networks. Between all of the assembly units there are connections, and from some of the assembly units there are connectors (to an external environment). The crude oil pipeline system assembly unit will be concretised next.

A Concretised Assembly Unit

Figure 3.9 on the following page shows a pipeline system. It consists of 32 units: fifteen (15) pipe units (shown as directed arrows and labelled p1–p15), four (4) input node units (shown as small circles, ∘, and labelled in*i*–in*ℓ*), four (4) flow pump units (shown as small circles, ∘, and labelled fp*a*–fp*d*), five (5) valve units (shown as

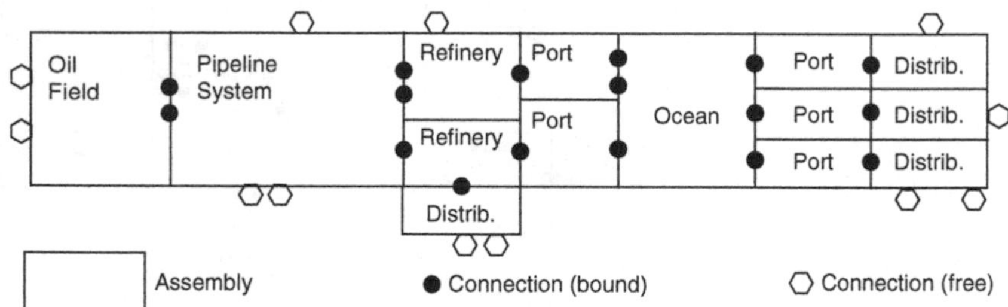

Fig. 3.8 A Schematic of an oil industry

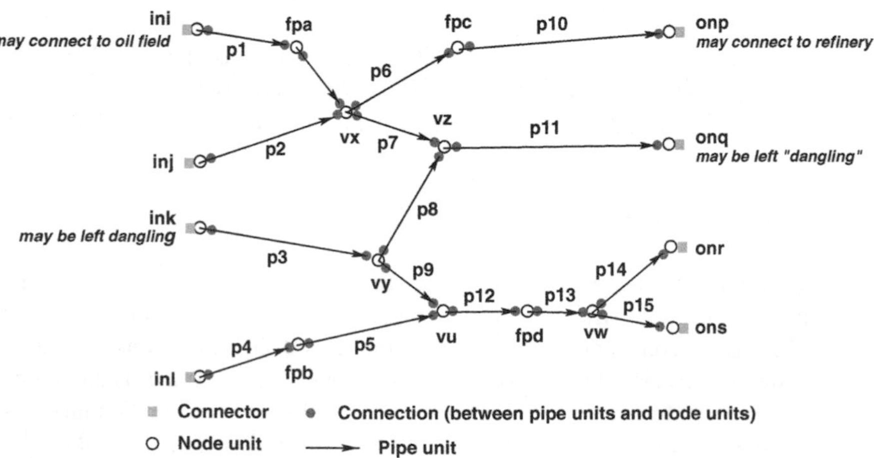

Fig. 3.9 A pipeline system

small circles, ∘, and labelled vx–vw), and four (4) output node units (shown as small circles, ∘, and labelled onp–ons). In this example the routes through the pipeline system start with node units and end with node units, alternates between node units and pipe units, and are connected as shown by fully filled-out red[2] disc connections. Input and output nodes have input, respectively, output connectors, one each, and shown with green.[3]

3.3.2.6 Railway Nets

Figure 3.10 on the next page diagrams four rail units, each with their two, three or four connectors. Multiple instances of these rail units can be assembled as shown on Fig. 3.11 on the facing page into proper rail nets.

Figure 3.11 on the next page diagrams an example of a proper rail net. It is assembled from the kind of units shown in Fig. 3.10. In Fig. 3.11 consider just the four dashed boxes: The dashed boxes are assembly units. Two designate stations, two designate lines (tracks) between stations. We refer to the caption four line text of Fig. 3.10 on the facing page for more "statistics". We could have chosen to show, instead, for each of the four "dangling" connectors, a composition of a connection, a special "end block" rail unit and a connector.

3.3.3 *Discussion*

It requires a somewhat more laborious effort, than just "flashing" and commenting on these diagrams, to show that the modelling of essential aspects of their structures can indeed be done by simple instantiation of the model given in the

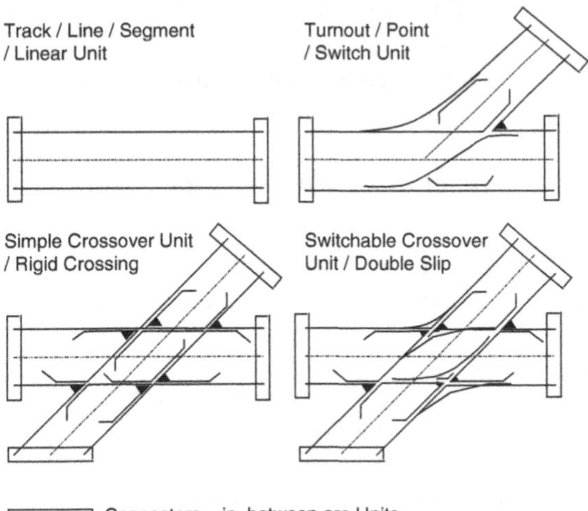

Fig. 3.10 Four example rail units

[2] This paper is most likely not published with colours, so red will be shown as darker colour.

[3] Shown as lighter coloured connections.

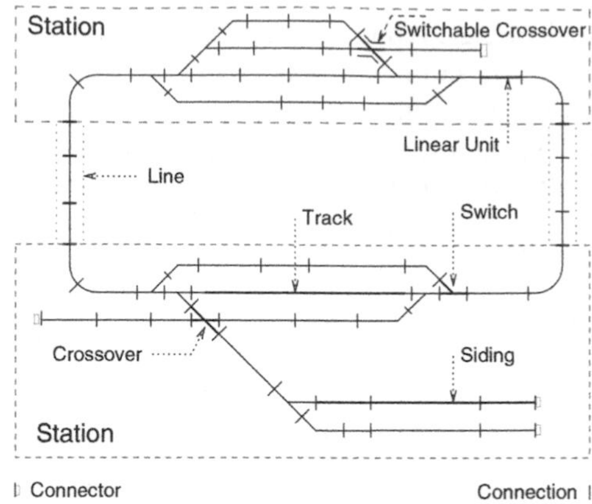

Fig. 3.11 A "model" railway net. An assembly of four Assemblies: two stations and two lines; *lines* here consist of linear rail units; stations of all the kinds of units shown in Fig. 3.10. There are 66 connections and four "dangling" connectors

previous section. We can refer to a number of documents which give rather detailed domain models of air traffic [1], container line industry [9],[4], financial service industry (banks, credit card companies, brokers, traders and securities and commodities exchanges, insurance companies, etc.),[5] health-care [16, Sects. 10.2.2 + 10.4.2], IT security [17], "the market" (consumers, retailers, wholesalers, producers and distribution chains) [2], "the" oil industry,[6] transportation nets,[7] railways [3, 4, 32, 33, 39] and [16, Sect. 10.6],[8] etc. Seen in the perspective of the present paper we claim that much of the modelling work done in those references can now be considerably shortened and trust in these models correspondingly increased.

3.4 Simple Entities

The reason for our interest in "simple entities" is that assemblies and units of systems possess static and dynamic properties which become contexts and states of the processes into which we shall "transform" simple entities.

3.4.1 Observable Phenomena

We shall just consider "simple entities". [9] By a simple entity we shall here understand a phenomenon that we can designate, viz. see, touch, hear, smell or taste, or

[4] http://www2.imm.dtu.dk/~db/container-paper.pdf

[5] http://www2.imm.dtu.dk/~db/fsi.pdf

[6] http://www2.imm.dtu.dk/~db/pipeline.pdf

[7] http://www2.imm.dtu.dk/~db/transport.pdf

[8] http://www.railwaydomain.org/

[9] We use the name "simple entities" in contrast to "entities" which we see as comprising all of simple entities, functions, events and behaviours. "Interesting" functions and normal events involve all forms of entities.

measure by some instrument (of physics, incl. chemistry). A simple entity thus has properties. A simple entity is either continuous or is discrete, and then it is either atomic or composite.

3.4.1.1 Attributes: Types and Values

By an attribute we mean a simple property of an entity. *A simple entity has properties* $p_i, p_j, \ldots, p_k$. Typically we express attributes by a pair of a type designator: *the attribute is of type* V, and a value: *the attribute has value* v (of type V, i.e., $v : V$). A simple entity may have many simple properties. A continuous entity, like "oil", may have the following attributes: type: *petroleum*, kind: *Brent-crude*, amount: *6 barrels*, price: *45 US \$/barrel*. An *atomic* entity, like a "person", may have the following attributes: gender: *male*, name: *Dines Bjørner*, birth date: *4. Oct. 1937*, marital status: *married*. A *composite* entity, like a railway system, may have the following attributes: country: *Denmark*, name: *DSB*, electrified: *partly*, owner: *independent public enterprise owned by Danish Ministry of Transport.*

3.4.1.2 Continuous Simple Entities

A simple entity is said to be continuous if, within limits, reasonably sizable amounts of the simple entity can be arbitrarily decomposed into smaller parts each of which still remain simple continuous entities of the same simple entity kind. Examples of continuous entities are: oil, i.e., any fluid, air, i.e., any gas, time period and a measure of fabric.

3.4.1.3 Discrete Simple Entities

A simple entity is said to be discrete if its immediate structure is not continuous. A simple discrete entity may, however, contain continuous sub-entities. Examples of discrete entities are: persons, rail units, oil pipes, a group of persons, a railway line and an oil pipeline.

Atomic Simple Entities

A simple entity is said to be atomic if it cannot be meaningfully decomposed into parts where these parts have a useful "value" in the context in which the simple entity is viewed and while still remaining an instantiation of that entity. Thus a "physically able person", which we consider atomic, can, from the point of physical ability, not be decomposed into meaningful parts: a leg, an arm, a head, etc. Other atomic entities could be a rail unit, an oil pipe, or a hospital bed. The only thing characterising an atomic entity are its attributes.

Composite Simple Entities

A simple entity, c, is said to be composite if it can be meaningfully decomposed into sub-entities that have separate meaning in the context in which c is viewed. We exemplify some composite entities. (1) A *railway net* can be decomposed into a set of one or more *train lines* and a set of two or more *train stations*. Lines and stations are themselves composite entities. (2) An *Oil industry* whose decomposition includes: one or more *oil fields*, one or more *pipeline systems*, one or more *oil refineries* and one or more *one or more oil product distribution systems*. Each of these sub-entities are also composite. Composite simple entities are thus characterisable by their attributes, their sub-entities, and the mereology of how these sub-entities are put together.

3.4.2 Mereology, Part III

Formula 3.15 on page 53 expresses that whenever an individual has one proper part then it has more than one. We mentioned there, Page 53, that we would comment on the fact that our model appears to allow that assemblies may have just one proper part. We now do so. We shall still allow assemblies to have just one proper part – in the sense of a sub-assembly or a unit – but we shall interpret the fact that an assembly always has at least one attribute. Therefore we shall "generously" interpret the set of attributes of an assembly to constitute a part. In Sect. 3.5 we shall see how attributes of both units and assemblies of the interpreted mereology contribute to the state components of the unit and assembly processes.

3.4.3 Discussion

In Sect. 3.3.2 we interpreted the model of mereology in six examples. The units of Sect. 3.2 which in that section were left uninterpreted now got individuality – in the form of aircraft, building rooms, rail units and oil pipes. Similarly for the assemblies of Sect. 3.2. They became pipeline systems, oil refineries, train stations, banks, etc. In conventional modelling the mereology of an infrastructure component, of the kinds exemplified in Sect. 3.3.2, was modelled by modelling that infrastructure component's special mereology together, "in line", with the modelling of unit and assembly attributes. With the model of Sect. 3.2 now available we do not have to model the mereological aspects, but can, instead, instantiate the model of Sect. 3.2 appropriately. We leave that to be reported upon elsewhere. In many conventional infrastructure component models it was often difficult to separate what was mereology from what were attributes.

3.5 A Semantic Model of a Class of Mereologies

3.5.1 The Mereology Entities ≡ Processes

The model of mereology presented in Sect. 3.2 (Pages 50–56) focused on the following simple entities (1) the assemblies, (2) the units and (3) the connectors. To assemblies and units we associate CSP processes, and to connectors we associate a CSP channels, one-by-one [28, 29, 34, 36]. The connectors form the mereological attributes of the model.

3.5.2 Channels

The CSP channels are each "anchored" into two parts: if a part is a unit then in "its corresponding" unit process, and if a part is an assembly then in "its corresponding" assembly process. From a system assembly we can extract all connector identifiers. They become indexes into an array of channels. Each of the connector channel identifiers is mentioned in exactly two unit or assembly processes.

value
  s:S
  kis:KI-**set** = xtr∀KIs(s)
type
  ChMap = AUI $\underset{m}{\rightarrow}$ KI-**set**
value
  cm:ChMap = [obs_AUI(p)↦obs_KIs(p)|p:P•p ∈ xtr_Ps(s)]
channel
  ch[i|i:KI•i ∈ kis] MSG

3.5.3 Process Definitions

value
  system: S → **Process**
  system(s) ≡ assembly(s)

  assembly: a:A→**in,out** {ch[cm(i)]|i:KI•i ∈ cm(obs_AUI(a))} **process**
  assembly(a) ≡
    $\mathcal{M}_{\mathcal{A}}$(a)(obs_A$\Sigma$(a)) ‖
    ‖ {assembly(a′)|a′:A•a′ ∈ obs_Ps(a)} ‖
    ‖ {unit(u)|u:U•u ∈ obs_Ps(a)}
  obs_AΣ: A → AΣ

$\mathcal{M}_\mathcal{A}$: a:A→AΣ→**in,out** {ch[cm(i)]|i:KI•i ∈ cm(obs_AUI(a))} **process**
$\mathcal{M}_\mathcal{A}$(a)(aσ) ≡ $\mathcal{M}_\mathcal{A}$(a)(A$\mathcal{F}$(a)(aσ))

A$\mathcal{F}$: a:A → AΣ → **in,out** {ch[em(i)]|i:KI•i ∈
cm(obs_AUI(a))}×AΣ

unit: u:U → **in,out** {ch[cm(i)]|i:KI•i ∈ cm(obs_UI(u))} **process**
unit(u) ≡ $\mathcal{M}_\mathcal{U}$(u)(obs_UΣ(u))
obs_UΣ: U → UΣ

$\mathcal{M}_\mathcal{U}$: u:U → UΣ → **in,out** {ch[cm(i)]|i:KI•i ∈ cm(obs_UI(u))} **process**
$\mathcal{M}_\mathcal{U}$(u)(uσ) ≡ $\mathcal{M}_\mathcal{U}$(u)(U$\mathcal{F}$(u)(uσ))

U$\mathcal{F}$: U → UΣ → **in,out** {ch[em(i)]|i:KI • i ∈ cm(obs_AUI(u))} UΣ

The meaning processes $\mathcal{M}_\mathcal{A}$ and $\mathcal{M}_\mathcal{U}$ are generic. Their sole purpose is to provide a never ending recursion. "In-between" they "make use" of assembly, respectively, unit specific functions here symbolised by $U\mathcal{A}$, respectively, $U\mathcal{F}$.

3.5.4 Mereology, Part IV

A little more meaning has been added to the notions of parts and connections. The within and adjacent to relations between parts (assemblies and units) reflects a phenomenological world of geometry, and the connected relation between parts (assemblies and units) reflects both physical and conceptual world understandings: physical world in that, for example, radio waves cross geometric "boundaries", and conceptual world in that ontological classifications typically reflect lattice orderings where *overlaps* likewise cross geometric "boundaries".

3.5.5 Discussion

3.5.5.1 Partial Evaluation

The assembly function "first" "functions" as a compiler. The "compiler" translates an assembly structure into three process expressions: the $\mathcal{M}_\mathcal{A}(a)(a\sigma)$ invocation, the parallel composition of assembly processes, a', one for each sub-assembly of a, and the parallel composition of unit processes, one for each unit of assembly a – with these three process expressions "being put in parallel". The recursion in assembly ends when a sub-. . . -assembly consists of no sub-sub-. . . -assemblies. Then the compiling task ends and the many generated $\mathcal{M}_\mathcal{A}(a)(a\sigma)$ and $\mathcal{M}_\mathcal{U}(u)(u\sigma)$ process expressions are invoked.

3.5.6 *Generalised Channel Processes*

We can refine the meaning of connectors. Each connector, so far, was modelled by a CSP channel. CSP channels serve both as a synchronisation and as a communication medium. We now suggest to model it by a process. A channel process can be thought of as having four channels and a buffering process. Connector, κ:K, may connect parts π_i, π_j. The four channels could be thought of as indexed by (κ, π_i), (π_i, κ), (κ, π_j) and (π_j, κ). The process buffer could, depending on parts p_i, p_j, be either queues, sets, bags, stacks or other.

3.6 Conclusion

3.6.1 *Summary*

We have proposed a simple model which we claim captures a large variety of structures of societal infrastructure components (Sect. 3.2). The model focused on parts, their within and next to one another relation as well as connections between parts. We have, rather briefly, held that model up against a variety of diagrammatic renditions of specific societal infrastructure components (Sect. 3.3) and claimed that the model is relevant for their formalisation. We have then reviewed the concepts of continuous (fluid, gaseous) and discrete (fixed, solid) simple entities and especially discussed the discrete atomic and composite simple entities (Sect. 3.4) and their attributes and sub-entities. We have done so in order first to [again] single out the topic of the mereology of composite (discrete) entities, and then to prepare for the next section's process states (and environments) – modelled from simple entity attributes. We have finally shown how one can relate simple entities to CSP processes and connectors to CSP channels (Sect. 3.5).

3.6.2 *What Have We Achieved?*

There is, as we indicated, in Sect. 3.3, a bewildering variety of societal infrastructure component and "gadget" structures – and these structures must be modelled. We claim that the mereology model (of Sect. 3.2) provides a common denominator for all of these: that the model is generic and can be simply instantiated for each of the shown, and, we again claim for many other domain examples. We claim that the model (of Sect. 3.2) can serve as a basis for investigating the axiom systems proposed for mereology [12] and a calculus of individuals [13]. We thus claim to have a simple model for the kind of mereologies presented in the literature.

3.6.3 Open Points

We have yet to carefully demonstrate two classes of things: (1) to properly refine our mereology model into models for the sub-entity structures of specific societal infrastructure components, etc.; and (2) to identify the exact relations between our model of mereology and the axiom systems presented in the literature [12, 13].

3.6.4 The Memorial and The Laudatio

On Douglas Taylor Ross:

> *It is possible his work in that direction became too pioneering or too advanced for his colleagues, including us. Who knows, the future may prove him right. At any rate, his reflections regularly made me think.*
>
> `Michel Sintzoff, 2007`

Acknowledgements I thank University of Saarland for hosting me during some of the time when I wrote this paper.

Bibliographical Notes

The present paper uses the `RAISE` Specification Language [5–7]. The concept of mereology appears to have been first studied by Leśniewski [31, 38]. Seminal mereology papers appears to be [12, 13, 30]. Since the present paper was first written and presented, April 16, 2009, and its revision for publication, I have thought more about the mereological issues and, at the instigation of Tony Hoare, combined these with a study of Bertrand Russell's *Philosophy of Logical Atomism* [35], [37, Vol. 8, Part III, Chap. 17, pp. 157–244]. The outcome became [8].

References

1. Bjørner, D.: Software systems engineering – from domain analysis to requirements capture: an air traffic control example. In: 2nd Asia-Pacific Software Engineering Conference (APSEC '95). IEEE Computer Society, 6–9 December 1995. Brisbane, Queensland, Australia.
2. Bjørner, D.: Domain models of "The Market" – in Preparation for e–transaction systems. In: Kilov, H., Baclawski, K. (eds.) Practical Foundations of Business and System Specifications, Kluwer Academic Press, The Netherlands, December 2002.
3. Bjørner, D.: Dynamics of railway nets: on an interface between automatic control and software engineering. In: Tsugawa, S., Aoki, M. (eds.) CTS2003: 10th IFAC Symposium on Control in Transportation Systems, Oxford, UK, August 4–6 2003. Elsevier Science Ltd. Symposium held at Tokyo, Japan.

4. Bjørner, D.: New results and trends in Formal techniques for the development of software for transportation systems. In: Tarnai, G., Schnieder, E. (eds.) FORMS2003: Symposium on Formal Methods for Railway Operation and Control Systems. Institut für Verkehrssicherheit und Automatisierungstechnik, Techn.Univ. of Braunschweig, Germany, 15–16 May 2003. Conf. held at Techn.Univ. of Budapest, Hungary, Germany.
5. Bjørner, D.: Software Engineering, Vol. 1: Abstraction and Modelling. Texts in Theoretical Computer Science, the EATCS Series. Springer, Berlin Heidelberg, Germany (2006).
6. Bjørner, D.: Software Engineering, Vol. 2: Specification of Systems and Languages. Texts in Theoretical Computer Science, the EATCS Series. Springer, Berlin Heidelberg, Germany (2006) Chapters 12–14 are primarily authored by Christian Krog Madsen.
7. Bjørner, D.: Software Engineering, Vol. 3: Domains, Requirements and Software Design. Texts in Theoretical Computer Science, the EATCS Series. Springer, Berlin Heidelberg, Germany (2006).
8. Bjørner, D.: An emerging domain science – a role for Stanisław Leśniewski's Mereology and Bertrand Russell's philosophy of logical atomism. Higher-Order and Symbolic Computation (2009).
9. Bjørner, D.: Domain Engineering. http://www2.imm.dtu.dk/~db/container-paper.pdf
10. Bjørner, D.: Domain Engineering: Technology Management, Research and Engineering. JAIST Press, March 2009. The monograph contains the following chapters: [15–24].
11. Bjørner, D., and Henson, M.C.: (eds.) Logics of Specification Languages. EATCS Series, Monograph in Theoretical Computer Science. Springer, Heidelberg, Germany (2008).
12. Casati, R. and Varzi, A.: Parts and Places: the Structures of Spatial Representation. MIT Press, Cambridge, Mass., USA (1999).
13. Clarke, B.L.: A calculus of individuals based on 'Connection'. Notre Dame J. Formal Logic **22**(3), 204–218 (1981).
14. Clarke, B.L.: Individuals and points. Notre Dame J. Formal Logic, **26**(1): 61–75 (1985).
15. Bjørner, D.: Chapter 5: The Triptych process model – process assessment and improvement, Domain Engineering: Technology Management, Research and Engineering, pp. 107–138. JAIST Press, Nomi, Ishikawa, Japan (March 2009).
16. Bjørner, D.: Chapter 10: Towards a family of script languages – licenses and contracts – incomplete sketch, Domain Engineering: Technology Management, Research and Engineering [10], pp. 283–328. JAIST Press, (March 2009).
17. Bjørner, D.: Chapter 9: Towards a model of IT security – the ISO information security code of practice – an incomplete rough sketch analysis, Domain Engineering: Technology Management, Research and Engineering [10], pp. 223–282. JAIST Press, (March 2009).
18. Bjørner, D.: Chapter 1: On domains and on domain engineering – prerequisites for trustworthy software – a necessity for believable management, Domain Engineering: Technology Management, Research and Engineering [10], pp. 3–38. JAIST Press (March 2009).
19. Bjørner, D.: Chapter 2: Possible collaborative domain projects – a management brief, Domain Engineering: Technology Management, Research and Engineering [10], pp. 39–56. JAIST Press (March 2009).
20. Bjørner, D.: Chapter 3: The role of domain engineering in software development, Domain Engineering: Technology Management, Research and Engineering [10], pp. 57–72. JAIST Press (March 2009).
21. Bjørner, D.: Chapter 4: Verified software for ubiquitous computing – a VSTTE ubiquitous computing project proposal, Domain Engineering: Technology Management, Research and Engineering [10], pp. 73–106. JAIST Press (March 2009).
22. Bjørner, D.: Chapter 6: Domains and problem frames – the triptych dogma and M.A.Jackson's PF paradigm, Domain Engineering: Technology Management, Research and Engineering [10], pp. 139–175. JAIST Press (March 2009).
23. Bjørner, D.: Chapter 7: Documents – A rough sketch domain analysis, Domain Engineering: Technology Management, Research and Engineering [10], pp. 179–200. JAIST Press (March 2009).

24. Bjørner, D.: Chapter 8: Public Government – a rough sketch domain analysis, Domain Engineering: Technology Management, Research and Engineering [10], pp. 201–222. JAIST Press (March 2009).
25. George, C. and Haxthausen, A.E.: Chapter The logic of the RAISE specification language, Logics of Specification Languages, pp. 349–399 in [11]. Springer, Berlin Heidelberg, Germany (2008).
26. George, C.W., Haff, P., Havelund, K., Haxthausen, A.E., Milne, R., Nielsen, C.B., Prehn, S. and Wagner, K.R. The RAISE Specification Language. The BCS Practitioner Series. Prentice-Hall, Hemel Hampstead, England (1992).
27. George, C.W., Haxthausen, A.E., Hughes, S., Milne, R. Prehn, S. and Pedersen, J.S. The RAISE Method. The BCS Practitioner Series. Prentice-Hall, Hemel Hampstead, England (1995).
28. Hoare, T.: Communicating Sequential Processes. C.A.R. Hoare Series in Computer Science. Prentice-Hall International, Hemel Hampstead, UK (1985).
29. Hoare, T.: Communicating Sequential Processes. Published electronically: http://www.usingcsp.com/cspbook.pdf, 2004. Second edition of [28]. See also http://www.usingcsp.com/.
30. Leonard, H.S. and Goodman, N.: The calculus of individuals and its uses. J. of Symbolic Logic, **5**: 45–44 (1940).
31. Luschei, E.C.: The Logical Systems of Leśniewksi. North Holland, Amsterdam, The Netherlands (1962).
32. Pěnička, M. and Bjørner, D.: From railway resource planning to train operation — a brief survey of complementary formalisations. In: Jacquart, R. (ed.) Building the Information Society, IFIP 18th World Computer Congress, Topical Sessions, 22–27 August, 2004, Toulouse, France, pp. 629–636. Kluwer Academic Publishers (August 2004).
33. Pěnička, M. Strupchanska, A.K. and Bjørner, D.: Train Maintenance Routing. In: Editors: Tarnai, G., Schnieder, E. (eds.) FORMS'2003: Symposium on Formal Methods for Railway Operation and Control Systems. L'Harmattan Hongrie, 15–16 May 2003. Conf. held at Techn.Univ. of Budapest, Hungary, Germany.
34. Roscoe, A.W.: Theory and Practice of Concurrency. C.A.R. Hoare Series in Computer Science. Prentice-Hall, Hemel Hampstead, UK (1997). Now available on the net: http://www.comlab.ox.ac.uk/people/bill.roscoe/publications/68b.pdf.
35. Russell, B.: The philosophy of logical atomism. The Monist: An Int. Quarterly J. General Philoso. Inqu., xxxviii–xxix:495–527, 32–63, 190–222, 345–380, 1918–1919.
36. Schneider, S.: Concurrent and Real-Time Systems – The CSP Approach. Worldwide Series in Computer Science. John Wiley & Sons, Baffins Lane, Chichester, West Sussex PO19 1UD, England (January 2000).
37. Slater, J.G.: (ed.), The Collected Papers of Bertrand Russel. Allen and Unwin, London, England (1986).
38. Srzednicki, J.T.J. and Stachniak, Z.: (eds.) Leśniewksi's Lecture Notes in Logic. Kluwer Academic, Dordrecht, The Netherlands (1988).
39. Strupchanska, A.K., Pěnička, M. and Bjørner, D.: Railway Staff Rostering. In: Tarnai, G., Schnieder, E. (eds.) FORMS2003: Symposium on Formal Methods for Railway Operation and Control Systems. L'Harmattan Hongrie, 15–16 May 2003. Conf. held at Techn.Univ. of Budapest, Hungary, Germany.

Chapter 4
Roles, Stacks, Histories: A Triple for Hoare

Johannes Borgström, Andrew D. Gordon, and Riccardo Pucella

Abstract Behavioural type and effect systems regulate properties such as adherence to object and communication protocols, dynamic security policies, avoidance of race conditions, and many others. Typically, each system is based on some specific syntax of constraints, and is checked with an ad hoc solver. Instead, we advocate types refined with first-order logic formulas as a basis for behavioural type systems, and general purpose automated theorem provers as an effective means of checking programs. To illustrate this approach, we define a triple of security-related type systems: for role-based access control, for stack inspection, and for history-based access control. The three are all instances of a refined state monad. Our semantics allows a precise comparison of the similarities and differences of these mechanisms. In our examples, the benefit of behavioural type-checking is to rule out the possibility of unexpected security exceptions, a common problem with code-based access control.

4.1 Introduction

4.1.1 Behavioural Type Systems

Type-checkers for behavioural type systems are an effective programming language technology, aimed at verifying various classes of program properties. We consider type and effect systems, typestate analyses, and various security analyses as being within the class of behavioural type systems. A few examples include memory management [28], adherence to object and communication protocols [16, 53], dynamic security policies [44], authentication properties of security protocols [30], avoidance of race conditions [23], and many more.

J. Borgström and A.D. Gordon (✉)
Microsoft Research, Cambridge, UK
e-mail: joborg@microsoft.com; adg@microsoft.com

R. Pucella
Department of Computer Science, Northeastern University, USA
e-mail: riccardo@ccs.neu.edu

C.B. Jones et al. (eds.), *Reflections on the Work of C.A.R. Hoare*,
DOI 10.1007/978-1-84882-912-1_4,

While the proliferation of behavioural type systems is a good thing – evidence of their applicability to a wide range of properties – it leads to the problem of fragmentation of both theory and implementation techniques. Theories of different behavioural type systems are based on a diverse range of formalisms, such as calculi of objects, classes, processes, functions, and so on. Checkers for behavioural type systems often make use of specialised proof engines for ad hoc constraint languages. The fragmentation into multiple theories and implementations hinders both the comparison of different systems, and also the sharing of proof engines between implementations.

We address this fragmentation. We show three examples of security-related behavioural type systems that are unified within a single logic-based framework. Moreover, they may be checked by invoking the current generation of automated theorem provers, rather than by building ad hoc solvers.

4.1.2 Refinement Types and Automated Theorem Proving

The basis for our work is the recent development of automatic type-checkers for pure functional languages equipped with refinement types. A *refinement type* $\{x : T|C\}$ consists of the values x of type T such that the formula C holds. Since values may occur within the formula, refinement types are a particular form of dependent type. Variants of this construction are referred to as refinement types in the setting of ML-like languages [22, 27, 56], but also as *subset types* [41] or *set types* [14] in the context of constructive type theory, and *predicate subtypes* in the setting of the interactive theorem prover PVS [50].

In principle, type-checking with refinement types may generate logical verification conditions requiring arbitrarily sophisticated proof. In PVS, for example, some verification conditions are implicitly discharged via automated reasoning, but often the user needs to suggest an explicit proof tactic.

Still, some recent type-checkers for these types use external solvers to discharge automatically the proof obligations associated with refinement formulas. These solvers take as input a formula in the syntax of first-order logic, including equality and linear arithmetic, and attempt to show that the formula is satisfiable. This general problem is known as *satisfiability modulo theories* (SMT) [47]; it is undecidable, and hence the solvers are incomplete, but remarkable progress is being made.

Three examples of type-checkers for refinement types are SAGE [22, 31], F7 [10], and Dsolve [49]. These type-checkers rely on the SMT solvers Simplify [17], Z3 [15], and Yices [18].

Our implementation experiments are based on the F7 type-checker, which checks programs in a subset of the Objective Caml and F# dialects of ML against a type system enhanced with refinements. The theoretical foundation for F7 and its type system is RCF, which is the standard Fixpoint Calculus (FPC, a typed call-by-value λ-calculus with sums, pairs, and iso-recursive types) [32, 45] augmented with message-passing concurrency and refinement types with formulas in first-order logic.

4.1.3 RIF: Refinement Types Meet the State Monad

Moggi [38] pioneered the *state monad* as a basis for the semantics of imperative programming. Wadler [54] advocated its use to obtain imperative effects within pure functional programming, as in Haskell, for instance. The state monad can be written as the following function type, parametric in a type state, of global imperative state.

$$\mathcal{M}(T) \triangleq \mathsf{state} \to (T \times \mathsf{state})$$

The idea is that $\mathcal{M}(T)$ is the type of a computation that, if it terminates on a given input state, returns an answer of type T, paired with an output state.

With the goal of full verification of imperative computations, various authors, including Filliâtre [21] and Nanevski et al. [39], consider the state monad of the form below, where P and Q are assertions about state. (We elide some details of variable binding.)

$$\mathcal{M}_{P,Q}(T) \triangleq (\mathsf{state} \mid P) \to (T \times (\mathsf{state} \mid Q))$$

The idea here is that $\mathcal{M}_{P,Q}(T)$ is the type of a computation returning T, with precondition P and postcondition Q. More precisely, it is a computation that, if it terminates on an input state satisfying the precondition P, returns an answer of type T, paired with an output state satisfying the postcondition Q. Hence, one can build frameworks for Hoare-style reasoning about imperative programs [20, 40], where $\mathcal{M}_{P,Q}(T)$ is interpreted so that $(\mathsf{state} \mid P)$ and $(\mathsf{state} \mid Q)$ are dependent pairs consisting of a state together with proofs of P and Q. (The recent paper by Régis-Gianas and Pottier [48] on Hoare logic reasoning for pure functional programs has a comprehensive literature survey on formalizations of Hoare logic.)

In this paper, we consider an alternative reading: let the *refined state monad* be the interpretation of $\mathcal{M}_{P,Q}(T)$ where $(\mathsf{state} \mid P)$ and $(\mathsf{state} \mid Q)$ are refinement types populated by states known to satisfy P and Q. In this reading, $\mathcal{M}_{P,Q}(T)$ is simply a computation that accepts a state known to satisfy P and returns a state known to satisfy Q, as opposed to a computation that passes around states paired with proof objects for the predicates P and Q.

This paper introduces and studies an imperative calculus in which computations are modelled as Fixpoint Calculus expressions in the refined state monad $\mathcal{M}_{P,Q}(T)$. More precisely, our calculus, which we refer to as *Refined Imperative FPC*, or RIF for short, is a generalization of FPC with dependent types, subtyping, global state accessed by get and set operations, and computation types refined with preconditions and postconditions. To specify correctness properties, we include assumptions and assertions as expressions. The expression **assume**$(s)C$ adds the formula $C\{^M/_s\}$, where M is the current state, to the *log*, a collection of formulas assumed to hold. The expression **assert**$(s)C$ always returns at once, but we say it *succeeds* when the formula $C\{^M/_s\}$, where M is the current state, follows from the log, and otherwise it *fails*. We define the syntax, operational semantics, and type system for RIF, and give a safety result, Theorem 1, which asserts that safety (the lack of all assertion failures) follows by type-checking. This theorem follows from a direct encoding of RIF within RCF, together with appeal to a safety theorem for RCF itself. For the sake of brevity, we relegate the direct encoding of RIF into RCF to a companion technical report [12], which contains various details and proofs omitted from this version of the paper.

Our calculus is similar in spirit to HTT [39] and YNot [40], although we use refinement types for states instead of dependent pairs, and we use formulas in classical first-order logic suitable for direct proof with SMT solvers, instead of constructive higher-order logic. Another difference is that RIF has a subtype relation, which may be applied to computation types to, for example, strengthen preconditions or weaken postconditions. A third difference is that we are not pursuing full program verification, which typically requires some human interaction, but instead view RIF as a foundation for automatic type-checkers for behavioural type systems.

If we ignore variable binding, both our refined type $\mathcal{M}_{P,Q}(T)$ and the constructive types in the work of Filliâtre and Marché [20] and Nanevski et al. [40] are instances of Atkey's [5] parameterised state monad, where the parameterization is over the formulas concerning the type state. When variable binding is included, the type $M_{P,Q}(T)$ is no longer a parameterized monad, since the preconditions and postconditions are of different types as the postcondition can mention the initial state.

4.1.4 Unifying Behavioural Types for Roles, Stacks, and Histories

Our purpose in introducing RIF is to show that the refined state monad can unify and extend several automatically checked behavioural type systems. RIF is parametric in the choice of the type of imperative state. We show that by making suitable choices of the type state, and by deriving suitable programming interfaces, we recover several existing behavioural type systems, and uncover some new ones.

We focus on security-related examples where run-time security mechanisms – based on roles, stacks, and histories – are used by trusted library code to protect themselves against less trusted callers. Unwarranted access requests result in security exceptions.

First, we consider role-based access control (RBAC) [19, 52] where the current state is a set of activated roles. Each activated role confers access rights to particular objects.

Second, we consider permission-based access control, where the current state includes a set of permissions available to running code. We examine two standard variants: stack-based access control (SBAC) [24, 29, 55] and history-based access control (HBAC) [2]. We implement each of the three access control mechanisms as an application programming interface (API) within RIF.

In each case, checking application code against the API amounts to behavioural typing, and ensures that application code causes no security exceptions. Hence, static checking prevents accidental programming errors in trusted code and both accidental and malicious programming errors in untrusted code.

Our results show the theoretical feasibility of our approach. We have type-checked all of the example code in this paper by first running a tool that implements a state-passing translation (described in Borgström et al. [12]) into RCF, and then type-checking the translated code with F7 and Z3.

The contents of the paper are as follows. Section 4.2 considers access control with roles. Section 4.3 considers access control with permissions, based either on stack inspection or a history variable. We use our typed calculus in these sections but postpone the formal definition to Section 4.4. Finally, Section 4.5 discusses related work and Section 4.6 offers some conclusions, and a dedication.

4.2 Types for Role-Based Access Control

In general, access control policies regulate access to resources based on information about both the resource and the entity requesting access to the resource, as well as information about the context of the request. In particular, RBAC policies base their decisions on the actions that an entity is allowed to perform within an organization – their role. Without loss of generality, we can identify resources with operations to access these resources, and therefore RBAC decisions concern whether a user can perform a given operation based on the role that the user plays. Thus, roles are a device for indirection: instead of assigning access rights directly to users, we assign roles to users, and access rights to roles.

In this section, we illustrate the use of our calculus by showing how to express RBAC policies, and demonstrate the usefulness of refinements on state by showing how to statically enforce that the appropriate permissions are in place before controlled operations are invoked. This appears to be the first-type system for RBAC properties – most existing studies on verifying RBAC properties in the literature use logic programming to reason about policies independently from code [8, 9, 36]. We build on the typeful approach to access control introduced by Fournet et al. [25] where the access policy is expressed as a set of logical assumptions; relative to that work, the main innovation is the possibility of de-activating as well as activating access rights.

As we mentioned in the introduction, our calculus is a generalization of FPC with dependent types and subtyping. As such, we will use an ML-like syntax for expressions in the calculus. The calculus also uses a global state to track security information, and computation types refined with preconditions and postconditions to express properties of that global state. The security information recorded in the global state may vary depending on the kind of security guarantees we want to provide. Therefore, our calculus is parameterized by the security information recorded in the global state and the operations that manipulate that information.

To use our calculus, we need to *instantiate* it with an extension API module that implements the security information tracked in the global state, and the operations to manipulate that information. The extension API needs to define a concrete state type that captures the information recorded in the global state. Functions in the extension

API are the only functions that can explicitly manipulate the state via the primitives **get**() and **set**(). Moreover, the extension API defines predicates by assuming logical formulas; this is the only place where assumptions are allowed.

We present an extension API for RBAC. In the simplest form of RBAC, permissions are associated with roles, and therefore we assume a type role representing the class of roles. The model we have in mind is that roles can be active or not. To be able to use the permissions associated with a role, that role must be active. Therefore, the security information to be tracked during computation is the set of roles that are currently active.

RBAC API

```
type state = role list

val activate : r:role → {(s)True} unit {(s')Add(s',s,r)}
val deactivate : r:role → {(s)True} unit {(s')Rem(s',s,r)}

assume ∀ts,x. Mem(x,ts) ⇔ (∃y, vs. ts = y::vs ∧ (x = y ∨ Mem (x,vs)))
assume ∀rs,ts,x. Add(rs,ts,x) ⇔ (∀y. Mem(y,rs) ⇔ (Mem(y,ts) ∨ x=y))
assume ∀rs,ts,x. Rem(rs,ts,x) ⇔ (∀y. Mem(y,rs) ⇔ (Mem(y,ts) ∧ ¬(x = y)))
assume ∀s. CurrentState(s) ⇒ (∀r. Active(r) ⇔ Mem(r,s))
```

An extension API supplies three kinds of information. First, it fixes a type for the global state. Based on the discussion above, the global state of a computation is the set of roles that are active, hence state $\triangleq$ role list, where role is the type for roles, which is a parameter to the API.

Second, an extension API gives functions to manipulate the global state. The extension API for primitive RBAC has two functions only: activate to add a role to the state of active roles, and deactivate to remove a role from the state of active roles.

We use **val** f:T to give a type to a function in an API. Expressions get *computation types* of the form $\{(s_0)C_0\}\, x{:}T\, \{(s_1)C_1\}$. Such a computation type is interpreted semantically using the refined state monad mentioned in Section 4.1.3, where it corresponds to the type $\mathcal{M}_{(s_0)C_0,(s_1)C_1}(T)$. In particular, a computation type states that an expression starts its evaluation with a state satisfying C_0 (in which s_0 is bound to that state in C_0) and yields a value of type T and a final state satisfying C_1 (in which s_0 is bound to the initial state of the computation in C_1, s_1 is bound to the final state of the computation, and x is bound to the value returned by the computation). Thus, for instance, activate is a function that takes role r as input and computes a value of type unit. That computation takes an unconstrained state (that is, satisfying True), and returning a state that is the union of the initial state and the newly activated role r – recall that a state here is a list of roles. Similarly, deactivate is a function that takes a role as input and computes a unit value in the presence of an unconstrained state and producing a final state that is simply the initial state minus the deactivated role.

The third kind of information contained in an API are logical axioms. Observe that the postconditions for activate and deactivate use predicates such as Add and Rem. We define such predicates using *assumptions*, which let us assume arbitrary formulas in our assertion logic, formulas that will be taken to be valid in any code using the API. Ideally, these assumed formulas would be proved sound in some external proof assistant, in terms of some suitable model, but here we follow an axiomatic approach. For the purposes of RBAC, we assume not only some set-theoretic predicates (using lists as a representation for sets), but also a predicate Active true exactly when a given role is currently active. To define Active, we rely on a predicate CurrentState, where CurrentState(s) captures the assumptions that s is the current set of active roles; Active then amounts to membership in the set of active roles. We can only reason about Active under the assumption of some CurrentState(s). We shall see that our formulas for reasoning about roles will always be of the form CurrentState(s)⇒ ..., where s is the current state.

RBAC API Implementation

```
// Set-theoretic operations (provided by a library)
val add: l:α list → e:α → {(s)True} r:α list {(s')s=s' ∧ Add(r,l,e)}
val remove : l:α list → e:α → {(s)True} r:α list {(s')s=s' ∧ Rem(r,l,e)}

let activate r = let rs = get() in let rs' = add rs r in set(rs')
let deactivate r = let rs = get() in let rs' = remove rs r in set(rs')
```

The implementation of activate and deactivate use primitive operations **get**() and **set**() to respectively get and set the state of the computation. We make the assumption that **get**() and **set**() may only be used in the implementation of API functions; in particular, user code cannot use those operations to arbitrarily manipulate the state. The API functions are meant to encapsulate all state manipulation. Beyond the use of **get**() and **set**(), the implementation of the API functions above also use set-theoretic operations add and remove to manipulate the content of the state. We only give the types of these operations – their implementations are the standard list-based implementations.

We associate permissions to roles via an access control policy expressed as logical assumptions. We illustrate this with a simple example, that of modelling access control in a primitive file system. We assume two kinds of roles: the superuser, and friends of normal users (represented by their login names):

```
type role = SuperUser | FriendOf of string
```

In this scenario, permissions concern which users can read which files. For simplicity, we consider a policy where a superuser can read all files, while other users can access specific files, as expressed in the policy. A predicate CanRead(f) expresses the "file f can be read" permission, given the currently active roles. Here is a simple policy in line with this description:

```
assume ∀file. Active(SuperUser) ⇒ CanRead(file)
assume Active(FriendOf("Andy")) ⇒ CanRead("andy.log")
```

This policy, aside from stating that the superuser can read all files, also states that if the role FriendOf("Andy") is active, then the file andy.log can be read. For simplicity, we consider only read permissions here. It is straightforward to extend the example to include write permissions or execute permissions.

The main function we seek to restrict access to is readFile, which intuitively requires that the currently active roles suffice to derive that the file to be read can in fact be read.

```
val readFile: file:string → {(rs) CurrentState(rs) ⇒ CanRead(file)} string {(s)s=rs}
let readFile file =
    assert (rs)(CurrentState(rs) ⇒ CanRead(file));
    primReadFile file
```

We express this requirement by writing an assertion in the code of readFile, before the call to the underlying system call primReadFile. The **assert** expression checks that the current state (bound to variable rs) proves that CanRead(file) holds, under the assumption that CurrentState(rs). Such an assertion *succeeds* if the formula is provable, and *fails* otherwise. The main property of our language is given by a *safety theorem*: if a program type-checks, then all assertions succeed. In other words, if a program that uses readFile type-checks, then we are assured that by the time we call primReadFile, we are permitted to read file, at least according to the access control policy. The type system, somewhat naturally, forces the precondition of readFile to ensure that the state can derive CanRead for the file under consideration.

Intuitively, the following expression type-checks:

```
activate(SuperUser); readFile "andy.log"
```

The expression first adds role SuperUser to the state, and the postcondition of activate notes that the resulting state is the union of the initial state (of which nothing is known) with SuperUser. When readFile is invoked, the precondition states that the current state must be able to prove CanRead("andy.log"). Because SuperUser is active and Active(SuperUser) implies CanRead(file) for any file, we get CanRead("andy.log"), and we can invoke readFile. The following examples type-check for similar reasons, since Active(FriendOf "Andy") can prove the formula CanRead("andy.log"):

```
activate(FriendOf "Andy"); readFile "andy.log"
activate(FriendOf "Andy"); deactivate(FriendOf "Jobo");
  readFile "andy.log"
```

In contrast, the following example fails to activate any role that gives a CanRead permission on file "andy.log", and therefore fails to type-check:

```
activate(FriendOf "Ric"); readFile "andy.log" // Does not type-check
```

After activating FriendOf "Ric", the postcondition of activate expresses that the state contains whatever was in the initial state along with the role FriendOf "Ric". When invoking readFile, the type system tries to establish the precondition, but it only knows that Active(FriendOf "Ric"), and the policy cannot derive the formula CanRead("andy.log") from it. Therefore, the type system fails to satisfy the precondition of readFile "andy.log", and reports a type error.

The access control policy need not be limited to a statically known set of files. Having a full predicate logic at hand affords us much flexibility. To express, for instance, that any file with extension .txt can be read by anyone, we can use a predicate Match:

```
assume ∀file.Match(file,"*.txt") ⇒ CanRead(file)
```

Rather than axiomatizing the Match predicate, we rely on a function glob that does a dynamic check to see if a file name matches the provided pattern, and in its postcondition fixes the truth value of the Match predicate on those arguments:

```
val glob : file:string → pat:string →
  {(rs) True} r:bool {(rs') rs=rs' ∧ (r=true ⇒ Match(file,pat))}
let glob file pat = if (* ... code for globbing ... *)
                        then assume Match(file,path); true
                     else false
```

The following code therefore type-checks, even when all the activated roles do not by themselves suffice to give a CanRead permission:

```
activate(FriendOf "Ric");
let f = "log.txt" in
  if (glob f "*.txt") then readFile f else "skipped"
```

Similarly, not only can we specify which roles give CanRead permissions for which files by saying so explicitly in the policy (as above), we can also dynamically check that a friend of some user can read a file by querying the physical file system through a primitive function primReadFSPerm(f,u) that checks whether a given user u (and therefore their friends) can access a given file f, and reflect the result of that dynamic check into the type system:

```
val hasFSReadPermission : f:string → u:string → {(rs) True}
    r:bool {(rs') rs=rs' ∧ (r=True ⇒ (Active(FriendOf(u)) ⇒ CanRead(f)))}
let hasFSReadPermission f u =
        if primReadFSPerm (f,u)
           then assume Active(FriendOf(u)) ⇒ CanRead(f); true
        else false
```

The following code now type-checks:

```
activate(FriendOf "Andy");
if (hasFSReadPermission "somefile" "Andy")
  then readFile "somefile"
else "cannot read file"
```

The code first activates the role FriendOf "Andy", and then dynamically checks, by querying the physical file system, that user "Andy" (and therefore his friends) can in fact read file "somefile". The type of hasFSReadPermission is such that if the result of the check is true, the new formula Active(FriendOf("Andy"))$\Rightarrow$ CanRead("somefile") can be used in subsequent expressions – in particular, when calling readFile "somefile". FriendOf "Andy" is active at that point, and therefore CanRead("somefile") holds.

4.3 Types for Permission-Based Access Control

The RBAC systems of the previous section are most applicable in an interactive setting, where principals inhabiting different roles can influence the computation as it is running. Without interaction, we can instead work with a static division of the program code based on its provenance. We assume that each function is assigned a set of static permissions that enable it to perform certain side effects, such as file system IO. A classical problem in this setting is the Confused Deputy [33], where untrusted code performs unauthorized side effects through exploiting a trusted API. This problem has been addressed through various mechanisms. In this section, we consider SBAC [29, 55] and HBAC [2].

The purpose of SBAC is to protect trusted functions from untrusted callers. Unless explicitly requested, a permission only holds at run-time if all callers on the call stack statically hold the permission.

HBAC also intends to protect trusted code from the untrusted code it may call, by ensuring that the run-time permissions depend on the static permissions of every function *called so far in the entire program.* In particular, when a function returns, the current run-time permissions can never be greater than the static permissions of that function. HBAC can be seen as a refinement of SBAC, in the sense that the run-time permissions at any point when using the HBAC calling conventions are less than those when using SBAC.

In this section, we show how the RIF calculus supports type-checking of both SBAC and HBAC policies. There are several formalizations of SBAC, some of which include type systems, Previous type systems for SBAC took a rather simple view of permissions. To quote Pottier et al. [46]: "In our model, privileges are identifiers, and expressions cannot compute privileges. It would be desirable to extend the static framework to at least handle first-class parameters of privileges, so for example, a Java FilePermission, which takes a parameter that is a specific file, could be modeled." Having both computation types and dependent types in our imperative calculus lets us treat not only parameters to privileges, but also have a general theory of partially ordered privileges. We can also type-check code that computes privileges, crucially including the privilege-manipulating API functions defined in Section 4.3.2.

As a side-effect, we can also investigate the differences between SBAC and HBAC as implemented in our framework. We show one (previously known) example where switching from SBAC to HBAC resolves a security hole by throwing a run-time exception; additionally, static type-checking discovers that the code is not safe to run under HBAC.

The use of type-checkers allows authors of trusted code to statically exclude run-time security exceptions relating to lack of privileges. As discussed above, we provide a more sensitive analysis than previous work, which facilitates the use of the principle of least privilege. Type-checking can also be applied to untrusted code before loading it, ensuring the lack of run-time security exceptions.

4.3.1 A Lattice of Permission Sets

As a running example, we introduce the following permissions. The ScreenIO permission is atomic. A FileIO permission is a tuple of an access right of type RW and a file scope of type Wildcard. The access rights are partially ordered: the owner of a file can both read and write it. The scope Any extends to any file in the system.

Partially Ordered Permissions

```
type α Wildcard = Any | Just of α
type RW = Read | Write | Owns
type Permission = ScreenIO | FileIO of RW * (string Wildcard)
type Perms = Permission list
```

When generalizing HBAC and SBAC to the setting where permissions are partially ordered, we run into a problem. Both HBAC and SBAC are built on taking unions and intersections of sets of atomic permissions. In our setting permissions are not atomic, but are built from partially ordered components, which makes set-theoretic union and (especially) intersection unsuitable. As an example, the greatest permission implied by both FileIO(Owns,Just(logFile)) and FileIO(Read,Any) is FileIO(Read,Just(logFile)), rather than the empty permission.

We encode the partial order on permissions as a predicate Holds(p,ps) that checks if a permission p is in the downward closure of the permission set ps. We define the predicate Subsumed in terms of Holds. The greatest lower bound (glb) of two permission sets ps and qs subsumes precisely those sets subsumed by both ps and qs. Dually, the least upper bound (lub) of two permission sets ps and qs is the smallest set subsuming both ps and qs. In the technical report [12], we show that these operations are well defined[1] on the poset of finite permission sets in this example.

[1] The general condition is that every pair of permissions must have a finite glb. This holds if the poset of permissions has no infinite subchains or if it forms a tree, where the latter is the case here.

Predicate Symbols and Their Definitions

assume ∀x,y,xs. Holds(FileIO(Owns,y),xs) ⇒ Holds(FileIO(x,y),xs)
assume ∀x,y,xs. Holds(FileIO(x,Any),xs) ⇒ Holds(FileIO(x,Just(y)),xs)
assume ∀x,xs. Holds(x,x::xs)
assume ∀x,y,xs. Holds(x,xs) ⇒ Holds(x,y::xs)
assume ∀xs. Subsumed(xs,xs) ∧ Subsumed([],xs)
assume ∀x,xs,ys. Holds(x,ys) ∧ Subsumed(xs,ys) ⇒ Subsumed(x::xs,ys)

We also define predicates for Lub and Glb, and assume the standard lattice axioms relating these to each other and to Subsumed (not shown). We then assume functions lub, glb, and subsumed that compute the corresponding operations for the permission language defined above, with the following types.

Types for Lattice Operations

val lub: ps:Perms → qs:Perms → {(s) True} res:Perms {(t) s=t ∧ Lub(res,ps,qs)}
val glb: ps:Perms → qs:Perms → {(s) True} res:Perms {(t) s=t ∧ Glb(res,ps,qs)}
val subsumed: ps:Perms → qs:Perms →
  {(s) True} x:bool {(t) s=t ∧ (x=True ⇔ Subsumed(ps,qs))}

4.3.2 Stack-Based Access Control

In order to compare history- and stack-based access control in the same framework, we begin by implementing API functions for requesting and testing permissions. We let state be a record type with two fields: state ≜ {ast:Perms; dy:Perms}. The ast field contains the current static permissions, which are used only when requesting additional dynamic permissions (see request below). The dy field contains the current dynamically requested permissions. Computations have type (α ;req) SBACcomp, for some return type α and required initial dynamic permissions req. An SBACthunk wraps a computation in a function with unit argument type.

The API functions have the following types and implementations. The become function is used (notionally by the run-time system) when calling a function that may have different static permissions from its caller. It first sets the static permissions to those of the called code. Then, since the called function may be untrusted, it reduces the dynamic permissions to the greatest lower bound of the current dynamic permissions and the static permissions of the called function. Dually, upon return the run-time system calls sbacReturn with the original permissions returned by become, restoring them. The request function augments the dynamic permissions, after checking that the static context (Subsumed(ps,st)) permits it. We check that the permissions ps dynamically hold using the function demand; it has type ps:Perms → (unit;ps)SBACcomp.

SBAC API and Calling Convention

```
type (α ;req:Perms) SBACcomp = {(s) Subsumed(req,s.dy)} α {(t) s=t}
type (α ;req:Perms) SBACthunk = unit → (α ;req) SBACcomp
val become: ps:Perms→ {(s)True}s':State{(t) s=s' ∧ t.ast = ps ∧ Glb(t.dy,ps,s.dy)}
val sbacReturn: olds:State → {(s) True} unit {(t) t=olds}
val permitOnly: ps:Perms→ {(s) True}unit{(t) s.ast = t.ast ∧ Glb(t.dy,ps,s.dy)}
val request: ps:Perms →
  {(s) Subsumed(ps,s.ast)} unit {(t) s.ast = t.ast ∧ Lub(t.dy,ps,s.dy)}
val demand: ps:Perms → (unit;ps) SBACcomp
```

The postcondition of an SBACcomp is that the state is unchanged. In order to recover formulas that hold about the state, we use subtyping. As usual, a subtype of a function type may return a subtype of the original computation type. In a subtype G of a computation type F, we can strengthen the precondition. The postcondition of G must also be weaker than (implied by) the precondition of G together with the postcondition of F. As an example, $\{(s)C\}\alpha\,\{(t)C\{^t/_s\}\}$ is a subtype of (α ;[])SBACcomp for every C, since $\vdash C \Rightarrow$ True and $\vdash (C \wedge s = t) \Rightarrow C\{^t/_s\}$. Subtyping is used to ensure that pre- and postconditions match up when sequencing computations using **let**. We also use subtyping to propagate assumptions that do not mention the state, such as the definitions of predicates.

In the implementations of request and demand below, we **assert** that subsumed always returns **true**. This corresponds to requiring that the caller has sufficient permissions. Since no **assert** fails in a well-typed program, any execution of such a program always has sufficient run-time permissions.

SBAC API Implementation

```
let sbacReturn s = set s

let become ps =
    let {ast=st;dy=dy} = get() in let dz = glb ps dy in
    set {ast=ps;dy=dz}; {ast=st;dy=dy}

let permitOnly ps =
   let {ast=st;dy=dy} = get() in let dz = glb ps dy in
   set ({ast=st;dy=dz})

let request ps =
    let {ast=st;dy=dy} = get() in let x = subsumed ps st in
    if x then let dz = lub ps dy in set {ast=st; dy=dz}
    else assert False ; failwith "SecurityException: request"

let demand ps =
    let {ast=_; dy=dy} = get() in let x = subsumed ps dy in
    if x then() else assert False; failwith "SecurityException:
    demand"
```

To exercise this framework, we work in a setting with two principals. Agent is untrusted, and can perform screen IO, read a version file and owns a temporary file. System can read and write every file. We define three trusted functions, that either run primitive (non-refined) functions or run as System. Function readFile demands that the read permission for its argument holds dynamically. Similarly deleteFile requires a write permission. Finally cleanupSBAC takes a function returning a file-name, and then deletes the file returned by the function.

```
let Applet = [ScreenIO;FileIO(Read,Just(version));FileIO(Owns,Just (tempFile))]
let System = [ScreenIO;FileIO(Write,Any);FileIO(Read,Any)]

val readFile: a:string → (string;[FileIO(Read,Just(a))]) SBACcomp
let readFile n = let olds = become System in demand [FileIO(Read,Just(n))];
  let res = "Content of "^n in sbacReturn olds; res

val deleteFile: a:string → (string;[FileIO(Write,Just(a))]) SBACcomp
let deleteFile n = let olds = become System in demand [FileIO(Write,Just(n))];
  let res = primitiveDelete n in sbacReturn olds; res

val cleanupSBAC: (string;[]) SBACthunk → (unit;[]) SBACcomp
let cleanupSBAC f = let olds = become System in request [FileIO(Write,Any)];
  let s = f () in let res = deleteFile s in sbacReturn olds; res
```

We now give some examples of untrusted code using these trusted functions and the SBAC calling conventions. In SBAC1, an applet attempts to read the version file. Since Applet has the necessary permission, this function is well typed at type unit SBACcomp. In SBAC2, the applet attempts to delete a password file. Since the applet does not have the necessary permissions, a run-time exception is thrown when executing the code – and we cannot type the function SBAC2 at type unit SBACcomp.

However, in SBAC3, the SBAC abstraction fails to protect the password file. Here the applet instead passes an untrusted function to cleanup. Since the permissions are reset after returning from the untrusted function, the cleanup function deletes the password file. Moreover, SBAC3 type-checks.

```
let SBAC1: (unit;[]) SBACthunk = fun () → let olds = become Applet in
  request [FileIO(Read,Just(version))]; readFile version; sbacReturn olds

 //Does not typecheck
let SBAC2 = fun () → let olds = become Applet in
  request [FileIO(Read,Just("passwd"))]; deleteFile "passwd";
  sbacReturn olds

let aFunSBAC: (string;[]) SBACthunk = fun () → let olds = become Applet in
  let res = "passwd" in sbacReturn olds; res
let SBAC3: (unit;[]) SBACthunk = fun () → let olds = become Applet in
  cleanupSBAC aFunSBAC; sbacReturn olds
```

4.3.3 History-Based Access Control

The HBAC calling convention was defined [2] to protect against the kind of attack that SBAC fails to prevent in SBAC3 above. To protect callers from untrusted functions, HBAC reduces the dynamic permissions after calling an untrusted function. A computation in HBAC of type (α ;req,pres) HBACcomp returning type α preserves the static permissions and does not increase the dynamic permissions. It also requires permissions req and preserves permissions pres. As above, a HBACthunk is a function from unit returning an HBACcomp. The HBAC calling convention is implemented by the function hbacReturn, whic resets the static condition and reduces the dynamic conditions to at most the initial ones.

The HBAC API extends the SBAC API with two functions for structured control of permissions, grant and accept, which can be seen as scoped versions of request. We use grant to run a subcomputation with augmented permissions. The second argument to grant ps is a (α ;ps,[]) HBACthunk, which may assume that the permissions ps hold upon entry. We can only call grant itself if the current static permissions subsume ps. Dually, accept allows us to recover permissions that might have been lost when running a subcomputation. accept ps takes an arbitrary HBACthunk, and guarantees that at least the glb (intersection) between ps and the initial dynamic permissions holds upon exit. As before, we can only call accept if the current static permissions subsume ps.

HBAC API and Calling Convention

```
type (α ;req:Perms,pres:Perms) HBACcomp =
    {(s) Subsumed(req,s.dy) } α {(t) s.ast = t.ast ∧ Subsumed(t.dy,s.dy)
     ∧ (∀qs. Subsumed(qs,pres) ∧ Subsumed(qs,s.dy) ⇒ Subsumed(qs,t.dy))}
type (α ;req:Perms,pres:Perms) HBACthunk = unit → (α ;req,pres) HBACcomp
val hbacReturn: os:State → {(s) True} unit {(t) t.ast=os.ast ∧ Glb(t.dy,s.dy,os.dy)}
val grant: ps:Perms → (α ;ps,[]) HBACthunk →
  {(s0) Subsumed(ps,s0.ast)} α {(s3) s3.ast=s0.ast ∧ Subsumed(s3.dy,s0.dy)}
val accept: ps:Perms → (α ;[],[]) HBACthunk →
  {(s) Subsumed(ps,s.ast)} α {(t)s.ast = t.ast ∧
   (∀qs. Subsumed(qs,ps) ∧ Subsumed(qs,s.dy) ⇒ Subsumed(qs,t.dy))}
```

Here (α ;req) SBACcomp is a subtype of (α ;req,pres) HBACcomp for every pres.

HBAC API Implementation

```
let hbacReturn s = let {ast=oldst; dy=oldy} = s in let {ast=st;dy=dy} = get() in
    let dz = glb dy oldy in set {ast=oldst;dy=dz}
private val getDy: unit → {(s) True} dy:Perms {(t) t = s ∧ t.dy = dy}
let getDy () = let {ast=_;dy=dy} = get() in dy
let grant ps a = let dy = getDy () in request ps; let res = a () in permitOnly dy; res
let accept ps a = let dy = getDy () in let res = a () in request ps; permitOnly dy; res
```

As seen above, the postcondition of an hbacComp does not set a lower bound for the dynamic permissions. Because of this, we cannot type-check the cleanup function with argument type string HBACcomp. Indeed, in this example, the dynamic permissions are reduced to at most Applet, which is not sufficient to delete the password file.

In example HBAC1 we instead use cleanup_grant. This function prudently checks the return value of its untrusted argument, and uses grant to give precisely the required permission to deleteFile. If the check fails, we instead give an error message (not to be confused with a security exception). For this reason, HBAC1 type-checks.

```
let cleanupHBAC f = let olds = become System in
request [FileIO(Write,Any)]; let s = f () in deleteFile s ; hbacReturn olds

let cleanup_grant : (string;[],[]) HBACthunk → (unit;[],[]) HBACcomp =
  fun f → let olds = become System; let s = f () in
  (if (s = tempFile) then let h = deleteFile s in grant [FileIO(Write,Just(s))] h
   else print "Check of untrusted return value failed.");
  hbacReturn olds

let aFunHBAC: (string;[],[]) HBACthunk = fun () →
    let olds = become Applet in let res = "passwd" in hbacReturn olds ; res
let HBAC1: (unit;[],[]) HBACthunk = fun () →
    let olds = become Applet in cleanup_grant Applet_fun ; hbacReturn olds
```

However, cleanupHBAC will delete the given file if the function it calls preserves the relevant write permission. This can cause a vulnerability. For instance, assume a library function expand that (notionally) expands environment variables in its argument. Such a library function would be statically trusted, and passing it to cleanup_HBAC will result in the sensitive file being deleted. Moreover, we can type-check expand at type string → cleanupArg, where a cleanupArg preserves all System permissions, including FileIO(Write,Just("passwd")), when run.

```
type cleanupArg: (string;[],System) HBACthunk

val cleanupHBAC: cleanupArg → (unit;[],System) HBACthunk

//Does not type-check, since aFunHBAC is not a cleanupArg
let HBAC2 = fun () → let olds = become Applet in
    cleanupHBAC aFunHBAC ; hbacReturn olds

let expand:string → cleanupArg = fun n → fun () →
  let olds = become System in let res = n in hbacReturn olds ; n
let HBAC3:(unit;[],[]) HBACthunk = fun () → let olds = become Applet in
    cleanup_HBAC (expand "passwd") ; hbacReturn olds
```

Here HBAC provides a middle ground when compared to SBAC on the one hand and taint-tracking systems on the other, in regard to accuracy and complexity.

In the examples above, well-typed code does not depend on the actual state in which it is run. Indeed, we could dispense with the state-passing entirely. However, we can also introduce a function which lets us check if we hold certain run-time permissions. When this function is part of the API, we need to keep an explicit permission state (in the general case).

API Function for Checking Run-Time Permissions

```
val check: ps:Perms → {(s)True} b:bool {(t)s=t ∧ (b=true ⇒ Subsumed(ps,t.dy))}
let check ps = let dy = getDy () in subsumed ps dy
```

We can use this function in the following (type-safe) way:

```
let HBAC4:(unit;[],[]) HBACthunk = fun () → let olds = become Applet in
  (if check [FileIO(Write,Just("passwd"))]
   then deleteFile "passwd"
   else print "Not enough permissions: giving up.");
  hbacReturn olds
```

4.4 A Calculus for the Refined State Monad

In this section, we present the formal definition of RIF, the calculus we have been using to model security mechanisms based on roles, stacks, and histories. We begin with its syntax and operational semantics in Sections 4.4.1 and 4.4.2. Section 4.4.3 describes the type system of RIF and its soundness with respect to the operational semantics. Finally, Section 4.4.4 describes how the calculus may be instantiated by suitable choice of the state type.

4.4.1 Syntax

Our starting point is the Fixpoint Calculus (FPC) [32, 45], a deterministic call-by-value λ-calculus with sums, pairs, and iso-recursive data structures.

Syntax of the Core Fixpoint Calculus

s, x, y, z	variable
h ::=	value constructor
inl	left constructor of sum type
inr	right constructor of sum type
fold	constructor of recursive type
M, N ::=	value
x	variable

$()$	unit
fun $x \to A$	function (scope of x is A)
(M,N)	pair
$h\,M$	construction
$A,B ::=$	expression
M	value
$M\,N$	application
$M = N$	syntactic equality
let $x = A$ **in** B	let (scope of x is B)
let $(x,y) = M$ **in** A	pair split (scope of x, y is A)
match M **with** $h\,x \to A$ **else** B	constructor match (scope of x is A)

We identify all phrases of syntax up to the consistent renaming of bound variables. In general, we write $\phi\{\psi/x\}$ for the outcome of substituting the phrase ψ for each free occurrence of the variable x in the phrase ϕ. We write fv(ϕ) for the set of variables occurring free in the phrase ϕ.

A value may be a variable x, the unit value $()$, a function **fun** $x \to A$, a pair (M,N), or a construction. The constructions $\mathsf{inl}\ M$ and $\mathsf{inr}\ M$ are the two sorts of value of sum type, while the construction $\mathsf{fold}\ M$ is a value of an iso-recursive type. A *first-order* value is any value not containing any instance of **fun** $x \to A$.

In our formulation of FPC, the syntax of expressions is in a reduced form in the style of A-normal form [51], where sequential composition of redexes is achieved by inserting suitable let-expressions. The other expressions are function application $M\ N$, equality $M = N$ (which tests whether the values M and N are syntactically identical), pair splitting **let** $(x,y) = M$ **in** A, and constructor matching **match** M **with** $h\,x \to A$ **else** B.

To complete our calculus, we augment FPC with the following operations for manipulating and writing assertions about a global state. The state is implicit and is simply a value of the calculus. We also assume an untyped first-order logic with equality over values, equipped with a *deducibility relation* $S \vdash C$, from finite multisets of formulas to formulas.

Completing the Syntax
Adding Global State to the Fixpoint Calculus

$A,B ::=$	expression
$\cdots$	expressions of the Fixpoint Calculus
get$()$	get current state
set(M)	set current state
assume $(s)C$	assumption of formula C (scope of s is C)
assert $(s)C$	assertion of formula C (scope of s is C)
$C ::=$	formula
$p(M_1,\ldots,M_n)$	predicate – p a predicate symbol
$M = M'$	equation
$C \wedge C' \mid \neg C \mid \exists x.C$	standard connectives and quantification

A formula C is first order if and only if it only contains first order values. A collection S is first order if and only if it only contains first order formulas.

The expression **get**() returns the current state as its value. The expression **set**(M) updates the current state with the value M and returns the unit value ().

We specify intended properties of programs by embedding assertions, which are formulas expected to hold with respect to the *log*, a finite multiset of assumed formulas. The expression **assume** $(s)C$ adds the formula $C\{^{M}/_{s}\}$ to the logged formulas, where M is the current state, and returns (). The expression **assert** $(s)C$ immediately returns (); we say the assertion *succeeds* if the formula $C\{^{M}/_{s}\}$ is deducible from the logged formulas, and otherwise that it *fails*. This style of embedding assumptions and assertions within expressions is in the spirit of the pioneering work of Floyd, Hoare, and Dijkstra on imperative programs; the formal details are an imperative extension of assumptions and assertions in RCF [10].

We use some syntactic sugar to make it easier to write and understand examples. We write $A;\ B$ for **let** _ $=$ A **in** B. We define boolean values as **false** $\triangleq$ inl () and **true** $\triangleq$ inr (). Conditional statements can then be defined as **if** M **then** A **else** B $\triangleq$ **match** M **with** inr $x \rightarrow A$ **else** B. We write **let rec** $f\ x = A$ **in** B as an abbreviation for defining a recursive function f, where the scope of f is A and B, and the scope of x is A. When s does not occur in C, we simply write C for $(s)C$. In our examples, we often use a more ML-like syntax, lessening the A-normal form restrictions of our calculus. In particular, we use **let** $f\ x = A$ for **let** f $=$ **fun** $x \rightarrow A$, **if** A **then** B_1 **else** B_2 for **let** $x = A$ **in if** x **then** B_1 **else** B_2 (where $x \notin \text{fv}(B_1, B_2)$), **let** $(x, y) = A$ **in** B for **let** $z = A$ **in let** $(x, y) = z$ **in** B (where $z \notin \text{fv}(B)$), and so on. See Bengtson et al. [10], for example, for a discussion of how to recover standard functional programming syntax and data types like Booleans and lists within the core FPC.

4.4.2 *Semantics*

We formalize the semantics of our calculus as a small-step reduction relation on configurations, each of which is a triple (A, N, S) consisting of a closed expression A, a state N, and a log S, which is a multiset of formulas generated by assumptions. A configuration (A, N, S) is first order if and only if N, S and all formulas occurring in A are first order.

We present the rules for reduction in two groups. The rules in the first group are independent of the current state, and correspond to the semantics of core FPC.

Reductions for the Core Calculus: $(A, N, S) \longrightarrow (A', N', S')$

$\mathcal{R}$ ::= [ ] | **let** $x = \mathcal{R}$ **in** A	evaluation context
$(\mathcal{R}[A], N, S) \longrightarrow (\mathcal{R}[A'], N', S')$ if $(A, N, S) \longrightarrow (A', N', S')$	(RED CTX)
$((\textbf{fun}\ x \rightarrow A)\ M, N, S) \longrightarrow (A\{^{M}/_{x}\}, N, S)$	(RED FUN)
$(M_1 = M_2, N, S) \longrightarrow (\textbf{true}, N, S)$ if $M_1 = M_2$	(RED EQ)
$(M_1 = M_2, N, S) \longrightarrow (\textbf{false}, N, S)$ if $M_1 \neq M_2$	(RED NEQ)

$(\textbf{let}\ x = M\ \textbf{in}\ A, N, S) \longrightarrow (A\{^M/_x\}, N, S)$	(RED LET)
$(\textbf{let}\ (x,y) = (M_1, M_2)\ \textbf{in}\ A, N, S) \longrightarrow (A\{^{M_1}/_x\}\{^{M_2}/_y\}, N, S)$	(RED SPLIT)
$(\textbf{match}\ (h\ M)\ \textbf{with}\ h\ x \to A\ \textbf{else}\ B, N, S) \longrightarrow (A\{^M/_x\}, N, S)$	(RED MATCH)
$(\textbf{match}\ (h'\ M)\ \textbf{with}\ h\ x \to A\ \textbf{else}\ B, N, S) \longrightarrow (B, N, S)$ if $h \neq h'$	(RED MISMATCH)

The second group of rules formalizes the semantics of assumptions, assertions and the get and set operators, described informally in the previous section.

Reductions Related to State: $(A,N,S) \longrightarrow (A',N',S')$

$(\textbf{get}(), N, S) \longrightarrow (N, N, S)$	(RED GET)
$(\textbf{set}(M), N, S) \longrightarrow ((), M, S)$	(RED SET)
$(\textbf{assume}\ (s)C, N, S) \longrightarrow ((), N, S \cup \{C\{^N/_s\}\})$	(RED ASSUME)
$(\textbf{assert}\ (s)C, N, S) \longrightarrow ((), N, S)$	(RED ASSERT)

We say an expression is safe if none of its assertions may fail at runtime. A configuration (A,N,S) has *failed* when $A = \mathcal{R}[\textbf{assert}\ (s)C]$ for some evaluation context $\mathcal{R}$, where $S \cup \{C\{^N/_s\}\}$ is not first order or we cannot derive $S \vdash C\{^N/_s\}$. A configuration (A,N,S) is *safe* if and only if there is no failed configuration reachable from (A,N,S), that is, for all (A',N',S'), if $(A,N,S) \longrightarrow^* (A',N',S')$ then (A',N',S') has not failed. The safety of a (first order) configuration can always be assured by carefully chosen assumptions (for example, **assume** (s)False). For this reason, user code should use assumptions with prudence (and possibly not at all).

The purpose of the type system in the next section is to establish safety by typing.

4.4.3 Types

There are two categories of type: *value types* characterize values, while *computation types* characterize the imperative computations denoted by expressions. Computation types resemble Hoare triples, with preconditions and postconditions.

Syntax of Value Types and Computation Types

$T, U, V ::=$	(value) type
α	type variable
unit	unit type
$\Pi x : T \cdot F$	dependent function type (scope of x is F)
$\Sigma x : T \cdot U$	dependent pair type (scope of x is U)
$T + U$	disjoint sum type
$\mu\, \alpha.T$	iso-recursive type (scope of α is T)
$F, G ::=$	computation type
$\{(s_0)C_0\}\, x{:}T\, \{(s_1)C_1\}$	(scope of s_0 is C_0, T, C_1, and scope of s_1, x is C_1)

Value types are based on the types of the FPC, except that function types $\Pi x : T \cdot F$ and pair types $\Sigma x : T \cdot U$ are dependent. In our examples we use the F7-style notations $x : T \to F$ and $x : T * U$ instead of $\Pi x : T \cdot F$ and $\Sigma x : T \cdot U$. If the bound variable x is not used, these types degenerate to simple types. In particular, if x is not free in U, we write $T * U$ for $x : T * U$, and if x is not free in F, we write $T \to F$ for $x : T \to F$. A value type T is first order if and only if T contains no occurrences of $\Pi x : U \cdot F$ (and hence contains no computation types). For the type $\Pi x : T \cdot F$ to be well formed, we require that either T is a first-order type or that x is not free in F. Similarly, for the type $\Sigma x : T \cdot U$ to be well formed, we require that either T is a first-order type or that x is not free in U.

A computation type $\{(s_0)C_0\}\, x{:}T\, \{(s_1)C_1\}$ means the following: if an expression has this type and it is started in an initial state s_0 satisfying the precondition C_0, and it terminates in final state s_1 with an answer x, then postcondition C_1 holds. As above, we write $\{(s_0)C_0\}\, T\, \{(s_1)C_1\}$ for $\{(s_0)C_0\}\, x{:}T\, \{(s_1)C_1\}$ if x is not free in C_1. If T is not first order, we require that x is not free in C_1.

When we write a type T in a context where a computation type is expected, we intend T as a shorthand for the computation type $\{(s_0)\mathsf{True}\}\, T\, \{(s_1)s_1 = s_0\}$. This is convenient for writing curried functions. Thus, the curried function type $x : T \to y : U \to F$ stands for $\Pi x : T \cdot \{(s_0')\mathsf{True}\}\, \Pi y : U \cdot F\, \{(s_1')s_1' = s_0'\}$.

Our calculus is parameterized by a type state representing the type of data in the state threaded through a computation, and which we take to be an abbreviation for a closed RIF type not involving function types – that is, a closed first-order type.

Our typing rules are specified with respect to *typing environments*, given as follows, which contain value types of variables, temporary subtyping assumptions for iso-recursive types, and the names of the state variables in scope.

Syntax of Typing Environments

$\mu ::=$	environment entry
$\quad \alpha <: \alpha'$	subtype ($\alpha \neq \alpha'$)
$\quad s$	state variable
$\quad x : T$	variable
$E ::= \varnothing \mid E, \mu$	environment

$\mathrm{dom}(\alpha <: \alpha') = \{\alpha, \alpha'\} \qquad \mathrm{dom}(s) = \{s\} \qquad \mathrm{dom}(x : T) = \{x\}$
$\mathrm{dom}(E, \mu) = \mathrm{dom}(E) \cup \mathrm{dom}(\mu) \qquad \mathrm{dom}(\varnothing) = \varnothing$
$\mathrm{fov}(E) = \{s \in E\} \cup \{x \in \mathrm{dom}(E) \mid (x : T) \in E,\ T \text{ is first-order}\}$

Our type system consists of several inductively defined judgments.

Judgments

$E \vdash \diamond$	E is syntactically well-formed
$E \vdash T$	in E, type T is syntactically well-formed
$E \vdash F$	in E, type F is syntactically well-formed
$E \vdash C$ fo	in E, formula C is first-order

$E \vdash T <: U$	in E, type T is a subtype of type U
$E \vdash F <: G$	in E, type F is a subtype of type G
$E \vdash M : T$	in E, value M has type T
$E \vdash A : F$	in E, expression A has computation type F

The rules defining these judgments are displayed in a series of groups. First, we describe the rules defining when environments, formulas, and value and computation types are well formed. An environment is well formed if its entries have pair-wise disjoint domains. A formula is well formed if all its free variables have first-order type in the environment. A type is well formed if its free variables have first-order type in the environment.

Rules of Well-Formedness

(ENV EMPTY)
$$\frac{}{\varnothing \vdash \diamond}$$

(ENV ENTRY)
$$\frac{E \vdash \diamond \quad \mathrm{fv}(\mu) \subseteq \mathrm{fov}(E) \quad \mathrm{dom}(\mu) \cap \mathrm{dom}(E) = \varnothing}{E, \mu \vdash \diamond}$$

(FORM)
$$\frac{E \vdash \diamond \quad C \text{ is first-order} \quad \mathrm{fv}(C) \subseteq \mathrm{fov}(E)}{E \vdash C \text{ fo}}$$

(ENV TYPE)
$$\frac{E \vdash \diamond \quad \mathrm{fv}(T) \subseteq \mathrm{fov}(E)}{E \vdash T}$$

First-order values may occur in types, but only within formulas; since our logic is untyped, these well-formedness rules need not constrain values occurring within types to be themselves well typed. We do constrain variables occurring in formulas to have first-order types.

General Rules for Expressions

(EXP RETURN)
$$\frac{E, s_0 \vdash M : T}{E \vdash M : \{(s_0)\mathsf{True}\}\,\_{:}T\,\{(s_1)s_0 = s_1\}}$$

(STATEFUL EXP LET)
$$\frac{E \vdash A : \{(s_0)C_0\}\,x_1{:}T_1\,\{(s_1)C_1\} \quad E, s_0, x_1 : T_1 \vdash B : \{(s_1)C_1\}\,x_2{:}T_2\,\{(s_2)C_2\} \quad \{s_1, x_1\} \cap \mathrm{fv}(T_2, C_2) = \varnothing}{E \vdash \mathbf{let}\ x_1 = A\ \mathbf{in}\ B : \{(s_0)C_0\}\,x_2{:}T_2\,\{(s_2)C_2\}}$$

(EXP EQ)
$$\frac{E \vdash M : T \quad E \vdash N : U \quad x \notin \mathrm{fv}(M,N) \quad E, s_0, s_1 \vdash C \text{ fo} \quad C = (s_0 = s_1) \wedge (x = \mathbf{true} \Leftrightarrow M = N) \quad T, U \text{ first-order}}{E \vdash M = N : \{(s_0)\mathsf{True}\}\,x{:}\mathsf{bool}\,\{(s_1)C\}}$$

In (EXP RETURN), when returning a value from a computation, the state is unchanged. In (EXP EQ), the return value of an equality test is refined with the logical formula expressing the test. The rule (STATEFUL EXP LET) glues together two computation types if the postcondition of the first matches the precondition of the second.

Assumptions and Assertions

(Exp Assume)

$$\frac{E, s_0, s_1 \vdash \diamond \quad E, s_0 \vdash C \text{ fo}}{E \vdash \textbf{assume } (s_0)C : \{(s_0)\mathsf{True}\}\, \mathsf{unit}\, \{(s_1)((s_0 = s_1) \wedge C)\}}$$

(Exp Assert)

$$\frac{E, s_0, s_1 \vdash \diamond \quad E, s_0 \vdash C \text{ fo}}{E \vdash \textbf{assert } (s_0)C : \{(s_0)C\}\, \mathsf{unit}\, \{(s_1)s_0 = s_1\}}$$

In (Exp Assume), an assumption **assume** $(s)C$ has C as postcondition, and does not modify the state. Dually, in (Exp Assert), an assertion **assert** $(s)C$ has C as precondition.

Rules for State Manipulation

(Stateful Get)

$$\frac{E, s_0, x_1 : \mathsf{state}, s_1 \vdash \diamond}{E \vdash \textbf{get}() : \{(s_0)\mathsf{True}\}\, x_1{:}\mathsf{state}\, \{(s_1)x_1 = s_0 \wedge s_1 = s_0\}}$$

(Stateful Set)

$$\frac{E \vdash M : \mathsf{state} \quad E, s_0, s_1 \vdash \diamond}{E \vdash \textbf{set}(M) : \{(s_0)\mathsf{True}\}\, \mathsf{unit}\, \{(s_1)s_1 = M\}}$$

In (Stateful Get), the type of **get**() records that the value read is the current state. In (Stateful Set), the postcondition of **set**(M) states that M is the new state. The postcondition of **set**(M) does not mention the initial state. We can recover this information through subtyping, below.

Subtyping for Computations

(Sub Comp)

$$\frac{\begin{array}{l} E, s_0 \vdash C_0 \text{ fo} \quad E, s_0 \vdash C_0' \text{ fo} \\ E, s_0, x{:}T, s_1 \vdash C_1 \text{ fo} \quad E, s_0, x{:}T', s_1 \vdash C_1' \text{ fo} \\ C_0' \vdash C_0 \quad E, s_0 \vdash T <: T' \quad (C_0' \wedge C_1) \vdash C_1' \end{array}}{E \vdash \{(s_0)C_0\}\, x{:}T\, \{(s_1)C_1\} <: \{(s_0)C_0'\}\, x{:}T'\, \{(s_1)C_1'\}}$$

(Exp Subsum)

$$\frac{E \vdash A : F \quad E \vdash F <: F'}{E \vdash A : F'}$$

In (Sub Comp), when computing the supertype of a computation type, we may strengthen the precondition, and weaken the postcondition relative to the strengthened precondition. For example, since $(C_0 \wedge C_1) \vdash (C_0 \wedge C_1)$, we have

$$E \vdash \{(s_0)C_0\}\, x{:}T\, \{(s_1)C_1\} <: \{(s_0)C_0\}\, x{:}T\, \{(s_1)C_0 \wedge C_1\}$$

Next, we present rules grouped by the different forms of value type. When type-checking values, we may gain information about their structure. We record this information by adding it to the precondition of the computation that uses the data, but only if the value being type-checked is first order.

Augmenting the Precondition of a Computation Type

$C \leadsto_T F \triangleq \{(s_1)C \wedge C_1\}\, x{:}U\, \{(s_2)C_2\}$ if T first-order

$C \leadsto_T F \triangleq F$ otherwise

where $F = \{(s_1)C_1\}\, x{:}U\, \{(s_2)C_2\}$ and $s_1 \notin \mathrm{fv}(C)$

Rules for Unit and Variables

(VAL UNIT)

$$\frac{E \vdash \diamond}{E \vdash () : \mathsf{unit}}$$

(VAL VAR)

$$\frac{E \vdash \diamond \quad (x : T) \in E}{E \vdash x : T}$$

The unit type has only one inhabitant (). The rule (VAL VAR) looks up the type of a variable in the environment.

Rules for Pairs

(VAL PAIR)

$$\frac{E \vdash M : T \quad E \vdash N : U\{M/x\}}{E \vdash (M, N) : (\Sigma x : T \cdot U)}$$

(STATEFUL EXP SPLIT)

$$\frac{\begin{array}{l} E \vdash M : (\Sigma x : T \cdot U) \\ E, x : T, y : U \vdash A : ((x, y) = M) \leadsto_{\Sigma x:T \cdot U} F \\ \{x, y\} \cap \mathrm{fv}(F) = \varnothing \end{array}}{E \vdash \mathbf{let}\ (x, y) = M\ \mathbf{in}\ A : F}$$

In (STATEFUL EXP SPLIT), when splitting a pair, we strengthen the precondition of the computation with the information derived from the pair split.

Rules for Sums and Recursive Types

$\mathsf{inl}{:}(T, T{+}U)$ $\quad \mathsf{inr}{:}(U, T{+}U)$ $\quad \mathsf{fold}{:}(T\{\mu\alpha.T/\alpha\}, \mu\alpha.T)$

(VAL INL INR FOLD)

$$\frac{h : (T, U) \quad E \vdash M : T \quad E \vdash U}{E \vdash h\, M : U}$$

(STATEFUL EXP MATCH INL INR FOLD)

$$\frac{\begin{array}{l} E \vdash M : T \quad h : (U, T) \quad x \notin \mathrm{fv}(F) \\ E, x : U \vdash A : (h\, x = M) \leadsto_T F \\ E \vdash B : (\forall x. h\, x \neq M) \leadsto_T F \end{array}}{E \vdash \mathbf{match}\ M\ \mathbf{with}\ h\, x \to A\ \mathbf{else}\ B : F}$$

The typing rules for dependent functions are standard.

Rules for Functions

(STATEFUL VAL FUN)

$$\frac{E, x : T \vdash A : F}{E \vdash \mathbf{fun}\, x \to A : (\Pi x : T \cdot F)}$$

(STATEFUL EXP APPL)

$$\frac{E \vdash M : (\Pi x : T \cdot F) \quad E \vdash N : T}{E \vdash M\, N : F\{N/x\}}$$

The rules for constructions $h\ M$ depend on an auxiliary relation $h : (T, U)$ that gives the argument T and result U of each constructor h. As in (STATEFUL EXP SPLIT), the rule (STATEFUL EXP MATCH INL INR FOLD) strengthens the preconditions of the different branches with information derived from the branching condition.

We complete the system with the following rules of subtyping for value types.

Subtyping for Value Types

(SUB UNIT)
$$\frac{E \vdash \diamond}{E \vdash \mathsf{unit} <: \mathsf{unit}}$$

(SUB SUM)
$$\frac{E \vdash T <: T' \quad E \vdash U <: U'}{E \vdash (T + U) <: (T' + U')}$$

(STATEFUL SUB FUN)
$$\frac{E \vdash T' <: T \quad E, x : T' \vdash F <: F'}{E \vdash (\Pi x : T \cdot F) <: (\Pi x : T' \cdot F')}$$

(SUB PAIR)
$$\frac{E \vdash T <: T' \quad E, x : T \vdash U <: U'}{E \vdash (\Sigma x : T \cdot U) <: (\Sigma x : T' \cdot U')}$$

(SUB VAR)
$$\frac{E \vdash \diamond \quad (\alpha <: \alpha') \in E}{E \vdash \alpha <: \alpha'}$$

(SUB REC)
$$\frac{E, \alpha <: \alpha' \vdash T <: T' \quad \alpha \notin \mathrm{fv}(T') \quad \alpha' \notin \mathrm{fv}(T)}{E \vdash (\mu\alpha.T) <: (\mu\alpha'.T')}$$

These rules are essentially standard [4, 13, 42]. In (SUB REC), when checking subtyping of recursive types, we use the environment to keep track of assumptions introduced when unfolding the types.

The main result of this section is that a well-typed expression run in a state satisfying its precondition is *safe*, that is, no assertions fail. Using this result, we can implement different type systems for reasoning about stateful computation in the calculus.

Theorem 1 (Safety) *If* $\varnothing \vdash A : \{(s)C\}\_ : T\{(s')\mathsf{True}\}$, $\varnothing \vdash C\{^M/_s\}$ *and* $\varnothing \vdash M :$ state *then the configuration* $(A, M, \varnothing)$ *is safe.*

The proof of this theorem uses a state-passing translation of RIF into RCF. In particular, a computation type $\{(s_0)C_0\}\, x{:}T\, \{(s_1)C_1\}$ is translated to the refined state monad $\mathcal{M}_{C_0,C_1}(\llbracket T \rrbracket)$ described in the introduction, where $\llbracket T \rrbracket$ is the translation of the value type T. We prove the translation to preserve types, allowing us to appeal to the safety theorem for well-typed RCF programs. The translation and the proof can be found in the technical report [12].

4.4.4 Pragmatics

We find it useful to organize our code into modules. Rather than formalize modules in the syntax, we follow the conventions of Bengtson et al. [10]. A module consists of a set of function names $f_1, \ldots, f_k$ with corresponding implementations $M_1, \ldots, M_k$ and associated types $T_1, \ldots, T_k$. It may also include predicate symbols p and an assumption **assume** $(s)C$. (Without loss of generality, we suppose there is a single such **assume** expression, but clearly multiple assume expressions can be reduced to a single **assume** expression with a conjunction of the assumed formulas.) A module is *well formed* if the functions type-check at the declared function types, under the given assumptions, that is, if for all $i \in [1..k]$: $f_1 : T_1, \ldots, f_k : T_k \vdash \textbf{let}\ \_ = \textbf{assume}\ (s)C\ \textbf{in}\ M_i : T_i$. All modules used in this paper are well formed. We use $\textbf{let} f = M$ to define the implementation of a function in a module, and $\textbf{val} f : T$ for its associated type. We sometimes also use $\textbf{let} f : T = M$ to capture the same information.

Type-checking a computation A (at type F) in the context of a module with functions $f_1, \ldots, f_k$ with implementations $M_1, \ldots, M_k$ and types $T_1, \ldots, T_k$ corresponds to type-checking $f_1 : T_1, \ldots, f_k : T_k \vdash \textbf{let}\ \_ = \textbf{assume}\ (s)C\ \textbf{in}\ A : F$ and executing A in the context of that module corresponds to executing the expression $\textbf{assume}\ (s)C;\ \textbf{let} f_1 = M_1\ \textbf{in}\ \ldots \textbf{let} f_n = M_n\ \textbf{in}\ A$.

As illustrated in previous sections, to use our calculus, we first *instantiate* it with an *extension API module* that embodies the behavioural type system that we want to capture. In particular, functions in an extension API module perform all the required state manipulations. These extension API functions are written in the internal language described earlier, using the state-manipulation primitives **get**() and **set**(). Moreover, the extension API defines a concrete state type.

4.5 Related Work

We discuss related work on type systems for access control. Pottier et al. [46] develop a type and effect system for SBAC. As in our work, the goal is to prevent security exceptions. Our work is intended to show that their type system may be generalized so that effects are represented as formulas. Hence, our work is more flexible in that we can deal with an arbitrary lattice of dependent permissions; their system is limited to a finite set of permissions.

Besson et al. [11] develop a static analysis for .NET libraries, to discover anomalies in the security policy implemented by stack inspection. The tool depends on a flow analysis rather than a type system.

A separate line of work investigates the information flow properties of stack-based and history-based access control [6, 7, 43]. We believe our type system could be adapted to check information flow, but this remains future work. Another line of future investigation is type inference; ideas from the study of refinement types may be helpful [35, 49].

Abadi et al. [3] initiated the study of logic for access control in distributed systems; they propose a propositional logic with a says-modality to indicate the intentions of different principals. This logic is used by Wallach et al. [55] to provide a logical semantics of stack inspection. Abadi [1] develops an approach to access control in which the formulas of a constructive version of the logic are interpreted as types. AURA Jia et al. [34] is a language that is based, in part, on this idea.

Fournet et al. [25] introduced the idea of type-checking code to ensure conformance to a logic-based authorization policy. A series of papers develops the idea for distributed systems modelled with process calculi [26, 37]. In this line of work, access rights may be granted but not retracted. Our approach in Section 4.2 is different in that we deal with roles that may be activated and deactivated.

4.6 Conclusion

We described a higher-order imperative language whose semantics is based on the state monad, refined with preconditions and postconditions. By making different choices for the underlying state type, and supplying suitable primitive functions, we gave semantics for standard access control mechanisms based on stacks, histories, and roles. Type-checking ensures the absence of security exceptions, a common problem for code-based access control.

This work is dedicated to Tony Hoare, in part in gratitude for his useful feedback over the years on various behavioural type systems for process calculi. Some of those calculi had a great deal of innovative syntax. So we hope he will endorse our general conclusion, that it is better to design behavioural type systems using types refined with logical formulas, than to invent still more syntax.

Acknowledgements We are grateful to Martín Abadi, Robert Atkey, Anindya Banerjee, Moritz Becker, Cliff Jones, David Naumann, Nikhil Swamy, and Wouter Swierstra for comments and discussions.

References

1. Abadi, M.: Access control in a core calculus of dependency. In: International Conference on Functional Programming (ICFP'06), pp. 263–273 (2006).
2. Abadi, M., Fournet, C.: Access control based on execution history. In: Network and Distributed System Security Symposium (NDSS'03), pp. 107–121. The Internet Society, ISOC, Reston, VA, USA (2003).
3. Abadi, M., Burrows, M., Lampson, B., Plotkin, G.: A calculus for access control in distributed systems. ACM Trans. Programming Languages Systems **15**(4), 706–734 (1993).
4. Aspinall, D., Compagnoni, A.: Subtyping dependent types. Theoret. Comput Sci. **266**(1–2), 273–309 (2001).
5. Atkey, R.: Parameterized notions of computation. J. Funct. Programm. **19**, 355–376 (2009).
6. Banerjee, A., Naumann, D.: History-based access control and secure information flow. In: Construction and Analysis of Safe, Secure, and Interoperable Smart Devices (CASSIS 2004), vol. 3362 of LNCS, pp. 27–48. Springer, Heidelberg, Germany (2005).
7. Banerjee, A., Naumann, D.: Stack-based access control and secure information flow. J. Funct. Programm. **15**(2), 131–177 (2005)
8. Becker, M.Y., Nanz, S.: A logic for state-modifying authorization policies. In: European Symposium on Research in Computer Security (ESORICS'07), vol. 4734 of LNCS, pp. 203–218. Springer, Heidelberg, Germany (2007).
9. Becker, M.Y., Sewell, P.: Cassandra: flexible trust management, applied to electronic health records. In: 17th IEEE Computer Security Foundations Workshop (CSFW'04), pp. 139–154 (June 2004).

10. Bengtson, J., Bhargavan, K., Fournet, C., Gordon, A.D., Maffeis, S.: Refinement types for secure implementations. Technical Report MSR-TR-2008-118, Microsoft Research (2008). A preliminary, abridged version appears in the proceedings of CSF'08.
11. Besson, F., Blanc, T., Fournet, C., Gordon, A.D.: From stack inspection to access control: A security analysis for libraries. In: Computer Security Foundations Workshop (CSFW'04), pp. 61–77 (2004).
12. Borgström, J., Gordon, A.D., Pucella, R.: Roles, stacks, histories: A triple for Hoare. Technical Report MSR-TR-2009-97, Microsoft Research (2009).
13. Cardelli, L.: Typechecking dependent types and subtypes. In: Foundations of Logic and Functional Programming, vol. 306 of LNCS, pp. 45–57. Springer (1986).
14. Constable, R.L., Allen, S.F., Bromley, H.M., Cleaveland, W.R., Cremer, J.F., Harper, R.W., Howe, D.J., Knoblock, T.B., Mendler, N.P., Panangaden, P., et al.: Implementing Mathematics with the Nuprl Proof Development System. Prentice-Hall, Hemel Hampstead, England (1986).
15. de Moura, L., Bjørner, N.: Z3: An efficient SMT solver. In: Tools and Algorithms for the Construction and Analysis of Systems (TACAS'08), vol. 4963 of LNCS, pp. 337–340. Springer (2008).
16. DeLine, R., Fähndrich, M.: Enforcing high-level protocols in low-level software. In: Programming Language Design and Implementation (PLDI'01), pp. 59–69 (2001).
17. Detlefs, D., Nelson, G., Saxe, J.B.: Simplify: a theorem prover for program checking. J. ACM **52**(3): 365–473 (2005).
18. Dutertre, B., de Moura, L.: The YICES SMT solver. Available at http://yices.csl.sri.com/tool-paper.pdf, 2006.
19. Ferraiolo, D.F., Kuhn, D.R.: Role based access control. In: Proc. National Computer Security Conference, pp. 554–563 (1992).
20. Filliâtre, J., Marché, C.: Multi-prover Verification of C Programs. In: International Conference on Formal Engineering Methods (ICFEM 2004), vol. 3308 of LNCS, pp. 15–29. Springer, Heidelberg, Germany (2004).
21. Filliâtre, J.-C.: Proof of imperative programs in type theory. In: Selected Papers from the International Workshop on Types for Proofs and Programs (TYPES '98), 1657, pp. 78–92. Springer (1999).
22. Flanagan, C.: Hybrid type checking. In: ACM Symposium on Principles of Programming Languages (POPL'06), pp. 245–256 (2006).
23. Flanagan, C., Abadi, M.: Types for safe locking. In: European Symposium on Programming (ESOP'99), vol. 1576 of LNCS, pp. 91–108, Springer (1999).
24. Fournet, C., Gordon, A.D.: Stack inspection: Theory and variants. ACM Trans. Programm. Languages Systems **25**(3): 360–399 (2003).
25. Fournet, C., Gordon, A.D., Maffeis, S.: A type discipline for authorization policies. In: 14th European Symposium on Programming (ESOP'05), vol. 3444 of LNCS, pp. 141–156. Springer, Heidelberg, Germany (2005).
26. Fournet, C., Gordon, A.D., Maffeis, S.: A type discipline for authorization policies in distributed systems. In: 20th IEEE Computer Security Foundation Symposium (CSF'07), pp. 31–45 (2007).
27. Freeman, T., Pfenning, F.: Refinement types for ML. In: Programming Language Design and Implementation (PLDI'91), pp. 268–277. ACM, New York, NY, USA (1991).
28. Gifford, D., Lucassen, J.: Integrating functional and imperative programming. In: ACM Conference on Lisp and Functional Programming, pp. 28–38, (1986).
29. Gong, L.: Inside Java 2 Platform Security: Architecture, API Design, and Implementation. Addison-Wesley (1999).
30. Gordon, A.D., Jeffrey, A.S.A.: Authenticity by typing for security protocols. J. Comput. Security **11**(4): 451–521 (2003).
31. Gronski, J., Knowles, K., Tomb, A., Freund, S.N., Flanagan, C.: Sage: hybrid checking for flexible specifications. In: R. Findler, (ed.) Scheme and Functional Programming Workshop, pp. 93–104, (2006).
32. Gunter, C.: Semantics of Programming Languages. MIT, Kluwer, Dordrecht, The Netherlands (1992).

33. Hardy, N.: The confused deputy (or why capabilities might have been invented). ACM SIGOPS Operat. Systems Rev., **22**, 36–38 (1988).
34. Jia, L., Vaughan, J.A., Mazurak, K., Zhao, J., Zarko, L., Schorr, J., Zdancewic, S.: AURA: Preliminary technical results. Technical Report MS-CIS-08-10, University of Pennsylvania (2008).
35. Knowles, K.W., Flanagan, C.: Type reconstruction for general refinement types. In: ESOP, vol. 4421 of LNCS, pp. 505–519. Springer (2007).
36. Li, N., Mitchell, J.C., Winsborough, W.H.: Design of a role-based trust management framework. In: IEEE Security and Privacy, pp 114–130, (2002).
37. Maffeis, S., Abadi, M., Fournet, C., Gordon, A.D.: Code-carrying authorization. In: European Symposium On Research In Computer Security (ESORICS'08), pp. 563–579 (2008).
38. Moggi, E.: Notions of computations and monads. Inform. Comput., **93**, 55–92 (1991).
39. Nanevski, A., Morrisett, G., Birkedal, L.: Polymorphism and separation in Hoare Type Theory. In: International Conference on Functional Programming (ICFP'06), pp. 62–73 (2006).
40. Nanevski, A., Morrisett, G., Shinnar, A., Govereau, P., Birkedal, L.: Ynot: dependent types for imperative programs. In: International Conference on Functional Programming (ICFP'08), pp. 229–240 (2008).
41. Nordström, B., Petersson, K., Smith, J.: Programming in Martin-Löf's Type Theory. Clarendon Press Oxford (1990).
42. Pierce, B., Sangiorgi, D.: Typing and subtyping for mobile processes. Math. Structures Comput. Sci., **6**(5) 409–454 (1996).
43. Pistoia, M., Banerjee, A., Naumann, D.: Beyond stack inspection: A unified access-control and information-flow security model. In: IEEE Security and Privacy, pp. 149–163 (2007).
44. Pistoia, M., Chandra, S., Fink, S.J., Yahav, E.: A survey of static analysis methods for identifying security vulnerabilities in software systems. IBM Syst. J. **46(2)**, 265–288 (2007).
45. Plotkin, G.D.: Denotational semantics with partial functions. Unpublished lecture notes, CSLI, Stanford University (July 1985).
46. Pottier, F., Skalka, C., Smith, S.: A systematic approach to static access control. ACM Trans. on Programm. Languages Systems **27**(2), 344–382 (2005).
47. Ranise S., Tinelli, C.: The SMT-LIB Standard: Version 1.2 (2006).
48. Régis-Gianas, Y., Pottier, F.: A Hoare logic for call-by-value functional programs. In: Mathematics of Program Construction (MPC'08), vol. 5133 of LNCS, pp. 305–335. Springer, Heidelberg, Germany (2008).
49. Rondon, P., Kawaguchi, M., Jhala, R.: Liquid types. In: Programming Language Design and Implementation (PLDI'08), pp. 159–169. ACM, New York, NY, USA (2008).
50. Rushby, J., Owre, S., Shankar, N.: Subtypes for specifications: Predicate subtyping in PVS. IEEE Trans. Software Eng., **24**(9), 709–720 (1998).
51. Sabry A., Felleisen, M.: Reasoning about programs in continuation-passing style. LISP and Symbolic Comput., **6**(3–4), 289–360 (1993).
52. Sandhu, R., Coyne, E.J., Feinstein, H.L., Youman, C.E.: Role-based access control models. IEEE Comput. **29**(2), 38–47 (1996).
53. Strom, R.E., Yemini, S.: Typestate: A programming language concept for enhancing software reliability. IEEE Trans. Software Eng. **12**, 157–171 (1986).
54. Wadler, P.: Comprehending monads. Math. Struct. Comput. Sci. **2**, 461–493 (1992).
55. Wallach, D.S., Appel, A.W., Felten, E.W.: SAFKASI: A security mechanism for language-based systems. ACM Trans. Software Eng. Methodo., **9**(4), pp. 341–378 (2000).
56. Xi, H., Pfenning, F., Dependent types in practical programming. In: Principles of Programming Languages (POPL'99), pp. 214–227 (1999).

Chapter 5
Forward with Hoare

Mike Gordon and Hélène Collavizza

Abstract Hoare's celebrated paper entitled "An Axiomatic Basis for Computer Programming" appeared in 1969, so the Hoare formula $P\{S\}Q$ is now 40 years old! That paper introduced Hoare Logic, which is still the basis for program verification today, but is now mechanised inside sophisticated verification systems. We aim here to give an accessible introduction to methods for proving Hoare formulae based both on the forward computation of postconditions and on the backward computation of preconditions. Although precondition methods are better known, computing postconditions provides a verification framework that encompasses methods ranging from symbolic execution to full deductive proof of correctness.

5.1 Introduction

Hoare logic [12] is a deductive system whose axioms and rules of inference provide a method of proving statements of the form $P\{S\}Q$, where S is a program statement[1] and P and Q are assertions about the values of variables. Following current practice, we use the notation $\{P\}S\{Q\}$ instead of $P\{S\}Q$. Such a 'Hoare triple' means that Q (the 'postcondition') holds in any state reached by executing S from an initial state in which P (the 'precondition') holds. Program statements may contain variables V (X, Y, Z, etc.), value expressions (E) and Boolean expressions (B). They are

[1] The word 'statement' is overused: Hoare statements $P\{S\}Q$ (or $\{P\}S\{Q\}$) are either true or false, but program statements are constructs that can be executed to change the values of variables. To avoid this confusion program statements are sometimes called commands.

M. Gordon (✉)
University of Cambridge Computer Laboratory William Gates Building,
15 JJ Thomson Avenue, Cambridge CB3 0FD, UK
e-mail: Mike.Gordon@cl.cam.ac.uk

H. Collavizza
Université de Nice–Sophia-Antipolis – I3S/CNRS, 930, route des Colles,
B.P. 145 06903 Sophia-Antipolis, France
e-mail: helen@polytech.unice.fr

C.B. Jones et al. (eds.), *Reflections on the Work of C.A.R. Hoare*,
DOI 10.1007/978-1-84882-912-1_5,

built out of the skip (SKIP) and assignment statements ($V := E$) using sequential composition ($S_1 ; S_2$), conditional branching (IF B THEN S_1 ELSE S_2) and WHILE-loops (WHILE B DO S). The assertions P and Q are formal logic formulae expressing properties of the values of variables.

Hoare explicitly acknowledges that his deductive system is influenced by the formal treatment of program execution due to Floyd [8].[2] There is, however, a difference, which is exhibited below using Hoare triple notation (where the notation $M[E/V]$, where M can be a formula or expression, denotes the result of substituting E for V in M).

Floyd's assignment axiom: $\vdash \{P\}\, V := E \{\exists v.\, (V = E[v/V]) \wedge P[v/V]\}$

Hoare's assignment axiom: $\vdash \{Q[E/V]\}\, V := E \{Q\}$

These are axiom schemes: any instance obtained by replacing P, Q, V, E by specific terms and formulae is an axiom. Example instances of the axiom schemes, using the replacements $P \mapsto (\mathtt{X}{=}\mathtt{Y})$, $Q \mapsto (\mathtt{X}{=}2{\times}\mathtt{Y})$, $V \mapsto \mathtt{X}$ and $E \mapsto (\mathtt{X}{+}\mathtt{Y})$, are:

Floyd: $\vdash \{\mathtt{X}{=}\mathtt{Y}\}\, \mathtt{X} := \mathtt{X}{+}\mathtt{Y} \{\exists v.\, (\mathtt{X} = ((\mathtt{X}{+}\mathtt{Y})[v/\mathtt{X}])) \wedge ((\mathtt{X}{=}\mathtt{Y})[v/\mathtt{X}])\}$

Hoare: $\vdash \{(\mathtt{X}{=}2{\times}\mathtt{Y})[(\mathtt{X}{+}\mathtt{Y})/\mathtt{X}]\}\, \mathtt{X} := \mathtt{X}{+}\mathtt{Y} \{\mathtt{X}{=}2{\times}\mathtt{Y}\}$

which become the following if the substitutions $M[E/V]$ are performed:

Floyd: $\vdash \{\mathtt{X}{=}\mathtt{Y}\}\, \mathtt{X} := \mathtt{X}{+}\mathtt{Y} \{\exists v.\, (\mathtt{X} = v{+}\mathtt{Y}) \wedge (v{=}\mathtt{Y})\}$

Hoare: $\vdash \{(\mathtt{X}{+}\mathtt{Y}){=}2{\times}\mathtt{Y}\}\, \mathtt{X} := \mathtt{X}{+}\mathtt{Y} \{\mathtt{X}{=}2{\times}\mathtt{Y}\}$

These are both equivalent to $\vdash \{\mathtt{X}{=}\mathtt{Y}\}\, \mathtt{X} := \mathtt{X}{+}\mathtt{Y} \{\mathtt{X}{=}2{\times}\mathtt{Y}\}$, but the reasoning in the Hoare case is a bit simpler since there is no existential quantification.

In general, the Floyd and Hoare assignment axioms are equivalent, but it is the Hoare axiom that is more widely used, since it avoids an accumulation of an existential quantifier – one for each assignment in the program.

The axioms of Hoare logic include all instances of the Hoare assignment axiom scheme given above. The rules of inference of the logic provide rules for combining Hoare triples about program statements into Hoare triples about the result of combining the statements using sequential composition, conditional branches and WHILE-loops.

5.2 Weakest Preconditions and Strongest Postconditions

A few years after Hoare's pioneering paper, Dijkstra published his influential book "A Discipline of Programming" [6] in which a framework for specifying semantics based on 'predicate transformers' – rules for transforming predicates on states – is

[2] The fascinating story of the flow of ideas between the early pioneers of programming logic is delightfully told in Jones' historical paper [16].

described. Dijkstra regarded assertions like preconditions (P above) and postconditions (Q above) as predicates on the program state, since for a given state such an assertion is either true or false. His book introduces 'weakest preconditions' as a predicate transformer semantics that treats assignment statements in a way equivalent to Hoare's assignment axiom. A dual notion of 'strongest postconditions' corresponds to Floyd's treatment of assignments. We do not know who first introduced the concept of strongest postconditions. They are discussed in Dijkstra's 1990 book with Scholten [7], but several recent papers (e.g. [11]) cite Gries' 1981 textbook [10], which only describes them in an exercise. Jones [16, p. 12] mentions that Floyd discusses a clearly related notion of 'strongest verifiable consequents' in his 1967 paper.

If $P \Rightarrow Q$ then P is said to be stronger than Q. The strongest postcondition predicate transformer for a statement S transforms a precondition predicate P to a postcondition predicate $\mathtt{sp}\, S\, P$, which is the 'strongest' predicate holding after executing S in a state satisfying precondition P. This is strongest in the sense that if Q has the property that it holds of any state resulting from executing S when P, then $\mathtt{sp}\, S\, P$ is stronger than Q – i.e. $\mathtt{sp}\, S\, P \Rightarrow Q$. The strongest postcondition predicate transformer semantics of $V := E$ is

$$\mathtt{sp}\,(V := E)\, P \;=\; \exists\, v.\,(V = E[v/V]) \wedge P[v/V]$$

The definition of strongest postcondition entails that $\{P\}\, V := E\, \{Q\}$ holds if and only if $\mathtt{sp}\,(V := E)\, P$ entails Q.

If $P \Rightarrow Q$ then Q is said to be weaker than P. The weakest precondition predicate transformer for a statement S transforms a postcondition predicate Q to a precondition predicate $\mathtt{wp}\, S\, Q$, which is the 'weakest' predicate that ensures that if a state satisfies it then after executing S the predicate Q holds.[3] This is weakest in the sense that if P has the property that executing S when P holds ensures that Q holds, then $\mathtt{wp}\, S\, Q$ is weaker than P – i.e. $P \Rightarrow \mathtt{wp}\, S\, Q$. The weakest precondition predicate transformer semantics of $V := E$ is

$$\mathtt{wp}\,(V := E)\, Q \;=\; Q[E/V]$$

The definition of weakest precondition entails that $\{P\}\, V := E\, \{Q\}$ holds if and only if P entails $\mathtt{wp}\,(V := E)\, Q$.

Equations satisfied by $\mathtt{sp}\, S\, P$ and $\mathtt{wp}\, S\, Q$ are listed in Fig. 5.1 (the equations for assignments are repeated there for convenience). These equations were originally taken as axioms. The axiomatic approach is discussed in Hoare's paper: it has the advantage of allowing a partial specification of meaning, which gives freedom to compiler writers and can make language standards more flexible. However, a purely axiomatic approach is hard to scale to complex programming constructs, as the

[3] Dijkstra defined 'weakest precondition' to require termination of S – what we are calling 'weakest precondition' he calls 'weakest liberal precondition'. Dijkstra also uses different notation: in his first book he uses $\mathtt{wlp}\,(S, Q)$ and $\mathtt{wp}\,(S, Q)$. In the later book with Scholten he uses $\mathtt{wlp}.S.Q$ and $\mathtt{wp}.S.Q$. Thus our $\mathtt{wp}\, S\, Q$ is Dijkstra's $\mathtt{wlp}\,(S, Q)$ (or $\mathtt{wlp}.S.Q$). However, our use of 'strongest postcondition' corresponds to Dijkstra's, though our notation differs.

$$\begin{aligned}
&\texttt{sp}\ \texttt{SKIP}\ P = P\\
&\texttt{wp}\ \texttt{SKIP}\ Q = Q\\[4pt]
&\texttt{sp}\ (V := E)\ P = \exists v.\,(V{=}E[v/V]) \wedge P[v/V]\\
&\texttt{wp}\ (V := E)\ Q = Q[E/V]\\[4pt]
&\texttt{sp}\ (S_1\,;S_2)\ P = \texttt{sp}\ S_2\ (\texttt{sp}\ S_1\ P)\\
&\texttt{wp}\ (S_1\,;S_2)\ Q = \texttt{wp}\ S_1\ (\texttt{wp}\ S_2\ Q)\\[4pt]
&\texttt{sp}\ (\texttt{IF}\ B\ \texttt{THEN}\ S_1\ \texttt{ELSE}\ S_2)\ P = (\texttt{sp}\ S_1\ (P \wedge B)) \vee (\texttt{sp}\ S_2\ (P \wedge \neg B))\\
&\texttt{wp}\ (\texttt{IF}\ B\ \texttt{THEN}\ S_1\ \texttt{ELSE}\ S_2)\ Q = ((\texttt{wp}\ S_1\ Q) \wedge B) \vee ((\texttt{wp}\ S_2\ Q) \wedge \neg B)\\[4pt]
&\texttt{sp}\ (\texttt{WHILE}\ B\ \texttt{DO}\ S)\ P = (\texttt{sp}\ (\texttt{WHILE}\ B\ \texttt{DO}\ S)\ (\texttt{sp}\ S\ (P \wedge B))) \vee (P \wedge \neg B)\\
&\texttt{wp}\ (\texttt{WHILE}\ B\ \texttt{DO}\ S)\ Q = (\texttt{wp}\ S\ (\texttt{wp}\ (\texttt{WHILE}\ B\ \texttt{DO}\ S)\ Q) \wedge B) \vee (Q \wedge \neg B)
\end{aligned}$$

Fig. 5.1 Equations defining strongest postconditions and weakest preconditions

axioms and rules get complicated and consequently hard to trust. It is now more common to give a formal semantics of programming constructs (either operational or denotational) and to derive Hoare logic axioms and rules and predicate transformer laws from this [24].

Computing $\texttt{sp}\,(S_1\,;S_2)\,P$ using the equations in Fig. 5.1 consists of starting from a precondition P, then first computing $\texttt{sp}\,S_1\,P$ and then applying $\texttt{sp}\,S_2$ to the resulting predicate. This is forwards symbolic execution. In contrast, computing $\texttt{wp}\,(S_1\,;S_2)\,Q$ proceeds backwards from a postcondition Q by first computing $\texttt{wp}\,S_2\,Q$ and then applying $\texttt{wp}\,S_1$ to the resulting predicate. We have more to say about forwards versus backwards later (e.g. in Section 5.6).

5.3 Proving Hoare Triples via Predicate Transformers

The relationship between Hoare triples, strongest postconditions and weakest preconditions is that $\{P\}S\{Q\}$ holds if and only if $(\texttt{sp}\,S\,P) \Rightarrow Q$ and also if and only if $P \Rightarrow \texttt{wp}\,S\,Q$. These implications are purely logical formulae, so a pure logic theorem prover can be used to prove them. Thus strongest postconditions and weakest preconditions each provide a way of 'compiling' the problem of verifying a Hoare triple to a purely logical problem.[4] For a loop-free program S, the equations in Fig. 5.1 can be used as left-to-right rewrites to calculate $\texttt{sp}\,S\,P$ and $\texttt{wp}\,S\,Q$ (if S contains a `WHILE`-loop then such rewriting may not terminate). The right-hand side of the equation for $\texttt{sp}\,(V := E)\,P$ contains an existentially quantified conjunction, whereas the right-hand side of the equation for $\texttt{wp}\,(V := E)\,Q$ is just $Q[E/V]$, thus

[4] Actually this is an oversimplification: mathematical constants might occur in the formula, e.g. $+$, $-$, $\times$ from the theory of arithmetic, so the theorem prover may need to go beyond pure logic and solve problems in mathematical theories.

```
R:=0;
K:=0;
IF I < J THEN K:=K+1 ELSE SKIP ;
IF K = 1 ∧ ¬(I = J) THEN R:=J − I ELSE R:=I − J
```

Fig. 5.2 The loop-free example program `AbsMinus`

the formulae generated by the equations for strongest postconditions will be significantly more complex than those for weakest preconditions. This is one reason why weakest preconditions are often used in Hoare logic verifiers. The reader is invited to compare the two proofs of $\{\texttt{I} < \texttt{J}\}\texttt{AbsMinus}\{\texttt{R} = \texttt{J}-\texttt{I} \wedge \texttt{I}<\texttt{J}\}$ (the loop-free program `AbsMinus` is given in Fig. 5.2) obtained by manually calculating `sp AbsMinus (I < J)` and `wp AbsMinus (R = J−I ∧ I<J)`.

Although the naive calculation of `sp` SP using the equations in Fig. 5.1 generates complicated formulae with nested existential quantifications, a more careful calculation strategy based on symbolic execution is possible. This can be used as a theoretical framework for symbolic execution in software model checking [11].

5.4 Symbolic Execution and Strongest Postconditions

Suppose all the variables in a program S are included in the list $X_1, \ldots, X_n$ (where if $m \neq n$ then $X_m \neq X_n$). We shall specify a set of states of the program variables symbolically by logical formulae of the form:

$$\exists x_1 \cdots x_n.\, X_1 = e_1 \,\wedge \cdots \wedge\, X_n = e_n \,\wedge\, \phi$$

where $x_1, \ldots, x_n$ are logical variables (think of x_i as symbolically representing the initial value of program variable X_i), $e_1, \ldots, e_n$ are expressions (e_i represents the current value of X_i) and ϕ is a logical formula constraining the relationships between the values of the variables. For reasons that will become clear later, it is required that neither $e_1, \ldots, e_n$ nor ϕ contain the program variables $X_1, \ldots, X_n$, though they may well contain the variables $x_1, \ldots, x_n$. For example, the formula

$$\exists i j.\, \texttt{I} = i \wedge \texttt{J} = j \wedge i < j$$

represents the set of states in which the value of program variable `I` (represented symbolically by i) is less than the value of program variable `J` (represented symbolically by j). This formula is logically equivalent to `I < J`. In general, any predicate P can be written as

$$\exists x_1 \cdots x_n.\, X_1 = x_1 \,\wedge \cdots \wedge\, X_n = x_n \,\wedge\, P[x_1, \ldots, x_n / X_1, \ldots, X_n]$$

where $P[x_1, \ldots, x_n / X_1, \ldots, X_n]$ (corresponding to ϕ above) denotes the result of replacing all occurrences of program variable X_i by variable x_i ($1 \leq i \leq n$) that symbolically represents its value. In these formulae, program variables X_i and variables x_i, representing symbolic values, are both just logical variables. Expressions in programs (e.g. the right-hand side of assignments) are logic terms and tests in conditionals are logic formulae. This identification of program language constructs with logic terms and formulae is one of the reasons why Hoare logic is so effective. Although this identification might appear to be confusing the different worlds of programming languages and logical systems, it does have a sound semantic basis [2, 4, 13]. The reason for adopting this form of symbolic representation is because the strongest postcondition for assignment preserves it and introduces no new existential quantifiers.

$$\mathtt{sp}\,(X_i := E)\,(\exists x_1 \cdots x_n.\, X_1 = e_1 \wedge \cdots \wedge X_n = e_n \wedge \phi)$$
$$\exists x_1 \cdots x_n.\, X_1 = e_1 \wedge \cdots \wedge X_i = E[e_1 \cdots e_n / X_1 \cdots X_n] \wedge \cdots \wedge X_n = e_n \wedge \phi$$

Thus calculating $\mathtt{sp}\,(X_i := E)$ consists of evaluating E in the current state (i.e. $E[e_1, \ldots, e_n / X_1, \ldots, X_n]$) and then updating the equation for X_i to specify that this is the new value after the symbolic execution of the assignment.

If $X_1, \ldots, X_n$, $x_1, \ldots, x_n$ and $e_1, \ldots, e_n$ are clear from the context, then they may be abbreviated to $\overline{X}$, $\overline{x}$ and $\overline{e}$ respectively. We may also write $\overline{X} = \overline{e}$ to mean $X_1 = e_1 \wedge \cdots \wedge X_n = e_n$. With this notation the equation above becomes

$$\begin{aligned}&\mathtt{sp}\,(X_i := E)\,(\exists \overline{x}.\, \overline{X} = \overline{e} \wedge \phi)\\ &= \exists \overline{x}.\, X_1 = e_1 \wedge \cdots \wedge X_i = E[\overline{e}/\overline{X}] \wedge \cdots \wedge X_n = e_n \wedge \phi\end{aligned}$$

The derivation of this equation follows below (an informal justification of each line is given in brackets just after the line). The validity of the equation depends on the restriction that neither $e_1, \ldots, e_n$ nor ϕ contain the program variables $X_1, \ldots, X_n$. In addition, we also need to assume below that v, $x_1, \ldots, x_n$ and $X_1, \ldots, X_n$ are all distinct and v, $x_1, \ldots, x_n$ do not occur in E. These restrictions are assumed from now on.

$$\mathtt{sp}\,(X_i := E)\,(\exists \overline{x}.\, \overline{X} = \overline{e} \wedge \phi)$$
$$= \exists v.\, \mathrm{X}_i{=}E[v/\mathrm{X}_i] \wedge (\exists \overline{x}.\, \overline{X} = \overline{e} \wedge \phi)[v/\mathrm{X}_i]$$
(Floyd assignment rule)
$$= \exists v.\, \mathrm{X}_i{=}E[v/\mathrm{X}_i] \wedge (\exists \overline{x}.\, \mathrm{X}_1{=}e_1 \wedge \cdots \wedge v{=}e_i \wedge \cdots \wedge \mathrm{X}_n{=}e_n \wedge \phi)$$
(distinctness of variables and X_i not in $e_1, \ldots, e_n$ or ϕ)
$$= \exists v\, \overline{x}.\, \mathrm{X}_i{=}E[v/\mathrm{X}_i] \wedge \mathrm{X}_1{=}e_1 \wedge \cdots \wedge v{=}e_i \wedge \cdots \wedge \mathrm{X}_n{=}e_n \wedge \phi$$
(pulling quantifiers to front: allowed as variables distinct, $\overline{x}$ not in E)
$$= \exists \overline{x}.\, \mathrm{X}_i{=}E[e_i/\mathrm{X}_i] \wedge \mathrm{X}_1{=}e_1 \wedge \cdots \wedge (\exists v.\, v{=}e_i) \wedge \cdots \wedge \mathrm{X}_n{=}e_n \wedge \phi$$
(restricting scope of v to the only conjunct containing v)
$$= \exists \overline{x}.\, \mathrm{X}_i{=}E[e_i/\mathrm{X}_i] \wedge \mathrm{X}_1{=}e_1 \wedge \cdots \wedge \mathsf{T} \wedge \cdots \wedge \mathrm{X}_n{=}e_n \wedge \phi$$
($\exists v.\, v{=}e_i$ is true)
$$= \exists \overline{x}.\, \mathrm{X}_1{=}e_1 \wedge \cdots \wedge \mathrm{X}_i{=}E[e_i/\mathrm{X}_i] \wedge \cdots \wedge \mathrm{X}_n{=}e_n \wedge \phi$$
(eliminate T and move equation for X_i to where it was in the conjunction)

$= \exists \overline{x}.\, X_1{=}e_1 \wedge \cdots \wedge X_i{=}E[e_1,\ldots,e_n/X_1,\ldots,X_n] \wedge \cdots \wedge X_n{=}e_n \wedge \phi$
($\overline{X} = \overline{e}$ justify replacing $X_1,\ldots,X_n$ in E by $e_1,\ldots,e_n$)

$= \exists \overline{x}.\, X_1{=}e_1 \wedge \cdots \wedge X_i{=}E[\overline{e}/\overline{X}] \wedge \cdots \wedge X_n{=}e_n \wedge \phi$
(definition of $[\overline{e}/\overline{X}]$ notation)

Since $\mathtt{sp}\,(S_1\,;S_2)\,P \;=\; \mathtt{sp}\,S_2\,(\mathtt{sp}\,S_1\,P)$, if S_1 and S_2 are assignments and P has the form $\exists \overline{x}.\overline{X} = \overline{e} \wedge \phi$, then to compute $\mathtt{sp}\,(S_1\,;S_2)\,P$, one just updates the equations in the conjunction corresponding to the variable being assigned by S_1 followed by that assigned by S_2.

For conditional branches, the equation for calculating strongest postconditions is: $\mathtt{sp}\,(\mathtt{IF}\,B\,\mathtt{THEN}\,S_1\,\mathtt{ELSE}\,S_2)\,P \;=\; (\mathtt{sp}\,S_1\,(P \wedge B)) \vee (\mathtt{sp}\,S_2\,(P \wedge \neg B))$. If P has the form $\exists \overline{x}.\overline{X} = \overline{e} \wedge \phi$ then $P \wedge B$ and $P \wedge \neg B$ can be put into this form. The derivation is below.

$P \wedge B = (\exists \overline{x}.\overline{X} = \overline{e} \wedge \phi) \wedge B$
(expanding P)
$= \exists \overline{x}.\overline{X} = \overline{e} \wedge (\phi \wedge B)$
(allowed if $x_1,\ldots,x_n$ do not occur in B, which is assumed)
$= \exists \overline{x}.\overline{X} = \overline{e} \wedge (\phi \wedge B[\overline{e}/\overline{X}])$
(conjuncts $\overline{X} = \overline{e}$ justify replacing $\overline{X}$ in B by $\overline{e}$)

Similarly: $P \wedge \neg B \;=\; \exists \overline{x}.\overline{X} = \overline{e} \wedge (\phi \wedge \neg B[\overline{e}/\overline{X}])$.

If a conditional is in a sequence then as $\mathtt{sp}\,S\,(P_1 \vee P_2) = \mathtt{sp}\,S\,P_1 \vee \mathtt{sp}\,S\,P_2$ for any program S, it follows that

$$\begin{aligned}&\mathtt{sp}\,((\mathtt{IF}\,B\,\mathtt{THEN}\,S_1\,\mathtt{ELSE}\,S_2)\,;S_3)\,P\\ &= \mathtt{sp}\,(S_1\,;S_3)\,(P \wedge B) \vee \mathtt{sp}\,(S_2\,;S_3)\,(P \wedge \neg B)\end{aligned}$$

thus the calculation of the strongest postcondition of a sequence starting with a conditional can proceed by separate symbolic evaluations of each arm.

If it can be shown that either $P \wedge B$ or $P \wedge \neg B$ are false (F) then, since for any S it is the case that $\mathtt{sp}\,S\,\mathsf{F} = \mathsf{F}$, one of the disjuncts can be pruned. If such pruning is not possible, then separate evaluations for each arm must be performed. These can be organised to maximise efficiency based on heuristics (e.g. depth-first or breadth-first). As an example illustrating how symbolic evaluation can be used to compute strongest postconditions, we calculate:

```
sp AbsMinus (I < J) =

sp(R := 0;
   K := 0;
   IF I < J THEN K := K + 1 ELSE SKIP;
   IF K = 1 ∧ ¬(I = J) THEN R := J − I ELSE R := I − J)
  (∃ijkr. I = i ∧ J = j ∧ K = k ∧ R = r ∧ i < j) =

sp(K := 0;
   IF I < J THEN K := K + 1 ELSE SKIP;
```

$$\begin{array}{l}
\quad\texttt{IF}\,\texttt{K} = 1 \wedge \neg(\texttt{I} = \texttt{J})\,\texttt{THEN}\,\texttt{R} := \texttt{J} - \texttt{I}\,\texttt{ELSE}\,\texttt{R} := \texttt{I} - \texttt{J})\\
\quad(\exists ijkr.\,\texttt{I} = i \wedge \texttt{J} = i \wedge \texttt{K} = k \wedge \texttt{R} = 0 \wedge i < j) \;=\\
\texttt{sp}(\texttt{IF}\,\texttt{I} < \texttt{J}\,\texttt{THEN}\,\texttt{K} := \texttt{K} + 1\,\texttt{ELSE}\,\texttt{SKIP};\\
\quad\texttt{IF}\,\texttt{K} = 1 \wedge \neg(\texttt{I} = \texttt{J})\,\texttt{THEN}\,\texttt{R} := \texttt{J} - \texttt{I}\,\texttt{ELSE}\,\texttt{R} := \texttt{I} - \texttt{J})\\
\quad(\exists ijkr.\,\texttt{I} = i \wedge \texttt{J} = i \wedge \texttt{K} = 0 \wedge \texttt{R} = 0 \wedge i < j) \;=\\
(\texttt{sp}(\texttt{K} := \texttt{K} + 1;\;\texttt{IF}\,\texttt{K} = 1 \wedge \neg(\texttt{I} = \texttt{J})\,\texttt{THEN}\,\texttt{R} := \texttt{J} - \texttt{I}\,\texttt{ELSE}\,\texttt{R} := \texttt{I} - \texttt{J})\\
\quad(\exists ijkr.\,\texttt{I} = i \wedge \texttt{J} = i \wedge \texttt{K} = 0 \wedge \texttt{R} = 0 \wedge (i < j \wedge (\texttt{I} < \texttt{J})[i,j/\texttt{I},\texttt{J}]))\\
\vee\\
\texttt{sp}(\texttt{SKIP};\;\texttt{IF}\,\texttt{K} = 1 \wedge \neg(\texttt{I} = \texttt{J})\,\texttt{THEN}\,\texttt{R} := \texttt{J} - \texttt{I}\,\texttt{ELSE}\,\texttt{R} := \texttt{I} - \texttt{J})\\
\quad(\exists ijkr.\,\texttt{I} = i \wedge \texttt{J} = i \wedge \texttt{K} = 0 \wedge \texttt{R} = 0 \wedge (i < j \wedge \neg(\texttt{I} < \texttt{J})[i,j/\texttt{I},\texttt{J}])))
\end{array}$$

Since $(\texttt{I} < \texttt{J})[i,j/\texttt{I},\texttt{J}] = i < j$ the precondition of the second disjunct above contains the conjunct $i < j \wedge \neg(i < j)$, which is false. Thus the second disjunct can be pruned:

$$\begin{array}{l}
(\texttt{sp}(\texttt{K} := \texttt{K} + 1;\;\texttt{IF}\,\texttt{K} = 1 \wedge \neg(\texttt{I} = \texttt{J})\,\texttt{THEN}\,\texttt{R} := \texttt{J} - \texttt{I}\,\texttt{ELSE}\,\texttt{R} := \texttt{I} - \texttt{J})\\
\quad(\exists ijkr.\,\texttt{I} = i \wedge \texttt{J} = i \wedge \texttt{K} = 0 \wedge \texttt{R} = 0 \wedge (i < j \wedge (\texttt{I} < \texttt{J})[i,j/\texttt{I},\texttt{J}]))\\
\vee\\
\texttt{sp}(\texttt{SKIP};\;\texttt{IF}\,\texttt{K} = 1 \wedge \neg(\texttt{I} = \texttt{J})\,\texttt{THEN}\,\texttt{R} := \texttt{J} - \texttt{I}\,\texttt{ELSE}\,\texttt{R} := \texttt{I} - \texttt{J})\\
\quad(\exists ijkr.\\
\qquad\texttt{I} = i \wedge \texttt{J} = i \wedge \texttt{K} = 0 \wedge \texttt{R} = 0 \wedge (i < j \wedge \neg(\texttt{I} < \texttt{J})[i,j/\texttt{I},\texttt{J}]))) \;=\\
\texttt{sp}(\texttt{K} := \texttt{K} + 1;\;\texttt{IF}\,\texttt{K} = 1 \wedge \neg(\texttt{I} = \texttt{J})\,\texttt{THEN}\,\texttt{R} := \texttt{J} - \texttt{I}\,\texttt{ELSE}\,\texttt{R} := \texttt{I} - \texttt{J})\\
\quad(\exists ijkr.\,\texttt{I} = i \wedge \texttt{J} = i \wedge \texttt{K} = 0 \wedge \texttt{R} = 0 \wedge i < j])) \;=\\
\texttt{sp}(\texttt{IF}\,\texttt{K} = 1 \wedge \neg(\texttt{I} = \texttt{J})\,\texttt{THEN}\,\texttt{R} := \texttt{J} - \texttt{I}\,\texttt{ELSE}\,\texttt{R} := \texttt{I} - \texttt{J})\\
\quad(\exists ijkr.\,\texttt{I} = i \wedge \texttt{J} = i \wedge \texttt{K} = (\texttt{K+1})[0/\texttt{K}] \wedge \texttt{R} = 0 \wedge i < j])) \;=\\
(\texttt{sp}(\texttt{R} := \texttt{J} - \texttt{I})\\
\quad(\exists ijkr.\,\texttt{I} = i \wedge \texttt{J} = i \wedge \texttt{K} = 1 \wedge \texttt{R} = 0 \wedge (i < j \wedge (1 = 1 \wedge \neg(i = j))))\\
\vee\\
\texttt{sp}(\texttt{R} := \texttt{I} - \texttt{J})\\
\quad(\exists ijkr.\\
\qquad\texttt{I} = i \wedge \texttt{J} = i \wedge \texttt{K} = 1 \wedge \texttt{R} = 0 \wedge (i < j \wedge \neg(1 = 1 \wedge \neg(i = j))))) \;=
\end{array}$$

The second disjunct is pruned as $i < j \wedge \neg(1 = 1 \wedge \neg(i = j))$ simplifies to F.

$$\begin{array}{l}
\texttt{sp}(\texttt{R} := \texttt{J} - \texttt{I})\\
\quad(\exists ijkr.\,\texttt{I} = i \wedge \texttt{J} = i \wedge \texttt{K} = 1 \wedge \texttt{R} = 0 \wedge i < j)\\
= (\exists ijkr.\,\texttt{I} = i \wedge \texttt{J} = i \wedge \texttt{K} = 1 \wedge \texttt{R} = (\texttt{J}-\texttt{I})[i,j/\texttt{I},\texttt{J}] \wedge i < j)
\end{array}$$

The right-hand side of this equation simplifies to $\texttt{R} = \texttt{J}-\texttt{I} \wedge \texttt{I} < \texttt{J}$ by performing the substitution and then using properties of existential quantifiers. Thus: $\texttt{sp}\ \texttt{AbsMinus}\ (\texttt{I} < \texttt{J}) = \texttt{R} = \texttt{J}-\texttt{I} \wedge \texttt{I} < \texttt{J}$ by the derivation above.

A similar calculation by symbolic execution (but pruning different branches of the conditionals) gives: $\texttt{sp}\ \texttt{AbsMinus}\ (\texttt{J} \leq \texttt{I}) = (\texttt{R} = \texttt{I}-\texttt{J} \wedge \texttt{J} \leq \texttt{I})$.

Since $\{P\}S\{Q\}$ if and only if $(\mathtt{sp}\,S\,P) \Rightarrow Q$ it follows from the results of calculations for `AbsMinus` above that $\{\mathtt{I} < \mathtt{J}\}\mathtt{AbsMinus}\{\mathtt{R} = \mathtt{J{-}I} \wedge \mathtt{I} < \mathtt{J}\}$ and $\{\mathtt{J} \leq \mathtt{I}\}\mathtt{AbsMinus}\{\mathtt{R} = \mathtt{I{-}J} \wedge \mathtt{J} \leq \mathtt{I}\}$. Hence by the disjunction rule for Hoare Logic

$$\frac{\vdash \{P_1\}S\{Q_1\} \qquad \vdash \{P_2\}S\{Q_2\}}{\vdash \{P_1 \vee P_2\}S\{Q_1 \vee Q_2\}}$$

we can conclude $\vdash \{\mathsf{T}\}\mathtt{AbsMinus}\{(\mathtt{R} = \mathtt{J{-}I} \wedge \mathtt{I} < \mathtt{J}) \vee (\mathtt{R} = \mathtt{I{-}J} \wedge \mathtt{J} \leq \mathtt{I})\}$.

This example suggests a strategy for proving Hoare triples $\{P\}S\{Q\}$. First split P into a disjunction $P \Leftrightarrow P_1 \vee \cdots \vee P_n$ where each P_i determines a path through the program S. Then, for each i, compute $\mathtt{sp}\,P_i\,S$ by symbolic execution. Finally check that $\mathtt{sp}\,P_i\,S \Rightarrow Q$ holds for each i. If these implications all hold, then the original Hoare triple follows by the disjunction rule above. This strategy is hardly new, but explaining it as strongest postcondition calculation implemented by symbolic evaluation with Hoare logic for combining the results of the evaluations provides a nice formal foundation and also provides a link from the deductive system of Hoare logic to automated software model checking, which is often based on symbolic execution.

5.5 Backwards with Preconditions

Calculating weakest preconditions is simpler than calculating strongest postconditions because the assignment rules need just one substitution and generate no additional quantifiers: $\mathtt{wp}\,(V\mathtt{:=}E)\,Q \;=\; Q[E/V]$. There is thus no need to use formulae of the form $\exists\overline{x}.\overline{X} = \overline{e} \wedge \phi$ as one can calculate with postconditions of any form. Furthermore, if the McCarthy conditional notation $(B \rightarrow P \mid Q)$ is defined by

$$(B \rightarrow P \mid Q) \;=\; (P \wedge B) \vee (Q \wedge \neg B)$$

then the `wp` rule for conditionals can be expressed as

$$\mathtt{wp}\,(\mathtt{IF}\,B\,\mathtt{THEN}\,S_1\,\mathtt{ELSE}\,S_2)\,Q \;=\; (B \rightarrow \mathtt{wp}\,S_1\,Q \mid \mathtt{wp}\,S_2\,Q)$$

which simplifies the calculation of `wp`. This is illustrated using the `AbsMinus` example (see Fig. 5.2). In the calculation that follows, assignment substitutions are performed immediately.

$\mathtt{wp}\,\mathtt{AbsMinus}\,(\mathtt{R} = \mathtt{J{-}I} \wedge \mathtt{I} < \mathtt{J}) \;=$

```
wp(R := 0;
   K := 0;
   IF I < J THEN K := K + 1 ELSE SKIP;
   IF K = 1 ∧ ¬(I = J) THEN R := J − I ELSE R := I − J)
  (R = J−I ∧ I < J) =
```

$$
\begin{array}{l}
\texttt{wp}(\texttt{R} := \texttt{0};\\
\quad \texttt{K} := \texttt{0};\\
\quad \texttt{IF I} < \texttt{J THEN K} := \texttt{K} + \texttt{1 ELSE SKIP})\\
\quad (\texttt{K} = 1 \wedge \neg(\texttt{I} = \texttt{J}) \rightarrow \texttt{J}{-}\texttt{I} = \texttt{J}{-}\texttt{I} \wedge \texttt{I}{<}\texttt{J} \mid \texttt{J}{-}\texttt{I} = \texttt{I}{-}\texttt{J} \wedge \texttt{I}{<}\texttt{J}) =
\end{array}
$$

$$
\begin{array}{l}
\texttt{wp}(\texttt{R} := \texttt{0};\\
\quad \texttt{K} := \texttt{0};\\
(\texttt{I}{<}\texttt{J} \rightarrow (\texttt{K}{+}1 = 1 \wedge \neg(\texttt{I} = \texttt{J}) \rightarrow \texttt{J}{-}\texttt{I} = \texttt{J}{-}\texttt{I} \wedge \texttt{I}{<}\texttt{J} \mid \texttt{J}{-}\texttt{I} = \texttt{I}{-}\texttt{J} \wedge \texttt{I}{<}\texttt{J})\\
\quad \mid (\texttt{K} = 1 \wedge \neg(\texttt{I} = \texttt{J}) \rightarrow \texttt{J}{-}\texttt{I} = \texttt{J}{-}\texttt{I} \wedge \texttt{I}{<}\texttt{J} \mid \texttt{J}{-}\texttt{I} = \texttt{I}{-}\texttt{J} \wedge \texttt{I}{<}\texttt{J})) =
\end{array}
$$

$$
\begin{array}{l}
(\texttt{I}{<}\texttt{J} \rightarrow (0{+}1 = 1 \wedge \neg(\texttt{I} = \texttt{J}) \rightarrow \texttt{J}{-}\texttt{I} = \texttt{J}{-}\texttt{I} \wedge \texttt{I}{<}\texttt{J} \mid \texttt{J}{-}\texttt{I} = \texttt{I}{-}\texttt{J} \wedge \texttt{I}{<}\texttt{J})\\
\quad \mid (0 = 1 \wedge \neg(\texttt{I} = \texttt{J}) \rightarrow \texttt{J}{-}\texttt{I} = \texttt{J}{-}\texttt{I} \wedge \texttt{I}{<}\texttt{J} \mid \texttt{J}{-}\texttt{I} = \texttt{I}{-}\texttt{J} \wedge \texttt{I}{<}\texttt{J}))
\end{array}
$$

This calculation can be simplified on-the-fly: $(\texttt{K} + 1 = 1)$ simplifies to $(\texttt{K} = 0)$, $(\texttt{J}{-}\texttt{I} = \texttt{J}{-}\texttt{I})$ simplifies to T and $(\texttt{J}{-}\texttt{I} = \texttt{I}{-}\texttt{J} \wedge \texttt{I}{<}\texttt{J})$ simplifies to F.

$$
\begin{array}{l}
\texttt{wp}(\texttt{R} := \texttt{0};\\
\quad \texttt{K} := \texttt{0};\\
\quad \texttt{IF I} < \texttt{J THEN K} := \texttt{K} + \texttt{1 ELSE SKIP};\\
\quad \texttt{IF K} = \texttt{1} \wedge \neg(\texttt{I} = \texttt{J})\ \texttt{THEN R} := \texttt{J} - \texttt{I ELSE R} := \texttt{I} - \texttt{J})\\
\quad (\texttt{R} = \texttt{J}{-}\texttt{I} \wedge \texttt{I}{<}\texttt{J}) =
\end{array}
$$

$$
\begin{array}{l}
\texttt{wp}(\texttt{R} := \texttt{0};\\
\quad \texttt{K} := \texttt{0};\\
\quad \texttt{IF I} < \texttt{J THEN K} := \texttt{K} + \texttt{1 ELSE SKIP})\\
\quad (\texttt{K} = 1 \wedge \neg(\texttt{I} = \texttt{J}) \rightarrow \texttt{I}{<}\texttt{J} \mid \mathsf{F}) =
\end{array}
$$

$$
\begin{array}{l}
\texttt{wp}(\texttt{R} := \texttt{0};\\
\quad \texttt{K} := \texttt{0};\\
\quad (\texttt{I}{<}\texttt{J} \rightarrow (\texttt{K} = 0 \wedge \neg(\texttt{I} = \texttt{J}) \rightarrow \texttt{I}{<}\texttt{J} \mid \mathsf{F})\\
\qquad \mid (\texttt{K} = 1 \wedge \neg(\texttt{I} = \texttt{J}) \rightarrow \texttt{I}{<}\texttt{J} \mid \mathsf{F})) =
\end{array}
$$

$$
(\texttt{I}{<}\texttt{J} \rightarrow (1 = 1 \wedge \neg(\texttt{I} = \texttt{J}) \rightarrow \texttt{I}{<}\texttt{J} \mid \mathsf{F}) \mid (0 = 1 \wedge \neg(\texttt{I} = \texttt{J}) \rightarrow \texttt{I}{<}\texttt{J} \mid \mathsf{F}))
$$

The last formula above is $\texttt{wp}\,\texttt{AbsMinus}\,(\texttt{R} = \texttt{J}{-}\texttt{I} \wedge \texttt{I} < \texttt{J})$ and simplifies to $(\texttt{I}{<}\texttt{J} \rightarrow \mathsf{T} \mid \mathsf{F})$, which simplifies to $\texttt{I}{<}\texttt{J}$.

The Hoare triple $\{\texttt{I}{<}\texttt{J}\}\texttt{AbsMinus}\{\texttt{R} = \texttt{J} - \texttt{I} \wedge \texttt{I}{<}\texttt{J}\}$ then follows from $\texttt{wp}\,\texttt{AbsMinus}\,(\texttt{R} = \texttt{J}{-}\texttt{I} \wedge \texttt{I} < \texttt{J}) = \texttt{I}{<}\texttt{J}$.

5.6 Forwards Versus Backwards

It seems clear from the example in the preceding section that proving $\{P\}S\{Q\}$ by calculating $\texttt{wp}\,S\,Q$ is simpler than proving it by calculating $\texttt{sp}\,S\,P$, indeed many automated Hoare logic verifiers work by calculating weakest preconditions. There are, however, several applications where strongest postconditions have a role.

One such application is 'reverse engineering' where, given a precondition, one tries to deduce what a program (e.g. legacy code) does by discovering a postcondition by symbolic execution [9]. Related to this is the use of symbolic execution for testing [18]. Yet another application is to verify a given Hoare triple by symbolically executing separate paths and combining the results (this approach has already been outlined at the end of Section 5.2). This is a form of software model checking, where loops are unwound some number of times to create loop-free straight line code, the strongest postcondition is calculated and then an automatic tool (like an SMT solver) used to show that this entails the given postcondition.[5] The hope is that one runs enough of the program to expose significant bugs. In general, code with loops cannot be unwound to equivalent straight line code, so although this approach is a powerful bug-finding method it cannot (without further analysis) be used for full proof of correctness. An advantage of symbolic evaluation is that one can use the symbolic representation of the current state to resolve conditional branches and hence prune paths. The extreme case of this is when the initial precondition specifies a unique starting state, so that symbolic execution collapses to normal 'ground' execution. Thus calculating strongest postconditions by symbolic execution provides a smooth transition from testing to full verification: by weakening the initial precondition one can make the verification cover more initial states.

5.7 Loops and Invariants

There is no general way to calculate strongest postconditions or weakest preconditions for `WHILE`-loops. Rewriting with the equations in Fig. 5.1 may not terminate, so if S contains loops then the strategies for proving $\{P\}S\{Q\}$ by calculating $\texttt{sp}\,P\,S$ or $\texttt{wp}\,S\,Q$ will not work. Instead, we define 'approximate' versions of `sp` and `wp` called, respectively, `asp` and `awp`, together with formulae ('verification conditions') $\texttt{svc}\,P\,S$ and $\texttt{wvc}\,S\,Q$ with the properties that

$$\vdash \texttt{svc}\,S\,P \Rightarrow \{P\}S\{\texttt{asp}\,S\,P\}$$

$$\vdash \texttt{wvc}\,S\,Q \Rightarrow \{\texttt{awp}\,S\,Q\}S\{Q\}$$

See Fig. 5.3 for equations specifying `asp` and `svc` and Fig. 5.4 for `awp` and `wvc`. Let ϕ be a formula and $x_1, \ldots, x_n$ all the free variables in ϕ. It is clear that if S is loop-free then $\texttt{svc}\,S\,P$ and $\texttt{wvc}\,S\,Q$ are true (T) and also $\texttt{asp}\,S\,P = \texttt{sp}\,S\,P$ and $\texttt{awp}\,S\,Q = \texttt{wp}\,S\,Q$. Thus for loop-free programs the 'approximate' predicate transformers are equivalent to the exact ones.

[5] State-of-the-art bounded model checkers [1,3] generate the strongest postcondition using similar rules to those given in Fig. 5.1. However, they first transform programs into SSA (Static Single Assignment) form [5] and avoid the explicit use of existential quantifiers generated by assignments. The approach in this paper seems equivalent to the use of SSA, but we have not worked out a clean account of this. A feature of our method is that it applies directly to programs without requiring any preprocessing.

$\texttt{asp}\,\texttt{SKIP}\,P = P$
$\texttt{svc}\,\texttt{SKIP}\,P = \mathsf{T}$

$\texttt{asp}\,(V\!:=\!E)\,P = \exists v.\,(V{=}E[v/V]) \wedge P[v/V]$
$\texttt{svc}\,(V\!:=\!E)\,P = \mathsf{T}$

$\texttt{asp}\,(S_1\,;S_2)\,P = \texttt{asp}\,S_2\,(\texttt{asp}\,S_1\,P)$
$\texttt{svc}\,(S_1\,;S_2)\,P = \texttt{svc}\,S_1\,P \wedge \texttt{svc}\,S_2\,(\texttt{asp}\,S_1\,P)$

$\texttt{asp}\,(\texttt{IF}\,B\,\texttt{THEN}\,S_1\,\texttt{ELSE}\,S_2)\,P = \texttt{asp}\,S_1\,(P \wedge B) \vee \texttt{asp}\,S_2\,(P \wedge \neg B)$
$\texttt{svc}\,(\texttt{IF}\,B\,\texttt{THEN}\,S_1\,\texttt{ELSE}\,S_2)\,P =$
$\quad(\texttt{UNSAT}(P \wedge B) \vee \texttt{svc}\,S_1\,(P \wedge B)) \wedge (\texttt{UNSAT}(P \wedge \neg B) \vee \texttt{svc}\,S_2\,(P \wedge \neg B))$

$\texttt{asp}\,(\texttt{WHILE}\,B\,\texttt{DO}\{R\}\,S)\,P = R \wedge \neg B$
$\texttt{svc}\,(\texttt{WHILE}\,B\,\texttt{DO}\{R\}\,S)\,P = (P \Rightarrow R) \wedge (\texttt{asp}\,S\,(R \wedge B) \Rightarrow R) \wedge \texttt{svc}\,S\,(R \wedge B)$

Fig. 5.3 Approximate strongest postconditions and verification conditions

$\texttt{awp}\,\texttt{SKIP}\,Q = Q$
$\texttt{wvc}\,\texttt{SKIP}\,Q = \mathsf{T}$

$\texttt{awp}\,(V\!:=\!E)\,Q = Q[E/V]$
$\texttt{wvc}\,(V\!:=\!E)\,Q = \mathsf{T}$

$\texttt{awp}\,(S_1\,;S_2)\,Q = \texttt{awp}\,S_1\,(\texttt{awp}\,S_2\,Q)$
$\texttt{wvc}\,(S_1\,;S_2)\,Q = \texttt{wvc}\,S_1\,(\texttt{awp}\,S_2\,Q) \wedge \texttt{wvc}\,S_2\,Q$

$\texttt{awp}\,(\texttt{IF}\,B\,\texttt{THEN}\,S_1\,\texttt{ELSE}\,S_2)\,Q = (B \rightarrow \texttt{awp}\,S_1\,Q \mid \texttt{awp}\,S_2\,Q)$
$\texttt{wvc}\,(\texttt{IF}\,B\,\texttt{THEN}\,S_1\,\texttt{ELSE}\,S_2)\,Q = \texttt{TAUT}(Q) \vee (\texttt{wvc}\,S_1\,Q \wedge \texttt{wvc}\,S_2\,Q)$

$\texttt{awp}\,(\texttt{WHILE}\,B\,\texttt{DO}\{R\}\,S)\,Q = R$
$\texttt{wvc}\,(\texttt{WHILE}\,B\,\texttt{DO}\{R\}\,S)\,Q = (R \wedge B \Rightarrow \texttt{awp}\,S\,R) \wedge (R \wedge \neg B \Rightarrow Q) \wedge \texttt{wvc}\,S\,R$

Fig. 5.4 Approximate weakest postconditions and verification conditions

In Fig. 5.3, the operator UNSAT is true if its argument is unsatisfiable: $\texttt{UNSAT}(\phi) = \neg\exists x_1 \cdots x_n.\,\phi$. The operator TAUT is true if its argument is a tautology: $\texttt{TAUT}(\phi) = \forall x_1 \cdots x_n.\,\phi$. The relation between UNSAT and TAUT is: $\texttt{UNSAT}(\phi) = \texttt{TAUT}(\neg\phi)$. Point 4 of the first proof in the appendix uses the fact that $\{P\}S\{Q\}$ holds vacuously if $\texttt{UNSAT}(P)$. Point 4 of the second proof in the appendix uses the dual fact that $\{P\}S\{Q\}$ holds vacuously if $\texttt{TAUT}(Q)$.

To establish $\{P\}S\{Q\}$, the Hoare logic 'Rules of Consequence' ensure that it is sufficient to prove either the conjunction $(\texttt{svc}\,S\,P) \wedge (\texttt{asp}\,S\,P \Rightarrow Q)$ or the conjunction $(\texttt{wvc}\,S\,Q) \wedge (P \Rightarrow \texttt{awp}\,S\,Q)$. The early development of mechanised program verification uses ideas similar to weakest preconditions to generate verification conditions [14, 15, 17, 19, 20, 23]. Strongest postconditions are less used for reasoning about programs containing loops, but generalisations of symbolic execution for them have been developed [22].

Reasoning about loops usually requires invariants to be supplied (either by a human or by some invariant-finding tool). Hoare logic provides the following `WHILE`-rule (which is a combination of Hoare's original 'Rule of Iteration' and his 'Rules of Consequence'). Following standard practice, we have added the invariant R as an annotation in curly brackets just before the body S of the `WHILE`-loop

$$\frac{\vdash P \Rightarrow R \qquad \vdash \{R \wedge B\}S\{R\} \qquad R \wedge \neg B \Rightarrow Q}{\vdash \{P\}\texttt{WHILE}\, B\, \texttt{DO}\{R\}\, S\{Q\}}$$

This rule is the logical basis underlying methods based on invariants for verifying `WHILE`-loops.

The ideas underlying `asp`, `svc`, `awp` and `wvc` are old and mostly very well known. The contribution here is a repackaging of these standard methods in a somewhat more uniform framework. The properties stated above connecting `asp` and `svc`, and `awp` and `wvc` are easily verified by structural induction. For completeness the proofs are given in an appendix.

The equations for `asp` in Fig 5.3 are the same as those for `sp` in Fig. 5.1, except for the additional equation for $\texttt{asp}\,\texttt{WHILE}\,B\,\texttt{DO}\{R\}\,S\,P$. For symbolic execution, as described in Section 5.4, this equation can be written as

$$\begin{aligned}&\texttt{asp}\,(\texttt{WHILE}\,B\,\texttt{DO}\{R\}\,S)\,(\exists \overline{x}.\,X_1 = e_1 \wedge \cdots \wedge X_n = e_n \wedge \phi)\\ &= \exists \overline{x}.\,\overline{X} = \overline{x} \wedge (R \wedge \neg B)[\overline{x}/\overline{X}]\end{aligned}$$

Thus symbolically executing $\texttt{WHILE}\,B\,\texttt{DO}\{R\}\,S$ consists in throwing away the precondition and restarting in a new symbolic state corresponding to the state specified as holding after the `WHILE`-loop by the Hoare rule. This is justified if the verification conditions for the `WHILE`-loop hold, namely:

$$\begin{aligned}&\texttt{svc}\,(\texttt{WHILE}\,B\,\texttt{DO}\{R\}\,S)\,(\exists \overline{x}.\,X_1 = e_1 \wedge \cdots \wedge X_n = e_n \wedge \phi)\\ &= ((\exists \overline{x}.\,X_1 = e_1 \wedge \cdots \wedge X_n = e_n \wedge \phi) \Rightarrow R)\\ &\quad \wedge (\texttt{asp}\,S\,(R \wedge B) \Rightarrow R) \wedge \texttt{svc}\,S\,(R \wedge B)\\ &= (\forall \overline{x}.\,\phi \Rightarrow R[\overline{e}/\overline{X}]) \wedge (\texttt{asp}\,S\,(R \wedge B) \Rightarrow R) \wedge \texttt{svc}\,S\,(R \wedge B)\end{aligned}$$

This says that the precondition must entail the invariant evaluated in the state when the loop is started ($R[\overline{e}/\overline{X}]$), the invariant R must really be an invariant ($\texttt{asp}\,S\,(R \wedge B) \Rightarrow R$) and any verification conditions when checking R is an invariant must hold ($\texttt{svc}\,S\,(R \wedge B)$). To verify that R is an invariant a recursive symbolic execution of the loop body, starting in a state satisfying $R \wedge B$, is performed. Note that:

$$\texttt{asp}\,S\,(R \wedge B) \;=\; \texttt{asp}\,S\,(\exists \overline{x}.\,\overline{X} = \overline{x} \wedge (R \wedge B)[\overline{x}/\overline{X}])$$

The equations for symbolic execution and verification conditions on symbolic state formulae are given in Fig 5.5. Note that $\text{UNSAT}(\exists \overline{x}.\,\overline{X} = \overline{e} \wedge \phi) = \text{UNSAT}(\phi)$.

As an example, consider the program `Div` in Fig. 5.6. For simplicity, assume the values of the variables in `Div` (i.e. `R`, `X` and `ERR`) are non-negative integers. First we compute `asp Div (Y=0)`.

$\mathtt{asp}\,\mathtt{SKIP}\,(\exists \overline{x}.\overline{X} = \overline{e} \wedge \phi) = (\exists \overline{x}.\overline{X} = \overline{e} \wedge \phi)$

$\mathtt{svc}\,\mathtt{SKIP}\,(\exists \overline{x}.\overline{X} = \overline{e} \wedge \phi) = \top$

$\mathtt{asp}\,(X_i := E)\,(\exists \overline{x}.\overline{X} = \overline{e} \wedge \phi)$
$\quad = \exists \overline{x}.X_1 = e_1 \wedge \ldots \wedge X_i = E[\overline{e}/\overline{X}] \wedge \ldots \wedge X_n = e_n \wedge \phi$

$\mathtt{svc}\,(X_i := E)\,(\exists \overline{x}.\overline{X} = \overline{e} \wedge \phi) = \top$

$\mathtt{asp}\,(S_1\,;S_2)\,(\exists \overline{x}.\overline{X} = \overline{e} \wedge \phi) = \mathtt{asp}\,S_2\,(\mathtt{asp}\,S_1\,(\exists \overline{x}.\overline{X} = \overline{e} \wedge \phi))$

$\mathtt{svc}\,(S_1\,;S_2)\,(\exists \overline{x}.\overline{X} = \overline{e} \wedge \phi) = \mathtt{svc}\,S_1\,(\exists \overline{x}.\overline{X} = \overline{e} \wedge \phi) \wedge \mathtt{svc}\,S_2\,(\mathtt{asp}\,S_1\,(\exists \overline{x}.\overline{X} = \overline{e} \wedge \phi))$

$\mathtt{asp}\,(\mathtt{IF}\,B\,\mathtt{THEN}\,S_1\,\mathtt{ELSE}\,S_2)\,(\exists \overline{x}.\overline{X} = \overline{e} \wedge \phi)$
$\quad = \mathtt{asp}\,S_1\,(\exists \overline{x}.\overline{X} = \overline{e} \wedge (\phi \wedge B[\overline{e}/\overline{X}])) \vee \mathtt{asp}\,S_2\,(\exists \overline{x}.\overline{X} = \overline{e} \wedge (\phi \wedge \neg B[\overline{e}/\overline{X}]))$

$\mathtt{svc}\,(\mathtt{IF}\,B\,\mathtt{THEN}\,S_1\,\mathtt{ELSE}\,S_2)\,(\exists \overline{x}.\overline{X} = \overline{e} \wedge \phi)$
$\quad = (\mathtt{UNSAT}(\phi \wedge B[\overline{e}/\overline{X}]) \vee \mathtt{svc}\,S_1\,(\exists \overline{x}.\overline{X} = \overline{e} \wedge (\phi \wedge B[\overline{e}/\overline{X}])))$
$\quad\ \wedge$
$\quad\ (\mathtt{UNSAT}(\phi \wedge \neg B[\overline{e}/\overline{X}]) \vee \mathtt{svc}\,S_2\,(\exists \overline{x}.\overline{X} = \overline{e} \wedge (\phi \wedge \neg B[\overline{e}/\overline{X}])))$

$\mathtt{asp}\,(\mathtt{WHILE}\,B\,\mathtt{DO}\{R\}\,S)\,(\exists \overline{x}.X_1 = e_1 \wedge \ldots \wedge X_n = e_n \wedge \phi)$
$\quad = \exists \overline{x}.\overline{X} = \overline{x} \wedge (R \wedge \neg B)[\overline{x}/\overline{X}]$

$\mathtt{svc}\,(\mathtt{WHILE}\,B\,\mathtt{DO}\{R\}\,S)\,(\exists \overline{x}.X_1 = e_1 \wedge \ldots \wedge X_n = e_n \wedge \phi) =$
$\quad = (\forall \overline{x}.\phi \Rightarrow R[\overline{e}/\overline{X}]) \wedge (\mathtt{asp}\,S\,(R \wedge B) \Rightarrow R) \wedge \mathtt{svc}\,S\,(R \wedge B)$

Fig. 5.5 Approximate strongest postconditions and verification conditions

```
R:=X; Q:=0; ERR:=0;
IF Y=0 THEN ERR:=1 ELSE WHILE Y < R DO{X = R + Y × Q} (R:=R−Y;Q:=1+Q)
```

Fig. 5.6 The example program `Div`

Let S be `WHILE Y < R DO{X = R + Y × Q} (R:=R−Y;Q:=1+Q)`, then:

$\mathtt{asp}$
$(\mathtt{R:=X;\ Q:=0;\ ERR:=0;\ IF\ Y{=}0\ THEN\ ERR:=1\ ELSE}\,S)$
$(\mathtt{Y}{=}0) =$

$\mathtt{asp}$
$(\mathtt{R:=X;\ Q:=0;\ ERR:=0;\ IF\ Y{=}0\ THEN\ ERR:=1\ ELSE}\,S)$
$(\exists xyqre.\,\mathtt{X}{=}x \wedge \mathtt{Y}{=}y \wedge \mathtt{Q}{=}q \wedge \mathtt{R}{=}r \wedge \mathtt{ERR}{=}e \wedge y{=}0) =$

$\mathtt{asp}$
$(\mathtt{IF\ Y{=}0\ THEN\ ERR:=1\ ELSE}\,S)$
$(\exists xyqre.\,\mathtt{X}{=}x \wedge \mathtt{Y}{=}y \wedge \mathtt{Q}{=}0 \wedge \mathtt{R}{=}x \wedge \mathtt{ERR}{=}0 \wedge y{=}0) =$

$\mathtt{asp}\,(\mathtt{ERR:=1})\,(\exists xyqre.\,\mathtt{X}{=}x \wedge \mathtt{Y}{=}y \wedge \mathtt{Q}{=}0 \wedge \mathtt{R}{=}x \wedge \mathtt{ERR}{=}0 \wedge y{=}0 \wedge (y{=}0))$
$\vee$
$\mathtt{asp}\,S\,(\exists xyqre.\,\mathtt{X}{=}x \wedge \mathtt{Y}{=}y \wedge \mathtt{Q}{=}0 \wedge \mathtt{R}{=}x \wedge \mathtt{ERR}{=}0 \wedge y{=}0 \wedge \neg(y{=}0)) =$

$\mathtt{asp}\,(\mathtt{ERR:=1})\,(\exists xyqre.\,\mathtt{X}{=}x \wedge \mathtt{Y}{=}y \wedge \mathtt{Q}{=}0 \wedge \mathtt{R}{=}x \wedge \mathtt{ERR}{=}0 \wedge y{=}0 \wedge (y{=}0)) =$

$(\exists xyqre.\,\mathtt{X}{=}x \wedge \mathtt{Y}{=}y \wedge \mathtt{Q}{=}0 \wedge \mathtt{R}{=}x \wedge \mathtt{ERR}{=}1 \wedge y{=}0 \wedge (y{=}0)) =$

$\mathtt{X}{=}\mathtt{R} \wedge \mathtt{Y}{=}0 \wedge \mathtt{ERR}{=}1$

Next we compute `svc Div (Y=0)` (simplifying $\mathsf{T} \wedge \phi$ to ϕ on-the-fly).

$$\begin{array}{l}
\texttt{svc} \\
\quad (\texttt{R:=X; Q:=0; ERR:=0; IF Y=0 THEN ERR:=1 ELSE}\, S) \\
\quad (\texttt{Y=0}) =
\end{array}$$

$$\begin{array}{l}
\texttt{svc} \\
\quad (\texttt{R:=X; Q:=0; ERR:=0; IF Y=0 THEN ERR:=1 ELSE}\, S) \\
\quad (\exists xyqre.\, \texttt{X}{=}x \wedge \texttt{Y}{=}y \wedge \texttt{Q}{=}q \wedge \texttt{R}{=}r \wedge \texttt{ERR}{=}e \wedge y{=}0) =
\end{array}$$

$$\begin{array}{l}
\texttt{svc} \\
\quad (\texttt{IF Y=0 THEN ERR:=1 ELSE}\, S) \\
\quad (\exists xyqre.\, \texttt{X}{=}x \wedge \texttt{Y}{=}y \wedge \texttt{Q}{=}0 \wedge \texttt{R}{=}x \wedge \texttt{ERR}{=}0 \wedge y{=}0) =
\end{array}$$

$$\begin{array}{l}
(\texttt{UNSAT}(y = 0 \wedge y = 0) \vee \texttt{svc}\,(\texttt{ERR:=1})\,(\cdots)) \\
\wedge \\
(\texttt{UNSAT}(y = 0 \wedge \neg(y = 0)) \vee \texttt{svc}\, S\,(\cdots)) \;=\; (\mathsf{F} \vee \mathsf{T}) \wedge (\mathsf{T} \vee \cdots) \;=\; \mathsf{T}
\end{array}$$

Thus $\{\texttt{Y=0}\}\texttt{Div}\{\texttt{X=R} \wedge \texttt{Y=0} \wedge \texttt{ERR=1}\}$, since $\forall\, S\, P.\, \texttt{svc}\, S\, P \Rightarrow \{P\}S\{\texttt{asp}\, S\, P\}$. Whilst this might seem to be a very heavyweight derivation of a trivial case, the point is that the derivation is a forward symbolic execution with some on-the-fly simplification. This simplification enables the calculation of `asp` and `svc` for the `WHILE`-loop to be avoided.

For the $\texttt{Y} > 0$ case, it is necessary to analyse the loop, which we now do.

$$\begin{array}{l}
\texttt{asp} \\
\quad (\texttt{R:=X; Q:=0; ERR:=0; IF Y=0 THEN ERR:=1 ELSE}\, S) \\
\quad (\texttt{Y>0}) =
\end{array}$$

$$\begin{array}{l}
\texttt{asp} \\
\quad (\texttt{R:=X; Q:=0; ERR:=0; IF Y=0 THEN ERR:=1 ELSE}\, S) \\
\quad (\exists xyqre.\, \texttt{X}{=}x \wedge \texttt{Y}{=}y \wedge \texttt{Q}{=}q \wedge \texttt{R}{=}r \wedge \texttt{ERR}{=}e \wedge y{>}0) =
\end{array}$$

$$\begin{array}{l}
\texttt{asp} \\
\quad (\texttt{IF Y=0 THEN ERR:=1 ELSE}\, S) \\
\quad (\exists xyqre.\, \texttt{X}{=}x \wedge \texttt{Y}{=}y \wedge \texttt{Q}{=}0 \wedge \texttt{R}{=}x \wedge \texttt{ERR}{=}0 \wedge y{>}0) =
\end{array}$$

$$\begin{array}{l}
\texttt{asp}\,(\texttt{ERR:=1})\,(\exists xyqre.\, \texttt{X}{=}x \wedge \texttt{Y}{=}y \wedge \texttt{Q}{=}0 \wedge \texttt{R}{=}x \wedge \texttt{ERR}{=}0 \wedge y{>}0 \wedge (y{=}0)) \\
\vee \\
\texttt{asp}\, S\,(\exists xyqre.\, \texttt{X}{=}x \wedge \texttt{Y}{=}y \wedge \texttt{Q}{=}0 \wedge \texttt{R}{=}x \wedge \texttt{ERR}{=}0 \wedge y{>}0 \wedge \neg(y{=}0)) \;=\\
\texttt{asp}\, S\,(\exists xyqre.\, \texttt{X}{=}x \wedge \texttt{Y}{=}y \wedge \texttt{Q}{=}0 \wedge \texttt{R}{=}x \wedge \texttt{ERR}{=}0 \wedge y{>}0 \wedge \neg(y{=}0))
\end{array}$$

Since S is $\texttt{WHILE Y} < \texttt{R DO}\{\texttt{X} = \texttt{R} + \texttt{Y} \times \texttt{Q}\}\,(\cdots)$, it follows (see Fig. 5.5) that

$$\begin{array}{l}
\texttt{asp Div (Y>0)} \;= \\
\texttt{asp}\, S\,(\exists xyqre.\, \texttt{X}{=}x \wedge \texttt{Y}{=}y \wedge \texttt{Q}{=}0 \wedge \texttt{R}{=}x \wedge \texttt{ERR}{=}0 \wedge y{>}0 \wedge \neg(y{=}0)) \;= \\
(\exists xyqre.\, \texttt{X}{=}x \wedge \texttt{Y}{=}y \wedge \texttt{Q}{=}q \wedge \texttt{R}{=}r \wedge \texttt{ERR}{=}e \wedge (x = r{+}y{\times}q \wedge \neg(y{<}r))) = \\
(\texttt{X} = \texttt{R} + \texttt{Y} \times \texttt{Q} \wedge \neg(\texttt{Y} < \texttt{R}))
\end{array}$$

Thus if `svc Div` (Y>0) holds (which it does, see below) then

$$\{\texttt{Y}{>}0\}\texttt{Div}\{\texttt{X} = \texttt{R} + \texttt{Y} \times \texttt{Q} \wedge \neg(\texttt{Y} < \texttt{R})\}$$

To verify `svc Div` (Y>0), first calculate:

$$\begin{array}{l} \texttt{svc} \\ (\texttt{R:=X; Q:=0; ERR:=0; IF Y=0 THEN ERR:=1 ELSE } S) \\ (\texttt{Y}{>}0) = \\[1ex] \texttt{svc} \\ (\texttt{R:=X; Q:=0; ERR:=0; IF Y=0 THEN ERR:=1 ELSE } S) \\ (\exists xyqre.\, \texttt{X}{=}x \wedge \texttt{Y}{=}y \wedge \texttt{Q}{=}q \wedge \texttt{R}{=}r \wedge \texttt{ERR}{=}e \wedge y{>}0) = \\[1ex] \texttt{svc} \\ (\texttt{IF Y=0 THEN ERR:=1 ELSE } S) \\ (\exists xyqre.\, \texttt{X}{=}x \wedge \texttt{Y}{=}y \wedge \texttt{Q}{=}0 \wedge \texttt{R}{=}x \wedge \texttt{ERR}{=}0 \wedge y{>}0) = \\[1ex] (\texttt{UNSAT}(y > 0 \wedge y = 0) \vee \texttt{svc}\,(\texttt{ERR:=1})\,(\cdots)) \\ \wedge \\ (\texttt{UNSAT}(y > 0 \wedge \neg(y = 0)) \vee \texttt{svc}\,S\,(\cdots)) = (\mathsf{T} \vee \mathsf{T}) \wedge (\mathsf{F} \vee \texttt{svc}\,S\,(\cdots)) = \\ \texttt{svc}\,S\,(\exists xyqre.\, \texttt{X}{=}x \wedge \texttt{Y}{=}y \wedge \texttt{Q}{=}0 \wedge \texttt{R}{=}x \wedge \texttt{ERR}{=}0 \wedge (y{>}0 \wedge \neg(y = 0))) \end{array}$$

S is a `WHILE`-loop; Fig. 5.5 shows the verification conditions generated:

1. $\forall xyqre.\, (y{>}0 \wedge \neg(y = 0)) \Rightarrow (\texttt{X} = \texttt{R} + \texttt{Y} \times \texttt{Q})[x, y, 0, x, 0/\texttt{X}, \texttt{Y}, \texttt{Q}, \texttt{R}, \texttt{ERR}]$
2. $\texttt{asp}\,(\texttt{R:=R-Y;Q:=1+Q})\,((\texttt{X} = \texttt{R} + \texttt{Y} \times \texttt{Q}) \wedge \texttt{Y} < \texttt{R}) \Rightarrow (\texttt{X} = \texttt{R} + \texttt{Y} \times \texttt{Q})$
3. $\texttt{svc}\,(\texttt{R:=R-Y;Q:=1+Q})\,((\texttt{X} = \texttt{R} + \texttt{Y} \times \texttt{Q}) \wedge \texttt{Y} < \texttt{R})$

The first (1) is $(y{>}0 \wedge \neg(y = 0)) \Rightarrow (x = x + y \times 0)$, which is clearly true. The third (3) is also clearly true as $\texttt{svc}\,S\,P = \mathsf{T}$ if S is loop-free. The second (2) requires a symbolic execution:

$$\begin{array}{l} \texttt{asp}\,(\texttt{R:=R-Y;Q:=1+Q})\,((\texttt{X} = \texttt{R+Y} \times \texttt{Q}) \wedge \texttt{Y} < \texttt{R}) = \\[1ex] \texttt{asp} \\ (\texttt{R:=R-Y;Q:=1+Q}) \\ (\exists x y q r.\, \texttt{X} = x \wedge \texttt{Y} = y \wedge \texttt{Q} = q \wedge \texttt{R} = r \wedge ((x = r + y{\times}q) \wedge y < r)) = \\[1ex] (\exists x y q r.\, \texttt{X} = x \wedge \texttt{Y} = y \wedge \texttt{Q} = 1{+}q \wedge \texttt{R} = r{-}y \wedge ((x = r + y{\times}q) \wedge y < r)) \end{array}$$

Thus to show verification condition 2 above, we must show:

$$\begin{array}{l} (\exists x y q r.\, \texttt{X} = x \wedge \texttt{Y} = y \wedge \texttt{Q} = 1{+}q \wedge \texttt{R} = r{-}y \wedge ((x = r + y{\times}q) \wedge y < r)) \\ \Rightarrow \\ (\texttt{X} = \texttt{R} + \texttt{Y}{\times}\texttt{Q}) \end{array}$$

i.e.: $(((x = r + y \times q) \wedge y < r)) \Rightarrow (x = (r{-}y) + y \times (1{+}q))$, which is true. So all three verification conditions, 1, 2 and 3 above, are true.

The application of weakest precondition methods (`wvc` and `awp`) to the `Div` example is completely standard and the details are well known, so we do not give them here. However, the general remarks made in Section 5.6 continue to apply when there are loops. In particular, using forward symbolic execution, one can separately explore non-looping paths through a program using software model checking methods. Deductive theorem proving needs only be invoked on paths with loops. The general framework based on `svc` and `asp` enables these separate analysis methods to be unified.

5.8 Discussion, Summary and Conclusion

Our goal has been to provide a review of some classical verification methods, especially Hoare logic, from the perspective of mechanical verification. We reviewed how both weakest preconditions and strongest postconditions could be used to convert the problem of verifying Hoare triples to problems in pure logic, suitable for theorem provers. Although 'going backwards' via weakest preconditions appears superficially simpler, we have tried to make a case for going forward using strongest postconditions. The benefits are that computing strongest postconditions can be formulated as symbolic execution, with loops handled via forward verification conditions. This provides a framework that can unify both deductive methods for full proof of correctness with automatic property checking based on symbolic execution.

Although the development in this paper has been based on classical Hoare logic, over the years there have been many advances that add new ideas. Notable examples are VDM [16] that generalises postconditions to relations between the initial and final states (rather than just predicates on the final state) and separation logic [21] that provides tractable methods for handling pointers. Separation logic tools are often based on symbolic execution (though it remains to to be seen whether anything here provides a useful perspective on this).

The contribution of this paper is to explain how old methods (Floyd-Hoare logic) and new ones (software model checking) can be fitted together to provide a spectrum of verification possibilities. There are no new concepts here, but we hope to have provided a clarifying perspective that shows that Hoare's pioneering ideas will be going strong for another 40 years!

References

1. Mantovani, J., Armando, A., Platania, L.: Bounded model checking of software using smt solvers instead of sat solvers. Int. J. Software Tools Technol. Transfer **11**(1), 69–83 February. (2009).
2. Apt, K.R.: Ten years of Hoare's logic: A survey – part I. ACM Trans. Program. Lang. Syst. **3**(4), 431–483 (1981).
3. Clarke E., Kroening, D., Lerda F.: A tool for checking ANSI-c programs. In: TACAS 2004, vol. 2988 of LNCS, pp. 168–176. Springer-verlag (2004).
4. Cook, S.A.: Soundness and completeness of an axiom system for program verification. SIAM J. Comput. **7**(1), 70–90 (1978).

5. Cytron, R., Ferrante, J., Rosen, B.K., Wegman, M.N., Zadeck, F.K.: Efficently computing static single assignment form and the control dependence graph. Trans. Program. Lang. Systems, **13**(4), 451–490 (1991).
6. Dijkstra, E.W.: A Discipline of Programming. Prentice Hall (October 1976).
7. Dijkstra, E.W., Scholten, C.S.: Predicate Calculus and Program Semantics. Texts and Monographs in Computer Science. Springer, New York, Inc., New York, NY, USA (1990).
8. Floyd, R.W.: Assigning meanings to programs. In: Procsedings of the. Sympos. Applied. Mathematics., Vol. XIX, pp. 19–32. Amer. Math. Soc., Providence, R.I., (1967).
9. Gannod, G.C., Cheng, B.H.C.: Strongest postcondition semantics as the formal basis for reverse engineering. In: WCRE '95: Proceedings of the Second Working Conference on Reverse Engineering, p. 188, IEEE Computer Society. Washington, DC, USA (1995).
10. Gries, D.: The Science of Programming. Springer (1981).
11. Henzinger, T.A., Jhala, R., Majumdar, R., McMillan, K.L.: Abstractions from proofs. In: Jones, N. D., Leroy, Xa. (eds.), POPL, pp. 232–244. ACM (2004).
12. Hoare, C.A.R.: An axiomatic basis for computer programming. Commun. the ACM **12**(10), 576–580 October (1969).
13. Hoare, C.A.R., Lauer, P.E.: Consistent and complementary formal theories of the semantics of programming languages. Acta Inf. **3**, 135–153 (1974).
14. Igarashi, S., London, R.L., Luckham, D.C.: Automatic program verification I: A logical basis and its implementation. Acta Inf. **4**, 145–182 (1975).
15. Igarashi, S., London, R.L., Luckham, D.C.: Automatic program verification i: a logical basis and its implementation. Technical report, Stanford University, Stanford, CA, USA (1973).
16. Jones, C.B.: The early search for tractable ways of reasoning about programs. IEEE Ann. Hist. Comput. **25**(2), 26–49, (2003).
17. King, J.C.: A program verifier. In: IFIP Congress (1), pp. 234–249 (1971).
18. King, J.C.: Symbolic execution and program testing. Commun. ACM **19**(7), 385–394 (July 1976).
19. Cornelius King, J.: A program verifier. PhD thesis, Carnegie Mellon University, Pittsburgh, PA, USA (1970).
20. Luckham, D.C.: A brief account: Implementation and applications of a pascal program verifier (position statement). In: ACM '78: Proceedings of the 1978 Annual conference, pp. 786–792 ACM, New York, NY, USA (1978).
21. O'Hearn, P.W., Reynolds, J.C., Yang, H.: Local reasoning about programs that alter data structures. In: Proceedings of 15th Annual Conference of the European Association for Computer Science Logic, vol. 2142 of Lecture Notes in Computer Science, pp. 1–19. Springer (September 2001).
22. Pasareanu, Co.S., Visser, W.: Verification of java programs using symbolic execution and invariant generation. In: Graf, S. Mounier, L. (eds.), SPIN, vol. 2989 of Lecture Notes in Computer Science, pp. 164–181. Springer (2004).
23. von Henke, F.W, Luckham, D.C.: A methodology for verifying programs. In: Proceedings of the International Conference on Reliable Software, pp. 156–164 ACM, New York, NY, USA (1975).
24. Winskel, G.: The Formal Semantics of Programming Languages: an Introduction. MIT, Cambridge, MA, USA (1993).

Appendix: Proofs Relating svc, asp, wvc, awp

Proof by Structural Induction on S that $\forall S\ P.\ \mathtt{svc}\,S\,P \Rightarrow \{P\}S\{\mathtt{asp}\,S\,P\}$

1. SKIP.
   Follows from $\vdash \{P\}\,\mathtt{SKIP}\,\{P\}$.
2. $V := E$.
   Follows from $\vdash \{P\}\,V := E\,\{\exists v.\,(V = E[v/V]) \wedge P[v/V]\}$.
3. $S_1\,;S_2$.
   Assume by induction:
   $\forall P.\ \mathtt{svc}\,S_1\,P \Rightarrow \{P\}S_1\{\mathtt{asp}\,S_1\,P\}$
   $\forall P.\ \mathtt{svc}\,S_2\,P \Rightarrow \{P\}S_2\{\mathtt{asp}\,S_2\,P\}$
   Specialising P to $\mathtt{asp}\,S_1\,P$ in the inductive assumption for S_2 yields:
   $\mathtt{svc}\,S_2\,(\mathtt{asp}\,S_1\,P) \Rightarrow \{\mathtt{asp}\,S_1\,P\}S_2\{\mathtt{asp}\,S_2\,(\mathtt{asp}\,S_1\,P)\}$
   Hence by inductive assumption for S_1 and the Hoare sequencing rule:
   $\mathtt{svc}\,S_1\,P \wedge \mathtt{svc}\,S_2\,(\mathtt{asp}\,S_1\,P) \Rightarrow \{P\}S_1\,;S_2\{\mathtt{asp}\,S_2\,(\mathtt{asp}\,S_1\,P)\}$
   Hence by definitions of $\mathtt{svc}\,(S_1\,;S_2)\,P$ and $\mathtt{asp}\,(S_1\,;S_2)\,P$:
   $\mathtt{svc}\,(S_1\,;S_2)\,P \Rightarrow \{P\}S_1\,;S_2\{\mathtt{asp}\,(S_1\,;S_2)\,P\}$.
4. $\mathtt{IF}\,B\,\mathtt{THEN}\,S_1\,\mathtt{ELSE}\,S_2$.
   Assume by induction:
   $\forall P.\ \mathtt{svc}\,S_1\,P \Rightarrow \{P\}S_1\{\mathtt{asp}\,S_1\,P\}$
   $\forall P.\ \mathtt{svc}\,S_2\,P \Rightarrow \{P\}S_2\{\mathtt{asp}\,S_2\,P\}$
   Specialising these with $P \wedge B$ and $P \wedge \neg B$, respectively, yields:
   $\mathtt{svc}\,S_1\,(P \wedge B) \Rightarrow \{P \wedge B\}S_1\{\mathtt{asp}\,S_1\,(P \wedge B)\}$
   $\mathtt{svc}\,S_2\,(P \wedge \neg B) \Rightarrow \{P \wedge \neg B\}S_2\{\mathtt{asp}\,S_2\,(P \wedge \neg B)\}$
   Applying the 'postcondition weakening' Hoare logic Rule of Consequence:
   $\mathtt{svc}\,S_1\,(P \wedge B) \Rightarrow \{P \wedge B\}S_1\{\mathtt{asp}\,S_1\,(P \wedge B) \vee \mathtt{asp}\,S_2\,(P \wedge \neg B)\}$
   $\mathtt{svc}\,S_2\,(P \wedge \neg B) \Rightarrow \{P \wedge \neg B\}S_2\{\mathtt{asp}\,S_1\,(P \wedge B) \vee \mathtt{asp}\,S_2\,(P \wedge \neg B)\}$
   Hence by definition of $\mathtt{asp}\,(\mathtt{IF}\,B\,\mathtt{THEN}\,S_1\,\mathtt{ELSE}\,S_2)\,P$:
   $\mathtt{svc}\,S_1\,(P \wedge B) \Rightarrow \{P \wedge B\}S_1\{\mathtt{asp}\,(\mathtt{IF}\,B\,\mathtt{THEN}\,S_1\,\mathtt{ELSE}\,S_2)\,P\}$
   $\mathtt{svc}\,S_2\,(P \wedge \neg B) \Rightarrow \{P \wedge \neg B\}S_2\{\mathtt{asp}\,(\mathtt{IF}\,B\,\mathtt{THEN}\,S_1\,\mathtt{ELSE}\,S_2)\,P\}$
   Since Hoare triples are true if the precondition is unsatisfiable:
   $\mathtt{UNSAT}(P \wedge B) \Rightarrow \{P \wedge B\}S_1\{\mathtt{asp}\,(\mathtt{IF}\,B\,\mathtt{THEN}\,S_1\,\mathtt{ELSE}\,S_2)\,P\}$
   $\mathtt{UNSAT}(P \wedge \neg B) \Rightarrow \{P \wedge \neg B\}S_2\{\mathtt{asp}\,(\mathtt{IF}\,B\,\mathtt{THEN}\,S_1\,\mathtt{ELSE}\,S_2)\,P\}$
   By definition of $\mathtt{svc}\,(\mathtt{IF}\,B\,\mathtt{THEN}\,S_1\,\mathtt{ELSE}\,S_2)\,P$ and Hoare logic rules:
   $\mathtt{svc}\,(\mathtt{IF}\,B\,\mathtt{THEN}\,S_1\,\mathtt{ELSE}\,S_2)\,P$
   $\Rightarrow \{P\}\,\mathtt{IF}\,B\,\mathtt{THEN}\,S_1\,\mathtt{ELSE}\,S_2\{\mathtt{asp}\,(\mathtt{IF}\,B\,\mathtt{THEN}\,S_1\,\mathtt{ELSE}\,S_2)\,P\}$
5. $\mathtt{WHILE}\,B\,\mathtt{DO}\{R\}\,S$.
   Assume by induction:
   $\forall P.\ \mathtt{svc}\,S\,P \Rightarrow \{P\}S\{\mathtt{asp}\,S\,P\}$

Specialise P to $R \wedge B$:
$\texttt{svc}\, S\, (R \wedge B) \Rightarrow \{R \wedge B\}\, S\, \{\texttt{asp}\, S\, (R \wedge B)\}$
By definition of $\texttt{svc}\, (\texttt{WHILE}\, B\, \texttt{DO}\{R\}\, S)\, P$ and Consequence Rules:
$\texttt{svc}\, (\texttt{WHILE}\, B\, \texttt{DO}\{R\}\, S)\, P \Rightarrow \{R \wedge B\}\, S\, \{R\}$
By definition of $\texttt{svc}\, (\texttt{WHILE}\, B\, \texttt{DO}\{R\}\, S)\, P$ and Hoare $\texttt{WHILE}$-rule:
$\texttt{svc}\, (\texttt{WHILE}\, B\, \texttt{DO}\{R\}\, S)\, P \Rightarrow \{P\}\, \texttt{WHILE}\, B\, \texttt{DO}\{R\}\, S\, \{R \wedge \neg B\}$
Hence by definition of $\texttt{asp}\, (\texttt{WHILE}\, B\, \texttt{DO}\{R\}\, S)\, P$:
$\texttt{svc}\, (\texttt{WHILE}\, B\, \texttt{DO}\{R\}\, S)\, P \Rightarrow$
$\{P\}\, \texttt{WHILE}\, B\, \texttt{DO}\{R\}\, S\, \{\texttt{asp}\, (\texttt{WHILE}\, B\, \texttt{DO}\{R\}\, S)\, P\}$

Proof by Structural Induction on S that: $\forall S\, Q.\ \texttt{wvc}\, S\, Q \Rightarrow \{\texttt{awp}\, S\, Q\}\, S\, \{Q\}$

1. $\texttt{SKIP}$.
   Follows from $\vdash \{Q\}\, \texttt{SKIP}\, \{Q\}$.
2. $V := E$.
   Follows from $\vdash \{Q[E/V]\}\, V := E\, \{Q\}$.
3. $S_1 ; S_2$.
   Assume by induction:
   $\forall Q.\, \texttt{wvc}\, S_1\, Q \Rightarrow \{\texttt{awp}\, S_1\, Q\}\, S_1\, \{Q\}$
   $\forall Q.\, \texttt{wvc}\, S_2\, Q \Rightarrow \{\texttt{awp}\, S_2\, Q\}\, S_2\, \{Q\}$
   Specialising Q to $\texttt{awp}\, S_2\, Q$ in the inductive assumption for S_1 yields:
   $\texttt{wvc}\, S_1\, (\texttt{awp}\, S_2\, Q) \Rightarrow \{\texttt{awp}\, S_1\, (\texttt{awp}\, S_2\, Q)\}\, S_1\, \{\texttt{awp}\, S_2\, Q\}$
   Hence by inductive assumption for S_2 and the Hoare sequencing rule:
   $\texttt{wvc}\, S_1\, (\texttt{awp}\, S_2\, Q) \wedge \texttt{wvc}\, S_2\, Q \Rightarrow \{\texttt{awp}\, S_1\, (\texttt{awp}\, S_2\, Q)\}\, S_1 ; S_2\, \{Q\}$
   Hence by definitions of $\texttt{wvc}\, (S_1 ; S_2)\, Q$ and $\texttt{awp}\, (S_1 ; S_2)\, Q$:
   $\texttt{wvc}\, (S_1 ; S_2)\, Q \Rightarrow \{\texttt{awp}\, (S_1 ; S_2)\, Q\}\, S_1 ; S_2\, \{Q\}$.
4. $\texttt{IF}\, B\, \texttt{THEN}\, S_1\, \texttt{ELSE}\, S_2$.
   Assume by induction:
   $\texttt{wvc}\, S_1\, Q \Rightarrow \{\texttt{awp}\, S_1\, Q\}\, S_1\, \{Q\}$
   $\texttt{wvc}\, S_2\, Q \Rightarrow \{\texttt{awp}\, S_2\, Q\}\, S_2\, \{Q\}$
   Strengthening the preconditions using the Rules of Consequence
   $\texttt{wvc}\, S_1\, Q \Rightarrow \{\texttt{awp}\, S_1\, Q \wedge B\}\, S_1\, \{Q\}$
   $\texttt{wvc}\, S_2\, Q \Rightarrow \{\texttt{awp}\, S_2\, Q \wedge \neg B\}\, S_2\, \{Q\}$
   Rewriting the preconditions using $\texttt{awp}\, (\texttt{IF}\, B\, \texttt{THEN}\, S_1\, \texttt{ELSE}\, S_2)\, Q$
   $\texttt{wvc}\, S_1\, Q \Rightarrow \{\texttt{awp}\, (\texttt{IF}\, B\, \texttt{THEN}\, S_1\, \texttt{ELSE}\, S_2)\, Q \wedge B\}\, S_1\, \{Q\}$
   $\texttt{wvc}\, S_2\, Q \Rightarrow \{\texttt{awp}\, (\texttt{IF}\, B\, \texttt{THEN}\, S_1\, \texttt{ELSE}\, S_2)\, Q \wedge \neg B\}\, S_2\, \{Q\}$
   Since Hoare triples are true if the postcondition is a tautology
   $\texttt{TAUT}(Q) \Rightarrow \{\texttt{awp}\, (\texttt{IF}\, B\, \texttt{THEN}\, S_1\, \texttt{ELSE}\, S_2)\, Q \wedge B\}\, S_1\, \{Q\}$
   $\texttt{TAUT}(Q) \Rightarrow \{\texttt{awp}\, (\texttt{IF}\, B\, \texttt{THEN}\, S_1\, \texttt{ELSE}\, S_2)\, Q \wedge \neg B\}\, S_2\, \{Q\}$

By the definition of $\texttt{wvc}\,(\texttt{IF}\,B\,\texttt{THEN}\,S_1\,\texttt{ELSE}\,S_2)\,Q$ and the Hoare conditional rule
$\texttt{wvc}\,(\texttt{IF}\,B\,\texttt{THEN}\,S_1\,\texttt{ELSE}\,S_2)\,Q$
$\Rightarrow \{\texttt{awp}\,(\texttt{IF}\,B\,\texttt{THEN}\,S_1\,\texttt{ELSE}\,S_2)\,Q\}\,\texttt{IF}\,B\,\texttt{THEN}\,S_1\,\texttt{ELSE}\,S_2\,\{Q\}$

5. $\texttt{WHILE}\,B\,\texttt{DO}\{R\}\,S$.
   Assume by induction:
   $\forall\,Q.\,\texttt{wvc}\,S\,Q \Rightarrow \{\texttt{awp}\,S\,Q\}\,S\{Q\}$
   Specialise Q to R. By $\texttt{wvc}\,(\texttt{WHILE}\,B\,\texttt{DO}\{R\}\,S)\,Q$ and Consequence Rule:
   $\texttt{wvc}\,(\texttt{WHILE}\,B\,\texttt{DO}\{R\}\,S)\,Q \Rightarrow \{R \wedge B\}\,S\{R\}$
   By Hoare $\texttt{WHILE}$-rule:
   $\texttt{wvc}\,(\texttt{WHILE}\,B\,\texttt{DO}\{R\}\,S)\,Q \Rightarrow \{R\}\,\texttt{WHILE}\,B\,\texttt{DO}\{R\}\,S\{R \wedge \neg B\}$
   By definitions of $\texttt{awp}$ and $\texttt{wvc}$ for $\texttt{WHILE}\,B\,\texttt{DO}\{R\}\,S$, and Consequence Rule:
   $\texttt{wvc}\,(\texttt{WHILE}\,B\,\texttt{DO}\{R\}\,S)\,Q \Rightarrow$
   $\{\texttt{awp}\,(\texttt{WHILE}\,B\,\texttt{DO}\{R\}\,S)\,Q\}\,\texttt{WHILE}\,B\,\texttt{DO}\{R\}\,S\{Q\}$

Chapter 6
Probabilistic Programming with Coordination

He Jifeng

Abstract Failure is the typical phenomenon of the execution of long-running transactions. To accommodate the random features of internet-based computing this paper concentrates on adding probabilistic behaviour to the Dijkstra's Guarded Command Language. We introduce probabilistic choice and coordination operators, and extend standard states to probabilistic states by replacing the final state with a final distribution. This paper explores algebraic properties of the new programming combinators, and shows how to convert programs to normal forms algebraically.

6.1 Introduction

A theory of programming is intended to aid the construction of programs that meet their specifications; for such a theory to be useful it should capture (only) the essential aspects of the program's behaviour, that is only those aspects which one wishes to observe. And it should do so in a mathematically elegant – hence tractable – way.

In recent years, in order to describe the infrastructure for carrying out long-running transactions, various business modeling languages have been introduced, such as XLANG, WSFL, BPEL4WS (BPEL) and StAC [1, 2, 6, 9]. Coordination and compensation mechanisms are vital in handling exception and failure which occur randomly during the execution of a long-running transaction. This paper is an attempt at taking a step forward to gain some perspectives on long-running transactions within the design calculus [4].

In [4], we give the relational meaning of a program by a pair of predicates p, R, with this syntax and interpretation:

$$p(s) \vdash R(s,s') =_{df} (ok \wedge p) \Rightarrow (ok' \wedge R)$$

He Jifeng (✉)
Shanghai Key Laboratory of Trustworthy Computing, East China Normal University, China
e-mail: jifeng@sei.ecnu.edu.cn

C.B. Jones et al. (eds.), *Reflections on the Work of C.A.R. Hoare*,
DOI 10.1007/978-1-84882-912-1_6,

where

- *ok* records the observation that the program has been properly started,
- ok' records the observation that the program has terminated normally (without "error messages") and
- s and s', respectively, denote the initial and final states of the program, mappings from the set of program variables to their values.

Thus if the program starts in an initial state satisfying the *precondition* p, it will terminate in a final state satisfying the *postcondition* R.

The effect of the "design" notation $\cdots \vdash \cdots$ is thus to adjoin a Boolean *ok* to the state space, for the description of proper termination: if the previous command has terminated (*ok* in the antecedent) and the precondition p holds of the passed-on state, then this command will establish relation R between s and s', and will itself terminate too (ok' in the consequent). The approach used in the refinement calculus and in VDM [5] gives semantics to programs by associating them with designs according to this scheme:

$$\bot =_{df} false \vdash true$$

$$\texttt{skip} =_{df} true \vdash (s' = s)$$

$$x := e =_{df} true \vdash (s' = s[e/x])$$

$$P \sqcap Q =_{df} P \vee Q$$

$$P \lhd b \rhd Q =_{df} (b \wedge P) \vee (\neg b \wedge Q)$$

$$P;\ Q =_{df} P \circ Q$$

$$(\mu X \bullet P(X)) =_{df} \bigvee \{Q \mid \forall ok, s, ok', s' \bullet (Q \Rightarrow P(Q))\}$$

where

$$P \circ Q =_{df} \exists\ \hat{ok}, \hat{s} \bullet P(\hat{ok}, \hat{s}/ok', s') \wedge Q(\hat{ok}, \hat{s}/ok, s)$$

and $s[e/x]$ denotes the new state obtained by updating s at x with e in the usual way.

A program *refines* another if it terminates more often and behaves less nondeterministically than the other. We write $\sqsubseteq$ for "is refined by"; for predicates P and Q it is defined by

$$P \sqsubseteq Q =_{df} \forall\ s, s', ok, ok' \bullet (Q \Rightarrow P)$$

In this paper we investigate two aspects of such semantic extensions, one general and one specific. The specific is that we concentrate on adding *probabilistic* behaviour to our programs. The more important general point however is to enrich the standard state space to deal with failure and rollback. There are two stages. In the first we extend the "base type" of the model by adding new logical variables to describe the control status of a program. The second stage is to determine what algebraic characteristics define the probabilistic behaviour of our programs. Such characteristics, often called "healthiness conditions", both reflect the behaviour of "real" programs and allow us to formulate and prove further algebraic laws that are of practical use in program derivation.

Our novel contributions include

- an enriched design model to handle exception and program failure,
- a set of new programming combinators in support of compensation and coordination and
- an algebraic system useful for program derivation and normal form reduction.

This paper presents a probabilistic model for coordination system, which is based on the UTP approach [4] developed by Tony Hoare. To celebrate the 75th birthday and many achievements of Tony Hoare, we write this paper as our gratitude to his encouragement, and in recognizing his great contribution to computer science.

6.2 Probabilistic Program Syntax

The language examined in this paper extends the Guarded Command Language [3] by including the probabilistic choice operator ${}_r\oplus$, compensation operator `cpens` and coordination operator `else`. The abstract syntax of the programming language is given below.

$P ::= \bot$	abort
$\mathtt{fail}$	primitive failure command
$\mathtt{skip}$	empty command
$x := e$	assignment
$P \lhd b \rhd P$	conditional
$P[\![p]\!]P$	probabilistic choice
$P\,\mathtt{caught-by}\,P$	exception handling
$P\,\mathtt{else}\,P$	coordination operator
$P;\ P$	sequential composition
$(\mu X \bullet F(X))$	recursion

where

- Program `fail` halts with indication of the failure of the execution.
- Let p be an expression satisfying $\forall\, v \bullet 0 \leq p \leq 1$. Program $P[\![p]\!]Q$ makes a choice between programs P and Q with probabilities p and $1-p$, respectively.
- Exception handling construct $P\,\mathtt{caught-by}\,Q$ runs program P first. If its execution fails, then Q will be invoked as the exception handler.
- Coordination construct $P\,\mathtt{else}\,Q$ behaves like P if its execution succeeds. Otherwise it will fire Q on the same initial state as P.

In the following sections, we will abbreviate the entire list of program variables $(x,\ y,\ ,\ ..,\ z)$ by the simple vector variable v.

6.3 Probabilistic Semantics

6.3.1 New State Ingredient

To equip a language with an exception handling mechanism, it is necessary to figure out the cases when the execution of a program fails. We add a new logical variable *eflag* (standing for error-flag) to the standard design model for the description of the current status of a program:

- $eflag' = false$ indicates it terminates successfully.
- $eflag' = true$ indicates it is forced to halt due to an exception case during its execution.

As a result, the enriched state space S used in later discussion has the type

$$(Var \rightarrow Val) \times (\{eflag\} \rightarrow Bool)$$

6.3.2 Final Distribution

We extend our standard states to probabilistic states by replacing the final state with a final *distribution* over S.

Definition (Probabilistic distribution)

A final distribution is a total function from S into the closed interval of reals [0, 1]. We define

$$\mathbf{PROB} =_{df} S \rightarrow [0,\ 1]$$

We insist further that for any member `prob` of **PROB** the probabilities must NOT exceed 1:

$$\Sigma_{s \in S}\,\mathtt{prob}(s) \ \leq\ 1$$

For any subset X of S we define

$$\mathtt{prob}(X) =_{df} \Sigma_{s \in X}\,\mathtt{prob}(s).$$

We use the notation **0** to denote the zero distribution $\lambda\, s \bullet 0$, and define

$$\mathtt{prob}_1 \leq \mathtt{prob}_2 \ =_{df}\ \forall\, s \in S \bullet (\mathtt{prob}_1(s) \leq \mathtt{prob}_2(s))$$

For any `prob` $\in$ **PROB** we have

$$\mathbf{0} \leq \mathtt{prob}$$

For any $s \in S$ we introduce its corresponding point-distribution η_s:

$$\eta_s =_{df} \lambda\, t : S \bullet \mathbf{int}(t = s)$$

where

$$\mathbf{int}(b) =_{df} 1 \lhd b \rhd 0$$

This paper identifies a probabilistic program as a function from S to **PROB**, and introduces the refinement relation $\leq$ between probabilistic programs as follows:

$$P \leq Q =_{df} \forall\, s \in S \bullet (P(s) \leq Q(s))$$

Lemma 3.1 *$\leq$ is a complete partial order with $\lambda\, s \bullet \mathbf{0}$ as its bottom.*

Proof For any increasing chain $\{P_n \mid 1 \leq n\}$ we can show that

$$\mathbf{sup}_n P_n =_{df} \lambda\, s : S \bullet \mathbf{sup}_n P_n(s)$$

is the least upper bound of the chain.

6.3.3 Healthiness Condition

Having introduced the logical variable *eflag* into the alphabet of our behavioural predicates, it becomes necessary to ask a program to remain idle when its predecessor throws an exception case, i.e., a probabilistic program must meet the following healthiness condition:

$(\mathbf{Req})P = \texttt{skip} \lhd \mathit{eflag} \rhd P$

where

$$P \lhd b \rhd Q =_{df} \mathbf{int}(b) \times P + \mathbf{int}(\neg b) \times Q$$

and

$$\texttt{skip} =_{df} \lambda\, s : S \bullet \eta_s$$

The healthiness condition is captured by the idempotent mapping

$$\mathcal{H} : (S \to \mathbf{PROB}) \to (S \to \mathbf{PROB})$$

where

$$\mathcal{H}(P) =_{df} \texttt{skip} \lhd \mathit{eflag} \rhd P$$

in the sense that a function from S to **PROB** is **Req** healthy if and only if it is a fixed point of $\mathcal{H}$.

Theorem 3.1 *Healthy functions form a complete partial order.*

In the following sections, we will confine ourselves to healthy mappings only.

6.4 Programs

This section provides a probabilistic semantics to our language. In the following discussion, v will represent the program variables cited in the alphabet of the program, and s the state variable of the type S defined in Section 6.3.1.

6.4.1 Primitive Commands

The execution of `fail` throws an exception case.

$$\texttt{fail} =_{df} \lambda s : S \bullet \eta_{s[true/eflag]}$$

Lemma 4.1

$\texttt{fail} = \mathcal{H}(\texttt{fail})$

The behaviour of the chaotic program $\bot$ is totally unpredictable

$$\bot =_{df} \mathcal{H}(\lambda s : S \bullet \mathbf{0})$$

6.4.2 Probabilistic Choice

Let P and Q be programs, and p an expression satisfying $\forall v \bullet 0 \leq p \leq 1$. Probabilistic choice $P[\![p]\!]Q$ selects P and Q with probability p and $1-p$, respectively.

$$P[\![p]\!]Q =_{df} p \times P + (1-p) \times Q$$

Healthy functions are closed under probabilistic choice operator:

Lemma 4.2

$\mathcal{H}(P)[\![p]\!]\mathcal{H}(Q) = \mathcal{H}(P[\![p]\!]Q)$

Probabilistic choice is symmetric, associative and idempotent.

Theorem 4.1

(1) $P\,[\![p]\!]\,Q = Q\,[\![1-p]\!]\,P$

(2) $P\,[\![1]\!]\,Q = P$

(3) $P\,[\![p]\!]\,P \;=\; P$

(4) $(P\,[\![p]\!]\,Q)\,[\![q]\!]\,R \;=\; P\,[\![(p \times q)]\!]\,(Q\,[\![(q - p \times q)/(1 \ominus p \times q)]\!]\,R)$

where

$$1 \ominus p =_{df} (1 - p) \lhd 0 \le p < 1 \rhd 1$$

Proof (4) When $p = q = 1$, the conclusion follows from (2). Otherwise we have

$$
\begin{array}{ll}
\quad LHS & \{\text{Def of } [\![r]\!]\} \\
= q \times (P[\![p]\!]Q) \;+\; (1-q) \times R & \{\text{Def of } [\![r]\!]\} \\
= q \times (p \times P \;+\; (1-p) \times Q) \;+\; (1-q) \times R & \{\text{calculation}\} \\
= (p \times q) \times P \;+\; (1 - p \times q) \times (q \times (1-p)/(1 - p \times q) \times Q & \\
\quad +(1-q)/(1 - p \times q) \times R & \{\text{Def of } [\![r]\!]\} \\
= RHS &
\end{array}
$$

Normal forms, which will be defined in Section 6.5, require us to add "generalised probabilistic choice" to our language. Let $\{p_i \mid 1 \le i \le n\}$ be a set of expressions satisfying

$$\forall v \bullet (0 \le \Sigma_{i \in \{1,..,n\}} p_i \;\le\; 1)$$

Let $\{P_i \mid 1 \le i \le n\}$ be a set of programs. We define the generalised probabilistic choice

$$\mathbf{pchoice}(p_1\&P_1, ..., p_n\&P_n) \;=_{df}\; \Sigma_{1 \le i \le n}(p_i \times P_i) \;+\; (1 - \Sigma_{1 \le i \le n} p_i) \times \bot$$

Theorem 4.2

(1) $\mathbf{pchoice}(p_1\&P_1, ..., p_n\&P_n) \;=\; \mathbf{pchoice}(p_{\pi(1)}\&P_{\pi(1)}, ..., p_{\pi(n)}\&P_{\pi(n)})$

for any permutation π *of* $\{1, ..., n\}$.

(2) $\mathbf{pchoice}(p_1\&\mathbf{pchoice}(q_1\&Q_1, .., q_k\&Q_k),\; ...\, p_n\&P_n)$

$\quad = \;\mathbf{pchoice}((p_1 \times q_1)\&Q_1, .., (p_1 \times q_k)\&Q_k, ..., p_n\&P_n)$

(3) $\mathbf{pchoice}(1\&P_1, ...) \;=\; P_1$

(4) $\mathbf{pchoice}(0\&P_1,\; p_2\&P_2, ...) \;=\; \mathbf{pchoice}(p_2\&P_2, ..)$

(5) $\mathbf{pchoice}(p_1\&P,\; p_2\&P, ...) \;=\; \mathbf{pchoice}((p_1 + p_2)\&P, ...)$

6.4.3 Conditional Choice

Conditional choice is defined by

$$P \lhd b \rhd Q =_{df} \quad \mathbf{int}(b) \times P \;+\; \mathbf{int}(\neg b) \times Q$$

It is actually a special type of probabilistic choice.

Theorem 4.3
$P \lhd b \rhd Q \;=\; P[\![\mathbf{int}(b)]\!]Q$

Proof *RHS* $\{\text{Def of } [\![p]\!]\}$

$= \mathbf{int}(b) \times P \,+\, (1 - \mathbf{int}(b)) \times Q$ $\{\mathbf{int}(\neg b) \;=\; 1 - \mathbf{int}(b)\}$

$= \mathbf{int}(b) \times P \,+\, \mathbf{int}(\neg b) \times Q$ $\{\text{Def of } \lhd b \rhd\}$

$= \mathit{LHS}$

6.4.4 Assignment

The execution of assignment $x := e$ assigns the value of e to variable x if e can be successfully evaluated. Otherwise it behaves like `fail`

$$(x := e) \;=_{df}\; (\lambda\, s : S \bullet \eta_{s[e/x]}) \lhd \mathcal{D}e \rhd \texttt{fail}$$

where $\mathcal{D}e$ is true in just those circumstances in which the evaluation of e will yield a value properly [8]. For example

$$\mathcal{D}x = \mathit{true}$$

$$\mathcal{D}(e + f) = \mathcal{D}e \wedge \mathcal{D}f$$

$$\mathcal{D}(e/f) = \mathcal{D}e \wedge \mathcal{D}f \wedge (f \neq 0)$$

$$\mathcal{D}(e \lhd b \rhd f) = \mathcal{D}b \wedge (b \Rightarrow \mathcal{D}e) \wedge (\neg b \Rightarrow \mathcal{D}f)$$

An expression e is well defined if $\mathcal{D}e \;\equiv\; \mathit{true}$. For example

$$e \lhd \mathcal{D}e \rhd x$$

is well defined.

Lemma 4.3
$x := e \;=\; \mathcal{H}(x := e)$

Definition 4.1
$x := e$ is a *total assignment* if e is well defined.

In the following sections we will confine ourselves to total assignments because an assignment $x := e$ can always be converted to a conditional with total assignment as its component

$$x := e \;=\; (x := (e \lhd \mathcal{D}e \rhd x)) \lhd \mathcal{D}e \rhd \texttt{fail}$$

6.4.5 Sequential Composition

For sequential composition we follow the Kleisli-triple approach to the semantics of programming languages [7], introducing a lift operator $\uparrow$ to map a function from S to **PROB** to a function from **PROB** to **PROB**.

Definition 4.2 (*Kleisli lifting*)

$$\uparrow P =_{df} \lambda\, \texttt{prob} : \mathbf{PROB} \bullet \Sigma_{s \in S}(\texttt{prob}(s) \times P(s))$$

Lemma 4.4
(1) $\uparrow \texttt{skip} = \lambda\, \texttt{prob} : \mathbf{PROB} \bullet \texttt{prob}$
(2) $\uparrow P \circ \texttt{skip} = P$
(3) $\uparrow (\uparrow Q \circ P) = \uparrow Q \circ \uparrow P$

Proof

(1) $\texttt{skip}$ $\{\text{Def of } \uparrow\}$

$= \lambda\, \texttt{prob} : \mathbf{PROB} \bullet \Sigma_{s \in S}\texttt{prob}(s) \times \texttt{skip}(s)$ $\{\text{Def of } \texttt{skip}\}$

$= \lambda\, \texttt{prob} : \mathbf{PROB} \bullet \Sigma_{s \in S}\texttt{prob}(s) \times \eta_s$ $\{\text{Def of } \eta_s\}$

$= \lambda\, \texttt{prob} : \mathbf{PROB} \bullet \texttt{prob}$

(2) $\uparrow P \circ \texttt{skip}$ $\{\text{Def of } \uparrow\}$

$= (\lambda\, \texttt{prob} : \mathbf{PROB} \bullet \Sigma_{s \in S}(\texttt{prob}(s) \times P(s))) \circ (\lambda\, s : S \bullet \eta_s)$ $\{\text{Def of composite}\}$

$= \lambda\, s : S \bullet (\Sigma_{t \in S}(\eta_s(t) \times P(t))$ $\{\text{Def of } \eta_s\}$

$= \lambda\, s : S \bullet P(s)$ $\{\text{Def of } P\}$

$= P$

(3) $\uparrow (\uparrow Q \circ P)$ $\{\text{Def of } \uparrow\}$

$= \lambda\, \texttt{prob} : \mathbf{PROB} \bullet \Sigma_{s \in S}(\texttt{prob}(s) \times (\uparrow Q \circ P)(s))$ $\{\text{Def of } \uparrow\}$

$= \lambda\, \texttt{prob} : \mathbf{PROB} \bullet \Sigma_{s \in S}(\texttt{prob}(s) \times \Sigma_{t \in S}(P(s)(t) \times Q(t)))$ $\{\text{calculation}\}$

$= \lambda\, \texttt{prob} : \mathbf{PROB} \bullet \Sigma_{t \in S}(\Sigma_{s \in S}(\texttt{prob}(s) \times P(s)(t)) \times Q(t))$ $\{\text{Def of } \uparrow\}$

$= \lambda\, \texttt{prob} : \mathbf{PROB} \bullet \Sigma_{t \in S}(\uparrow P(\texttt{prob})(t) \times Q(t))$ $\{\text{Def of } \uparrow\}$

$= \lambda\, \texttt{prob} : \mathbf{PROB} \bullet \uparrow Q(\uparrow P(\texttt{prob}))$ $\{\text{Def of composite}\}$

$= \uparrow Q \circ \uparrow P$

We define

$$P;\, Q =_{df} (\uparrow Q) \circ P$$

Healthy functions are closed under sequential composition

Lemma 4.5
$\mathcal{H}(P);\ \mathcal{H}(Q)\ =\ P(s)(eflag = true) \times (eflag = false) \lhd Q(s)$

$\mathcal{H}(P;\ \mathcal{H}(Q))$
where

$$(X \lhd \mathtt{prob})(s) =_{df}\ = \mathtt{prob}(s) \lhd s \in X \rhd 0$$

Because sequential composition adopts a new definition, we are obliged to reestablish its well-known properties.

Theorem 4.4
(1) $\mathtt{skip};\ P\ =\ P\ =\ P;\ \mathtt{skip}$

(2) $P;\ (Q;\ R)\ =\ (P;\ Q);\ R$

(3) $\mathbf{pchoice}(p_1\&P_1, ..., p_n\&P_n);\ Q\ =\ \mathbf{pchoice}(p_1\&(P_1;\ Q), ..., p_n\&(P_n;\ Q))$

(4) $(x := e)\ ;\ \mathbf{pchoice}(p_1(x)\&P_1, ..., p_n(x)\&P_n)\ =$
$\quad \mathbf{pchoice}(p_1(e)\&(x := e\ ;\ P_1), ..., p_n(e)\&(x := e\ ;\ P_n))$

provided that $\forall\, v \bullet \Sigma_{1 \le i \le n}\, p_i\ =\ 1.$

Proof

$$
\begin{array}{ll}
(1)\ \mathtt{skip};\ P & \{\text{Def of };\ \} \\
=\ \uparrow P \circ \mathtt{skip} & \{\text{Lemma 4.4(2)}\} \\
=\ P & \{\text{Lemma 4.4(1)}\} \\
=\ \uparrow \mathtt{skip} \circ P & \{\text{Def of };\ \} \\
=\ P;\ \mathtt{skip} &
\end{array}
$$

$$
\begin{array}{ll}
(2)\ P;\ (Q;\ R) & \{\text{Def of };\ \} \\
=\ \uparrow (\uparrow R \circ Q) \circ P & \{\text{Lemma 4.4(3)}\} \\
=\ \uparrow R \circ \uparrow Q \circ P & \{\text{Def of };\ \} \\
=\ \uparrow R \circ (P;\ Q) & \{\text{Def of };\ \} \\
=\ (P;\ Q);\ R &
\end{array}
$$

$$
\begin{array}{ll}
(3)\ LHS & \{\text{Def of };\ \} \\
=\ \lambda\, s : S \bullet \Sigma_{t \in S}(\Sigma_{1 \le i \le n} p_i(s) \times P_i(s)(t) & \\
\quad +\, (1 - \Sigma_{1 \le i \le n} p_i(s)) \times \bot(s)(t)) \times Q(t) & \{\Sigma_{t \in S} \circ + = + \circ\ \Sigma_{t \in S}\} \\
=\ \lambda\, s : S \bullet \Sigma_{1 \le i \le n}\, \lambda\, s : S \bullet & \\
\quad (p_i(s) \times \Sigma_{t \in S}(P_i(s)(t)) \times Q(t)) & \\
\quad +\, (1 - \Sigma_{1 \le i \le n} p_i(s)) \times \Sigma_{t \in S}(\bot(s)(t) \times Q(t)) & \{\text{Def of } \uparrow\} \\
=\ \Sigma_{1 \le i \le n}\, \lambda\, s : S \bullet (p_i(s) \times \uparrow Q(P_i(s))) + & \\
\quad \lambda\, s : S \bullet (1 - \Sigma_{1 \le i \le n} p_i(s)) \times \uparrow Q(\bot(s)) & \{\text{Def of };\ \}
\end{array}
$$

$= \Sigma_{1\leq i\leq n}\ \lambda\, s : S \bullet (p_i(s) \times (P_i;\ Q)(s))$

$\quad + \lambda\, s : S \bullet (1 - \Sigma_{1\leq i\leq n} p_i(s)) \times (\bot;\ Q)(s))$ {Def of **pchoice**}

$= RHS$

Both $\bot$ and `fail` act as left zero of sequential composition

Theorem 4.5
(1) `fail`; P = `fail`

(2) $\bot;\ P = \bot$

Proof

(1) `fail`; P {Def of ; }

$= \uparrow P \circ$ `fail` {Def of composite}

$= \lambda\, s : S \bullet \Sigma_{t\in S}\mathtt{fail}(s)(t) \times P(t)$ {Def of `fail`}

$= \lambda\, s : S \bullet P(s[true/eflag])$ **{Req}**

$= \lambda\, s : S \bullet \mathtt{skip}(s[true/eflag])$ {Def of `skip`}

$= \lambda\, s : S \bullet \eta_{s[true/flag]}$ {Def of `fail`}

$=$ `fail`

6.4.6 Exception Handling

Let P and Q be programs. The program $P\,\mathtt{caught-by}\,Q$ runs P first. If it fails, then Q is fired to handle the exception thrown by P.

$$P\,\mathtt{caught-by}\,Q = \mathcal{H}(P;\ \Psi(Q))$$

where

$$\Psi(Q) =_{df} Q[false/eflg] \lhd eflag \rhd \mathtt{skip}$$

Exception handling operator is associative, and has $\bot$ and $x := e$ as its left zeros. It also distributes probabilistic choices.

Theorem 4.6
(1) $P\,\mathtt{caught-by}\,(Q\,\mathtt{caught-by}\,R) = (P\,\mathtt{caught-by}\,Q)\,\mathtt{caught-by}\,R$

(2) $\bot\,\mathtt{caught-by}\,Q = \bot$

(3) $(x := e)\,\mathtt{caught-by}\,Q = x := e$

(4) $(x := e;\ \mathtt{fail})\,\mathtt{caught-by}\,Q = (x := e;\ Q)$

(5) $\mathbf{pchoice}(p_1\&P_1, ..., p_n\&P_n)\,\mathtt{caught-by}\,Q$

$\quad = \mathbf{pchoice}(p_1\&(P_1\,\mathtt{caught-by}\,Q), ..., p_n\&(P_n\,\mathtt{caught-by}\,Q))$

provided that $\forall\, v \bullet (\Sigma_{i\in\{1,..,n\}} p_i = 1)$

Proof

(1) LHS {Def of **caught – by**}

$= \mathcal{H}(P;\ \Psi(\mathcal{H}_1(Q;\ \Psi(R))))$ $\{\Psi(\mathcal{H}(X)) = \Psi(X)\}$

$= \mathcal{H}(P;\ \Psi(Q;\ \Psi(R)))$ $\{\Psi(Q;\ \Psi(R)) = \Psi(Q);\ \Psi(R)\}$

$= \mathcal{H}(P;\ \Psi(Q);\ \Psi(R))$ $\{\mathcal{H}$ is idempotent$\}$

$= \mathcal{H}(\mathcal{H}_1(P;\ \Psi(Q);\ \Psi(R)))$ {Def of $\mathcal{H}$}

$= \mathcal{H}((\neg efalg)_\perp;\ \mathcal{H}_1(P;\ \Psi(Q);\ \Psi(R)))$ $\{P \lhd false \rhd Q = Q\}$

$= \mathcal{H}((\Psi(R) \lhd eflag \rhd (P;\ \Psi(Q);\ \Psi(R))))$ $\{\lhd b \rhd\ --;$ distributive$\}$

$= \mathcal{H}(\mathcal{H}_1(P\Psi(Q));\ \Psi(R))$ {Def of `caught – by`}

$= RHS$

6.4.7 Coordination

Let P and Q be programs. The coordination construct P `else` Q behaves like P if its execution succeeds. Otherwise it behaves like Q.

$$P\,\texttt{else}\,Q =_{df} \lambda\, s : S \bullet (eflag = false) \lhd P(s)\ +\ P(s)(eflag = true) \times Q(s)$$

From the definition it follows that

$(eflag = false) \lhd (P\,\texttt{else}\,Q)(s)$

$= (eflag = false) \lhd P(s)\ +\ P(s)(eflag = true) \times (eflag = false) \lhd Q(s)$

$(P\,\texttt{else}\,Q)(eflag = true)$

$= P(s)(eflag = true) \times Q(s)(eflag = true)$ $(*)$

Lemma 4.6

$\mathcal{H}(P)\,\texttt{else}\,\mathcal{H}(Q) = \mathcal{H}(P\,\texttt{else}\,Q)$

Coordination operator is associative, and has both $\perp$ and $x := e$ as its left zeroes and `fail` *as its left unit. It also distributes over probabilistic choice.*

Theorem 4.7

(1) $P\,\texttt{else}\,(Q\,\texttt{else}\,R) = (P\,\texttt{else}\,Q)\,\texttt{else}\,R$

(2) $\perp\texttt{else}\,Q = \perp$

(3) $(x := e)\,\texttt{else}\,Q = (x := e)$

(4) $(x := e;\ \texttt{fail})\,\texttt{else}\,Q = Q$

(5) **pchoice**$(p_1\&P_1, ..., p_n\&P_n)\,\texttt{else}\,Q =$

pchoice$(p_1\&(P_1\,\texttt{else}\,Q), ..., p_n\&(P_n\,\texttt{else}\,Q))$

provided that $\forall\, v \bullet (\Sigma_{1\le i\le n}\, p_i = 1)$

Proof

$$
\begin{aligned}
&(1)\ LHS && \{\text{Def of } \mathtt{else}\}\\
&= \lambda s : S \bullet ((eflag = false) \lhd P(s) + \\
&\quad P(s)(eflag = true) \times (Q \,\mathtt{else}\, R)(s) && \{\text{Def of } \mathtt{else}\}\\
&= \lambda s : S \bullet ((eflag = false) \lhd P(s) + \\
&\quad P(s)(eflag = true) \times (eflag = false) \lhd Q(s) + \\
&\quad P(s)(eflag = true) \times Q(s)(eflag = true) \times R(s) && \{\text{Conclusion } (*)\}\\
&= \lambda s : S \bullet (eflag = false) \lhd (P \,\mathtt{else}\, Q)(s) + \\
&\quad (P \,\mathtt{else}\, Q)(s)(eflag = true) \times R(s) && \{\text{Def of } \mathtt{else}\}\\
&= RHS
\end{aligned}
$$

$$
\begin{aligned}
&(2)\ LHS && \{\text{Def of } \mathtt{else}\}\\
&= \lambda s : S \bullet (eflag = false) \lhd \mathbf{0} \ + \ \mathbf{0}(eflag = true) \times Q(s) && \{\text{Def of } \mathbf{0}\}\\
&= \lambda s : S \bullet \mathbf{0} && \{\text{Def of } \bot\}\\
&= RHS
\end{aligned}
$$

6.4.8 Recursion

Recursive program $\mu X \bullet F(X)$ is defined as the least upper bound of the increasing chain $\{F^n(\bot) \mid 1 \le n\}$:

$$\mu X \bullet F(X) \ = \ \mathbf{sup}_n F^n(\bot)$$

where

$$
\begin{aligned}
F^0(X) &=_{df} \bot\\
F^{n+1}(X) &=_{df} F(F^n(\bot))
\end{aligned}
$$

Theorem 4.8
$\mu X \bullet F(X) \ = \ F(\mu X \bullet F)$

Proof We are required to show that all programming combinators are continuous. Let $\{P_n \mid n \ge 1\}$ be an increasing chain.

$$
\begin{aligned}
&Q;\ \mathbf{sup}_n P_n && \{\text{Def of } ;\ \}\\
&= \lambda s : S \bullet \Sigma_{t \in S}(Q(s)(t) \times (\mathbf{sup}_n P_n)(t)) && \{\text{Lemma 3.1}\}\\
&= \lambda s : S \bullet \Sigma_{t \in S}(Q(s)(t) \times \mathbf{sup}_n P_n(t)) && \{\times \text{ is continuous}\}\\
&= \lambda s : S \bullet \Sigma_{t \in S}(\mathbf{sup}_n (Q(s)(t) \times P_n(t))) && \{\text{calculation}\}
\end{aligned}
$$

$$= \lambda\, s : S \bullet \mathbf{sup}_n(\Sigma_{t \in S}(Q(s)(t) \times P_n(t)) \qquad \{\text{Def of};\ \}$$

$$= \mathbf{sup}_n(Q;\ P_n)$$

$$(\mathbf{sup}_n P_n)\ ;\ Q \qquad \{\text{Def of};\ \}$$

$$= \lambda\, s \bullet \Sigma_{t \in S}(\mathbf{sup}_n P_n)(s)(t) \times Q(t)) \qquad \{\text{Lemma 3.1}\}$$

$$= \lambda\, s : S \bullet \Sigma_{t \in S}(\mathbf{sup}_n(P_n(s)(t)) \times Q(t))) \qquad \{\times \text{ is continuous}\}$$

$$= \lambda\, s \bullet \Sigma_{t \in S}(\mathbf{sup}_n(P_n(s)(t) \times Q(t))) \qquad \{\text{Calculation}\}$$

$$= \mathbf{sup}_n(\lambda\, s : S \bullet\ (\Sigma_{t \in S}(P_n(s)(t) \times Q(t))) \qquad \{\text{Def of};\ \}$$

$$= \mathbf{sup}_n(P_n;\ Q)$$

$$(\mathbf{sup}_n P_n)\, [\![r]\!] Q \qquad \{\text{Def of } [\![r]\!]\}$$

$$= r \times (\mathbf{sup}_n P_n)\ +\ (1 - r) \times Q \qquad \{\times \text{ is continuous}\}$$

$$= \mathbf{sup}_n(r \times P_n\ +\ (1 - r) \times Q) \qquad \{\text{Def of } [\![r]\!]\}$$

$$= \mathbf{sup}_n(P_n\, [\![r]\!]\, Q)$$

$$\mathbf{sup}_n P_n\ \texttt{else}\ Q \qquad \{\text{Def of } \texttt{else}\}$$

$$= \lambda\, s : S \bullet (\mathit{eflag} = \mathit{false}) \lhd (\mathbf{sup}_n P_n)(s) +$$
$$(\mathbf{sup}_n P_n)(s)(\mathit{eflag} = \mathit{true})) \times Q(s) \qquad \{\text{Lemma 3.1}\}$$

$$= \lambda\, s : S \bullet \mathbf{sup}_n((\mathit{eflag} = \mathit{false}) \lhd P_n(s)) +$$
$$\mathbf{sup}_n(P_n(s)(\mathit{eflag} = \mathit{true}) \times Q(s)) \qquad \{\text{calculation}\}$$

$$= \mathbf{sup}_n(\lambda\, s : S \bullet (\mathit{eflag} = \mathit{false}) \lhd P_n(s) +$$
$$P_n(s)(\mathit{eflag} = \mathit{true}) \times Q(s)) \qquad \{\text{Def of } \texttt{else}\}$$

$$= \mathbf{sup}_n(P_n\ \texttt{else}\ Q)$$

6.5 Normal Form

The normal form of our language is of the form

$$\mathbf{pchoice}\begin{pmatrix} p_1\&(v := e_1), ..., p_m\&(v := e_m), \\ q_1\&(v := f_1;\ \texttt{fail}), ..., q_n\&(v := f_n;\ \texttt{fail}) \\ r\&\bot \end{pmatrix}$$

where v stands for the vector of program variables $< x,\ y,\ .., z >$, and all expressions e_i, f_j are well defined, and

$$\forall\, v \bullet (\Sigma_{1 \le i \le m} p_i\ +\ \Sigma_{1 \le j \le n} q_j\ +\ r)\, y =\ 1$$

Theorem 5.1 *$\bot$, `fail` and total assignment can be converted to normal forms.*

Proof
(1) $\bot = \mathbf{pchoice}(1\&\bot)$

(2) `fail` $= \mathbf{pchoice}(1\&(v := v;\ \texttt{fail}))$

(3) $x := e = \mathbf{pchoice}(1\&(x, y, .., z := e, y, .., z))$

Proof Conclusions (1) and (2) follow from Theorem 4.2(3).

$$
\begin{array}{lll}
(3) & LHS & \{(x := e) = (x,\ y := e,\ y)\} \\
= & x,\ y,\ ..., z := e,\ y,\ .., z & \{\text{Theorem 4.2(3)}\} \\
= & RHS &
\end{array}
$$

Theorem 5.2 *Normal forms are closed under all programming operators.*

Proof Let

$$P = \mathbf{pchoice}\begin{pmatrix} a_1\&(v := e_1), ..., a_j\&(v := e_j), \\ b_1\&(v := f_1;\ \texttt{fail}), ..., b_k\&(v := f_k;\ \texttt{fail}) \\ c\&\bot \end{pmatrix}$$

$$Q = \mathbf{pchoice}\begin{pmatrix} p_1\&(v := g_1), ..., p_m\&(v := g_m), \\ q_1\&(v := h_1;\ \texttt{fail}), ..., q_n\&(v := h_n;\ \texttt{fail}) \\ r\&\bot \end{pmatrix}$$

$P[\![d]\!]Q$

{Theorem 4.3(2)}

$$= \mathbf{pchoice}\begin{pmatrix} (a_1 \times d)\&(v := e_1), ..., (a_j \times d)\&(v := e_j), \\ (b_1 \times d)\&(v := f_1;\ \texttt{fail}), ..., (b_k \times d)\&(v := f_k;\ \texttt{fail}) \\ (c \times d)\&\bot \\ (p_1 \times (1-d))\&(v := g_1), ..., (p_m \times (1-d))\&(v := g_m), \\ (q_1 \times (1-d))\&(v := h_1;\ \texttt{fail}) \\ ... \\ (q_n \times (1-d))\&(v := h_n;\ \texttt{fail}) \\ (r \times (1-d))\&\bot \end{pmatrix}$$

{Theorem 4.3(5)}

$$= \mathbf{pchoice}\begin{pmatrix} (a_1 \times d)\&(v := e_1), ..., (a_j \times d)\&(v := e_j), \\ (p_1 \times (1-d))\&(v := g_1), ..., (p_m \times (1-d))\&(v := g_m), \\ (b_1 \times d)\&(v := f_1;\ \texttt{fail}), ..., (b_k \times d)\&(v := f_k;\ \texttt{fail}) \\ (q_1 \times (1-d))\&(v := h_1;\ \texttt{fail}), ..., \\ (q_n \times (1-d))\&(v := h_n;\ \texttt{fail}) \\ (c \times d\ +\ r \times (1-d))\&\bot \end{pmatrix}$$

$P\,\texttt{caught}-\texttt{by}\,Q$

$\{\text{Theorem}\,4.6\}$

$$= \textbf{pchoice}\begin{pmatrix} a_1\&(v := e_1), ..., a_j\&(v := e_j), \\ b_1\&(v := f_1;\ Q), ..., b_k\&(v := f_k;\ Q) \\ c\&\bot \end{pmatrix}$$

$\{\text{Theorem}\,4.4(4)\}$

$$= \textbf{pchoice}\begin{pmatrix} a_1\&(v := e_1), ..., a_j\&(v := e_j), \\ b_1\&\textbf{pchoice}\begin{pmatrix} p_1(f_1)\&(v := g_1(f_1)), ..., \\ p_m(f_1)\&(v := g_m(f_1)), \\ q_1(f_1)\&(v := h_1(f_1);\ \texttt{fail}), ..., \\ q_n(f_1)\&(v := h_n(f_1);\ \texttt{fail}) \\ r(f_1)\&\bot \end{pmatrix} \\ , ..., \\ b_k\&\textbf{pchoice}\begin{pmatrix} p_1(f_k)\&(v := g_1(f_k)), ..., p_m\&(v := g_m(f_k)), \\ q_1(f_k)\&(v := h_1(f_k);\ \texttt{fail}), ..., \\ q_n(f_k)\&(v := h_n(f_k);\ \texttt{fail}) \\ r(f_k)\&\bot \end{pmatrix} \\ c\&\bot \end{pmatrix}$$

$\{\text{Theorem}\,4.2(2)\}$

$$= \textbf{pchoice}\begin{pmatrix} a_1\&(v := e_1), ..., a_j\&(v := e_j), \\ (b_1 \times p_1(f_1))\&(v := g_1(f_1)), ..., (b_1 \times p_m(f_1))\&(v := g_m(f_1)), \\ (b_1 \times q_1(f_1))\&(v := h_1(f_1);\ \texttt{fail}) \\ ... \\ (b_1 \times q_n(f_1))\&(v := h_n(f_1);\ \texttt{fail}) \\ (b_1 \times r(f_1))\&\bot, \\ ..., \\ (b_k \times p_1(f_k))\&(v := g_1(f_k)), ..., (b_k \times p_m(f_k))\&(v := g_m(f_k)), \\ (b_k \times q_1(f_k))\&(v := h_1(f_k);\ \texttt{fail}) \\ ... \\ (b_k \times q_n(f_k))\&(v := h_n(f_k);\ \texttt{fail}) \\ (b_k \times r(f_k))\&\bot \\ c\&\bot \end{pmatrix}$$

{Theorem 4.2(1) and (5)}

$$= \textbf{pchoice}\begin{pmatrix} a_1\&(v := e_1), ..., a_j\&(v := e_j), \\ b_1\&(b_1 \times p_1(f_1))\&(v := g_1(f_1)), ..., \\ (b_1 \times p_m(f_1))\&(v := g_m(f_1)), \\ ......, \\ (b_k \times p_1(f_k))\&(v := g_1(f_k)), ..., (b_k \times p_m(f_k))\&(v := g_m(f_k)), \\ (b_1 \times q_1(f_1))\&(v := h_1(f_1);\ \texttt{fail}) \\ ... \\ (b_1 \times q_n(f_1))\&(v := h_n(f_1);\ \texttt{fail}) \\ ......, \\ (b_k \times q_1(f_k))\&(v := h_1(f_k);\ \texttt{fail}) \\ ... \\ (b_k \times q_n(f_k))\&(v := h_n(f_k);\ \texttt{fail}) \\ (\Sigma_{1\le i\le k}(b_i \times r(f_i)) + c)\&\bot \end{pmatrix}$$

$P\,\texttt{else}\,Q$

{Theorem 4.7}

$$= \textbf{pchoice}\begin{pmatrix} a_1\&(v := e_1), ..., a_j\&(v := e_j), \\ b_1\&Q, ..., b_k\&Q \\ c\&\bot \end{pmatrix}$$

{Theorem 4.2(2)}

$$= \textbf{pchoice}\begin{pmatrix} a_1\&(v := e_1), ..., a_j\&(v := e_j), \\ (b_1 \times p_1)\&(v := g_1), ..., (b_1 \times p_m)\&(v := g_m), \\ (b_1 \times q_1)\&(v := h_1;\ \texttt{fail}), ..., (b_1 \times q_n)\&(v := h_n;\ \texttt{fail}) \\ (b_1 \times r)\&\bot \\ ......, \\ (b_k \times p_1)\&(v := g_1), ..., (b_k \times p_m)\&(v := g_m), \\ (b_k \times q_1)\&(v := h_1;\ \texttt{fail}), ..., (b_k \times q_n)\&(v := h_n;\ \texttt{fail}) \\ (b_k \times r)\&\bot \\ c\&\bot \end{pmatrix}$$

{Theorem 4.2(1) and (5)}

$$= \textbf{pchoice}\begin{pmatrix} a_1\&(v := e_1), ..., a_j\&(v := e_j), \\ (b_1 \times p_1)\&(v := g_1), ..., (b_1 \times p_m)\&(v := g_m), \\ ....., \\ (b_k \times p_1)\&(v := g_1), ..., (b_k \times p_m)\&(v := g_m), \\ (b_1 \times q_1)\&(v := h_1;\ \texttt{fail}), ..., (b_1 \times q_n)\&(v := h_n;\ \texttt{fail}) \\ ......, \\ (b_k \times q_1)\&(v := h_1;\ \texttt{fail}), ..., (b_k \times q_n)\&(v := h_n;\ \texttt{fail}) \\ (\sigma_{1 \le i \le k} b_i \times r + c)\& \bot \end{pmatrix}$$

$P;\ Q$

{Theorem 4.4(3)}

$$= \textbf{pchoice}\begin{pmatrix} a_1\&(v := e_1;\ Q), ..., a_m\&(v := e_j;\ Q), \\ b_1\&(v := f_1;\ \texttt{fail};\ Q), ..., b_k\&(v := f_k;\ \texttt{fail};\ Q) \\ c\&(\bot;\ Q) \end{pmatrix}$$

{Theorem 4.5}

$$= \textbf{pchoice}\begin{pmatrix} a_1\&(v := e_1;\ Q), ..., a_m\&(v := e_j;\ Q), \\ b_1\&(v := f_1;\ \texttt{fail}), ..., b_k\&(v := f_k;\ \texttt{fail}) \\ c\&\bot \end{pmatrix}$$

{Theorem 4.4(4)}

$$= \textbf{pchoice}\begin{pmatrix} a_1\&\textbf{pchoice}\begin{pmatrix} p_1(e_1)\&(v := g_1(e_1)), ..., \\ p_m(e_1)\&(v := g_m(e_1)), \\ q_1(e_1)\&(v := h_1(e_1);\ \texttt{fail}), ..., \\ q_n(e_1)\&(v := h_n(e_1);\ \texttt{fail}) \\ r(e_1)\&\bot \end{pmatrix} \\ ......, \\ a_m\&\textbf{pchoice}\begin{pmatrix} p_1(e_m)\&(v := g_1(e_m)), ..., \\ p_m(e_m)\&(v := g_m(e_m)), \\ q_1(e_m)\&(v := h_1(e_m);\ \texttt{fail}), ..., \\ q_n(e_m)\&(v := h_n(e_m);\ \texttt{fail}) \\ r(e_m)\&\bot \end{pmatrix} \\ b_1\&(v := f_1;\ \texttt{fail}), ..., b_k\&(v := f_k;\ \texttt{fail}) \\ c\&\bot \end{pmatrix}$$

{Theorem 4.2(2)}

$$= \mathbf{pchoice}\left(\begin{array}{l}(a_1 \times p_1(e_1))\&(v := g_1(e_1)), ..., \\ (a_1 \times p_m(e_1))\&(v := g_m(e_1)), \\ (a_1 \times q_1(e_1))\&(v := h_1(e_1);\ \texttt{fail}), ..., \\ (a_1 \times q_n(e_1))\&(v := h_n(e_1);\ \texttt{fail}) \\ (a_1 \times r(e_1))\&\bot ......, \\ (a_m \times p_1(e_m))\&(v := g_1(e_m)), ..., \\ (a_m \times p_m(e_m))\&(v := g_m(e_m)), \\ (a_m \times q_1(e_m))\&(v := h_1(e_m);\ \texttt{fail}), ..., \\ (a_m \times q_n(e_m))\&(v := h_n(e_m);\ \texttt{fail}) \\ (a_m \times r(e_m))\&\bot \\ b_1\&(v := f_1;\ \texttt{fail}), ..., b_k\&(v := f_k;\ \texttt{fail}) \\ c\&\bot\end{array}\right)$$

{Theorem 4.2(1) and (5)}

$$= \mathbf{pchoice}\left(\begin{array}{l}(a_1 \times p_1(e_1))\&(v := g_1(e_1)), ..., \\ (a_1 \times p_m(e_1))\&(v := g_m(e_1)), \\ ......, \\ (a_m \times p_1(e_m))\&(v := g_1(e_m)), ..., \\ (a_m \times p_m(e_m))\&(v := g_m(e_m)), \\ (a_1 \times q_1(e_1))\&(v := h_1(e_1);\ \texttt{fail}), ..., \\ (a_1 \times q_n(e_1))\&(v := h_n(e_1);\ \texttt{fail}) \\ ......, \\ (a_m \times q_1(e_m))\&(v := h_1(e_m);\ \texttt{fail}), ..., \\ (a_m \times q_n(e_m))\&(v := h_n(e_m);\ \texttt{fail}) \\ b_1\&(v := f_1;\ \texttt{fail}), ..., b_k\&(v := f_k;\ \texttt{fail}) \\ (\Sigma_{1\le i\le m} a_i \times r(e_i)\ +\ c)\&\bot\end{array}\right)$$

Theorem 5.3 *All finite programs can be converted to normal forms.*

Proof From Theorems 5.1 and 5.2.

6.6 Conclusion

This paper presents a probabilistic model to an extended guarded command language. A new logical variable *eflag* is added to the standard design model to describe the failure state of a program. We introduce the probabilistic choice operator to "implement" the nondeterministic choice operator by providing the probability with which the alternatives are selected randomly. Aiming to reduce the failure rate of programs, we introduce the notion of coordination construct whose second operand acts as the assistant of its first operand when the latter fails during its execution.

Acknowledgement This work was supported by the National Basic Research Program of China (Grant No. 2005CB321904), National Natural Science Foundation of China (No. 90718004) and Shanghai Leading Academic Discipline Project B412.

References

1. Bulter, M.J., Ferreria, C.: An Operational Semantics for StAC: a Language for Modelling Long-Running Business Transactions. Lecture Notes in Computer Science, vol. 2949, pp. 87–104, Springer (2004).
2. Curbera, F., Goland, Y., Klein, J., et al.: Business Process Execution Language for Web Service. http://www.siebei.com/bpel. (2003).
3. Dijkstra, E.W.: A Discipline of Programming. Prentice Hall, Englewood Cliffs, NJ (1976).
4. Hoare, C.A.R., He Jifeng.: Unifying Theories of Programming. Prentice Hall, London (1998)
5. Jones, C.B.: Systematic Software Development Using VDM. Prentice-Hall, New York (1986).
6. Leymann, F.: Web Service Flow Language (WSFL1.0). IBM, (2001)
7. Moggi, E.: Notations of computation and monads. Inform. Comput. **93**, 55–92 (1986).
8. Morris, J.M.: Non-deterministic expressions and predicate transformers. Inform. Process. Lett. **61**, 241–246 (1997).
9. Thatte, S.: XLANG: Web Service for Business Process Design. Microsoft, Redmond (2001).

Chapter 7
The Operational Principle and Problem Frames

Michael Jackson

Abstract In the problem frames approach to software development – as its name indicates – analysis of the *problem* precedes construction of the *solution*. The problem analysis rests on certain ideas of structure and simplicity, including a general recommendation that composition should be postponed until the parts to be composed are well understood in their preliminary isolated forms. These ideas are discussed in the light of Michael Polanyi's notion of the *operational principle* of a machine or *contrivance*, and his account of the relationship between scientific knowledge and understanding of machines. Criteria are suggested for simplicity in problem decomposition. The outline structure of the associated development approach is sketched, and the relationship between formal development methods and problem structuring is clarified.

7.1 Complexity and Simplicity

In software development complexity is the mother of failure. As C A R Hoare famously said, speaking of Algol W and Algol 68 in his Turing Award lecture [4]: "I conclude that there are two ways of constructing a software design: One way is to make it so simple that there are *obviously* no deficiencies and the other way is to make it so complicated that there are no *obvious* deficiencies." The emphasis on what is *obvious* shows clearly that Hoare was talking about complexity in a subjective human sense – about a particular kind of obstacle to human understanding. It is intellectual complexity, that manifests itself as difficulty in designing, writing and understanding software – in developing a dependable system and achieving confidence that it will provide the required functionality.

M. Jackson (✉)
Department of Computing, The Open University, UK
e-mail: jacksonma@acm.org

C.B. Jones et al. (eds.), *Reflections on the Work of C.A.R. Hoare*,
DOI 10.1007/978-1-84882-912-1_7,

7.1.1 Computer-Based Systems

The theme of this paper is mastery of this kind of complexity as it is encountered in software development for *software-intensive* or *computer-based systems*. These are systems in which computers interact with the physical world in order to bring about certain desired effects there. For example: a system for a lending library, intended to control library membership and the acquisition, cataloguing and lending of books, and to provide information about these activities; an avionics system, designed to help the pilot to fly the plane safely and efficiently; or a lift control system, whose purpose is to provide convenient and safe transport from floor to floor in a tall building. In all of these systems, the success of the development is judged by the effects in the physical world. The true subject matter of the software development activity is not the computations carried out inside the computer, but the desired behaviour that these computations evoke and control in the world outside.

Realistic systems of this kind are complex. The world with which the computer interacts is usually a heterogeneous assemblage of physical *domains*. For the avionics system these domains include the earth's atmosphere, the pilot, the airport runways, the aircraft's engines and its control surfaces. For the lending library system they include the library staff, the members, the books and the barcode labels stuck on their covers, and the membership swipe cards. For the lift-control system the domains include the lift shafts and the building's floors, the lift cars, the request buttons, the users, the lift and lobby doors, the lift position display and so on. Further complexity arises from the proliferation of features, along with their inescapable feature interactions, in response to market pressures. At the same time, the highest possible level of automation is sought, even within critical systems. The development process, then, must address the software's interactions with many physical domains of different natures, exploiting the multiple properties of each domain in the service of each of many interacting features. It is in the understanding and development of such complex systems that we seek simplicity.

Much of the complexity in these systems springs from the interactions of relatively simple constituents brought together to form complex wholes. Mastering this complexity demands the unravelling – and subsequently the analysis and reconstruction – of these interactions. Formal languages, analysis, reasoning and calculation are vital tools in this task; and so too is a sound technique of formalising a non-formal reality so that it can be reasoned about as reliably as possible. But these tools alone are not sufficient. They must be applied within a conceptual framework which supports and guides both a decomposition of a complex whole into simple parts and an analysis of the interactions among those parts that must be accommodated when they are recombined into the desired whole. Proposing and clarifying such a framework is the purpose of this paper.

7.1.2 Problem Frames and the Operational Principle

The conceptual framework proposed in this paper is that of the problem frames approach [1] to software development. Development of a system is regarded as a *problem*: the task is to devise a software behaviour that will satisfy the *requirement* – that is, will produce the required effects in the physical *problem world*. The complexity of the problem is addressed by decomposition into *subproblems*, and so on recursively, until the subproblems obtained are sufficiently simple to be understood and solved without further decomposition. A subproblem is simple when the argument necessary to justify a solution is itself simple by certain specific criteria.

Each simple subproblem can be regarded as defining a small system to be developed – with its own software behaviour, problem world, and requirement. The subproblem and its associated system are regarded as closed: they are to be analysed in isolation, temporarily ignoring interactions with other subproblems. The subsequent recombination of the analysed subproblems, to give the analysis of the original whole problem, is a substantial task in its own right. Naturally, the decomposition into simple subproblems proceeds top-down, while their recombination proceeds bottom-up.

Support for the ideas on which this conceptual framework is based, and clarification of its consequences, can be drawn from the notion of the *operational principle* of a machine or *contrivance*, extensively discussed by the philosopher and physical chemist Michael Polanyi in his book Personal Knowledge [9]. Each small system defined by a simple subproblem can be regarded as a contrivance in Polanyi's sense, the software and the problem domains constituting the characteristic parts of the contrivance. Polanyi lays great stress on the human and individual nature of knowledge and understanding, which are central to the practical work of developing a computer-based system. He emphasises the distinction between scientific knowledge and the understanding of machines. This distinction has a clear parallel in software development: formal scientific and mathematical knowledge are to be distinguished from the understanding of problem and system structures within which they can be deployed. The relationship between them is discussed here in the context of the conceptual framework of the problem frames approach.

7.1.3 A Caveat

A caveat is necessary before the substance of the paper is presented in the sections that follow. Success in software development, as in any human activity, is often to be sought by identifying and following successful precedents – in short, by practising *normal design* as discussed by the aeronautical engineer Vincenti [10]. The focus of the development work is then the instantiation and improvement of an existing accepted design: the developer rarely has reason to reconsider the decomposition into components or to devise a new configuration of the components and their interactions. In effect, the long evolution of the normal design has gradually stimulated, and then absorbed, successive steps in a mastery of the problem complexities: in a normal practice it is unnecessary to recapitulate that evolution.

In this paper, however, mastery of complexity is the central topic. The discussion will therefore implicitly assume that the development problem is – at least to a large extent – novel, and that the developer cannot rely chiefly on precedent but must draw on general principles to master the problem complexity. The practical justification for adopting this assumption is that many areas of software development are regrettably lacking in established and acknowledged normal designs. The intellectual justification is that mastery of complexity ab initio is a topic of intrinsic interest.

7.2 The Operational Principle

Polanyi elaborates the notion of an operational principle as it applies in several fields. He discusses operational principles in language, mathematics, biology, psychology and even in logic. He also applies and illustrates it in the field of *machines* such as clocks, locomotives, telephones and cameras, and other *contrivances* of a like nature, which are assemblages of physical parts. This is where the notion is most directly applicable to the development of computer-based systems and to the theme of this paper.

7.2.1 A Machine Example

The operational principle of a machine specifies [9] how "its characteristic parts – its organs – fulfil their special function in combining to an overall operation which achieves the purpose of the machine". For example, we may describe the operational principle of the weight-driven pendulum clock in terms of the weights, the gear train, the hands, the escapement, the pendulum and the passage of time. In the style of a *problem diagram* [6], the interactions among these parts, together with the purpose of the whole machine, are sketched in Fig. 7.1.

The operational principle is as follows. The weights, under gravity, apply power (a1) to turn the gear train. The escapement wheel turns (a2), being fixed to a shaft in the gear train. The pendulum is connected to the escapement lever. Through the

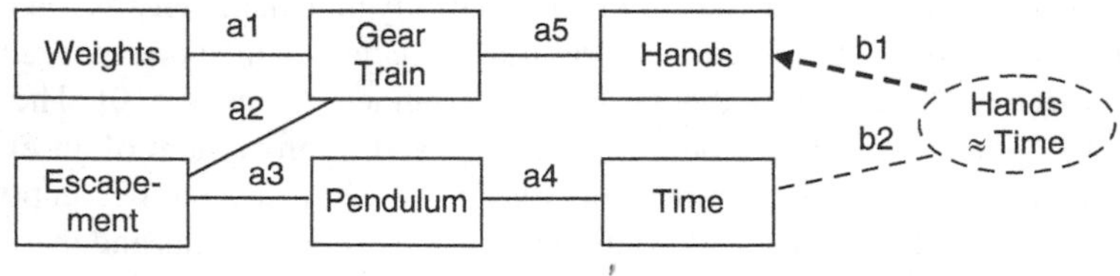

Fig. 7.1 A pendulum clock and its purpose

lever each swing of the pendulum allows the escapement wheel to advance by one unit for each swing (a3) and also to give a small impulse (a3) to keep the pendulum swinging. The gear train shafts therefore turn proportionally to the number of swings of the pendulum, and the rotating hands, fixed to appropriate shafts in the train (a5), count the pendulum swings (a4) and so effectively indicate the passage of time. The purpose of the machine is shown in the dashed oval: it is to govern the angular positions of the hands (b1) to correspond to the elapsed time (b2). The arrowhead on the dashed line b1, and its absence from the line b2, indicates that the purpose of the contrivance is to constrain the hands, not to constrain the passage of time.

7.2.2 Science and the Operational Principle

Polanyi is at pains to stress the difference between knowledge and understanding of the operational principle of a contrivance, and knowledge of the relevant natural science and mathematics. He goes so far as to write:

> ... Indeed, the understanding of the structure and operation of a machine require as a rule very little knowledge of physics and chemistry. Hence the two kinds of knowledge, the technical and the scientific, largely by-pass each other.
>
> But the relation of the two kinds of knowledge is not symmetrical. If any object—such as for example a machine—is essentially characterised by a comprehensive feature, then our understanding of this feature will grant us a true knowledge of what the object is. It will reveal a machine as a machine. But the observation of the same object in terms of physics and chemistry will spell complete ignorance of what it is. Indeed, the more detailed knowledge we acquire of such a thing, the more our attention is distracted from seeing what it is.

The "understanding of the structure and operation of the machine" does not itself explain in mathematical and scientific terms the detailed conditions necessary for the clock to achieve its purpose. Rather, it provides an intellectual and practical structure within which such an explanation can be formulated and given. This explanation must rest on two foundations. First, on a scientific understanding of the physical properties of the characteristic parts of the clock. The pendulum swings with an approximately constant period that depends – in accordance with the mathematical analysis of the forces acting on it – on its length and the acceleration due to gravity. The impulses imparted to the pendulum are strong enough to compensate for the effects of friction and air resistance. The weight is heavy enough to drive the whole mechanism. The escapement mechanism exploits the mechanical principle of the lever to minimise disturbance of the pendulum and wear on the contact surfaces. The gear ratios of the shafts for the hands and the escapement are correctly matched to the pendulum's period – and so on. Second, the scientific explanation depends for its applicability on the assumed *context* of the machine operation. The clock must be located in the earth's gravitational field; it must be positioned close to sea level; it must be stably located on *terra firma* and not tossed about on a ship at sea; the centre of the pendulum swing must be at the vertical position; and so on. The scientific and mathematical explanations given need be valid only in the specific local context for which the machine has been devised. If this local context is familiar, or readily understood, the contrivance and its operational principle are easily grasped: they provide the intellectual structure for the scientific and mathematical explanations and for their understanding and validation.

7.3 The Operational Principle in Computer-Based Systems

Polanyi's discussion returns more than once to the description of the contrivance as it would be – or is – presented in a patent, because he sees the patent claim as a document in which the inventor will "... always try to obtain a patent in the widest possible terms; he will therefore try to cover all conceivable embodiments of its operational principle by avoiding the mention of the physical or chemical particulars of any actually constructed machine, unless these are strictly indispensable to the operations claimed for the machine." The patent applicant, in short, is trying to give the most abstract specification of the invention that is consistent with the conditions on which patents can be issued, excluding inessential implementation detail that would limit the scope of the patent.

7.3.1 The Given Problem World

Practical software development, unlike a patent application, is usually concerned with operational principles in a very specific concrete form. A computer-based system brings together the *software*, executed by one or more computers, with a *problem world* – which is a heterogeneous assemblage of physical *problem domains*. The purpose of the software[1] is to govern the interactions of the computers with the world and, through these interactions, to achieve some observable effects in the world: these observable effects are the *functional requirement* for the system.

In the design of a contrivance such as a clock, the designer is in principle free to choose any assemblage of parts, and to arrange any interaction paths among them, that can achieve the purpose of the contrivance. In a computer-based system the parts are the computer (executing the software to be developed) and the problem domains, and the interaction paths are the interfaces of phenomena they share. For software development per se, this configuration of parts and interfaces is largely – or even entirely – given: that is, it is not open to the software developers to introduce additional or replacement problem domains, or to introduce new

[1] In the usual presentation of the problem frames approach [6] the software and computer are regarded as together constituting the *machine*. Here we avoid this term because Polanyi uses it for what we consider to be the whole system, comprising both the software and the problem world.

interaction paths between problem domains or between the computer and the problem domains. These given parts and interfaces determine the arrangement of the system's parts in a very concrete way. The problem to be solved by the software developers is to devise a software behaviour that will achieve the system's purpose within this given configuration.

7.3.2 A Zoo Turnstile

Figure 7.2 depicts a very small example. The system is intended to control entry to a zoo, ensuring that each visitor pays for entry.

Entry is protected by a turnstile barrier controlled by the software, which is also interfaced to a coin acceptor into which entry fees are to be inserted. The parts of the system are the given problem domains – the People, the Coin Acceptor, the Coins, and the Entry Barrier – and the Turnstile Software, which is to be developed. These parts and their interfaces are identified in Figure 7.2: people may insert coins into the acceptor (a4); they may enter through the barrier when the barrier allows entry (a3); the software controls the entry barrier (a2) and detects coins inserted into the acceptor (a1). The purpose of the system, represented by the dashed oval, is to achieve *Convenient Paid Entry*, by controlling people's entry (b2) with respect to the insertion of coins (b1); the insertion of coins (b1) is not constrained. The operational principle is readily expressed in terms of the system parts. People can insert coins (a4) into the acceptor; the turnstile software detects (a1) coin insertions and releases the entry barrier (a2) accordingly to allow people to enter (a3).

Evidently, within this operational principle, there is room for variation in the purpose of the system and in the realisation of the operational principle, even when the problem world is given. For example, depending on the relative positions of the coin acceptor and entry barrier, there may be neither the intent nor the possibility of ensuring that each person admitted is the person who most recently inserted a coin. The purpose must then specify which possible interleavings of coin insertion and barrier release events are acceptable. There are arguments in favour of strict alternation; but a schoolteacher equipped with a handful of coins to pay for pupils on a school outing may be grateful for a looser scheduling that ensures only that cumulatively the number of entries does not exceed the number of coins inserted.

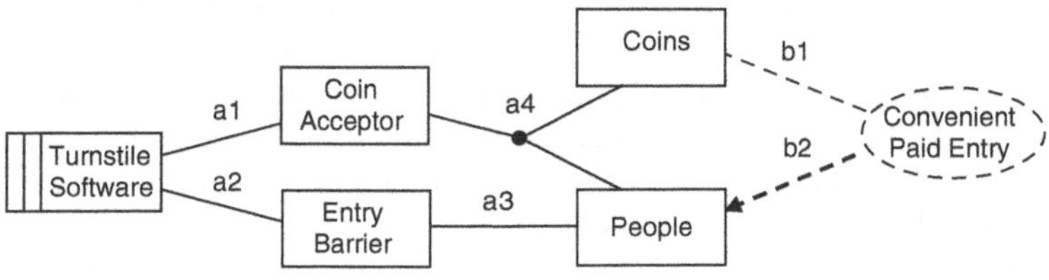

Fig. 7.2 Controlling a zoo turnstile

7.3.3 Understanding the Operational Principle

Although there is room for variation, the system's purpose and its operational principle are simple enough to be humanly intelligible. This simplicity is vital, because it provides a clear structure within which the detailed examination and analysis can be made of the given domain properties, and of the possibilities they offer for satisfying the system's functional requirements. Polanyi boldly asserts:

> Unless I believe a purpose to be reasonable or at least conceivably reasonable, I cannot endorse an operational principle which teaches how to achieve this purpose.

Putting the same point differently: the developers will be more liable to confusion and error in their work unless they have both accepted the functional requirement and clearly understood the operational principle of the system by which the requirement is to be achieved. Although the eventual development will embrace many details that must be dealt with exactly, the acceptance and understanding spoken of here do not depend on exactness. They depend more on the recognition of components of familiar kinds, interacting in familiar structures and configurations. It is with this clear recognition that the detailed work of modelling the problem world domains and their interactions, and of devising a satisfactory software behaviour, can be most reliably conducted.

7.3.4 Solving the Problem

Solving the software development problem depends on detailed investigation, formalisation and analysis of the properties and behaviours of the problem domains, and of the shared phenomena by which they interact with each other and with the software. For example, it is necessary to understand not only the interface (a2) at which the software can control the entry barrier, but also the interactions at (a3) between a visitor trying to enter and the possible states of the barrier. To enter it may be necessary to *push* on the barrier, indicating at (a2) that entry is requested; if the software then *releases* the barrier (a2) the visitor can *enter* by pushing the barrier further, whereupon the barrier reverts to its *locked* state to prevent a further entry until there has been a further pair of push and release events. This barrier behaviour is operationally similar to the behaviour of the clock escapement, and may similarly involve some matters of timing in the interactions of the system's parts.

When the development is complete, the developers must be able to show that they have produced an adequate solution. This adequacy argument will involve formal descriptions of the requirement and of the properties and behaviours of the problem domains and the software. For example, it may include a finite state machine description of the given behaviour of the entry barrier, from which the effects at (a3) of possible visitor behaviours at (a3) combined with the software's control behaviour at (a2) can be formally deduced. The operational principle of the system gives an outline structure for the adequacy argument. The argument will include reasoning along causal chains in the system, both within the software and the problem domains and at their interaction interfaces. The formal descriptions of properties and behaviours of the software and of problem domains, and the reasoning based on them, furnish the lemmas that allow some detail to be hidden and the structure of the whole argument to be clearly visible. Local invariants may provide succinct links between behaviours of adjacent domains. Some aspects of the system requirements may be captured formally in global invariants that can be shown to hold over the operation of the whole system. In essence, the role of the adequacy argument is to show that the system embodies its operational principle, not only in the large, but in the small also; and that it does so in a way that achieves its purpose.

7.4 Problems and Solutions

The zoo turnstile system is unrealistically small and simple, permitting a simple relationship between the problem and its solution. The functional requirement – the purpose – of the system can be easily understood and tersely expressed, and its operational principle is easily grasped and easily referred to the behaviour of the problem domains and the software.

7.4.1 Refinement

Development of the solution can proceed by a kind of refinement, successively stepping across the problem diagram of Fig. 7.2 from right to left, appealing at each step to the given properties of the relevant problem domain [7]. The requirement is expressed in terms of coin insertions (b1) and entries (b2). The coin insertions are elementary events (a4), but each entry event (a3) is the culmination of a little protocol executed by the visitor and the entry barrier. The given properties of the coin acceptor allow the coin insertions to be refined to events at the interface (a1) between the software and the coin acceptor. The given properties of the turnstile allow the entry protocol for the visitor to be refined to a protocol of events at the interface (a2) between the software and the entry barrier. In the final refinement steps the software itself can be developed in detail to maintain the required relationship between events at (a1) and events at (a2).

Subject to developer trial and error, this kind of development is a monotonic progression from problem to solution, refining and elaborating the requirement until it becomes the software solution. The structure of the requirement is elaborated to respect and exploit the given problem world properties (which must, of course, be explicitly described in documentation referenced in the refinement steps), and becomes the structure of the solution. There is no well-defined point in the development at which the developer shifts attention from problem analysis to construction of the solution.

7.4.2 Limitations of Refinement

The advantages of refinement as a technique for developing a program from a formal program specification are well known. Here we are arguing that a form of refinement can also be used in developing the software of a small and simple system. However, it is not fully and directly applicable to realistically large and complex computer-based systems. The immediately obvious obstacle is that neither the operational principle nor the functional requirement of such a system can be captured in a terse formal specification, even at a high level of abstraction. What is the purpose of the global telephone network system? Of the lending library system? Of an avionics system? Of a chemical process control system? Of a banking system?

Of course, it is easy enough to choose some salient, centrally important, function. "The purpose of the telephone system is to enable people to talk to each other," we may say. But such a large purpose, unlike the turnstile requirement, gives no useful purchase on the first refinement step. It is simultaneously too large to grasp as a development objective, and too small to encompass the whole of the required functionality. What about billing? What about conference calls, call forwarding and wake-up calls? Or automatic callback, call blocking and credit card calls? Some decomposition and structuring of the purpose or requirement must take place before it can form a basis for solution development.

7.4.3 Problem Structuring

In the problem frames approach, structuring the purpose or requirement of the system is regarded as structuring the *problem*. The problem is regarded as having the general form exemplified by Fig. 7.2. That is: it defines a small system to be developed, having a problem world comprising given problem domains, a software part, interaction paths among them and a system functional requirement, which stipulates the effects to be brought about in the problem world by the execution of the software. If the requirement is very complex, as it will be in a realistic computer-based system, then the problem must be decomposed into subproblems, each subproblem itself having the general form of a problem. Decomposition continues recursively until the problems at the leaves of the decomposition tree have clear and easily understandable purposes and operating principles, and are sufficiently simple – like the turnstile problem – to be solved directly.

This is a decomposition of the problem, not of the solution. The small systems defined by the subproblems are not, in general, structural *subsystems* of the whole system to be built. Nor can the problem structure that results from the decomposition be confidently expected to serve as a solution structure: the software in each subproblem is not expected to become a module of the software of the whole system when it is eventually completed. Rather, the small systems defined by the subproblems should be regarded as *projections* of the whole system. The behaviours of the subproblems' software are projections of the behaviour of the completed software;

the domain behaviours which the subproblems evoke are projections of the domain behaviours in the completed system; and the requirements of the subproblems, when fleshed out by the subproblem analysis, are projections of the functional requirement of the whole system.

There is a little paradox here. The problem frames approach aims to be firmly anchored in the physical problem world: the software in each subproblem must evoke a physical system behaviour that exemplifies the subproblem's operational principle. Yet the software parts of these small systems are not expected to fit together snugly as subsystems of the completed software. The source of the paradox is the pursuit of simplicity and understanding in problem structure and analysis, deferring considerations of software architecture – which are concerned with the structure of the solution rather than the problem. A realistic computer-based system can be understood from many points of view and dissected and structured in many dimensions. For example, in a particular business system development, it may be clear that the eventual implementation will be based on a three-tier architecture: the architectural view then has the three parts *ClientPresentation*, *BusinessLogic* and *ServerDatabase*. The architecture of an embedded system may have four parts: *AcceptStimuli*; *ProcessStimuli*; *ControlOutputs*; *ManageDisplay*. These may be excellent structures for the software; but they are likely to be an obstacle – not an aid – to understanding the problems that the systems are intended to solve. From the point of view of problem analysis, they separate what should be brought together, and bring together what should be separated. Useful problem structures will be quite different. A simple correspondence between problem and solution structures is desirable, but may often be unachievable without doing violence to one of the two. The malleability – even fluidity – of software allows a rich repertoire of transformations: when the time comes the old wine of the problem-structured analyses can be carefully poured into the new bottles of the chosen implementation architecture.

7.4.4 Two Sources of Complexity

Each subproblem to be identified in a problem decomposition will correspond broadly to an identifiable useful functionality of the whole system: for example, in the library system *BookLending* and *MembershipManagement* may be identified as two subproblems. Decomposition to a much finer granularity will not increase understandability, because the resulting fragments of functionality, when considered individually, will have no intelligible purpose or operational principle. The point is readily illustrated by the analysis of a large finite-state machine. Understanding may be achievable by factoring into smaller quotient machines, or by identifying nearly decomposable regions. But decomposition into individual state transitions will hinder understanding, not help it. A single transition arc, considered individually, can have no intelligible purpose.

The complexity of any subproblem in a realistic system arises from contributions from two sources: from the intrinsic complexity of the subproblem function itself; and from the modification – perhaps even the distortion – of the function due to its interactions with other functions. The *BookLending* subproblem must deal with the basic events in which members borrow and return books, renew loans when they want to keep the book for longer than the standard loan period, reserve a book that is currently out on loan, cancel a reservation and so on. In addition the subproblem must deal with such possibilities as the loss, theft or destruction of books. The *MembershipManagement* subproblem must handle initiating, renewing and resigning membership, payment of subscriptions, changes in members' circumstances – such as bankruptcy, emigration, change of name, prolonged illness – and so on.

Each of these subproblems, then, has its own intrinsic complexity. Additionally, the subproblems interact because books are to be borrowed only by members. A further potential contribution to the complexity of both subproblems is therefore the need to handle this interaction. Can a book be lent if the borrower's membership is due to expire within the standard loan period? Can a member be permitted to resign while still holding a borrowed book? What must happen if a member's name changes while a book is reserved but not yet borrowed?

7.4.5 Top-Down Decomposition, Bottom-Up Recombination

In the proposed approach to problem analysis, the two sources of subproblem complexity are separated. The decomposition into subproblems is carried out top-down. Each identified subproblem is regarded as defining a small closed system, ignoring its interactions with other subproblems of the system. For example, the *BookLending* subproblem may ignore the interaction with the *MembershipManagement* subproblem by assuming a context in which memberships, and the properties of individual members, are constant. The *recombination* of the subproblems, after their respective analyses, is carried out bottom-up. In the library system, the recombination will address the complexities arising from the interactions between the book lending and membership management processes.

Deferring the subproblem interactions in this way allows the intrinsic complexities of each subproblem to be studied and sufficiently well understood before the interaction complexities are addressed. Recognising the need for recombination as a distinct development task has implications for the whole development process. Because the subproblems identified in decomposition are oversimplified, some of the analysis may need to be reconsidered and possibly modified. By design, therefore, the development process is non-monotonic.

The decomposition is also unconventional in two other ways. First, because it ignores the interactions of the identified subproblems, the decomposition does not formally specify any relationship among them. In particular, if a problem *P* is decomposed into two subproblems *S1* and *S2*, the decomposition says nothing about *P* itself except that *S1* and *S2* will – eventually – contribute to its solution.[2] Second,

---

[2] There is an exception to this statement, explained in the following section. In some cases a local variable of the software of *P* is identified by which *S1* and *S2* will communicate.

the decomposition is not exhaustive: it does not exhaust the subproblems that will eventually make up the whole problem. The task of recombining the subproblems will, in general, reveal the existence of additional subproblems concerned with the analysis and management of interactions among the subproblems to be recombined.

Naturally there are opportunities and motivations for modifying this process; and judgment must be exercised in deciding how far the analysis of each subproblem should be carried before its combination with its siblings can be addressed. These judgments are made in the light of the general principle that the parts of a whole must be both identified and well understood before they can be recombined. The seventeenth-century clockmaker could not begin the design work for the first pendulum clock by designing the clock's frame. It was necessary first to design the parts – the weight, the pendulum and its suspension, the gear train, the escapement and the hands – before the necessary dimensions and properties of the frame could be determined.

7.5 Requirement Decomposition and Instrumental Decomposition

So far, the discussion of decomposition here has emphasised the identification of subproblems concerned with distinct functions that the system is required to provide. Each subproblem's requirement is a separate projection of the whole requirement, and its problem world is a projection of the whole problem world. This may be called *requirement decomposition*. It differs from *instrumental decomposition*, in which the responsibility for satisfying one requirement projection is divided between two loosely communicating subproblems. The difference is explained in this section.

7.5.1 Requirement Decomposition

Figure 7.3 shows a sketch of a system to control a lift in a hotel.

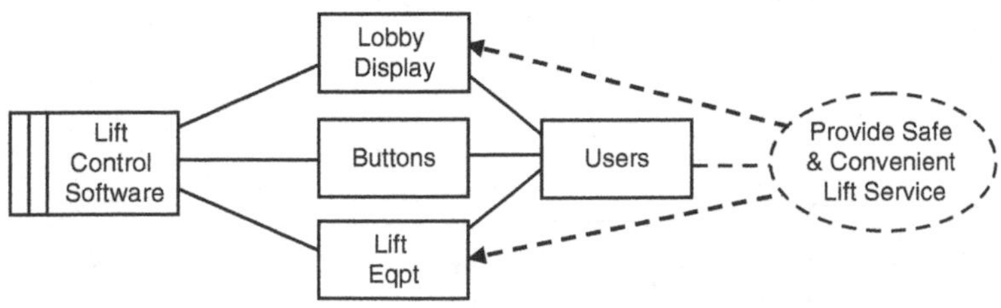

Fig. 7.3 A lift control system

The stated system purpose is to provide safe and convenient lift service; but this is not a simple purpose readily associated with a simply expressed and understood operational principle. On investigation, it appears, rather, to be some combination of at least three smaller purposes:

- To provide lift service in the usual sense, transporting users from floor to floor on request
- To maintain safety by detecting equipment faults such as hoist motor failure, breakage of the hoist cable, or a stuck floor sensor, and taking appropriate action to avoid disaster
- To maintain a display in the hotel lobby, showing which floor the lift car is currently at and which floors have pending requests

If this view holds, the decomposition must take the form of capturing these three identified subproblems. The first is shown in Fig. 7.4.

In this projection, the lobby display is not relevant and has been omitted. Also, a local assumption has been made about the lift equipment problem domain. It is assumed that the equipment is healthy in the sense that it is sufficiently free from malfunctions to provide the behaviours necessary to the lift service function. That is: when the software sets the hoist motor state to *upwards* and *on*, the lift car rises at the expected rate in the shaft; when the car reaches and leaves a floor the floor sensor state switches to *on* and *off* accordingly; and so on. This assumption, that fault-free behaviour is a given property of the lift equipment, is, of course, a strictly local assumption about the context of the subproblem.

The second subproblem is shown in Fig. 7.5.

The purpose of this subproblem is to monitor the behaviour of the lift equipment in order to detect faults that could potentially endanger the lift users, and to take appropriate action when such a fault is detected. Here, of course, the local context does not assume healthy equipment. On the contrary, it assumes that the equipment is liable to faults. The given domain properties of the lift equipment are therefore those that allow faults – including incipient and impending faults – to occur: when the hoist motor state is *upwards* and *on*, the lift car may fail to rise at the expected

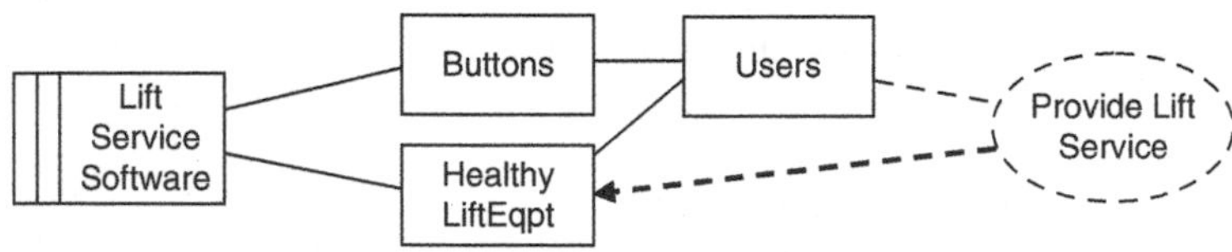

Fig. 7.4 Lift service subproblem

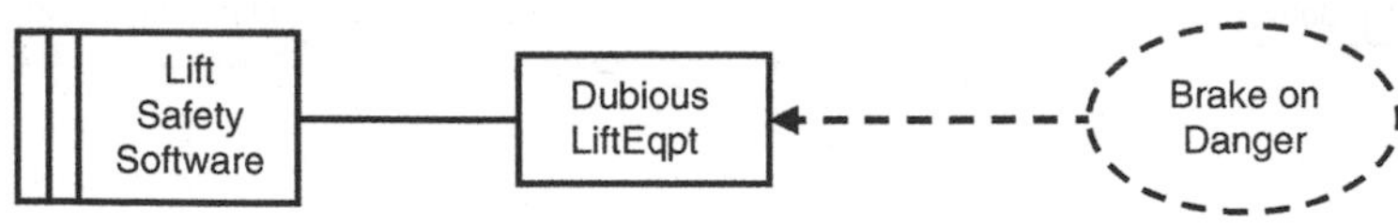

Fig. 7.5 A simple lift safety subproblem

rate in the shaft. To the extent that is possible and desirable, the given properties also allow faults to be detected, and the necessary precautionary action to be taken. Here we may suppose that the action to be taken is always the same: the hoist motor state is set to off and the emergency brake is applied, locking the lift car in the shaft so that it cannot fall freely.

7.5.2 Instrumental Decomposition

A different form of decomposition is *instrumental decomposition.* Requirement decomposition answers the question: What are the smaller and simpler purposes that contribute to the larger purpose of this problem? Instrumental decomposition answers the question: How can the intrinsic complexity of this problem's purpose be mastered? In an instrumental decomposition some internal interface of the undecomposed software – a structure of otherwise hidden phenomena – is exposed to serve as a medium of communication between the decomposed subproblems. For example, this interface may be a shared data structure, or a set of shared events. Unlike requirement decomposition, instrumental decomposition therefore has a substantial design aspect. In the lift control system, for example, the safety system may be decomposed as shown in Fig. 7.6.

In the safety subproblem the exposed interface is the LiftEqptModel. It is a shared data structure written by one of the subproblems and read by the other, functioning as a *model* – or software surrogate – of the lift equipment. The upper subproblem's software monitors the behaviour of the lift equipment (excluding the emergency brake, which is assumed to be fully reliable), and builds and maintains a dynamic representation in the LiftEqptModel of the equipment's current history and state, with particular focus on potential failures. The lower subproblem's software monitors the history and state of the model; it detects any dangerous situation recognisable in the model, and takes the necessary action. The primary design task arising from the decomposition is to design the data structure – probably as an instance of

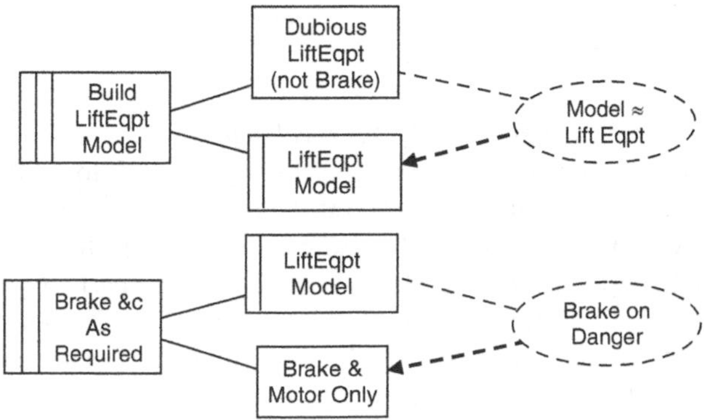

Fig. 7.6 Instrumental decomposition of a safety subproblem

an abstract data type. The design will be determined by the information needed by the lower subproblem, and by the extent to which the upper subproblem's software can maintain a data structure from whose current value that information is directly available or can be derived.

The motive for this decomposition is to make a separation that is instrumental in satisfying the safety requirement. The separation is not in any way inherent in the safety requirement: it is a chosen instrument to simplify satisfaction of the requirement by separating two concerns. One concern is to monitor the behaviour of the lift equipment, continually checking the sensor states in relation to each other and to the current and recent motor settings, and maintaining a partially summarised record – that is, the model – from which existing, incipient and impending faults can be inferred. The other concern is to draw appropriate inferences from the model state as it changes, and to take any necessary action. The justification for this separation is the complexity of these two concerns.

7.6 Simple Operational Principles

The discussion so far has merely asserted the simplicity of the chosen subproblems. If problem complexity is to be mastered by decomposition into simple subproblems, practical criteria are needed to distinguish the complex from the simple. The operational principle of a proposed subproblem provides the context for applying such criteria. When the subproblem purpose is elaborated or refined in the process of solving the subproblem – that is, specifying a software behaviour that can ensure satisfaction of that purpose – the operational principle provides a structure for the process. Traversing that structure, considering the subproblem requirement and the given properties of its domains, the developer may encounter points at which simplicity appears seriously compromised, and the choice of the subproblem in hand must be reconsidered. In this section some criteria of simplicity are mentioned and briefly discussed. These criteria are not disjoint. In the presence of complexity more than one criterion of simplicity is likely to be compromised.

7.6.1 One Level of Purpose

A simple operational principle has only *one level of purpose*. In many systems a cascading requirement stipulates a primary goal to be achieved, together with one or more levels of weaker goals to be achieved if the primary goal is unattainable. This is common in systems that must exhibit some degree of fault-tolerance. It may be recognised also in systems where the behaviour of a human participant in the problem world may fall short of what is normally expected. The criterion suggests that distinct levels of the requirement cascade should be treated in separate subproblems. For example, a bank loan customer may pass through several successive levels of delinquency by failing to meet the bank's loan conditions. Separating the treatment of the different levels will both clarify the conditions applicable to each level and expose the concerns to be addressed when the customer moves to a higher or lower level.

7.6.2 One Level of Abstraction

A simple operational principle is based on *one level of abstraction* of the phenomena of the problem domains. Suppose, for example, that in a system to control a car park the shared phenomena by which the software normally controls the raising and lowering of the barrier are abstracted as the events {*Raise* and *Lower*}; in some circumstances a finer-grained abstraction of the same phenomena – {*MotorOn*, *MotorOff*, *MotorUp*, *MotorDown*, *Open* and *Closed*} – may be appropriate. The two abstractions should not be applied in the service of the same operational principle; they should be applied in different subproblems.

To provide the more abstract interface {*Raise* and *Lower*} it will be necessary to translate between the two levels: the translation separates the car park management requirement from the detail of operating the barrier hardware. The translation is itself a distinct subproblem resulting from an instrumental decomposition. Both levels of abstraction will appear in the translation subproblem, but as phenomena of distinct problem domains. Only the fine-grained level appear as phenomena of the barrier domain; the more abstract {*Raise* and *Lower*} appear as phenomena of a domain introduced in the decomposition, behaving as a source of commands issued to the barrier. The stream of these commands is the structure of exposed phenomena of the undecomposed software.

7.6.3 Uniform Given Domain Properties

A simple operational principle assumes *uniform given properties* for each problem domain. For example, in the lift control example, the lift service subproblem must assume healthy operation of the lift equipment to the degree that is necessary to provide service. For the lift safety system, by contrast, the operational principle rests specifically on the potential for faults in the equipment, and on the relationships between internal equipment faults – such as a stuck sensor – and the evidence of that fault detectable at the interface with the software. This consideration alone indicates that the lift service and lift safety requirements are to be handled by distinct subproblems.

7.6.4 Synchronicity

Every system has a temporal dimension of execution. This temporal dimension may embrace asynchronous concurrent processes: it is then necessary to separate the concurrent processes into distinct subproblems. (In the turnstile problem the stream of coin insertions and the protocol by which each visitor negotiates the barrier may be regarded as concurrent processes.)

In the absence of true concurrency, a system may still perform functions of different periodicities. The tempi of these functions may be synchronised by nesting, just as the gear train of the pendulum clock has shafts rotating at different, but synchronised, speeds. In some cases, however, the tempi may be incompatible and cannot be nested – for example, if one behaviour is synchronised with calendar months and another with seven-day weeks, or one with lunar months and another with solar years. Incompatible tempi should be separated for treatment in distinct subproblems. An application of this idea to the spatial periodicity of iterative stream structures is found in the notion of a *structure clash* in the JSP design method [5] for sequential programs.

7.6.5 Uniform Domain Roles

In a simple operational principle each problem domain plays essentially *one role*. For example, in a system in which clerical workers edit documents, and management information is provided about the work they do, the workers are playing two roles. In one role they are the users in a document editing problem; in the other they are the subjects of an information display problem. The two roles should be separated into distinct subproblems.

7.6.6 Single Operational Phase

Many systems have distinct *phases* of operation. For example, in an avionics system the phases may be: pull-back from departure gate; taxing; take-off; climbing; cruising; descent; landing; pull-in to arrival gate; and so on. Each phase is likely to have its own local assumptions of problem domain properties, and its own operational principle. To maintain simplicity of the operational principle, each phase should therefore be separated into distinct subproblems.

7.6.7 Completeness

A subproblem can embody a simple operational principle, and achieve an intelligible purpose which the developer can easily endorse, only if its problem world is in some sense closed and complete. First, in a closed problem world every state or event is regarded as controlled by some problem domain included in the problem world. This is an assumption of the local subproblem context: for example, in the lift safety subproblem shown in Fig. 7.5 the changes in the motor state are regarded as spontaneous behaviour of the lift equipment, although in the lift service subproblem of Fig. 7.3 they are regarded as controlled by the lift control software. Second, the problem world must be complete in the same sense as a CSP process must be complete. That is: if the alphabet of a problem domain includes any events of a class, then all events of that class must be accounted for in the described domain properties.

In some software application areas it is common to find a style of requirement description by isolated fragments that make this criterion hard to satisfy. For example, the following requirement appeared in a large specification of a chemical manufacturing plant [2]: "When the temperature is maximum, the system should display a message on the screen, unless no operator is on the site except when $T < 60°$." The apparent intention is to relate the dynamic behaviour of the temperature, the possible presence and absence of an operator, and the desired message display. Taken alone, this isolated statement cannot define an intelligible purpose for a subproblem: its satisfaction cannot be the purpose of a contrivance embodying an intelligible operational principle.

7.7 Bottom-Up Recombination

In identifying very simple subproblems, the decomposition oversimplifies by ignoring the eventual need for recombination. Each subproblem can then be analysed and understood in isolation. For example, when a subproblem associated with one mode or phase of the system is analysed, the local context of the subproblem treats that mode or phase as if it persisted over the whole operational life of the system. This approach flouts the dictum ascribed to Albert Einstein: "Everything should be as simple as possible, but no simpler," the oversimplification being justified by the easier understanding of each subproblem in isolation. But in the end the dictum cannot be gainsaid, and the price is paid when the parts are recombined to constitute the whole. Recombination is itself to be regarded as a distinct task, in which the subproblems to be combined constitute the problem world.

7.7.1 Requirement Recombination

Subproblem recombination includes the task of bringing the subproblem requirements together in a coherent overall requirement.

Some recombinations may fall into the ambit of well-known techniques. For example, the combination of the two parts of the safety system – one building and the other using the LiftEqpt model – is a relatively straightforward case of managing access by a writer and a reader to a shared variable: the granularity of the interleaved accesses must take account of both syntactic and semantic properties of the model.

Sequential recombinations of parts associated with distinct phases are, in general, concerned with identifying and establishing a compatible state which can serve both as the termination state of the preceding phase and the initial state of the subsequent phase. It may be necessary to modify the phase subproblems to ensure this orderly switchover; or an additional subproblem may be identified that is responsible for reaching the compatible state before the switchover takes place.

Some recombinations demand the reconciliation of a conflict between the parts to be combined. For example, the lift service and lift safety requirements come into conflict when an equipment fault has been detected. The safety requirement demands that the motor be switched off; the service requirement demands that the motor continues to be available for sending the lift car to requested floors. In such a case it is necessary to concede priority to one part over another.

Where two subproblems have requirements that overlap in time, but make inconsistent local assumptions about problem domain properties, the inconsistency may be removed by suitable elaboration of one or both subproblems. For example, in the library system, the book lending subproblem may have assumed that membership is effectively static. In reality, the status of each member may change during the currency of one episode of lending. Both the lending and the membership subproblems have already been well understood and analysed in their simplified forms: in particular, the possible behaviours and event sequences have been elaborated for the lending subproblem, and the various member statuses and the transitions between them have been analysed in the membership subproblem. Viewing both subproblems as defining finite state machines, the developer can in principle construct their product machine. The states and events of the product machine can then be examined to identify impossible or undesirable events and transitions, and the software behaviours of the subproblems can be modified to eliminate them.

7.7.2 Software Recombination

A system comprising only one subproblem can be implemented by executing the subproblem's software. Where the system has more than one subproblem the subproblems' software must be recombined into a suitable architecture. In general, this recombination will involve transforming each subproblem's software. For example: the software of one subproblem may be dismembered and distributed in the text of the software of another subproblem; two similar but not identical models of a problem domain may be merged into one; a software behaviour including operations to read from an input stream of events or messages may be transformed into a procedure to be invoked as each element of the stream becomes available.[3]

Because the topic of this paper is problem analysis rather than software implementation, these transformations will not be further discussed here. Their

[3] An example of this transformation is the *program inversion* scheme described in [5].

significance for this paper is that the possibility of transformation releases the problem analysis from the obligation to fit the Procrustean bed of the eventual software architecture.

7.8 Formal Reasoning and Operational Principles

Polanyi stresses the distinction between science and mathematics on the one hand and operational principles of contrivances on the other, even when they are applied to the same physical objects:

> The first thing to realize is that a knowledge of physics and chemistry would in itself not enable us to recognize a machine. Suppose you are faced with a problematic object and try to explore its nature by a meticulous physical or chemical analysis of all its parts. You may thus obtain a complete physico-chemical map of it. At what point would you discover that it is a machine (if it is one), and if so, how it operates? Never. For you cannot even put this question, let alone answer it, though you have all physics and chemistry at your finger-tips, unless you already know how machines work. Only if you know how clocks, typewriters, boats, telephones, cameras, etc. are constructed and operated, can you even enquire whether what you have in front of you is a clock, typewriter, boat, telephone, etc. The questions: 'Does the thing serve any purpose, and if so, what purpose, and how does it achieve it?' can be answered only by testing the object practically as a possible instance of known, or conceivable, machines. The physico-chemical topography of the object may in some cases serve as a clue to its technical interpretation, but by itself it would leave us completely in the dark in this respect.

In the development of computer-based systems, similarly, the role of science and mathematics is not to propose, or select, or establish operational principles of contrivances. Rather, it is to operate within the framework determined by the informally identified operational principles of the subproblems and their recombination in the system which is to embody them. Formal software development should be based on non-formal, clearly articulated, structures and operational principles.

7.9 Concluding Remarks

The fundamental technique for mastering complexity is division of the complex object of study into simple parts. This technique has been known in principle since antiquity, and was compellingly reiterated [1] in one of Descartes' four principles:

> ...to divide each of the difficulties under examination into as many parts as possible, and as might be necessary for its adequate solution.

but as Leibnitz pointed out [8]:

> This rule of Descartes is of little use as long as the art of dividing remains unexplained. ...By dividing his problem into unsuitable parts, the inexperienced problem-solver may increase his difficulty.

The central theme of this paper is that the problem frames approach can help to reduce difficulty, and also to place formal and structural aspects of development in their proper relationship. Polanyi's notion of the operational principle of a machine or contrivance offers both justification and support for this approach, and clarifies the relationship between natural science and mathematics on one side, and what Polanyi calls "the logic of contriving" on the other. The applicability of this notion to software development has been argued here at length. Applicability in another field is evidenced by its enthusiastic adoption by the aeronautical engineer Walter Vincenti. He wrote [10]:

> Finally, the operational principle provides an important point of difference between technology and science – it originates outside the body of scientific knowledge and comes into being to serve some innately technological purpose. The laws of physics may be used to analyze such things as air foils, propellers, and rivets once their operational principle has been devised, and they may even help in devising it; they in no way, however, contain or by themselves imply the principle.

The broad structure proposed in this paper, in which the development problem is decomposed top-down and the decomposed parts subsequently recombined bottom-up, reflects the character of human understanding as a dynamic process. Just as developers gain in general understanding of their field during their individual working lifetimes, so in the same way they gain in specific understanding of each system to be developed during the progress of its development. The top-down initial identification and analysis of isolated simplified systems, followed by bottom-up recombination – demanding some adjustment and rework of what has already been done on the way down – can be seen as an instance of this learning process. Descartes' well-known principle of overcoming complexity by division into parts is accompanied [1] by three other principles. Perhaps the most apposite here is this:

> ... to conduct my thoughts in such order that, by commencing with objects the simplest and easiest to know, I might ascend by little and little, and, as it were, step by step, to the knowledge of the more complex; assigning in thought a certain order even to those objects which in their own nature do not stand in a relation of antecedence and sequence.

The "top-down, then bottom-up" sequence of problem analysis and understanding is valuable in itself, and is well supported by careful attention to the operational principle of each identified subproblem. For some readers, surely, this paper will have done no more than articulate a form of development process that they will recognise as their own usual practice.

Acknowledgements This paper has been much improved by Daniel Jackson's comments and suggestions.

References

1. Descartes, R.: Discourse on the Method of Rightly Conducting the Reason, and Seeking Truth in the Sciences. Leyden, 1637. Available as Project Gutenberg Etext #59 at http://www.gutenberg.org/etext/59 [accessed April 2009].

2. Harel, D.: Statecharts in the making: a personal account. Commun. ACM **52**(3), 67–75 (2009).
3. Hoare, C.A.R., Jones., C.B.: Essays in Computing Science. Prentice Hall International, Hemel Hempstead, Herts, UK (1989).
4. Hoare, C.A.R.: The emperor's old clothes. Commun. ACM **24**(2), 75–83 (1981). Reprinted in [3].
5. Jackson, M.A.: Principles of Program Design. Academic, Orlando, FL, USA (1975).
6. Jackson, M.: Problem Frames: Analyzing and Structuring Software Development Problems. Addison-Wesley Longman Publishing, Boston, MA, USA (2001).
7. Jackson, M., Zave, P.: Deriving specifications from requirements: An example. In ICSE '95: Proceedings of the 17th International Conference on Software Engineering, pp. 15–24 ACM, New York, NY, USA (1995).
8. Leibnitz, G.W.: In: Gerhardt, C.I. (ed.), Philosophical Writings (Die philosophischen Schriften) Volume IV, p. 331. 1857–1890.
9. Polanyi, M.: Personal Knowledge: Towards a Post-Critical Philosophy. Routledge and Kegan Paul, London (1958). Reprinted by University of Chicago & Press (1974).
10. Vincenti, W.G.: What Engineers Know and How They Know It: Analytical Studies from Aeronautical History. The Johns Hopkins University Press, Baltimore, MD (1993). Paperback edition.

Chapter 8
The Role of Auxiliary Variables in the Formal Development of Concurrent Programs

C.B. Jones

Abstract So called "auxiliary variables" are often used in reasoning about concurrent programs. They can be useful – but they can also be undesirable in that they can undermine the hard won property of "compositionality". This paper explores the issue of auxiliary variables and tries to set concerns about overuse in a wider context; it concludes with an attempt to recommend constraints on their use.

8.1 Introduction

There have been a number of "X considered harmful" papers, the most famous being [14]. The position taken here is that the use – or rather overuse – of "auxiliary variables" (sometimes referred to as "ghost variables") can be harmful in the development of concurrent programs.

The reason that concurrent programs are difficult to think about is the interference that comes from their environment. Interference is the reason that it is difficult to find compositional ways of formally developing concurrent programs; rely/guarantee ideas offer a way to achieve a notion of "compositionality" that enables separate development of programs that run in parallel. In most cases, rely conditions express assumptions about how variables written in another process (or "thread") change. Auxiliary variables are often used in reasoning about concurrent programs; typically each such variable is changed in exactly one process and only used in assertions of other processes. The alternative phrase "ghost variables" emphasises the fact that they can subsequently be erased without affecting the behaviour of a program.

There is, however, a danger inherent in the use of ghost or auxiliary variables in reasoning about concurrency. In the extreme, they can be used to record the entire history of execution of a process; if the rely conditions of other processes use this history, there is no abstraction of the interference. One could not, for example,

C.B. Jones (✉)
School of Computing Science, Newcastle University, UK
e-mail: cliff.jones@ncl.ac.uk

C.B. Jones et al. (eds.), *Reflections on the Work of C.A.R. Hoare*,
DOI 10.1007/978-1-84882-912-1_8,

reuse the proof with a slightly different split. More importantly, there is no sense in which a design decision to split a system into two or more parallel threads would facilitate separate development.

The next two sections include a review of known material. At first sight, this might appear to be a digression but, on the one hand, it builds up to some key issues about concurrency and, on the other hand, identifies via a rather different route a basis for believing that abstraction is best served by minimising auxiliary variables. The discussion of rely/guarantee thinking in Section 8.2 also serves to make the paper relatively self-contained. Section 8.4 discusses the search for a general approach to "atomicity refinement" and, finally, Section 8.5.2 sets out my current views on using auxiliary variables.

8.2 Rely/Guarantee "Thinking"

8.2.1 For Comparison: the Sequential Case

Today, it is second nature to talk about specifications in the form of pre - and post-conditions but this was not always the case. Tony Hoare's "axiomatic basis" paper led to what might reasonably be classed a "paradigm shift" in the way computer scientists think about programs.[1] The move from the flow charts of Floyd [17] or King [44] to thinking about programs in non-operational terms is clear in [22] and crucial for the intellectual shift that has followed.

In fact, the most important point about pre/postconditions was not really explicitly recognised in Tony's papers until he presented a development of $FIND$ in [23] in which he shows how the axiomatic approach offers a useful notion of separating development choices. Items that are specified (and are to be implemented by a program) are referred to as "operations" as in VDM (the B method uses the same term, Event-B uses "events"). Assuming that one has some specified operation S and makes a design decision to split it into a sequential composition of operations $S1$ and $S2$ (thus $S = S1;\ S2$) – of course specifying $S1$ and $S2$ with pre- and postconditions, the key property is that the development of $S1$ can be independent of S and $S2$. Once the proof rule for "semicolon" is discharged, that step of the argument does not need to be revisited (unless there is some broader change to be made). This property of a development method is often referred to as "compositionality" and this term is used below. To find compositional development rules for sequential programs is reasonably straightforward. A top-down documentation of design can introduce design decisions in many layers but the proofs at each layer are independent of each other and the development of sibling operations.

[1] My view of the importance of Hoare's paper led me to take [22] as the "fulcrum" for [39]; that discussion links the prior work of Floyd, Naur and van Wijngaarden (and remarks on the lack of what could have been an interesting link back to Turing's work).

Before the discussion moves to concurrent programming, there are several points to be made about the above approach to sequential programs – the message is that, although facing concurrency magnifies some problems, their seeds are present even with sequential reasoning.

First, there is the issue of whether one should strive for one, definitive, set of rules. Even within Hoare's framework, there are choices about how to present the rules for programming constructs. For example, one version might include a specific rule to weaken pre- and postconditions – alternatively, such weakening can be built into the rules for each construct by adding implications.

Another issue is that misnamed "partial correctness" (vs. "total correctness"): termination was not handled in [22]. Ignoring termination was lampooned by McCarthy's "millionaire's algorithm" (to become a millionaire, walk along the street – pick up every piece of paper on the sidewalk – if it's a check – made out to you – for a million dollars then cash it; otherwise, discard the piece of paper and continue).

VDM [37] rules are about "total correctness" – that is, they require termination. They also differ from some other approaches such as "weakest preconditions" [15, 16] in that VDM's postconditions are relational (they are predicates of two states: initial and final).[2] Relevant to the issue of auxiliary variables is that relational postconditions have the advantage that they obviate the need to use free (logical) variables in weakest preconditions approaches to define constraints on the final state that are relative to values in the initial state.

The proof rules in [34] were – in Peter Aczel's polite phrase – "unmemorable"; his unpublished note [3] gave a presentation of the VDM rules that is close to Hoare's original rules but deals with relational postconditions and termination (these rules are used in [37]):[3]

$$\boxed{while - I}\ \frac{\{P \wedge b\}\ S\ \{P \wedge W\}}{\{P\}\ \textbf{while}\ b\ \textbf{do}\ S\ \textbf{od}\ \{P \wedge \neg b \wedge W^*\}}$$

The use of postconditions (especially when presented as relations) yields a natural way of writing specifications that do not determine a unique outcome, somewhat loosely, these are often referred to as "non-deterministic specifications". It has become clear with usage that such specifications are a very good way of structuring the introduction of decisions during the design process. For example, the properties of a free storage manager are easily documented before a specific algorithm is designed.

---

2 Both points were true not only in the early book on program development in VDM [34] but also the earlier IBM reports [31, 32].

3 In the rule, P is a predicate of one state; W a predicate of two that is well founded (thus establishing termination without the need for a "variant function"); W^* is the reflexive and transitive closure of W. See [37] for the honest form of this rule which has an additional hypothesis on definedness – but this paper is not about partial functions.

One last, but important, point (that is magnified considerably by concurrency) is "expressive weakness". In common with some other approaches, it is a requirement in VDM that the set of states defined by the precondition of any operation should be a subset of the domain of the relation characterised by the postcondition of the operation. One might say that if an operation is required to terminate on some state, the postcondition should constrain the result state. This prompts a satisfaction relation that a valid step of development can widen the precondition or restrict the non-determinacy in the postcondition (subject to the aforementioned "satisfiability" condition). In most situations, these guidelines fit and are not even noticed but there are applications like security where non-determinacy has to play a different role and in "action systems" semantics are not preserved by widening "guards" – some of the alternatives are explored in [8].

8.2.2 Onwards to the Concurrent Case

It is worth taking a careful look at why it is much harder to achieve compositionality for concurrent, than sequential, program development. Postconditions are enough to characterise sequential operations because the latter can be considered to execute atomically. In contrast, if two parallel processes share variables, each process can have an effect on the other. Such effects (viewed from the recipient) are "interference". Once this point is recognised, it becomes obvious that a development method for concurrent programs must support documentation of – and reasoning about – interference. As with other formalisations of development, the quest is then for tractability: we know that we need to record more than the input/output relation for an operation but recording the full history of execution is clearly not going to yield a compositional development method.

Rely/guarantee "thinking" is about finding this sweet point. A possible way to record a specification of a shared variable program is to add to:

$$pre\text{-}OP_i : \Sigma \to \mathbb{B}$$
$$post\text{-}OP_i : \Sigma \times \Sigma \to \mathbb{B}$$

a predicate that records what can happen to the shared state when the environment interferes:

$$rely\text{-}OP_i : \Sigma \times \Sigma \to \mathbb{B}$$

and one that records the interference that OP_i will inflict on the environment:

$$guar\text{-}OP_i : \Sigma \times \Sigma \to \mathbb{B}$$

An execution, in which the environment makes the state transition from σ_i to σ_{i+1} and the component makes the transition from σ_j to σ_{j+1}, is pictured in Figure 8.1.

It was perhaps not fully appreciated at the time of [22] that the roles of pre-and postconditions differ in that a precondition gives *permission* to a developer to ignore

$$\overbrace{\sigma_0}^{pre} \quad \cdots \quad \overbrace{\sigma_i \; \sigma_{i+1}}^{rely} \quad \cdots \quad \underbrace{\sigma_j \; \sigma_{j+1}}_{guar} \quad \cdots \quad \sigma_f$$
$$\text{(the whole execution from } \sigma_0 \text{ to } \sigma_f \text{ is marked } post\text{)}$$

Fig. 8.1 Illustrative execution under interference

certain possibilities; the onus is on a user to prove that a component will not be initiated in a state that does not satisfy its precondition. In contrast a postcondition is an *obligation* on the code that is created according to the specification. This Deontic view carries over: just as preconditions should be viewed as assumptions that the developer can make about where the finished code will be deployed, rely conditions are assumptions that the developer can make on the limit of interference that the code will have to endure (i.e. permission to ignore the possibility of arbitrary interference). Similarly, a guarantee condition is like a postcondition in that it is a commitment on the code finally created from the development process; in the case of a guarantee condition, the finished code must not generate interference that does not satisfy the specified relation.

Typical clauses that occur in rely and guarantee conditions are:

- Some variable x is unchanged.[4]
- A variable changes in some monotonic way – notice that the ordering need not be over numbers, the example in Section 8.3.3 uses $s \subseteq s'$-.
- The truth/falsity of some flag implies some condition similar to one of the above.
- And, of course, ensuring that such a flag behaves as expected is an example of monotonic change.

It is interesting that, even in fairly complicated concurrent programs, most variables are changed in only one thread even though many processes might access their values. The most common exception to this observation is in fact flag-like variables.

In [35] and several subsequent papers, rely and guarantee conditions are constrained to be both transitive and reflexive: this corresponds to the observation that there can be zero or multiple steps of interference. This is only one of the points on which there is flexibility in choosing specific rules for reasoning about interference. This flexibility prompts the use of the term "rely/guarantee thinking" to make clear that we are not limiting the discussion to one specific set of rules.

It is worth looking at a representative rule. If one wishes to decompose the operation S into the parallel composition of S_l and S_r, it is clear that the interference generated by S_l can affect the outcome of S_r. In the spirit of presenting Hoare-like rules as $\{P\}\ S\ \{Q\}$ one can write: $\{P, R\}\ S\ \{G, Q\}$; a sound rule is:

[4] Rely/guarantee conditions are quite capable of recording "no change" but Section 8.2.3 discusses how the read/write frames of VDM simplify such descriptions.

$$\boxed{\text{Par-I}}\ \frac{\begin{array}{l}\{P, R \vee G_r\}\ S_l\ \{G_l, Q_l\} \\ \{P, R \vee G_l\}\ S_r\ \{G_r, Q_r\} \\ G_l \vee G_r \ \Rightarrow\ G \\ \overleftarrow{P} \wedge Q_l \wedge Q_r \wedge (R \vee G_l \vee G_r)^* \ \Rightarrow\ Q\end{array}}{\{P, R\}\ S_l\ ||\ S_r\ \{G, Q\}}$$

There are a number of issues that could be addressed at this point but, for the immediate purpose of cuing discussion of auxiliary variables, the most pressing of these issues is the "expressive weakness" of rely/guarantee conditions. Basically, the decision to record potential interference in a single relation makes it difficult or impossible to state certain behaviours. For example, consider a sequence of instructions that can be viewed as progressing through two phases: in the first phase, some variable x is monotonically increased; whereas in the second phase, x is monotonically decreased. The union of the two behaviours $\overleftarrow{x} \leq x$ and $\overleftarrow{x} \geq x$ tells us nothing other than that x might change! Unfortunately, there are contexts that require something more useful than this nugatory information. Section 8.5.2 indicates that this specific example can often be finessed. Be that as it may, expressive weakness is one of the issues that the rely/guarantee rules for concurrency magnify (over the sequential case) and the question must be faced as to whether this forces the use of auxiliary variables. The answer is, however, deferred to Section 8.5.2 pending explanation of the distaste of such variables.

8.2.3 Conclusions So Far

It is, perhaps, worth first repeating the point that the attempt here is to learn from "rely/guarantee thinking": the point has been made that there is considerable freedom in the presentation of such rules – far more than there is with Hoare logic of sequential programs (but, freedom – Section 8.2.2 points out – is already there). There is a significant literature on extensions and variants of rely/guarantee rules (see [41]). One interesting extension is the use of "dynamic invariants" in [11]. There are also some odd variants including those that try to get by with predicates of single states for rely and guarantee conditions; stirling [58][5] even restricts post-conditions to being predicates of a single state. In each case, for practical application, the move away from relations creates the need for extra auxiliary or logical variables.

Turning now to the lessons themselves, they fall under the headings of abstraction, compositionality and granularity. The abstraction with *pre/post* might be described as "what – not how" (e.g. it is not only easier to write and/or read a specification of *SORT* than an implementation but the latter is also much harder to use for subsequent reasoning because algorithm equivalence is more difficult than showing an algorithm satisfies some property). Rely/guarantee thinking retains this viewpoint as far as it can but needs to face the extra abstraction of "interference" which it is

[5] Colin Stirling was interested in meta results more than usability in applications.

argued is the essence of concurrency. The question which has to be addressed below (cf. Section 8.5) is whether the abstraction using relations is well chosen.[6]

The main motivation behind the inception [35] of rely/guarantee conditions was the lack of compositionality in [50]. Both multi-level decomposition and even changes of data representation work compositionally with rely/guarantee conditions. Thus, we have a design method that allows the designer to make and record design decisions in a stepwise form. As with introducing loops and sequential composition in sequential program design, definite design decisions to use parallel composition are difficult to undo in the sense that designers should avoid putting themselves back into the problems of equivalence proofs.

In concurrent program design, the issue of granularity is closely linked to compositionality: a guarantee condition must be respected at the level of granularity at which the final code executes. This, in fact, works well but it must be tackled with awareness. Making rash granularity decisions can necessitate locking of variables and this can destroy the performance advantages of parallel execution. In general, it is far better to avoid locking. Section 8.3.2 and the example in Section 8.3.3 offer interesting insight on the topic of granularity; further discussion can be found in [12, 13].

8.3 Abstract Objects

Although this section covers what might be classed as well-known territory, there is in the first sub-section a useful warning about "clutter" in specifications and an indication of how abstraction can be used to avoid it. Perhaps most importantly for the analysis of auxiliary variables, a precise test is given for where complexity is actually "clutter". Section 8.3.2 moves on to an important link between data reification and rely/guarantee thinking.

8.3.1 Why Use a Relation if a Retrieve Function Will Do?

The story of using abstract data objects to obtain short and perspicuous specifications is traced in [36]. In passing, I might comment that I am proud of having included data abstraction in the early book on VDM [34] and of promoting it to its rightful place ahead of operation decomposition in the 1986 first edition of [37]. The essence of the abstraction is to use, in a specification, data types that match the

[6] There are those who argue that the root of the problem is, in fact, shared variable concurrency. Another of Tony Hoare's major contributions is, of course, the development of CSP [26, 27]. Although the concept of communicating processes has yielded considerable insight into the nature of concurrency, it is by no means immune from interference. The interference just comes from communication. This is manifest in any process algebra in which shared variables can be simulated by a process that holds their current value.

problem rather than the implementation. Typically, these are finite mathematical objects with pleasing algebras. It is revealing that quite diverse specification languages such as Z [18], VDM and SETL [6] all build on some form of sets, sequences, maps and records.

The use of the abstraction leaves the two questions of how good it is (as an abstraction) and how to get from the abstraction to the implementation. It is useful to tackle the second of these issues first for reasons that become clear below.

Given two descriptions of a collection of operations, one needs to be able to determine if they exhibit the same "behaviour". Peter Lucas faced this problem in looking at two operational models of the PL/I programming language: did they give the same semantics? In [45], he used a "twin machine" proof. In essence, he defined a large machine with state elements from both descriptions and linked them by what we might call today a "gluing invariant"; he then proved that the combined machine preserved this data type invariant. The argument was then that either set of variables could be regarded as "ghost variables" and be erased without changing the behaviour. It is possible to argue that this was the mother and father of all auxiliary variable ideas! The contribution of [30][7] was to capitalise on the fact that – in most cases – one model is more abstract than the other in that it "has less information". Where this is the case, it is reasonable to take the model with less information as the specification and simplify the reification proof by recording a function from the (more populous) implementation type back to the abstraction. In VDM, these were called "retrieve" functions because they extracted the abstraction from the details of the representation. This homomorphic idea is, of course, the same as in [46][8] and [24]. The VDM rules for data reification include an "adequacy" proof obligation that determines whether there is at least one representation for each abstract state. Failures of adequacy frequently indicate missed invariants. We have not laboured data type invariants here – although extremely important, they have little to add to the discussion of "auxiliary variables". Suffice it to say that an additional heuristic is to prefer – of two isomorphic models – the one with simpler invariants. Heinrich Hertz wrote:

> Various models of the same objects are possible, and these may differ in various respects. We should at once denote as inadmissible all models which contradict our laws of thought. We shall denote as incorrect any permissible models, if their essential relations contradict the relations of the external things. But two permissible and correct models of the same external objects may yet differ in respect of appropriateness. Of two models of the same object ... the more appropriate is the one which contains the smaller number of superfluous or empty relations; the simpler of the two.

The question of how good an abstraction is can now be addressed. It is easy to see that the retrieve function idea offers a partial ordering on models: model S is at least as abstract as I if there is a retrieve function from $I \rightarrow S$. There are, however, "equivalently abstract" models where there are retrieve functions in both directions.

[7] Far too much of the Vienna Lab's work was only published as technical reports.

[8] The community was denied a journal version of this paper because it was rejected by JACM.

The question of how to know if one has found one of the "sufficiently abstract" models is settled in [33] by saying that a specification is "biased" if the equality on the underlying states cannot be computed in terms of the operations of the type. (Worked examples are provided in [34, Chapter 15] and [37, Section 9.3]).

One could, in fact, get by with a biased specification by adding "ghost variables" to the implementation and later erasing them as in Lucas' twin machine proofs but there is a real sense in which abstraction can be listed as a virtue – a virtue for which there is a precise test. This situation led to a certain smugness in the model-oriented camp. One should never be smug! The claim that any biased specification could, and should, be replaced by one that is appropriately abstract was challenged by Lyn Marshall who was writing a large VDM specification (of the then standard of the "Graphics Kernel System"). Lyn claimed that bias was required in her specification. After much discussion, she was proved right. The problem boils down to there being non-determinacy in the specification that, once a designer makes design choices, obviates the need for some state values. Together with Tobias Nipkow we boiled this down to a tiny example that illustrated the point beautifully. In parallel (and partially in cooperation) with researchers from Oxford, Tobias came up with a data refinement rule that he proved to be complete in a useful sense (see [20,47,48]). This rule uses a relation and thus evokes shades of the twin machine idea. More details of this story are given in [36] (and both rules are described in (even the first edition of) [37]); what matters for the discussion of auxiliary variables in concurrency are the points:

- The essence of design is that it introduces "bias" (cf. decisions made in decomposition of operations)
- But for specifications, *prefer the simpler model*
- Abstraction should be used to avoid bias because equivalence is harder than reification
- There is a test for "goodness"
- Where there is a specific technical problem, it might be possible to devise a new proof method

8.3.2 Linking Rely/Guarantee with Reification

There is a very interesting connection between rely/guarantee development and data reification. Surprisingly, this was not made explicit in any of the early rely/guarantee proofs. In fact, as far as I'm aware, the first written reference is in [40]. The observation is that *often* obligations from guarantee conditions can only be realised without excessive locking by choosing a clever data representation. So, just like the comment on non-determinacy being a good abstraction of design choices, guarantee conditions are a way of postponing a design decision. Of course, postponement can be perilous if the designer has no idea how to solve the problem.

A very simple example can be made of the *FINDP* problem for Sue Owicki's thesis [50]. The top level specification states that the task is to find the minimum value of an array index such that the indexed element satisfies some predicate.[9] A sequential algorithm simply searches the array indices from the minimum index upwards. The interest is how to use concurrency – an "n-fold" split of the indices is no more technically difficult, but the description is shorter if two processes are considered. Suppose one process searches the odd – and the other the even – indices. If these two processes do not communicate, it is easy to see that there is a trap where the parallel algorithm could be slower than the sequential alternative. To avoid this, either process should terminate if its sibling process has detected an array element with a lower index that has the required condition. An obvious abstraction is to have the two processes share a variable, say t, in which they record any index for which it is detected that the array element at that index satisfies the given predicate. At this level of abstraction, both processes need a sub-operation whose specification involves setting t to the minimum of the current value of t and some variable local to that process. Mental warning lights (should) flash when writing down a rely condition that specifies that neither process can live with the other lying (in the sense that they temporarily reduce t then increase it again): the process on which this dishonesty is inflicted might have terminated prematurely. At this level of abstraction, it is not difficult to describe the honesty requirement in a rely condition.

One possible implementation strategy is for both processes to lock t when they need to access it but this could also make a concurrent implementation slower than the simpler sequential approach. In this example, it is not difficult to spot that equipping each process with a local variable means that t can be reified to the minimum of these values. The troublesome guarantee condition of monotonic reduction is now trivial because each local variable is read but not written by the partner process.

The same story of the interplay of reification with satisfying guarantee conditions can be seen with the *SIEVE* example of Section 8.3.3 – but here it is more interesting:

- Each of n processes removes elements from a set s.
- Assuming the designer does not want to lock s (it's big!).
- The designer must find a representation that helps realise rely/guarantee conditions $s \subseteq \overleftarrow{s}$.
- The (less obvious) representation of s as a bit vector meets the need.

This example is spelled out in the next section.

Yet more interesting is the example discussed in Section 8.5.1. Simpson's so-called "four-slot" implementation of Asynchronous Communication Methods (ACMs) is an intriguing and very clever piece of programming whose correctness is far from easy to prove. Even more challenging is the task of presenting the development and its formalisation in a way that conveys Simpson's contribution. The claim made in [42] is that this is achieved by the use of data reification combined with rely and guarantee conditions. Before more detail is given, Section 8.4 adds one more idea to our armoury.

The above three examples are identified in [40] and are expanded on in [53].

[9] In the case that there is no such value, the program can either return an indicator or add a sentinel that does have the property.

8.3.3 An Example

The example in this section is a parallel version of the "Sieve of Eratosthenes" which finds all prime numbers – up to some required n – by removing composite numbers. The first reference that I am aware of to a concurrent version is [25].

We can use an abstract object containing a set of numbers to make the overall problem clear:[10]

$$post-PRIMES(\overleftarrow{s}, s) \triangleq s = \{1 \leq i \leq n \mid is-prime(i)\}$$

It is equally straightforward to make (and record) the decision to split *SIEVE* into two sequentially decomposed sub-operations: one for initialisation of s to contain all natural numbers up to the required limit(n); the other operation removes all composites from s. One might think that the specification of the sub-operations *INIT* and *SIEVE* is best written as follows:

$(INIT;\ SIEVE)$ **satisfies** $PRIMES$
$post-INIT(\overleftarrow{s}, s) \triangleq s = \{1, \ldots, n\}$

$pre\text{-}SIEVE(s) \triangleq s = \{1, \ldots, n\}$
$post\text{-}SIEVE(\overleftarrow{s}, s) \triangleq post\text{-}Primes(\overleftarrow{s}, s)$

But this would be a mistake – in two ways *SIEVE* is being too tightly specified to fit its context. A better split is to recognise that sieving can be performed on any set and that the removal need not necessarily end up with all primes (consider the case where the starting state for *SIEVE* is the empty set) – so:

$pre\text{-}SIEVE \triangleq true$
$post\text{-}SIEVE(\overleftarrow{s}, s) \triangleq s = \overleftarrow{s} - \bigcup\{mults(i) \mid 2 \leq i \leq \lfloor\sqrt{n}\rfloor\}$

creates a much cleaner separation of *SIEVE* from its context. Here, in the sequential case, the earlier definition might not be disastrous but in more complex cases it could be; moreover, the issue of separation is certainly one that is magnified by the move to concurrency.

As pointed out in Section 8.2, the step of introducing sequential constructs as in $PRIMES = (INIT;\ SIEVE)$ marks a clear design decision. If a sequential implementation is sought, it is now straightforward to make – and justify – further design decisions for *SIEVE* to use nested loops as in:

for $i \leftarrow \cdots$
  $post\text{-}BODY: s = \overleftarrow{s} - mults(i)$
  for $j \leftarrow \cdots$
    $s \leftarrow s - mults(i * j)$

[10] VDM notation [37] is used; the only item that might be unfamiliar is the use of $\overleftarrow{s}$ for the initial (and undecorated s for the final) state in relational postconditions. Furthermore, the predicate $is-prime$ should be obvious and the function *mults* delivers the set of multiples (by 2 and above) of its argument.

The fact that repeated execution of the removal of composites $(i * j)$ eventually ensures the postcondition $s = \overleftarrow{s} - mults(i)$ relies on there being no interference and this is a reasonable assumption in sequential programs.

The real interest here is to use the design of a concurrent *SIEVE* to illustrate points about the trade-off between the various predicates in a rely/guarantee specification. So, implementing *SIEVE* as:

$$||_i REM(i)$$

One might first try copying the idea from $post - BODY$ above and write:

$$post - REM(\overleftarrow{s}, s) \triangleq s = \overleftarrow{s} - mults(i)$$

but this exact definition of the elements to be removed cannot be achieved in the situation where it is the intention that sibling processes are removing elements of s. This points to the idea of specifying in the postcondition only that certain elements must be absent after $REM(i)$ has executed:

$$post - REM(\overleftarrow{s}, s) \triangleq s \cap mults(i) = \emptyset$$

A moment's thought however indicates that even the lower bound on removal of elements can be achieved in the presence of arbitrary interference – the reliance on the fact that no sibling will re-insert deleted elements can be easily recorded in

$$rely - REM(\overleftarrow{s}, s) \triangleq s \subseteq \overleftarrow{s}$$

An attempt to use (an n-ary form of) the $Par - I$ proof rule of Section 8.2.2 shows that too much was given away in the above relaxation to the postcondition of *REM*: this lower bound on removal could in fact be achieved by setting s to the empty set which will clearly not lead to satisfying the specification of the overall *SIEVE* process. So the guarantee condition can be used to outlaw such over zealousness

$$guar\text{-}REM(\overleftarrow{s}, s) \triangleq (\overleftarrow{s} - s) \subseteq mults(i) \wedge \cdots$$

This pattern of shifting conditions that might fit the post condition of a sequential process back into the guarantee conditions of concurrent specifications is both common and useful.

Finally, since the sibling processes of $REM(i)$ are actually twins, the guarantee condition is completed by conjoining a copy of the rely condition (cf. $Par-I$) giving the overall specification of each $REM(i)$ to be

$REM(i)$
pre *true*
rely $s \subseteq \overleftarrow{s}$
guar $(\overleftarrow{s} - s) \subseteq mults(i) \wedge s \subseteq \overleftarrow{s}$
post $s \cap mults(i) = \emptyset$

Thus far, the example has been used to illustrate both the fact that – even in sequential programs – care in divorcing a sub-operation from its context produces a more useful specification; and furthermore the sometimes delicate trade-off between the predicates used in the description of a concurrent program (not surprisingly, this balance is more interesting in complex examples – see [11]).

The largest lesson from this example is however to illustrate the point made in Section 8.3.2. To set the scene, Hoare writes in his discussion of the problem in [25]:

> Of course, when a variable is a large data structure, as in the example given above, the apparently atomic operations upon it may in practice require many actual atomic machine operations. In this case an implementation must ensure that these operations are not interleaved with some other operation on that same variable

As Hoare goes on to mention, placing all updates to s in critical regions is certainly one way of ensuring that the guarantee condition is met but it is an implementation that is unlikely to give high performance.

An alternative is to choose a data representation in which such updates can be made safely without locking. As hinted in Section 8.3.2, this can be achieved by representing the set as a vector of n bits.

To emphasise how subtle the issue of granularity can be, it is worth mentioning that there could still be a dependency on the machine architecture if the implementer packs bits in such a way that it is impossible to set one bit atomically.

8.4 Abstraction Using a "Fiction of Atomicity"

Just as postconditions abstract from "how" to achieve an objective, and abstract data objects offer a way to abstract from details of machine representations honed for efficiency, a "fiction of atomicity" can be a powerful abstraction that achieves far more perspicuous descriptions than is possible when considering the actual interleaving of steps in an algorithm. Far from being a completely new idea, this very convenient fiction is well known in computing. In particular, it is key to the whole idea of database transactions: a user of a DBMS can picture transactions as "atomic" and it is the responsibility of the system both to overlap transactions and to disguise that fact that it has done so. (Furthermore, it has to do so in the presence of failures in hardware.)

Although by no means the first attempt, what is perhaps unusual is the extent to which [40] attempts to elevate the atomicity abstraction – and approaches around splitting – to tools to be used alongside, and in concert with, the other development approaches of Sections 8.2 and 8.3. It is indicated below that compositionality can be achieved by deploying rely/guarantee conditions.

Some of the ideas here were enhanced by two Schloß Dagstuhl workshops[11] on the topic of atomicity. The objective was to bring together researchers from different fields that use atomicity in one form or another. In particular [29] draws up a "manifesto" that compares and contrasts views and approaches from database, hardware, fault-tolerance and formalism research.

The genesis of my own research on splitting atoms was an acceptance that rely/guarantee reasoning was bound to be heavier than proofs in terms of pre- and

---

[11] Some papers from the 2004 workshop appear in *Journal of Universal Computing Science*, Vol. 11, No.5; similarly (and in the same journal), Vol. 13, No. 8 for the 2006 workshop.

postconditions. More generally, it is inevitable that development of algorithms that interfere will be more difficult than those that (appear to) run in isolation. The higher level advice must be to use concurrency only where it is really required either by the problem itself or to make really telling performance gains.

The acceptance that one needed to be able to limit the areas of reasoning using rely/guarantee conditions came when trying to write a joint paper with Ketil Stølen after he submitted his PhD thesis [59]. Our paper was never completed – but we learned a lot. In fact, it was the start of my search for ways of limiting interference.[12] In particular, the power of object oriented (OO) programming languages to control interference appeared promising: Pierre America's POOL language [5] proved to be a good basis for further investigation.

The avenue I followed in the $\pi o\beta\,\lambda$ research was to offer "equivalence rules" that facilitated transforming OO programs with large (atomic) steps into equivalent programs where many objects were active concurrently. The argument was that, if there were many processors to run threads for different objects, performance would improve. The notion of "equivalence" was, of course, crucial: the $\pi o\beta\,\lambda$ language was designed to be expressively weak so that its observations were a sensible approximation to what a user might want. The work on proving these equivalences correct showed that being precise about acceptable observations was crucial. This research (and pointers to more detailed papers – especially on the semantics to justify the equivalences) is summarised in [38].

The general proposal in [40] is to use the "fiction of atomicity" as an abstraction with the corresponding development method called "splitting (software) atoms safely" (or "atomicity refinement"). In the $\pi o\beta\,\lambda$ proposal, the fission was supported by equivalence rules. More generally, if one starts with an abstraction of atomicity, it is essential to have a notion of observation power to determine whether decomposed (and overlapping) sub-operations offer the expected behaviour to an observer. After all, to an all powerful observer, the behaviour is manifestly different.

Recall also the emphasis in earlier sections on compositionality: there will be cases where splitting can occur at more than one stage of design. If we look for cases where separation is not the answer, it will clearly be necessary to have a handle on any potential interference that can occur with the decomposed sub-operations.

The foregoing observations all point to reasons to investigate how useful rely and/or guarantee conditions can be in atomicity refinement. The general argument looks quite strong: guarantee conditions state what the outside world can rely on – any decomposition must preserve this but is at liberty to decompose operations on any variables not so constrained. To give a trivial example, an operation whose postcondition requires the value of a variable x to be increased by, say, 10 can be decomposed into any number of assignments whose accumulated effect is that increment if there are no guarantee conditions on x; if there is a guarantee condition that x increases monotonically some decompositions such as $x \leftarrow x-2;\ x \leftarrow x+12$ are ruled out.

[12] My valued friends working on Separation Logic [28, 55] for concurrency [10, 49, 51, 52, 56] should remember that this was back in the early 1990s.

The far more complex example in Section 8.5.1 offers more evidence for the usefulness of rely and guarantee conditions in atomicity refinement. It is perhaps worth contrasting this approach to the interesting "event refinement" in [1]. The need to introduce the concept of some events "refining skip" is a consequence of not having rely conditions.

8.5 Limiting the Use of Auxiliary Variables

The essence of the argument here is that abstraction is a better tool than auxiliary variables. The example in Section 8.5.1 not only illustrates the techniques outlined above; the frank account of two attempts to present an informative development underlies the conclusions in Section 8.5.2.

8.5.1 Development of ACMs

This section indicates how the ideas in Sections 8.2–8.4 are used in concert to provide a rational reconstruction of a very intricate algorithm. A development of Simpson's "four-slot" implementation of "Asynchronous Communication Mechanisms" (ACMs) is given in [42]; the fact that the authors discovered flaws in the original development and the investigation of whether auxiliary variables are needed to complete the proof is of relevance to the key message of the current paper.

The objective in writing yet another paper on Simpson's algorithm was precisely to provide insight as to what is going on in its design. The extremely tight code is difficult to prove correct, but somehow treatments like [19, 57] (and even the more recent [2, 7]) fail to utilise fully abstraction in their proofs.

ACMs are used to communicate values between two processes which are asynchronous in the sense that it is not allowed for either to hold up the other. Thus, in the ACM world, locking a shared variable is certainly not an option. A little thought shows that it is possible for the *Read* process to see the same value more than once and for the reader to miss values that are written. There is a requirement that the reader gets the freshest reasonable value and most importantly that the reader never sees a value older than one already read.

The first challenge is to provide a specification to act as a reference point that is clear enough that a user can have confidence that he/she understands the properties. We based the specification in [42] around an abstraction (Σ^a) of a sequence of all *Value*s written. This is clearly redundant but precisely in the way discussed in Section 8.3.1: the redundancy admits non-determinacy and the state can be specialised once the choices are narrowed.

More controversially, the specifications of *Read* and *Write* in [42] are each split into two phases. In the terms of the current paper, this is a design commitment: it would be messy to justify further development that was not a specialisation of these phases. In fact, the split *start-Write*, *commit-Write*, *start-Read* and *end-Read* not only holds good for the development, it also makes the behaviour of reader/writer values easy to comprehend. Furthermore, this "phasing" makes it possible to record simpler rely and guarantee conditions than would work with the unsplit operations. Another key aid to clear rely and guarantee conditions is the use of VDM's read-/write frames.

The first step of development in [42] shows that it is not necessary for the state to hold the whole history of values input. This is a classic example of using Nipkow's rule [48] to show that an otherwise "inadequate" representation gives acceptable behaviour. The states Σ^i are mappings from some arbitrary index set X to the *Values* to be transmitted. In fact, if X is the natural numbers, this model could be identical to Σ^a but the intermediate step establishes properties required of the set X. It is clear from the formal descriptions that the cardinality of X must be at least three. The key to Simpson's choice of *four* slots is actually about communication between the *Read* and *Write* threads: the only atomicity assumption is on the setting and reading of single control bits.

At the Σ^i stage of development, there are still unacceptable atomicity assumptions on updates to the state. The step to Simpson's actual design (Σ^r) uses the fact that four variables (with clever control flags) suffice. The final essence of Simpson's inspiration is presented (cf. Section 8.3.2 above) as choosing a representation that makes the guarantee conditions realisable. The residual atomicity assumptions are limited to the ability to update single bit flags without corruption.

Unfortunately, when filling in more detailed proofs to write a journal version of [42], we detected flaws in two of the proofs. Initially, I could only see how to fix these by adding deprecated auxiliary variables and this led me on this odyssey to understand how to constrain their use. The revised development has been submitted to a journal and a version (prerefereeing) is available at [43].

One flaw in the development in [42] was a postcondition which stated that a local variable could acquire either the initial or final value of a variable changed by the other thread. In fact, because the relative progress of the threads is not synchronised, the other thread could potentially change this value many times. A short term fix is to use an auxiliary variable to record all possible values. This is the resolution presented in [53]. The solution in [43] is more radical: a new specification concept of the set of possible values of a variable is introduced. Thus, in a postcondition, $\widehat{var}$ is a set of all values that this variable has during the execution of the specified operation. This concept not only avoids the need to introduce an auxiliary variable in this case, it also provides a specification concept that is of use in other circumstances.

The other place where [53] and [43] differ is the way they handle the crucial avoidance of a clash of the *Read* and *Write* processes on a single position in the four slots. This also points to a surprising conclusion about the respective strengths of the rely/guarantee approach and separation logic.

The classical idea of *mutual exclusion* is one of the core concepts in concurrency. Interestingly, Simpson's algorithm does not fit the classic pattern. One reason for this is that mutual exclusion leads to blocking which is inimical with the requirements of ACMs. There is however an issue that might be called "mutual data exclusion": the *Read* and *Write* processes must not interfere on the same cell. In [53], this is proved by adding auxiliary variables at the Σ^r level; the approach in [43] establishes the relevant conditions at the more abstract level (Σ^i). This is a useful illustration of the proposal to use abstraction in preference to auxiliary variables.

The deeper aspects of this are even more interesting. John Reynolds pointed out verbally at MFPS in 2005: "separation logic lets one reason about avoiding races; rely/guarantee conditions support reasoning about racy programs". Like so much that Reynolds says, this shows great insight but the example in hand points to a further observation. Simpson's final code does not "race"; in fact, the whole point is to avoid conflicting reads/writes. The use of rely/guarantee conditions makes it possible to present a key abstraction in which there appear to be races.

8.5.2 Auxiliary Variables: a Position

The expressive weakness of rely/guarantee conditions is conceded in Section 8.2 but it is also made clear in discussing pre/postcondition specifications that there is always a trade-off between being able to express everything and having a tractable method that makes good engineering sense: abstraction must have a part. In particular, compositionality dictates that detail must be postponed by abstraction.

Coming back to auxiliary variables, it is worth looking in more detail at what we have learnt. It should be clear from Sections 8.2 and 8.3 that it is easier to show that a reification step fills in detail than to prove that two detailed algorithms are equivalent. Specifically, with respect to abstract data types, one feels on solid ground if there is a precise test for unnecessary detail.

Before going further, it is worth pinning down the origin of the expressive weakness: is it a facet of rely/guarantee conditions? I concede that I assumed this to be the case for some time. In fact, this is incorrect! If one considers Owicki's "Einmischungsfrei" proof obligation [50], it requires that no step of s_r can interfere with the proof of a step between any two statements of s_l. In fact, the issue is already there in the earlier approach proposed in [4]. Even though neither of these methods is compositional in the sense set out in Section 8.2, they have no way of describing different behaviour during the progress of a sibling process.[13]

So, given the widespread expressive weakness, is it acceptable to plug it with auxiliary variables and can we put precise limits on their use? Two further data points are given before I, tentatively, give positive answers to both questions.

The apparent weakness of rely conditions has an interesting role in the soundness proof for rely/guarantee rules given in [12]. Essentially, the fact that a rely condition must be broad enough to capture *any* interference means that it can be used in the

[13] This is the source of the difficulty in [50] in proving that two parallel instances of $< x \leftarrow x+1 >$ achieve the obvious result.

induction proof of a parallel construct even though interference can come either from a sibling process *or from any contextual process*. (The language in [12], unlike that in the Isabelle-checked proofs of [54], permits nested parallelism; our paper and [13] also accommodate fine grained interleaving of expression evaluation.)

What is the evidence that one can *not* avoid auxiliary variables? It is plausible that a process will go through phases in which different conditions are guaranteed. For example, one process might, under the control of a flag p, guarantee

$$\begin{array}{l} p \Rightarrow \overleftarrow{x} \leq x \\ \neg p \Rightarrow \overleftarrow{x} \geq x \end{array}$$

Although this might be viewed as internal information of the process, if the joint behaviour depends on it, the rely condition must record it. Actually, so far, there is no problem in its recordability. In fact, it is reasonable to see it as an extension of the "phasing" idea of Section 8.5.1. The problem comes where there is no convenient variable p to demarcate the phases.

The position taken here is that, in such circumstances, it is reasonable to add an auxiliary variable in place of the missing p. This introduces no more dependence on the other process, no more loss of compositionality, than if the variable were actually present in the first place. Clearly, parallelism that does not depend on distinct phasing in its sibling processes is more robust but, in examples like that in Section 8.5.1, the mutual dependencies are very intimate.

In spite of conceding this use of auxiliary variables, in all cases, I would prefer a better abstraction to the use of such coding tricks. The key reason for this preference is that it is difficult to retain compositionality without severe constraints on the use of ghost variables.

There is one remaining question – prompted by the history above of reification of data types – and that is whether the whole issue of auxiliary variables points to new proof rules and/or languages. I venture to suggest that process algebras will not resolve the issue. Nor do I expect anything like our current temporal logics to be the source of a solution; but Amir Pnueli[14] who heard the talk from which this paper is derived did make the point that past-time temporal logic could cover some cases.

Acknowledgements I have had the pleasure of knowing Tony Hoare since the 1960s and my DPhil research was done under his supervision in 1979–1981. The process of editing "Essays" [21] enhanced our collaboration after I left Oxford. As was said (repeatedly) at the Cambridge meeting in April, 2009 Tony has inspired and supported many of us over decades.

This paper was not actually presented at the Cambridge meeting to mark Tony's birthday because Bill Roscoe and I had held ours as "makeweights" in case any speakers could not get there. The material was actually presented at the PSY workshop at CAV Grenoble (June 2009).

I am grateful for comments on drafts of this paper from Joey Coleman, Linas Laibinis, Thai Son Hoang and Bill Roscoe; and to my ever-patient proof reader Ms. Allison. This is also a nice opportunity to give belated thanks to Schloß Dagstuhl for (among other pleasurable visits) the two on "Atomicty". The staff in Dagstuhl, the environment and the stimulating participants always make trips there rewarding and refreshing.

[14] Amir was of course co-author of the first paper to apply rely/guarantee thinking to temporal logic [9].

My research is currently funded by the EU "Deploy" project, the (UK) EPSRC "TrAmS" platform grant and the ARC project (that brings together Ian Hayes, Keith Clark, Alan Burns and myself) "Time Bands for Teleo-Reactive Programs".

References

1. Abrial, J.-R.: The Event-B Book. Cambridge University Press, Cambridge, UK (2010),
2. Abrial J.-R., Cansell, D.: Development of a concurrent program, private communication (2008).
3. Aczel, P.: A note on program verification. (Private communication) Manuscript, Manchester (January 1982).
4. Ashcroft, E.A., Manna, Z.: Formalization of properties of parallel programs. In: Meltzer, B., Michie, D. (eds.), Machine Intelligence, 6, pp. 17–41. Edinburgh University Press (1971).
5. America, P.: Issues in the design of a parallel object-oriented language. Formal Aspects Comput. **1**(4), 366–411 (1989).
6. Anon. SETL: main page, Oct 2009. www.setl-lang.org.
7. Bornat, R., Amjad, H.: Inter-process buffers in separation logic with rely-guarantee, 2008. (private communication) Submitted to Formal Aspects Comput doi:10.1007/s00165-009-0141-8.
8. Bicarregui, J.: Intra-Modular Structuring in Model-Oriented Specification: Expressing Non-Interference with Read/Write Frames. PhD thesis, Manchester University (1995).
9. Barringer, H., Kuiper, R., Pnueli, A.: Now you can compose temporal logic specification. In: Proceedings of 16th ACM STOC, Washington (May 1984).
10. Brookes, S.D.: A semantics of concurrent separation logic. Theoret. Comput. Sci. (Reynolds Festschrift) **375**(1–3), 227–270 (2007). (Preliminary version appeared in CONCUR'04, LNCS 3170, pp. 16–34.)
11. Collette, P., Jones, C.B.: Enhancing the tractability of rely/guarantee specifications in the development of interfering operations. In: Plotkin, G., Stirling, C., Toft, M., (eds.), Proof, Language and Interaction, chapter 10, pp. 277–307. MIT (2000).
12. Coleman, J.W., Jones, C.B.: A structural proof of the soundness of rely/guarantee rules. J. Logic Comput. **17**(4), 807–841 (2007).
13. Coleman, J.W.: Constructing a Tractable Reasoning Framework upon a Fine-Grained Structural Operational Semantics. PhD thesis, Newcastle University (January 2008).
14. Dijkstra, E.W.: Go to statement considered harmful. Commun. ACM **11**(3), 147–148 (1968).
15. Dijkstra, E.W.: A Discipline of Programming. Prentice-Hall, Englewood Cliffs, NJ, USA (1976).
16. Dijkstra, E.W., Scholten, C.S.: Predicate Calculus and Program Semantics. Springer, New York, NY, USA (1990). ISBN 0-387-96957-8, 3-540-96957-8.
17. Floyd, R.W.: Assigning meanings to programs. In: Proc. Symp. in Applied Mathematics, vol. 19: Mathematical Aspects of Computer Science, pp. 19–32. American Mathematical Society (1967).
18. Hayes, I., (ed.), Specification Case Studies, 2nd edn. Prentice Hall International, Englewood Cliffs, NJ, USA (1993).
19. Henderson, N.: Formal Modelling and Analysis of an Asynchronous Communication Mechanism. PhD thesis, University of Newcastle upon Tyne (2004).
20. Hoare, C.A.R., Hayes, I.J., He, J., Morgan, C., Roscoe, A.W., Sanders, J.W., Sørensen, I.H., Spivey, J.M., Sufrin, B.A.: The laws of programming. Commun. ACM **30**, 672–687 (1987). See Corrigenda in ibid 30:770.
21. Hoare, C.A.R., Jones, C. B.: Essays in Computing Science. Prentice Hall International, Hemel Hempstead, UK (1989).
22. Hoare, C.A.R.: An axiomatic basis for computer programming. Commun. ACM **12** (10) 576–580, 583 (October 1969).

23. Hoare, C.A.R.: Proof of a program: FIND. Commun. ACM **14**, 39–45 (January 1971).
24. Hoare, C.A.R.: Proof of correctness of data representations. Acta Inform. **1** 271–281 (1972).
25. Hoare, C.A.R.: Parallel programming: An axiomatic approach. Comput. Lang., **1**(2) 151–160 (June 1975).
26. Hoare, C.A.R.: Communicating sequential processes. Commun. ACM **21**, 666–677 (August 1978).
27. Hoare, C.A.R.: Communicating Sequential Processes. Prentice-Hall, Hemel Hempstead, UK (1985).
28. Isthiaq, S., O'Hearn, P.W.: BI as an assertion language for mutable data structures. In: 28th POPL, pp. 36–49 (2001).
29. Jones, C.B., Lomet, D., Romanovsky, A., Weikum, G.: The atomic manifesto. J. Universal Comput. Sci. **11**(5), 636–650 (2005).
30. Jones, C.B.: A technique for showing that two functions preserve a relation between their domains. Technical Report LR 25.3.067, IBM Laboratory, Vienna (April 1970).
31. Jones, C.B.: Formal development of correct algorithms: an example based on Earley's recogniser. In: SIGPLAN Notices, vol. 7, Number 1, pp. 150–169. ACM (January 1972).
32. Jones, C.B.: Operations and formal development. Technical Report TN 9004, IBM Laboratory, Hursley (September 1972).
33. Jones, C.B.: Implementation bias in constructive specification of abstract objects typescript (September 1977).
34. Jones, C.B.: Software Development: A Rigorous Approach. Prentice Hall International, Englewood Cliffs, NJ, USA (1980).
35. Jones, C.B.: Development Methods for Computer Programs including a Notion of Interference. PhD thesis, Oxford University, June 1981. Printed as: Programming Research Group, Technical Monograph 25.
36. Jones, C.B.: Computer-aided formal reasoning for software design, March 1989. talk at: TAPSOFT'89, Barcelona.
37. Jones, C.B.: Systematic Software Development Using VDM 2nd edn., Prentice Hall International, (1990).
38. Jones, C.B.: Accommodating interference in the formal design of concurrent object-based programs. Formal Methods System Design **8**(2), 105–122 (March 1996).
39. Jones, C.B.: The early search for tractable ways of reasoning about programs. IEEE, Ann. History Comput. **25**(2), 26–49 (2003).
40. Jones, C.B.: Splitting atoms safely. Theoret. Comput. Sci. **357**, 109–119 (2007).
41. Jones, C.B.: Annotated bibliography on rely/guarantee conditions (Oct 2009). http://homepages.cs.ncl.ac.uk/cliff.jones/ftp-stuff/rg-hist.pdf.
42. Jones, C.B., Pierce, K.G.: Splitting atoms with rely/guarantee conditions coupled with data reification. In: ABZ2008, vol. LNCS 5238, pp. 360–377 (2008).
43. Jones, C.B., Pierce, K.G.: Elucidating concurrent algorithms via layers of abstraction and reification. Technical Report CS-TR-1166, School of Computing Science, Newcastle University (2009).
44. King, J.C.: A Program Verifier. PhD thesis, Department of Computer Science Carnegie-Mellon University (1969).
45. Lucas, P.: Two constructive realizations of the block concept and their equivalence. Technical Report TR 25.085, IBM Laboratory Vienna (June 1968).
46. Milner, R.: An algebraic definition of simulation between programs. Technical Report CS-205, Computer Science Dept, Stanford University (February 1971).
47. Nipkow, T.: Non-deterministic data types: Models and implementations. Acta Inform. **22**, 629–661 (1986).
48. Nipkow, T.: Behavioural Implementation Concepts for Nondeterministic Data Types. PhD thesis, University of Manchester (May 1987).
49. O'Hearn, P.W.: Resources, concurrency and local reasoning. Theoret. Comput. Science (Reynolds Festschrift) **375** (1–3), 271–307 (May 2007). Preliminary version appeared in CONCUR'04, LNCS 3170, 49–67.

50. Owicki, S.: Axiomatic Proof Techniques for Parallel Programs. PhD thesis, Department of Computer Science, Cornell University (1975).
51. O'Hearn, P.W., Yang, H., Reynolds, J. C.: Separation and information hiding. ACM TOPLAS **31** (3) (April 2009). Preliminary version appeared in 31st POPL, pp. 268–280 (2004).
52. Parkinson, M., Bierman, G.: Separation logic and abstraction. In: POPL '05: Proceedings of the 32nd ACM SIGPLAN-SIGACT Symposium on Principles of Programming Languages, pp. 247–258, New York, NY, USA (2005). ACM.
53. Ken Pierce: Enhancing the Usability of Rely-Guaranteee Conditions for Atomicity Refinement. PhD thesis, University of Newcastle upon Tyne. (2009).
54. Prensa Nieto, L.: Verification of Parallel Programs with the Owicki-Gries and Rely-Guarantee Methods in Isabelle/HOL. PhD thesis, Institut für Informatic der Technischen Universitaet München (2001).
55. Reynolds, J.C.: Intuitionistic reasoning about shared mutable data structure. In: Davies, J. Roscoe, B. and Woodcock, J. (eds.) Millennial Perspectives in Computer Science, pp. 303–321, Palgrave, Houndsmill, Hampshire (2000).
56. Reynolds, J.C.: Separation logic: A logic for shared mutable data structures. In: Proceedings of 17th LICS, pp. 55–74. IEEE (2002).
57. Simpson, H.R.: New algorithms for asynchronous communication. IEE, Proc. of Comput. Digital Technol. **144** (4), 227–231 (1997).
58. Stirling, C.: A compositional reformulation of Owicki-Gries' partial correctness logic for a concurrent while language. In: ICALP'86. Springer (1986). LNCS 226.
59. Stølen, K.: Development of Parallel Programs on Shared Data-Structures. PhD thesis, Manchester University (1990). Available as UMCS-91-1-1.

Chapter 9
Avoid a Void: The Eradication of Null Dereferencing

Bertrand Meyer, Alexander Kogtenkov, and Emmanuel Stapf

Abstract All object-oriented programs, but also those in C or Pascal as soon as they use pointers, are subject to the risk of run-time crash due to "null pointer dereferencing". Until recently this was the case even in statically typed languages. Tony Hoare has called this problem his "billion-dollar mistake".

In the type system of ISO-standard Eiffel, the risk no longer exists: void safety (the absence of null pointer dereferencing) has become a property guaranteed by the type system and enforced by the compiler. The mechanism is fully implemented and major libraries and applications have been made void-safe.

This presentation describes the principles of Eiffel's void safety, their implementation and the lessons gained.

9.1 Repairing the One-Billion-Dollar Mistake

Tony Hoare recently spoke [6] about the issue of null dereferencing:

> *I call it my billion-dollar mistake. It was the invention of the null reference in 1965. At that time, I was designing the first comprehensive type system for references in an object oriented language (ALGOL W). My goal was to ensure that all use of references should be absolutely safe, with checking performed automatically by the compiler. But I couldn't resist the temptation to put in a null reference, simply because it was so easy to implement. This has led to innumerable errors, vulnerabilities, and system crashes, which have probably caused a billion dollars of pain and damage in the last forty years.*

The present note (a modest attempt at a 75th birthday present) describes how a statically typed object-oriented programming language has, 4 decades after Algol W

A. Kogtenkov and E. Stapf
Eiffel Software, www.eiffel.com

B. Meyer (✉)
Chair of Software Engineering, ETH Zurich, Clausiusstrasse 59, 8092 ETH Zentrum, Zurich, Switzerland
and
Eiffel Software, www.eiffel.com
e-mail: Bertrand.Meyer@inf.ethz.ch

C.B. Jones et al. (eds.), *Reflections on the Work of C.A.R. Hoare*,
DOI 10.1007/978-1-84882-912-1_9,

and half a century after the appearance of NIL in Lisp, liberated its users from the scourge of null-dereferencing failures.

Hoare's statement seems to hint that just a little more care and discipline in the design of Algol W would have prevented the problem from even arising. Even in light of Hoare's record of finding brilliantly simple solution to problems that had eluded other researchers, our experience makes us doubt that null dereferencing could have vanished at the stroke of a pen. The problem indeed is not the *null reference*, a concept that appears as necessary to the type systems of usable programming languages as zero – another troublemaker, the tormentor of division – to the number system of mathematics. What threatens to make programs crash is the risk of *null dereferencing* (or "void call"): a run-time attempt to apply to a null (void) reference an operation that can only work if the reference denotes an object – in other words, if it is not void. In mathematics we want zero and we also want to divide numbers (by non-zero denominators); the difficulty is to avoid ever applying a division to a zero denominator. In programming, we want void references and we also want to apply operations to objects (through the associated non-void references); the difficulty is to avoid ever applying a call to a void reference, a property we shall call **void safety**. This need to reconcile two desirable but conflicting goals explains that a void-safety policy requires not only a sound theoretical concept but also careful engineering. As often in language design, success involves a delicate balancing act between programmer expressiveness and run-time safety.

Devising, refining and documenting the concept behind the mechanism presented here took a few weeks. The engineering took 4 years.

This article describes the concept, the same in its essence as first presented in the original article [10] and ISO language standard [5] but with important simplifications, and discusses the engineering of the implemented solution. All the mechanisms presented are in use today as part of EiffelStudio (commercial and open-source licenses), which has offered them since version 6.4 (May 2009); in particular, the libraries have been updated to void safety.

While the authors take responsibility for the present article and the implementation, any credit for the design of the mechanism must be shared with other members of the ECMA TC49-TG4 committee, in particular Éric Bezault, Karine Bezault and Mark Howard. ECMA provided an ideal framework for the difficult task of standardizing the language while continuing to innovate.

We are grateful to Erik Meijer, Rustan Leino, Manuel Fähndrich, Wolfram Schulte and other members of Microsoft Research for introducing us to the Spec# non-null type mechanism [1,4], which provided the decisive influence on our work. From the many people whose comments helped improve the mechanism we should cite Peter Müller, Piotr Nienaltowski (for applications to concurrency not detailed in this article), Kim Waldén, David Hollenberg, Bernd Schoeller, Paul-Georges Crismer, Ian King and Jocelyn Fiat.

Section 9.2 presents the problem and a general overview of the solution (sufficient to understand its essential elements). Section 9.3 details the background, listing in particular the constraints on any satisfactory approach. Section 9.4 presents the basic language mechanisms for void safety, and Section 9.5 some of the specific elements that make the result practical. Section 9.6 addresses the delicate problem of genericity, and Section 9.7 the solution to the final remaining need: handling arrays. The final sections present the pragmatic perspective: an estimate of the conversion, based on our experience in making the Eiffel libraries void-safe (8); and lessons learned (9).

9.2 Overview

We start with a description of the problem and an outline of the solution.

9.2.1 The Void-Safety Issue

Finding a practical solution to void safety may be delicate, but describing the problem is easy. In an object-oriented language, the basic computational mechanism is a feature call (also known as method call and as message passing) of the form

$x.f(a,\ b,\ \ldots)$	**/E1/**

where x is expected to denote an object and f is a feature (operation). The arguments $a,\ b,\ \ldots$ play no role here and the discussion will ignore them. If x is of a *reference* type, its possible run-time values are references; a reference is either *attached* to an object or *void*. If the value of x is attached to an object, /E1/ will apply f to that object. A *void call* arises if the value of x is void. Void safety is the avoidance of void calls.

In a language that does not guarantee void safety, the run-time effect of a void call is either to crash the program or, if the language supports exception handling, to trigger an exception. (The difference is not necessarily significant in practice, since programs seldom provide sophisticated exception handling for such cases: if a programmer detects the risk of a void call, he will generally find it just as simple to remove it than to let an exception happen and try to recover through an exception handler.)

The risk of void calls is already present in Pascal and C programs, where f takes no argument and denotes a field. It is even more acute in O-O languages since /E1/ is the basic form of object-oriented computation. In the absence of a void-safety mechanism, the risk of void call is a Sword of Damocles potentially threatening the execution of every O-O program.

With the possible exception of some arithmetic overflows, it is the *last* such risk. By adopting static typing, most modern O-O languages have ruled out *type mismatch*, the other potential source of run-time failure. Type mismatch would arise in /E1/ if x were dynamically attached to an object on which no appropriate feature f is available, or the feature exists but cannot accept $a,\ b,\ \ldots$ as arguments. The type system of such languages as Eiffel, Java and C# excludes this through simple rules enforced at compile time: every variable and expression must have an explicit type; this type must be based on a class that includes a feature f; the types of the actual arguments a, b, ... must conform to those of the formal arguments of f; and in any assignment $x := y$ (or actual-formal argument association) the type of y must conform to the type of x.

Static typing ensures type safety. The goal of the present discussion is to replicate that success story for void safety.

9.2.2 Sketch of the Solution

The basic elements of the mechanism detailed below are the following. "Attached", as defined so far, is a property of run-time values (references). To be more explicit we may call it "*dynamically* attached". The void-safety mechanism defines another property, "*statically* attached", applicable to variables and expressions; compilers (and human readers) can determine static attachment through a simple analysis of the program text. The goal is to ensure the following property:

Attachment consistency: If x is statically attached, its possible run-time values are dynamically attached.

The language rule is then simply:

Void safety rule: A call $x.f(\ldots)$ is only permitted if x is statically attached.

This rule will only ensure void safety, and hence deserve its name, if the language mechanism satisfies attachment consistency. The mechanism appears to meet this requirement; at present, however, we have not performed a mathematical proof.

The rest of this discussion uses the word "attached" without specifying "statically" or "dynamically", since the context removes any ambiguity: static attachment is a property of program elements (variables and expressions); dynamic attachment is a property of run-time values.

The void-safety mechanism provides three ways to ensure that a variable or expression x, of some type T, is (statically) attached:

- T is an *attached type*. An attached type is devised so that all its values will be dynamically attached; in other words, it does not admit **Void** as one of its values. Using an attached type is in principle the most effective way to guarantee the absence of void calls; the disadvantage is that any attached type must possess an initialization mechanism ensuring that the corresponding variables have a non-void value on first use. The remaining two cases assume that T is a *detachable* (not-attached) type.
- The context of a call may guarantee that x has a non-void value. For example, if x is a local variable the call in

if $x /=$ **Void then** $x.f(\ldots)$ **end**	**/E2/**

is void-safe. The language definition includes a small number of such schemes, known as **certified attachment patterns** or CAPs.

- More delicate cases may use the *object test* construct to guarantee safety. /E2/ is not necessarily void-safe if x is an arbitrary expression, because of the possibility of side effects and also in the presence of multi-threading. The scheme becomes void-safe if rewritten as

if attached x **as** l **then** $l.f(\ldots)$ **end**	**/E3/**

The boolean expression **attached** x **as** l is the object test; it has value True if an only if the value of x is dynamically attached to an object, and also has the effect of binding l (a fresh name) to that object over the *scope* of the object test, which in this case is the **then** clause.

In addition, special care must be taken when handling variables of generic types.

These rules are the core of the void-safety mechanism and will be reviewed in detail below.

9.3 Background

To understand the language mechanism it is necessary to review the constraints that apply to any solution, and the precise role of void references in practical programming.

9.3.1 Constraints on the Solution

The following constraints governed the design of the solution:

Requirements on the void-safety mechanism

1	*Static*: compile-time mechanism ensuring full void safety.
2	*General*: applicable to generic types and concurrent programming.
3	*Simple*: no mysterious rules; for programmers, easy to learn; for compiler writers, realistically implementable.
4	*Compatible*: minimal language extension; respects the spirit of the language; fits well with other constructs; does not limit programmer expressiveness; minimum change for existing code.

Constraint 1 prescribes an entirely static mechanism, like type safety. If a compiler accepts a program, it must guarantee the absence of void calls in any execution of the generated code.

Constraint 2 requires support for advanced language mechanisms:

- A class may be **generic**. In the class *LIST* [*G*], the name *G* represents an arbitrary type; a call of the form /E1/ is more delicate to handle if x of type *G* than if it is of a known type, since *G* represents many possible actual types, as in the "generic derivations" *LIST* [*INTEGER*], *LIST* [*SOME_REFERENCE_TYPE*], *LIST* [*LIST* [*INTEGER*]] and so on.
- The mention of **concurrency** illustrates how perversely language mechanisms can interact with each other. Void safety might at first seem independent from concurrency issues, but it is not. In particular, scheme /E2/ is not void-safe if x is an attribute (representing object fields) rather than a local variable as previously assumed: in the presence of multi-threading, another thread can make x void between the time the current thread ascertains that $x /=$ **Void** and the time it takes advantage of that finding to execute $x\,.\,f(\ldots)$. This problem is the major irritant in the practical use of the void-safety mechanism. Its presence is particularly frustrating to us since the SCOOP concurrency mechanism [11] designed for Eiffel handles multi-threading at a higher level of abstraction and removes such fine-grain interference; since SCOOP is not yet available as part of standard Eiffel implementations, programmers today must use traditional multi-threading techniques, which may cause interference in schemes such as /E2/ and as a result complicate the void-safety mechanism.

Constraint 3 states that void safety should not come at the expense of simplicity. Professional programmers should learn the new mechanisms easily, and the language should still be teachable to novices. (In a university setting we rely on object-oriented techniques for first-semester introductory programming and like to present the language as used in industry.) This constraint also cautions against making the language too hard to implement; we can be tougher on compiler writers than on language users, but within reason.

Relevant to both language users and compiler writers is the avoidance of *mysterious rules*. Today's compilers may use sophisticated techniques to determine that certain schemes are void-safe; such an approach is only acceptable if it relies on clear criteria which can be explained in the form of simple language rules. Otherwise programmers have to rely blindly on their compiler, not understanding what is going on; and one compiler may reject a program that another accepts.

Constraint 4 covers compatibility. It was a critical requirement for the work described here, whose goal was not to design a language from scratch but to make an existing language void-safe. There are several aspects to compatibility:

- *Minimal language extension*: additions to the programming language – constructs, keywords – should be kept to a minimum.
- *Respecting the spirit of the existing language design*: new mechanisms should fit with existing ones. In the Eiffel case, the language design follows a number of explicit principles, such as "Provide *one* good way to do anything important"; they should be retained.

- *Not limiting programmers' power of expression*: the void-safety mechanism should avoid bothering programmers unless their code demonstrably causes a risk of void call. This requirement is one of the hardest to satisfy.
- *Minimum change for existing code*: we need the best possible mechanism for future generations, but we also have to contend with millions of lines of existing production code.

This final requirement causes the worst headaches. Some of the existing programs may contain sources of potential void calls (if programmers only ever wrote void-perfect code, there would be no need for any new mechanism); the problem is to avoid false alarms. As much as possible, we would like to accept existing code unchanged except for elements that are demonstrably void-unsafe. This goal has only been reached in part; we have succeeded in minimizing change to existing code, but not in eliminating it.

The adaptation of the standard Eiffel libraries themselves took up the better part of a release cycle (6 months). This measure is not representative, since the circumstances were peculiar: we were performing such an effort for the first time, learning along the way; we did not have a conversion guide (but as a by-product of the effort developed such a guide [3], facilitating the tasks of others who need to adapt their programs); and we were still refining the mechanism as we went, improving the end result but causing delays in the process. Still, migration of existing code continues to require a significant effort.

9.3.2 *Void and Attached References*

A literal reading of Hoare's comment might suggest that void references are dispensable. One may indeed wish for a language design that magically gets rid of them. Unfortunately, this is only a dream; attempts have been made, as in the Self language [2], but they do not remove the underlying problem.

This problem is, at its core, the need to terminate linked structures. In the same way that numbers need a zero to denote the number that can be added to another without changing it, linked representations of data structures such as lists and trees need **Void** to denote the reference that can be included in an object to refer to no other object. Linked lists are the archetypal example:

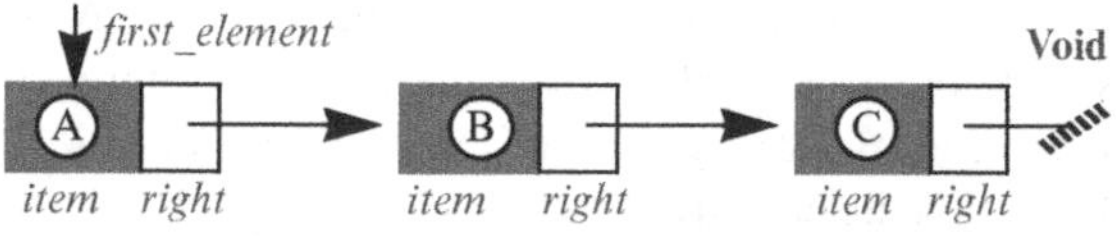

In the figure, the list is represented by three cells (of type *LINKABLE* [*CHARACTER*] in the EiffelBase library), each with a field *item* giving the value and a reference field *right* leading to the next cell. The *right* field in the last cell cannot lead to any object and hence must be void.

The presence of such possibly void references immediately introduces the risk of void calls. For example, if *first_element* is the reference to the first list cell (*first_element* is indeed the name of the corresponding attribute in the *LINKED_LIST* class), and we assume *first_element* itself has a non-void value, then *first_element.right* might be void, so an attempt to evaluate *first_element.right.right* may cause a void call. This result is not a nasty side-effect of introducing an ill-conceived notion (void references) into the programming language, but the expression of an incontrovertible property: the expression does not make sense if the list has fewer than two elements – just as $1/(m - n)$, in ordinary mathematics, does not make sense if m happens to be equal to n.

Because void calls result from logical impossibilities, not artifacts of language design, simplistic attempts to remove void references disguise the problem rather than removing it. Two such ideas are:

- Prohibit void references and use some trick to represent structure termination; for example, in linked lists, the last *right* reference would point to the cell itself. This breaks the acyclic nature of linked lists, and requires checking every use of *right*, for example in a list traversal, to determine whether it is truly a reference to another element or an artificial self-reference marker.
- Use inheritance to distinguish between two kinds of *LINKABLE* cells: proper linkables and end markers. The last *right* would be of the second kind. This complicates the inheritance structure, and requires checking every use of *right* for its type. The effect on performance (in particular the extra load on the garbage collector) can also be noticeable.

Such solutions replace void checks (**if** *right*/=**Void then**...) by checks of another kind, with no clear benefit. They cause the risk that a wrong dereferencing, such as *first_element.right.right.item* applied to a one-element list, will yield an incorrect result (in the first solution, the value of the first element) instead of an exception. In erroneous cases, it is generally preferable to crash than to continue and deliver wrong results.

This discussion dashes any hope of casting off the void-safety problem by simply casting off void references. It also includes some good news. Terminating linked structures seems to be the *only* case that truly requires void references. That case occurs in system-oriented parts of programs, typically in libraries that implement fundamental data structures; in the more application-oriented parts of a program, void references are generally unnecessary. Consider a program manipulating bank accounts objects, each with an *owner* field denoting a *PERSON*. To represent the notion of a bank account by an unknown owner, a void reference is usually not the best solution; instead, the program can define a special object representing a *PERSON* with incomplete information.

This observation suggests a software design guideline: confine void references to specific parts of a system, largely preserving the application-oriented layers from having to worry about the issues discussed in this article. It also confirms our expectation that the conversion of typical user applications will require significantly less effort than our initial experiences, which involved system-level libraries.

9.4 Basic Language Mechanisms

We now review the three major techniques for ensuring void safety: attached types in the present section, CAP and object test in the next two.

9.4.1 Attached Types

The void-safety mechanism introduces into the type system an attachment qualifier for types. A reference type is either *attached* or *detachable*. The difference is that **Void** is a valid value for detachable types only.

Syntactically, a detachable type is indicated by the keyword **detachable**, as in

```
right: detachable LINKABLE [G]
```

Attached types can similarly use the keyword **attached**, but this is usually not needed as "attached" is the default status; a declaration

```
owner: PERSON        – In class BANK_ACCOUNT
```

has the same meaning as *owner*: **attached** *PERSON*. This policy follows from the above observation that application-oriented types do not normally need a void value. Experience has shown it to be the right decision, even though it raises compatibility issues (see constraint 4) since previous code followed the inverse convention.

The explicit form **attached** *PERSON* is mostly useful during the transition period. The EiffelStudio compiler provides a compatibility option with three possible values, settable class-by-class to help programmers migrate existing code progressively:

- Enforce void safety. This is the default for the future.
- Do not enforce void safety; ignore **attached** and **detachable** type marks. This is the full-backward-compatibility option.
- Enforce void safety rules, but only for attached types; leave detachable types alone (void calls will still be possible in the corresponding cases). This is a transition option.

Defining a type *T* as attached – using any syntactic convention – is only a declaration; the important part of the language mechanism is the set of semantic rules that ensure the *attachment consistency* property introduced earlier: any run-time use of a variable *x* of type *T* must find *x* attached to an object. This requires the mechanism to enforce two properties:

A1 The value of *x* on first use, as defined by language initialization rules, must be non-void.

A2 Any assignment to *x* must leave the value of *x* non-void.

Objective A2 is the easier of the two, achieved through the following rule:

Attachment Preservation rule

An attachment operation of source *y* and target *x*, where the type of *x* is attached, is permitted only if the type of *y* is also attached.

An "attachment operation" is either an assignment $x := y$ or an argument passing $f(\ldots, y, \ldots)$ where the corresponding formal argument is *x*. (This meaning of the word "attachment" to denote an operation predates its use to describe, as in the rest of this article, the status of a reference.)

This leaves the issue of initialization (A1). Eiffel (followed in this respect by other modern object-oriented languages) includes initialization rules for all types; for example, all integer variables are initialized to zero and all booleans to False. For reference types, the earlier initialization value was **Void**: the most obvious one, and indeed the only one applicable to all (detachable) reference types – but also the worst possible choice for an attached type! The void-safety mechanism requires a new policy.

The key notion is that of a variable being *properly set*, meaning that it has been given a non-void value. It figures in the rule for variables of attached types:

Attached Type Initialization rule

If a program uses the variable at a certain position, one of the following properties must hold:

- The variable is properly set at that position. This possibility applies to both kinds of variable: attributes of a class, and local variables of a routine.
- The variable is an attribute, and is properly set at the end position of every creation procedure of the class.

The *creation procedures* of a class, also known as its *constructors*, are the initialization operations associated with the class. A variable *x* of type *T* is properly set at a certain position if one of the instructions preceding that position is an assignment to *x* (which, thanks to the Attachment Preservation rule, gives it an attached value if *T* is an attached type) or a creation instruction of target *x* (of the form **create** *x*...).

As an example, the use of *x* in the last instruction of the following routine is valid:

```
r
    do
            create y
            ...
            x := y
            print (x)
    end
```

This assumes that *x* and *y* are variables of the same type. In the last instruction, *x* is properly set since the preceding instruction is an assignment to *x*. In that assignment, the source *y* itself is properly set since it was earlier the target of a creation instruction; without this property, the assignment *x* := *y* would be invalid as it is uses the value of *y*.

This discussion and the rule do not apply to formal arguments of routines, which are not variables (they cannot be the target of assignments). In a routine *r*(*x*: *T*), the Attachment Preservation rule guarantees that the formal argument *x* will always be attached since in any call *r*(*y*) the actual argument *y* must be attached.

As stated, the condition guaranteeing that a variable is properly set is over-conservative; for example, it does not imply that *x* is properly set after

```
if c then create x else x := y end      – With y properly set   /E4/
```

In moving library code to void safety we realized that scheme /E4/ is fairly common, and added it, along with a few others, to those accepted by EiffelStudio as void-safe. Since these cases fall outside of the current language definition, a compiler option is available to disable them for portability; we will submit them to the standards committee for inclusion in the initialization rule. The challenge – in line with constraint 3, "No mysterious rules" – is to replace operational, compiler-oriented descriptions of specific cases by general language rules, lending themselves to clear, abstract definitions.

The simplicity of the rules governing attached types suggests using these types as much as possible; as noted, the business-oriented parts of a program should limit themselves almost exclusively to attached types. This will spare them the difficulties of ensuring void safety for detachable types – the topic of the remaining sections.

9.4.2 Certified Attachment Patterns

In the interest of simplicity and compatibility (constraints 3 and 4), it is desirable to accept without change some program schemes that are demonstrably void-safe even though they involve detachable variables or expressions. Such a scheme is called a Certified Attachment Pattern or CAP. The language standard currently defines a single CAP, which covers a number of useful cases. It is phrased as follows:

Basic CAP

A call *x*.*f* (...), where *x* is a formal argument or local variable of a routine, is void-safe if this call both:

- Appears in the scope of a void test involving *x*.
- Is not preceded, in that scope, by a setter for *x*.

The arguments, variables and expressions considered in this rule and the rest of the discussion are all of detachable types, since no further rules are necessary for the attached case. A *void test* is one of the following, possibly involving a boolean expression e:

- Positive void test: the simple form $x =$ **Void**, or the composite form $x =$ **Void or else** e
- Negative void test: the simple form $x /=$ **Void**, or the composite form $x /=$ **Void and then** e

(The operators **and then** and **or else** are the non-commutative variants of **and** and **or**: if a is False, evaluating a **and then** b will not evaluate b; if a is True, evaluating a **or else** b will not evaluate b.) The scope of a void test v includes:

S1 If v is of a composite form: the rest of the expression, e
S2 If v is a negative void test appearing in a conditional instruction **if** v **then** … **end** (where the instruction may include **elseif** clauses and an **else** clause): the **then** clause
S3 If v is a positive void test appearing in a conditional instruction **if** v **then** … **else** … **end** (where the instruction may include **elseif** clauses): the **else** and **elseif** clauses
S4 If v is a positive void test appearing in a loop instruction **from** … **until** v **loop** … **end**: the loop body (**loop** clause)

A "setter for x" is an assignment to x or a control structure that (recursively) includes a setter for x.

The CAP makes it possible to sanction a wide range of fundamental programming schemes. Examples, accepted as void-safe, include not only the simple conditional /E2/ but algorithms for traversing or searching linked structures, such as:

```
from
        l := first_element
until
        l = Void or else l.item ~ sought        -- ~ is object equality
loop
        l := l.right
end
```

Such schemes occur frequently in basic libraries of data structures and algorithms and reflect natural ways of expressing search and other traversal operations. It was critical, as part of the compatibility and simplicity of use requirements, to accept them without change.

Case S1 allows other frequent schemes, arising in boolean expressions:

```
x /= Void and then x.some_property            /E5/
x = Void or else x.some_property              /E6/
```

/E5/ is widely used in contracts: preconditions, postconditions and class invariants. It expresses a requirement that an object, *if it exists*, satisfies a certain property. For example, the equality operation on two references *a* and *b* has the postcondition

```
Result =
    (a = Void and b = Void) or else ((a / = Void and b / = Void) and then
a.is_equal (b))
```

defining them to be equal if they are either both void or attached to equal objects. The operation *is_equal* ascertains the equality of two objects, and hence can only be applied to a non-void target and a non-void argument. Case S1 of the CAP certifies this postcondition as void-safe.

These results extend to contracts consisting of several clauses; the language semantics treats them as if they were separated by **and then**, so that if a routine starts with

```
r (x: detachable T)                                    /E7/
        require
                x/= Void
                x.some_property
```

its precondition is equivalent to /E5/; as a consequence, the second clause is void-safe.

The CAP is limited to formal arguments and local variables, excluding attributes. Cases such as the following are indeed not void-safe if *x* is an attribute:

```
if x/= Void then                                       /E8/
        routine_call
        x. f(...)
end
```

One of the reasons why this example could lead to a void call was mentioned in connection with the simpler variant /E2/: in a multi-threading execution, another thread could falsify the property x / = **Void** before the call. Another risk, even with single threading, is that a routine call may perform an assignment to the attribute *x*.

Similarly, the second precondition clause in the following variant of /E7/ is not void-safe if *x* is an attribute rather than a formal argument:

```
r                                                      /E9/
      require
              x/= Void
              x.some_property
```

Achieving void safety in such cases may require a specific technique: object test.

9.4.3 Object Test

The "object test" language construct provides, under a simple syntax, a general solution to the problem known as *run-time type identification* (or RTTI), with particular application to void safety.

In object-oriented languages, it is generally not necessary to query an object directly for its type; the preferred technique [8] is to use inheritance, polymorphism and dynamic binding. In a call $x.\ f(\ldots)$, the target x may be polymorphic, meaning that it may at run time become attached to objects of different types, all descending from a common ancestor. Any of these classes may provide a specific version of f; then dynamic binding ensures that each call will select the appropriate version, based on the type of the object actually to x. For the simplicity and ease of change of the software's architecture these techniques are preferable to letting the program test explicitly for the type of the object and select the appropriate variant of f through a conditional instruction.

Techniques of run-time type identification, also known as "type narrowing" and "downcasting", are necessary for more complex cases where these standard object-oriented techniques do not apply. The most obvious example is that of an object obtained from the outside world (a file, a network): the program has no choice but to posit a certain type and dynamically find out whether the object matches it.

Object test provides a general mechanism for run-time type identification, which we find preferable to existing approaches, including the construct previously available in Eiffel (assignment attempt, introduced in 1988). An object test checks that a reference is attached to an object of a specified type, and if so catches the object under a local name to avoid safe processing over a certain syntactic scope.

An object test on a given expression *exp* of a detachable type may appear as follows, here as part of a conditional instruction

```
if attached {T} exp as l then                                         /E10/
        ... Operations on l, such as l.f(...) ...
end
```

The object test is **attached** $\{T\}$ *exp* **as** l. It is a boolean expression, evaluating to True if and only if the value of *exp* is a reference attached to an object of type T or conforming. Then the "object-test local" l, a fresh name (distinct from the names of all variables in the context), will denote a reference to that object throughout the *scope* of the object-test local, defined by the same rules as the scope of a void test.

Here, the scope is the **then** clause; the effect of the conditional instruction is to determine whether *exp* is attached to an object of type T and, if so, to apply the given operations to that object. Because the object is captured under the temporary name l at the time of the object test, no interference may arise from multi-threading or from operations that could cause the value of *exp* to change.

In such uses of an object test for void safety rather than general run-time type identification, the type T is often just the (static) type of *exp*; for that reason the qualifier {*T*} is optional. We may indeed write the object test in /E10/ as just **attached** *exp* **as** *l*. (The "**as** *l*" part can also be omitted for RTTI uses that need the object only to test its type, but in void-safety applications it is necessary.)

An object test will achieve void safety in the second variant of the precondition example /E9/, which involved an attribute and hence was not covered by the CAP. A void-safe version is

```
r                         – Void-safe version of /E9/                    /E11/
    require
        x /= Void
        attached x as l and then l.some_property
```

The second clause is void-safe thanks to clause S1 of the CAP.

Although the first clause *x* /= **Void** is now redundant, we have retained it for the (frequent) occurrences of this pattern in our library conversions so far. The reason is to help testing and debugging. In the case of a contract violation, the run-time contract monitoring tools identify the violated clause; for a void *x*, it is clearer to see a violation of the first clause, since a violation of the second one does not distinguish between a void *x* (no object) and an object that exists but does not satisfy *some_property*.

9.5 Fine-Tuning the Mechanism

Object test would in principle provide, just by itself, a general solution to void safety: protect every feature call *x*.*f*(...) with an object test on *x*. This would be an extreme solution, and indeed the general design guideline, consistent with the object-oriented method's reluctance to use RTTI except when polymorphism and dynamic binding are not applicable, is to minimize the use of object test.

We have already seen two alternatives, superior to object test whenever they can be applied: attached types and CAPs. Two other facilities, the Check instruction and stable attributes, help limit the use of object test.

9.5.1 The Check Instruction

The Check instruction – not a new construct, but an existing part of Eiffel's Design by Contract mechanism [8] – expresses that a certain property is assumed always to hold at a certain program position, whether or not a proof exists. It is particularly relevant for void safety, addressing cases where a detachable expression is known from the context to be non-void.

The following example is typical. Class *LINKED_LIST* describes lists in a linked implementation, with list cells implemented as instances of *LINKABLE* as discussed above. *LINKED_LIST* itself describes a list as a whole and includes a notion of "cursor", which can be moved to a list item, as well as to the positions immediately to the left of the first item if any and to the right of the last item if any:

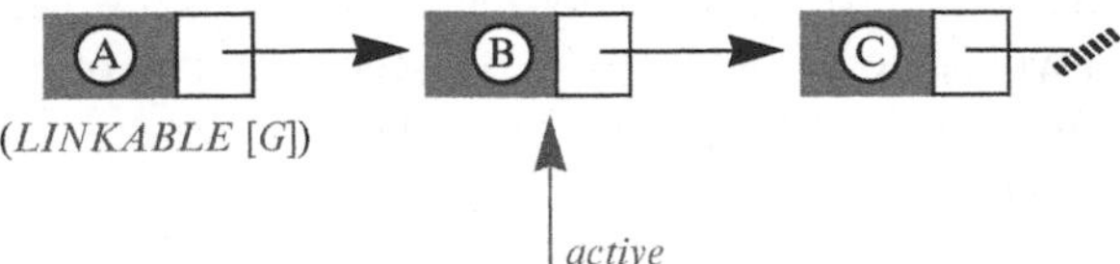

The attribute *active* represents the cursor position. By convention, *active* is always attached to a list cell, except if the list is empty; this is reflect by a clause of the class invariant:

(*active* = **Void**) **implies** *is_empty*

Now consider a routine of the class with the precondition **not** *is_empty*. From the invariant, it also satisfies *active* /= **Void**. With the rules given so far, however, the following version will be rejected:

```
r
    require
            not is_empty
    do
            active.some_operation
    end
```

The attribute *active* is of type **detachable** *LINKABLE* [*G*] and it is not used as part of a void-safe CAP, so the value of *active* at the place of the call is not known to be attached. There is no easy way to address this problem through a solution based only on the type system. We can protect the call with an object test, through one of the forms

if attached *active* **as** *l* **then** *l.some_operation* **else** "Raise an exception" **end** **/E12/**
if attached *active* **as** *l* **then** *l.some_operation* **end** **/E13/**

In both cases we test for a property that we expect always to hold; the difference is that if it does not /E12/ raises an exception whereas /E13/ does nothing. Neither variant is satisfactory: the object test is in principle unnecessary; if there is a mistake, doing nothing is not an appropriate solution. The recommended scheme in such a case is

check attached *active* **as** *l* **then** *l.some_operation* **end** **/E14/**

The semantics of **check** *e* **then** *Instructions* **end** (inspired, in its current form, by Spec#'s "assert" instruction) is that the construct requires any compiler to either:

- Prove that *e* will always hold. (This assumes a "verifying compiler" equipped with proof capabilities – another concept promoted by Tony Hoare [7].)
- Generate code with the effect of /E12/, triggering an exception if *e* is dynamically not satisfied.

The first solution is the desirable one, but places high demands on the compiler (see "realistically implementable" in constraint 3). The second solution, currently implemented in EiffelStudio, is open to criticism: one can argue that it simply replaces one kind of exception, void call, with another. To refute this criticism we note that there exists in practice a fundamental difference: a program written prior to the introduction of void safety is chock-full with potentially unsafe calls; adapted to obey the void-safety rules, it may still contain a few **check** constructs in the style of /E14/, which may cause exceptions but are clearly identified; they will be the natural target of quality assurance efforts intended to demonstrate that the condition will never be True during execution.

9.5.2 Stable Attributes

As described, the void-safety mechanism does a reasonable job of not bothering programmers (especially, not forcing them to write object tests) when there is no real risk of void call; the annoying case that remain is scheme /E2/ applied to an attribute:

if $x /=$ **Void then** $x.f(\ldots)$ **end**	**/E2/**

This is not void-safe and requires an object test. The culprit, as noted, is multi-threading, and the annoyance will remain as long as SCOOP-based concurrency is not fully available. In one case, however, the annoyance can be avoided. The technique relies on the following notion:

Definition: stable attribute
A detachable attribute is *stable* if it does not appear as target of an assignment whose source is a detachable expression.

("Detachable attribute" and "detachable expression" are abbreviations for attribute and expression of a detachable type.) A stable attribute might have a void value on object creation, but once it becomes attached it will remain attached, since every value that gets assigned to it will be attached. The definition is restrictive: the source of an attachment cannot just be stable, it has to be attached. Even so, however, stable attributes do constitute a substantial share of detachable attributes; detecting them is useful since /E2/ is void-safe for a stable attribute, avoiding an object test.

A compiler can easily determine, when seeing a pattern such as /E2/, that x is a stable attribute (just check all the assignments in the class). In spite of this property, a recently adopted language extension introduces an explicit **stable** marker in the syntax for attribute declarations

stable x: **detachable** *SOME_TYPE*

The reason for this decision is that in the implicit approach, where the compiler silently blesses /E2/ when it determines that x is stable, a small change to a class, such as adding an assignment in a routine, may suddenly cause the program no longer to compile because of a void-safety violation in a seemingly unrelated part of the code.

It remains an open question in the standards committee whether – for the sake of minimizing programmer annoyance – /E2/ should be accepted anyway, possibly with a compiler warning, for an attribute that happens to be stable but has not been declared as such.

9.6 Handling Genericity

All the types considered so far were explicit, and known directly from the program text. A typed object-oriented language will also provide a generic mechanism, with classes such as *LIST* [*G*] where *G* represents an arbitrary type. A particular use of the class uses a type obtained as a *generic derivation*, using a type as actual generic parameter; an example is *LIST*[*CHARACTER*]. The question of void safety arises here too: for *x* declared of type *G* in a class *C* [*G*], under what conditions is a call `x.`*f*(...) void-safe? The techniques that we have seen are different for attached and detachable types; but within the class we do not know whether the actual generic parameter *T* of any particular generic derivation *C* [*T*] will be of one kind or the other.

To obtain a suitable solution, we should first note the general convention regarding genericity. The basic form is *constrained* genericity, whereby a class is declared as

```
class C[G−> CT]...
```

for some type *CT* known as the *constraint* (or "constraining type"). This means that the only valid generic derivations are of the form *C* [*T*] where *T* conforms (according to inheritance-based rules) to the constraint *CT*. *Unconstrained* genericity, as in *LIST* [*G*], is simply an abbreviation for a special case of constrained genericity, *LIST* [*G*− > *ANY*], where *ANY* is the library class serving as ancestor to all programmer-defined classes (*ANY* is called Object in some object-oriented languages).

The introduction of void safety leads to a slight adaptation of this convention: unconstrained genericity *C* [*G*] is now an abbreviation for *C* [*G*−> **detachable** *ANY*]. The type system, as implied by the discussion in previous sections, ensures that *T* (synonym for **attached** *T*) conforms to **detachable** *T* but not the other way around. Within the class *C* [*G*], then, *G* represents a detachable type; with *x* declared of type *G*, the call `x.`*f*(...) is not void-safe and must be protected through a CAP, an object test, a Check instruction or a stable attribute status for *x*.

It is also possible to declare *x* of type **attached** *G*; then the call is void-safe, but *x* is subject to the initialization constraints on attributes of attached types.

As another possibility, the class declaration may read *C* [*G*−> *ANY*] or more generally *C* [*G*−> *T*] for some attached type *T* (remember again that these are synonyms for *C* [*G*−> **attached** *ANY*] and *C* [*G*−> **attached** *T*]). Then *G* represents an attached type and the call is void-safe.

These rules make it possible to write void-safe generic container classes – representing structures such as lists, stacks queues and many others – in a convenient fashion. One of the goals defined for the design of the void safety mechanism was indeed to enable a smooth and easy conversion of the EiffelBase library of fundamental data structures and algorithms, involving as little rewrite as possible.

One generic structure, however, remains beyond the scope of these techniques: arrays.

9.7 Arrays

The language definition is engineered in such a way that programmers get the advantages of two complementary views of arrays:

- The traditional view, with the performance benefits of direct-access, contiguous-memory representation and usual array syntax such as

```
a[i] := a[i] + p                                    /E15/
```

- The object-oriented view, where *ARRAY* [*G*] has all the prerogatives of a normal generic class: it is characterized by features (so that /E15/ is simply an abbreviation for the object-oriented form *a*.*put* (*a*.*item* (*i*) + *p*)), has preconditions, postconditions and a class invariant, and can be used by other classes, for example as ancestor in inheritance.

ARRAY, however, is a special class because its implementation relies on a contiguous memory area that cannot be entirely managed by the program. For void safety, this means that it is impossible without a further mechanism to accept a declaration

```
a: ARRAY [T]
```

where *T* is an attached type. Normally, an array is created through the *make* creation procedure, as

```
create a.make (l, h)
```

where the arguments *l* and *h* are the initial bounds, low and high, of the array. After that creation, any operation is possible on the array, including an access to *a* [*i*] as in /E15/ – assuming in this case that *T* has a "+" operation, so that the right side of /E15/ is an abbreviation for *a* [*i*].*plus* (*p*). But this call is not void-safe: the creation procedure *make* has no provision for initializing the array elements; there is no guarantee that *a* [*i*] will be non-void.

We see here a fundamental consequence of making the language void-safe: language-specified automatic initialization of variables, mentioned at the beginning of this article as a key property of modern object-oriented languages, is no longer possible, or at least not in a simple form. Previously every type had a default value, which was **Void** for all reference types; this property is still applicable to detachable types and to *expanded* types (non-reference types, including basic types such as *INTEGER*), but not to attached reference types.

If *T* is detachable, the items of an *ARRAY* [*T*] will be initialized to **Void**; for expanded types, they will be initialized to the default value such as zero for integers; but for attached *T* no such universal default is available.

This property does not cause any particular problem for ordinary generic classes such as *LINKED_LIST*, since they are entirely under the control of the programmer, who can also take care of initialization for any type, in accordance with rules of the previous section. But creating an array allocates a memory area that lies beyond the programmer's direct control. Another way to express this observation is that arrays remain a system-level island in a modern high-level language.

As a result of this situation, arrays require special treatment. The solution is simple: for attached reference types (as opposed to detachable types and expanded types), array creation may no longer use the *make* creation procedure, with its two arguments representing bounds; it must instead use a newly introduced creation procedure, *make_filled*, with an extra argument representing a default value. Its signature in *ARRAY* [*G*] is

```
make_filled (low, high: INTEGER; value: G)
```

allowing creation instructions of the form

```
create a.make (l, h, val)
```

where *val* is a value of the appropriate type; if that type is attached, the type rules guarantee that *val* must be attached as well – a reference to an actual object. Upon creation of the array, every one of its entries will be a reference to that object. More precisely, the abstract requirement is that for an entry that has not been explicitly initialized *a* [*i*] must yield such a reference; the implementation can achieve it in smarter ways than physically copying the reference. The implementation should also consider the needs of garbage collection (to make sure that the shared object can be freed if no longer useful).

To avoid making up a specific default value for every array, a mechanism is under consideration that would allow defining a default value for any type, under the form {*T*}.*set_default* (*val*). (The notation {*T*}, a reflection mechanism, denotes an object representing the type *T*.) The creation procedure *make* would then be applicable to an *ARRAY* [*T*].

The current solution to the problem of making arrays void-safe is clearly sound, and is generally acceptable, at least for new code. In practice it causes some unpleasantness in only one case: when there is no obvious default *value*, and the program's makeup guarantees that no array entry will be accessed without having been set. The most important example we know is the *HASH_TABLE* class of EiffelBase: an implementation of hash tables using an array controls the array entirely, and can guarantee the set-before-accessing property; but it requires a default value to placate the void-safe type system.

Even though the solution works, it is an example of the worst possible nightmare for a language designer: having to change the usage instructions for a fundamental mechanism – arrays in this case – used by every single program in existence.

9.8 Measuring the Conversion Effort

The recently completed library conversion process provides a basis for assessing the amount of work needed to adapt code. Out of thousands of converted classes, the following measures apply to 215 fundamental classes of Free ELKS (the Eiffel Library Kernel Standard, a subset of EiffelBase common to all implementations):

- Introduction of object tests: before conversion, the code included 100 occurrences of the assignment attempt instruction, the predecessor to object test. After conversion, it contains 115 object tests. All the added object tests are in contract elements, specifically postconditions and class invariants.
- Introduction of check instructions: there were 71 Check instructions; the number is now 90.

It is encouraging to note that no object test had to be added outside of contract elements. In the case of contracts, many of the changes were of the kind illustrated with /E9/ and /E11/; for example the insertion routine *put_left* from *LINKED_LIST* now has the postcondition clauses

```
previous /= Void
attached previous as q and then q.item = v
```

with the redundancy noted in Section 9.4.3. Another example of an added object test is the following clause in the postcondition of *put_right*, now reading:

```
(old before) implies (attached active as c and then c.item = v)
```

(**old**, in a postcondition, denotes the value of an expression on entry to the routine). In this case the object test causes no redundancy; indeed the previous version of the class had the clause as just

```
(old before) implies (active.item = v)
```

but no clause stating that *active* /= **Void**. In the absence of a proof that *active* cannot be void on routine exit, this expression was not void-safe.

Altogether, the percentage of lines changed in EiffelBase between versions 6.1 and 6.4 is 11% (9,093 out of 82,459). This is probably not a reliable indicator of future conversion efforts as the changes span three release cycles over an 18-month period, during which many non-void-safety-related changes also took place (but are not separately identified in the change record). The reason an analysis of EiffelBase changes requires going back that far is that EiffelBase served as a testbed for the progressive implementation of void safety, starting with 6.2. Since the library covers fundamental data structures, it makes extensive use of void references and is probably a worst-case example.

The EiffelVision multi-platform graphical library was converted in a single shot between versions 6.3 and 6.4, with almost no other changes. The figures may be more generally relevant since EiffelVision is more similar to application libraries. It is also much larger than EiffelBase. In EiffelVision the number of changed lines was 10,909 out of 376,592 – less than 3%.

The conversion efforts that have occurred until now have mostly been applied to libraries. To maintain compatibility for existing client code, the converted versions must declare all externally visible reference types as *detachable*: using attached types would make existing client code invalid whenever it passes actual arguments – possibly void – to the corresponding routines. This policy goes against the general recommendation of using attached types as much as possible. No such precaution is necessary for converting non-library code and for writing *new* code; this is one of the reasons why we expect that the change effort in the future will be less than the above figures.

While there is not enough concrete experience to offer a definitive estimate, the experience so far is encouraging. It suggests that the effort of adapting existing software to void safety is tractable, and that requiring void safety for new code will not impose an undue burden on programmers.

Conversion is a temporary hurdle. What is clearly emerging from our experience is that writing **new** code so that it is void-safe implies no particular effort once one has mastered the concepts. For daily programming in our groups at Eiffel Software and ETH, void safety has become a self-evident part of the process.

9.9 Assessment and Conclusion

Initial user reactions to the void-safety mechanism were not all positive. Predictably, the need to convert existing code caused some concerns among users, including long-time Eiffel programmers who feared that it would take them back to "defensive programming", at the antipodes of Desing by Contract and the Eiffel method. At the time of writing, these objections have largely subsided. Many experienced users appreciate that the cost of conversion is justified; and like our own groups they now write new code so that it is void-safe from the start.

The preceding sections have illustrated the challenges of language evolution, discussed in more general terms in a previous contribution to a Hoare anniversary volume [9]. Research on language design often focuses on inventing language constructs and trying them out separately. Such experimentation is obviously useful; but it may miss the difficulties faced by language designers who are in charge of an existing language, having existing users and an existing code base.

The development of the void-safety mechanism and its insertion into a full-fledged, industrially used language are a reminder of some of these difficulties:

- *Interaction Between Language Features* Two of the major obstacles to void safety turned out to be multi-threading and arrays. It was not clear to us, at the beginning of this effort, that they would even figure in the discussion. The original article [10] does not mention them; their importance became clear as we started applying the mechanism to the mass conversion of existing programs and libraries. The need to use object tests to protect simple accesses to attributes is, for us, one more incentive to complete the implementation of the SCOOP mechanism, which unlike today's multithreading mechanisms provides a concurrency framework at a level of abstraction that matches the expressive power of modern programming and modern programming languages.

- *Engineering Considerations* The most clever language design ideas will fail unless they can be properly engineered into compilers, explained to programmers and retrofitted into existing designs.
- *Compatibility and Migration* Whenever possible, new mechanisms should remain compatible with existing ones. Failing this goal, a migration path should be devised, enabling users to adapt their code progressively. We have repeatedly found, in the evolution of Eiffel, that users are not adverse to change; but the change must be justified, and a clear path charted. This starts with providing compatibility options in compilers, which will process existing code unchanged, and continues with providing migration guides (or, when possible, conversion tools).

The process is not always perfect; our own experience with void safety has involved many trials and many errors. We hope that the results will be useful to others: not just the lessons of that experience but, concretely, the availability for the first time of guaranteed void safety in a mainstream programming language.

References

1. Barnett, M., Leino, R., Schulte, W.: The Spec# Programming System; CASSIS 2004, Lecture Notes in Computer Science 3362, Springer, Heidelberg (2004).
2. Chambers, C. et al.: Papers on the Self language at research.sun.com/self/papers/papers.html.
3. Eiffel community: Void safety migration guide, at dev.eiffel.com/Void-Safe_Library_Status.
4. Fähndrich, M., Leino, R.: Declaring and Checking Non-null Types in an Object-Oriented Language; in OOPSLA 2003, SIGPLAN Notices, vol. 38, no. 11, pp. 302–312. ACM, New York (November 2003).
5. ECMA Technical Group TG49-TG4 (Eiffel) of ECMA Technical Committee 49 (Programming Languages): Standard ECMA-367 and ISO/IEC 25436:2006, Eiffel Analysis, Design and Programming Language, 2nd edition. ECMA International and International Standards Organization, Geneva (June 2006).
6. Hoare, C.A.R.: Null References: The Billion Dollar Mistake, abstract of talk at QCon London, 9–12 March 2009, at qconlondon.com/london-2009/presentation/Null+References:+The+Billion+Dollar+Mistake.
7. Hoare, C.A.R., Misra, J.: In: Meyer, B., Woodcock, J. (eds.) Verified Software: Theories, Tools, Experiments, Vision of a Grand Challenge Project, pp. 1–18. VSTTE 2005. Lecture Notes in Computer Science 4171. Springer, Heidelberg (2008).
8. Meyer, B.: Object-Oriented Software Construction, 2nd edn. Prentice Hall, Upper Saddle River, NJ (1997).
9. Meyer, B.: In: Davies, J., Roscoe, B., Woodcock, J. (eds.) Principles of Language Design and Evolution, in Millenial Perspectives in Computer Science (Proceedings of the 1999 Oxford-Microsoft Symposium in Honour of Sir Tony Hoare), pp. 229–246. Cornerstones of Computing. Palgrave, Basingstoke-New York (2000).
10. Meyer, B.: In: Black, A. (ed.) Attached Types and Their Application to Three Open Problems of Object-Oriented Programming, pp. 1–32. In ECOOP 2005 (Proceedings of European Conference on Object-Oriented Programming, Edinburgh, 25–29 July 2005). Lecture Notes in Computer Science 3586. Springer, Heidelberg (2005).
11. SCOOP concurrency mechanism, see references at se.ethz.ch/research/scoop.

Chapter 10
Unfolding CSP

Mikkel Bundgaard and Robin Milner

Dedicated to Sir Tony Hoare for his 75th birthday

Appreciation from the second author Tony Hoare and I have exchanged ideas on concurrent processes for three decades. To a sufficiently distant observer it has seemed that we were doing the same thing, and that therefore we should not have made it look different. A closer view shows this to be false. Complementary things, yes; and both have been enriched by the cross-fertilisation.

A little history shows something of these different approaches. Around 1979 we first discovered our complementary interests in concurrency. Tony at first expressed his ideas through the medium of a programming language [6], and I through a prototypical algebraic theory [8]. The difference became plainer as time went on. Tony was keen to find a single formalism in which specifications of concurrent systems could be refined into programs. I, on the other hand, was keen to find a mathematical concept of *process* that could stand in analogy with the familiar notion of (single valued) *function*, and I was happy that specification should be done in an associated logic. We enjoyed discussing these things. I recall one discussion at a blackboard (or was it a whiteboard?) where Tony hinted to me his first ideas about failures semantics.

The present short paper, in honour of Tony and continuing our long, friendly and sometimes rivalrous collaboration, is another step towards harmonising our approaches.

Abstract This paper demonstrates that a wide range of the CSP operators, in particular parallel composition, hiding, general choice, interleaving, and the non-deterministic OR, can be represented by confluent unfolding to a normal form. The relevant normal form is an enrichment of the CSP choice construction by the inclusion of non-determinism and silent actions. It is demonstrated that the majority of the equational laws presented by Hoare for these operators are valid not only for the failures equivalence but even for strong bisimilarity. This work is a prelude to embedding CSP in the bigraph model, a recent generic model for ubiquitous computing in which other process calculi have been faithfully embedded. The authors

M. Bundgaard (✉)
IT University of Copenhagen, Rued Langgaards Vej 7
e-mail: mikkelbu@itu.dk

R. Milner
University of Cambridge, 15 JJ Thomson Avenue

C.B. Jones et al. (eds.), *Reflections on the Work of C.A.R. Hoare*,
DOI 10.1007/978-1-84882-912-1_10,

hope by this means to elucidate the differences and similarities between CSP and other calculi. The present paper presents the main ideas of the embedding in the formalism of CSP itself, and makes no use of bigraphs in doing so.

10.1 Motivation

Over the past decade a topographical process model called *Bigraphs* [11] has been developed, aiming to provide a rigorous definitional platform for ubiquitous computing. A first priority has been to show how existing process calculi can be embedded faithfully in the bigraphical framework. This effort has been largely successful, and the effort on bigraphs is now broadening into the experimental modelling of real ubiquitous systems.

An exception to this success has, hitherto, been the attempt to accommodate CSP [7] within the bigraphical framework. Why has this seemed difficult? (Readers not familiar with bigraphs can safely skim, or even ignore, the rest of this section, since bigraphs are hardly mentioned thereafter.)

The difficulty is not due to the semantic treatment. CSP favours a preorder based upon the notions of refusals and failures, thus providing process specifications as well as fully defined processes. On the other hand, CCS [9] emphasises the equivalence relation of bisimilarity, relying on other means, such as an associated logic, to provide specification. However, this difference is no barrier to accommodating CSP-style specifications in the bigraphical framework, where both semantic treatments fit comfortably.

More significant are two features special to CSP: channel ownership and a large repertoire of operations on processes. Consider the latter first. The bigraph model is a symmetric partial monoidal (spm) category, and the main operations of parallel composition in both CCS and CSP can be modelled essentially by the tensor product, which is a structural operation central to such categories. However, it was not clear how to model other CSP operations, such as general choice or interleaving. It seemed that a more cumbersome categorical structure would be needed, and this would not do justice to the inherent simplicity of CSP. But the appearance is unfounded; by the device of *unfolding* – a special case of parametric recursion – these operations (many, perhaps all) can be defined by reduction to a normal form, a device present in the bigraph model.

Turning to channel ownership: In CSP, one can maintain the distinction among the channel-sets owned by several processes by careful limitation of the use of non-injective renaming; for example, in his book [7] Hoare uses process labelling. In bigraphs it appears that similar control can be exercised by careful restriction of the use of substitutions, which are themselves elementary bigraphs. This is achieved by defining a so-called *sorting*, a device inspired by many-sorted algebra to determine a sub-spm-category of bigraphs for any particular application.

In a future paper we shall identify the sorted bigraphical model for CSP. Here we confine ourselves to the representation of CSP operators by unfolding, which can be presented independently of bigraphs.

10.2 Outline and Disclaimer

As we have already declared, we hope in a future paper to represent CSP as a bigraphical reactive system. Here, we wish to demonstrate the complementarity between the CSP approach and one that features bisimilarity. We avoid any judgement that one or the other approach is superior. Our main focus here is upon finding how the richly various set of CSP operators can be defined so as to harmonise with bisimilarity.

Let us make explicit the differing concerns of the two approaches. CSP defines the *failures* preorder that allows specifications, as well as their refinement into implementations, to be expressed within a single syntactic framework. The emphasis is upon refinement. On the other hand, the aim in CCS [9] is to characterise the notion of *process* as an equivalence class of process expressions, respecting the order in which non-deterministic choices are made as the process progresses. This equivalence relation is the (strong) bisimilarity – introduced by Park [12], an improvement on the equivalence originally given for CCS.

Bisimilarity is a congruence, i.e. preserved by syntactic context. Furthermore bisimilarity is also preserved by the transition relation between processes. This latter property – preservation by transition – is not satisfied by the CSP failures preorder or its variants; it could not be, since these preorders allow a specification to be refined into process expressions that differ in when they make non-deterministic choices. To achieve complementarity between these approaches we must, as far as possible, define any CSP operator $\textsc{op}$ to 'make sense' for bisimilarity; i.e. (for binary $\textsc{op}$) if $P_1 \sim Q_1$ and $P_2 \sim Q_2$ then $\textsc{op}(P_1, P_2) \sim \textsc{op}(Q_1, Q_2)$. We believe that this can be achieved for all the operators; here we shall ensure it for a selection of them. Moreover, the equational laws of CSP declared in Hoare's book for the operators we examine (except those involving $\sqcap$, non-deterministic 'or') are almost all satisfied not just for failures equivalence, but for strong bisimilarity.

Now, since the failures preorder includes strong bisimilarity, the preorder can be understood to be over processes themselves, not only over the expressions that denote them. It is therefore possible to combine the theories of CCS and CSP.

To define the CSP operators over processes, we shall work with a new head normal form. This will be based upon a generalisation of the CSP choice construction. We can then define the operators quite simply, using the *unfolding* of process expressions. This notion of unfolding (related to that already studied for bigraphs, see [11]) turns out to be confluent. Moreover, the equivalence induced by unfolding is closely related to bisimilarity, even coinciding with it in the absence of recursively defined processes.

Roscoe [15] has already defined a head normal form for CSP, and thence a full normal form following De Nicola [5]. These forms depend crucially upon the way

$\sqcap$ (non-deterministic 'or') distributes over other operators. Thus, at least for finite processes (those without recursion), two process expressions in normal form are essentially identical if and only if they are *failures-equivalent*.[1] However, our purpose is to achieve a similar result for *bisimilarity equivalence*, where we regard non-deterministic 'or' as an action that does not in general commute with other actions. We therefore unfold the $\sqcap$ operator in the same way as the other operators.

Let us repeat: the failures model and the notion of bisimilarity are not in competition; each has a rationale with independent value.

10.3 CSP with Enriched Syntax

Recall the well-known CSP syntax, employing several binary operators. The constructions were designed to introduce the phenomena of choice, concurrency, non-determinism, hiding, etc., one-by-one.

Channel names $x, y, \ldots$ (also called channels) are drawn from an infinite vocabulary $\mathcal{X}$. Each process P has a finite[2] alphabet $\alpha P \subset \mathcal{X}$. CSP has many process constructions, often binary operators. We shall not model them all here; for example, we shall not consider the sequential composition $P;\ Q$ nor the interrupt operator $P \bigtriangleup Q$. We consider the following six process constructions, and conjecture that our treatment can be extended to some or all of the others:

P, Q	$::=$		
	$(x_1 \to P_1 \mid \cdots \mid x_n \to P_n)$	choice	$\alpha P = \alpha P_i \supseteq \{x_1, \ldots, x_n\}$ (x_i distinct)
	$P_1 \parallel P_2$	parallel	$\alpha P = \alpha P_1 \cup \alpha P_2$
	$Q \setminus Y$	hiding	$\alpha P = \alpha Q \setminus Y$
	$P_1 \,\Box\, P_2$	general choice	$\alpha P = \alpha P_1 = \alpha P_2$
	$P_1 \,\vert\vert\vert\, P_2$	interleave	$\alpha P = \alpha P_1 = \alpha P_2$
	$P_1 \sqcap P_2$	'or'	$\alpha P = \alpha P_1 = \alpha P_2$

The n-ary choice construction is deterministic in the sense that there is a unique choice of action for each channel $x \in \alpha P$.

The important intuition of parallel composition $P \parallel Q$ is that on the shared channels $x \in \alpha P \cap \alpha Q$ the actions of P and Q are synchronised, while on unshared channels only the unique possessor acts, the other remain unchanged. Thus the parallel composition preserves determinism.

The other operators introduce non-determinism in various ways. In particular, the hiding construction $Q \setminus Y$ renders the actions in $\alpha Q \cap Y$ unobservable. Hence the actions are able to occur without further participants.

[1] Roscoe's normal form also caters explicitly for divergence; this lies beyond the scope of our paper.

[2] For simplicity, we assume alphabets to be finite. Later work may relax this restriction.

In his book, Hoare avoids formalising the operational behaviour of CSP. It has been formalised by others, probably first by Brookes et al. [3], employing the structural operational semantics pioneered by Plotkin [13]. However, we adopt a different approach here, defining the behaviour by unfolding each syntactic construction to a *head normal form.* As we shall see, this unfolding is a confluent reduction system. Indeed, for finite CSP (i.e. no user-defined recursions) this unfolding terminates in a *normal form*; moreover, two process terms unfold to the same normal form if and only if they are strongly bisimilar.

In the next section we shall define how each of the several operators unfolds. But first we have to define our head normal forms. To understand our definition better, it is helpful to recall an equation that records how parallel composition 'unfolds' into a choice among alternatives. It was first introduced as a law [8], and later became the expansion theorem of CCS [9]. Recall that the parallel composition of two CCS processes is written $P \mid Q$, and that this allows P and Q each to perform an input action x or output action $\overline{x}$ independently or to communicate – creating a hidden action τ – if P can do x and Q do $\overline{x}$ or vice versa. Thus interaction in CCS involves exactly two participants, unlike in CSP.

The expansion theorem then captures the behaviour of the parallel composition of two 'summations' (or choice forms, in CSP terminology), expressing it again as a summation. Each summand takes the form $\mu \cdot P$, where the prefix μ takes the form x, $\overline{x}$ or τ. (A summand $\mu \cdot P$ corresponds to a choice element $\mu \rightarrow P$ in CSP.) We declare that $\overline{\overline{x}} = x$. Letting $P = \sum_i \lambda_i \cdot P_i$ and $Q = \sum_j \mu_j \cdot Q_j$ the expansion theorem asserts:

$$\sum_i \lambda_i \cdot P_i \Big| \sum_j \mu_j \cdot Q_j \quad \sim \quad \sum_i \lambda_i \cdot (P_i \mid Q) + \sum_j \mu_j \cdot (P \mid Q_j) + \sum_{\lambda_i = \overline{\mu_j}} \tau \cdot (P_i \mid Q_j)$$

where $\sim$ denotes strong equivalence, later improved to strong bisimilarity by Park [12].

This theorem arose from the semantics of CCS defined by structured operational semantics [13], i.e. by an inference system over labelled transitions. But it suggests another way to formulate the semantics. Let us convert the expansion theorem into a rewriting rule

$$\sum_i \lambda_i \cdot P_i \Big| \sum_j \mu_j \cdot Q_j \quad \hookrightarrow \quad \sum_i \lambda_i \cdot (P_i \mid Q) + \sum_j \mu_j \cdot (P \mid Q_j) + \sum_{\lambda_i = \overline{\mu_j}} \tau \cdot (P_i \mid Q_j)$$

where the directed relation $\hookrightarrow$ unfolds a parallel composition into a summation. CCS would also need such an unfolding rule for restriction (hiding); then bisimilarity, and other semantic equivalences or preorders, can be defined in terms of such rules.

We propose to adopt this approach in the bigraph model; it will be especially useful for process calculi like CSP which have many operators, each giving rise to an unfolding rule. We shall do this here for CSP directly, in terms of its familiar syntax.

Thus we avoid further reference to bigraphs, but we pave the way for a simple embedding of CSP in bigraphs, allowing the insights of CSP to be conferred upon other calculi.

For this to work, we must enrich the choice construction

$$P = (\mu_1 \rightarrow P_1 \mid \cdots \mid \mu_n \rightarrow P_n)$$

to allow non-determinism; this entails allowing the actions μ_i to be not necessarily distinct, and also to be drawn from $\alpha P \cup \{\tau\}$, where τ represents a hidden action. For simplicity, since the order of choices is immaterial, we shall define $\mathsf{Procsets}_X$ to mean the set of finite[3] sets of process expressions over alphabet X, and enrich the choice construction to a so-called *head normal form* (hnf):

$$P = F : \alpha P \cup \{\tau\} \longrightarrow \mathsf{Procsets}_{\alpha P}$$

Thus a hnf F is a function mapping each action $\mu \in \alpha P \cup \{\tau\}$ to a finite set of possible successor processes. For example, the hnf

$$F : x \mapsto \{P_1, P_2\}, y \mapsto \{Q\}, \tau \mapsto \{R_1, R_2\}$$

could be written in an extension of the CSP choice notation as

$$F = (x \rightarrow P_1 \mid x \rightarrow P_2 \mid y \rightarrow Q \mid \tau \rightarrow R_1 \mid \tau \rightarrow R_2)$$

We conjecture that sequential composition $P; Q$ can be treated by introducing a special hnf $\text{S}\textsc{kip}_X$, for each alphabet X, to represent successful termination. We define a process P to be in *normal form* if and only if the only constructions in P are enriched choices.

Definition 1 (Normal Form) A process P is a *normal form* iff the only process operators in P are enriched choices.

In the rest of the paper we will present several relations on CSP terms, and we will tacitly assume that these relations only relate terms with the same alphabet.

10.4 Unfolding

We now define all the CSP operators listed above by means of unfolding to hnfs. Let us use F, G, H to range over hnfs, P, Q, R over arbitrary processes, and S, T over finite sets of processes. Furthermore we extend the operators to sets of processes by defining, for example,

$$P \parallel S \stackrel{\text{def}}{=} \{P \parallel Q : Q \in S\} \qquad \text{and} \qquad S \parallel T \stackrel{\text{def}}{=} \{P \parallel Q : P \in S, Q \in T\}$$

[3] Here again, it may be possible to remove the finiteness constraint for some purposes.

For each operator we give a single axiom that defines its unfolding for arguments that are themselves hnfs. In the following we assume $\alpha F = X$ and $\alpha G = Y$, and to avoid too many parentheses we assume that set union $\cup$ binds less tightly than all the operators. Note that $X = Y$ in the case of the operators $\Box$ (general choice), $|||$ (interleaving) and $\sqcap$ (or).

$$F \parallel G \hookrightarrow H \text{ where } H(z) = \begin{cases} F(z) \parallel G & (z \in X \setminus Y) \\ F \parallel G(z) & (z \in Y \setminus X) \\ F(z) \parallel G(z) & (z \in X \cap Y) \end{cases}$$
$$\text{and } H(\tau) = F(\tau) \parallel G \cup F \parallel G(\tau)$$

$$F \Box G \hookrightarrow H \text{ where } H(x) = F(x) \cup G(x) \quad (x \in X)$$
$$\text{and } H(\tau) = F(\tau) \Box G \cup F \Box G(\tau)$$

$$F \,|||\, G \hookrightarrow H \text{ where } H(\mu) = F(\mu) \,|||\, G \cup F \,|||\, G(\mu) \quad (\mu \in X \cup \{\tau\})$$

$$F \setminus Z \hookrightarrow H \text{ where } H(x) = F(x) \setminus Z \quad (x \in X \setminus Z)$$
$$\text{and } H(\tau) = F(\tau) \setminus Z \cup \textstyle\bigcup_{x \in X \cap Z} F(x) \setminus Z$$

$$F \sqcap G \hookrightarrow H \text{ where } H(\mu) = F(\mu) \cup G(\mu) \quad (\mu \in X \cup \{\tau\})$$

In addition, we allow unfolding to occur in any context; that is:

$$\text{for any process context } \mathcal{C}[\cdot], \text{ if } P \hookrightarrow P' \text{ then } \mathcal{C}[P] \hookrightarrow \mathcal{C}[P']$$

For finite CSP, this defines unfolding fully. Infinite CSP allows mutually recursive definitions of any number of process identifiers. For each such identifier A there is a unique defining expression P_{A}, and the definition augments the unfolding operation with the axiom

$$\mathsf{A} \hookrightarrow P_{\mathsf{A}}$$

Each P_{A} may contain occurrences of any of the process identifiers, but these occurrences must be guarded – i.e. must be within the body of some enriched choice construction.

Now recall that a (directed) relation $\rightarrow$ is *confluent* if, whenever $a \rightarrow^* a_1$ and $a \rightarrow^* a_2$, then there exists a' such that $a_1 \rightarrow^* a'$ and $a_2 \rightarrow^* a'$.

Theorem 1 (Confluence) *The unfolding relation $\hookrightarrow$ is confluent.*

Proof The proof will be given fully in a later paper. Intuitively, it relies on the intuition that unfolding loses none of the non-determinism represented in each operation.

In summary, the proof uses a generalisation of the *Parallel Moves Lemma* for term rewriting, which may be found as Lemma 4.3.3 in [17]. This asserts that a reduction relation on terms is confluent provided its rules are left-linear (no repeated parameter variables on the left-hand side of a rule) and non-overlapping (no preemption of one rule by another). These conditions are satisfied by our set of unfolding rules. The lemma is slightly generalised since it originally applies to terms, whose syntax consists of strings of symbols, and we have introduced the syntax of enriched choice constructions, which are finite maps to sets. □

Although unfolding is confluent, it may fail to terminate. One reason is the recursive unfolding of process identifiers; indeed, the single recursive rule $\mathsf{A} \hookrightarrow \{x \mapsto \{\mathsf{A}\}\}$ repeats the action x ad infinitum. Perhaps surprisingly, this is the only reason for non-termination. To see this, we first define strong normalisation.

Definition 2 (Strong Normalisation) A process P is *strongly normalising* if it has no infinite unfolding.

Theorem 2 (Strong Normalisation) *Recursion-free processes are strongly normalising.*

Proof In outline, we assign to each term a multiset, consisting of the heights of all the process operators in the term, except for enriched choice operators. For instance, the term

$$((F \parallel F) \,|||\, F) \,\square\, ((F \parallel F) \,|||\, F)$$

– where F is an empty hnf – will be assigned the multiset $\{2,2,3,3,4\}$, since there are two operator occurrences (both $\parallel$) with height 2, two (both $|||$) with height 3, and one ($\square$) with height 4. (For convenience, leaves have height 1.)

Now it is known [4] that if an ordering on a set C is well founded, then so is its extension to an ordering on finite multisets over C. Here, take C to be the natural numbers; then the ordering extends to finite multisets as follows: $B \succ B'$ if B' can be obtained from B by replacing some elements by finitely many smaller elements.

It remains to prove that every unfolding strictly decreases this ordering. Indeed, an unfolding does not increase the height of a term; and it replaces a single process operator with a finite number of process operators, but of smaller height. □

For the next section we shall need to use the transitive reflexive closure of unfolding, written $\hookrightarrow^*$. We shall also need the transitive reflexive symmetric closure of unfolding which we will call structural congruence.

Definition 3 (Structural Congruence) *Structural congruence*, denoted by $\equiv$, is the transitive reflexive symmetric closure of unfolding $(\hookleftarrow \cup \hookrightarrow)^*$.

This concludes the properties of unfolding that we need.

10.5 Bisimilarity

We shall now introduce transition relations labelled by actions $\mathcal{X} \cup \{\tau\}$; we shall let μ range over these labels. The simplest case is for a hnf F; we want $F \searrow_{\mu} P'$ whenever $P' \in F(\mu)$. However, we want transitions for an arbitrary process term P, not necessarily a hnf; so we allow P to unfold into a hnf first. Thus transitions are defined by the following rule:

$$\frac{P \hookrightarrow^* F \qquad P' \in F(\mu)}{P \searrow_\mu P'}$$

Having defined transitions, we can now define strong bisimilarity in the usual way.

Definition 4 (Bisimulation, Bisimilarity) A strong bisimulation is a binary relation $\mathcal{R}$ over processes such that, whenever $(P, Q) \in \mathcal{R}$ and $P \searrow_\mu P'$ then there exists Q' such that $Q \searrow_\mu Q'$ and $(P', Q') \in \mathcal{R}$, and conversely when $Q \searrow_\mu Q'$ then there exists P' such that $P \searrow_\mu P'$ and $(P', Q') \in \mathcal{R}$. Bisimilarity, denoted by $\sim$, is the largest bisimulation; that is, it is the union of all bisimulations.

A weaker equivalence relation, *weak bisimilarity*, places less constraint upon τ actions $P \searrow_\tau P'$; for example, two τ actions in sequence are equivalent to one. We are only concerned here with the strong version; its role is to provide one answer to the question 'What is a process?'; the answer is 'A bisimilarity-class of process expressions'. This recalls the definition of a natural number, attributed to Bertrand Russell, as 'an equivalence class of sets under bijection'.

CSP places emphasis on the failures preorder on process expressions; this is – intentionally – much weaker than strong bisimilarity, and as a preorder it represents the way in which a process may be said to satisfy a specification. A point relevant to the present work is that, since the failures preorder includes the strong bisimilarity equivalence, it can be understood as a relation on *processes*, i.e. bisimilarity classes of process expressions, rather than on the process expressions themselves. In other words, the CSP semantics can be factored into two; first we determine which expressions denote the same process, and second we determine whether one process *satisfies* or *implements* another considered as a specification.

The remainder of this paper therefore has two concerns: First, how does (strong) bisimilarity relate to structural congruence as we have defined it, namely as the transitive reflexive symmetric closure of unfolding? Second, which of the well-known equations of CSP – as for instance listed in Hoare [7] – already hold for bisimilarity, and which hold only for failures equivalence?

Our first result is that bisimilarity is no stronger than structural congruence:

Theorem 3 (Bisimilarity Includes Structural Congruence) $\equiv \subseteq \sim$.

Proof It is enough to show that $\equiv$ is a bisimulation, and this is straightforward. □

The second result is more surprising, since we are used to thinking of structural congruence as a demanding (i.e. small) congruence. But the version of structural congruence introduced here places more emphasis upon similar *behaviour*, and less upon *syntactic* similarity. In fact:

Theorem 4 (Structural and Behavioural Congruence) *In finite (i.e. recursion-free) CSP, structural congruence and strong bisimilarity coincide; that is,* $\equiv = \sim$.

Proof It only remains to prove that $\sim \subseteq \equiv$. Unfolding in finite CSP is both confluent and strongly normalising, so each term unfolds uniquely to a normal form (i.e. containing no process constructions except for enriched choice). Hence it is enough to prove that if two normal forms are bisimilar, they are structurally congruent. This can be proved by induction on the structure of normal forms. □

Why does this result fail in the presence of recursion? It is enough to find two recursively defined processes that are bisimilar but not structurally congruent. This is easy; consider the two recursive definitions

$$\mathsf{A} \hookrightarrow \{x \mapsto \{\mathsf{A}\}\} \text{ and } \mathsf{B} \hookrightarrow \{x \mapsto \{\mathsf{B}\}\}$$

They are not structurally congruent, since they never unfold to the same process, but they are bisimilar; indeed, consider the singleton bisimulation $\{(\mathsf{A}, \mathsf{B})\}$.

Since bisimilarity does not coincide with structural congruence in the presence of recursion, we have to prove it to be a congruence by other means. In fact we must prove that it is preserved by each of the operators. This, though a little tedious, is straightforward.

Theorem 5 (Congruence of Bisimilarity) *Strong bisimilarity is a congruence.*

Proof (outline) We shall be content to present the case that one operator, $\|$, preserves bisimilarity. The proof of congruence of the other operators follows the same template.

We wish to prove that if $P_1 \sim P_2$ then $P_1 \| Q \sim P_2 \| Q$. For this, it is enough to prove that $\mathcal{B} \stackrel{\text{def}}{=} \{(P_1 \| Q, P_2 \| Q) \mid P_1 \sim P_2\}$ is a bisimulation.

Let $P_1 \| Q \searrow_\mu R_1$. We must find R_2 such that $P_2 \| Q \searrow_\mu R_2$ and $(R_1, R_2) \in \mathcal{B}$. Now by definition of transition we have $P_1 \| Q \hookrightarrow^* H$, with $R_1 \in H(\mu)$.

We consider only the case in which $\mu = z \in \alpha P_1 \setminus \alpha Q$ (other cases are similar). By the definition of unfolding for $\|$, we have $P_1 \hookrightarrow^* F_1$ and $Q \hookrightarrow^* G$, with $H(z) = F_1(z) \| G$, and $R_1 = P_1' \| G$ where $P_1' \in F_1(z)$.

From this we first deduce that $P_1 \searrow_z P_1'$. But $P_1 \sim P_2$, so there exists P_2' such that $P_2 \searrow_z P_2'$ and $P_1' \sim P_2'$. This implies that $P_2 \hookrightarrow^* F_2$, with $P_2' \in F_2(z)$.

It follows that $P_2 \| Q \hookrightarrow^* F_2 \| G$ and $F_2 \| G \hookrightarrow H'$ for some (unique) H'; so, by the transition rule, $P_2 \| Q \searrow_z R_2'$ for any R_2' in $H'(z)$. But $H'(z) = F_2(z) \| G$ in this case, and $P_2' \| G$ is in $F_2(z) \| G$. Hence $P_2 \| Q \searrow_z P_2' \| G$. So we are done by taking R_2 to be $P_2' \| G$. □

What are we to make of our 'discovery' that, for finite CSP, bisimilarity ($\sim$) agrees with what we have called structural congruence ($\equiv$)? We have to admit that there is no unique notion of structure – and hence of structural congruence – for processes. This amounts to saying that, given a syntax of process terms, like CSP or CCS or ACP [2], there is no unique congruence on its terms such that we all agree that its congruence classes are processes. For some people, process structure involves a causal relationship among actions; in that case a process in which an action x causes an action y differs from one in which x merely precedes y. For other people, process structure will involve duration of action or locality of agents, and so on.

Our definition of unfolding commits us to an abstract notion of process in which causality, timing and placing are all ignored; the only remaining structure is that of non-determinism, recording the possible transitions in any state, whether or not under control of the process's environment. This structure is captured for finite CSP by the congruence based upon unfolding, and – as we have seen – strong bisimilarity equally captures it.

How does this generalise to infinite CSP, where recursive definitions enable infinite unfolding? An infinitely proceeding process, one that enables an infinite sequence

$$P_1 \searrow_{\mu_1} P_2 \searrow_{\mu_2} P_3 \searrow_{\mu_3} \cdots\cdots$$

of transitions, corresponds closely to an infinite chain

$$S_1 \ni S_2 \ni S_3 \ni \cdots\cdots$$

of inverse membership of sets, in the theory of non-well-founded sets. Peter Aczel, in his book [1], argues that equality of such sets coincides with bisimilarity, i.e. it is the largest symmetric relation $\mathcal{R}$ such that

$$\text{if } S \mathrel{\mathcal{R}} T \text{ and } S' \in S, \text{ then } S' \mathrel{\mathcal{R}} T' \text{ for some } T' \in T$$

The bisimilarity of process terms differs only in that transition is a little more complex than inverse membership; indeed the relation $\ni$ is replaced by the compound relation $\hookrightarrow^{*}\ni$. Therefore, even for infinite CSP, we are justified in interpreting bisimilarity as a structural congruence.

10.6 Equational Theory

In this section we examine the equational laws of CSP as given in Hoare's book [7], for concurrency ($\|$), general choice ($\Box$), hiding ($\backslash Z$), interleaving ($|||$) and non-deterministic 'or' ($\sqcap$). They all hold when equality is interpreted as failures equivalence; that is the intention in CSP. We indicate which of them hold also for strong bisimilarity ($\sim$); in fact, we tag with the symbol $\div$ all those – a minority – which do *not* so hold. As is well known, the discrepancy between these two interpretations is largely due to the τ-transitions, which matter more in strong bisimilarity than in the failures model. They are relevant to the failures model in a negative sense: a *failure* of P is a pair (t, S), where $t \in \mathcal{X}^*$ and $S \subseteq \mathcal{X}$, such that P can perform t to reach a state in which no τ-transitions are possible and in which no action in S can be performed.

Each law that holds for strong bisimilarity, $\sim$, can be established by exhibiting a suitable bisimulation; we omit these to avoid boring the reader. As mentioned above, a law is tagged with $\div$ if it does not hold for $\sim$, and in each case we sketch a concrete counter-example. Many of these laws involve the non-deterministic 'or' ($\sqcap$); we will discuss this a little further at the end of this section.

Of course it has long been known that such laws do not hold for $\sim$. The point of this section is to add detail to our claim that the theory of CSP can be factorised into two complementary parts: first, we quotient the class of CSP expressions by the congruence $\sim$, calling each congruence class a *process*, and we identify an algebraic theory of these processes; second, we assert further laws that hold for the failures preorder over processes as so defined.

For the purpose of this section, let us first define the well-known CSP processes $\mathtt{STOP}_X$ and $\mathtt{RUN}_X$ as hnfs:

$$\mathtt{STOP}_X \stackrel{\Delta}{=} \{\mu \mapsto \emptyset \mid \mu \in X \cup \{\tau\}\}$$
$$\mathtt{RUN}_X \stackrel{\Delta}{=} \{x \mapsto \{\mathtt{RUN}_X\} \mid x \in X\} \cup \{\tau \mapsto \emptyset\}$$

As described in [7], $\mathtt{STOP}_X$ is the process with alphabet X which never actually engages in any of the events of X. On the other hand $\mathtt{RUN}_X$ is the process which at all times can engage in any event of its alphabet X. We shall discuss these definitions further at the end of the section.

In Table 10.1 we list the equational laws for $\|$ as presented in section 2.3.1 in [7]. We note that all the laws hold for $\sim$ except for *L3A*. The reason for the latter is that if P can perform a τ-transition then $P \parallel \mathtt{STOP}_{\alpha P}$ can perform one, whereas $\mathtt{STOP}_{\alpha P}$ cannot.

In Table 10.2 we list the equational laws for the general choice $\Box$ from section 3.3.1. For this operator several of the laws do not hold for $\sim$. For *L*1, the reason is that the process $P \Box P$ can possibly perform two τ-transitions when P can only perform one.

As expected the laws relating $\Box$ and $\sqcap$ do not hold for $\sim$. For *L*5, the left-hand side must choose either $P(a)$ or $Q(a)$ when performing a shared event a whereas this choice is 'delayed' in the right-hand side. For *L*6, if $P \searrow_\tau P'$ then the left-hand side may become $P' \Box (Q \sqcap R)$, while the right-hand side becomes either $P' \Box Q$ or $P' \Box R$. Similarly, we can find a counter-example to *L*7 by letting Q perform a τ-transition.

Table 10.1 Equational laws for $\|$ from section 2.3.1 in [7]

*L*1	$P \parallel Q = Q \parallel P$	
*L*2	$P \parallel (Q \parallel R) = (P \parallel Q) \parallel R$	
L3A	$P \parallel \mathtt{STOP}_{\alpha P} = \mathtt{STOP}_{\alpha P}$	÷
L3B	$P \parallel \mathtt{RUN}_{\alpha P} = P$	
Let $a \in (\alpha P \setminus \alpha Q)$, $b \in (\alpha Q \setminus \alpha P)$, and $\{c, d\} \subseteq (\alpha P \cap \alpha Q)$.		
L4A	$(c \to P) \parallel (c \to Q) = c \to (P \parallel Q)$	
L4B	$(c \to P) \parallel (d \to Q) = \mathtt{STOP}$ if $c \neq d$	
L5A	$(a \to P) \parallel (c \to Q) = a \to (P \parallel (c \to Q))$	
L5B	$(c \to P) \parallel (b \to Q) = b \to ((c \to P) \parallel Q)$	
*L*6	$(a \to P) \parallel (b \to Q) = (a \to (P \parallel (b \to Q)) \mid b \to ((a \to P) \parallel Q))$	
Let $P = (x : X \to P(x))$ and $Q = (y : Y \to Q(y))$.		
*L*7	$(P \parallel Q) = (z : Z \to P' \parallel Q')$ where $\begin{cases} Z = (X \cap Y) \cup (X \setminus \alpha Q) \cup (Y \setminus \alpha P) \\ P' = P(z) \text{ if } z \in X \text{ otherwise } P' = P \\ Q' = Q(z) \text{ if } z \in Y \text{ otherwise } Q' = Q. \end{cases}$	

Table 10.2 Equational laws for $\Box$ from section 3.3.1 in [7]

$L1$	$P \Box P = P$	$\div$
$L2$	$P \Box Q = Q \Box P$	
$L3$	$P \Box (Q \Box R) = (P \Box Q) \Box R$	
$L4$	$P \Box \mathtt{STOP} = P$	
$L5$	$(x : X \rightarrow P(x)) \Box (y : Y \rightarrow Q(y)) = (z : (X \cup Y) \rightarrow \begin{cases} P(z) & \text{if } z \in (X \setminus Y) \\ Q(z) & \text{if } z \in (Y \setminus X) \\ P(z) \sqcap Q(z) & \text{if } z \in (X \cap Y) \end{cases}$	$\div$
$L6$	$P \Box (Q \sqcap R) = (P \Box Q) \sqcap (P \Box R)$	$\div$
$L7$	$P \sqcap (Q \Box R) = (P \sqcap Q) \Box (P \sqcap R)$	$\div$

Table 10.3 Equational laws for $\setminus$ from section 3.5.1 in [7]

$L1$	$P \setminus \{\} = P$	
$L2$	$(P \setminus Y) \setminus Z = P \setminus (Y \cup Z)$	
$L3$	$(P \sqcap Q) \setminus Z = (P \setminus Z) \sqcap (Q \setminus Z)$	
$L4$	$\mathtt{STOP}_X \setminus Z = \mathtt{STOP}_{X \setminus Z}$	
$L5$	$(x \rightarrow P) \setminus Z = \begin{cases} x \rightarrow (P \setminus Z) & \text{if } x \notin Z \\ P \setminus Z & \text{if } x \in Z \end{cases}$	$\div$
$L6$	If $\alpha P \cap \alpha Q \cap \alpha Z = \{\}$, then$(P \parallel Q) \setminus Z = (P \setminus Z) \parallel (Q \setminus Z)$	
$L8$	If $Y \cap Z = \{\}$, then$(x : Y \rightarrow P(x)) \setminus Z = (x : Y \rightarrow (P(x) \setminus Z))$	
$L9$	If $Y \subseteq Z$, and Y is finite and not empty, then $(x : Y \rightarrow P(x)) \setminus Z = \sqcap_{x \in Y}(P(x) \setminus Z)$	$\div$

Table 10.4 Equational laws for $|||$ from section 3.6.1 in [7]

$L1$	$P \,|||\, (Q \sqcap R) = (P \,|||\, Q) \sqcap (P \,|||\, R)$	$\div$
$L2$	$P \,|||\, Q = Q \,|||\, P$	
$L3$	$P \,|||\, (Q \,|||\, R) = (P \,|||\, Q) \,|||\, R$	
$L4$	$P \,|||\, \mathtt{STOP} = P$	
$L5$	$P \,|||\, \mathtt{RUN} = \mathtt{RUN}$ Provided P does not diverge	$\div$
$L6$	$(x \rightarrow P) \,|||\, (y \rightarrow Q) = (x \rightarrow (P \,|||\, (y \rightarrow Q))) \Box (y \rightarrow ((x \rightarrow P) \,|||\, Q))$	
$L7$	*If* $P = (x : X \rightarrow P(x))$ and $Q = (y : Y \rightarrow Q(y))$ then $P \,|||\, Q = (x : X \rightarrow (P(x) \,|||\, Q)) \Box (y : Y \rightarrow (P \,|||\, Q(y)))$	

Table 10.3 contains the laws governing the hiding operator. All of the laws hold for $\sim$, except for two. For $L5$, suppose that the choice x is hidden by Z, i.e. $x \in Z$. Then the left-hand side can perform a τ-transition to become $P \setminus Z$, but this τ-transition is not possible for the right-hand side of the equation. For $L9$ we tacitly assume that we have generalised the binary non-deterministic 'or' operator into an n-ary operator. The law contravenes $\sim$ for the same reason as $L5$.

Table 10.4 contains the laws for the interleaving operator. As expected the law $L1$ does not hold for $\sim$. A simple counter-example can be constructed by making P perform any transition. For $L5$, $P \,|||\, \mathtt{RUN}$ can possibly perform a τ-transition (if P can) which cannot be matched by $\mathtt{RUN}$.

Table 10.5 Equational laws for $\sqcap$ from section 3.2.1 in [7]

$L1$	$P \sqcap P = P$	
$L2$	$P \sqcap Q = Q \sqcap P$	
$L3$	$P \sqcap (Q \sqcap R) = (P \sqcap Q) \sqcap R$	
$L4$	$x \to (P \sqcap Q) = (x \to P) \sqcap (x \to Q)$	$\div$
$L5$	$(x : X \to (P(x) \sqcap Q(x))) = (x : X \to P(x)) \sqcap (x : X \to Q(x))$	$\div$
$L6$	$P \parallel (Q \sqcap R) = (P \parallel Q) \sqcap (P \parallel R)$	$\div$
$L7$	$(P \sqcap Q) \parallel R = (P \parallel R) \sqcap (Q \parallel R)$	$\div$

Finally, Table 10.5 contains the laws for non-deterministic 'or'. Due to the simple unfolding rule for $\sqcap$, we are in fact able to prove that the three first laws hold even for structural congruence ($\equiv$), by reducing both sides to the same hnf. However, laws $L4$ and $L5$ do not hold for $\sim$ since the left-hand side has not made the choice between the processes, whereas the choice has been made in the right-hand side. For laws $L6$ and $L7$ we can find simple counter-examples by letting respectively P or R perform a transition. This will leave the non-deterministic 'or' unchanged in the left-hand side of the equation, but enforce a choice in the right-hand side.

We note that we cannot redefine $\sqcap$ in such a way that these laws hold for $\sim$. That is because the laws take advantage of the properties of the failures preorder, which intentionally conflates what may be regarded as two kinds of non-determinism: the dynamic kind arising from uncontrolled decisions at run-time, and the static kind arising from lack of knowledge of what process is running. The latter kind is what lies behind the failures preorder. But bisimilarity aims to define the notion of non-deterministic process (irrespective of how much we know about it), so it is only concerned with the former kind.

We conjecture that further CSP operators – for example sequential composition and interrupt – are amenable to definition by unfolding, and that certain of the laws they satisfy will hold for $\sim$. Recall our conjecture that the constant $\mathtt{SKIP}_X$, essential for sequential composition, can be treated as a special normal form, whose character is determined by unfolding rules. We also conjecture that both $\mathtt{STOP}_X$ and $\mathtt{RUN}_X$, which we defined above, can instead be treated as special normal form constants, in such a way that the laws listed for them will all hold for $\sim$.

10.7 Conclusion

This paper is motivated by the wish to represent CSP as a bigraphical reactive system. This is to ensure that the bigraph model, which aspires to be a generic framework for process modelling, can indeed represent the phenomena that are special to CSP. This will not only add validity to the bigraph model; it will also allow other bigraphical reactive systems to benefit from the specific insights of CSP.

In this paper we have therefore handled some of CSP's repertoire of operators in a way that reflects how they will be defined in bigraphs, while remaining close to CSP's syntactic framework. In bigraphs, we expect to define these operators by generalising a notion of unfolding already present in bigraphs (see [11]). This generalisation has already been mooted, and the CSP encoding will add motivation for it.

Indeed, the work presented here suggests a class of unfolding relations for which unfolding in bigraphs is guaranteed to be confluent, though it is not yet clear how broad this class may be. After doing the present work the authors have become aware of Roscoe's [16] proposed definition for 'CSP-like' operators; it will be interesting to compare CSP-like operators with those that unfold confluently.

The second CSP phenomenon which we have mentioned, the ownership of channels, has not been discussed further in this paper. It will be handled in bigraphs by imposing a constraint on what bigraphs are admitted in the encoding. As mentioned in the motivation, such a constraint in bigraphs is called a *sorting*; a sorting is usually needed when encoding a calculus, because of the generality of bigraphical contexts.

Let us renew our claim that the present approach complements, rather than contravenes, the original presentation of CSP. It enriches the choice construction, making it non-deterministic. Hoare's original choice construction preserves determinism, thus allowing the phenomena of concurrency to be introduced one-by-one as the repertoire of operators is extended. But the original choice construction is still available as a special case of the enriched one. Also, our hnfs provide a simple formal understanding of many of CSP's wide range of operators, and a simple way to define the bisimilarity of CSP process expressions. As we have noted, most of CSP's equational properties, not involving $\sqcap$, hold not just for the failures preorder, but even for strong bisimilarity.

In doing this work we have gained a more intimate understanding of the power and beauty of CSP, such as cannot be gained by just reading about it. We would be grateful for any feedback from those who have worked closely with CSP, in the hope of a better integrated theory of concurrent processes.

References

1. Aczel, P.: Non-well-founded Sets, CSLI Lecture Notes 14. Center for the Study of Language and Information, Stanford University, Stanford, CA (1988).
2. Baeten, J., Weijland, W.P.: Process Algebra Cambridge University Press, (1990).
3. Brookes, S., Roscoe, A.W., Walker, D.J.: An operational semantics for CSP (Manuscript). Available from http://www.cs.cmu.edu/afs/cs.cmu.edu/user/brookes/www/papers/OperationalSemanticsCSP.pdf (1988).
4. Dershowitz, N., Manna, Z.: Proving termination with multiset orderings. Commun. ACM **22**(8), 465–476 (1979).
5. De Nicola, R.: Two complete axiom systems for a theory of communicating sequential processes. Inform. Control, **64**, 136–172 (1985).
6. Hoare, C.A.R.: Communicating sequential processes. Commun. ACM **21**(8), 666–777 (1978).
7. Hoare, C.A.R.: Communicating sequential processes. Prentice Hall (1985).

8. Milner, R.: Synthesis of Communicating Behaviour. Proc. 7th Symposium on Mathematical Foundations of Computer Science, Lecture Notes in Computer Science, vol. 64, Springer, Zakopane, Poland (1978).
9. Milner, R.: A Calculus of Communicating Systems. Lecture Notes in Computer Science, vol 92, Springer (1980).
10. Milner, R.: Communicating and Mobile Systems: the π-Calculus. Cambridge University Press (1999).
11. Milner, R.: The Space and Motion of Communicating Agents. Cambridge University Press (2009).
12. Park, D.: Concurrency and Automata on Infinite Sequences Proc. 5th GI-Conference on Theoretical Computer Science, Karlsruhe, Germany, March 23–25, Lecture Notes in Computer Science, vol. 104, Springer (1980).
13. Plotkin, G.D.: A structural approach to operational semantics. Report DAIMI-FN-19, Computer Science Department, Århus University, Denmark (1981). Reprinted as [14].
14. Plotkin, G.D.: A structural approach to operational semantics. J. Logic Algebra. Program. **60–61**, 17–139 (2004).
15. Roscoe, A.W.: The Theory and Practice of Concurrency. Prentice Hall (1998); revised (2005).
16. Roscoe, A.W.: On the expressiveness of CSP, Submitted for publication.
17. TeReSe, Term Rewriting Systems. Cambridge Tracts in Theoretical Computer Science 55. Cambridge University Press (2003).

Chapter 11
Quicksort: Combining Concurrency, Recursion, and Mutable Data Structures

David Kitchin, Adrian Quark, and Jayadev Misra

Abstract Quicksort (Commun. ACM 4(7):321–322, 1961) remains one of the most studied algorithms in computer science. It is important not only as a practical sorting method, but also as a splendid teaching aid for introducing recursion and systematic algorithm development. The algorithm has been studied extensively; so, it is natural to assume that everything that needs to be said about it has already been said. Yet, in attempting to code it using a recent programming language of our design, we discovered that its structure is more clearly expressed as a concurrent program that manipulates a shared mutable store, without any locking or explicit synchronization. In this paper, we describe the essential aspects of our programming language Orc (Proceedings of FMOODS/FORTE, vol. 5522 of *LNCS*, pp. 1–25. Springer 2009), show a number of examples that combine its features in various forms, and then develop a concise description of Quicksort. We hope to highlight the importance of including concurrency, recursion and mutability within a single theory.

11.1 Introduction

Quicksort [5] remains one of the most studied algorithms in computer science. Its performance has been studied extensively by Knuth [11] and Sedgewick [17] in particular. A variety of implementations exist on different architectures, and many variants of Quicksort have been developed that improve its performance for specific platforms.

D. Kitchin
University of Texas at Austin
e-mail: dkitchin@cs.utexas.edu

A. Quark
University of Texas at Austin
e-mail: quark@cs.utexas.edu

J. Misra (✉)
University of Texas at Austin
e-mail: misra@cs.utexas.edu

C.B. Jones et al. (eds.), *Reflections on the Work of C.A.R. Hoare*,
DOI 10.1007/978-1-84882-912-1_11,

The structure of the algorithm has also been studied extensively. It presents three important ideas in computing – mutable store, recursion, and concurrency – making it attractive as a teaching tool. These aspects cross the usual boundaries of programming languages: pure functional programs typically do not admit in situ permutation of data elements, imperative programs are typically sequential and do not highlight concurrency, and typical concurrency constructs do not combine well with recursion.

We have recently designed a process calculus [14] and a programming language based on it, called Orc [8]. We believe that the Orc coding of Quicksort, in Section 11.5, highlights all three of these aspects while remaining faithful to the original intent of the algorithm.

This paper first presents Orc, starting with the Orc calculus, and then the programming language designed around the calculus. The calculus starts with the premise that concurrency is fundamental; sequential programming is a special case. The calculus itself is extremely small, consisting of four combinators (only three of which are essential for this paper) and a definition mechanism. It contains no data structuring, nor any notion of process, thread or communication.

The calculus is next enhanced with a small functional language to ease writing of practical programs. The language includes basic operators, conditionals, some primitive data types, and pattern matching mechanisms. The enhancements are mere syntactic sugar; they can all be translated to the core Orc calculus, and that is how they are actually implemented. The programming model draws its power from external services, called *sites*, which may encode functionalities that are better expressed in other programming paradigms. The combinators allow these sites to be integrated into a full concurrent program.

The paper is structured as follows. In Section 11.2, we review the Orc concurrency calculus. Section 11.3 shows its expansion into a functional concurrent programming language, with a library of sites supporting time, mutable state, communication, and synchronization. Section 11.4 presents a series of example programs using concurrency, recursion, and the additional capabilities provided by the site library. In Section 11.5, we present the Quicksort algorithm in Orc. Section 11.6 includes brief concluding remarks.

For a more thorough review of the Orc language, see [8], from which Sections 11.2, 11.3, and 11.4 borrow substantially. We also encourage the reader to visit our web site [16]; it hosts a comprehensive user guide [9], a community wiki, and a web-based interface for experimenting with Orc.

11.2 The Orc Concurrency Calculus

The Orc calculus is based on the execution of *expressions*. Expressions are built up recursively using Orc's concurrency *combinators*. When executed, an Orc expression invokes services and may *publish* values. Different executions of the same expression may have completely different behaviors; they may call different services, receive different responses from the same service, and publish different values. An expression is *silent* if it never publishes a value.

In order to invoke services, Orc expressions call *sites*. A site may be implemented on the client's machine or a remote machine. A site may provide any service; it could run sequential code, transform data, communicate with a web service, or be a proxy for interaction with a human user.

We describe three of the four concurrency combinators of Orc in this paper. Notable omissions in this paper are treatments of logical time (using site `Ltimer`) and halting (using the fourth concurrency combinator `;`). The operational and denotational semantics of the calculus appear in [7].

11.2.1 Site Calls

The simplest Orc expression is a *site call* $M(\overline{p})$, where M is a site name and $\overline{p}$ is a list of parameters, which are values or variables. The execution of a site call invokes the service associated with M, sending it the parameters $\overline{p}$. If the site responds, the call publishes that response. A site responds with at most one value.

Here are some examples of site calls.

`add(3,4)`	Add the numbers 3 and 4.
`CNN(d)`	Get the CNN news headlines for date `d`.
`Prompt("Name:")`	Prompt the user to enter a name on the console.
`random(10)`	Generate a random integer in the range 0..9.
`email(a,m)`	Send message `m` to email address `a`

11.2.1.1 Fundamental Sites

Though the Orc calculus itself contains no sites, there are a few fundamental sites that are so essential to writing useful programs that we always assume they are available. The site `let` is the identity site; when passed one argument, it publishes that argument, and when passed multiple arguments it publishes them as a tuple. The site `if` responds with a signal (a value which carries no information) if its argument is `true`, and otherwise it does not respond. The site call `Rtimer(t)` responds with a signal after exactly `t` time units.

11.2.1.2 `signal` and `stop`

For convenience, we allow two additional expressions: **`signal`** and **`stop`**. The expression **`signal`** just publishes a signal when executed; it is equivalent to `if(true)`. The expression **`stop`** is simply silent; it is equivalent to `if(false)`.

11.2.2 Combinators

Orc has four combinators to compose expressions: the parallel combinator `|`, the sequential combinator `>x>`, the pruning combinator[2] `<x<`, and the otherwise combinator `;`. We discuss only the first three in this paper; see [8] for more information on the otherwise combinator.

When composing expressions, the `>x>` combinator has the highest precedence, followed by `|`, then `<x<`.

11.2.2.1 Parallel Combinator

In *F* | *G*, expressions *F* and *G* execute independently. The sites called by *F* and *G* are the ones called by *F* | *G* and any value published by either *F* or *G* is published by *F* | *G*. There is no direct communication or interaction between *F* and *G*.

For example, evaluation of `CNN(d) | BBC(d)` initiates two independent computations; up to two values will be published depending on the number of responses received.

The parallel combinator is commutative and associative.

11.2.2.2 Sequential Combinator

In *F* >x> *G*, expression *F* is first evaluated. Each value published by *F* initiates a separate execution of *G* wherein `x` is bound to that published value. Execution of *F* continues in parallel with these executions of *G*. If *F* publishes no value, no execution of *G* occurs. The values published by the executions of *G* are the values published by *F* >x> *G*. The values published by *F* are consumed.

As an example, the following expression calls sites `CNN` and `BBC` in parallel to get the news for date `d`. Responses from either of these calls are bound to `x` and then site `email` is called to send the information to address `a`. Thus, `email` may be called 0, 1 or 2 times, depending on the number of responses received.

```
( CNN(d) | BBC(d) ) >x> email(a, x)
```

The sequential combinator is right associative, i.e. *F* >x> *G* >y> *H* is *F* >x> (*G* >y> *H*). When `x` is not used in *G*, one may use the short-hand *F* >> *G* for *F* >x> *G*.

The sequential combinator generalizes the sequential composition of the traditional imperative languages for a concurrent world: if *F* publishes a single value and does nothing further, then *F* >> *G* behaves like an imperative sequential program, *F* followed by *G*.

[2] In previous publications, *F* <x< *G* was written as *F* **where** $x :\in G$.

11.2.2.3 Pruning Combinator

In *F* <x< *G*, both *F* and *G* execute in parallel. Execution of parts of *F* that do not depend on x can proceed, but site calls in *F* for which x is a parameter are suspended until x has a value. If *G* publishes a value, then x is assigned that value, *G*'s execution is terminated and the suspended parts of *F* can proceed. This is the only mechanism in Orc to block or terminate parts of a computation.

In contrast to sequential composition, the following expression calls `email` at most once.

```
email(a, x) <x< ( CNN(d) | BBC(d) )
```

The pruning combinator is left associative, i.e. *F* <x< *G* <y< *H* is (*F* <x< *G*) <y< *H*. When x is not used in *F*, one may use the short-hand *F* << *G* for *F* <x< *G*.

The pruning combinator introduces eager concurrent evaluation. Later, we will see that expressions in the Orc language are often converted to pure Orc calculus using the pruning combinator; this introduces concurrency, even in the evaluation of arithmetic expressions, without programmer intervention.

11.2.3 Algebraic Properties of the Combinators

An operational semantics of Orc based on a labeled transition system appears in [18]. Employing bisimulation, we have proven the following algebraic properties of the combinators, some of which resemble laws of Kleene algebra (see [19] for these proofs). Below, we write "*f* is *x*-free" to mean that *x* does not occur as a free variable in *f*.

(Unit of |) $f \mid \mathbf{stop} = f$
(Commutativity of |) $f \mid g = g \mid f$
(Associativity of |) $(f \mid g) \mid h = f \mid (g \mid h)$

(Left zero of $\gg$) $\mathbf{stop} > x > f = \mathbf{stop}$
(Left unit of $\gg$) $\mathbf{signal} \gg f = f$
(Right unit of $\gg$) $f > x > let(x) = f$
(Associativity of $\gg$) $(f > x > g) > y > h = f > x > (g > y > h)$, if h is x-free
(Distributivity of | over $\gg$) $(f \mid g) > x > h = (f > x > h \mid g > x > h)$
(Right unit of $\ll$) $f \ll \mathbf{stop} = f$
(Commutativity of | with $\ll$) $(f \mid g) < x < h = (f < x < h) \mid g$, if g is x-free
(Commutativity of $\gg$ with $\ll$) $(f > y > g) < x < h = (f < x < h) > y > g$, if g is x-free
(Commutativity of $\ll$ with $\ll$) $((f < x < g) < y < h) = ((f < y < h) < x < g)$, if g is y-free and h is x-free

We can prove, for example, that $(f$ <x< $g) = f$ | (**stop** <x< g), if f is x-free. This follows from unit of | , commutativity of | , and commutativity of | over $\ll$.

11.2.4 Definitions

An Orc expression may be preceded by a sequence of definitions of the form:

def $E(\overline{x}) = F$

This defines a function named E whose formal parameter list is $\overline{x}$ and body is expression F. Definitions may be recursive.

A call $E(\overline{p})$ executes the body F with the actual parameters $\overline{p}$ substituted for the formal parameters $\overline{x}$. A function call may publish more than one value; it publishes every value published by the execution of F. If multiple concurrent calls are made to a function E, all instances of the body F execute concurrently.

Unlike a site call, a function call does not require all of its arguments to have values. Suppose E is called when an actual parameter q, corresponding to a formal parameter y, does not have a value. As in the pruning combinator, the executions of parts of F that do not depend on y may proceed, and the parts that depend on y will block until q has a value, which is then substituted for y.

11.3 The Orc Programming Language

In the preceding section, we introduced a small concurrency calculus, which serves well as a formal model, but is not a practical language for writing larger programs. Now we describe a language by introducing constructs familiar from functional programming. We show how each construct can be represented in the Orc calculus, so that every program can be translated directly into an equivalent expression in the calculus that uses a small set of primitive sites for arithmetic or data structuring operations. We conclude with an example program and its translation into the calculus. For the details of the full language, see the Orc User Guide [9].

11.3.1 Functional Aspects of the Language

11.3.1.1 Values and Operators

The Orc language has three types of constants: numbers (5, −1, 2.71828, ⋯), strings (`"orc"`, `"ceci n'est pas une |"`, ⋯), and booleans (`true` and `false`). It provides typical arithmetic (`+ - * /` ⋯), logical (`&& ||` ⋯), and comparison (`= < >` ⋯) operators. They are written infix with Java-like operator precedence. Parentheses can be used to override this precedence.

`(98+2)*17`	evaluates to `1700`.
`4 = 20 / 5`	evaluates to `true`.
`"leap" + "frog"`	evaluates to `"leapfrog"`.

The arithmetic, logical, and comparison operators translate directly to site calls; for example, `2+3` translates to `add(2,3)`, where `add` is simply a site that performs addition. A value `v` which occurs as an expression on its own becomes a site call `let(v)`.

11.3.1.2 Nested Expressions and Implicit Concurrency

The Orc language allows nested expressions, such as `2+(3+4)`. However, `2+(3+4)` cannot be translated directly to `add(2, add(3,4))` as described above; the Orc calculus does not allow expressions, such as `add(3,4)`, to appear as arguments. Instead, we use a fresh variable `z` as the argument, and then use a pruning combinator to bind the result of `add(3,4)` to `z`. Thus the expression `2+(3+4)` translates to `add(2,z) <z< add(3,4)`.

Any expression may be nested in this way, even expressions using concurrency combinators. For example, we allow the expression `2 + (3 | 4)`; it translates to `add(2,z) <z< (3 | 4)`. Since the pruning combinator `<z<` binds only the first value published by `3 | 4` to `z`, the expression could evaluate to either 5 or 6. Furthermore any depth of nesting is allowed, and unfolded in the same way; `2+(3+(4+5))` becomes `add(2,z) <z< add(3,y) <y< add(4,5)`.

This is the fundamental link between Orc as a concurrency calculus and Orc as a functional concurrent language. Since we use the pruning combinator in this translation, all subexpressions are executed concurrently, providing massive implicit parallelism without any additional work by the programmer. See Sections 11.3.2 and 11.4.1 for examples.

11.3.1.3 Conditionals

A conditional expression is of the form **if** *E* **then** *F* **else** *G*. If *E* evaluates to `true`, then *F* is evaluated. If *E* evaluates to `false`, then *G* is evaluated. If *E* does not publish a value, neither *F* nor *G* is evaluated.

`if true then 4 else 5`	evaluates to `4`.
`if 0 < 5 then 0/5 else 5/0`	evaluates to `0`.
`if 1 < 1/0 then 2 else 3`	is silent.

The conditional expression **if** *E* **then** *F* **else** *G* translates to:

```
( if(b) >> F' | not(b) >c> if(c) >> G' ) <b< E'
```

where E', F' and G' are translations of *E*, *F* and *G*, respectively.

Recall that `if(true)` publishes a signal and `if(false)` is silent. The site `not` performs boolean negation.

11.3.1.4 Variables

We introduce and bind variables using a **`val`** declaration, as follows. Below, `x` and `y` are bound to `3` and `6`, respectively.

```
val x = 1 + 2
val y = x + x
```

Variables cannot be reassigned. If the same variable is bound again, subsequent references to that variable will use the new binding, but previous references remain unchanged. Variable bindings obey the rules of lexical scope.

The declaration **`val`** `x =` *G*, followed by expression *F*, translates to:

F' `<x<` G'

where F' and G' are translations of *F* and *G*, respectively.

All the rules that apply to the pruning combinator apply to `val`, and it is permissible to write any Orc expression, even one that publishes multiple values, in a `val`. One of the most common Orc programming idioms is to write a `val` to choose the first available publication of a concurrent expression:

```
val url = Google("search term") | Yahoo("search term")
```

11.3.1.5 Data Structures

The Orc language supports two types of data structures: *tuples*, such as `(3, 7)` or `("tag", true, false)`, and finite *lists*, such as `[4,4,1]` or `["example"]` or `[]`. A tuple or list containing expressions to be evaluated is itself an expression; each of the expressions is evaluated, and the result is a tuple or list of those results.

`[1,2+3]`	evaluates to `[1,5]`.
`(3+4, if true then "yes" else "no")`	evaluates to `(7, "yes")`.

Tuples and lists can contain any value, including other tuples or lists.

The prepend (*cons*) operation on lists is written `x:xs`, where `xs` is a list and `x` is some element to be prepended to that list.

`[3,5] >t> 1:t` evaluates to `[1,3,5]`.

Data structures are created by site calls. The site `let` creates tuples directly. The site `nil` returns the empty list when called. The site `cons` implements the cons operator and is also used to construct list expressions. For example, `[1,2]` translates to `cons(1,s) <s< cons(2,t) <t< nil()`.

11.3.1.6 Patterns

We can bind parts of data structures to variables using *patterns*. We write _ for the wildcard pattern.

Patterns may replace variables in the `>x>` and `<x<` combinators. If a publication does not match the pattern of a `>x>` combinator, the publication is ignored, and no new instance of the right hand expression is executed. For the `<x<` combinator, the publication is ignored, and the right-hand expression continues to run.

```
(3,4) >(x,y)> x+y                 publishes 7.
x <(0,x)< ((1,0) | (0,1))         publishes 1.
```

Since the `val` declaration is simply a different form of the `<x<` combinator, patterns may replace variables in `val` as well:

```
val (x,y) = (2+3,2*3)
```
binds `x` to `5` and `y` to `6`.

```
val [a,_,c] = "one":["two", "three"]
```
binds `a` to `"one"` and `c` to `"three"`.

```
val ((a,b),c) = ((1, true), (2, false))
```
binds `a` to `1`, `b` to `true`, and `c` to `(2,false)`.

Patterns can be translated into a set of calls to pattern deconstruction sites followed by a set of variable bindings to match up each of the pieces with the appropriate variable names.

11.3.1.7 Functions

Functions are defined using the keyword **def**, and are identical to definitions in the Orc calculus. Definitions may be recursive, and groups of definitions may be mutually recursive.

```
def sumto(n) = if n <= 0 then 0 else n + sumto(n-1)
```

Functions can be defined as a series of *clauses*, each of which has a different list of patterns for its formal parameters. When such a function is called, the function body used for the call is that of the first clause whose formal parameter patterns match the actual parameters.

```
def fib(0) = 0
def fib(1) = 1
def fib(n) = if (n < 0) then 0 else fib(n-1) + fib(n-2)
```

The function `fib` may also be written more efficiently, as follows:

```
def fibpair(0) = (0,1)
def fibpair(n) = fibpair(n-1) >(a,b)> (b,a+b)
def fib(n) = if (n < 0) then 0 else fibpair(n) >(x,_)> x
```

Defining a function creates a value called a *lexical closure*; the name of the function is a variable and its bound value is the closure, which records all of the current bindings for free variables in the function body.

Since a closure is a value, it can be passed as an argument to another function, thus allowing us to define *higher-order* functions. As an example, here is the classic `map` function; see additional examples in Sections 11.4.1.3 and 11.4.3.3.

```
def map(f,[])   = []
def map(f,x:xs) = f(x):map(f,xs)
```

Note the important distinction between `f` and `f(x)`; the former is a variable whose bound value is a function (closure), and the latter is a call to that function.

11.3.2 Implicit Concurrency: An Example

We show an Orc program that does not use any of the concurrency combinators explicitly. In fact, the program is entirely functional, with the sole exception of the site call `random(6)`, which returns a random integer between `0` and `5`. Yet, each nested expression translates into a use of the pruning combinator, making this program implicitly concurrent without any programmer intervention.

The program runs a series of experiments. Each experiment consists of rolling a pair of dice. An experiment succeeds if the total shown by the two dice is `c`. The function `exp(n,c)` returns the number of successes in `n` experiments.

```
-- return a random number between 1 and 6
def toss() = random(6) + 1

def exp(0,_) = 0
def exp(n,c) = exp(n-1,c) + (if toss()+toss() = c then 1 else 0)
```

In `exp(n,c)`, the two expressions `exp(n-1,c)` and `if toss()+toss() = ...` may be executed concurrently; both calls to `toss` may also be executed concurrently. Therefore, all 2*n* calls to `toss` may be executed concurrently. This is clearly seen in the translation, given below, of this program into the Orc calculus. Here, site `add` returns the sum of its arguments, `sub(x,y)` returns `x-y`, `not(b)` returns the negation of `b`, and `equals` returns `true` iff its two arguments are equal.

```
def toss() = add(x,1) <x< random(6)

def exp(n,c) =
    ( if(b) >> let(0)
    | not(b) >nb> if(nb) >>
      ( add(x,y)
           <x< ( exp(m,c) <m< sub(n,1) ) )
           <y< ( ( if(bb) >> 1 | not(bb) >nbb> if(nbb) >> 0 )
                     <bb< equals(p,c)
                       <p< add(q,r)
                         <q< toss()
                         <r< toss() )

    ) <b< equals(n,0)
```

11.3.3 Site Library

We have implemented a library of useful sites. We introduce a few essential sites here, and we also note a few properties of sites that were not previously discussed.

11.3.3.1 Sites Are First-Class Values

In both the Orc calculus and the Orc programming language, sites are first-class values; they may be bound to variables, passed as arguments, published, and returned by site calls. It is very important that sites can be published by other sites, as this allows the use of "factory" sites, which create new sites such as mutable references or communication channels.

11.3.3.2 Sites May Have Methods

Sites may represent objects with multiple methods, in an object-oriented style. We access methods on sites using a special form of site call, as in `c.put(4)`, which accesses the `put` method of channel `c` and calls it as a site, with argument `4`.

This call form, like every other new syntactic form introduced so far, can be encoded in the Orc calculus. The site `c` is sent a special value called a *message*, in this case the `"put"` message. The site responds to that message with another site which will execute the desired method when called. So `c.put(4)` translates to `c("put") >x> x(4)`.

11.3.3.3 Time

Orc is designed to communicate with the external world, and one of the most important characteristics of the external world is the passage of time. Orc implicitly accounts for the passage of time by interacting with external services that may take time to respond. However, Orc can also explicitly wait for a specific amount of time, using the special site `Rtimer`. The call `Rtimer(t)`, where `t` is an integer, responds with a signal exactly `t` milliseconds later.[3]

We can use `Rtimer` together with the `<x<` combinator to enforce a timeout. Continuing with the example from Section 11.2.2, we can query `BBC` for a headline, but allow a default response if `BBC` does not respond within 5 seconds.

```
email(a, x) <x< (BBC(d) | Rtimer(5000) >> "BBC timed out.")
```

[3] An implementation can only approximate this guarantee.

11.3.3.4 References

Orc does not have mutable variables. Mutable state is provided by sites instead. The `Ref` site is used to create new mutable references, which are used in a style similar to Standard ML's `ref` [15].

A call to `Ref` may include an argument specifying the initial contents of the reference; if none is given, then the reference's value is undefined. Given a reference `r`, `r.write(v)` overwrites the current value stored in `r`, changing it to `v`, and returns a signal; `r.read()` publishes the current value stored in `r`. If `r` is undefined, `r.read()` blocks until a value is written into `r`.

We write `r := v` as syntactic sugar for `r.write(v)`, and `r?` for `r.read()`.

11.3.3.5 Arrays

The `Array` site creates new mutable arrays. Calling `Array(n)`, where `n` is the size of the array to be created, returns an array `a` with indices `0` through `n-1`, where the element values are undefined. Elements of array `a` are accessed by a site call, `a(i)`, which returns a reference to the *i*th element. That reference can then be read or written just like any reference created by `Ref`. The expression `a.length()` returns the length of the array.

```
Array(3) >a> a(0):= true >> a(1):= false >> a(1)?
```

publishes `false`.

```
Array(3) >a> a(a.length()-1)?
```

blocks until `a(2)` has a value.

11.3.3.6 Semaphores

Unlike other concurrent languages, Orc does not have any built-in locking mechanisms. Instead, it uses the `Semaphore` site to create semaphores which enable synchronization and mutual exclusion. `Semaphore(k)` creates a semaphore with the initial value `k` (i.e. it may be acquired by up to `k` parties simultaneously). Given a semaphore `s`, `s.acquire()` attempts to acquire `s`, reducing its value by one if it is positive, or blocking if its value is zero. The call `s.release()` releases `s`, increasing its value by one. The implementation of `Semaphore` guarantees strong fairness, i.e. if the semaphore value is infinitely often non-zero, then every call to `acquire` will eventually succeed.

We show below a function that returns an array of `n` semaphores, each with initial value 0.

```
def semArray(n) =
  val a = Array(n)
  def populate(0) = signal
  def populate(i) = a(i-1) := Semaphore(0) >> populate(i-1)
  populate(n) >> a
```

In practice, semaphores and other synchronization sites are only needed when resolving resource conflicts, i.e. concurrent calls to a site that has mutable state. Orc programs with implicit concurrency do not require these arbitration mechanisms.

11.3.3.7 Channels

Orc has no communication primitives like π-calculus channels [13] or Erlang mailboxes [1]. Instead, it makes use of sites to create channels of communication.

The most frequently used of these sites is `Buffer`, which publishes a new asynchronous FIFO channel. That channel is a site with two methods: `get` and `put`. The call `c.get()` takes the first value from channel `c` and publishes it, or blocks until a value becomes available. The call `c.put(v)` puts `v` as the last item of `c` and publishes a signal. A channel is a value, so it can be passed as an argument.

11.4 Example Programs

In this section, we present a number of small programs, demonstrating how Orc combines concurrency and recursion, integrates real time, manipulates mutable state, and performs complex synchronizations.

11.4.1 Examples Using Concurrency and Recursion

These examples implement some common idioms of concurrent and functional programming. Despite the austerity of Orc's combinators, we are able to encode a variety of idioms concisely.

11.4.1.1 Fork-Join

One of the most common concurrent idioms is a *fork-join*: evaluate two expressions F and G concurrently and wait for a result from both before proceeding. Thanks to the unfolding of nested expressions described on page 235, this is easily expressed in Orc using just a tuple:

```
(F,G)
```

This expands to:

```
(x,y) <x< F <y< G
```

We take advantage of the fact that a tuple is constructed by a site call, which must wait for all of its arguments to become available. In fact, any operator or site call may serve to join forked expressions. For example, if F and G each publish a number and we wish to output their maximum value, we simply write `max(F,G)`, where `max` returns the maximum of its arguments. We extend this example below.

Simple Parallel Auction

Orc programs often use fork-join together with recursion to dispatch many tasks in parallel and wait for all of them to complete. Suppose we have a list of bidders in a sealed-bid, single-round auction. Calling `b.ask()` requests a bid from the bidder `b`. We want to ask for one bid from each bidder and then publish the highest bid. The function `auction` performs this task:

```
def auction([]) = 0
def auction(b:bs) = max(b.ask(), auction(bs))
```

Note that all bidders are called simultaneously. Also note that if some bidder fails to return a bid, then the auction will never complete. Section 11.4.2.1 presents a different solution that addresses the issue of non-termination by using timeout.

11.4.1.2 Parallel Or

"Parallel or" is a classic idiom of parallel programming. The "parallel or" operation executes two expressions *F* and *G* in parallel, each of which may publish a single boolean, and returns the disjunction of their publications as soon as possible. If one of the expressions publishes `true`, then the disjunction is `true`, so it is not necessary to wait for the other expression to publish a value. This holds even if one of the expressions never publishes a value.

The "parallel or" of expressions *F* and *G* may be expressed in Orc as follows:

```
val result =
  val a = F
  val b = G
  (a || b) | if(a) >> true | if(b) >> true
result
```

The expression `(a || b)` waits for both `a` and `b` to become available and then publishes their disjunction. However, if either `a` or `b` is true we must publish `true` immediately, regardless of whether the other variable has a value. Therefore we run `if(a) >> true` and `if(b) >> true` in parallel. Since more than one of these expressions may publish `true`, we bind only the first result to `result`. The value of the whole expression is simply the value bound to `result`.

Note that *F* and *G* are evaluated within the binding of `result`, so that when `result` becomes bound, *F* and *G* are terminated. If `val a =` *F* and `val b =` *G* were written above `val result = ...`, their executions would continue.

11.4.1.3 Fold

We consider various concurrent implementations of the classic "list fold" function, defined by `fold(f, [`x_1`, ... ,` x_n`]) = f(`x_1`, f(`x_2`, ... f(`x_{n-1}`,` x_n`) ... )`. Here is a simple functional implementation:

```
def fold(_, [x])    = x
def fold(f, x:xs)  = f(x, fold(f, xs))
```

This is a seedless fold (sometimes called `foldl`) which requires that the list be non-empty, and uses its first element as the seed. This implementation is short-circuiting – it may finish early if the reduction operator `f` does not use its second argument – but it is not concurrent; no two calls to `f` can proceed in parallel. However, if `f` is associative, we can overcome this restriction and implement fold concurrently. If `f` is also commutative, we can further increase concurrency.

Associative Fold

We define `afold(f,xs)` where `f` is an associative binary function and `xs` is a non-empty list. The implementation iteratively reduces `xs` to a single value. Each iteration applies the auxiliary function `step`, which reduces adjacent pairs of items to single values.

```
def afold(f, [x]) = x
def afold(f, xs) =
  def step([]) = []
  def step([x]) = [x]
  def step(x:y:xs) = f(x,y):step(xs)
  afold(f, step(xs))
```

Notice that `f(x,y):step(xs)` is an implicit fork-join, as described in Section 11.4.1.1. Thus, the call `f(x,y)` executes concurrently with the recursive call `step(xs)`. As a result, all calls to `f` execute concurrently within each iteration of `afold`.

Associative, Commutative Fold

We can make the implementation even more concurrent when the fold operator is both associative and commutative. We define `cfold(f,xs)`, where `f` is an associative and commutative binary function and `xs` is a non-empty list. The implementation initially copies all list items into a buffer in arbitrary order using the auxiliary function `xfer`, counting the total number of items copied. The auxiliary function `combine` repeatedly pulls pairs of items from the buffer, reduces them, and places the result back in the buffer. Each pair of items is reduced in parallel as they become available. The last item in the buffer is the result of the overall fold.

```
def cfold(f, xs) =
  val c = Buffer()

  def xfer([])    = 0
  def xfer(x:xs)  = c.put(x) >> stop | xfer(xs)+1

  def combine(0)  = stop
  def combine(1)  = c.get()
```

```
def combine(m) = c.get() >x> c.get() >y>
                 ( c.put(f(x,y)) >> stop | combine(m-1))

xfer(xs) >n> combine(n)
```

11.4.2 Examples Using Time

These examples demonstrate how Orc programs can integrate real time to detect time outs, and execute expressions at regular time intervals, using the site `Rtimer` described in Section 11.3.3.

11.4.2.1 Timeout

Timeout, the ability to execute an expression for at most a specified amount of time, is an essential ingredient of fault-tolerant and distributed programming. Orc accomplishes timeout using pruning and the `Rtimer` site, as we saw in Section 11.3.3; we further develop that technique in these examples.

Auction with Timeout

The auction example in Section 11.4.1.1 may never finish if one of the bidders does not respond. We add a timeout so that each bidder has at most 8 seconds to respond:

```
def auction([]) = 0
def auction(b:bs) = max(b.ask() | Rtimer(8000) >> 0, auction(bs))
```

This version of the auction is guaranteed to complete within 8 seconds.[4]

Priority

We can use `Rimer` to give a window of priority to one computation over another. In this example, we run expressions *F* and *G* concurrently, each of which may publish a single result. For a time interval of 1 second, *F* has priority; *F*'s result is published immediately if it is produced within 1 second; otherwise, the first value from *F* or *G* is published after the time interval.

```
val result =
  val a = F
  val b = G
  a | Rtimer(1000) >> b
result
```

[4] An implementation can only approximate this guarantee.

Detecting Timeout

Sometimes, rather than just yielding a default value, we would like to determine whether an expression has timed out, and if so, perform some other computation. To detect the timeout, we pair the result of the original expression with `true` and the result of the timer with `false`. Thus, if the expression does time out, then we can distinguish that case using the boolean value.

Here, we run expression *F* with a time limit `t`. If it publishes within the time limit, we bind its result to `r` and execute *G*. Otherwise, we execute *H*.

```
val (r, b) = (F, true) | (Rtimer(t), false)
if b then G else H
```

11.4.2.2 Metronome

A timer can be used to execute an expression repeatedly at regular intervals. We define a function `metronome(t)`, which publishes a signal every `t` time units.

```
def metronome(t) = signal | Rtimer(t) >> metronome(t)
```

The following example publishes "tick" once per second, and "tock" once per second after a half-second delay. The publications alternate: "tick tock tick tock ...". Note that this code is not recursive; the recursion is entirely contained within `metronome`.

```
metronome(1000) >> ("tick" | Rtimer(500) >> "tock")
```

11.4.3 Examples Using Mutable State

These examples show how Orc can manipulate mutable state, such as the reference cells and arrays described in Section 11.3.3. Recall that `x?` is syntactic sugar for `x.read()`, and `x := y` for `x.write(y)`. Also recall that the expression `a(i)` returns a reference to the element of array `a` at index `i`; array indices start from 0.

11.4.3.1 Simple Swap

The following function takes two references as arguments, exchanges their values, and returns a signal.

```
def swap(a, b) = (a?, b?) >(x,y)> (a := y, b := x) >> signal
```

11.4.3.2 Array Permutation

The following function randomly permutes the elements of an array in place. It uses the helper function `randomize`, which for each index `i` in the array generates a random number `j` between `0` and `(i-1)` inclusive, and swaps `a(i-1)` with `a(j)`.

```
def permute(a) =
  def randomize(0) = signal
  def randomize(i) = random(i) >j>
                     swap(a(i-1),a(j)) >>
                     randomize(i-1)
  randomize(a.length())
```

Since `random` returns values from a uniform distribution, each possible permutation of the array is equally likely. This algorithm originally appears in [3, 10].

The technique we use here – traversing an array recursively and calling `swap` to exchange its elements – is crucial for our Quicksort implementation.

11.4.3.3 Applicative Map

The `map` function, shown in Section 11.3.1, applies a function to each element in a list and returns a new list populated with the results; it is a common idiom in pure functional programming. When manipulating mutable arrays, it is often helpful to perform a map operation in place: apply the function to each element of the array overwriting the previous contents. The function `inplacemap(f,a)`, defined below, applies the function `f` to the array `a` in this way. The helper function `mapstep(i)` applies `f` to each element of `a` with index less than `i`.

```
def inplacemap(f,a) =
  def mapstep(0) = signal
  def mapstep(i) =
    val rest = mapstep(i-1)
    a(i-1) := f(a(i-1)?) >> rest
  mapstep(a.length())
```

A call to `mapstep(i)` applies the function `f` to element `a(i-1)`, and concurrently maps the remainder of the array by calling `mapstep(i-1)`. When `mapstep(i-1)` completes, `rest` is bound to a signal, and then `mapstep(i)` returns.

The following expression increments the value of each element of `a` by 1:

```
def inc(x) = x+1
inplacemap(inc,a)
```

11.4.4 Examples Using Synchronization and Communication

Synchronization and communication are fundamental to concurrent computing. We implement some examples of synchronization – the rendezvous mechanism [6, 12] and a solution to the readers–writers problem [2] – and show how communicating processes [6] may be programmed in Orc.

11.4.4.1 Rendezvous

The concept of *rendezvous* between two parties was first introduced by Hoare and Milner as a form of process synchronization. Orc does not include rendezvous as a primitive concept, but we can program it using semaphores. First, we show a two-party rendezvous, and then generalize it to $(n + 1)$-party rendezvous, for $n \geq 1$.

A rendezvous occurs between a sender and a receiver when both of them are waiting to perform their respective operations. They each wait until they complete the rendezvous, and then they can proceed with their computations. A rendezvous involves synchronization and data transfer. In the solution below, first we show only the synchronization, and later data transfer. Potentially many senders and receivers may simultaneously wait to rendezvous, but each can rendezvous with exactly one other party.

Senders and receivers call the functions `send` and `receive`, respectively, when they are ready to rendezvous. The solution employs two semaphores, `up` and `down`, which are acquired and released in a symmetric manner. (The roles of sender and receiver are symmetric; so the two function bodies may be exchanged.) It can be shown that this solution synchronizes a pair of sender and receiver, each of them receives a signal following a synchronization, and that it leaves the semaphores in their original states (with value 0) following the synchronization. We expect each semaphore to be binary-valued, yet this is not a requirement. For general semaphores, there is still pairwise synchronization, though it cannot be ascertained which sender has synchronized with which receiver.

```
val up   = Semaphore(0)
val down = Semaphore(0)
def send() = up.release() >> down.acquire()
def recv() = up.acquire() >> down.release()
```

In order for the sender to send data value `v`, replace semaphore `up` by buffer `b`, and modify the programs:

```
def send(v)    = b.put(v) >> down.acquire()
def receive() = b.get() >x> down.release() >> x
```

The given solution can be generalized to the case where the senders and receivers belong to specific groups, and a rendezvous occurs only between members of a group. In that case, each group uses its own pair of semaphores and corresponding definitions.

$(n + 1)$-party Rendezvous

We generalize the rendezvous algorithm given above to synchronize $n + 1$ parties (processes), $n \geq 1$, using $2n$ semaphores. We create two arrays of semaphores, `up` and `down`, using the `semArray` function defined in Section 11.3.3. The algorithm is reminiscent of 2-phase commit protocol in databases. Each of the $n + 1$ parties calls a function when it is ready to synchronize, like the sender and the receiver above. The process with index n is designated the coordinator, and it calls function `coord`; all others call `ready`. Function call `ready(i)`, where `0 ≤ i < n`, first releases semaphore `up(i)` and then waits to acquire `down(i)`. Function `coord` first acquires all the `up` semaphores and then releases all the `down` semaphores. The 2-party rendezvous is a special case where the receiver played the role of the coordinator.

```
val up = semArray(n)
val down = semArray(n)
def ready(i) = up(i).release >> down(i).acquire
def coord() =
  def Acq(0) = signal
  def Acq(k) = up(k-1).acquire >> Acq(k-1)
  def Rel(0) = signal
  def Rel(k) = (down(k-1).release,Rel(k-1)) >> signal
  Acq(n) >> Rel(n)
```

11.4.4.2 Readers–Writers Synchronization

We present a solution to the classical Readers–Writers synchronization problem [2]. Processes, called *readers* and *writers*, share a resource such that concurrent reading is permitted but a writer needs exclusive access. We present a starvation-free solution consisting of three functions: `start`, `end`, and `manager`. Readers and writers call `start`, a blocking operation, to request access; readers call `start(true)` and writers call `start(false)`. Function `start` publishes a signal when the resource can be granted. Readers and writers call `end()` to release the resource. Function `manager` runs concurrently with the rest of the program to grant the requests.

A call to `start(b)` adds a request to channel `q`. Function `manager` reads from `q`, decides when the request can be granted, and then calls back the requester. We employ semaphores for callback. Specifically,

```
val q = Buffer()
def start(b) = Semaphore(0) >s> q.put((b,s)) >> s.acquire()
```

Function `manager` releases `s` when it can grant the request. Since `s` has initial value 0, `s.acquire()` blocks until the request is granted.

To count the number of active readers and writers, we employ a *counter* `c`, a mutable object on which three methods are defined: (1) `c.inc()` adds 1 to the counter value, (2) `c.dec()` subtracts 1 from the counter value, and (3) `c.onZero()` sends a signal only when the counter value is 0. The first two are non-blocking operations, and the last one is blocking. Though `onZero()` sends a signal only when the counter value is 0, the value may be non-zero by the time the recipient receives the signal. There is a weak fairness guarantee: if the counter value remains 0 continuously, a signal is sent to some caller of `onZero()`. The counter is initially 0. The site call `Counter()` creates and returns a new counter.

The code for `end` merely decrements the counter:

```
val c = Counter()
def end() = c.dec()
```

The manager is an eternal loop structured as follows:

```
def manager() =
  q.get() >(b,s)> if b then read(s) else write(s) >> manager()
```

The invariants in each iteration of `manager` are that (1) there are no current writers, and (2) the counter value is the number of current readers. We use these invariants in the implementations of `read` and `write`.

A reader can always be granted permission to execute, from invariant (1). To satisfy invariant (2), the counter value must be incremented.

```
def read(s) = c.inc() >> s.release()
```

A writer can be granted permission only if there are no active readers. To satisfy invariant (1), the execution of `write` terminates only when there are no active writers.

```
def write(s) = c.onZero() >> c.inc() >> s.release() >> c.onZero()
```

We start execution of an instance of `manager` by writing:

```
val _ = manager()
```

The Readers–Writers program in its entirety is shown below.

```
val q = Buffer()
def start(b) = Semaphore(0) >s> q.put((b,s)) >> s.acquire()
val c = Counter()
def end() = c.dec()
def manager() =
  q.get() >(b,s)> if b then read(s) else write(s) >> manager()
def read(s) = c.inc() >> s.release()
def write(s) = c.onZero() >> c.inc() >> s.release() >> c.onZero()
val _ = manager()
```

11.4.4.3 Process Network

Process networks [6] and actors [1,4] are popular models for concurrent programming. Their popularity derives from the structure they impose on a concurrent computation. Different aspects of the computation are partitioned among different processes (actors), and the processes communicate through messages over channels. This simple programming model allows a programmer to focus attention on one aspect of a problem at a time, corresponding to a process. Additionally, interference and race conditions among processes, the bane of concurrent programming, are largely eliminated by restricting communication to occur through messages.

We show how this programming model can be incorporated within Orc. Channels are created by calls to `Buffer`. Processes are represented as Orc definitions, which share these channels. The entire process network is the parallel composition of these processes. Below, we restrict ourselves to FIFO channels though other communication protocols can be defined in Orc.

As an example, consider a transformer process `P` that reads inputs one at a time from channel `in`, transforms each input to a single output by calling function (or site) `transform`, writes the result on channel `out`, and repeats these steps forever.

```
def P(c,d) = c.get() >x> transform(x) >y> d.put(y) >> P(c,d)
P(in,out)
```

Next, we build a small network of such processes. The network has two processes, and both read from `in` and write to `out`.

```
P(in,out) | P(in,out)
```

Here, the two processes may operate at arbitrary speeds in removing items from `in` and writing to `out`. Therefore, the order of items in the input channel is not necessarily preserved with the corresponding outputs in `out`.

Probabilistic Load Balancing

Consider adding a *balancer* process that reads from `in` and randomly assigns the input to one of the processes for transformation, as a form of load balancing. Again, the processes write their results to `out`, and they may not preserve the input order. We define two internal channels `in'` and `in''` which link *balancer* to the transformer processes.

```
def balancer(c,c',c'') =
  c.get() >x>
  (if random(2) = 0 then c'.put(x) else c''.put(x)) >>
  balancer(c,c',c'')

val (in', in'') = (Buffer(), Buffer())

  balancer(in,in',in'')
| P(in',out) | P(in'',out)
```

Deterministic Load Balancing

Now consider a load balancing network in which the order of inputs is preserved in the output. We replace the *balancer* process with a *distributor* process that sends alternate input items along `in'` and `in''`. The transformer processes write their outputs to two internal channels `out'` and `out''`. And, we add a *collector* process that copies the values from `out'` and `out''` alternately to `out`.

```
def distributor(c,c',c'') =
  c.get() >x> c'.put(x) >>
  c.get() >y> c''.put(y) >>
  distributor(c,c',c'')

def collector(d',d'',d) =
  d'.get() >x> d.put(x) >>
  d''.get() >y> d.put(y) >>
  collector(d',d'',d)

val (in',in'') = (Buffer(), Buffer())
val (out',out'') = (Buffer(), Buffer())

  distributor(in,in',in'')
| P(in',out') | P(in'',out'')
| collector(out',out'',out)
```

We have shown some very simple networks here; in particular, the networks are acyclic and a priori bounded in size. See [16] for networks in which arbitrarily many processes are dynamically initiated, interrupted, resumed, or terminated. The networks may be structured in a hierarchy where a process itself may be a network to any arbitrary depth, and connections among network components are established statically by naming explicit channels as shown, or dynamically by sending a channel name as a data item.

11.5 Quicksort in Orc

The Quicksort algorithm focuses on three core ideas in computing: recursion, mutable store, and concurrency. We present an implementation of Quicksort in Orc, in which we show how Orc expresses all three of these ideas. The program is recursive and largely functional in its structure. It uses fork-join when partitioning the array and sorting subarrays, making both the partitioning process and the recursive subsorts implicitly parallel throughout. Furthermore, it manipulates the array elements in place, avoiding the overhead of maintaining extra copies.

We define a `quicksort` function, which takes as its only argument an array `a`, and sorts that array in place. When the sort is complete, it returns a signal.

```
def quicksort(a) = ...
```

Within the body of `quicksort`, we define an auxiliary function `part(p,s,t)` that partitions the subarray of `a` defined by indices `s` through `t` into two partitions, one containing values ≤`p` and the other containing values >`p`. One of the partitions may be empty. The call `part(p,s,t)` returns an index `m` such that `a(i) ≤ p` for all `s ≤ i ≤ m`, and `a(j) > p` for all `m < j ≤ t`.

```
def part(p, s, t) = ...
```

To create the partitions, `part` calls two auxiliary functions `lr` and `rl`. These functions scan the subarray from the left and right, respectively, looking for the first out-of-place element. Function `lr` returns the index of the leftmost item that exceeds `p`, or simply `t` if there is none. Function `rl` returns the index of the rightmost item that is less than or equal to `p`, or simply `s-1` if there is none (the value at `a(s-1)` is assumed to be ≤`p`).

```
def lr(i) = if i < t && a(i)? <= p then lr(i+1) else i
def rl(i) = if a(i)? > p then rl(i-1) else i
```

Observe that `lr` and `rl` may safely be executed concurrently, since they do not modify the array elements.

Once two out-of-place elements have been found, they are swapped using the function `swap` defined in Section 11.4.3.1, and then the unscanned portion of the subarray is partitioned further. Partitioning is complete when the entire subarray has been scanned. Here is the body of the `part` function:

```
(lr(s), rl(t)) >(s', t')>
  ( if(s' + 1 < t') >> swap(a(s'), a(t')) >> part(p, s'+1, t'-1)
  | if(s' + 1 = t') >> swap(a(s'), a(t')) >> s'
  | if(s' + 1 > t') >> t'
  )
```

Observe that in the body of `part`, we use three parallel calls to the `if` site, with mutually exclusive conditions, each followed by >> and another expression. This is a representation of Dijkstra's *guarded commands* in Orc, using `if` to represent a guard, followed by >> and a consequent. Also observe that the second guarded command can be eliminated by replacing the first guard by `s' + 1 <= t'`; this incurs a slight performance penalty.

The main sorting function `sort(s,t)` sorts the subarray given by indices `s` through `t` by calling `part` to partition the subarray and then recursively sorting the partitions concurrently. It publishes a signal on completion.

```
def sort(s, t) =
     if s >= t then signal
     else part(a(s)?, s+1, t) >m>
          swap(a(m), a(s)) >>
          (sort(s, m-1), sort(m+1, t)) >>
          signal
```

The body of `quicksort` is just a call to `sort`, selecting the whole array:

```
sort(0, a.length()-1)
```

Here is the `quicksort` program in its entirety.

```
def quicksort(a) =

  def part(p, s, t) =
    def lr(i) = if i < t && a(i)? <= p then lr(i+1) else i
    def rl(i) = if a(i)? > p then rl(i-1) else i

    (lr(s), rl(t)) >(s', t')>
    ( if (s' + 1 < t') >> swap(a(s'),a(t')) >> part(p,s'+1,t'-1)
    | if (s' + 1 = t') >> swap(a(s'),a(t')) >> s'
    | if (s' + 1 > t') >> t'
    )

  def sort(s, t) =
     if s >= t then signal
     else part(a(s)?, s+1, t) >m>
          swap(a(m), a(s)) >>
          (sort(s, m-1), sort(m+1, t)) >>
          signal

  sort(0, a.length()-1)
```

11.6 Why Orc?

Much like other process algebras, the Orc calculus was designed to study the appropriateness of certain combinators for concurrent computing. Unlike most other process algebras, the calculus relies on external sites to deal with non-concurrency issues. Many of the lower-level problems, such as management of locks and shared state, are delegated to sites in Orc. The Orc language was designed to provide a minimal base to experiment with the Orc combinators. Therefore, the language includes only the basic data types and structuring mechanisms. A site library provides additional capabilities for creating references, arrays, and channels, for example. Such a combination has proved fruitful, as we have demonstrated in programming a classic example, Quicksort.

We hope that designers of future languages will adopt the fundamental principle we have espoused in the design of Orc: seamless integration of concurrency, structure, and interaction with the external world.

Acknowledgements Jayadev Misra is deeply grateful to Tony Hoare for research ideas, inspiration, and personal friendship spanning over 3 decades. It is no exaggeration that he would not have pursued certain research directions, that have ultimately proved quite successful, had it not been for Tony's encouragement. This paper is a small token of appreciation.

The authors are indebted to Doug McIlroy and Manuel Serrano for their careful reading of this manuscript and many perceptive comments and suggestions. Our long-time collaborators, Albert Benveniste, Claude Jard, and Jose Meseguer have helped us refine the underlying ideas of Orc.

This work is partially supported by National Science Foundation grant CCF-0811536.

References

1. Armstrong, J., Virding, R., Wikström, C., Williams, M.: Concurrent Programming in ERLANG 2nd edn. Prentice Hall International (UK) Ltd., Hertfordshire, UK, (1996).
2. Courtois, P.J., Heymans, F., Parnas, D.L.: Concurrent control with "readers" and "writers". Commun. ACM **14**(10)667–668 (1971).
3. Fisher, R., Yates, F.: Statistical Tables for Biological, Agricultural and Medical Research. Oliver and Boyd, London, 3rd edn. (1948).
4. Hewitt, C., Bishop, P., Steiger, R.: A universal modular actor formalism for artificial intelligence. International Joint Conference on Artificial Intelligence (1973).
5. Hoare, C.A.R.: Partition: Algorithm 63, quicksort: Algorithm 64, and find: Algorithm 65. Commun. the ACM **4**(7)321–322 (1961).
6. Hoare, C.A.R.: Communicating sequential processes. Commun. ACM **21**(8)666–677 (1978).
7. Kitchin, D., Cook, W.R., Misra, J.: A language for task orchestration and its semantic properties. In: CONCUR, pp. 477–491 (2006).
8. Kitchin, D., Quark, A., Cook, W., Misra, J.: The Orc programming language. In Lee, D., Lopes, A., Poetzsch-Heffter, A: (eds.) Formal Techniques for Distributed Systems; Proceedings of FMOODS/FORTE, vol. 5522 of LNCS, pp. 1–25. Springer, Lisbon (2009).
9. Kitchin, D., Quark, A., Cook, W.R., Misra, J.: Orc user guide. http://orc.csres.utexas.edu/userguide/html/index.html.
10. Knuth, D.E.: Seminumerical Algorithms, vol. 2 of The Art of Computer Programming, 3rd edn. Addison-Wesley, Reading, (1997).

11. Knuth, D.E.: Sorting and Searching, vol. 2 of The Art of Computer Programming, 2nd edn. Addison-Wesley, Reading, MA (1998).
12. Milner, R.: A Calculus of Communicating Systems. Springer LNCS Vol. 12, Springer-Verlag (1980).
13. Milner, R.: Communicating and Mobile Systems: the π-Calculus. Cambridge University Press, Cambridge (May 1999).
14. Misra, J.: Computation orchestration: A basis for wide-area computing. In Broy, M: (ed.) Proc. of the NATO Advanced Study Institute, Engineering Theories of Software Intensive Systems, NATO ASI Series, Marktoberdorf, Germany, (2004).
15. Paulson, L.C.: ML for the Working Programmer. Cambridge University Press, Cambridge (1991).
16. Quark, A., Kitchin, D., Cook, W.R., Misra, J.: Orc language project website. http://orc.csres.utexas.edu.
17. Sedgewick, R.: Quicksort. PhD thesis, Stanford University (1975).
18. Wehrman, I., Kitchin, D., Cook, W., Misra, J.: A timed semantics of Orc. Theoret. Comput. Sci. **402**(2–3)234–248 (August 2008).
19. Wehrman, I., Kitchin, D., Cook, W.R., Misra, J.: Properties of the timed operational and denotational semantics of Orc. Technical Report TR-07-65, The University of Texas at Austin, Department of Computer Sciences (December 2007).

Chapter 12
The Thousand-and-One Cryptographers

A.K. McIver and C.C. Morgan

Abstract Chaum's *Dining Cryptographers* protocol crystallises the essentials of security just as other famous diners once demonstrated deadlock and livelock: it is a benchmark for security models and their associated verification methods.

Here we give a correctness proof of the Cryptographers in a new style, one in which stepwise refinement plays a prominent role. Furthermore, our proof applies to arbitrarily many diners: that is unusually general.

The proof is based on the *Shadow Security Model*, which integrates non-interference and program refinement: with it, we try to make a case that stepwise development of security protocols is not only possible but also actually to be recommended. It benefits from more than 3 decades of experience of how layers of abstraction can both simplify the design process and make its outcomes more likely to be correct.

12.1 Introduction: Refinement of Security Properties

Program development by stepwise refinement [34] is widely accepted as a good idea in theory, but it is often a late arrival in practice. Indeed, with some notable exceptions [1, 5] most current approaches and tools for correctness concentrate on proving[1] that a single system has certain desirable properties, whereas a refinement-based approach would rather prove that one (real, i.e. implementation) system had all the desirable properties of another (ideal, i.e. specification) system.

For example, we note the frequent claims that downgrading is a challenging issue in the non-interference model of security [12]. In that model a program is secure if

[1] We include model checking as a form of proving, at this informal level.

A.K. McIver
Dept. of Computing, Macquarie University, NSW 2109 Australia
e-mail: annabelle.mciver@mq.edu.au

C.C. Morgan (✉)
School of Comp. Sci. and Eng., Univ. NSW, NSW 2052 Australia
e-mail: carrollm@cse.unsw.edu.au

C.B. Jones et al. (eds.), *Reflections on the Work of C.A.R. Hoare*,
DOI 10.1007/978-1-84882-912-1_12,

observation of its "low-security" visible outputs does not reveal anything about its "high-security" hidden inputs; thus in the context of visible integer variable v and hidden variable h the program $v{:=}\, 0{\times}h$ is secure but $v{:=}\, 1{\times}h$ is not. As an intermediate option there is the program $v{:=}\, h{\div}2$ that "downgrades" the security, revealing in this case most bits of v but not all, yet it is not considered to be "intermediately" secure: like $v{:=}\, 1 \times h$, it is considered (simply) insecure.

Now in a real system we might find the code

$$v{:=}\,0;\;\; \textbf{while}\, v+2 \leq h\, \textbf{do}\, \langle \textit{send two bytes} \rangle;\; v{:=}\, v+2\, \textbf{end}\,, \tag{12.1}$$

in which v counts the number of bytes sent, ensuring no more than h can be sent overall. If the sent messages are observed and counted, then this program also reveals – to anyone aware of the source code – all but the low-order bit of h. Like $v{:=}\, h \div 2$ above, it is considered insecure in the non-interference model.

Downgrading is inescapable in practice, and it is to reason about it effectively – in spite of the black-or-white judgement of the original non-interference model – that downgrading extensions to that model are introduced [7, 20] in which one can express, by annotations of the code, the information leaks that are to be considered acceptable. The proof of correctness is then relative to those annotations.

But there is an alternative to concentrating on downgrading exclusively: instead we concentrate on refinement, with downgrading then a special case. In this approach we would describe a downgrading policy for the loop of (12.1) as a requirement of there being a refinement, saying that

$$v{:=}\, 2(h \div 2)\; \sqsubseteq v{:=}\,0;\;\; \textbf{while}\, v+2 \leq h\, \textbf{do} \langle\, \textit{send} \rangle;\; v{:=}\, v+2\, \textbf{end}, \tag{12.2}$$

i.e. that the *lhs* "is refined by" the *rhs* and meaning that the desirable properties of the specification on the left – including its not revealing h's low-order bit – are shared by its implementation on the right. The downgrading aspect is that the *rhs* can indeed reveal the higher-order bits of h – because the *lhs* does just that. We feel that a refinement-based approach to security has many advantages, demonstrated over the years by its success generally (in those places where it has, after all, been adopted). In this particular case, for example, using it would mean that we require neither annotations nor an explicit notion of downgrading.

Integrating refinement and security is exactly what we do here: we make (12.2) precise by giving an appropriately extended definition of refinement, one which is "security aware." It is explained below (and earlier [25, 27]). In doing so we join a small number of other researchers – from the large security community – who have similar aims [2, 9, 21]; we compare our work with theirs in Section 12.9. In the meantime, we highlight some of the conspicuous aspects of our approach.

Refinement is complementary to abstraction, and abstraction can be viewed in turn as demonic nondeterministic choice resolved at design-time; but it is well known that there are conceptual benefits to conflating abstraction with run-time demonic choice [4, 8, 17, 23] and so it is natural to include demonic choice in our security model in both the design- and run-time senses. Where this has been done by others, in some cases the non-interference model has been extended so that the "full range of nondeterminism" of the hidden variables must not be dependent on visible variables' observed values, but the nondeterminism cannot subsequently be reduced as refinement would ordinarily allow [19, 32]; and in other cases the requirement has been imposed that – while nondeterminism is allowed in the model – in the final implementation program there must be none of it remaining [31]. *One aspect* of our work is that, in contrast, we include both features: nondeterminism can be reduced; and some of it can remain in the implementation. This requires careful treatment of hidden-versus visible nondeterminism, and is how we solved the Refinement Paradox [18, 24].

A second aspect is that our notion of adversary is quite strong: we allow perfect recall [11] that intermediate values of visible variables can be observed even if they subsequently are overwritten; and we allow an attacker's observation of control flow, that conditionals' Booleans expressions are (implicitly) leaked. We assume also that the program code is known. Doing all these effectively, while avoiding an infinite regress to "quark-level attacks," requires explicit treatment of atomicity at some point. We define that.

The reason for the strong adversary is that refinements must be effective locally: refinement of a small fragment in a large program must refine the whole program even if the refinement was proved only for the fragment. This is monotonicity – and without it no scaled-up development is possible. Since for some fresh local visible variable v' it is a refinement to insert assignment $v'{:=}\,v$ willy-nilly at almost any place in a program, we must live with the fact that v's value at that point will possibly be preserved (in some local v') in spite of v's subsequent overwriting: that is, although the unfortunate $v'{:=}\,v$ might not be there "now," one developer must accept that a second developer in some other building might put it there "later" without asking. After all, if it's a refinement (and it is) then he does not *need* to ask.

Rather than making refinements unworkable, the strong-adversary assumptions make them more applicable. Distributed protocols (such as the Dining Cryptographers) can be treated as single "sequential" programs because the information hiding normally implied by non-interference's end-to-end analysis does not apply. Indeed, if it did, the sequential formulation would seem to be hiding the transfer of messages and the interleaving of concurrent threads, and that would make it unsound. For example, if Agent A executes $v{:=}\,h$ and Agent B then executes $v{:=}\,0$ we can analyse this as the single sequential program $v{:=}\,h;\ v{:=}\,0$ without having accidentally (and incorrectly) ignored the fact that A can observe v (and hence learn h) before B's thread has begun the execution that would overwrite it.

A third aspect of our approach is that we concentrate on algebraic reasoning for proving refinement: although we do have both an operational model (Section 12.2) and a language of logical assertions (Section 12.3) for refinement-based security, we use those mainly for proving schematic program-fragment equalities and refinements (Section 12.4). Those schemes, rather than the logic or the model, are then what is used in the derivation of specific programs. For this we need a program-level indication of information escape, analogous to the way in which the *assert* statement can embed Hoare-Logic pre- and post-conditions within program code [16, 23, 35].

This is our **reveal** E statement that publishes E's value for all to read, but does not change any program variable: its purpose is to bring an extra expressivity that helps formulate general algebraic (in)equalities. Since functionally it acts as **skip** on program variables (having no effect at all), but *wrt* secrecy it does not act as **skip** (it releases information but **skip** does not), its behaviour considered alone will capture much of the flavour of what we intend to do.

Section 12.2 gives our relational-style operational model; Section 12.3 describes a corresponding modal logic based on the logic of knowledge; and Section 12.4 introduces our program algebra. Sections 12.5–12.8 demonstrate the approach on examples of increasing complexity.

Throughout we use left-associating dot for function application, so that $f.x.y$ means $(f(x))(y)$ or $f(x,y)$, and comprehensions/quantifications are written uniformly, as $(\mathsf{Q}x\colon T \mid R \cdot E)$ for quantifier Q, bound variable(s) x of type(s) T, range predicate R (probably) constraining x and element-constructor E in which x (probably) appears free. For sets the opening "(Q" is "{" and the closing ")" is "}" so that, e.g. the comprehension $\{x,y\colon \mathbb{N} \mid y = x^2 \cdot z + y\}$ is the set of all natural numbers that exceed z by a perfect square exactly, that is $\{z, z{+}1, z{+}4, \cdots\}$.

12.2 The Shadow Model of security

12.2.1 Introduction; Non-interference; Logic of Knowledge

Our operational model is loosely based on non-interference [12] and on the Kripke structures associated with the (modal) Logic of Knowledge [11]: it extends the former with concepts of the latter, and is targetted specifically at development of secure programs (in its terms) via a process of stepwise refinement. The "shadow" of the title refers to an extra semantic component that tracks a postulated attacker's inferred knowledge, or ignorance, of hidden (high-security) variables.

The non-interference approach (in its simplest form) partitions variables into high-security- and low-security classes: we call them *hidden* and *visible*, respectively. A "non-interference -secure" program then prevents an attacker's inferring hidden variables' initial values from initial and/or final visible variables' values. Assuming for simplicity just two variables v, h of class visible, hidden, respectively we consider in this simple approach a possibly nondeterministic program r that takes initial states (v,h), to sets of final visible states v' and is thus of type $\mathcal{V} \to \mathcal{H} \to \mathbb{P}\mathcal{V}$, where $\mathcal{V}, \mathcal{H}$ are the value sets corresponding to the types of v, h, respectively; note that we are ignoring final hidden values at this point. Such a program r is *non-interference secure* just when for any initial visible value the set of possible final visible values is independent of the initial hidden value [19, 28, 32] as expressed here:

$$(\forall\, v\colon \mathcal{V};\ h_0, h_1\colon \mathcal{H} \cdot r.v.h_0 = r.v.h_1)\,.$$

Our first extension of the simple approach is to concentrate on final- (rather than initial) hidden values and therefore to model programs by the slightly more elaborate type $\mathcal{V} \to \mathcal{H} \to \mathbb{P}(\mathcal{V} \times \mathcal{H})$. For two such programs $r_{\{1,2\}}$ we say that $r_1 \sqsubseteq r_2$, that r_1 "is (securely) refined by" r_2, just when the following both hold:

(i) For any initial state v, h each possible r_2 outcome is also a possible r_1 outcome, that is

$$(\forall\, v{:}\,\mathcal{V};\ h{:}\,\mathcal{H} \cdot r_1.v.h \supseteq r_2.v.h)\,.^2$$

This is the normal "can reduce nondeterminism" form of refinement, i.e. it is the classical form.

(ii) For any initial state v, h and final state v' possible for r_2 (i.e. for which there exists a compatible h'_2), each h'_1 that r_1 can produce with that v, v' can also be produced by r_2 with that same v, v', that is

$$\left(\begin{array}{ll}\forall\, v, v'{:}\,\mathcal{V};\ h, h'_1, h'_2{:}\,\mathcal{H} \cdot & (v', h'_2) \in r_2.v.h \wedge (v', h'_1) \in r_1.v.h \\ & \Rightarrow (v', h'_1) \in r_2.v.h\end{array}\right).$$

This second condition says that for any particular visible final v' the attacker's "ignorance" of h''s compatible with that v' cannot be decreased by the refinement from r_1 to r_2: whenever we must consider out of ignorance that some h'_1 is possible for r_1, we must be forced to consider that same h'_1 to be possible for r_2 as well. This is the extended "secure" refinement that we use to restrict the classical.

In fact, in this moderately extended approach, the two conditions (i), (ii) together do not allow ignorance strictly to increase: refinement then boils down to a simple policy of allowing decrease of nondeterminism in v but not in h. But strict increase of hidden nondeterminism will be possible (12.3) in the more ambitious approach we introduce below.

As an example of the above we restrict all our variables' types so that $\mathcal{V} = \mathcal{H} = \{0, 1\}$, and we let r_1 be the maximally nondeterministic program that can produce from any initial values (v, h) any one of the four possible (v', h') final values in $\mathcal{V} \times \mathcal{H}$. Then the program r_2 that produces only the two final values in $\{(0, 0), (0, 1)\}$ is a refinement of r_1 that strictly reduces nondeterminism in v but not in h, and is (therefore) still secure. But the program r'_2 that produces only the two final values in $\{(0, 0), (1, 1)\}$ is not a secure refinement, because it reduces nondeterminism in h (as well).

Thus r_1 allows any behaviour, and r_2 simply reduces the nondeterminism by limiting its outputs to $v' = 0$ only; but, even with the limited outputs, an attacker of r_2 can gain no more knowledge of h''s value than it would have had from attacking

[2] Some researchers [2] do not consider the final h here: for our purposes that would make our program operators non-monotonic for refinement (thus a failure of compositionality). That is, if for hidden h the assignments $h{:=}\,0$ and $h{:=}\,1$ are the same, then for visible v the compositions $h{:=}\,0;\ v{:=}\,h$ and $h{:=}\,1;\ v{:=}\,h$ should not be different.

r_1 instead. So $r_1 \sqsubseteq r_2$. An attacker of r_2' however can deduce h''s value from having seen v''s, since that program guarantees they will be equal. Since that attack is not possible on r_1, we have $r_1 \not\sqsubseteq r_2'$.

12.2.2 The Shadow of h

In r_1 above, when the final value v' was 0 the corresponding set of associated possible values of h' was $\{0, 1\}$. This set $\{0, 1\}$ is called "*The Shadow,*" and represents explicitly an attacker's ignorance of the hidden variables' values. In r_2 that shadow was the same (for $v' = 0$); but in r_2' the shadow was smaller, and that is why we don't consider r_2' to be a refinement of r_1 as far as security is concerned.

In the shadow semantics we model this ignorance-set explicitly, so that our final program state is extended to a triple (v', h', H') with H' a subset of $\mathcal{H}$ – in each triple the H' contains exactly those (other) values that h' might have had. The (extended) output-triples of the three example programs are then respectively

$$
\begin{array}{ll}
r_1 - & \{(0,0,\{0,1\}),\ (0,1,\{0,1\}),\ (1,0,\{0,1\}),\ (1,1,\{0,1\})\} \\
r_2 - & \{(0,0,\{0,1\}),\ (0,1,\{0,1\})\} \\
r_2' - & \{(0,0,\{0\}),\quad (1,1,\{1\})\}\,,
\end{array}
$$

and we can see $r_1 \sqsubseteq r_2$ because r_1's set of outcomes includes all of r_2's. But, e.g. the outcome $(0, 0, \{0\})$ of r_2' does not occur among r_1's outcomes, nor is there even an r_1-outcome $(0, 0, H')$ with $H' \subseteq \{0\}$ that would satisfy (ii). That is why we say that $r_1 \not\sqsubseteq r_2'$ for security.

Now – the final step – to enable the sequential composition of shadow-enhanced programs also initial triples (v, h, H) must be dealt with, since the final triples of some first component become initial triples for a second component following it. We therefore define the full shadow semantics, in the next section, by showing how those triples are related by program execution.

12.2.3 The Shadow Semantics of Atomic Programs

A "non-shadow," call it *classical* program r is effectively an input–output relation between $\mathcal{V} \times \mathcal{H}$ -pairs. Its shadow version $\langle r \rangle$ is a relation between $\mathcal{V} \times \mathcal{H} \times \mathbb{P}\mathcal{H}$ -triples and is defined as follows:

Definition 1. *Atomicity* Given a standard program $r{:}\, \mathcal{V} \rightarrow \mathcal{H} \rightarrow \mathbb{P}(\mathcal{V} \times \mathcal{H})$ we define its *atomic shadow version* $\langle r \rangle{:}\, \mathcal{V} \rightarrow \mathcal{H} \rightarrow \mathbb{P}\mathcal{H} \rightarrow \mathbb{P}(\mathcal{V} \times \mathcal{H} \times \mathbb{P}\mathcal{H})$ so that $\langle r \rangle.v.h.H \ni (v', h', H')$ just when

(i) we have both $r.v.h \ni (v', h')$.
(ii) and $H' = \{h'{:}\,\mathcal{H} \mid (\exists h{:}\, H \cdot r.v.h \ni (v', h'))\}$.

The final shadow component is thus generated from the initial shadow component and any nondeterminism present in the program. □

As a first example, let the syntax $x{:\in}\, S$ denote the standard program that chooses variable x's value from a set S, which we assume to be non-empty. From Definition 1 we have that

(i) A choice of visible v has no effect on h, H
because $\langle v{:\in}\, S\rangle.v.h.H = \{v'{:}\,S \cdot (v', h, H)\}$

(ii) But choice of hidden h introduces ignorance
because $\langle h{:\in}\, S\rangle.v.h.H = \{h'{:}\,S \cdot (v, h', S)\}$

(iii) And finally an assignment of hidden to visible "collapses" any ignorance that might be there because $\langle v{:=}\, h\rangle.v.h.H = \{(h, h, \{h\}\}$

From (ii) and (iii) above we can therefore see that in the sequential composition $\langle h{:\in}\, S\rangle;\ \langle v{:=}\, h\rangle$ the first statement introduces ignorance – we do not know h's exact value "at the semicolon" – but the second statement then removes it because we can deduce h's value, at the end, by observing v. The composition as a whole is nondeterministic, because v, h's common final value is drawn arbitrarily from S; but the nondeterminism is observable.

In general, atomicity is not preserved by composition (indeed one expects it not to be); but in many simple cases it is preserved.

Lemma 1. *atomicity and composition* Given two programs $r_{\{1,2\}}$ over v, h we have $\langle r_1;\ r_2\rangle = \langle r_1\rangle;\ \langle r_2\rangle$ just when v's *intermediate* value, i.e. "at the semicolon," can be deduced from its *endpoint* values, i.e. initial and final, possibly in combination. The semicolon denotes relational composition in both cases, of pairs on the left and of triples on the right.

Proof. Given in [22 App. 1.10]. □

In fact this lemma is more significant when its conditions are *not* met than when they are. It means, for example, that we cannot conclude from Lemma 1 that $\langle v{:=}\, h;\ v{:=}\, 0\rangle = \langle v{:=}\, h\rangle;\ \langle v{:=}\, 0\rangle$, since on the left the intermediate value of v cannot be deduced from its endpoint values: for h is not visible at the beginning and v itself has been "erased" at the end. And indeed from Definition 1

(i) On the left we have $\langle v{:=}\, h;\ v{:=}\, 0\rangle.v.h.H = \{(0, h, H)\}$, whereas
(ii) On the right we have $(\langle v{:=}\, h\rangle;\ \langle v{:=}\, 0\rangle).v.h.H = \{(0, h, \{h\})\}$.

This phenomenon is called *perfect recall* [11] – that v's temporary receipt of h is seen by an attacker even though it is subsequently overwritten – and it is a feature (not a bug). It is due to our refinement-oriented point of view, as we now explain.

12.2.4 Refinement Versus Atomicity: Gedanken *Experiments*

Perfect recall is necessary because refinement must be *monotonic*, i.e. (A) that refinement of a program portion must refine the whole program; and we insist additionally (B) that classical refinements involving v only must remain valid even when we take security into account. Both principles (A, B) are required in order to be able to develop large programs via local reasoning over small portions.

For example, without perfect recall the overwriting of v would prevent program $v{:=}\,h;\;\; v{:\in}\,\{0,1\}$ from revealing h. Yet from (B) we have $v{:\in}\,\{0,1\} \sqsubseteq v{:=}\,v$; and then from (A) we have $(v{:=}\,h;\;\; v{:\in}\,\{0,1\}) \sqsubseteq (v{:=}\,h;\;\; v{:=}\,v)$ – and it is a contradiction of secure refinement that the *lhs* does not reveal h but the *rhs* does. Thus the premise – that recall is not perfect – is false.

There is a similar experiment for conditionals: because (A, B) imply the refinement

$$\begin{array}{ll} & \textbf{if}\ h=0\ \textbf{then}\ v{:\in}\,\{0,1\}\ \textbf{else}\ \ v{:\in}\,\{0,1\}\ \textbf{fi} \\ \sqsubseteq & \textbf{if}\ h=0\ \textbf{then}\ v{:=}\,0 \qquad\ \textbf{else}\ \ v{:=}\,1 \qquad\ \textbf{fi}\,, \end{array}$$

we must accept that the **if**-test reveals its outcome, in this case whether $h = 0$ holds. And nondeterministic choice $P_1 \sqcap P_2$ is visible to the attacker because each of the two branches $P_{\{1,2\}}$ can be refined separately in a similar way.

12.2.5 Declared Atomicity

If there is a code fragment P that we know will be executed atomically at runtime, we can write it $\langle P \rangle$ using the notation of Definition 1. This will however have two consequences:

(i) At runtime the atomicity must be guaranteed for P's execution, and
(ii) At design-time only equality reasoning can be used within P.

With respect to (2) we mean that $P \sqsubseteq P'$ does not allow us to conclude the refinement $\langle P \rangle \sqsubseteq \langle P' \rangle$. We can however conclude the equality $\langle P \rangle = \langle P' \rangle$ from $P{=}P'$.

12.2.6 Summary of Semantics

The Shadow Semantics of a small imperative language is given in Fig. 12.1 for non-looping constructs. The only non-traditional command is **reveal** that gives the value of some expression to the attacker directly, but changes no program variables; note it does change the shadow.

Refinement between programs is defined as follows:

Definition 2. *Refinement* For programs $P_{\{1,2\}}$ we say that P_1 *is refined by* P_2 and write $P_1 \sqsubseteq P_2$ just when for all v, h, H we have

$$\begin{array}{l} (\forall (v',h',H_2') \colon [\![P_2]\!].v.h.H \,\cdot \\ \qquad (\exists H_1' \colon \mathbb{P}\mathcal{H} \mid H_1' \subseteq H_2' \cdot \quad (v',h',H_1') \in [\![P_1]\!].v.h.H))\,. \end{array}$$

	Program P	Semantics $[\![P]\!].v.h.H$	
Publish a value	**reveal** $E.v.h$	$\{\ (v,\ h,\ \{h'{:}H \mid E.v.h' = E.v.h\})\ \}$	
Assign to visible	$v{:=}\,E.v.h$	$\{\ (E.v.h,\ h,\ \{h'{:}H \mid E.v.h' = E.v.h\})\ \}$	$*$
Assign to hidden	$h{:=}\,E.v.h$	$\{\ (v,\ E.v.h,\ \{h'{:}H \bullet E.v.h'\})\ \}$	$*$
Choose visible	$v{:\in}\,S.v.h$	$\{v'{:}S.v.h \bullet\ (v',\ h,\ \{h'{:}H \mid v' \in S.v.h'\})\ \}$	$*$
Choose hidden	$h{:\in}\,S.v.h$	$\{h'{:}S.v.h \bullet\ (v,\ h',\ \{h'{:}H;\ h''{:}S.v.h' \bullet h''\})\ \}$	$*$
Sequential composition	$P_1;\ P_2$	$([\![P_1]\!];\ [\![P_2]\!]).v.h.H$	
Demonic choice	$P_1 \sqcap P_2$	$[\![P_1]\!].v.h.H \cup [\![P_2]\!].v.h.H$	
Conditional	**if** $E.v.h$ **then** P_t **else** P_f **fi**	$[\![P_t]\!].v.h.\{h'{:}H \mid E.v.h' = \mathbf{true}\}$ $\lhd\ E.v.h\ \rhd$ $[\![P_f]\!].v.h.\{h'{:}H \mid E.v.h' = \mathbf{false}\}$	

The commands P marked $*$ satisfy $[\![P]\!] = (\text{"}\textit{classical semantics of } P\text{"})$, and we call them the *atomic* commands, meaning semantically so. Note that **reveal** is therefore not security-atomic, even though it is a syntactic atom.

Fig. 12.1 Semantics of non-looping commands

This means that for each initial triple (v,h,H) every final triple (v',h',H'_2) produced by P_2 must be "justified" by a triple (v',h',H'_1), with equal or smaller ignorance, produced by P_1.[3] □

For example, from Fig. 12.1 we have that $[\![h{:=}\,0 \sqcap h{:=}\,1]\!].v.h.H$ produces the outome $\{(v,0,\{0\}),(v,1,\{1\})\}$, whereas $[\![h{:\in}\{0,1\}]\!].v.h.H$ produces the outcome $\{(v,0,\{0,1\}),(v,1,\{0,1\})\}$. Thus

$$h{:=}\,0 \sqcap h{:=}\,1 \quad \sqsubset \quad h{:\in}\{0,1\} \tag{12.3}$$

is an example of a strict refinement where the two commands differ only by a strict increase of ignorance: they have equal nondeterminism functionally, but in one case ($\sqcap$) it can be observed by the attacker and in the other case ($:\in$) it cannot. For example, the "more ignorant" triple $(v,0,\{0,1\})$ is strictly justified by the "less ignorant" triple $(v,0,\{0\})$, where we say "strictly" because $\{0\} \subset \{0,1\}$.

12.3 The Logic of Ignorance

With the (v,h,H)-triple semantics of Section 12.2.6 comes an assertion logic over the triples; it is based on the Logic of Knowledge and its interpretation over Kripke structures [11]. We call it *The Logic of Ignorance*.

[3] This is the Smyth Order [33] on sets of outcomes that is induced by the order on individual outcomes given by $(v,h,H_1) \sqsubseteq (v,h,H_2)$ iff $H_1 \subseteq H_2$.

As in Hoare Logic for sequential programs [16] we interpret first-order predicate formulae over program states by making the program variables act as constants in the logic. To that we add a *possibility modality* so that $P\phi$ means (roughly) that ϕ holds for some "possible" value $h{\in}H$ rather than necessarily for the actual current value of h, where ϕ is a classical formula. In fact we have $\phi \Rightarrow P\phi$ because a property of our semantics is that $h{\in}H$ for all triples (v, h, H) we consider: what is true must also be possible. In general, however, we do not have $P\phi \Rightarrow \phi$, since what is possible is not necessarily true.

12.3.1 Interpretation of Modal Formulae

The assertion language contains function- (including constant-) and relation symbols as needed, among which we distinguish the (program-variable) constant symbols *visibles* in some set V and *hiddens* in H; as well there are the usual (logical) variable symbols in L over which we allow $\forall, \exists$ quantification. The visibles, hiddens and variables are collectively the *scalars* $\mathsf{X}{:=}\mathsf{V} \cup \mathsf{H} \cup \mathsf{L}$ with $\mathsf{V}, \mathsf{H}, \mathsf{L}$ assumed disjoint.

A *structure* comprises a non-empty domain $\mathcal{D}$ of values, together with functions and relations over it that interpret the function- and relation symbols mentioned above; within the structure we name the partial functions v, h that interpret visibles and hiddens, respectively; we write their types $\mathsf{V} \nrightarrow \mathcal{D}$ and $\mathsf{H} \nrightarrow \mathcal{D}$, respectively (where the "crossbar" indicates the potential partiality of the function). We don't bother naming the interpretations of function- and relation symbols, as they do not vary from one program state to another.

A *valuation* is a partial function from scalars to $\mathcal{D}$, thus typed $\mathsf{X} \nrightarrow \mathcal{D}$; one valuation w' can override another w so that for scalar x we have that $(\mathsf{w}{\lhd}\mathsf{w}').x$ is $\mathsf{w}'.x$ if w' is defined at x and is $\mathsf{w}.x$ otherwise. The valuation $x{\mapsto}d$ is defined only at variable x, where it takes value d.

A *state* $(\mathsf{v}, \mathsf{h}, \mathsf{H})$ comprises a visible- v, hidden- h and *shadow*- part H; the last, in $\mathbb{P}(\mathsf{H} \nrightarrow \mathcal{D})$, is a *set* of valuations over hiddens only. All the states that we consider satisfy $\mathsf{h}{\in}\mathsf{H}$.

We define truth of Φ at $(\mathsf{v}, \mathsf{h}, \mathsf{H})$ under valuation w by induction in the usual style, writing $(\mathsf{v}, \mathsf{h}, \mathsf{H}), \mathsf{w} \models \Phi$. For term t let $[\![t]\!].\mathsf{v}.\mathsf{h}.\mathsf{w}$ be its value interpretation determined inductively from the valuation $\mathsf{v}{\lhd}\mathsf{h}{\lhd}\mathsf{w}$ and the (implicit) interpretation of function symbols. Then our formula interpretation is as defined in Fig. 12.2 [11, pp. 79, 81].

12.3.2 Shadow-Sensitive Hoare-Triples; Revelations

As is normal, we say that $\{\Phi\}prog\{\Psi\}$ just when any initial state $(\mathsf{v}, \mathsf{h}, \mathsf{H}) \models \Phi$ can lead via $[\![prog]\!]$ only to final states $(\mathsf{v}', \mathsf{h}', \mathsf{H}') \models \Psi$; typically Φ is called the *precondition* and Ψ is called the *postcondition*.

- $(\mathsf{v},\mathsf{h},\mathsf{H}),\mathsf{w} \models R.t_1.\cdots.t_K$ for relation symbol R and terms $t_{\{1\cdots K\}}$ iff the tuple $([\![t_1]\!].\mathsf{v}.\mathsf{h}.\mathsf{w},\cdots,[\![t_K]\!].\mathsf{v}.\mathsf{h}.\mathsf{w})$ is an element of the interpretation of R in $\mathcal{D}^K$.
- $(\mathsf{v},\mathsf{h},\mathsf{H}),\mathsf{w} \models t_1 = t_2$ iff $[\![t_1]\!].\mathsf{v}.\mathsf{h}.\mathsf{w} = [\![t_2]\!].\mathsf{v}.\mathsf{h}.\mathsf{w}$.
- $(\mathsf{v},\mathsf{h},\mathsf{H}),\mathsf{w} \models \neg\Phi$ iff $(\mathsf{v},\mathsf{h},\mathsf{H}),\mathsf{w} \not\models \Phi$.
- $(\mathsf{v},\mathsf{h},\mathsf{H}),\mathsf{w} \models \Phi_1 \wedge \Phi_2$ iff $(\mathsf{v},\mathsf{h},\mathsf{H}),\mathsf{w} \models \Phi_1$ and $(\mathsf{v},\mathsf{h},\mathsf{H}),\mathsf{w} \models \Phi_2$.
- $(\mathsf{v},\mathsf{h},\mathsf{H}),\mathsf{w} \models (\forall x \cdot \Phi)$ iff $(\mathsf{v},\mathsf{h},\mathsf{H}),\mathsf{w}\lhd(x\mapsto d) \models \Phi$ for all d in $\mathcal{D}$.
- $(\mathsf{v},\mathsf{h},\mathsf{H}),\mathsf{w} \models P\Phi$ iff $(\mathsf{v},\widehat{\mathsf{h}},\mathsf{H}),\mathsf{w} \models \Phi$ for some $\widehat{\mathsf{h}}$ in H.

We write just $(\mathsf{v},\mathsf{h},\mathsf{H}) \models \Phi$ when w is empty, and $\models \Phi$ when $(\mathsf{v},\mathsf{h},\mathsf{H}) \models \Phi$ for all $(\mathsf{v},\mathsf{h},\mathsf{H})$ with $\mathsf{h}{\in}\mathsf{H}$, and we take advantage of the usual "syntactic sugar" for other operators. Thus, for example, we can show $\models \Phi \Rightarrow P\Phi$ for all Φ, a fact which we mentioned earlier. Similarly we can assume *wlog* that modalities are not nested, since we can remove nestings via the validity $\models P\Phi \equiv (\exists c \cdot \Phi_{h\leftarrow c} \wedge P(h{=}c))$.

As a convenience we allow 0-subscripted hidden variables (e.g. h_0) within the modality to refer to the actual rather than potential hidden value; for that we extend the last clause above to read

- $(\mathsf{v},\mathsf{h},\mathsf{H}),\mathsf{w} \models P\Phi$ iff $(\mathsf{v},\widehat{\mathsf{h}},\mathsf{H}),\mathsf{w}\lhd(h_0\mapsto\mathsf{h}.h) \models \Phi$ for some $\widehat{\mathsf{h}}$ in H.

Thus, for example, $P(h{=}\neg h_0)$ means that whatever value Boolean h might have, we must consider also its negation to be possible: we do not (cannot, if that formula holds) know it exactly.

Fig. 12.2 Interpretation of logic of Ignorance

We illustrate Shadow-sensitive Hoare-triples with the **reveal** E command: we have for any classical ϕ that[4]

$$\{P(E{=}E_0 \wedge \phi)\}\ \textbf{reveal}\ E\ \{P\phi\}\,, \qquad \text{where } E_0 \text{ is } E \text{ with all its hidden variables 0-subscripted.} \tag{12.4}$$

It is verified as follows:

$$
\begin{array}{lll}
 & (\mathsf{v},\mathsf{h},\mathsf{H}) \models P(E{=}E_0 \wedge \phi) & \\
 & \text{and } [\![\textbf{reveal}\,E]\!].\mathsf{v}.\mathsf{h}.\mathsf{H} \ni (\mathsf{v}',\mathsf{h}',\mathsf{H}') & \\
\text{iff} & & \text{“Fig. 12.2, for some } \widehat{\mathsf{h}} \in \mathsf{H} \text{ and } \mathsf{h}_0 = (h_0\mapsto\mathsf{h}.h)\text{”} \\
 & (\mathsf{v},\widehat{\mathsf{h}},\mathsf{H}),(\mathsf{w}\lhd\mathsf{h}_0) \models E{=}E_0 \wedge \phi & \\
 & \text{and } [\![\textbf{reveal}\,E]\!].\mathsf{v}.\mathsf{h}.\mathsf{H} \ni (\mathsf{v}',\mathsf{h}',\mathsf{H}') & \\
\text{iff} & (\mathsf{v},\widehat{\mathsf{h}},\mathsf{H}),(\mathsf{w}\lhd\mathsf{h}_0) \models E{=}E_0 & \text{“Fig. 12.2”} \\
 & \text{and } (\mathsf{v},\widehat{\mathsf{h}},\mathsf{H}),(\mathsf{w}\lhd\mathsf{h}_0) \models \phi & \\
 & \text{and } [\![\textbf{reveal}\,E]\!].\mathsf{v}.\mathsf{h}.\mathsf{H} \ni (\mathsf{v}',\mathsf{h}',\mathsf{H}') & \\
\text{iff} & E.\mathsf{v}.\widehat{\mathsf{h}} = E.\mathsf{v}.\mathsf{h} & \text{“Fig. 12.2; Fig. 12.1”} \\
 & \text{and } (\mathsf{v},\widehat{\mathsf{h}},\mathsf{H}),(\mathsf{w}\lhd\mathsf{h}_0) \models \phi & \\
 & \text{and } \mathsf{v}'{=}\mathsf{v} \wedge \mathsf{h}'{=}\mathsf{h} \wedge \mathsf{H}'{=}\{\mathsf{h}'{:}\,\mathsf{H} \mid E.\mathsf{v}.\mathsf{h}' = E.\mathsf{v}.\mathsf{h}\} &
\end{array}
$$

[4] We use upper case for modal formulae, and lower case for classical.

iff $\quad \widehat{\mathsf{h}} \in \mathsf{H}'$ "third line simplifies first; equalities"
and $(\mathsf{v}', \widehat{\mathsf{h}}, \mathsf{H}), (\mathsf{w} \triangleleft \mathsf{h}'_0) \models \phi$
and $\mathsf{v}' = \mathsf{v} \wedge \mathsf{h}' = \mathsf{h} \wedge \mathsf{H}' = \{\mathsf{h}' : \mathsf{H} \mid E.\mathsf{v}.\mathsf{h}' = E.\mathsf{v}.\mathsf{h}\}$

iff $\quad \widehat{\mathsf{h}} \in \mathsf{H}'$ "classical ϕ has shadow-independent interpretation: thus can replace H by H'"
and $(\mathsf{v}', \widehat{\mathsf{h}}, \mathsf{H}'), (\mathsf{w} \triangleleft \mathsf{h}'_0) \models \phi$
and $\mathsf{v}' = \mathsf{v} \wedge \mathsf{h}' = \mathsf{h} \wedge \mathsf{H}' = \{\mathsf{h}' : \mathsf{H} \mid E.\mathsf{v}.\mathsf{h}' = E.\mathsf{v}.\mathsf{h}\}$

implies $(\mathsf{v}', \widehat{\mathsf{h}}, \mathsf{H}'), (\mathsf{w} \triangleleft \mathsf{h}'_0) \models \phi$ "for some $\widehat{\mathsf{h}} \in \mathsf{H}'$"

iff $(\mathsf{v}', \mathsf{h}', \mathsf{H}'), \mathsf{w} \models P\phi$. "Fig. 12.2"

That was not a pretty calculation but, having done it once, we can use (12.4) forever.

In fact the precondition in (12.4) is the *weakest* such with respect to postcondition $P\phi$, and we thoroughly explore ignorance-based weakest preconditions elsewhere [8, 25, 27]. Using that, we can give some examples of assertion-based reasoning about revelations.

In the items below, let Ψ be the assertion $P((h \textbf{ mod } 2 = h_0 \textbf{ mod } 2) \wedge h{=}3)$, generated by (12.4) applied to **reveal** $(h$ **mod** $2)$ $\{P(h{=}3)\}$, which we can simplify as follows:

$$
\begin{array}{ll}
 & P((h \textbf{ mod } 2 = h_0 \textbf{ mod } 2) \wedge h{=}3) \\
= & P((3 \textbf{ mod } 2 = h_0 \textbf{ mod } 2) \wedge h{=}3) \\
= & P((1 = h_0 \textbf{ mod } 2) \wedge h{=}3) \\
= & (h \textbf{ mod } 2){=}1 \wedge P(h{=}3)\,,
\end{array}
$$

that is **odd** $h \wedge P(h{=}3)$. With that we consider the following examples:

(i) Does $h{:}{\in}\{1,3\}$; **reveal** $(h$ **mod** $2)$ establish $P(h{=}3)$? *Yes* ✓
Command $h{:}{\in}\{1,3\}$ establishes both conjuncts of Ψ.

(ii) Does $h{:}{\in}\{1,5\}$; **reveal** $(h$ **mod** $2)$ establish $P(h{=}3)$? *No* ×
Command $h{:}{\in}\{1,5\}$ does not establish $P(h{=}3)$, which is the second conjunct of Ψ. Given the source code, it is obvious that h cannot be 3 finally.

(iii) Does $h{:}{\in}\{2,3\}$; **reveal** $(h$ **mod** $2)$ establish $P(h{=}3)$? *No* ×
Command $h{:}{\in}\{1,5\}$ does not establish **odd** h, which is the first conjunct of Ψ. One possible outcome is that 0 is revealed, which precludes h's being finally 3.

(iv) Does $(h{:=}\,1 \sqcap h{:=}\,3)$; **reveal** $(h$ **mod** $2)$ establish $P(h{=}3)$? *No* ×
The left-hand command $h{:=}\,1$ – a demonic possibility which we must take into account – establishes the first conjunct of Ψ but not the second. Because the nondeterminism is visible (unlike Case (1)), if the left branch is taken – and it might be – then from the source code we know that h cannot be 3.

Note especially the difference between (i) and (iv). In the former, the nondeterminism occurs within an atomic command, and is therefore hidden; but, in the latter, it occurs between atomic commands, and is therefore observable.

12.4 The Algebra of Ignorance

12.4.1 Assertions: The Historical Motivation

The Hoare-logic method of program correctness involves "hybrid" formulae (the triples) that are built from two formal languages: the programming language, and the assertion language. Thus $\{\phi\}prog\{\psi\}$ in its partial correctness interpretation holds just when every terminating execution of *prog* from an initial state satisfying ϕ is guaranteed to deliver a final state satisfying ψ.

The command **assert** ϕ is typically defined to act as **skip** in states satisfying ϕ and to "abort" (or give some error message) otherwise [23, 35]. Assuming that "abort" is refined by anything, we can see that the classical program-algebraic inequality

$$\textbf{assert}\,\phi;\ prog \ \sqsubseteq\ prog;\ \textbf{assert}\,\psi$$

has the same meaning as $\{\phi\}prog\{\psi\}$ does. It *encodes* the Hoare-triple entirely within the programming language and its in-built notion of refinement, thus within the program algebra: if ϕ does not hold in the initial state, then the refinement goes through because the entire left side aborts; if ϕ does hold, then the refinement goes though only if the right-hand side does *not* abort – it must deliver only final states of *prog* for which the subsequent **assert** ψ does not abort.

12.4.2 Revelations: The Modern Analogue of Assertions for Security

By analogy with Section 12.3.2 we can express ignorance-logical properties of program fragments entirely within the programming language by using a special-purpose command encoding the ignorance formulae. There are two main idioms.

In the first we have

$$\textbf{assert}\,\phi;\ prog \ \sqsubseteq\ \textbf{reveal}\,E;\ prog, \tag{12.5}$$

where of course refinement is now understood in the sense of Definition 2, that is non-classically because it preserves ignorance as well as functional properties. If ϕ does not hold in the initial state, then the refinement goes through; otherwise, it goes through only if *prog* reveals the initial value of E "anyway" (so that the explicit **reveal** E on the right "does no further damage"). Thus (12.5) expresses "If ϕ holds initially, then *prog* reveals the initial value of E."

In the second we have

$$\textbf{assert}\,\phi;\ prog \ \sqsubseteq\ prog;\ \textbf{reveal}\,E\,,$$

expressing "If ϕ holds initially, then *prog* reveals the final value of E."

Here are some examples, in which our variables take numeric values. We have the refinement

$$\textbf{assert}\, v{\neq}0;\;\; v{:=}\, v{\times}h \;\;\sqsubseteq\;\; \textbf{reveal}\, h;\;\; v{:=}\, v{\times}h$$

because h's initial value can be deduced by dividing v's final value by its initial value, provided that initial value was not zero. The refinement does not go through without the assertion, since in the v-initially-zero case we cannot deduce h's value. For final values we have

$$\textbf{assert}\, v{=}0;\;\; h{:=}\, v{\times}h \;\;\sqsubseteq\;\; h{:=}\, v{\times}h;\;\; \textbf{reveal}\, h$$

because when v is zero we can see that h's final value must be zero too, although in that case $h{:=}\, v{\times}h$ still tells us nothing about h's initial value. The refinement does not go through without the assertion, since in the v-initially-nonzero case we cannot deduce h's final value without knowing what its initial value was.

Further idioms are possible, for example, with revelations on both sides.

12.4.3 A Calculus of Revelations [5]

We now set out some of the program-algebra associated with revelations; much use of the identities will be made later.

12.4.3.1 Replacing One Revelation by Another

Provided that truth of ϕ implies the equality $F = f(E)$ for some function f depending (optionally) on other visible variables, we have

$$\textbf{assert}\, \phi;\;\; \textbf{reveal}\, E \;\;\sqsubseteq\;\; \textbf{reveal}\, F\,. \tag{12.6}$$

These are some examples:

$\textbf{assert}\, h{=}0;\;\; \textbf{skip} \sqsubseteq \textbf{reveal}\, h$		Here f is the constant function 0.
$\textbf{reveal}\, h \sqsubseteq \textbf{reveal}\, h{\ominus}1$		... that is $h{-}1$ **max** 0.
$\textbf{reveal}\, h{\ominus}1 \not\sqsubseteq \textbf{reveal}\, h$		Initial values 0,1 not distinguished.
$\textbf{assert}\, h{>}0;\;\; \textbf{reveal}\, h{\ominus}1 \sqsubseteq \textbf{reveal}\, h$		If $h{>}0$ then $({\ominus}1)$ is injective.

[5] This is the title of the presentation on which the current paper is based [26].

12.4.3.2 Combining Revelations

In all cases we have

$$\textbf{reveal}\, E;\ \ \textbf{reveal}\, F \quad = \quad \textbf{reveal}\,(E,F)\,. \tag{12.7}$$

Here is an example over Booleans and exclusive-or:

$$\begin{array}{lll} & \textbf{reveal}\, x \oplus y;\ \ \textbf{reveal}\, y \oplus z & \text{“Write } \oplus \text{ for exclusive-or”} \\ = & \textbf{reveal}\,(x \oplus y, y \oplus z) & \text{“(12.7)”} \\ = & \textbf{reveal}\,(x \oplus y, x \oplus z) & \text{“(12.6) in both directions”} \\ = & \textbf{reveal}\, x \oplus y;\ \ \textbf{reveal}\, x \oplus z\,. & \text{“(12.7) in both directions”} \end{array}$$

12.4.3.3 Equivalence with Assignment to Local Visible

In all cases we have

$$\textbf{reveal}\, E \quad = \quad [\![\, \textbf{vis}\, v \cdot v{:=}\, E \,]\!]\,, \tag{12.8}$$

highlighting the fact that scope (local vs global) and visibility (**vis** vs **hid**) are orthogonal: in spite of the fact that v is temporary, ultimately “popped from the stack and discarded,” assigning to it while it is there does reveal the value assigned.

An example of this is given in Section 12.4.4.

12.4.4 Example: Specifications and the Encryption Lemma

For Booleans, or isomorphically $\{0,1\}$-valued variables x, y we write $x{\oplus}y{:=}\,E$ to abbreviate the specification statement $x, y{:}[x{\oplus}y = E]$ in the style of the Refinement Calculus [1, 3, 23], thus a command that sets x, y nondeterministically to make their exclusive-or equal to E. We define the command to be atomic, so that $[\![x{\oplus}y{:=}\,E]\!] = \langle x, y{:}[x{\oplus}y = E]\rangle$.

A common pattern for this is $[\![\, \textbf{vis}\, v;\ \ \textbf{hid}\, h' \cdot v{\oplus}h'{:=}\, h \,]\!]$ in the context of a declaration **hid** h. It is functionally equivalent to **skip** because it assigns only to local variables; we show it is Shadow-equivalent to **skip** also, i.e. that its effect of assigning to visible v reveals nothing about h. We have

$$\begin{array}{lll} & [\![\, \textbf{vis}\, v;\ \ \textbf{hid}\, h' \cdot v{\oplus}h'{:=}\, h \,]\!] & \\ = & [\![\, \textbf{vis}\, v;\ \ \textbf{hid}\, h' \cdot \langle v, h'{:}[v{\oplus}h' = h]\rangle \,]\!] & \text{“defined above”} \\ = & [\![\, \textbf{vis}\, v;\ \ \textbf{hid}\, h' \cdot \langle v{:\in}\, \{0,1\};\ \ h'{:=}\, h{\oplus}v\rangle \,]\!] & \text{“standard equality *”} \\ = & [\![\, \textbf{vis}\, v;\ \ \textbf{hid}\, h' \cdot \langle v{:\in}\, \{0,1\}\rangle;\ \ \langle h'{:=}\, h{\oplus}v\rangle \,]\!] & \text{“Lemma 1”} \\ = & [\![\, \textbf{vis}\, v;\ \ \textbf{hid}\, h' \cdot v{:\in}\, \{0,1\};\ \ h'{:=}\, h{\oplus}v \,]\!] & \text{“Fig. 12.1”} \\ = & [\![\, \textbf{vis}\, v \cdot v{:\in}\, \{0,1\};\ \ [\![\, \textbf{hid}\, h' \cdot h'{:=}\, h{\oplus}v \,]\!]]\!] & \text{“move scopes”} \end{array}$$

$$
\begin{array}{lll}
= & [\![\, \mathbf{vis}\, v \cdot v{:}\in\{0,1\}]\!] & \text{“assignment to local hidden is } \mathbf{skip}\text{”} \\
= & \mathbf{skip}\,. & \text{“assignment of visibles to local visible is } \mathbf{skip}\text{”}
\end{array}
$$

But at $*$ we could have written instead

$$
\begin{array}{lll}
= & [\![\, \mathbf{vis}\, v;\ \mathbf{hid}\, h' \cdot \langle h'{:}\in\{0,1\};\ v{:=}\,h'\oplus h\rangle\,]\!] & \text{“standard equality”} \\
= & & \text{“Lemma 1; Fig. 12.1; move scopes } \dagger\text{”} \\
 & [\![\, \mathbf{hid}\, h' \cdot h'{:}\in\{0,1\};\ [\![\, \mathbf{vis}\, v \cdot v{:=}\,h'\oplus h\,]\!]]\!] & \\
= & [\![\, \mathbf{hid}\, h' \cdot h'{:}\in\{0,1\};\ \mathbf{reveal}\, h'\oplus h\,]\!]\,, & \text{“(12.8) } \ddagger\text{”}
\end{array}
$$

with both $\dagger, \ddagger$ being interesting formulations often used in protocols: they too are therefore equal to **skip**. Each sets a hidden local Boolean h' randomly and publishes its exclusive-or with some global hidden h; the reasoning above shows rigorously (and formally) that no information about h is released by doing that.

We call that *The Encryption Lemma* and make much use of it below.

12.5 The Two Cryptographers [6]

Two cryptographers are about to choose from the trolley, but there are only two desserts there: a lavish cream cake, and a small biscuit. To avoid a series of insincere "after you" exchanges, they engage in this simple protocol: a single coin is flipped privately between them; each secretly writes his dessert choice on his own napkin if the coin shows heads, or the opposite choice if it shows tails; then they hand their folded-over napkins to the waiter.

If the waiter tells them their napkin-choices differ, they can safely take the two desserts and select their actual preferences once the waiter has gone away; otherwise, to avoid embarrassment, they will forego dessert altogether.

The protocol ensures that neither cryptographer knows the other's choice before he makes his own choice; and, whatever happens, the waiter does not find out which of them greedily chose the cream cake.[7]

Here is a Shadow-analysis of the protocol. Let the two cryptographers be A and B with Boolean variables a, b recording whether each wants the cream cake, respectively. Boolean c is the shared coin. We do not model the waiter explicitly, because his function of ensuring "oblivious choices" is outside our terms of reference: we

[6] While based on Chaum's *Dining Cryptographers* [6], the story for this tiny example has been especially invented to illustrate piecewise construction of a protocol that ultimately will be quite complex. This is the smallest portion, the first step.

[7] The original story ends differently. Without a protocol, the two diners do engage in "after you" protestations, each believing that the one who eventually chooses first will out of politeness have to take the small cracker; but in fact one diner finally chooses the cake. Outraged, the other diner protests "If *I* had chosen first, I'd have taken the cracker!" "Well," replies the first, "That's exactly what you've got."

do not address the issue of possible protocol violations. The *specification* of the protocol is just

$$\textbf{hid}\ a, b{:}\ \textbf{Bool}\ \cdot$$
$$\quad \textbf{reveal}\ a{\equiv}b\ ,$$

where the declarations of the hidden a, b are global: we assume them in subsequent manipulations of this example.

The specification says clearly that whether a and b agree is to be revealed but nothing else, and in fact it is hard to think of a clearer way of saying this. And although revealing $a{\equiv}b$ reveals a's value to B by implication (and vice versa), this does not need any special treatment: it cannot be avoided, and so there is no need to mention it. [8] Thus "but nothing else" above, an informal phrase, carries the sense of "unless unavoidable."

With the declarations as given, both a, b hidden, the observer is "the public" who thus cannot observe either one directly. The *implementation* under those same declarations, that is the protocol above, is derived algebraically as follows:

$$\textbf{reveal}\ a{\equiv}b$$

$=$ $\textbf{skip}$; "classical reasoning"
$\quad \textbf{reveal}\ a{\equiv}b$

$=$ $[\![\ \textbf{hid}\ c{:}\ \textbf{Bool}\ \cdot$ "Encryption Lemma, Section 12.4.4, and that ($\textbf{reveal}\ a{\equiv}b$) $=$ ($\textbf{reveal}\ a{\oplus}b$) by (12.6)"
$\qquad c{:}{\in}\ \textbf{Bool}$;
$\qquad \textbf{reveal}\ a{\equiv}c$
$\quad]\!]$;
$\quad \textbf{reveal}\ a{\equiv}b$

$=$ $[\![\ \textbf{hid}\ c{:}\ \textbf{Bool}\ \cdot$ "adjust scopes"
$\qquad c{:}{\in}\ \textbf{Bool}$;
$\qquad \textbf{reveal}\ a{\equiv}c$;
$\qquad \textbf{reveal}\ a{\equiv}b$
$\quad]\!]$

$=$ $[\![\ \textbf{hid}\ c{:}\ \textbf{Bool}\ \cdot$ "Reveal Calculus, example following (12.7): $(a{\equiv}c, a{\equiv}b)$ determines $(a{\equiv}c, b{\equiv}c)$ and vice versa"
$\qquad c{:}{\in}\ \textbf{Bool}$;
$\qquad \textbf{reveal}\ a{\equiv}c$;
$\qquad \textbf{reveal}\ b{\equiv}c$
$\quad]\!]$.

[8] We formalise this observation by observing that with the altered declarations **hid** a; **vis** b, that is B's point of view, we have the equality ($\textbf{reveal}\ a{\equiv}b$) $=$ ($\textbf{reveal}\ a{\equiv}b$; $\textbf{reveal}\ a$) from (12.6) and b's being visible.

Note (and recall from the introduction) that our strong assumptions for the adversary mean that it is sound to model this distributed protocol with a single sequential program: adversaries' access to the individual threads is modelled by the assumption of perfect recall.

In [22, App. 1.11] we illustrate some conventions for abbreviating the presentation of derivations like the one above.

12.6 The Three Cryptographers [9]

Three cryptographers have just had lunch, and ask for the bill. The waiter says that the bill has already been paid; and the cryptographers want to determine whether one of them paid it or whether it was paid by the NSA. In the case that one of them paid, none of the other cryptographers nor anyone else is to be able to determine which one it was. They proceed as follows.

They are sitting at a round table, [10] and each of the three adjacent pairs flips a coin between them that only that pair can see; thus each cryptographer can see two coins, because he is a member of two such pairs.

Each cryptographer then announces whether he paid; but if the two coins he sees show different faces, he lies. If an odd number of cryptographers claim to have paid, then indeed one did, but no-one (except him) knows who it was; otherwise the lunch was paid for by the NSA.

12.6.1 Helping Three Cryptographers by Considering One at a Time

Rather than giving a direct derivation in the style of Section 12.5, we build this protocol up from smaller components. We imagine a single cryptographer X with Boolean x who has access to two coins l, r on his left and right. The left one is already flipped; the right one he must flip himself; and then he reveals the exclusive-or of all three values. That amounts to the fragment

$$\begin{array}{l} \textbf{var}\ l, r\colon \textbf{Bool};\ \ \textbf{hid}\ x\colon \textbf{Bool}\ \cdot \\ \quad \left.\begin{array}{l} r{:\in}\ \textbf{Bool}; \\ \textbf{reveal}\ l \oplus x \oplus r\,, \end{array}\right\}\ \text{Protocol}\ X \end{array}$$

in which for the moment we are not giving the visibility type of l, r.

Now if we instantiate the X-fragment to A and B in turn, and introduce a hidden "middle" coin m: **Bool**, with both fragments we can get

[9] Three diners is Chaum's example exactly.

[10] This Arthurian concept is one of Formal Methods' great contributions to computing.

$$
\begin{array}{l}
\textbf{var}\ l, r\colon \textbf{Bool};\ \ \textbf{hid}\ a, b\colon \textbf{Bool}\ \cdot \\
\quad [\![\ \textbf{hid}\ m\colon \textbf{Bool}; \\
\qquad \left.\begin{array}{l} m{:}\in \textbf{Bool}; \\ \textbf{reveal}\ l \oplus a \oplus m; \end{array}\right\}\ \text{First instance of } X \\
\\
\qquad \left.\begin{array}{l} r{:}\in \textbf{Bool}; \\ \textbf{reveal}\ m \oplus b \oplus r \end{array}\right\}\ \text{Second instance of } X \\
\quad]\!] \,,
\end{array}
\tag{12.9}
$$

and this – by similar reasoning to Section 12.5 – can be shown [11] to implement the specification

$$
\begin{array}{l}
\textbf{var}\ l, r\colon \textbf{Bool};\ \ \textbf{hid}\ a, b\colon \textbf{Bool}\ \cdot \\
\quad r{:}\in \textbf{Bool}; \\
\quad \textbf{reveal}\ l \oplus (a \oplus b) \oplus r\,.
\end{array}
\tag{12.10}
$$

Again only $a \oplus b$ is revealed, and nothing about a or b individually. But the point of doing it in this way is that it suggests how the protocol can be extended to any number of participants. So far we have dealt with two out of three.

For the third cryptographer (or final, when there are more than three in total) we must use a slightly different approach. It is no more complex, but must be "backwards" since he cannot assume that some coin is already flipped: the process must begin somewhere; and the two "extremal" coins must be hidden. Thus Cryptographer C executes

$$
\begin{array}{l}
[\![\ \textbf{hid}\ l, r\colon \textbf{Bool}\ \cdot \\
\quad l{:}\in \textbf{Bool}; \\
\quad \left.\begin{array}{l} r{:}\in \textbf{Bool}; \\ \textbf{reveal}\ l \oplus (a \oplus b) \oplus r \end{array}\right\}\ \begin{array}{l}\text{specification from (12.10)} \\ \text{implemented by (12.9)}\end{array} \\
\quad \textbf{reveal}\ l \oplus c \oplus r \\
]\!] \,,
\end{array}
\tag{12.11}
$$

in which we have embedded the *specification* of the A, B protocol as the middle two commands. That is, Cryptographer C flips a coin l and says to A, B "now execute your protocol," finally making his own revelation using the coin l he flipped himself (now some time ago) and the "output" coin r provided by the A, B protocol he arranged to have executed. This is the right thing to do, because in two easy steps from the above we can reason

[11] Think of A's secret in Section 12.5 being $l \oplus a$ and B's secret being $b \oplus r$, and re-instantiate the derivation on that basis, replacing $\equiv$ by $\oplus$.

$$
\begin{array}{ll}
(12.11) = & \text{“Revelation Calculus; adjust scopes”} \\
\quad [\![\, \textbf{hid}\; l, r\colon \textbf{Bool} \cdot & \\
\qquad l{:}{\in}\, \textbf{Bool}; & \\
\qquad r{:}{\in}\, \textbf{Bool}; & \\
\qquad \textbf{reveal}\; l \oplus (a \oplus b) \oplus r & \\
\quad]\!]; & \\
\quad \textbf{reveal}\; a \oplus b \oplus c & \\
& \\
= \quad \textbf{reveal}\; a \oplus b \oplus c\,, & \text{“Encryption Lemma for } l, r \text{ together”}
\end{array}
$$

which is our specification for the Three Cryptographers.

To finish the three cryptographers' protocol we now simply replace the specification of A, B's sub-protocol by its implementation, which was given earlier. Because the monotonicity property of refinement, actually equality in this case, we do not need to do any further checking. The immediate result, thus obtained "for free" from (12.10) $\sqsubseteq$ (12.9), is

$$
\begin{array}{ll}
\quad \textbf{hid}\; a, b, c\colon \textbf{Bool} \cdot & \\
& \\
\qquad \textbf{reveal}\; a \oplus b \oplus c & \\
& \\
= \quad [\![\, \textbf{hid}\; l, m, r\colon \textbf{Bool} \cdot & \text{“replace } A, B \text{ specification above} \\
\qquad l{:}{\in}\, \textbf{Bool}; & \text{by its implementation from earlier”} \\
\qquad m{:}{\in}\, \textbf{Bool}; & \\
\qquad \textbf{reveal}\; l \oplus a \oplus m; & \\
\qquad r{:}{\in}\, \textbf{Bool}; & \\
\qquad \textbf{reveal}\; m \oplus b \oplus r; & \\
\qquad \textbf{reveal}\; l \oplus c \oplus r & \\
\quad]\!]\,. &
\end{array}
$$

In Section 12.8 we will do the same step-by-step construction within a loop, thus dealing with arbitrarily many cryptographers.

12.6.2 On Expressiveness and "Caveats"

An informal specification of the Three Cryptographers might state that whether the NSA paid is to be learned without at the same time learning whether any particular cryptographer paid. Except of course the paying cryptographer himself, who knows it anyway... Similarly, as we saw, it is unavoidable that in the Two Cryptographers protocol, each learns what the other chose, given that he knows his own choice and comes to know whether the other's differs.

Thus if the first sentence above were formalised, as a logical assertion to be met by the implemented code, it would be too strong. The *caveat* (A) is that when we write (somehow) "for all i,j: 1..3 cryptographer$_i$ does not know whether cryptographer$_j$ paid," we must add (when we remember) "provided $i \neq j$."

Similarly there is an implicit assumption that at most one cryptographer paid (where "implicit" means "probably we forgot to mention that the first time around"). If two cryptographers paid (B), then the outcome will be "NSA paid" when in fact it did not: two of the three cryptographers did. So another caveat is added: "Assuming that at most one cryptographer paid..."

In fact neither of these two problems bother us if we use refinement. In both cases (A, B) it is obvious from the *specification* **reveal** $a \oplus b \oplus c$ what behaviour we should expect in all situations, no matter how bizarre, and we do not have to add extra "caveat" clauses to some assertion in order to accommodate them. More importantly, we do not have to worry about whether we have added *enough* caveat clauses. A similar situation occurs in the *Obvlivious Transfer Protocol* [10,29,30], specified $a := b_i$ and in which A reads into a his choice indexed i: $\{1,2\}$ of one of two messages $b_{1,2}$ that B holds, without A's learning anything about the message he did not choose and without B's learning anything about the index i of the choice A made. Except that in the case $m_1 = m_2$ we must accept (C) that A does learn about the message he did not choose, because it is equal to the one he did choose...

Again, from the specification $a := b_i$ it is obvious what happens in (C), and we do not have to introduce caveats to accommodate it. (We gave a rigorous derivation of the Oblivious Transfer Protocol in our earlier report [27].)

12.6.3 *On Points of View*

In the derivation of Section 12.6.1 all three variables a, b, c are declared hidden, and so our conclusions apply only to adversaries for whom they actually *are* all-three hidden: the general public. To show that as well that no cryptographer learns the thoughts of another, say that C does not learn about whether A or B paid (unless of course C did pay, in which case he knows that A and B did not... another caveat we can ignore), we would vary the declarations **hid** a, b; **vis** c and do the derivation under those conditions.

In general, sometimes the same derivation steps go through for all viewpoints; but sometimes they do not, and then we must choose different intermediate refinement steps depending on "who's looking." When that happens, it's equivalent to a case analysis and can fairly be considered a disadvantage: thus we try to find derivations that go through for all viewpoints in the same way.

12.7 Loops and Fixed-Points

As an example of how loops are treated, the code of (12.1) in Section 12.1, slightly modified, is shown to satisfy a simple specification: we will prove the equality

$\quad$ **hid** h: ℕ ·

$\qquad$ **reveal** $h{\div}2$;
$\qquad$ $h{:=}\ h$ **mod** 2

$=\quad$ **while** $h{>}1$ **do**
$\qquad$ $h{:=}\ h-2$
$\quad$ **end** .

That is, not only does the loop change the value of h (in an obvious way), but, also the repeated conditional tests reveal all but the low bit of h's original value. This leaking occurs because it is a refinement (an equality) to unfold a loop, which produces an **if** command, and we have already seen how refinement causes leakage in the conditionals of **if**'s.

Terminating loops are the unique fixed-points of their associated program functionals, and so to prove equality between a loop and some specification it is enough to show the specification satisfies the loop's functional. In the example above, that means we show

$\quad$ **hid** h: ℕ ·

$\qquad$ **reveal** $h{\div}2$;
$\qquad$ $h{:=}\ h$ **mod** 2

$=\quad$ **if** $h{>}1$ **then**
$\qquad$ $h{:=}\ h-2$;
$\qquad$ **reveal** $h{\div}2$;
$\qquad$ $h{:=}\ h$ **mod** 2
$\quad$ **fi** ,

for which the techniques we have already will suffice.

We start with the right-hand side, since it has more structure (thus suggesting appropriate moves), and the left-hand side is a smaller target:

$\quad$ **if** $h{>}1$ **then**
$\qquad$ $h{:=}\ h-2$;
$\qquad$ **reveal** $h{\div}2$;
$\qquad$ $h{:=}\ h$ **mod** 2
$\quad$ **fi**

$=\quad$ **if** $h{>}1$ **then** $\qquad$ "add assertion"
$\qquad$ **assert** $h{>}1$;
$\qquad$ $h{:=}\ h{-}2$;
$\qquad$ **reveal** $h{\div}2$;
$\qquad$ $h{:=}\ h$ **mod** 2
$\quad$ **fi**

$=$ **if** $h{>}1$ **then** "commute commands"
  assert $h{>}1$;
  reveal $(h{-}2) \div 2$;
  $h{:=}\,h{-}2$;
  $h{:=}\,h$ **mod** 2
fi

$=$ **if** $h{>}1$ **then** "Revelation calculus; classical reasoning; remove assertion"
  reveal $h{\div}2$;
  $h{:=}\,h$ **mod** 2
fi

$=$ **if** $h{>}1$ **then** "Add assertion; Revelation Calculus; classical reasoning"
  reveal $h{\div}2$;
  $h{:=}\,h$ **mod** 2
else
  assert $0{\leq}h{\leq}1$;
  reveal $h{\div}2$;
  $h{:=}\,h$ **mod** 2
fi

$=$ **if** $h{>}1$ **then skip else skip fi**; "Remove assertion; classical reasoning"
reveal $h{\div}2$;
$h{:=}\,h$ **mod** 2

$=$ **reveal** $h{>}1$; "Revelation calculus"
reveal $h{\div}2$;
$h{:=}\,h$ **mod** 2

$=$ **reveal** $h{\div}2$; "Revelation calculus"
$h{:=}\,h$ **mod** 2 ,

and we are done.

An abbreviated derivation is given in [22 App. 1.12].

12.8 The Thousand-and-One Cryptographers [12]

With the tools introduced in earlier sections, we can now derive a looping program that implements the Dining Cryptographers' specification for as many participants as we like. Let the cryptographers be numbered $0..N$ inclusive (thus $N+1$ of them)

---

[12] This is in the Arabian sense: "as many as you like."

and let their did-pay states be recorded as indexed Boolean variables $a[0..N]$: **Bool**. Our specification is then

$$\textbf{vis}\, N\colon \mathbb{N};\;\; \textbf{hid}\, a[0..N]\colon \textbf{Bool}\,\cdot$$

$$\textbf{reveal}\,(\oplus n\colon \mathbb{N} \mid 0\le n\le N \cdot a[n])\,,$$

Having learned in Section 12.6.1 that the last cryptographer is treated specially, we make that special treatment our first development step, reasoning

$$\begin{array}{ll} = & [\![\; \textbf{hid}\; l, r\colon \textbf{Bool}\,\cdot \\ & \quad \textbf{reveal}\; l \oplus (\oplus n\colon \mathbb{N} \mid 0\le n<N \cdot a[n]) \oplus r; \quad | \\ & \quad \textbf{reveal}\; l \oplus a[N] \oplus r \\ &]\!]\,, \end{array} \qquad \text{“As in Section 12.6.1”}$$

intending to implement the right-barred portion (i.e. having a “|” at right) as a loop.

For that loop, we refer again to Section 12.6.1, which suggests using a loop body built on the fragment

$$\begin{array}{l} r{:\in}\, \textbf{Bool}; \\ \textbf{reveal}\; l \oplus a[n] \oplus r; \\ n{:=}\, n{+}1, \end{array}$$

and it turns out that a **repeat-until** works better in this instance. With that in mind we propose as the next step for the right-barred portion, above, the code

$$\begin{array}{ll} = & [\![\; \textbf{vis}\; n\colon \mathbb{N};\;\; \textbf{hid}\; m\,\cdot \\ & \quad m, n{:=}\, l, 0; \\ & \quad \textbf{repeat} \\ & \qquad r{:\in}\, \textbf{Bool}; \\ & \qquad \textbf{reveal}\; m \oplus a[n] \oplus r; \\ & \qquad m, n{:=}\, r, n{+}1 \\ & \quad \textbf{until}\; n{=}N \\ &]\!]\,, \end{array}$$

where we have had to introduce a temporary variable m to avoid over writing the initially flipped l that will be needed at the end by Cryptographer N. In order to establish this equality, we use the techniques of Section 12.7 to show that the right-barred **repeat-until** is equal to this straight-line fragment:

$$\begin{array}{l} r{:\in}\, \textbf{Bool}; \\ \textbf{reveal}\; m \oplus (\oplus i\colon \mathbb{N} \mid n\le i<N \cdot a[i]) \oplus r \\ m, n{:=}\, r, N \end{array}$$

For the loop (and its functional) as given, that means we must work towards the program fragment immediately above from this fragment below:

```
vis N: ℕ;  hid a[0..N]: Bool ·

  reveal (⊕n: ℕ | 0≤n≤N · a[n])

=  ⟦ vis n: ℕ;  hid l, m, r: Bool ·               "Reasoning in this section"
     l:∈ Bool;
     m, n:= l, 0;
     repeat
       r:∈ Bool;
       reveal m ⊕ a[n] ⊕ r;
       m, n:= r, n+1
     until n=N;
     reveal l ⊕ a[N] ⊕ r
   ⟧
```

Fig. 12.3 Specification and implementation for the thousand-and-one cryptographers

```
r:∈ Bool;
reveal m ⊕ a[n] ⊕ r;
m, n:= r, n+1;

if n<N then
  r:∈ Bool;
  reveal m ⊕ (⊕i: ℕ | n≤i<N · a[i]) ⊕ r;
  m, n:= r, N
fi .
```

Since this derivation is "more of the same" material that we have illustrated in earlier sections, we put it elsewhere [22, App. 1.13].

As we remarked in Section 12.6.1, monotonicity of refinement (equivalently, the congruence of our program operators) means that no further reasoning is necessary when we pull the pieces of this section together. That gives the overall equality shown in Fig. 12.3.

12.9 Advantages; Disadvantages; Comparisons; Conclusions

Provable program refinement is the established scientific technique relating specifications to software code; it is hard to achieve, but brings with it a recognised quality to the workmanship of the code it produces. "Provable security refinement" – or something very like – is the technique we propose here with similar implications of quality.

Our proposed mathematical model for secure refinement has been inspired by a number of other works; our contribution has been to select and fuse several well-known techniques to produce a reasoning tool that can be applied at the source level, and our focus on reasoning *at the level of source code* is the most obvious feature setting us apart from other researchers. Earlier work setting out the theory [25, 26] outlined in more detail how this approach relates to other techniques. In summary, it shares many similarities with the Logic of Knowledge [15] but is less general. The semantic technique is based on a version of noninterference, which distinguishes "high-security" variables from "low security," and similar techniques have been suggested by Leino [19] and Sabelfeld [32].

However, our overriding motivation is to be able to prove security properties about program code relative to specific assumptions about the operating context. But code – even without security implications – is hard to understand; with security in the mix it can rise to a higher order of impenetrability, and finding security flaws in such code is an unending task. In 1988 Goldwasser, Micali and Rivest [13] were the first to introduce the idea of "provable security"; it was highly innovative for its time but set the foundations to place security on a scientific footing, and has led to many theoretical results about cryptographic protocols and their relationship to their underlying cryptographic primitives. Although we do not claim a technique as general or widely applicable as Goldwasser and Micali's work, we do claim a source-level method following its fundamental principles, which is applicable to some security properties. Here our attacker – a feature of their work – is the programmer who might (maliciously or not) attempt to use a program in a context for which it was not designed; secure refinement means exactly that the implemented code has the same (or better) security properties as the specification. The crucial advantage of this is that the specification suffers exactly the same security flaws as the implementation, whatever they might be, and is exposed to *the same attacks*. Specifications by tradition only state the designer's ideal requirements and avoid the issues of implementation, and – as with traditional functional properties – it is only at the abstract level that designers have any chance of understanding their designs: this is where security issues should be considered.

References

1. Abrial, J.-R.: The B Book: Assigning Programs to Meanings. Cambridge University Press, (1996)
2. Alur, R., Černý, P., Zdancewic, S.: Preserving secrecy under refinement. In: ICALP '06: Proceedings (Part II) of the 33rd International Colloquium on Automata, Languages and Programming, pp. 107–118. Springer (2006)
3. Back, R.-J.R.: On the correctness of refinement steps in program development. Report A-1978-4, Dept Comp Sci, Univ Helsinki (1978)
4. Back, R.-J.R.: A calculus of refinements for program derivations. Acta Inf. **25**, 593–624 (1988)
5. Broadfoot, P J., Roscoe, A.W.: Tutorial on FDR and its applications. In: Havelund, K., Penix, J., Visser, W. (eds.), SPIN, volume 1885 of Lecture Notes in Computer Science, pp. 322. Springer (2000)

6. Chaum, D.: The dining cryptographers problem: unconditional sender and recipient untraceability. J. Cryptol. **1**(1), 65–75 (1988)
7. Chong, S., Myers, A.C.: Security policies for downgrading. In: CCS '04: Proceedings of the 11th ACM Conference on Computer and Communications Security, pp 198–209, New York, USA (2004). ACM
8. Dijkstra, E.W.: A Discipline of Programming. Prentice-Hall (1976)
9. Engelhardt, K., Moses, Y., van der Meyden, R.: Unpublished report, Univ NSW (2005)
10. Even, S., Goldreich, O., Lempel, A.: A randomized protocol for signing contracts. Commun. ACM, **28**(6), 637–647 (1985)
11. Fagin, R., Halpern, J., Moses, Y., Vardi, M.: Reasoning about Knowledge. MIT Press (1995)
12. Goguen J.A., Meseguer, J.: Unwinding and inference control. In: Proc IEEE Symp on Security and Privacy, pp. 75–86 (1984)
13. Goldwasser, S., Micali, S., Rivest, R.: A digital signature scheme secure against adaptive chosen message attacks. SIAM J. Comput. **17**, 281–308 (1988)
14. Probabilistic Systems Group. Collected publications. `www.cse.unsw.edu.au/~carrollm/probs`
15. Halpern, J.Y., O'Neill, K.R.: Anonymity and information hiding in multiagent systems. In: Proc 16th IEEE Computer Security Foundations Workshop, pp. 75–88 (2003)
16. Hoare, C.A.R.: An axiomatic basis for computer programming. Comm. ACM **12**(10), 576–80, 583 (October 1969)
17. Hoare, C.A.R.: Communicating Sequential Processes. Prentice Hall (1985)
18. Jacob. J.: Security specifications. In: IEEE Symposium on Security and Privacy, pp. 14–23 (1988)
19. Leino, K.R.M., Joshi, R.: A semantic approach to secure information flow. Science Comput. Program. **37**(1–3), 113–38 (2000)
20. Li, P., Zdancewic, S.: Downgrading policies and relaxed noninterference. In: POPL '05: Proc. 32nd ACM SIGPLAN-SIGACT Symp. on Princ. of Prog. Lang., pp. 158–170, New York, USA (2005) ACM
21. Mantel, H.: Preserving information flow properties under refinement. In: Proc IEEE Symp Security and Privacy, pp. 78–91 (2001)
22. McIver, A.K., Morgan, C.C.: The thousand-and-one cryptographers. At [14, `McIver:10web`]; includes appendices (April 2009)
23. Morgan, C.C.: Programming from Specifications, 2nd ed Prentice-Hall, (1994). `web.comlab.ox.ac.uk/oucl/publications/books/PfS/`
24. Morgan, C.C.: Of probabilistic wp and CSP. In: Abdallah, A., Jones, C.B., Sanders, J.W. (eds.), Communicating Sequential Processes: The First 25 Years. Springer (2005)
25. Morgan, C.C.: The Shadow Knows: Refinement of ignorance in sequential programs. In: Uustalu, T. (ed.), Math Prog. Construction, volume 4014 of Springer, pp. 359–78. Springer (2006) Treats Dining Cryptographers
26. Morgan, C.C.: A calculus of revelations (2008). Presented at VSTTE '08, Toronto. `http://www.cs.stevens.edu/~naumann/vstte-theory-2008/`
27. Morgan, C.C.: The Shadow Knows: refinement of ignorance in sequential programs. Sci. Comput. Program. **74**(8) (2009) Treats Oblivious Transfer
28. Morgan, C.C., McIver, A.K.: Unifying wp and wlp. Inf. Proc. Lett., **20**(3), 159–164 (1996). Available at [14, key MM95]
29. Rabin, M. O.: How to exchange secrets by oblivious transfer. Technical Report TR-81, Harvard University (1981). Available at `eprint.iacr.org/2005/187`
30. Rivest, R.: Unconditionally secure commitment and oblivious transfer schemes using private channels and a trusted initialiser. Technical report, MIT press (1999). `//theory.lcs.mit.edu/~rivest/Rivest-commitment.pdf`
31. Roscoe, A.W., Woodcock, J.C.P., Wulf, L.: Non-interference through determinism. Journal of Computer Security, **4**(1), 27–54, (1996)
32. Sabelfeld, A., Sands, D.: A PER model of secure information flow. Higher-Order Symb. Comput., **14**(1), 59–91 (2001)

33. Smyth, M.B.: Power domains. Jnl. Comp. Sys. Sci. **16**, 23–36 (1978)
34. Wirth, N.: Program development by stepwise refinement. Comm. ACM **14**(4), 221–7 (1971)
35. Wirth, N., Hoare, C.A.R.: A contribution to the development of ALGOL. Commun. ACM **9**(6), 413–432 (June 1966)

Chapter 13
On Process-Algebraic Extensions of Metric Temporal Logic

Christoph Haase, Joël Ouaknine, and James Worrell

Abstract It is known that the satisfiability problem for Metric Temporal Logic (MTL) is decidable over finite timed words. In this chapter we study the satisfiability problem for extensions of this logic by various process-algebraic operators. On the negative side we show that satisfiability becomes undecidable when any of hiding, renaming, or asynchronous parallel composition are added to the logic. On the positive side we show decidability with the addition of alphabetised parallel composition and fixpoint operators. We use one-clock Timed Propositional Temporal Logic (TPTL(1)) as a technical tool for the decidability results and show that TPTL(1) with fixpoints provides a logical characterisation of the class of languages accepted by one-clock timed alternating automata.

13.1 Introduction

The model of time usually adopted in computer-aided verification and process algebra is *qualitative*: it offers an ordering of the various events a given system may go through, but abstracts away from *quantitative*, or *metric*, information regarding the precise timing of these events. If such information is required, one must adopt a more sophisticated framework, modelling time using real numbers, for example. Over the last two decades, much work has gone into developing and studying such frameworks, both in the model-checking and in the process-algebraic communities.

This chapter studies extensions of the linear dense-time specification formalism *Metric Temporal Logic (MTL)*. MTL, introduced by Koymans in 1990 [13], is one of the most prominent logics for reasoning about real-time systems. MTL formulas can either be interpreted in a *state-based* semantics, in which observations are made continuously, or in an *event-based* semantics, in which observations are recorded

C. Haase, J. Ouaknine (✉), and J. Worrell
Oxford University Computing Laboratory, UK
e-mail: chrh@comlab.ox.ac.uk; joel@comlab.ox.ac.uk; jbw@comlab.ox.ac.uk

C.B. Jones et al. (eds.), *Reflections on the Work of C.A.R. Hoare*,
DOI 10.1007/978-1-84882-912-1_13, © Springer-Verlag London Limited 2010

as instantaneous "snapshots" whenever a discrete change, or "event," occurs. In the latter, models of formulas are *timed words*, i.e., sequences of events together with associated real-valued timestamps.

Unfortunately, it has long been known that MTL satisfiability is undecidable in the state-based semantics [2, 9]. Moreover, it was shown more recently that over infinite timed words, MTL is also undecidable [19]. Surprisingly, MTL turned out to be decidable – albeit with non-primitive recursive complexity – over finite timed words [20]. Subsequent to this discovery, various fragments of MTL – over both semantics and over both finite and infinite behaviours – were shown to be decidable; for a recent survey of these results, we refer the reader to [5, 21].

This chapter focuses on extensions of MTL by various natural process-algebraic operators, from the point of view of computability. Accordingly, we are exclusively interested in the event-based semantics over finite timed words, as all other semantics immediately result in undecidability. We consider MTL augmented with the following various operators:

- *Hiding.* This operator, which corresponds to existential quantification, provides a convenient way to abstract away unimportant events (as regards a particular property of interest).
- *Renaming.* Similarly to hiding, the renaming operator is useful for expressing specifications and constructing abstractions of systems; it can be used, for example, to group the various possible events into a small number of categories.
- *Asynchronous parallel composition.* Also known as *interleaving* or *shuffle product*; this operator combines the behaviours of two systems in as liberal a way as possible; in particular, each system is entirely oblivious to the other one.
- *Alphabetised parallel composition.* Also known as *(partially) synchronous parallel composition*. Two systems thus composed will synchronise over their common events, and otherwise proceed independently of each other. This operator is particularly useful to model communication over a well-defined interface.
- *Fixpoints.* Fixpoint operators are omnipresent in process algebra and model checking, enhancing the expressiveness of various formalisms and allowing one, for example, to model recursion.

The results of this chapter are twofold. On the negative side, we show that MTL augmented with any of hiding, renaming or asynchronous parallel composition becomes undecidable. The main result, however, is that we can augment MTL with both alphabetised parallel composition and least fixpoint operators and still retain decidability over finite words. The key technical tools we use to obtain decidability are the one-clock (or one-variable) fragment of Timed Propositional Temporal Logic, denoted TPTL(1) [3], and one-clock Timed Alternating Automata (1TAA) [15, 20]. Moreoever, we show that the extension of TPTL(1) with fixpoints provides a complete logical characterisation of 1TAA, which is of independent interest.

The process-algebraic operators listed above originate from Tony Hoare's Communicating Sequential Processes (CSP), undoubtedly the most prominent linear-time process algebra. These operators, or slight variations thereof, have also figured in other process algebras and in the context of temporal and dynamic logics. For example, Lange [14] considers LTL with fixpoint operators, showing that it is expressively equivalent to finite alternating automata with weak parity acceptance conditions. Hiding also appears in temporal logic in the guise of existential quantification over propositional variables. Sistla, Vardi, and Wolper [26] show that LTL with existential quantification can express all ω-regular languages. Over real time, it is known that Metric Interval Temporal Logic (MITL) with existential quantification can express all languages that are accepted by timed automata [11]. Propositional Dynamic Logic with interleaving has been considered in [16].

One of the key contributions of Tony Hoare's work on CSP has been a deeper understanding of the central phenomenon of *nondeterminism* in semantics. Hoare's classic text *Communicating Sequential Processes* [12], for example, devotes an entire chapter to the subject; his perspective on nondeterminism, in particular as a mechanism of underspecification, but also as an inevitable consequence of concurrency, has proven enormously influential.

From a semantic standpoint, it seems fair to say that the development of the standard failures divergences model for CSP [6] arose principally as a solution to the problem of adequately handling nondeterminism in a denotational setting. The problems turned out considerably more resilient in the timed world, and a fully satisfactory understanding of nondeterminism in Timed CSP has not yet been reached [25]. Nonetheless, one of the pivotal notions to emerge from the study of nondeterminism in both the untimed and timed settings is that of *operators that preserve determinism.* It is remarkable – although perhaps not entirely surprising – that in the present chapter, the operators that preserve decidability turn out to be precisely those that preserve determinism (quite independently of the fact that basic MTL formulas do exhibit native "nondeterminism" through disjunction in any case).

Nondeterminism was also studied around the same time as Tony Hoare by Robin Milner, and features in his seminal work *A Calculus of Communicating Systems* [17]. Milner was, however, exclusively concerned with operational semantics at the time, and consequently his outlook had a very different flavour. Outside of process algebra and semantics, nondeterminism has an even older history, going back (at least) some two millennia in philosophy, and half a century in other areas of computer science [22], notably formal language theory, algorithms and complexity. Modern applications of nondeterminism can be found, among others, in computer security, artificial intelligence and software engineering.

Most proofs have been omitted from this chapter and can be found in the technical report [8].

13.2 Preliminaries

Let $\mathbb{R}_+$ denote the set of non-negative real numbers, $\mathbb{Q}_+$ the set of non-negative rational numbers, and $\mathbb{N}$ the set of positive integers. The set $\mathbb{N}_n$ is the set of positive integers up to and including n, i.e., $\mathbb{N}_n := \{1, \ldots, n\}$. For an interval $\mathcal{I} \subseteq \mathbb{R}_+$ and

$r \in \mathbb{R}_+$, $\mathcal{I} + r := \{u + r \mid u \in \mathcal{I}\}$. By $Id_X := \{(x,x) \mid x \in X\}$ we denote the identity relation on a set X. Given a binary relation $R \subseteq X \times Y$, we define its functional lifting $R : X \to \mathcal{P}(Y)$ as $R(x) := \{y \mid (x,y) \in R\}$. We call R *total* if $R(x) \neq \emptyset$ for all $x \in X$. Given a function $f : X \to Y$, its update $f[x \mapsto y] : X \to Y$ is defined as $f[x \mapsto y](z) := y$ if $z = x$ and $f[x \mapsto y](z) := f(z)$ otherwise.

In the untimed world, traces of systems are usually modelled as finite or infinite words over some alphabet of events Σ. However, as discussed in Section 13.1, this model does not allow one to make quantitative assertions regarding *when* events occur. A natural way to overcome this drawback, first proposed by Reed and Roscoe in the development of Timed CSP [23, 24], is to model traces of timed systems as finite or infinite words over the event alphabet together with timestamps indicating the time of occurrence of events. In the remainder of this chapter we focus exclusively on finite timed words.

Definition 1 (Timed words). Let Σ be a nonempty finite set of events. A **time sequence** τ is a finite sequence $\tau_1\tau_2\ldots\tau_n$ of time values from $\mathbb{R}_+$ such that $\tau_i \leq \tau_{i+1}$ for all $1 \leq i < n$. A **timed word** ρ over Σ is a tuple (σ, τ) where τ is a time sequence and $\sigma = \sigma_1\sigma_2\ldots\sigma_n$ is a word over Σ of the same length as τ.

The set of all finite timed words over Σ is written $T\Sigma^*$. Note that our notion of time is *weakly monotonic*, in that we allow several events to share the same timestamp. Similar results to the ones presented here also hold for *strongly monotonic* time, although as pointed out in [10], awkward complications arise when disallowing the possibility of simultaneous events in the presence of parallel composition operators. Note that we do not require the first element of a time sequence to be zero.

The *length* of a timed word ρ is denoted by $\mid \rho \mid$ and is the length of the underlying time sequence. Alternatively, we can represent a timed word as a sequence of *timed events* by writing $\rho = (\sigma_1, \tau_1)(\sigma_2, \tau_2)\ldots(\sigma_n, \tau_n)$. For convenience, we also define auxiliary functions as follows: for $1 \leq i \leq \mid \rho \mid$, $\sigma_i(\rho) := \sigma_i$ and $\tau_i(\rho) := \tau_i$, where (σ_i, τ_i) is the i-th timed event of ρ. Given a timed word ρ, denote by $\rho^{i,j}$ the timed word $(\sigma_i, 0)(\sigma_{i+1}, \tau_{i+1} - \tau_i)\ldots(\sigma_j, \tau_j - \tau_i)$, $1 \leq i \leq j \leq \mid \rho \mid$. Moreover $\rho^i := \rho^{i,|\rho|}$ and for $j > \mid \rho \mid$, $\rho^{i,j} := \rho^i$. Given $E \subseteq \Sigma$, the timed word $\rho \setminus E$ is obtained from ρ by deleting all timed events (σ_i, τ_i) from ρ with $\sigma_i \in E$.

Definition 2 (TPTL(1) syntax). TPTL(1) formulas are defined inductively according to the following grammar:

$$\varphi ::= a \mid \varphi_1 \vee \varphi_2 \mid \neg\varphi \mid \bigcirc\varphi \mid \varphi_1 \mathcal{U} \varphi_2 \mid x \sim c \mid x.\varphi$$

Here, $a \in \Sigma$ is an event, $\bigcirc$ is the **next** operator, $\mathcal{U}$ is the **until** operator, x is a **clock variable**, $c \in \mathbb{Q}_+$ and $\sim \in \{\leq, <, =, \neq, >, \geq\}$. Note that TPTL(1) makes use of a single-clock variable, x.

We define the standard Boolean abbreviations $\varphi_1 \wedge \varphi_2 := \neg(\neg\varphi_1 \vee \neg\varphi_2)$, $\varphi_1 \to \varphi_2 := \neg\varphi_1 \vee \varphi_2$, $\top := a \vee \neg a$, and $\bot := \neg\top$. The *eventually* operator is defined as $\Diamond\varphi := \top \mathcal{U} \varphi$ and the *globally* operator as $\Box\varphi := \neg\Diamond\neg\varphi$. The clock variable in TPTL(1) formulas is the key reference for making quantitative statements about the evolution of time. It allows one to "freeze" (or record) time points along a timed word, which can later be compared to the current time. When $x.\varphi$ holds at some time point τ, x is bound to τ in φ and when the clock constraint $x \sim c$ is evaluated at some later time point τ', it is checked whether or not $\tau' - \tau \sim c$. This can be seen this *resetting* the clock x at time point τ.

Originally, TPTL as introduced in [3] allowed for multiple clock variables. However, that logic has an undecidable satisfiability problem and we therefore only consider its one-variable fragment TPTL(1) in this chapter.

We now give a non-standard presentation of the semantics of TPTL(1), which can however easily be shown to be equivalent to that commonly found in the literature. Its main advantage is to ease the definition of fixpoint operators later on.

Given a timed word ρ and a TPTL(1) formula φ, the semantic function $[\![-]\!]^\rho$ maps φ to an element of the set $\mathcal{V}(\rho) := \mathcal{P}(\mathbb{N}_{|\rho|} \times \mathbb{R}_+)$. Intuitively, $(i, r) \in [\![\varphi]\!]^\rho$ if φ holds at position i in ρ when the value of the clock variable x is r.

Definition 3 (TPTL(1) semantics). The semantics of a TPTL(1) formula φ is defined by induction on the structure of φ, as follows:

$$
\begin{aligned}
[\![a]\!]^\rho &:= \{(i,r) \mid \sigma^i = a, i \in \mathbb{N}_{|\rho|}, \text{ and } r \in \mathbb{R}_+\} \\
[\![\varphi_1 \vee \varphi_2]\!]^\rho &:= [\![\varphi_1]\!]^\rho \cup [\![\varphi_2]\!]^\rho \\
[\![\neg\varphi]\!]^\rho &:= \{(i,r) \mid i \in \mathbb{N}_{|\rho|} \text{ and } r \in \mathbb{R}_+\} \setminus [\![\varphi]\!]^\rho \\
[\![\bigcirc\varphi]\!]^\rho &:= \{(i,r) \mid (i+1, r') \in [\![\varphi]\!]^\rho \text{ and } r = r' + \tau_i - \tau_{i+1}\} \\
[\![\varphi_1 \,\mathcal{U}\, \varphi_2]\!]^\rho &:= \{(i,r) \mid \exists j. i \leq j \leq \mid \rho \mid \text{ and } (j, r + \tau_j - \tau_i) \in [\![\varphi_2]\!]^\rho \text{ and} \\
&\qquad \forall k. i \leq k < j \text{ implies } (k, r + \tau_k - \tau_i) \in [\![\varphi_1]\!]^\rho\} \\
[\![x \sim c]\!]^\rho &:= \{(i,r) \mid i \in \mathbb{N}_{|\rho|}, r \in \mathbb{R}_+, \text{ and } r \sim c\} \\
[\![x.\varphi]\!]^\rho &:= \{(i,r) \mid (i,0) \in [\![\varphi]\!]^\rho \text{ and } r \in \mathbb{R}_+\}
\end{aligned}
$$

We write $\rho \models \varphi$ iff $(1, \tau_1(\rho)) \in [\![\varphi]\!]^\rho$, and $L(\varphi) := \{\rho \mid \rho \models \varphi\}$ for the timed language defined by φ. A TPTL(1) formula φ is called *satisfiable* iff $L(\varphi) \neq \emptyset$. The problem of checking whether a formula φ is satisfiable has been shown to be decidable with non-primitive recursive complexity in [20], by translating TPTL(1) formulas into one-clock timed alternating automata (1TAA), introduced subsequently.[1]

The real-time logic MTL can be defined as a syntactic fragment of TPTL(1). It is known to be strictly less expressive than TPTL(1) [4].

Definition 4 (MTL). MTL formulas are defined according to the following grammar, where $a \in \Sigma$ and $\mathcal{I}$ is an open, half-open, or closed interval with endpoints in $\mathbb{Q}_+$:

$$\varphi ::= a \mid \varphi_1 \vee \varphi_2 \mid \neg\varphi \mid \bigcirc_{\mathcal{I}}\varphi \mid \varphi_1 \,\mathcal{U}_{\mathcal{I}}\, \varphi_2$$

---

[1] Technically speaking, [20] deals with Metric Temporal Logic rather than TPTL(1). The proof techniques however carry over straightforwardly.

The semantics of MTL formulas is given by a translation function $(-)^\dagger$ that maps MTL formulas to TPTL(1) formulas, as follows:

$$
\begin{aligned}
a^\dagger &:= a & (\bigcirc_{\mathcal{I}}\varphi)^\dagger &:= x.\bigcirc(x \in \mathcal{I} \wedge \varphi^\dagger) \\
(\varphi_1 \vee \varphi_2)^\dagger &:= \varphi_1^\dagger \vee \varphi_2^\dagger & (\varphi_1 \,\mathcal{U}_{\mathcal{I}}\, \varphi_2)^\dagger &:= x.(\varphi_1^\dagger \,\mathcal{U}\, (x \in \mathcal{I} \wedge \varphi_2^\dagger)) \\
(\neg\varphi)^\dagger &:= \neg(\varphi^\dagger)
\end{aligned}
$$

where $x \in \mathcal{I}$ denotes the obvious corresponding conjunction of inequalities.

We call $\bigcirc_{\mathcal{I}}$ the *time-constrained next* and $\mathcal{U}_{\mathcal{I}}$ the *time-constrained until* operators. The *time-constrained eventually* operator $\Diamond_{\mathcal{I}}$ and *globally* operator $\Box_{\mathcal{I}}$ are defined similarly to their TPTL(1) counterparts. We also sometimes abuse notation and use pseudo-arithmetic expressions, such as '$=1$', to denote intervals.

Let S be a finite set of *locations*, and define the set $\Phi(S)$ of formulas as follows:

$$\varphi ::= \mathbf{tt} \mid \mathbf{ff} \mid \varphi_1 \wedge \varphi_2 \mid \varphi_1 \vee \varphi_2 \mid s \mid x \sim c \mid x.\varphi$$

where $s \in S$, $c \in \mathbb{Q}_+$ and $\sim \in \{<, \leq, =, \neq, \geq, >\}$. As in TPTL(1), $x \sim c$ is a clock constraint and the expression $x.\varphi$ resets the clock variable x, i.e., binds x to 0 in φ.

Definition 5 (1TAA). A **one-clock timed alternating automaton** or **1TAA** is a five-tuple $\mathcal{A} = (\Sigma, S, s_0, F, \delta)$ where Σ is a **finite alphabet**, S is a finite set of **locations**, s_0 is the **initial location**, $F \subseteq S$ is a finite set of **accepting locations** and $\delta : S \times \Sigma \to \Phi(S)$ is the **transition function**.

Given a 1TAA $\mathcal{A}$, a *state* of $\mathcal{A}$ is a tuple (s, v), where s is a location and $v \in \mathbb{Q}_+$ a clock value. A *configuration* C of $\mathcal{A}$ is a finite set of states, and $\{(s_0, 0)\}$ is the *initial configuration* of $\mathcal{A}$. By $C + r$ we denote the configuration $\{(s, v + r) \mid (s, v) \in C\}$. We call a configuration C *accepting* if $s \in F$ for every location s occurring in C. For convenience, given a 1TAA $\mathcal{A}_i = (\Sigma_i, S_i, s_0^i, F_i, \delta_i)$ we introduce functions for accessing each of the components of $\mathcal{A}_i$, e.g., $S(\mathcal{A}_i) = S_i$, $s_0(\mathcal{A}_i) = s_0^i$, etc.

Given a configuration C and a clock value v, we define a Boolean valuation on $\Phi(S)$ as follows:

$$
\begin{aligned}
&C \models_v \mathbf{tt} \\
&C \models_v \varphi_1 \wedge \varphi_2 && \text{iff } C \models_v \varphi_1 \text{ and } C \models_v \varphi_2 \\
&C \models_v \varphi_1 \vee \varphi_2 && \text{iff } C \models_v \varphi_1 \text{ or } C \models_v \varphi_2 \\
&C \models_v s && \text{iff } (s, v) \in C \\
&C \models_v x \sim c && \text{iff } v \sim c \\
&C \models_v x.\varphi && \text{iff } C \models_0 \varphi
\end{aligned}
$$

Definition 6 (Run). Given a finite timed word ρ of length n, define $d_j := \tau_j - \tau_{j-1}$ for $1 \leq j \leq n$ with $\tau_0 := 0$. A **run** of a 1TAA $\mathcal{A}$ on ρ is a finite sequence of configurations

$$C_0 \overset{d_1}{\rightsquigarrow} C_1 \overset{\sigma_1}{\longrightarrow} C_2 \overset{d_2}{\rightsquigarrow} C_3 \overset{\sigma_2}{\longrightarrow} \cdots \overset{d_n}{\rightsquigarrow} C_{2n-1} \overset{\sigma_n}{\longrightarrow} C_{2n}$$

such that $C_{2j+1} = C_{2j} + d_{j+1}$ and for $C_{2j+1} = \{(s_i, v_i)\}_{i \in I}$, $C_{2j+2} = \bigcup_{i \in I} C'_i$, where $C'_i \models_{v_i} \delta(s_i, \sigma_{j+1})$ with $0 \leq j < n$. Here, $C_{2j} \overset{d_{j+1}}{\rightsquigarrow} C_{2j+1}$ is called a delay step and $C_{2j+1} \xrightarrow{\sigma_{j+1}} C_{2j+2}$ is a discrete step. A run is **accepting** if C_{2n} is accepting.

A finite timed word ρ is accepted by a 1TAA $\mathcal{A}$ with respect to an initial clock value v if $\mathcal{A}$ has an accepting run starting from $C_0 = \{(s_0, v)\}$. The language accepted by $\mathcal{A}$, $L(\mathcal{A}) \subseteq T\Sigma^*$, is the set of all finite timed words accepted by $\mathcal{A}$ with respect to the initial clock value zero.

13.3 Decidable Cases

In this section we establish the decidability of satisfiability for TPTL(1) augmented with least fixpoint and alphabetised parallel operators. Our strategy is to translate a formula φ in the extension under consideration to a 1TAA $\mathcal{A}_\varphi$ such that $L(\varphi) = L(\mathcal{A}_\varphi)$.

13.3.1 Least Fixpoints

Introducing the least fixpoint operator offers a natural way to express recursive specifications in TPTL(1). The resulting logic μTPTL(1) is strictly more expressive than TPTL(1).

In order to guarantee the existence of fixpoints, we restrict μTPTL(1) formulas to be in negation normal form, i.e., with negations only occurring in front of events from Σ. We moreover drop the until operator, since it can be expressed with the least fixpoint operator.

Definition 7 (μTPTL(1) syntax). The set of μTPTL(1) formulas is defined inductively according to the following grammar:

$$\varphi ::= \top \mid \bot \mid \dashv \mid a \mid \neg a \mid Z \mid x \sim c \mid x.\varphi \mid \bigcirc\varphi \mid \varphi_1 \wedge \varphi_2 \mid \varphi_1 \vee \varphi_2 \mid \mu Z.\varphi$$

Here, Z is a *propositional variable* from a finite set $\mathcal{Z}$, μZ is the *least fixpoint* operator, and $\dashv$ is an end-marker that is only true at the last position of a timed word, i.e. is equivalent to $\neg \bigcirc \top$. A μTPTL(1) formula φ is *closed* if every Z in φ occurs within the scope of a least fixpoint operator μZ. Otherwise, the formula is deemed to be *open* and we may write $\varphi(Z_1, \ldots, Z_k)$ to indicate that $Z_1, \ldots, Z_k$ occur unbound in φ. If $Z \in \mathcal{Z}$ is bound in φ, we require without loss of generality that there be exactly one least fixpoint quantifier μZ occurring in φ. By *fpd*(φ) we denote the *fixpoint depth* of φ, which is the maximum nesting depth of least fixpoint operators, e.g. *fpd*$(\mu Y.(\bigcirc(a \vee Y) \vee \mu Z.(b \vee \bigcirc(Y \wedge Z)))) = 2$. Note that the until operator $\varphi_1 \mathcal{U} \varphi_2$ can be introduced as an abbreviation for $\mu Z.(\varphi_2 \vee (\varphi_1 \wedge \bigcirc Z))$.

The semantics of μTPTL(1) formulas is given with respect to an *environment* ξ, which enables one to evaluate open μTPTL(1) formulas. Given a timed word ρ, ξ is a mapping from the propositional variables in $\mathcal{Z}$ to $\mathcal{V}(\rho)$.

The clauses of Definition 3, which prescribe the semantics of TPTL(1) formulas, carry over to μTPTL(1) formulas whose outermost connective is in TPTL(1). The additional clauses specific to μTPTL(1) are as follows:

$$\begin{aligned}
[\![\dashv]\!]^{\rho}_{\xi} &:= \{(|\rho|, r) \mid r \in \mathbb{R}_{+}\} \\
[\![Z]\!]^{\rho}_{\xi} &:= \xi(Z) \\
[\![\mu Z.\psi(Z)]\!]^{\rho}_{\xi} &:= \bigcap\{M \in \mathcal{V}(\rho) \mid [\![\psi(Z)]\!]^{\rho}_{\xi[Z\mapsto M]} \subseteq M\}
\end{aligned}$$

Thus, $[\![\mu Z.\psi(Z)]\!]^{\rho}_{\xi}$ is the least fixpoint of the function $F_{\psi,Z,\rho,\xi}(M) := [\![\psi]\!]^{\rho}_{\xi[Z\mapsto M]}$.

Before we show the decidability of μTPTL(1) by translation to 1TAA, we give an example of the usefulness of this extension of TPTL(1).

Example 1. The formula $\mathit{even}(\varphi)$ expresses the property that φ is true on a timed word an even number of times. The untimed language of $L(\mathit{even}(\varphi))$ is not counter-free and not expressible in TPTL(1).

$$\mathit{even}(\varphi) = \mu\, Y.((\neg\varphi \wedge (\dashv \vee \bigcirc Y)) \vee (\varphi \wedge \bigcirc\, \mu Z.((\neg\varphi \wedge \bigcirc Z) \vee (\varphi \wedge (\dashv \vee \bigcirc Y)))))$$

(Of course, one would need to put $\neg\varphi$ in negation normal form, which can readily be done as soon as a concrete φ is supplied.)

The existence of least fixpoints is a consequence of the subsequent lemma and the Knaster-Tarski fixpoint theorem.

Lemma 1. *For any timed word ρ, μTPTL(1) formula $\varphi(Z, Z_1, \ldots, Z_k)$, and valuation of the propositional variables ξ, the function $F_{\varphi,Z,\rho,\xi}$ is monotone with respect to $\subseteq$.*

Let $\varphi[Z/\psi]$ be the μTPTL(1) formula obtained from φ in which every occurrence of Z in φ is replaced by ψ. Approximants of a formula $\mu Z.\psi(Z)$ are inductively defined for any $i \in \mathbb{N}$ as:

$$\begin{aligned}
\mu^{0}\, Z.\psi(Z) &:= \bot \\
\mu^{i+1}\, Z.\psi(Z) &:= \psi[Z/\,\mu^{i}\, Z.\psi(Z)]
\end{aligned}$$

The next lemma is a standard result about approximants:

Lemma 2. *For any timed word ρ and μTPTL(1) formula $\varphi = \mu\, Z.\psi(Z)$, $M = [\![\varphi]\!]^{\rho}_{\xi}$ iff there exists an $i \in \mathbb{N}$ such that $M = [\![\mu^{i}\, Z.\psi(Z)]\!]^{\rho}_{\xi}$.*

Given a μTPTL(1) formula $\varphi(Z, Z_1, \ldots, Z_k)$, Z is *guarded* in φ if it occurs in the scope of a next operator. We call a formula φ *proper* if for every subformula $\mu Z.\psi(Z)$ in φ, Z is guarded in $\psi(Z)$. Properness of μTPTL(1) formulas will be assumed in the following without loss of generality, since $\mu Z.(Z \vee \psi(Z))$ is equivalent to $\mu Z.\psi(Z)$ and $\mu Z.(Z \wedge \psi(Z))$ is equivalent to $\bot$. Since we are dealing with finite timed words the fixpoint of $F_{\varphi,Z,\rho,\xi}$ is unique for proper formulas. It therefore follows that least and greatest fixpoints coincide for μTPTL(1), obviating the need for two distinct fixpoint operators.

Lemma 3. *Let ρ be a timed word and $\varphi(Z, Z_1, \ldots, Z_k)$ be a formula such that Z occurs guarded in $\varphi(Z)$. Then for all ξ, M^*, N^*, $F_{\varphi,Z,\rho,\xi}(M^*) = M^*$ and $F_{\varphi,Z,\rho,\xi}(N^*) = N^*$ implies $M^* = N^*$.*

Although we have not explicitly allowed for arbitrary negation, μTPTL(1) still is closed under complement. Given a formula φ, we define its complement $\overline{\varphi}$ by induction on the structure of φ, where, $\overline{\sim}$ maps the relation $\sim$ to its complementary relation, e.g., $<$ to $\geq$, $=$ to $\neq$ etc.

$$
\begin{array}{llll}
\overline{\top} := \bot & \overline{a} := \neg a & \overline{x \sim c} := x \overline{\sim} c & \overline{\varphi_1 \vee \varphi_2} := \overline{\varphi_1} \wedge \overline{\varphi_2} \\
\overline{\bot} := \top & \overline{\neg a} := a & \overline{\bigcirc \varphi} := \dashv \vee \bigcirc \overline{\varphi} & \overline{\mu Z.\varphi} := \mu Z.\overline{\varphi} \\
\overline{\dashv} := \bigcirc \top & \overline{Z} := Z & \overline{\varphi_1 \wedge \varphi_2} := \overline{\varphi_1} \vee \overline{\varphi_2} &
\end{array}
$$

Lemma 4. *Let φ be a proper μTPTL(1) formula. Then $(i, r) \in [\![\varphi]\!]^{\rho}_{\xi}$ iff $(i, r) \notin [\![\overline{\varphi}]\!]^{\rho}_{\overline{\xi}}$, where $\overline{\xi}(Z) := \{(i, r) \mid i \in \mathbb{N}_{|\rho|}$ and $r \in \mathbb{R}_+\} \setminus \xi(Z)$.*

The lemma can be proved straightforwardly by induction on the structure of φ using the properness of the subformulas $\mu Z.\psi(Z)$ of φ and the resulting unique fixpoint property.

The translation of a μTPTL(1) formula φ into a 1TAA $\mathcal{A}_\varphi$ is given by induction on *fpd*(φ) and is somewhat similar to the untimed case considered in [14]. Recall that Z is assumed to be guarded in $\psi(Z)$ for any subformula $\mu Z.\psi(Z)$ of φ. For *fpd*(φ) $= 0$, we define $\mathcal{A}_\varphi$ by induction on the structure of φ:

- *Case* $\varphi = a$. Define $\mathcal{A}_\varphi = (\Sigma, \{s_\varphi\}, s_\varphi, \emptyset, \delta)$ with $\delta(s_\varphi, a) = \mathbf{tt}$ and $\delta(s_\varphi, b) = \mathbf{ff}$ if $b \neq a$.
- *Case* $\varphi = \dashv$. Define $\mathcal{A}_\varphi = (\Sigma, \{s_\varphi, s_\dashv\}, s_\varphi, \{s_\dashv\}, \delta)$ with $\delta(s_\varphi, a) = s_\dashv$ and $\delta(s_\dashv, a) = \mathbf{ff}$ for all $a \in \Sigma$.
- *Case* $\varphi = Z$. Define $\mathcal{A}_\varphi = (\Sigma, \{s_\varphi\}, s_\varphi, \emptyset, \delta)$ with $\delta(s_\varphi, a) = \mathbf{tt}$ for all $a \in \Sigma$. Note that we will refer to s_φ as s_Z in the induction step $\varphi = \mu Z.\psi(Z)$.
- *Case* $\varphi = x \sim c$. Define $\mathcal{A}_\varphi = (\Sigma, \{s_\varphi\}, s_\varphi, \emptyset, \delta)$ with $\delta(s_\varphi, a) = x \sim c$ for all $a \in \Sigma$.
- *Case* $\varphi = x.\psi$. Define $\mathcal{A}_\varphi = (\Sigma, \{s_\varphi\} \cup S(\mathcal{A}_\psi), s_\varphi, F(\mathcal{A}_\psi), \delta)$ with $\delta(s_\varphi, a) = x.\delta(\mathcal{A}_\psi)(s_0(\mathcal{A}_\psi), a)$ and $a \in \Sigma$ and $\delta(s, a) = \delta(\mathcal{A}_\psi)(s, a)$ for all $s \in S(\mathcal{A}_\psi)$.
- *Case* $\varphi = \psi_1 \wedge \psi_2$. Define $\mathcal{A}_\varphi = (\Sigma, \{s_\varphi\} \cup S(\mathcal{A}_{\psi_1}) \cup S(\mathcal{A}_{\psi_2}), s_\varphi, F(\mathcal{A}_{\psi_1}) \cup F(\mathcal{A}_{\psi_2}), \delta)$ with $\delta(s_\varphi, a) = \delta(\mathcal{A}_{\psi_1})(s_0(\mathcal{A}_{\psi_1}), a) \wedge \delta(\mathcal{A}_{\psi_2})(s_0(\mathcal{A}_{\psi_2}), a)$ and $\delta(s, a) = \delta(\mathcal{A}_{\psi_i}, a)$ if $s \in S(\mathcal{A}_{\psi_i})$ for all $a \in \Sigma$.
- *Case* $\varphi = \bigcirc\psi$. Define $\mathcal{A}_\varphi = (\Sigma, \{s_\varphi\} \cup S(\mathcal{A}_\psi), s_\varphi, F(\mathcal{A}_\psi), \delta)$ with $\delta(s_\varphi, a) = s_0(\mathcal{A}_\psi)$ and $\delta(s, a) = \delta(\mathcal{A}_\psi)(s, a)$ for all $s \in S(\mathcal{A}_\psi)$ and $a \in \Sigma$.

The cases when φ is $\top, \bot, \neg a$, or $\psi_1 \vee \psi_2$ are defined in a similar way. In the construction above we assume different subformulas to have disjoint sets of states, but that $\mathcal{A}_\varphi = \mathcal{A}_\psi$ if $\varphi = \psi$. In particular, if Z is a free variable in φ, then $\mathcal{A}_\varphi$ contains exactly one state s_Z corresponding to Z.

Now for $fpd(\varphi) = n + 1$, we consider the only relevant case $\varphi = \mu Z.\psi(Z)$; the construction for the remaining cases can be done along similar lines as the above. Define $\mathcal{A}_\varphi = (\Sigma, \{s_\varphi\} \cup S(\mathcal{A}_{\psi(Z)}), F(\mathcal{A}_{\psi(Z)}), \delta)$ with $\delta(s_\varphi, a) = \delta(\mathcal{A}_{\psi(Z)})(s_0(\mathcal{A}_{\psi(Z)}), a)$, $\delta(s_Z, a) = \delta(s_\varphi, a)$, and $\delta(s, a) = \delta(\mathcal{A}_{\psi(Z)})(s, a)$ for all s distinct from s_φ and s_Z. Here, $a \in \Sigma$ and s_Z is the state obtained from the 1TAA corresponding to Z during the inductive construction of $\psi(Z)$. The transition function is well-defined since Z occurs guarded in $\psi(Z)$.

Lemma 5. *Let φ be a closed μTPTL(1) formula and ρ a timed word. Then $(i, r) \in [\![\varphi]\!]^\rho$ iff $\mathcal{A}_\varphi$ has an accepting run on ρ^i with initial clock value r.*

Theorem 1. *Satisfiability in μTPTL(1) over finite words is decidable with non-primitive recursive complexity.*

The translation from μTPTL(1) formulas to 1TAA also works in the other direction, i.e. for any 1TAA there exists a closed μTPTL(1) formula $\varphi_\mathcal{A}$ such that $\rho \in L(\mathcal{A})$ iff $\rho \models \varphi_\mathcal{A}$, as we now demonstrate. The translation has the same structure as the analogous construction of μ-calculus formulas from alternating automata in the untimed case.

At this point it is helpful to extend the definition of μTPTL(1) to allow fixed points in *vectorial form*. Given an n-dimensional vector of variables $\mathbf{Z} = (Z_1, \ldots, Z_n)$ and an n-dimensional vector of formulas $(\varphi_1, \ldots, \varphi_n)$, we allow for vectorial fixpoints $\mu\, \mathbf{Z}.(\varphi_1, \ldots, \varphi_n)$. Given a timed word ρ, such a vectorial fixed point is interpreted as an element of the n-fold product $\mathcal{V}(\rho)^n$ according to the following rule, where M_i is the i-th component of $\mathbf{M}$:

$$[\![\mu\, \mathbf{Z}.(\varphi_1, \ldots, \varphi_n)]\!]^\rho_\xi := \bigcap \{\mathbf{M} \in \mathcal{V}(\rho)^n \mid [\![\varphi_i]\!]^\rho_{\xi[\mathbf{Z} \mapsto \mathbf{M}]} \subseteq M_i \text{ for all } 1 \le i \le n\}\,.$$

Let ρ be a timed word and let π_i denote the i-th projection $\mathcal{V}(\rho)^n \to \mathcal{V}(\rho)$ for $1 \le i \le n$.

Proposition 1. *Given a vectorial fixed point formula $\mu\, \mathbf{Z}.(\varphi_1, \ldots, \varphi_n)$, for each $i \in \{1, \ldots, n\}$ there is a corresponding μTPTL(1) formula ψ_i such that $\pi_i([\![\varphi]\!]^\rho_\xi) = [\![\psi_i]\!]^\rho_\xi$.*

Proof. The proof is by repeated application of the Bekić identity

$$\pi_1 [\![\mu(Y, \mathbf{Z}).(\varphi_1, \ldots, \varphi_n)]\!]^\rho_\xi = [\![\mu\, Y.\varphi_1[\mathbf{Z}/\, \mu\, \mathbf{Z}.(\varphi_2, \ldots, \varphi_n)]]\!]^\rho_\xi\,.$$

This identity is valid in any complete lattice, so holds for our semantics.

Now let $\mathcal{A} = (\Sigma, S, s_0, F, \delta)$ be a 1TAA. Let $\mathbf{Z} = (Z_s \mid s \in S)$ be a vector of variables indexed by the set of locations of $\mathcal{A}$. Recall from Definition 5 that the transition function δ of $\mathcal{A}$ takes values in the set of expressions $\Phi(S)$. The first step in defining $\varphi_{\mathcal{A}}$ is to give a translation mapping each expression φ in $\Phi(S)$ to a corresponding μTPTL(1) formula $\varphi^{\ddagger}$ with free variables in $\mathbf{Z}$. To this end we write:

$$\mathbf{tt}^{\ddagger} = \top \qquad (\varphi_1 \wedge \varphi_2)^{\ddagger} = \varphi_1^{\ddagger} \wedge \varphi_2^{\ddagger} \qquad (x \sim c)^{\ddagger} = x \sim c$$
$$\mathbf{ff}^{\ddagger} = \bot \qquad (\varphi_1 \vee \varphi_2)^{\ddagger} = \varphi_1^{\ddagger} \vee \varphi_2^{\ddagger} \qquad (x.\varphi)^{\ddagger} = x.\varphi^{\ddagger}$$
$$s^{\ddagger} = \bigcirc Z_s$$

For each location $s \in S$ we define a μTPTL(1) formula $\varphi_s(\mathbf{Z})$, where

$$\varphi_s(\mathbf{Z}) = \begin{cases} \bigvee_{a \in \Sigma}(a \wedge \delta(s,a)^{\ddagger}) & \text{if } s \text{ is not accepting} \\ \dashv \vee \bigvee_{a \in \Sigma}(a \wedge \delta(s,a)^{\ddagger}) & \text{if s is accepting} \end{cases}$$

Recall that $s_0 \in S$ is the initial location of $\mathcal{A}$. We define $\varphi_{\mathcal{A}}$ to be the μTPTL(1) formula that is equivalent to the s_0-th component of the vectorial fixed point $\mu\,\mathbf{Z}.(\varphi_s \mid s \in S))$. Such a formula is guaranteed to exist by Proposition 1.

Theorem 2. *Let $\mathcal{A}$ be a 1TAA and $\varphi_{\mathcal{A}}$ its corresponding μTPTL(1) formula φ. Then $L(\mathcal{A}) = L(\varphi_{\mathcal{A}})$.*

This result, together with the construction underlying Theorem 1, shows that μTPTL(1) characterises the class of languages accepted by one-clock timed alternating automata.

13.3.2 Alphabetised Parallel Composition of TPTL(1) Formulas

In this section we consider TPTL(1) extended with the alphabetised parallel composition operator $\|$ and show the decidability of the augmented logic. This extension is useful for specifying systems that run independently subject to sharing some events in common. For example, consider the following specification:

$$(\Box(\mathit{processed} \to \bigcirc_{\leq 1}\mathit{queued})) \parallel (\Box(\mathit{queued} \to \bigcirc_{=1}\mathit{send})).$$

It describes a system consisting of a processor and a sender that run independently of each other and only synchronise on the *queued* event. The specification requires that a processed item be queued by the processor in the *next* step within one time unit, and that each queued item be sent by the sender in the *next* step one time unit later. However, in the timed trace of the composed system internal events from the sender may occur between a *processed* and *queue*-event of the processor. This issue is resolved by the $\|$ operator which ensures that the events unrelated to each specification do not interfere with it.

Formally, we augment the syntax of TPTL(1) in Definition 2 with an additional term for the *alphabetised parallel composition* $\varphi_1 \parallel \varphi_2$. The *alphabetised parallel composition* of timed words ρ_1 and ρ_2 over the alphabets Σ_1 and Σ_2 respectively is defined as follows: $\rho \in \rho_1 \parallel \rho_2 \subseteq T(\Sigma_1 \cup \Sigma_2)^*$ iff $\rho_1 = \rho \setminus (\Sigma_2 - \Sigma_1)$

and $\rho_2 = \rho \setminus (\Sigma_1 - \Sigma_2)$. Informally speaking, the timed events from ρ_1 and ρ_2 are merged in ρ with the requirement that the timed events from $\Sigma_1 \cap \Sigma_2$ occur at the same time points in both ρ_1 and ρ_2. The semantics of TPTL(1) together with alphabetised parallel composition is obtained by adding the following clause to Definition 3:

$$[\![\varphi_1 \parallel \varphi_2]\!]^\rho := \{(i,r) \mid \exists \rho_1, \rho_2.\rho^i \in \rho_1 \parallel \rho_2, (1,r) \in [\![\varphi_1]\!]^{\rho_1}, (1,r) \in [\![\varphi_2]\!]^{\rho_2}\}$$

We have seen in the previous section how to construct a 1TAA from a TPTL(1) formula φ. We now extend this construction to show decidability of TPTL(1) with alphabetised parallel composition. For $i \in \{1,2\}$, given TPTL(1) formulas φ_i with their corresponding event alphabets Σ_i and 1TAA $\mathcal{A}_i$, we show how to construct a 1TAA $\mathcal{A}_1 \parallel \mathcal{A}_2$ such that $L(\mathcal{A}_1 \parallel \mathcal{A}_2) = L(\varphi_1 \parallel \varphi_2)$. Let $\mathcal{A}_1 = (\Sigma_1, S, s_0, F, \delta)$, define $\mathcal{A}_1$ extended with Σ_2 as $\mathcal{A}_1^{\Sigma_2} := (\Sigma_1 \cup \Sigma_2, S, s_0, F, \delta')$, where $\delta'(s,a) = \{s\}$ for all $a \in \Sigma_2 - \Sigma_1$ and $\delta'(s,a) = \delta(s,a)$ otherwise. Without loss of generality we assume the set of states of $\mathcal{A}_1$ and $\mathcal{A}_2$ to be disjoint. Define $\mathcal{A}_1 \parallel \mathcal{A}_2 := (\Sigma_1 \cup \Sigma_2, S(\mathcal{A}_1) \cup S(\mathcal{A}_2) \cup \{s_\parallel\}, \{s_\parallel\}, F(\mathcal{A}_1) \cup F(\mathcal{A}_2), \delta)$, where

$$\delta(s,a) = \begin{cases} \delta(\mathcal{A}_1^{\Sigma_2})(s,a) & \text{if } s \in S(\mathcal{A}_1) \\ \delta(\mathcal{A}_2^{\Sigma_1})(s,a) & \text{if } s \in S(\mathcal{A}_2) \\ \delta(\mathcal{A}_1^{\Sigma_2})(s_0(\mathcal{A}_1),a) \wedge \delta(\mathcal{A}_2^{\Sigma_1})(s_0(\mathcal{A}_2),a) & \text{if } s = s_\parallel \end{cases}$$

Decidability of TPTL(1) + alphabetised parallel composition is then a consequence of the following lemma.

Lemma 6. *Let $\mathcal{A}_1$ and $\mathcal{A}_2$ be two 1TAA over the alphabets Σ_1 and Σ_2 respectively. Then $\mathcal{A}_1 \parallel \mathcal{A}_2$ has an accepting run on ρ iff $\mathcal{A}_1$ has an accepting run on $\rho \setminus (\Sigma_2 - \Sigma_1)$ and $\mathcal{A}_2$ has an accepting run on $\rho \setminus (\Sigma_1 - \Sigma_2)$.*

Proof. Given an accepting run $C_0 \overset{d_1}{\rightsquigarrow} C_1 \overset{\sigma_1}{\longrightarrow} \dots \overset{\sigma_n}{\longrightarrow} C_{2n}$ of $\mathcal{A}_1 \parallel \mathcal{A}_2$ on ρ, by exhaustively replacing $C_{2i-2} \overset{d_i}{\rightsquigarrow} C_{2i-1} \overset{\sigma_i}{\longrightarrow} C_{2i} \overset{d_{i+1}}{\rightsquigarrow} C_{2i+1}$ with $C_{2i-2} \overset{d_i+d_{i+1}}{\rightsquigarrow} C_{2i+1}$ if $\sigma_i \in \Sigma_2 - \Sigma_1$, intersecting each remaining C_i with $\{(s,r) \mid s \in S(\mathcal{A}_1), r \in \mathbb{R}_+\}$, and replacing C_0 with $\{(s_0(\mathcal{A}_1), 0)\}$, we obtain an accepting run of $\mathcal{A}_1$. The construction works, since $C'_{2i-2} \cap \{(s,r) \mid s \in S(\mathcal{A}_1), r \in \mathbb{R}_+\} = C'_{2i+1} \cap \{(s,r) \mid s \in S(\mathcal{A}_1), r \in \mathbb{R}_+\}$ ensures that we obtain a valid run of $\mathcal{A}_1$ on $\rho \setminus (\Sigma_2 - \Sigma_1)$. Similarly, we obtain an accepting run of $\mathcal{A}_2$ on $\rho \setminus (\Sigma_1 - \Sigma_2)$.

Conversely, let $C_0 \overset{d_1}{\rightsquigarrow} C_1 \overset{\sigma_1}{\longrightarrow} \dots \overset{\sigma_n}{\longrightarrow} C_{2n}$ be an accepting run of $\mathcal{A}_1$ on ρ_1. This run can be altered to become an accepting run of $\mathcal{A}_1^{\Sigma_2}$ on ρ. In general, for $(\sigma_j, \tau_j)(\sigma_{j+1}, \tau_{j+1}) \dots (\sigma_k, \tau_k)$ in ρ with $\sigma_j, \sigma_k \in \Sigma_1$, $\sigma_\ell \in \Sigma_2 - \Sigma_1$ for $j < \ell < k$ and (σ_j, τ_j) equal to (σ_i, τ_i) in ρ_1, $C_{2i-1} \overset{\sigma_i}{\longrightarrow} C_{2i} \overset{\tau_{i+1}(\rho_1)-\tau_i(\rho_1)}{\rightsquigarrow} C_{2i+1}$ can be exhaustively replaced with $C_{2i-1} \xrightarrow{\sigma_i(\rho_1)} C_{2i} \overset{\tau_{j+1}(\rho)-\tau_j(\rho)}{\rightsquigarrow} C_{2i} + \tau_{j+1}(\rho) - \tau_j(\rho) \xrightarrow{\sigma_{j+1}} \dots \overset{\tau_{i+1}(\rho_1)-\tau_{k-1}(\rho)}{\rightsquigarrow} C_{2i+1} \xrightarrow{\sigma_{i+1}(\rho_1)} C_{2i+2}$ in order to obtain an accepting run of $\mathcal{A}_1^{\Sigma_2}$ on ρ. Then by joining the accepting runs of $\mathcal{A}_1^{\Sigma_2}$ and $\mathcal{A}_2^{\Sigma_1}$ and setting $C_0 = \{(s_\parallel, 0)\}$ we obtain an accepting run of $\mathcal{A}_1 \parallel \mathcal{A}_2$ on ρ.

Theorem 3. *Satisfiability in TPTL(1) augmented with alphabetised parallel composition is decidable over finite words with non-primitive recursive complexity.*

It is not hard to see that it is possible to combine the inductive constructions of 1TAA from μTPTL(1) and TPTL(1) together with alphabetised parallel composition. Hence satisfiability for TPTL(1) augmented both with fixpoint operators and alphabetised parallel composition is decidable.

Theorem 4. *Satisfiability for TPTL(1) augmented with fixpoint operators and alphabetised parallel composition is decidable over finite words, with non-primitive recursive complexity.*

13.4 Undecidable Cases

In this section we show that augmenting MTL (and a fortiori also TPTL(1)) with any of hiding, renaming or asynchronous parallel composition renders the corresponding satisfiability problem undecidable.

To establish these results, we reduce the reachability problem for deterministic two-counter machines (2CM) to satisfiability for MTL with the extensions under consideration. A 2CM $\mathcal{M} = (S, init, \delta)$ is a finite-state automaton augmented with two counters over the naturals, where S is a finite set of states, $init \in S$ is the initial location and δ is the transition function. A configuration of $\mathcal{M}$ is a triple $(s, n_0, n_1) \in S \times \mathbb{N} \times \mathbb{N}$. From a given configuration, the transition function can test each of the counters for zero and accordingly change configurations by jumping to a new location and incrementing, decrementing or leaving each of the counters untouched. A run of a 2CM is a finite sequence of configurations that is consistent with the transition function. The reachability problem asks whether for a given 2CM $\mathcal{M}$ it is possible to reach a configuration $(s, 0, 0)$ starting from the initial configuration $(init, 0, 0)$. This problem is well-known to be undecidable [18].

Following [1] and [7], we can encode a run of an m-location 2CM $\mathcal{M}$ as a timed word ρ over the alphabet $\Sigma = \{a, b_1, \ldots, b_m, c\}$. The a-events are used to encode the value of the counters in unary, each b_i represents a location of $\mathcal{M}$, and c is used as a marker. The i-th configuration (s_j, v_1, v_2) of a run is stored in the interval $[i, i+1)$ of ρ. The event b_j occurs at time i, representing the current location s_j. In the following, let $\mathcal{I} := (0, 0.25)$. The number of a-events in the interval $\mathcal{I} + i$ encodes the value of the first counter. Likewise, the value of the second counter is encoded in the interval $\mathcal{I} + i + 0.5$. The marker c occurs at time $i + 0.5$ and the remaining intervals in $[i, i + 1)$ do not contain any a- or b_i-events. We assume that $init = s_1$, so that b_1 is the first event to occur. It is not hard to see that we can construct an MTL[2] formula $\varphi_{\mathcal{M}}$ such that $\varphi_{\mathcal{M}} \wedge \Diamond b_i$ is satisfiable if $(s_i, 0, 0)$ is reachable. The converse, however, does not hold, since MTL is incapable of detecting *insertion errors*.

[2] This even holds for the until-free fragment of MTL, which is obtained from Definition 4 by dropping the $\mathcal{U}_{\mathcal{I}}$-definition and introducing $\Box_{\mathcal{I}}$ and $\Diamond_{\mathcal{I}}$ as primitives.

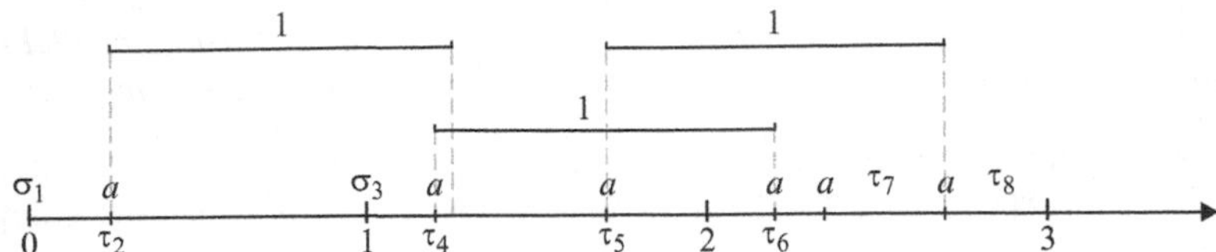

Fig. 13.1 Illustration of a timed word suffering from insertion errors

Definition 8. Let $\rho \models \varphi_{\mathcal{M}}$ be a timed word representing a run of $\mathcal{M}$. Then ρ **suffers from insertion errors** if there are $1 \leq i < j \leq |\rho|$ and $\sigma_i, \sigma_j \in \Sigma$ such that ρ contains $(\sigma_i, \tau_i)(a, \tau_{i+1})$ and $(\sigma_j, \tau_i + 1)(a, \tau_{j+1})$ with $\tau_{j+1} < \tau_{i+1} + 1$.

An illustration of this definition is presented in Fig. 13.1. First, consider the events $(\sigma_1, 0)$ and (a, τ_2). We have that $(\sigma_1, 0)$ is followed one time unit later by $(\sigma_3, 1)$ which itself is followed by (a, τ_4). However, $\tau_4 < \tau_2 + 1$ and hence (a, τ_4) is wrongly inserted. Observe that (a, τ_2) does not have any corresponding event one time unit later. Second, the a-event at time τ_7 is also wrongly inserted, since it lies strictly between $\tau_4 + 1$ and $\tau_5 + 1$.

D'Souza and Prabhakar show in [7] that MTL augmented with any extension that is able to characterise a slightly more restricted version of the language from Definition 8 has an undecidable satisfiability problem. We now use their observation to establish undecidability of satisfiability of MTL extended with any of hiding, renaming or asynchronous parallel composition. For each extension, we define a formula φ_{ie} that is capable of detecting insertion errors. Whence there exists a run of $\mathcal{M}$ reaching s_i iff $\varphi_{\mathcal{M}} \wedge \Diamond b_i \wedge \neg\varphi_{ie}$ is satisfiable.

13.4.1 Hiding

Let $E \subseteq \Sigma$ be a set of events. We augment the syntax of TPTL(1) in Definition 2 with an additional term for the *hiding* operator $\backslash E$. In designing specifications, hiding is used to abstract away irrelevant events. For example, given a set $I \subseteq \Sigma$, the formula $(\Box(\varphi \rightarrow \bigcirc_{<1}\psi)) \setminus I$ specifies a bounded response property that "ignores" events from I that could occur between φ and ψ. Formally, the semantic mapping for hiding is obtained by adding the following clause to Definition 3:

$$[\![\varphi \setminus E]\!]^{\rho} := \{(i, r) \mid \exists \rho'.\rho^i = \rho' \setminus E \text{ and } (1, r) \in [\![\varphi]\!]^{\rho'}\}$$

It has been observed in [10] that hidden propositions lead to an undecidable satisfiability problem for real-time logics when the underlying time model is dense. In order to detect insertion errors, we add d to the event alphabet and use the hiding operator in the following way: ρ suffers from insertion errors (following Definition 8) iff we can insert a d-event into ρ immediately preceding an a-event, in such a way that d is followed exactly one time unit later by an a. Formally:

Lemma 7. *Let* $\varphi_{ie} = (\varphi_{sm} \wedge \Diamond(d \wedge \Diamond_{\mathcal{I}} a \wedge \Diamond_{=1} a)) \setminus \{d\}$ *and* $\rho \models \varphi_{\mathcal{M}}$ *be a timed word representing a run of* $\mathcal{M}$. *Then* ρ *suffers from insertion errors iff* $\rho \models \varphi_{ie}$.

(In the above, φ_{sm} stands for a formula that captures precisely all strongly monotonic timed words, i.e. words in which no two events share the same timestamp.)

The lemma shows that hiding renders the satisfiability problem undecidable even if applied at the outermost level, i.e. checking satisfiability of $\varphi \setminus E$ is undecidable for MTL formulas φ. This is not the case for MITL, where checking satisfiability of $\varphi \setminus E$ for some MITL formula φ still is decidable [10].

13.4.2 Renaming

Let $R \subseteq \Sigma \times \Sigma$ be a total renaming relation over Σ. We augment the syntax of TPTL(1) in Definition 2 with an additional term for the *renaming* operator $[R]$. Let us write that $\rho \in \rho'[R]$ iff $|\rho| = |\rho'|$, $\tau_i(\rho) = \tau_i(\rho')$, and $\sigma_i(\rho) \in R(\sigma_i(\rho'))$ for all $1 \leq i \leq |\rho|$. The semantics of TPTL(1) together with renaming is obtained by adding the following clause to Definition 3:

$$[\![\varphi[R]]\!]^{\rho} := \{(i, r) \mid \exists \rho'.\rho^i \in \rho'[R] \text{ and } (1, r) \in [\![\varphi]\!]^{\rho'}\}$$

The effect of renaming is less drastic than that of hiding, since it does not delete timed events from timed words. It, however, still provides a convenient means of abstraction in specifications. For example, given a set $I \subseteq \Sigma$ of internal events and renaming relation $R := \{i/b\}_{i \in I} \cup Id_{\Sigma \setminus I}$, the formula $(\Box(\varphi \rightarrow (b\ \mathcal{U}_{<1}\ \psi))[R]$ expresses a bounded response property that treats all events from I in the same way by grouping them into a single event b.

Using the renaming operator to detect insertion errors is slightly more involved than in the previous case, and we describe the procedure with the help of an example given in Fig. 13.2. Observe that the a-event at time τ_3 is wrongly inserted in the timed word shown in the lower part of Fig. 13.2. Our tactic is to nondeterministically rename some a-events to d-events in this timed word in such a way as to identify the wrongly inserted a-event. Such a renaming is shown in the upper part of the figure. There we have that the a-event at time τ_1 is immediately followed by exactly one d-event, which itself is followed exactly one time unit later by a d-event. For the event at time τ_1, we can then check that there is in strictly more than one time unit later an a-event followed immediately by a d-event – which identifies the wrongly inserted a-event.

The formulas below also have to take account of the case in which the a-event at time τ_2 does not have a corresponding a-event one time unit later and are therefore somewhat trickier to read. However, it is not hard to check that they capture the intuition described above.

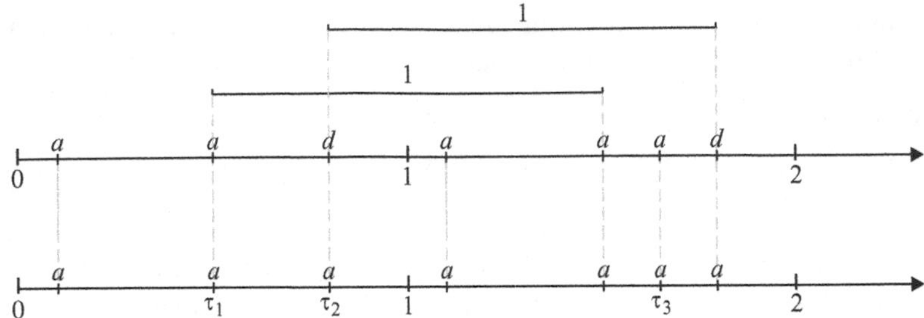

Fig. 13.2 On the bottom, a timed word suffering from an insertion error, and above its renaming that allows one to detect it

Lemma 8. *Let $\rho \models \varphi_{\mathcal{M}}$ be a timed word representing a run of $\mathcal{M}$, and let*

$$\psi := \Box_{\mathcal{I}}((a \vee d) \rightarrow \Box_{\mathcal{I}}\neg d) \wedge \Diamond_{\mathcal{I}}(d \wedge (\Diamond_{=1}(d \wedge \Box_{\mathcal{I}}\neg d) \vee \Box_{[1,1.25)}\bot))$$
$$\varphi_{ie} := \Diamond(\psi \wedge \Diamond_{=1}((\Diamond_{\mathcal{I}}(a \wedge \Diamond_{\mathcal{I}} d) \vee (\Box_{\mathcal{I}}\neg d \wedge \Diamond_{\mathcal{I}} a))))[\{(d,a)\} \cup Id_{\Sigma\setminus\{d\}}]$$

Then ρ suffers from insertion errors iff $\rho \models \varphi_{ie}$.

13.4.3 Asynchronous Parallel Composition

We augment the syntax of TPTL(1) in Definition 2 with an additional term for the *asynchronous parallel composition* operator $|||$, also known as *interleaving* and *(timed) shuffle product*. This operator is similar to its alphabetised counterpart in that it allows one to express specifications on systems that run concurrently.

Given timed words ρ, ρ_1, and ρ_2 with $|\rho| = n$, $|\rho_1| = n_1$, and $|\rho_2| = n_2$, we let $\rho \in \rho_1 ||| \rho_2$ iff the set of positions $\{1, \ldots, n\}$ of ρ can be partitioned into disjoint sets $\{i_1, \ldots, i_{n_1}\}$ and $\{j_1, \ldots, j_{n_2}\}$ such that $\sigma_k(\rho_1) = \sigma_{i_k}(\rho)$, $\tau_k(\rho_1) = \tau_{i_k}(\rho)$ for $1 \leq k \leq n_1$, and $\sigma_\ell(\rho_2) = \sigma_{j_\ell}(\rho)$, $\tau_\ell(\rho_2) = \tau_{j_\ell}(\rho)$ for $1 \leq \ell \leq n_2$.

The semantics of TPTL(1) together with asynchronous parallel composition is obtained by adding the following clause to Definition 3:

$$[\![\varphi_1 ||| \varphi_2]\!]^\rho := \{(i,r) \mid \exists\, \rho_1, \rho_2 . \rho^i = \rho_1 ||| \rho_2, (1,r) \in [\![\varphi_1]\!]^{\rho_1}, (1,r) \in [\![\varphi_2]\!]^{\rho_2}\}$$

In order to show undecidability, we use the fact $\varphi_{\mathcal{M}}$ holds on timed words with *and* without insertion errors. Consequently, the interleaving $\varphi_{\mathcal{M}} ||| a$ only holds on timed words *with* insertion errors.

Lemma 9. *Let $\rho \models \varphi_{\mathcal{M}}$ be a timed word representing a run of $\mathcal{M}$ and let $\varphi_{ie} := \varphi_{\mathcal{M}} ||| a$. Then ρ suffers from insertion errors iff $\rho \models \varphi_{ie}$.*

We sum up the results of this section in the following theorem.

Theorem 5. *The satisfiability problem for MTL augmented with any of hiding, renaming or asynchronous parallel composition is undecidable.*

13.5 Conclusion

In this chapter, we have considered various extensions of the central timed specification formalism of Metric Temporal Logic by process-algebraic operators originating from Tony Hoare's Communicating Sequential Processes. We have argued that such extensions, each of which strictly enhances the expressive power of MTL, allow for more natural and versatile specification of timed systems.

On the positive side, we have shown that MTL augmented with both fixpoint operators and alphabetised parallel composition remains decidable. On the other hand, the addition of any of hiding, renaming or asynchronous parallel composition (also known as interleaving and shuffle product) immediately yields undecidability.

One of our main technical tools has been the one-clock fragment of Timed Propositional Temporal Logic, TPTL(1). We have shown that extending this formalism with fixpoint operators provides a precise logical characterisation of the class of languages accepted by one-clock timed alternating automata, a result of independent interest. An intriguing question is whether the fixpoint-extension of the n-clock fragment of TPTL precisely characterises the class of languages accepted by n-clock timed alternating automata, thereby extending Theorem 2 (notwithstanding the fact that such languages are in general not recursive).

An interesting avenue for future work would be to investigate more thoroughly the methodological applications of our decidability results towards the specification of timed systems themselves built from recursive and concurrent components, such as Timed CSP processes.

References

1. Alur, R., Dill, D.L.: A theory of timed automata. Theor. Comput. Sci. **126**(2), 183–235 (1994)
2. Alur, R., Henzinger, T.A.: Real-time logics: complexity and expressiveness. Technical report, Stanford University (1990)
3. Alur, R., Henzinger, T.A.: A really temporal logic. J. ACM **41**(1), 181–203 (1994)
4. Bouyer, P., Chevalier, F., Markey, N.: On the expressiveness of TPTL and MTL. In: Proceedings of FSTTCS, volume 3821 of Lecture Notes in Computer Science, pp. 432–443. Springer (2005)
5. Bouyer, P., Markey, N., Ouaknine, J., Worrell, J.: On expressiveness and complexity in real-time model checking. In: Proceedings of ICALP, volume 5126 of Lecture Notes in Computer Science, pp 124–135. Springer (2008)
6. Brookes, S.D., Hoare, C.A.R., Roscoe, A.W.: A theory of communicating sequential processes. J. ACM **31**(3), 560–599 (1984)

7. D'Souza, D., Prabhakar, P.: On the expressiveness of MTL in the pointwise and continuous semantics. STTT **9**(1), 1–4 (2007)
8. Haase, C., Ouaknine, J., Worrell, J.: On extensions of metric temporal logic. Technical report, Oxford University Computing Laboratory (2009). http://www.comlab.ox.ac.uk/files/2180/how-09.pdf
9. Henzinger, T.A.: The temporal specification and verification of real-time systems. Ph.D, thesis, Stanford University (1992)
10. Henzinger, T.A.: Its about time: real-time logics reviewed. In: Proceedings of CONCUR, volume 1466 of Lecture Notes in Computer Science, pp. 439–454 (1998)
11. Henzinger, T.A., Raskin, J.-F., Schobbens, P.-Y.: The regular real-time languages. In: Proceedings of ICALP, volume 1443 of Lecture Notes in Computer Science, pp. 580–591. Springer (1998)
12. Hoare, C.A.R.: Communicating Sequential Processes. Prentice-Hall (1985)
13. Koymans, R.: Specifying real-time properties with Metric Temporal Logic. Real-Time Syst. **2**(4), 255–299 (1990)
14. Lange, M.: Weak automata for the linear time μ-calculus. In: Proceedings of VMCAI, volume 3385 of Lecture Notes in Computer Science, pp. 267–281. Springer (2005)
15. Lasota, S., Walukiewicz, I.: Alternating timed automata. ACM Trans. Comput. Logic **9**(2), 1–27 (2008)
16. Mayer, A.J., Stockmeyer, L.J.: The complexity of PDL with interleaving. Theor. Comput. Sci. **161**(1–2), 109–122 (1996)
17. Milner, R.: A Calculus of Communicating Systems, volume 92 of Lecture Notes in Computer Science. Springer (1980)
18. Minsky, M.L.: Computation: Finite and Infinite Machines. Prentice-Hall., Upper Saddle River, NJ (1967)
19. Ouaknine, J., Worrell, J.: On Metric Temporal Logic and Faulty turing machines. In: Proceedings of FoSSaCS, volume 3921 of Lecture Notes in Computer Science, pp. 217–230. Springer (2006)
20. Ouaknine, J., Worrell, J.: On the decidability complexity of Metric Temporal Logic over finite words. Logic. Meth. Comp. Sci. **3**(1) (2007)
21. Ouaknine, J., Worrell, J.: Some recent results in Metric Temporal Logic. In: Proceedings of FORMATS, volume 5215 of Lecture Notes in Computer Science, pp. 1–13. Springer (2008)
22. Rabin, M.O., Scott, D.: Finite automata and their decision problems. IBM J. Res. Dev. **3**(2), 115–125 (1959)
23. Reed, G.M., Roscoe, A.W.: A timed model for Communicating Sequential Processes. In: Proceedings of ICALP, volume 226 of Lecture Notes in Computer Science, pp. 314–323. Springer (1986)
24. Reed, G.M., Roscoe, A.W.: Metric spaces as models for real-time concurrency. In: Proceedings of MFPS, volume 298 of Lecture Notes in Computer Science, pp. 331–343. Springer (1987)
25. Reed, G.M., Roscoe, A.W.: The timed failures-stability model for CSP. Theor. Comput. Sci. **211**(1–2), 85–127 (1999)
26. Sistla, A.P., Vardi, M.Y., Wolper, P.: The complementation problem for Büchi automata with applications to temporal logic (extended abstract). In: Proceedings of ICALP, volume 194 of Lecture Notes in Computer Science, pp. 465–474. Springer (1985)

Chapter 14
Fun with Type Functions

Oleg Kiselyov, Simon Peyton Jones, and Chung-chieh Shan

Abstract Tony Hoare has always been a leader in writing down and proving properties of programs. To prove properties of programs automatically, the most widely used technology today is the ubiquitous type checker. Alas, static type systems inevitably exclude some good programs and allow some bad ones. Thus motivated, we describe some fun we have been having with Haskell, by making the type system more expressive without losing the benefits of automatic proof and compact expression. Specifically, we offer a programmer's tour of so-called *type families*, a recent extension to Haskell that allows functions on types to be expressed as straightforwardly as functions on values. This facility makes it easier for programmers to effectively extend the compiler by writing functional programs that execute during type checking.

Source code for all the examples is available at
http://research.microsoft.com/simonpj/papers/assoc-types/fun-with-type-funs.zip.

14.1 Introduction

The type of a function specifies (partially) what it does. Although weak as a specification language, static types have compensating virtues: they are

- *Lightweight*, so programmers use them
- *Machine-checked*, with minimal programmer assistance
- *Ubiquitous*, so programmers cannot avoid them.

O. Kiselyov
FNMOC, Monterey, CA, USA
e-mail: oleg@pobox.com

S.L. Peyton Jones (✉)
Microsoft Research Ltd, 7 JJ Thomson Avenue, Cambridge CB3 0FB, England
e-mail: simonpj@microsoft.com

C.-c. Shan
Rutgers University, USA
e-mail: ccshan@rutgers.edu

C.B. Jones et al. (eds.), *Reflections on the Work of C.A.R. Hoare*,
DOI 10.1007/978-1-84882-912-1_14,

As a result, static type checking is by far the most widely used verification technology today.

Every type system excludes some "good" programs and permits some "bad" ones. For example, a language that lacks polymorphism will reject this "good" program:

```
f :: [Int] -> [Bool] -> Int
f is bs = length is + length bs
```

Why? Because the `length` function cannot apply to both a list of `Int`s and a list of `Bool`s. The solution is to use a more sophisticated type system in which we can give `length` a polymorphic type.

Conversely, most languages will accept the expression

```
speed + distance
```

where `speed` is a variable representing speed and `distance` represents distance, even though adding a speed to a distance is as much nonsense as adding a character to a boolean.

The type-system designer wants to accommodate more good programs and exclude more bad ones, without going overboard and losing the virtues mentioned above. In this chapter we describe *type families*, an experimental addition to Haskell with precisely this goal. We start by using type families to accommodate more good programs, then turn in Section 14.5 to excluding more bad programs. We focus on the programmer, and our style is informal and tutorial. The technical background can be found elsewhere [5–7, 42].

14.2 Associated Types: Indexing Types by Types

Haskell has long offered two ways to express *relations* on types. Multiparameter type classes express arbitrary, many-to-many relations, whereas type constructors express specifically *functional* relations, where one type (the "argument") uniquely determines the other. For example, the relation between the type of a list and the type of that list's elements is a functional relation, expressed by the type constructor `[] :: * -> *`, which maps an arbitrary type `a` to the type `[a]` of lists of `a`. A type constructor maps its argument types *uniformly*, incorporating them into a more complex type without inspecting them. Type functions, the topic of this chapter, also establish functional relations between types, but a type function may perform case analysis on its argument types.

For example, consider the relation between a monad that supports mutable state and the corresponding type constructor for reference cells. The `IO` monad supports the following operations on reference cells of type `IORef a`:

```
newIORef   :: a -> IO (IORef a)
readIORef  :: IORef a -> IO a
writeIORef :: IORef a -> a -> IO ()
```

Similarly, the `ST s` monad supports the analogous operations on reference cells of type `STRef s a`:

```
newSTRef   :: a -> ST s (STRef s a)
readSTRef  :: STRef s a -> ST s a
writeSTRef :: STRef s a -> a -> ST s ()
```

It is tempting to overload these operations using a multiparameter type class:

```
class Mutation m r where
  newRef   :: a -> m (r a)
  readRef  :: r a -> m a
  writeRef :: r a -> a -> m ()

instance Mutation IO IORef where
  newRef = newIORef
  ...etc...

instance Mutation (ST s) (STRef s) where
  newRef = newSTRef
  ...etc...
```

This approach has two related disadvantages. First, the types of `newRef` and the other class operations are too polymorphic: one could declare an instance such as

```
instance Mutation IO (STRef s) where ...
```

even though we intend that the `IO` monad has *exactly one* reference type, namely `IORef`. Second, as a result, it is extremely easy to write programs with ambiguous typings, such as

```
readAndPrint :: IO ()
readAndPrint = do { r <- newRef 'x'
                  ; v <- readRef r
                  ; print v }
```

We know, from the type signature, that the computation is performed in the `IO` monad, but the type checker cannot select the type of `r`, since the `IO` monad could have reference cells of many different types. Therefore, we must annotate `r` with its type explicitly. Types are no longer lightweight when they have to be explicitly specified even for such a simple function.

The standard solution to the second problem is to use a *functional dependency*:

```
class Mutation m r | m -> r where ...
```

The "`m -> r`" part says that every `m` is related to at most one `r`. Functional dependencies have become a much-used extension of Haskell, and we return to a brief comparison in Section 14.6. Meanwhile, the main purpose of this chapter is to explain an alternative approach in which we express the functional dependency at the type level in an explicitly functional way.

14.2.1 Declaring an Associated Type

The class `Mutation` does not *really* have two type parameters: it has one type parameter, associated with another type that is functionally dependent. Type families allow one to say this directly:

```
class Mutation m where
  type Ref m :: * -> *
  newRef   :: a -> m (Ref m a)
  readRef  :: Ref m a -> m a
  writeRef :: Ref m a -> a -> m ()

instance Mutation IO where
  type Ref IO = IORef
  newRef   = newIORef
  readRef  = readIORef
  writeRef = writeIORef

instance Mutation (ST s) where
  type Ref (ST s) = STRef s
  newRef   = newSTRef
  readRef  = readSTRef
  writeRef = writeSTRef
```

The `class` declaration now introduces a *type function* `Ref` (with a specified kind) alongside the usual *value functions* such as `newRef` (each with a specified type). Similarly, each `instance` declaration contributes a clause defining the type function at the instance type alongside a witness for each value function.

We say that `Ref` is a *type family*, or an *associated type* of the class `Mutation`. It behaves like a function at the type level, so we also call `Ref` a *type function*. Applying a type function uses the same syntax as applying a type constructor: `Ref m a` above means to apply the type function `Ref` to `m`, then apply the resulting type constructor to `a`.

The types of `newRef` and `readRef` are now more perspicuous:

```
newRef  :: Mutation m => a -> m (Ref m a)
readRef :: Mutation m => Ref m a -> m a
```

Furthermore, by omitting the functionally determined type parameter from `Mutation`, we avoid the ambiguity problem exemplified by `readAndPrint` above. When performing type inference for `readAndPrint`, the type of `r` is readily inferred to be `Ref IO Char`, which the type checker reduces to `IORef Char`. In general, the type checker reduces `Ref IO` to `IORef`, and `Ref (ST s)` to `STRef s`.

These type equalities aside, `Ref` behaves like any other type constructor and it may be used freely in type signatures and data type declarations. For example, this declaration is fine:

```
data T m a = MkT [Ref m a]
```

14.2.2 Arithmetic

In the class `Mutation` of Section 14.2.1, we used an associated type to avoid a two-parameter type class, but that is not to say that associated types obviate multiparameter type classes. By declaring associated types in multiparameter type classes, we introduce type functions that take multiple arguments. One compelling use of such type functions is to make type coercions implicit, especially in arithmetic. Suppose we want to be able to write `add a b` to add two numeric values `a` and `b` even if one is an `Integer` and the other is a `Double` (without writing `fromIntegral` explicitly). We also want to add a scalar to a vector represented by a list without writing `repeat` explicitly to coerce the scalar to the vector type. The result type should be the simplest that is compatible with both operands. We can express this intent using a two-parameter type class, whose parameters are the argument types of `add` and whose associated type `SumTy` is the result:

```
class Add a b where
  type SumTy a b
  add :: a -> b -> SumTy a b

instance Add Integer Double where
  type SumTy Integer Double = Double
  add x y = fromIntegral x + y

instance Add Double Integer where
  type SumTy Double Integer = Double
  add x y = x + fromIntegral y

instance (Num a) => Add a a where
  type SumTy a a = a
  add x y = x + y
```

In other words, `SumTy` is a two-argument type function that maps the argument types of an addition to the type of its result. The three instance declarations explain how `SumTy` behaves on arguments of various types. We can then write `add (3::Integer) (4::Double)` to get a result of type `SumTy Integer Double`, which is the same as `Double`.

The same technique lets us conveniently build homogeneous lists out of heterogeneous but compatible components:

```
class Cons a b where
  type ResTy a b
  cons :: a -> [b] -> [ResTy a b]

instance Cons Integer Double where
  type ResTy Integer Double = Double
  cons x ys = fromIntegral x : ys

-- ...
```

With instances of this class similar to those of the class `Add`, we can `cons` an `Integer` to a list of `Doubles` without any explicit conversion.

14.2.3 Graphs

Garcia et al. [15] compare the support for generic programming offered by Haskell, ML, C++, C#, and Java. They give a table of qualitative conclusions, in which Haskell is rated favourably in all respects except associated types. This observation was one of the motivations for the work we describe here. Now that GHC supports type functions, we can express their main example as follows:

```
class Graph g where
  type Vertex g
  data Edge g
  src, tgt :: Edge g -> Vertex g
  outEdges :: g -> Vertex g -> [Edge g]

newtype G1 = G1 [Edge G1]
instance Graph G1 where
  type Vertex G1 = Int
  data Edge   G1 = MkEdge1 (Vertex G1) (Vertex G1)
  -- ...definitions for methods...

newtype G2 = G2 (Map (Vertex G2) [Vertex G2])
instance Graph G2 where
  type Vertex G2 = String
  data Edge   G2 = MkEdge2 Int (Vertex G2) (Vertex G2)
  -- ...definitions for methods...
```

The class `Graph` has two associated types: `Vertex` and `Edge`. We show two representative instances. In `G1`, a graph is represented by a list of its edges and a vertex is represented by an `Int`. In `G2`, a graph is represented by a mapping from each vertex to a list of its immediate neighbours, a vertex is represented by a `String`, and an `Edge` stores a weight (of type `Int`) as well as its end points. As these instance declarations illustrate, the declaration of a `Graph` instance is free to use the type functions `Edge` and `Vertex`.

14.2.4 Associated Data Types

The alert reader will notice in the class `Graph` that the associated type for `Edge` is declared using "`data`" rather than "`type`." Correspondingly, the `instance` declarations give a `data` declaration for `Edge`, complete with data constructors `MkEdge1` and `MkEdge2`. The reason for this use of `data` is somewhat subtle.

A type constructor such as `[]` expresses a functional relation between types that is *injective*, mapping different argument types to different results. For example, if two list types are the same, then their element types must be the same, too. This injectivity does not generally hold for type functions. Consider this function to find the list of vertices adjacent to the given vertex `v` in the graph `g`:

```
neighbours g v = map tgt (outEdges g v)
```

We expect GHC to infer the following type:

```
neighbours :: Graph g => g -> Vertex g -> [Vertex g]
```

Certainly, `outEdges` returns a `[Edge g1]` (for some type `g1`), and `tgt` requires its argument to be of type `Edge g2` (for some type `g2`). So, GHC's type checker requires that `Edge g1` $\sim$ `Edge g2`, where "$\sim$" means type equality.[1] Does that mean that `g1` $\sim$ `g2`, as intuition might suggest? Not necessarily! If `Edge` were an associated `type`, rather than `data`, we could have written these instances:

```
instance Graph G3 where
  type Edge G3 = (Int,Int)
instance Graph G4 where
  type Edge G4 = (Int,Int)
```

so that `Edge G3` $\sim$ `Edge G4` even though `G3` and `G4` are distinct. In that case, the inferred type of `neighbours` would be:

```
neighbours :: (Graph g1, Graph g2, Edge g1 ~ Edge g2)
           => g1 -> Vertex g1 -> [Vertex g2]
```

Although correct, this type is more general and complex than we want. By declaring `Edge` with `data`, we specify that `Edge` is injective, that `Edge g1` $\sim$ `Edge g2` indeed implies `g1` $\sim$ `g2`.[2] GHC then infers the simpler type we want.

---

[1] "=" is used for too many other things.

[2] A possible extension, not currently implemented by GHC, would be to allow an associated `type` synonym declaration optionally to specify that it should be injective, and to check that this property is maintained as each `instance` is added.

14.2.5 Type Functions Are Open

Value-level functions are *closed* in the sense that they must be defined all in one place. For example, if one defines

```
length :: [a] -> Int
```

then one must give the *complete* definition of `length` in a single place:

```
length []     = 0
length (x:xs) = 1 + length xs
```

It is not legal to put the two equations in different modules.

In contrast, a key property of type functions is that, like type classes themselves, they are *open* and can be extended with additional instances at any time. For example, if next week we define a new type `Age`, we can extend `SumTy` and `add` to work over `Age` by adding an instance declaration:

```
newtype Age = MkAge Int

instance Add Age Int where
  type SumTy Age Int = Age
  add (MkAge a) n = MkAge (a+n)
```

We thus can add an `Int` to an `Age`, but not an `Age` or `Float` to an `Age` without another instance.

14.2.6 Type Functions May Be Recursive

Just as the instance for `Show [a]` is defined in terms of `Show a`, a type function is often defined by structural recursion on the input type. Here is an example, extending our earlier `Add` class with a new instance:

```
instance (Add Integer a) => Add Integer [a] where
  type SumTy Integer [a] = [SumTy Integer a]
  add x y = map (add x) y
```

Thus

`SumTy Integer [Double]` $\sim$ `[SumTy Integer Double]` $\sim$ `[Double]`.

In a similar way, we may extend the `Mutation` example of Section 14.2.1 to *monad transformers*. Recall that a monad transformer `t :: (* -> *) -> (* -> *)` is a higher-order type constructor that takes a monad `m` into another monad `t m`.

```
class MonadTrans t where
  lift :: Monad m => m a -> t m a
```

At the value level, `lift` turns a monadic computation (of type `m a`) into one in the transformed monad (of type `t m a`). Now, if a monad `m` is an instance of `Mutation`, then we can make the transformed monad `t m` into such an instance too:

```
instance (Monad m, Mutation m, MonadTrans t)
      => Mutation (t m) where
  type Ref (t m) = Ref m
  newRef   = lift . newRef
  readRef  = lift . readRef
  writeRef = (lift .) . writeRef
```

The equation for `Ref` says that the type of references in the transformed monad is the same as that in the base monad.

14.3 Optimised Container Representations

A common optimisation technique is to represent data of different types differently (rather than uniformly as character strings, for example). This technique is best known when applied to container data. For example, we can use the same array container to define a `Bool` array and to define an `Int` array, yet a `Bool` array can be stored more compactly and negated elementwise faster when its elements are tightly packed as a bit vector. C++ programmers use template meta-programming to exploit this idea to great effect, for example, in the Boost library [47]. The following examples show how to express the same idea in Haskell, using type functions to map among the various concrete types that represent the same abstract containers.

14.3.1 Type-Directed Memoisation

To memoise a function is to improve its future performance by recording and reusing its past behaviour in a *memo table* [35]. The memo table augments the concrete representation of the function without affecting its abstract interface. A typical way to implement memoisation is to add a lookup from the table on entry to the function and an update to the table on exit from the function. Haskell offers an elegant way to express memoisation, because we can use lazy evaluation to manage the lookup and update of the memo table. But type functions offer a new possibility: *the type of the memo table can be determined automatically from the argument type of the memoised function* [12, 19].

We begin by defining a type class `Memo`. The constraint `Memo a` means that the behaviour of a function from an argument type `a` to a result type `w` can be represented as a memo table of type `Table a w`, where `Table` is a type function that maps a type to a constructor.

```
class Memo a where
  data Table a :: * -> *
  toTable   :: (a -> w) -> Table a w
  fromTable :: Table a w -> (a -> w)
```

For example, we can memoise any function from `Bool` by storing its two return values as a lazy pair. This lazy pair is the memo table.

```
instance Memo Bool where
  data Table Bool w = TBool w w
  toTable f = TBool (f True) (f False)
  fromTable (TBool x y) b = if b then x else y
```

To memoise a function `f :: Bool -> Int`, we simply replace it by `g`:

```
g :: Bool -> Int
g = fromTable (toTable f)
```

The first time `g` is applied to `True`, the Haskell implementation computes the first component of the lazy pair (by applying `f` in turn to `True`) and remembers it for future reuse. Thus, if `f` is defined by

```
f True  = factorial 100
f False = fibonacci 100
```

then evaluating `(g True + g True)` will take barely half as much time as evaluating `(f True + f True)`.

Generalising the `Memo` instance for `Bool` above, we can memoise functions from any sum type, such as the standard Haskell type `Either`:

```
data Either a b = Left a | Right b
```

We can memoise a function from `Either a b` by storing a lazy pair of a memo table from `a` and a memo table from `b`. That is, we take advantage of the isomorphism between the function type `Either a b -> w` and the product type `(a -> w, b -> w )`.

```
instance (Memo a, Memo b) => Memo (Either a b) where
  data Table (Either a b) w = TSum (Table a w)
                                   (Table b w)
  toTable f = TSum (toTable (f . Left))
                   (toTable (f . Right))
  fromTable (TSum t _) (Left  v) = fromTable t v
  fromTable (TSum _ t) (Right v) = fromTable t v
```

Of course, we need to memoise functions from `a` and `b`; hence the "`(Memo a, Memo b) =>`" part of the declaration. Dually, we can memoise functions from the product type `(a,b)` by storing a memo table from `a` whose entries are memo tables from `b`. That is, we take advantage of the currying isomorphism between the function types `(a,b) -> w` and `a -> b -> w`.

```
instance (Memo a, Memo b) => Memo (a,b) where
  newtype Table (a,b) w
    = TProduct (Table a (Table b w))
  toTable f = TProduct (toTable (\x ->
                           toTable (\y -> f (x,y))))
  fromTable (TProduct t) (x,y)
    = fromTable (fromTable t x) y
```

14.3.2 Memoisation for Recursive Types

What about functions from recursive types, like lists? No problem! A list is a combination of a sum, a product, and recursion:

```
instance (Memo a) => Memo [a] where
  data Table [a] w = TList w (Table a (Table [a] w))
  toTable f = TList (f [])
                    (toTable (\x -> toTable
                                (\xs -> f (x:xs))))
  fromTable (TList t _) []     = t
  fromTable (TList _ t) (x:xs) = fromTable
                                   (fromTable t x) xs
```

As in Section 14.3.1, the type function `Table` is recursive. Since a list is either empty or not, `Table [Bool] w` is represented by a pair (built with the data constructor `TList`), whose first component is the result of applying the memoised function `f` to the empty list, and whose second component memoises applying `f` to non-empty lists. A non-empty list `(x:xs)` belongs to a product type, so the corresponding table maps each `x` to a table that deals with `xs`. We merely combine the memoisation of functions from sums and from products.

It is remarkable how laziness takes care of the recursion in the type `[a]`. A memo table for a function `f` maps *every possible argument* `x` of `f` to a result `(f x)`. When the argument type is finite, such as `Bool` or `(Bool,Bool)`, the memo table is finite as well, but what if the argument type is infinite, such as `[Bool]`? Then, of course, the memo table is infinite: in the instance declaration above, we define `toTable` for `[a]` not only using `toTable` for `a` but also using `toTable` for `[a]` recursively. Just as each value `(f x)` in a memo table is evaluated only if the function is ever applied to that particular `x`, so each sub-table in this memo table is expanded only if the function is ever applied to a list with that prefix. So the laziness works at two distinct levels.

Now that we have dealt with sums, products and recursion, we can deal with any data type at all. Even base types like `Int` or `Integer` can be handled by first converting them (say) to a list of digits, say `[Bool]`. Alternatively, it is equally easy to give a specialised instance for `Table Integer` that uses some custom (but infinite!) tree representation for `Integer`.

More generally, if we define Memo instances – once and for all – for sum types, product types, and fixpoint types, then we can define a Memo instance for some new type just by writing an isomorphism between the new type and a construction out of sum types, product types, and fixpoint types. These boilerplate Memo instances can in fact be defined generically, with the help of functional dependencies [8] or type functions.[3]

14.3.3 Generic Finite Maps

A *finite map* is a partial function from a domain of *keys* to a range of *values*. Finite maps can be represented using many standard data structures, such as binary trees and hash tables, that work uniformly across all key types. However, our memo-table development suggests another possibility, that of representing a finite map using a memo table:

```
type Map key val = Table key (Maybe val)
```

That is, we represent a *partial* function from `key` to `val` as a *total* function from `key` to `Maybe val`. But we get two problems. The smaller one is that whereas `Table` did not need an `insert` method – once we construct the memo table, we never need to update it – `Map` needs `insert` and many other methods including `delete` and `union`. These considerations might lead us to add `insert`, `delete`, etc. to the `Table` interface, where they appear quite out of place. A nicer alternative would be to define a sub-class of `Table`.

The second, more substantial problem is that `Table` is unnecessarily inefficient in the way it represents keys that map to `Nothing`. An extreme case is an *empty* map whose key type is `Integer`. An efficient finite map would represent an empty map as an empty trie, so that the `lookup` operation returns immediately with `Nothing`. If instead we represent the empty map as an (infinite) `Table` mapping every `Integer` to `Nothing`, each lookup will explore a finite path in the potentially infinite tree, taking time proportional the number of bits in the `Integer`. Furthermore, looking up many `Integers` in such a `Table` would force many branches of the `Table`, producing a large tree in memory, with `Nothing` in every leaf! Philosophically, it seems nicer to distinguish the mapping of a key to `Nothing` from the *absence* of the mapping for that key.

For these reasons, it makes sense to implement Map afresh [19, 22]. As with `Memo`, we define a class `Key` and an associated data type `Map`:

```
class Key k where
  data Map k :: * -> *
  empty  :: Map k v
  lookup :: k -> Map k v -> Maybe v
  -- ...many other methods could be added...
```

[3] http://hackage.haskell.org/cgi-bin/hackage-scripts/package/pointless-haskell

Now the instances follow in just the same way as before:

```
instance Key Bool where
  data Map Bool elt = MB (Maybe elt) (Maybe elt)
  empty = MB Nothing Nothing
  lookup False (MB mf _) = mf
  lookup True  (MB _ mt) = mt

instance (Key a, Key b) => Key (Either a b) where
  data Map (Either a b) elt = MS (Map a elt)
                                 (Map b elt)
  empty = MS empty empty
  lookup (Left  k) (MS m _) = lookup k m
  lookup (Right k) (MS _ m) = lookup k m

instance (Key a, Key b) => Key (a,b) where
  data Map (a,b) elt = MP (Map a (Map b elt))
  empty = MP empty
  lookup (a,b) (MP m) = case lookup a m of
                          Nothing -> Nothing
                          Just m' -> lookup b m'
```

The fact that this is a *finite* map makes the instance for `Int` easier than before, because we can simply invoke an existing data structure (a Patricia tree, for example) for finite maps keyed by `Int`:

```
instance Key Int where
  newtype Map Int elt = MI (Data.IntMap.IntMap elt)
  empty = MI Data.IntMap.empty
  lookup k (MI m) = Data.IntMap.lookup k m
```

Implementations of other methods (such as `insert` and `union`) and instances at other types (such as lists) are left as exercises for the reader.

Hutton describes another example with the same flavour [24].

14.3.4 Session Types and Their Duality

We have seen a recursively defined correspondence between the type of keys and the type of a finite map over those keys. The key and the lookup function of a finite map can be regarded as a pair of *processes* that communicate in a particular way: the key sends indices to the lookup, then the lookup responds with the element's value. In this section, we generalise this correspondence to the relationship between a pair of processes that communicate with each other by sending and receiving values in a *session*.

For example, consider the following definitions:

```
data Stop = Done
newtype In  a b = In (a -> IO b)
data    Out a b = Out a   (IO b)

add_server :: In Int (In Int (Out Int Stop))
add_server = In $ \x -> return $ In $ \y ->
             do { putStrLn "Thinking"
                ; return $ Out (x + y) (return Done) }
```

The function-like value add_server accepts two Ints in succession, then prints "Thinking" before responding with an Int, their sum. We call add_server a *process*, whose interface protocol is specified by its type – so-called *session type*. We write session types explicitly in this section, but they can all be inferred.

We may couple two processes whose protocols are complementary, or *dual*:

```
class Session a where
  type Dual a
  run :: a -> Dual a -> IO ()
```

Of course, to write down the definition of run we must also say what it means to be dual. Doing so is straightforward:

```
instance (Session b) => Session (In a b) where
  type Dual (In a b) = Out a (Dual b)
  run (In f) (Out a d) = f a >>= \b -> d >>= \c -> run b c

instance (Session b) => Session (Out a b) where
  type Dual (Out a b) = In a (Dual b)
  run (Out a d) (In f) = f a >>= \b -> d >>= \c -> run c b

instance Session Stop where
  type Dual Stop = Stop
  run Done Done = return ()
```

The type system guarantees that the protocols of the two processes match. Thus, if we write a suitable client add_client, like

```
add_client :: Out Int (Out Int (In Int Stop))
add_client = Out 3 $ return $ Out 4 $
             do { putStrLn "Waiting"
                ; return $ In $ \z -> print z >> return Done }
```

we may couple them (either way around):

```
> run add_server add_client
Thinking
Waiting 7
> run add_client add_server
Thinking
Waiting 7
```

However, `run` will not allow us to couple two processes that do not have dual protocols. Suppose that we write a negation server:

```
neg_server :: In Int (Out Int Stop)
neg_server = In $ \x ->
             do { putStrLn "Thinking"
                ; return $ Out (-x) (return Done) }
```

Then `(run add_client neg_server)` will fail with a type error. Just as the `Memo` class represents functions of type `a -> w` by memo tables of the matching type `Table a w`, this `Session` class represents consumers of type `a -> IO ()` by producers of the matching type `Dual a`.

These protocols do not allow past communication to affect the type and direction of *future* exchanges. For example, it seems impossible to write a well-typed server that begins by receiving a `Bool`, then performs addition if `True` is received and negation if `False` is received. However, we can express a protocol that chooses between addition and negation (or more generally, a protocol that chooses among a finite number of ways to continue). We simply treat such a binary choice as a distinct sort of protocol step. The receiver of the choice has a product type, whereas the sender has a sum type:

```
instance (Session a, Session b) => Session (Either a b) where
  type Dual (Either a b) = (Dual a, Dual b)
  run (Left  y) (x,_) = run y x
  run (Right y) (_,x) = run y x

instance (Session a, Session b) => Session (a, b) where
  type Dual (a,b) = Either (Dual a) (Dual b)
  run (x,_) (Left  y) = run x y
  run (_,x) (Right y) = run x y
```

These additional instances let us define a combined addition-negation server, along with a client that chooses to add. The two new processes sport (inferable) types that reflect their initial choice.

```
server :: (In Int (Out Int Stop),
           In Int (In Int (Out Int Stop)))
server = (neg_server, add_server)

client :: Either (Out Int (In Int Stop))
                 (Out Int (Out Int (In Int Stop)))
client = Right add_client
```

To connect `server` and `client`, we can evaluate either `run server client` or `run client server`. The session type of the client hides which of the two choices the client eventually selects; the choice may depend on user input at run time, which the type checker has no way of knowing. The type checker does statically verify that the corresponding server can handle either choice.

With the instances defined above, each protocol allows only a finite number of exchanges, so a server cannot keep looping until the client disconnects. This restriction is not fundamental: recursion in protocols can be expressed, for example using an explicit fixpoint operator at the type level [38].

We can also separate the notion of a *process* from that of a *channel*, and associate a protocol with the channel rather than the process. This and other variants have been explored in other works [26, 27, 36, 38, 41], from which we draw the ideas of this section in a simplified form.

In principle, we can require that `Dual` be an involution (i.e. `Dual` be its own inverse) by adding a *equality constraint* as a superclass of `Session`:

```
class (Dual (Dual a) ~ a) => Session a where ...
```

We can then invoke `run` on a pair of processes without worrying about which process is known to be the dual of which other process. More generally, this technique lets us express bijections between types. However, such equality superclasses are not yet implemented in the latest release of GHC (6.12).

14.4 Typed Sprintf and Sscanf

We conclude the first half of the chapter, about using type functions to accommodate more good programs, with a larger example: typed `sprintf` and `sscanf`.

A hoary chestnut for typed languages is the definition of `sprintf` and `sscanf`. Although these handy functions are present in many languages (such as C and Haskell), they are usually not type-safe: the type checker does not stop the programmer from passing to `sprintf` more or fewer arguments than required by the format descriptor. The typing puzzle is that we want the following to be true:

```
sprintf "Name=%s"              :: String -> String
sprintf "Age=%d"               :: Int -> String
sprintf "Name=%s, Age=%d" :: String -> Int -> String
```

That is, the *type* of `(sprintf fs)` depends on the *value* of the *format descriptor* `fs`. Supporting such dependency directly requires a full-spectrum dependently typed language, but there is a small literature of neat techniques for getting close without such a language [1, 9, 20]. Here we show one technique using type families. In fact, we accomplish something more general: typed `sprintf` and `sscanf` *sharing the same format descriptor*. Typed `sprintf` has received a lot more attention than typed `sscanf`; it is especially rare for an implementation of both to use the same format descriptor.

14.4.1 Typed Sprintf

We begin with two observations:

- Format descriptors in C are just strings, which leaves the door wide open for malformed descriptors that `sprintf` does not recognise (e.g. `sprintf "%?"`).

The language of format descriptors is a small domain-specific language; the type checker should reject ill-formed descriptors.

- In Haskell, we cannot make the type of `(sprintf f)` depend on the value of the format descriptor `f`. However, using type functions, we can make it depend on the *type* of `f`.

Putting these two observations together suggests that we use a now-standard design pattern: a domain-specific language expressed using a generalised algebraic data type (GADT) indexed by a type argument. Concretely, we can define the type of format descriptors `F` as follows:

```
data F f where
  Lit :: String -> F L
  Val :: Parser val -> Printer val -> F (V val)
  Cmp :: F f1 -> F f2 -> F (C f1 f2)

data L
data V val
data C f1 f2

type Parser  a = String -> [(a,String)]
type Printer a = a -> String
```

So `F` is a GADT with three constructors, `Lit`, `Val`, and `Cmp`.[4] Our intention is that `(sprintf f)` should behave as follows:

- If `f` = `Lit s`, then print (that is, return as the output string) `s`.
- If `f` = `Cmp f1 f2`, then print according to descriptor `f1` and continue according to descriptor `f2`.
- If `f` = `Val r p`, then use the printer `p` to convert the first argument to a string to print. (The `r` argument is used for parsing in Section 14.4.2 below.)

If `fmt :: F ty`, then the *type* `ty` encodes the *shape* of the term `fmt`. For example, given `int :: F (V Int)`, we may write the following format descriptors:

```
f_ld  = Lit "day"                                  :: F L
f_lds = Cmp (Lit "day") (Lit "s")                  :: F (C L L)
f_dn  = Cmp (Lit "day ") int                       :: F (C L (V Int))
f_nds = Cmp int (Cmp (Lit " day") (Lit "s")) :: F (C (V Int) (C L L))
```

In each case, the type encodes an abstraction of the value. (We have specified the types explicitly, but they can be inferred.) The types `L`, `V` and `C` are type-level abstractions of the terms `Lit`, `Val` and `Cmp`. These types are uninhabited by any value, but they index values in the GADT `F` and they are associated with other, inhabited types by two type functions. We turn to these type functions next.

We want an interpreter `sprintf` for this domain-specific language, so that:

```
sprintf :: F f -> SPrintf f
```

[4] "`Cmp`" is short for "compose".

where `SPrintf` is a type function that transforms the (type-level) format descriptor `f` to the type of `(sprintf f)`. For example, the following should all work:

```
sprintf f_ld          -- Result: "day"
sprintf f_lds         -- Result: "days"
sprintf f_dn 3        -- Result: "day 3"
sprintf f_nds 3       -- Result: "3 days"
```

It turns out that the most convenient approach is to use continuation-passing style, at both the type level and the value level. At the type level, we define `SPrintf` above using an auxiliary type function `TPrinter`. Because `TPrinter` has no accompanying value-level operations, a type class is not needed. Instead, GHC allows the type function to be defined directly, like this:[5]

```
type SPrintf f = TPrinter f String

type family TPrinter f x
type instance TPrinter L          x = x
type instance TPrinter (V val)    x = val -> x
type instance TPrinter (C f1 f2) x = TPrinter f1 (TPrinter f2 x)
```

So `SPrintf` is just a vanilla type synonym, which calls the type function `TPrinter` with second parameter `String`. Then `TPrinter` transforms the type as required. For example:

```
SPrintf (C L (V Int)) ~ TPrinter (C L (V Int)) String
                      ~ TPrinter L (TPrinter (V Int) String)
                      ~ TPrinter (V Int) String
                      ~ Int -> String
```

At the value level, we proceed thus:

```
sprintf :: F f -> SPrintf f
sprintf p = printer p id

printer :: F f -> (String -> a) -> TPrinter f a
printer (Lit str)     k = k str
printer (Val _ show) k = \x -> k (show x)
printer (Cmp f1 f2)  k = printer f1 (\s1 ->
                          printer f2 (\s2 ->
                          k (s1++s2)))
```

[5] GHC requires the alarming flag `-XAllowUndecidableInstances` to accept the `(C f1 f2)` instance for `TPrinter`, because the *nested* recursive call to `TPrinter` does not "obviously terminate." Of course, every call to `TPrinter` does terminate, because the second argument (where the nested recursive call is made) is not scrutinised by any of the equations, but this is a non-local property that GHC does not check. The flag promises the compiler that `TPrinter` will terminate; the worst that can happen if the programmer makes an erroneous promise is that the type checker diverges.

It is interesting to see how `printer` type-checks. Inside the `Lit` branch, for example, we know that `f` is `L` and hence that the desired result type `TPrinter f a` is `TPrinter L a`, or just `a`. Since `k str :: a`, the actual result type matches the desired one. Similar reasoning applies to the `Val` and `Cmp` branches.

14.4.2 Typed sscanf

We can use the same domain-specific language of format descriptors for parsing as well as printing. That is, we can write

```
sscanf :: F f -> SScanf f
```

where `SScanf` is a suitable type function. For example, reusing the format descriptors defined above, we may write:

```
sscanf f_ld  "days long"   -- Result: Just ((), "s long")
sscanf f_ld  "das long"    -- Result: Nothing
sscanf f_lds "days long"   -- Result: Just ((), " long")
sscanf f_dn  "day 4."      -- Result: Just (((),4), ".")
```

In general, `sscanf f s` returns `Nothing` if the parse fails and `Just (v,s')` if it succeeds, where `s'` is the unmatched remainder of the input string and `v` is a (left-nested) tuple containing the parsed values. The details are now fairly routine:

```
type SScanf f = String -> Maybe (TParser f (), String)

type family TParser f x
type instance TParser L          x = x
type instance TParser (V val)    x = (x,val)
type instance TParser (C f1 f2) x = TParser f2 (TParser f1 x)

sscanf :: F f -> SScanf f
sscanf fmt inp = parser fmt () inp

parser :: F f -> a -> String -> Maybe (TParser f a, String)
parser (Lit str)      v s = parseLit str v s
parser (Val reads _) v s = parseVal reads v s
parser (Cmp f1 f2)    v s = case parser f1 v s of
                                Nothing -> Nothing
                                Just (v1,s1) -> parser f2 v1 s1

parseLit :: String -> a -> String -> Maybe (a, String)
parseLit str v s = case prefix str s of
                       Nothing -> Nothing
                       Just s' -> Just (v, s')

parseVal :: Parser b -> a -> String -> Maybe ((a,b), String)
parseVal reads v s = case reads s of
                         [(v',s')] -> Just ((v,v'),s')
                         _         -> Nothing
```

14.4.3 Reflections

We conclude with a few reflections on the design.

- Our `Val` constructor makes it easy to add printers for new types. For example:

```
newtype Dollars = MkD Int

dollars :: F (V Dollars)
dollars = Val read_dol show_dol
  where
    read_dol ('$':s) = [ (MkD d, s) | (d,s) <- reads s ]
    read_dol _       = []
    show_dol (MkD d) = '$' : show d
```

- Our approach is precisely that of Hinze [20], except that we use type functions and GADTs (unavailable when Hinze wrote) to produce a much more elegant result.
- It is (just) possible to take the domain-specific-language approach *without* using type functions, albeit with less clarity and greater fragility [31].
- Defining `F` as a GADT makes it easy to define new interpreters beyond `sprintf` and `sscanf`, but hard to add new format-descriptor combinators. A dual approach [33], which makes it easy to add new descriptors but hard to define new interpreters, is to define `F` as a record of operations:

```
data F f = F {
  printer :: forall a. (String -> a) -> TPrinter f a,
  parser  :: forall a. a -> String
                            -> Maybe (TParser f a, String) }
```

  Instead of being a GADT, `F` becomes a higher-rank data constructor – that is, its arguments are polymorphic functions. The type functions `TPrinter` and `TParser` are unchanged. The format-descriptor combinators are no longer data constructors but ordinary functions instead:

```
lit :: String -> F I
lit str = F { printer = \k -> k str,
              parser  = parseLit str }

int :: F (V Int)
int = F { printer = \k i -> k (show i),
          parser  = parseVal reads }
```

- If we consider only `sprintf` or only `sscanf`, then the type-level format descriptor is the result of *defunctionalising* a type-level function, and `TPrinter` or `TParser` is the *apply function* [10, 39]. Considering `sprintf` and `sscanf` together takes format descriptors out of the image of defunctionalisation.

In general, type functions let us easily express a parser that operates on types (and produces corresponding values). In this way, we can overlay our own domain-specific, variable-arity syntax onto Haskell's type system.[6] For example, we can concisely express XML documents,[7] linear algebra,[8] and even keyword arguments.[9]

14.5 Fun with Phantom Types

Each type function we have seen so far returns types that are actually used in the value-level computations. In other words, type functions are necessary to type-check the overloaded functions above. For example, it is thanks to the type function `Ref` that the value functions `newIORef` and `newSTRef` can be overloaded under the name `newRef`. In contrast, this section considers type functions that operate on so-called *phantom types*.

Phantom types enforce distinctions among values with the same run-time representation, such as numbers with different units [30] and strings for different XML elements. Functions on phantom types propagate these distinctions through a static approximation of the computation. Phantom types and functions on them thus let us reason more precisely about a program's behaviour before running it, essentially by defining additional type-checking rules that refine Haskell's built-in ones. The reader may find many applications of phantom types elsewhere [13, 14, 21]; our focus here is on the additional expressiveness offered by type families – to exclude more bad programs.

14.5.1 Pointer Arithmetic and Alignment

The refined distinctions afforded by phantom types are especially useful in embedded and systems programming, where a Haskell program (or code it generates) performs low-level operations such as direct memory access and interacts with hardware device drivers [11, 32]. It is easy to use phantom types to enforce access permissions (read versus write), but we take the example of pointer arithmetic and alignment to illustrate the power of type functions.

Many hardware operations require pointers that are properly aligned (i.e., divisible) by a statically known small integer, even though every pointer, no matter how aligned, is represented by a machine word at run time. Our goal is to distinguish the types of differently aligned pointers and thus prevent the use of misaligned pointers.

[6] http://okmij.org/ftp/Haskell/types.html#polyvar-fn

[7] http://okmij.org/ftp/Haskell/typecast.html#solving-read-show

[8] http://okmij.org/ftp/Haskell/typecast.html#is-function-type

[9] http://okmij.org/ftp/Haskell/keyword-arguments.lhs

Before we can track pointer alignment, we first need to define natural numbers at the type level. The type `Zero` represents 0; if the type `n` represents n then the type `Succ n` represents $n + 1$.

```
data Zero
data Succ n
```

For convenience, we also define synonyms for small type-level numbers.

```
type One   = Succ Zero
type Two   = Succ One
type Four  = Succ (Succ Two )
type Six   = Succ (Succ Four)
type Eight = Succ (Succ Six )
```

These type-level numbers belong to a class `Nat`, whose value member `toInt` lets us read off each number as an `Int`:

```
class Nat n where
  toInt :: n -> Int
instance Nat Zero where
  toInt _ = 0
instance (Nat n) => Nat (Succ n) where
  toInt _ = 1 + toInt (undefined :: n)
```

In this code, `toInt` uses a standard Haskell idiom called *proxy arguments*. As the underscores in its `instances` show, `toInt` never examines its argument. Nevertheless, it must *take* an argument, as a proxy that specifies which instance to use. Here is how one might call `toInt`:

```
Prelude> toInt (undefined :: Two)
2
```

We use Haskell's built-in `undefined` value and specify that it has type `Two`, thereby telling the compiler which instance of `Nat` to use. There is exactly such a call in the `(Succ n)` instance of `Nat`, only in that case the proxy argument is given the type `n`, a lexically scoped type variable.

As promised above, we represent a pointer or offset as a machine word at run time, but use a phantom type at compile time to track how aligned we know the pointer or offset to be.

```
newtype Pointer n = MkPointer Int
newtype Offset  n = MkOffset  Int
```

Thus a value of type `Pointer n` is an `n`-byte-aligned pointer; and a value of type `Offset n` is a multiple of `n`. For example, a `Pointer Four` is a 4-byte-aligned pointer. `Pointer n` is defined as a `newtype` and so the data constructor `MkPointer` has no run-time representation. In other words, the phantom-type alignment annotation imposes no run-time overhead.

To keep this alignment knowledge sound, the data constructors `MkPointer` and `MkOffset` above must not be exported for direct use by clients. Instead, clients must construct `Pointer` and `Offset` values using "smart constructors." One such constructor is `multiple`:

```
multiple :: forall n. (Nat n) => Int -> Offset n
multiple i = MkOffset (i * toInt (undefined :: n))
```

So `(multiple i)` is the `i`-th multiple of the alignment specified by the return type. For example, evaluating `multiple 3 :: Offset Four` yields `MkOffset 12`, the third multiple of a `Four`-byte alignment.

When a pointer is incremented by an offset, the resulting pointer is aligned by the greatest common divisor (GCD) of the alignments of the original pointer and the offset. To express this fact, we define a type function `GCD` to compute the GCD of two type-level numbers. Actually, `GCD` takes three arguments: `GCD d m n` computes the GCD of `d+m` and `d+n`. We will define `GCD` in a moment, but assuming we have it we can define `add`:

```
add :: Pointer m -> Offset n -> Pointer (GCD Zero m n)
add (MkPointer x) (MkOffset y) = MkPointer (x + y)
```

Thus, if `p` has the type `Pointer Eight` and `o` has the type `Offset Six`, then `add p o` has the type `Pointer Two`.

The type checker does not check that `x + y` is indeed aligned by the GCD. Like `multiple`, the function `add` is trusted code and its type expresses claims that its programmer must guarantee. Once she does so, however, the clients of `add` have complete security. If `fetch32` is an operation that works on 4-aligned pointers only, then we can give it the type

```
(GCD Zero n Four ~ Four) => Pointer n -> IO ()
```

In words, `fetch32` works on any pointer whose alignment's GCD with 4 is 4. It is then a type error to apply `fetch32` to `add p o`, but it is acceptable to apply `fetch32` to `p`.

Because the type function `GCD` has no accompanying value-level operations, we can define it without a type class:

```
type family GCD d m n
type instance GCD d Zero Zero = d
type instance GCD d (Succ m) (Succ n) = GCD (Succ d) m n
type instance GCD Zero (Succ m) Zero = Succ m
type instance GCD (Succ d) (Succ m) Zero = GCD (Succ Zero) d m
type instance GCD Zero Zero (Succ n) = Succ n
type instance GCD (Succ d) Zero (Succ n) = GCD (Succ Zero) d n
```

14.5.2 *Tracking State and Control in a Parameterised Monad*

Because actions in Haskell are values as well, phantom types can be used to enforce properties on actions and control flow as well as on values and data flow. In particular, we can express the preconditions and postconditions of monadic actions by generalising monads to *parameterised monads* [2]. A parameterised monad is a type constructor that takes three arguments, reminiscent of a Hoare triple: an initial state, a final state, and the type of values produced by the action. As shown in the following class definition (generalising the `Monad` class), a pure action does not change the state and concatenating two actions identifies the final state of the first action with the initial state of the second action.

```
class PMonad m where
  unit :: a -> m p p a
  bind :: m p q a -> (a -> m q r b) -> m p r b
```

The precise meaning of states depends on the particular parameterised monad: they could describe files open, time spent, or the shape of a managed heap [32]. In this example, we use a parameterised monad to track the locks held among a given (finite) set.

A lock can be acquired only if it is not currently held, and released only if it is currently held. Furthermore, no lock is held at the beginning of the program and no lock should be held at the end. We encode a set of locks and whether each is held by a type-level list of booleans. The spine of the list is made of `Cons` cells and `Nil`; each element of the list is either `Locked` or `Unlocked`. For example, suppose we are tracking three locks. If only the first and last are held, then the state is the type `Cons Locked (Cons Unlocked (Cons Locked Nil))`.

```
data Nil
data Cons l s

data Locked
data Unlocked
```

The run-time representation of our parameterised monad is simply that of Haskell's `IO` monad, so it is easy to implement a `PMonad` instance.

```
newtype LockM p q a = LockM { unLockM :: IO a }

instance PMonad LockM where
  unit x   = LockM (return x)
  bind m k = LockM (unLockM m >>= unLockM . k)
```

It is also easy to lift an `IO` action that does not affect locks to become a `LockM` action whose initial and final states are the same and arbitrary.

```
lput :: String -> LockM p p ()
lput = LockM . putStrLn
```

To manipulate boolean lists at the type level, we define type functions `Get` and `Set`. Given a type-level natural number `n` and a list `p`, the type `Get n p` is the `n`-th element of that list, and the type `Set n e p` is the result of replacing the `n`-th element of `p` by `e`. The first element of a list is indexed by `Zero`. It is a type error if the element does not exist because the list is too short.

```
type family Get n p
type instance Get Zero (Cons e p) = e
type instance Get (Succ n) (Cons e p) = Get n p

type family Set n e' p
type instance Set Zero e' (Cons e p) = Cons e' p
type instance Set (Succ n) e' (Cons e p) = Cons e (Set n e' p)
```

We represent a lock as a mutex handle (here caricatured by an `Int`), with a phantom type `n` attached to identify the lock at compile time. The phantom type `n` is an index into a type-level list.

```
newtype Lock n = Lock Int deriving Show

mkLock :: forall n. Nat n => Lock n
mkLock = Lock (toInt (undefined::n))
```

The data constructor introduced by the `newtype` declaration has no run-time representation and so this wrapping imposes no run-time overhead. We make one lock, `lock1`, for the sake of further examples.

```
lock1 = mkLock :: Lock One
```

We can now define actions to acquire and release locks. The types of the actions reflect their constraints on the state.

```
acquire :: (Get n p ~ Unlocked) =>
           Lock n -> LockM p (Set n Locked p) ()
acquire l = LockM (putStrLn ("acquire " ++ show l))

release :: (Get n p ~ Locked) =>
           Lock n -> LockM p (Set n Unlocked p) ()
release l = LockM (putStrLn ("release " ++ show l))
```

In the type of `acquire`, the constraint `Get n p ~ Unlocked` is the *precondition* on the state before acquiring the lock: the lock to be acquired must not be already held. The final state of the `LockM` action returned by `acquire` specifies the *postcondition*: the lock just acquired is `Locked`. For the `release` action, the pre- and postconditions are the converse. To keep the example simple, we do not manipulate any real locks; rather, we print our intentions.

At the top level, a `LockM` action is executed by applying the function `run` to turn it into an `IO` action. The type of `run` below requires that the action begin and end with no lock held among three available.

```
type ThreeLocks = Cons Unlocked (Cons Unlocked (Cons Unlocked Nil))
run :: LockM ThreeLocks ThreeLocks a -> IO a
run = unLockM
```

For example, given any action `a`, the action `with1 a` defined below acquires lock 1, performs `a`, then releases lock 1 and returns the result of `a`.

```
with1 a = acquire lock1 `bind` \_ ->
          a `bind` \x ->
          release lock1 `bind` \_ ->
          unit x
```

Therefore, we can execute `run (with1 (lput "hello"))` by itself.

```
> run (with1 (lput "hello"))
acquire Lock 1
hello
release Lock 1
```

Multiple locks can be held at the same time and need not be released in the opposite order as they were acquired. However, the type system prevents us from nesting `with1` inside `with1`, because such an action would try to acquire lock 1 twice. Indeed, the expression `run (with1 (with1 (lput "hello")))` does not type-check. We also cannot acquire a lock without releasing it subsequently. For example, the expression `run (acquire lock1)` is rejected.

We can also introduce actions that do not change the state of locks yet require that a certain lock be held:

```
critical1 :: (Get One p ~ Locked) => LockM p p ()
critical1 = LockM (putStrLn "Critical section 1")
```

An attempt to run such an action without holding the required lock, as in `run critical1`, is rejected by the type checker. On the other hand, the program `run (with1 critical1)` type checks and can be successfully executed. Likewise, we can define potentially blocking actions, to be executed only when a lock is not held; the type checker will then prevent such actions within a critical section protected by the lock.

14.5.3 Keeping the Kinds Straight

It will not have escaped the reader's notice that we are doing *untyped* functional programming at the type level. For example, the kind of `GCD` is

```
GCD :: * -> * -> * -> *
```

so the compiler would accept the nonsensical type `(GCD Int Zero Bool)`. The same problem occurs with `Pointer n` and other types defined in this section. We can alleviate the problem using the `Nat n` constraint. For example, we could define `Pointer n` as

```
newtype Nat n => Pointer n = MkPointer Int
```

so that, for example, `Pointer Bool` becomes invalid and will raise a compile-time error. The constraint `Nat n` is a *kind predicate*, specifying the set of types that constitute natural numbers – just as the type `Int` specifies a set of values.

We wish for the convenience and discipline of algebraic data kinds when writing type-level functions, just as we are accustomed to algebraic data types in conventional, term-level programs. One possibility is to "lift"' the ordinary data type declaration

```
data N = Zero | Succ N
```

to the kind level. Alternatively, we may want to declare algebraic data kinds like this:

```
data kind N = Zero | Succ N
```

Here `N` is a kind constant and `Zero` and `Succ` are type constructors. Now `GCD` could have the kind

```
GCD :: N -> N -> N -> N
```

Similarly, `Pointer` and `Offset` should both have kind `N -> *`. Much the same applies in the discussion of state and control, where we would rather write:

```
data kind ListLS = Nil | Cons LockState ListLS
data kind LockState = Locked | Unlocked
```

then give a decent kind to `Get`:

```
Get :: N -> ListS -> LockState
```

Furthermore, unlike the earlier examples in which it was crucial that our type functions were open (Section 14.2.5), type functions such as `GCD` and `Get` are *closed*, in that all their equations are given in one place.

These are shortcomings of GHC's current implementation, but there is no technical difficulty with algebraic data kinds; indeed they are fully supported by the Ω language [43].

14.5.4 Type-Preserving Compilers

A popular, if incestuous, application of Haskell is for writing compilers. If the object language is statically typed, then one can index a GADT by a phantom type to ensure that only well-typed object programs can be represented in the compiler [37]:

```
data Exp a where
  Enum :: Int -> Exp Int
  Eadd :: Exp Int -> Exp Int -> Exp Int
  Eapp :: Exp (a->b) -> Exp a -> Exp b
  ...
```

Now an optimiser and an evaluator might have types

```
optimise :: Exp a -> Exp a
evaluate :: Exp a -> a
```

which compactly express the facts that (a) the optimiser need only deal with well-typed object terms, (b) optimising a term does not change its type, and (c) evaluating a term yields a value of the correct type.

But what about transforming programs into continuation-passing style? In that case, the type of the result term is a *function of* the type of the argument term:

```
cpsConvert :: Exp a -> Exp (CpsT a)
```

Here `CpsT` maps a type `a` to its CPS-converted version [34]. Guillemette and Monnier express `CpsT` as a type-level function [18], whereas Carette et al. show how to do without type-level functions [4].

14.6 Related Work and Reflections

The goal of type families is to build on the success of static type systems, by extending their power and expressiveness without losing their brevity and comprehensibility to programmers. (Of course, there is an implicit tension between these goals and the reader will have to judge how successful we have been.) There are other designs with similar goals:

- Functional dependencies took the Haskell community by storm when Mark Jones introduced them [29], because they met a real need. Many, perhaps all, of the examples in this tutorial can also be programmed using functional dependencies, but the programming style at the type level feels like logic programming rather than functional programming. The reader may find a programmer's-eye comparison of the two approaches in [6]. Jones showed recently how the stylistic question can be at least partly addressed by a notational device [28] but, more fundamentally, the interaction of functional dependencies with other type-level features such as existentials and GADTs is not well understood and possibly problematic. In fact, one may see type families as a way to understand functional dependencies in these more general settings.
- Ω [43] is a prototype programing language that specifically aims to provide the programmer with type-level computation. It goes quite a bit further than GHC's type families (e.g., Ω has an infinite tower of kinds and supports closed type functions), but lacks type classes and much of the other Haskell paraphernalia. Ω comes with a number of excellent papers giving many a motivating example [44–46].

These designs, along with GHC's type families, can be thought of as helping programmers prove more interesting theorems that characterise their programs. Meanwhile, the theorem-proving and type-theory community has been drawing from its long history of type-level computation to help mathematicians write more interesting programs that witness their theorems [3].

The motivation for type-level computations comes from the Curry-Howard correspondence [17, 23] that underlies Martin-Löf's intuitionistic type theory: propositions are types and proofs are terms. The more expressive a type system, the more propositions we can state and prove in it, such as properties involving numbers and arithmetic. Hence expressive languages such as those of NuPRL, Coq, Epigram, and Agda permit types involving numbers and arithmetic. For example, the following type in Agda states that addition is commutative:

```
(n m : Nat) -> n + m == m + n
```

To prove this proposition is to write a term of this type, and to check the proof is the job of the type checker. To do its job, the type checker may need to simplify a type like `(Zero + m)` to `m`, so type checking involves type-level computations. Because a proof checker should always terminate, it is natural to insist that type-level computations also always terminate.

Since proof assistants based on type theory implement a (richly typed) λ-calculus, they can be used to program – that is, to write terms that compute interesting values, not just inhabit interesting types. To this end, an expressive type system lets us state and prove more interesting properties about programs – of the sort we have shown in this chapter. Tools such as Coq, Epigram, and Agda thus cater increasingly to the use of theorem proving for practical programming. This convergence of theory and practice renews our commitment to Tony Hoare's ideal of simple, reliable software.

Acknowledgements We would like to thank people who responded to our invitation to suggest interesting examples of programming with type families, or commented on a draft of the chapter: Lennart Augustsson, Neil Brown, Toby Hutton, Ryan Ingram, Chris Kuklewicz, Dave Menendez, Benjamin Moseley, Hugh Pacheco, Conrad Parker, Bernie Pope, Tom Schrijvers, Josef Svenningsson, Paulo Tanimoto, Magnus Therning, Ashley Yakeley and Brent Yorgey.

References

1. Asai, K.: On typing delimited continuations: three new solutions to the printf problem. Higher-Order and Symbolic Computation. **22**(3), 275–291 (2009)
2. Atkey, R.: Parameterised notions of computation. J. Funct. Program. **19**(3&4), 355–376 (2009)
3. Bove, A., Dybjer, P.: Dependent types at work. In: International summer school on language engineering and rigorous software development. Lecture Notes in Computer Science 5520 (2009)
4. Carette, J., Kiselyov, O., Shan, C.-c.: Finally tagless, partially evaluated: tagless staged interpreters for simpler typed languages. J. Funct. Program. **19**(5), 509–543 (2009)
5. Chakravarty, M.M.T.: Type families. http://haskell.org/haskellwiki/GHC/Indexed_types (2008)
6. Chakravarty, M.M.T., Keller, G., Peyton Jones, S.L.: Associated type synonyms. In: ICFP '05: Proc. ACM international conference on functional programming, pp. 241–253. ACM Press, New York (2005)
7. Chakravarty, M.M.T., Keller, G., Peyton Jones, S.L., Marlow, S.: Associated types with class. In: Palsberg, J., Abadi, M. (eds.), POPL '05: Conference Record of the Annual ACM Symposium on Principles of Programming Languages, pp. 1–13. ACM Press, New York (2005)
8. Cunha A., Pinto, J.S., Proença, J.: A framework for point-free program transformation. In: Butterfield, A., Grelck, C., Huch, F. (eds.), Revised selected papers from IFL 2005: Implementation and application of functional languages, pp. 1–18. Lecture Notes in Computer Science 4015, Springer, Berlin (2006)
9. Danvy, O.: Functional unparsing. J. Funct. Program. **8**(6), 621–625 (1998)

10. Danvy, O., Nielsen, L.R.: Defunctionalization at work. In: Proceedings of the 3rd international conference on principles and practice of declarative programming, pp. 162–174. ACM Press, New York (2001)
11. Diatchki, I.S., Jones, M.P.: Strongly typed memory areas: programming systems-level data structures in a functional language. In: Proceedings of the 2006 Haskell Workshop. ACM Press, New York (2006)
12. Elliott, C.: Elegant memoization with functional memo tries. http://conal.net/blog/posts/elegant-memoization-with-functional-memo-tries (2008)
13. Fluet, M., Pucella, R.: Practical datatype specializations with phantom types and recursion schemes. In: Proceedings of the 2005 Workshop on ML. Electronic Notes in Theoretical Computer Science (2005)
14. Fluet, M., Pucella, R.: Phantom types and subtyping. J. Funct. Program. **16**(6), 751–791 (2006)
15. Garcia, R., Järvi, J., Lumsdaine, A., Siek, J., Willcock, J.: An extended comparative study of language support for generic programming. J. Funct. Program. **17**(2), 145–205 (2007)
16. Gill, A. (ed.): Proceedings of the 1st ACM SIGPLAN symposium on Haskell. ACM Press, New York (2008)
17. Girard, J.-Y., Taylor, P., Lafont, Y.: Proofs and types. Cambridge University Press, Cambridge (1989)
18. Guillemette, L.-J., Monnier, S.: A type-preserving compiler in Haskell. In [25], 75–90 (2008)
19. Hinze, R.: Generalizing generalized tries. J. Funct. Program. **10**(4), 327–351 (2000)
20. Hinze, R.: Formatting: a class act. J. Funct. Program. **13**(5), 935–944 (2003)
21. Hinze, R.: Fun with phantom types. In: Gibbons, J., de Moor, O. (eds.), The fun of programming, pp. 245–262. Palgrave (2003)
22. Hinze, R., Jeuring, J., Löh, A.: Type-indexed data types. In: Proceedings of the Sixth International Conference on Mathematics of Program Construction (MPC 2002), pp. 148–174. Lecture Notes in Computer Science 2386, Springer Verlag (2002)
23. Howard, W.A.: The formulae-as-types notion of construction. In: Seldin, J.P., Hindley, J.R. (eds.), To H. B. Curry: Essays on Combinatory Logic, Lambda Calculus and Formalism, pp. 479–490. Academic Press, San Diego, CA (1980).
24. Hutton, T.: Fun with type functions. http://www.haskell.org/pipermail/haskell-cafe/2008-November/051105.html (2008)
25. Hook, J., Thiemann, P. ICFP '08: Proc. ACM international conference on functional programming. ACM Press, New York (2008)
26. Imai, K., Yuen, S., Agusa, K.: A full implementation of session types in Haskell. In: PPL2009: 11th Programming and Programming Languages Workshop. http://www.agusa.i.is.nagoya-u.ac.jp/person/sydney/fullsession-ppl2009/20090224/imai-ppl2009-submitted1.pdf (2009)
27. Ingram, R.: Fun with type functions. http://www.haskell.org/pipermail/haskell-cafe/2008-November/051108.html (2008)
28. Jones, M.P.: Languages and program design for functional dependencies. In [16], 87–98 (2008)
29. Jones, M.P.: Type classes with functional dependencies. In: Programming Languages and Systems: Proceedings of ESOP 2000, 9th European Symposium on Programming, Smolka, G. (ed.), pp. 230–244. Lecture Notes in Computer Science 1782, Springer, Berlin (2000)
30. Kennedy, A.: Programming languages and dimensions. Ph.D. thesis, University of Cambridge (1995)
31. Kiselyov, O.: Formatted IO as an embedded DSL: the initial view. http://okmij.org/ftp/typed-formatting/#DSL-In (2008)
32. Kiselyov, O., Shan, C.-c.: Lightweight static resources: sexy types for embedded and systems programming. In: Morazán, M.T., Nilsson, H. (eds.), Draft Proceedings of TFP 2007: 6th Symposium on Trends in Functional Programming. Tech. Rep. TR-SHU-CS-2007-04-1, Department of Mathematics and Computer Science, Seton Hall University (2007)
33. Krishnamurthi, S., Felleisen, M., Friedman, D.P.: Synthesizing object-oriented and functional design to promote re-use. In: Jul, E. (ed.), Proceedings of ECOOP'98: 12th European Conference on Object-oriented Programming, pp. 91–113. Lecture Notes in Computer Science 1445, Springer, Berlin (1998)

34. Meyer, A.R., Wand, M.: Continuation semantics in typed lambda-calculi (summary). In: Logics of programs, Parikh, R. (ed.), pp. 219–224. Lecture Notes in Computer Science 193, Springer, Berlin (1985)
35. Michie, D.: "Memo" functions and machine learning. Nature **218**:19–22 (1968)
36. Neubauer, M., Thiemann, P.: An implementation of session types. In: Practical Aspects of Declarative Languages: 6th International Symposium, PADL 2004, Jayaraman, B. (ed.), pp. 56–70. Lecture Notes in Computer Science 3057, Springer, Berlin (2004)
37. Peyton Jones, S.L., Vytiniotis, D., Weirich, S., Washburn, G.A.: Simple unification-based type inference for GADTs. In: ICFP '06: Proc. ACM international conference on functional programming, pp. 50–61. ACM Press, New York (2006)
38. Pucella, R., Tov, J.: Haskell session types with (almost) no class. In [16], 25–36 (2008)
39. Reynolds, J.C.: Definitional interpreters for higher-order programming languages. In: Proceedings of the ACM National Conference, vol. 2, pp. 717–740. ACM Press, New York. Reprinted as [40] (1972)
40. Reynolds, J.C.: Definitional interpreters for higher-order programming languages. Higher-Order and Symbolic Computation **11**(4), 363–397 (1998)
41. Sackman, M.: A tutorial for session types. http://www.wellquite.org/sessions/tutorial_1.html (2008)
42. Schrijvers, T., Peyton Jones, S.L., Chakravarty, M.M.T., Sulzmann, M.: Type checking with open type functions. In: [25], 51–62 (2008)
43. Sheard, T.: Languages of the future. Onward Track, OOPSLA'04. Reprinted in: ACM SIGPLAN Notices, Dec. 2004. **39**:116–119. OOPSLA Companion Volume (2004)
44. Sheard, T.: Generic programming in Ω. In: Backhouse, R., Gibbons, J., Hinze, R., Jeuring, J. (eds.), Datatype-generic programming, vol. 4719 of Lecture Notes in Computer Science, pp. 258–284. Springer (2006)
45. Sheard, T., Linger, N.: Programming in Ω. In: Horváth, Z., Plasmeijer, R., Soós, A., Zsók, V. (eds.), 2nd Central European Functional Programming School, vol. 5161 of Lecture Notes in Computer Science, pp. 158–227. Springer (2007)
46. Sheard, T., Pasalic, E.: Meta-programming with built-in type equality. In: Proceedings of the fourth international workshop on logical frameworks and meta-languages (LFM'04) (2004)
47. Siek, J., Lee, L.-Q., Lumsdaine, A.: The Boost Graph Library User Guide and Reference Manual. Addison-Wesley (2001)

Chapter 15
On CSP and the Algebraic Theory of Effects

Rob van Glabbeek and Gordon Plotkin*

Abstract We consider CSP from the point of view of the algebraic theory of effects, which classifies operations as effect *constructors* or effect *deconstructors*; it also provides a link with functional programming, being a refinement of Moggi's seminal monadic point of view. There is a natural algebraic theory of the constructors whose free algebra functor is Moggi's monad; we illustrate this by characterising free and initial algebras in terms of two versions of the stable failures model of CSP, one more general than the other. Deconstructors are dealt with as homomorphisms to (possibly non-free) algebras.

One can view CSP's action and choice operators as constructors and the rest, such as concealment and concurrency, as deconstructors. Carrying this programme out results in taking deterministic external choice as constructor rather than general external choice. However, binary deconstructors, such as the CSP concurrency operator, provide unresolved difficulties. We conclude by presenting a combination of CSP with Moggi's computational λ-calculus, in which the operators, including concurrency, are polymorphic. While the paper mainly concerns CSP, it ought to be possible to carry over similar ideas to other process calculi.

15.1 Introduction

We examine Hoare's CSP [9,13,29] from the point of view of the algebraic theory of effects [14,22,23,25], a refinement of Moggi's seminal "monads as notions of computation" [3,18,19]. This is a natural exercise as the algebraic nature of both points

---

*This work was done with the support of a Royal Society-Wolfson Award.

R.J. van Glabbeek
NICTA, Sydney, Australia
and
University of New South Wales, Sydney, Australia
e-mail: rvg@cs.stanford.edu

G.D. Plotkin (✉)
Laboratory for the Foundations of Computer Science, School of Informatics,
University of Edinburgh, UK
e-mail: gdp@inf.ed.ac.uk

C.B. Jones et al. (eds.), *Reflections on the Work of C.A.R. Hoare*,
DOI 10.1007/978-1-84882-912-1_15,

to a possibility of commonality. In the algebraic theory of effects all operations do not have the same character. Some are effect *constructors*: they create the effects at hand; some are effect *deconstructors*: they respond to effects created. For example, raising an exception creates an effect – the exception raised – whereas exception-handling responds to effects – exceptions that have been raised. It may therefore be interesting, and even useful, to classify CSP operators as constructors or deconstructors. Considering CSP and the algebraic theory of effects together also raises the possibility of combining CSP with functional programming in a principled way, as Moggi's monadic approach provides a framework for the combination of computational effects with functional programming. More generally, although we mainly consider CSP, a similar exercise could be undertaken for other process calculi as they have a broadly similar algebraic character.

The theory of algebraic effects starts with the observation that effect constructors generally satisfy natural equations, and Moggi's monad T is precisely the free algebra monad for these equations (an exception is the continuations monad, which is of a different character). Effect deconstructors are treated as homomorphisms from the free algebra to another algebra, perhaps with the same carrier as the free algebra but with different operations. These operations can be given by combinations of effect constructors and previously defined deconstructors. The situation is much like that of primitive recursive definitions, although we will not present a formal definitional scheme.

We mainly consider that part of CSP containing action, internal and external choice, deadlock, relabelling, concealment, concurrency and interleaving, but not, for example, recursion (we do, albeit briefly, consider the extension with termination and sequencing). The evident constructors are then action prefix, and the two kinds of choice, internal and external, the latter together with deadlock. The evident deconstructors are relabelling, concealment, concurrency and interleaving. There is, however, a fly in the ointment, as pointed out in [25]. Parallel operators, such as CSP's concurrency and interleaving, are naturally binary, and respond to effects in both arguments. However, the homomorphic approach to deconstructors, as sketched above, applies only to unary deconstructors, although it is possible to extend it to accommodate parameters and simultaneous definitions. Nonetheless, the natural definitions of concurrency and interleaving do not fall within the homomorphic approach, even in the extended sense. This problem has nothing to do with CSP: it applies to all examples of parallelism of which we are aware.

Even worse, when we try to carry out the above analysis for CSP, it seems that the homomorphic approach cannot handle concealment. The difficulty is caused by the fact that concealment does not commute with external choice. Fortunately this difficulty can be overcome by changing the effect constructors: we remove external choice and action prefix and replace them by the deterministic external choice operator $(a_1 \rightarrow P(a_1) \mid \ldots \mid a_n \rightarrow P(a_n))$, where the a_i are all different. Binary external choice then becomes a deconstructor.

With that we can carry out the program of analysis, finding only the expected difficulty in dealing with concurrency and interleaving. However, it must be admitted that the n-ary operators are somewhat clumsy to work with, and it is at least a priori odd to take binary external choice as a deconstructor. On the other hand, in [13] Section 1.1.3 Hoare writes:

> The definition of choice can readily be extended to more than two alternatives, e.g.,
>
> $$(x \to P \mid y \to Q \mid \ldots \mid z \to R)$$
>
> Note that the choice symbol $\mid$ is *not* an operator on processes; it would be syntactically incorrect to write $P \mid Q$, for processes P and Q. The reason for this rule is that we want to avoid giving a meaning to
>
> $$(x \to P \mid x \to Q)$$
>
> which appears to offer a choice of first event, but actually fails to do so.

which might be read as offering some support to a treatment, which takes deterministic external choice as a primitive (here = constructor), rather than general external choice. On our side, we count it as a strength of the algebraic theory of effects that it classifies effect-specific operations and places constraints on them: that they either belong to the basic theory or must be defined according to a scheme that admits inductive proofs.

Turning to the combination with functional programming, consider Moggi's computational λ-calculus. Just as one accommodates imperative programming within functional programming by treating commands as expressions of type `unit`, so it is natural to treat our selection of CSP terms as expressions of type `empty` as they do not terminate normally, only in deadlock. For process languages such as ACP [4, 5] which do have the possibility of normal termination, or CSP with such a termination construct, one switches to regarding process terms as expressions of type `unit`, when a sequencing operator is also available.

As we have constructors for every $T(X)$, it is natural to treat them as polymorphic constructs, rather than just as process combinators. For example, one could have a binary construction for internal choice, with typing rule:

$$\frac{M:\sigma \qquad N:\sigma}{M \sqcap N:\sigma}$$

It is natural to continue this theme for the deconstructors, as in:

$$\frac{M:\sigma}{M\backslash a:\sigma} \qquad\qquad \frac{M:\sigma \qquad N:\tau}{M||N:\sigma\times\tau}$$

where the thought behind the last rule is that M and N are evaluated concurrently, terminating normally only if they both do, when the pair of results returned individually by each is returned.

In the case of CSP a functional programming language CSPM incorporating CSP processes has been given by Scattergood [31]; it is used by most existing CSP tools including the Failures Divergences Refinement Checker (FDR), see [28]. Scattergood's CPSM differs from our proposal in several respects. Most significantly, processes are not treated on a par with other expressions: in particular, they cannot be taken as arguments in functions, and CSP constructors and deconstructors are only available for processes. It remains to be seen if such differences are of practical relevance.

In Section 15.3 we take deadlock, action, binary internal and external choice as the constructors. We show, in Theorem 1, that, with the standard equational theory, the initial algebra is the "finitary part" of the original Brookes-Hoare-Roscoe failures model [9]; which is known to be isomorphic to the finitary, divergence- and ✓-free part of the failures/divergences model, as well as the finitary, divergence- and ✓-free part of the stable failures model, both of which are described in [29]. In Section 15.4 we go on to consider effect deconstructors, arriving at the difficulty with concealment and illustrating the problems with parallel operators in the (simpler) context of Milner's synchronisation trees. A reader interested in the problem of dealing with parallel operators algebraically need only read this part, together with [25].

We then backtrack in Section 15.5, making a different choice of constructors, as discussed above, and giving another characterisation of the finitary failures model as an initial algebra in Theorem 3. With that, we can carry out our programme, failing only where expected: with the binary deconstructors. In Section 15.6 we add a zero for the internal choice operator to our algebra; this can be interpreted as divergence in the stable failures model, and permits the introduction of a useful additional deterministic external choice constructor. Armed with this tool, in Section 15.7, we look at the combination of CSP and functional programming, following the lines hinted at above. In order to give a denotational semantics we need, in Theorem 7, to characterise the free algebras rather than just the initial one.

As remarked above, termination and sequencing are accommodated within functional programming via the type `unit`; in Section 15.7.1 we therefore also give a brief treatment of our fragment of CSP extended with termination and sequencing, modelling it in the free algebra over the one-point set.

Section 15.8 contains a brief discussion of the general question of combining process calculi, or parallelism with a global store, with functional programming. The case of CSP considered here is just one example of the many such possible combinations. Throughout this paper we do not consider recursion; this enables us to work within the category of sets. A more complete treatment would deal with recursion working within, say, the category of ω-cpos (i.e., partial orders with lubs of increasing ω-sequences) and continuous functions (i.e., monotone functions preserving lubs of increasing ω-sequences). This is discussed further in Section 15.8. The appendix gives a short presentation of Moggi's computational λ-calculus.

15.2 Technical Preliminaries

We give a brief sketch of finitary equational theories and their free algebra monads. For a fuller explanation see, e.g., [2, 8]. Finitary equational theories Th are derived from a given set of axioms, written using a signature Σ consisting of a set of operation symbols op: n, together with their arities $n \geq 0$. One forms terms t from the signature and variables and the axioms then consist of equations $t = u$ between the terms; there is a natural equational logic for deducing consequences of the axioms; and the theory consists of all the equations derivable from the axioms. A *ground* equation is one where both terms are *closed*, meaning that they contain no variables.

For example, we might consider the fragment of CSP with signature $\Box : 2$, `Stop`:0 and the following axioms for a semilattice (the first three axioms) with a zero (the last):

Associativity	$(x \Box y) \Box z = x \Box (y \Box z)$
Commutativity	$x \Box y = y \Box x$
Idempotence	$x \Box x = x$
Zero	$x \Box \texttt{Stop} = x$

A Σ-*algebra* is a structure $\mathcal{A} = (X, (\mathrm{op}_{\mathcal{A}} : X^n \to X)_{\mathrm{op}:n \in \Sigma})$; we say that X is the *carrier* of $\mathcal{A}$ and the $\mathrm{op}_{\mathcal{A}}$ are its *operations*. We may omit the subscript on operations when the algebra is understood. When we are thinking of an algebra as an algebra of processes, we may say "operator" rather than "operation." A homomorphism between two algebras is a map between their carriers respecting their operations; we therefore have a category of Σ-algebras.

Given such a Σ-algebra, every term t has a *denotation* $[\![t]\!](\rho)$, an element of the carrier, given an assignment ρ of elements of the carrier to every variable; we often confuse terms with their denotation. The algebra *satisfies* an equation $t = u$ if t and u have the same denotation for every such assignment. If $\mathcal{A}$ satisfies all the axioms of a theory Th, it is called a Th-algebra; the Th-algebras form a subcategory of the category of Σ-algebras. Any equation provable from the axioms of a theory Th is satisfied by any Th-algebra. We say that a theory Th is *(ground) equationally complete* with respect to a Th-algebra if a (ground) equation is provable from Th if, and only if, it is satisfied by the Th-algebra.

Any finitary equational theory Th determines a free algebra monad T_{Th} on the category of sets, as well as operations

$$\mathrm{op}_X : T_{\mathrm{Th}}(X)^n \to T_{\mathrm{Th}}(X)$$

for any set X and op: $n \in \Sigma$, such that $(T_{\mathrm{Th}}(X), (\mathrm{op}_X : X^n \to X)_{\mathrm{op}:n \in \Sigma})$ is the free Th-algebra over X. Although $T_{\mathrm{Th}}(X)$ is officially just a set, the carrier of the free algebra, we may also use $T_{\mathrm{Th}}(X)$ to denote the free algebra itself. In the above example the monad is the finite powerset monad:

$$\mathcal{F}(X) = \{u \subseteq X \mid u \text{ is finite}\}$$

with $\Box_X$ and $\texttt{Stop}_X$ being union and the empty set, respectively.

15.3 A First Attempt at Analysing CSP

We consider the fragment of CSP with deadlock, action prefix, internal and external choice, relabelling and concealment, and concurrency and interleaving. Working over a fixed alphabet A of *actions*, we consider the following operation symbols:

Deadlock

$$\texttt{Stop}:0$$

Action

$$a \to -:1 \qquad (a \in A)$$

Internal and External Choice

$$\sqcap, \Box:2$$

Relabelling and Concealment

$$f(-), -\backslash a:1$$

for any *relabelling function* $f: A \to A$ and action a. If A is infinite, this makes the syntax infinitary; as that causes us no problems, we do not avoid it.

Concurrency and Interleaving

$$||, |||:2$$

The signature of our (first) equational theory CSP ($\Box$) for CSP only has operation symbols for the subset of these operators, which are naturally thought of as constructors, namely deadlock, action and internal and external choice. Its axioms are those given by de Nicola in [10]. They are largely very natural and modular, and are as follows:

- $\Box$, Stop is a semilattice with a zero (i.e., the above axioms for a semilattice with a zero).
- $\sqcap$ is a semilattice (i.e., the axioms stating the associativity, commutativity and idempotence of $\sqcap$).
- $\Box$ and $\sqcap$ distribute over each other:

$$x \Box (y \sqcap z) = (x \Box y) \sqcap (x \Box z) \qquad x \sqcap (y \Box z) = (x \sqcap y) \Box (x \sqcap z)$$

- Actions distribute over $\sqcap$:

$$a \to (x \sqcap y) = a \to x \sqcap a \to y$$

and:

$$a \to x \Box a \to y = a \to x \sqcap a \to y$$

All these axioms are mathematically natural except the last which involves a relationship between three different operators.

We adopt some useful standard notational abbreviations. For $n \geq 1$ we write $\bigsqcap_{i=1}^{n} t_i$ to abbreviate $t_1 \sqcap \ldots \sqcap t_n$, intending t_1 when $n = 1$. We assume that parentheses associate to the left; however as $\sqcap$ is associative, the choice does not matter. As $\sqcap$ is a semilattice, we can even index over nonempty finite sets, as in $\bigsqcap_{i \in I} t_i$, assuming some standard ordering of the t_i without repetitions. As $\Box$ is a semilattice with a zero, we can adopt analogous notations $\Box_{i=1}^{n} t_i$ and $\Box_{i \in I} t_i$ but now also allowing n to be 0 and I to be $\emptyset$.

As $\sqcap$ is a semilattice we can define a partial order for which it is the greatest lower bound by writing $t \sqsubseteq u$ as an abbreviation for $t \sqcap u = t$; then, as $\Box$ distributes over $\sqcap$, it is monotone with respect to $\sqsubseteq$: that is, if $x \sqsubseteq x'$ and $y \sqsubseteq y'$ then $x \Box y \sqsubseteq x' \Box y'$. (We mean all these in a formal sense, for example, that if $t \sqsubseteq u$ and $u \sqsubseteq v$ are provable, so is $t \sqsubseteq v$, etc.) We note the following, which is equivalent to the distributivity of $\sqcap$ over $\Box$, given that $\sqcap$ and $\Box$ are semilattices, and the other distributivity, that $\Box$ distributes over $\sqcap$:

$$x \sqcap (y \Box z) = x \sqcap (y \Box z) \sqcap (x \Box y) \tag{15.1}$$

The equation can also be written as $x \sqcap (y \Box z) \sqsubseteq (x \Box y)$. Using this one can derive another helpful equation:

$$(x \Box a \to z) \sqcap (y \Box a \to w) = (x \Box a \to (z \sqcap w)) \sqcap (y \Box a \to (z \sqcap w)) \tag{15.2}$$

We next rehearse the original refusal sets model of CSP, restricted to finite processes without divergence; this provides a convenient context for identifying the initial model of CSP ($\Box$) in terms of failures.

A *failure (pair)* is a pair (w, W) with $w \in A^*$ and $W \subseteq_{\text{fin}} A$. For every set F of failure pairs, we define its set of *traces* to be

$$\text{tr}_F = \{w \mid (w, \emptyset) \in F\}$$

and for every $w \in \text{tr}_F$ we define its set of *futures* to be:

$$\text{fut}_F(w) = \{a \mid wa \in \text{tr}_F\}$$

With that a *refusal set* F (aka a *failure set*) is a set of failure pairs, satisfying the following conditions:

1. $\varepsilon \in \text{tr}_F$
2. $wa \in \text{tr}_F \Rightarrow w \in \text{tr}_F$
3. $(w, W) \in F \wedge V \subseteq W \Rightarrow (w, V) \in F$
4. $(w, W) \in F \wedge a \notin \text{fut}_F \Rightarrow (w, W \cup \{a\}) \in F$

A refusal set is *finitary* if its set of traces is finite.

The collection of finitary refusal sets can be turned into a CSP (□)-algebra $\mathcal{R}_f$ by the following standard definitions of the operators:

$$\begin{aligned}
\mathtt{Stop}_{\mathcal{R}_f} &= \{(\varepsilon, W) \mid W \subseteq_{\text{fin}} A\} \\
a \rightarrow_{\mathcal{R}_f} F &= \{(\varepsilon, W) \mid a \notin W\} \cup \{(aw, W) \mid (w, W) \in F\} \\
F \sqcap_{\mathcal{R}_f} G &= F \cup G \\
F \,\Box_{\mathcal{R}_f}\, G &= \{(\varepsilon, W) \mid (\varepsilon, W) \in F \cap G\} \cup \{(w, W) \mid w \neq \varepsilon,\ (w, W) \in F \cup G\}
\end{aligned}$$

The other CSP operation symbols also have standard interpretations over the collection of finitary refusal sets:

$$\begin{aligned}
f(F) &= \{(f(w), W) \mid (w, f^{-1}(W) \cap \text{fut}_F(w)) \in F\} \\
F \backslash a &= \{(w \backslash a, W) \mid (w, W \cup \{a\}) \in F\} \\
F \,||\, G &= \{(w, W \cup V) \mid (w, W) \in F,\ (w, V) \in G\} \\
F \,|||\, G &= \{(w, W) \mid (u, W) \in F,\ (v, W) \in G,\ w \in u \,|\, v\}
\end{aligned}$$

with the evident action of f on sequences and sets of actions, and where $w \backslash a$ is obtained from w by removing all occurrences of a, and where $u \mid v$ is the set of interleavings of u and v.

Lemma 1. *Let F be a finitary refusal set. Then for every $w \in \text{tr}_F$ there are $V_1, \ldots, V_n \subseteq \text{fut}_F(w)$, including $\text{fut}_F(w)$, such that $(w, W) \in F$ iff $W \cap V_i = \emptyset$ for some $i \in \{1, \ldots, n\}$.*

Proof. The closure conditions imply that (w, W) is in F iff $(w, W \cap \text{fut}_F(w))$ is. Thus we only need to be concerned about pairs (w, W) with $W \subseteq \text{fut}_F(w)$. Now, as $\text{fut}_F(w)$ is finite, for any relevant $(w, W) \in F$, of which there are finitely many, we can take V to be $\text{fut}_F(w) \backslash W$, and we obtain finitely many such sets. As $(w, \emptyset) \in F$, these include $\text{fut}_F(w)$. □

Lemma 2. *All finitary refusal sets are definable by closed* CSP (□) *terms.*

Proof. Let F be a finitary refusal set. We proceed by induction on the length of the longest trace in F. By the previous lemma there are sets $V_1, \ldots, V_n$, including $\text{fut}_F(\varepsilon)$, such that $(\varepsilon, W) \in F$ iff $W \cap V_i = \emptyset$ for some $i \in \{1, \ldots, n\}$. Define F_a, for $a \in \text{fut}_F(\varepsilon)$, by:

$$F_a = \{(w, W) \mid (aw, W) \in F\}$$

Then it is not hard to see that each F_a is a finitary refusal set, and that

$$F = \bigsqcap_i \mathop{\Box}_{a \in V_i} a \rightarrow F_a$$

As the longest trace in F_a is strictly shorter than the longest one in F, the proof concludes, employing the induction hypothesis. □

We next recall some material from de Nicola [10]. Let $\mathcal{L}$ be a collection of sets; we say it is *saturated* if whenever $L \subseteq L' \subseteq \bigcup \mathcal{L}$, for $L \in \mathcal{L}$ then $L' \in \mathcal{L}$. Then a closed CSP ($\Box$)-term t is in *normal form* if it is of the form:

$$\bigsqcap_{L \in \mathcal{L}} \Box_{a \in L} a \to t_a$$

where $\mathcal{L}$ is a finite non-empty saturated collection of finite sets of actions and each term t_a is in normal form. Note that the concept of normal form is defined recursively.

Proposition 1. CSP ($\Box$) *is ground equationally complete with respect to* $\mathcal{R}_f$.

Proof. Every term is provably equal in CSP ($\Box$) to a term in normal form. For the proof, follow that of Proposition A6 in [10]; alternatively, it is a straightforward induction in which Eqs. 15.1 and 15.2 are helpful. Further, it is an immediate consequence of Lemma 4.8 in [10] that if two normal forms have the same denotation in $\mathcal{R}_f$ then they are identical (and Lemma 6 below establishes a more general result). The result then follows. □

Theorem 1. *The finitary refusal sets algebra* $\mathcal{R}_f$ *is the initial* CSP ($\Box$) *algebra.*

Proof. Let the initial such algebra be I. There is a unique homomorphism $h : \mathrm{I} \to \mathcal{R}_f$. By Lemma 2, h is a surjection. By the previous proposition, $\mathcal{R}_f$ is complete for equations between closed terms, and so h is an injection. So h is an isomorphism, completing the proof. □

15.4 Effect Deconstructors

In the algebraic theory of effects, the semantics of effect *deconstructors*, such as exception handlers, is given using homomorphisms from free algebras. In this case we are interested in $T_{\mathrm{CSP}\ (\Box)}(\emptyset)$. This is the initial CSP ($\Box$) algebra, $\mathcal{R}_f$, so given a CSP ($\Box$) algebra:

$$\mathcal{A} = (T_{\mathrm{CSP}\ (\Box)}(\emptyset), \sqcap_{\mathcal{A}}, \mathtt{Stop}_{\mathcal{A}}, (a \to_{\mathcal{A}}), \Box_{\mathcal{A}})$$

there is a unique homomorphism:

$$h : \mathcal{R}_f \to \mathcal{A}$$

Relabelling We now seek to define $f(-) : T_{\mathrm{CSP}\ (\Box)}(\emptyset) \to T_{\mathrm{CSP}\ (\Box)}(\emptyset)$ homomorphically. Define an algebra Rl on $T_{\mathrm{CSP}\ (\Box)}(\emptyset)$ by putting, for refusal sets F, G:

$$\mathtt{Stop}_{Rl} = \mathtt{Stop}_{\mathcal{R}_f}$$

$$(a \rightarrow_{Rl} F) = (f(a) \rightarrow_{\mathcal{R}_f} F)$$

$$F \sqcap_{Rl} G = F \sqcap_{\mathcal{R}_f} G \qquad F \,\Box_{Rl}\, G = F \,\Box_{\mathcal{R}_f}\, G$$

One has to verify this gives a CSP ($\Box$)-algebra, which amounts to verifying that the two action equations hold, for example that, for all F, G:

$$a \rightarrow_{Rl} (F \sqcap_{Rl} G) = (a \rightarrow_{Rl} F) \sqcap_{Rl} (a \rightarrow_{Rl} G)$$

which is equivalent to:

$$f(a) \rightarrow_{\mathcal{R}_f} (F \sqcap_{\mathcal{R}_f} G) = (f(a) \rightarrow_{\mathcal{R}_f} F) \sqcap_{\mathcal{R}_f} (f(a) \rightarrow_{\mathcal{R}_f} G)$$

We therefore have a unique homomorphism

$$\mathcal{R}_f \xrightarrow{h_{Rl}} Rl$$

and so the following equations hold over the algebra $\mathcal{R}_f$:

$$h_{Rl}(\mathtt{Stop}) = \mathtt{Stop}$$

$$h_{Rl}(a \rightarrow F) = f(a) \rightarrow h_{Rl}(F)$$

$$h_{Rl}(F \sqcap G) = h_{Rl}(F) \sqcap h_{Rl}(G) \qquad h_{Rl}(F \,\Box\, G) = h_{Rl}(F) \,\Box\, h_{Rl}(G)$$

Informally one can use these equations to define h_{Rl} by a "*principle of equational recursion*," but one must remember to verify that the implicit algebra obeys the required equations.

We use h_{Rl} to interpret relabelling. We then immediately recover the familiar CSP laws:

$$f(\mathtt{Stop}) = \mathtt{Stop}$$

$$f(a \rightarrow x) = f(a) \rightarrow f(x)$$

$$f(x \sqcap y) = f(x) \sqcap f(y) \qquad f(x \,\Box\, y) = f(x) \,\Box\, f(y)$$

which we now see to be restatements of the homomorphism of relabelling.

Concealment There is a difficulty here. We do not have that

$$(F \,\Box\, G)\backslash a = F\backslash a \,\Box\, G\backslash a$$

but rather have the following two equations (taken from [10]):

$$((a \rightarrow F) \,\Box\, G)\backslash a = F\backslash a \sqcap ((F \,\Box\, G)\backslash a) \tag{15.3}$$

$$\left(\Box_{i=1}^{n} a_i F_i\right) \Big\backslash a = \Box_{i=1}^{n} a_i(F_i \backslash a) \tag{15.4}$$

where no a_i is a. Furthermore, there is no direct definition of concealment via an equational recursion, i.e., there is no suitable choice of algebra, $\Box_{\mathcal{A}}$ etc. For, if there were, we would have:

$$(F \Box G)\backslash a = F\backslash a \Box_{\mathcal{A}} G\backslash a \tag{15.5}$$

So if a does not occur in any trace of F' or G' we would have:

$$\begin{aligned} F' \Box_{\mathcal{A}} G' &= F'\backslash a \Box_{\mathcal{A}} G'\backslash a \\ &= (F' \Box G')\backslash a \\ &= F' \Box G' \end{aligned}$$

but, returning to Eq. 15.5, a certainly does not occur in any trace of $F\backslash a$ or $G\backslash a$ and so we would have:

$$\begin{aligned} (F \Box G)\backslash a &= F\backslash a \Box_{\mathcal{A}} G\backslash a \\ &= F\backslash a \Box_{\mathcal{R}_f} G\backslash a \end{aligned}$$

which is false. It is conceivable that although there is no direct homomorphic definition of concealment, there may be an indirect one where other functions (possibly with parameters – see below) are defined homomorphically and concealment is definable as a combination of those.

15.4.1 Concurrency Operators

Before trying to recover from the difficulty with concealment, we look at a further difficulty, that of accommodating binary deconstructors, particularly parallel operators. We begin with a simple example in a strong bisimulation context, but rather than a concurrency operator in the style of CCS we consider one analogous to CSP's $||$.

We take as signature a unary action prefix, $a.-$, for $a \in A$, a nullary `NIL` and a binary sum $+$. The axioms are that $+$ is a semilattice with zero `NIL`; the initial algebra is then that of finite synchronisation trees ST. Every synchronisation tree τ has a finite depth and can be written as

$$\sum_{i=1}^{n} a_i.\tau_i$$

for some $n \geq 0$, where the τ_i are also synchronisation trees (of strictly smaller depth), and where no pair (a_i, τ_i) occurs twice. The order of writing the summands makes no difference to the tree denoted.

One can define a binary synchronisation operator $||$ on synchronisation trees $\tau = \sum_i a_i.\tau_i$ and $\tau' = \sum_j b_j.\tau_j$ by induction on the depth of τ (or τ'):

$$\tau \mid\mid \tau' = \sum_{a_i = b_j} a_i.(\tau_i \mid\mid \tau_j')$$

Looking for an equational recursive definition of $||$, one may try a "mutual (parametric) equational recursive definition" of $||$ and a certain family $||^a$ with x, y, z varying over ST:

$$\begin{aligned} \mathtt{NIL} \mid\mid z &= \mathtt{NIL} \\ (x+y) \mid\mid z &= (x \mid\mid z) + (y \mid\mid z) \\ a.x \mid\mid z &= x \mid\mid^a z \end{aligned}$$

and

$$\begin{aligned} z \mid\mid^a \mathtt{NIL} &= \mathtt{NIL} \\ z \mid\mid^a (x+y) &= (z \mid\mid^a x) + (z \mid\mid^a y) \\ z \mid\mid^a b.x &= \begin{cases} a.(z \mid\mid x) & (\text{if } b = a) \\ \mathtt{NIL} & (\text{if } b \neq a) \end{cases} \end{aligned}$$

Unfortunately, this definition attempt is not an equational recursion. Mutual (parametric) equational recursions are single ones to an algebra on a product. Here we wish a map: $ST \to ST \times ST$. Informally we would write such clauses as:

$$\langle (x+y) \mid\mid z,\ z \mid\mid^a (x+y) \rangle = \langle (x \mid\mid z) + (y \mid\mid z),\ (z \mid\mid^a x) + (z \mid\mid^a y) \rangle$$

with the recursion variables, here x, y, on the left for $||$ and on the right for $||^a$. However:

$$\langle a.x \mid\mid z,\ z \mid\mid^a b.x \rangle = \begin{cases} \langle x \mid\mid^a z,\ a.(z \mid\mid x) \rangle & (\text{if } b = a) \\ \langle x \mid\mid^a z,\ \mathtt{NIL} \rangle & (\text{if } b \neq a) \end{cases}$$

does not respect this discipline: the recursion variable, here x, (twice) switches places with the parameter z.

We are therefore caught in a dilemma. One can show, by induction on the depth of synchronisation trees, that the above definitions, viewed as equations for $||$ and $||^a$ have a unique solution: the expected synchronisation operator $||$, and the functions $||^a$ defined on synchronisation trees τ and $\tau' = \sum_j b_j.\tau_j$ by:

$$\tau \mid\mid^a \tau' = \sum_{b_j = a} a.(\tau \mid\mid \tau_j)$$

So we have a correct definition not in equational recursion format. So we must find either of the following:

- A different correct definition in the equational recursion format
- Another algebraic format into which the correct definition fits

When we come to the CSP parallel operator we do not even get as far as we did with synchronisation trees. The problem is like that with concealment: the distributive equation:

$$(F \,\Box\, F') \,||\, G = (F \,||\, G) \,\Box\, (F' \,||\, G)$$

does not hold. One can show that there is no definition of $||$ analogous to the above one for synchronisation trees, i.e., there is no suitable choice of algebra, $\Box_{\mathcal{A}}$ etc, and functions $||^a$. The reason is that there is no binary operator $\Box'$ on (finitary) failure sets such that, for all F, G, H we have:

$$(F \,\Box\, F') \,||\, G = (F \,||\, G) \,\Box'\, (F' \,||\, G)$$

For suppose, for the sake of contradiction, that there is such an operator. Then, fixing F and F', choose G such that $F \,||\, G = F$, $F' \,||\, G = F'$ and $(F\Box F') \,||\, G = (F\Box F')$. Then, substituting into the above equation, we obtain that $F \,\Box\, F' = F \,\Box'\, F'$ and so the above equation yields distributivity, which, in fact, does not hold. As in the case of concealment, there may nonetheless be an indirect definition of $||$.

A similar difficulty obtains for the CSP interleaving operator. It too does not commute with $\Box$, and it too does not have any direct definition (the argument is like that for the concurrency operator but a little simpler, taking $G = \mathtt{Stop}$). As in the case of the concurrency operator, there may be an indirect definition.

15.5 Another Choice of CSP Effect Constructors

Equations 15.3 and 15.4 do not immediately suggest a recursive definition of concealment. However, one can show that, for distinct actions a_i $(i = 1, n)$, the following equation holds between refusal sets:

$$\left(\mathop{\Box}_{i=1}^{n} a_i \to F_i\right) \Big\backslash a_j = (F_j \backslash a_j) \sqcap \left((F_j \backslash a_j) \,\Box\, \mathop{\Box}_{i \neq j} a_i \to (F_i \backslash a_j)\right)$$

where $1 \leq j \leq n$. Taken together with Eq. (15.4), this suggests a recursive definition in terms of deterministic external choice. We therefore now change our choice of constructors, replacing binary external choice, action prefix and deadlock by deterministic external choice.

So as our second signature for CSP we take a binary operation symbol $\sqcap$ of internal choice and, for any *deterministic action sequence* **a** (i.e., any sequence of actions a_i $(i = 1, n)$, with the a_i all different and $n \geq 0$), an n-ary operation symbol $\Box_{\mathbf{a}}$ of deterministic external choice. We write $\Box_{\mathbf{a}}(t_1, \ldots, t_n)$ as $\Box_{i=1}^{n} a_i t_i$ although it is more usual to use Hoare's notation $(a_1 \to t_1 \mid \cdots \mid a_n \to t_n)$; we also use $\mathtt{Stop}$ to abbreviate $\Box_{\mathbf{a}}()$.

We have the usual semilattice axioms for $\sqcap$. Deterministic external choice is commutative, in the sense that:

$$\Box_i a_i x_i = \Box_i a_{\pi(i)} x_{\pi(i)}$$

for any permutation π of $\{1, \ldots, n\}$. Given this, we are justified in writing deterministic external choices over finite, possibly empty, sets of actions, $\Box_{a \in I} a t_a$, assuming some standard ordering of pairs (a, t_a) without repetitions.

For the next axiom it is convenient to write $(a_1 \to t_1) \Box \Box_{i=2}^{n} a_i t_i$ for $\Box_{i=1}^{n} a_i t_i$ (for $n \geq 0$). The axiom states that deterministic external choice distributes over internal choice:

$$(a_1 \to (x \sqcap x')) \Box \Box_{i=2}^{n} a_i x_i = \left((a_1 \to x) \Box \Box_{i=2}^{n} a_i x_i \right) \sqcap \left((a_1 \to x') \Box \Box_{i=2}^{n} a_i x_i \right)$$

This implies that deterministic external choice is monotone with respect to $\sqsubseteq$.

We can regard a, possibly nondeterministic, external choice, in which the a_i need not be all different, as an abbreviation for a deterministic one, via:

$$\Box_i a_i t_i = \Box_{b \in \{a_1, \ldots, a_n\}} b \left(\bigsqcap_{a_i = b} t_i \right) \tag{15.6}$$

With that convention we may also write $a_1 \to t_1 \Box \Box_{i=2}^{n} a_i t_i$ even when a_1 is some a_i, for $i > 1$. We can now write our final axiom:

$$\left(\Box_i a_i x_i \right) \sqcap \left((b_1 \to y_1) \Box \Box_{j=2}^{n} b_j y_j \right) \sqsubseteq (b_1 \to y_1) \Box \Box_i a_i x_i \tag{15.7}$$

Restricting the external choice $(b_1 \to y_1) \Box \Box_j b_j y_j$ to be deterministic gives an equivalent axiom, as does restricting $\Box_i a_i x_i$ (in the presence of the others).

Let us call this equational theory CSP($|$). The finitary refusal sets form a CSP($|$)-algebra $\mathcal{R}_{df}$ with the evident definitions:

$$\begin{aligned} F \sqcap_{\mathcal{R}_{df}} G &= F \cup G \\ (\Box_{\mathbf{a}})_{\mathcal{R}_{df}} (F_1, \ldots, F_n) &= \{(\varepsilon, W) \mid W \cap \{a_1, \ldots, a_n\} = \emptyset\} \\ &\quad \cup \{(a_i w, W) \mid (w, W) \in F_i\} \end{aligned}$$

Theorem 2. *The finitary refusal sets algebra $\mathcal{R}_{df}$ is complete for equations between closed* CSP($|$) *terms.*

Proof. De Nicola's normal form can be regarded as written in the signature of CSP($|$), and a straightforward induction proves that every CSP($|$) term can be reduced to such a normal form using the above axioms. But two such normal forms have the same denotation whether they are regarded as CSP ($\Box$) or as CSP($|$) terms, and in the former case, by Lemma 4.8 of [10], they are identical. $\Box$

Theorem 3. *The finitary refusal sets algebra $\mathcal{R}_{df}$ is the initial* CSP($|$) *algebra.*

Proof. Following the proof of Lemma 2 we see that every finitary refusal set is definable by a closed CSP($|$) term. With that, initiality follows from the above completeness theorem, as in the proof of Theorem 1. $\Box$

Turning to the deconstructors, relabelling again has a straightforward homomorphic definition: given a relabelling function $f : A \to A$, $h_{Rl} : T_{\mathrm{CSP}(|)}(\emptyset) \to T_{\mathrm{CSP}(|)}(\emptyset)$ is defined homomorphically by:

$$h_{Rl}(F \sqcap G) = h_{Rl}(F) \sqcap h_{Rl}(G)$$

$$h_{Rl}\left(\Box_i a_i F_i\right) = \Box_i f(a_i) h_{Rl}(F_i)$$

As always one has to check that the implied algebra satisfies the equations, here those of CSP($|$).

There is also now a natural homomorphic definition of concealment, $-\backslash a$, but, surprisingly perhaps, one needs to assume that $\Box$ is available. For every $a \in A$ one defines $h_a : T_{\mathrm{CSP}(|)}(\emptyset) \to T_{\mathrm{CSP}(|)}(\emptyset)$ homomorphically by:

$$h_a(F \sqcap G) = h_a(F) \sqcap h_a(G)$$

$$h_a\left(\Box_{i=1}^{n} a_i F_i\right) = \begin{cases} h_a(F_j) \sqcap (h_a(F_j) \Box \Box_{i \neq j} a_i h_a(F_i)) & (\text{if } a = a_j,\ j \in \{1 \ldots n\} \\ \Box_{i=1}^{n} a_i h_a(F_i) & (\text{if } a \neq \text{any } a_i) \end{cases}$$

Verifying that the implicit algebra obeys satisfies the required equations is quite a bit of work. We record the result, but omit the calculations:

Proposition 2. *One can define a* CSP($|$)*-algebra Con on $T_{\mathrm{CSP}(|)}(\emptyset)$ by:*

$$F \sqcap_{Con} G = F \sqcap G$$

$$(\Box_{\mathbf{a}})_{Con}(F_1, \ldots, F_n) = \begin{cases} F_j \sqcap (F_j \Box \Box_{i \neq j} a_i F_i) & (\textit{if } a = a_j) \\ \Box_i a_i F_i & (\textit{if } a \neq \textit{any } a_i) \end{cases}$$

The operator $\Box$ is, of course, no longer available as a constructor. However, it can alternatively be treated as a binary deconstructor. While its treatment as such is no more successful than our treatment of parallel operators, it is also no less successful. We define it simultaneously with $(n+1)$-ary functions $\Box^{a_1 \cdots a_n}$ on $T_{\mathrm{CSP}(|)}(\emptyset)$, for $n \geq 0$, where the a_i are all distinct. That we are defining infinitely many functions simultaneously arises from dealing with the infinitely many deterministic choice operators (there would be be infinitely many even if we considered them as parameterised on the a's). However, we anticipate that this will cause no real difficulty, given that we have overcome the difficulty of dealing with binary deconstructors.

Here are the required definitions:

$$
\begin{aligned}
(F \sqcap F') \,\square\, G &= (F \,\square\, G) \sqcap (F' \,\square\, G) \\
\left(\square_i a_i F_i\right) \square\, G &= (F_1, \ldots, F_n) \,\square^{a_1 \ldots a_n}\, G \\
(F_1, \ldots, F_n) \,\square^{a_1 \ldots a_n}\, (G \sqcap G') &= ((F_1, \ldots, F_n) \,\square^{a_1 \ldots a_n}\, G) \\
&\quad \sqcap ((F_1, \ldots, F_n) \,\square^{a_1 \ldots a_n}\, G') \\
(F_1, \ldots, F_n) \,\square^{a_1 \ldots a_n} \left(\square_j b_j G_j\right) &= (a_1 \rightarrow F_1) \\
&\quad \square \left(\ldots \left((a_n \rightarrow F_n) \,\square\, \square_j b_j G_j\right) \ldots\right)
\end{aligned}
\tag{15.8}
$$

where, in the last equation, the notational convention $(a_1 \rightarrow t_1) \,\square\, \square_{i=2}^{n} a_i t_i$ is used n times. It is clear that $\square$ together with the functions

$$\square^{a_1 \ldots a_n} : T_{\mathrm{CSP}(|)}(\emptyset)^{n+1} \rightarrow T_{\mathrm{CSP}(|)}(\emptyset)$$

defined by:

$$\square^{a_1 \ldots a_n}(F_1, \ldots, F_n, G) = \left(\square_i a_i F_i\right) \square\, G \tag{15.9}$$

satisfy the equations, and, using the fact that all finitary refusal sets are definable by normal forms, one sees that they are the unique such functions.

We can treat the CSP parallel operator $||$ in a similar vein following the pattern given above for parallel merge operators in the case of synchronisation trees. We define it simultaneously with $(n+1)$-ary functions $||^{a_1 \ldots a_n}$ on $T_{\mathrm{CSP}(|)}(\emptyset)$, for $n \geq 0$, where the a_i are all distinct:

$$
\begin{aligned}
(F \sqcap F') \,||\, G &= (F \,||\, G) \sqcap (F' \,||\, G) \\
\left(\square_i a_i F_i\right) ||\, G &= (F_1, \ldots, F_n) \,||^{a_1 \ldots a_n}\, G \\
(F_1, \ldots, F_n) \,||^{a_1 \ldots a_n}\, (G \sqcap G') &= ((F_1, \ldots, F_n) \,||^{a_1 \ldots a_n}\, G) \\
&\quad \sqcap ((F_1, \ldots, F_n) \,\square^{a_1 \ldots a_n}\, G') \\
(F_1, \ldots, F_n) \,||^{a_1 \ldots a_n} \left(\square_j b_j G_j\right) &= \square_{a_i = b_j} a_i (F_i \,||\, G_j)
\end{aligned}
\tag{15.10}
$$

Much as before, $||$ together with the functions $||^{a_1 \ldots a_n}\colon T_{\mathrm{CSP}(|)}(\emptyset)^{n+1} \rightarrow T_{\mathrm{CSP}(|)}(\emptyset)$ defined by:

$$||^{a_1 \ldots a_n}\,(F_1, \ldots, F_n, G) = \left(\square_i a_i F_i\right) ||\, G$$

are the unique functions satisfying the equations.

Finally, we consider the CSP interleaving operator $|||$. We define this by following an idea, exemplified in the ACP literature [4, 5], of splitting an associative operation into several parts. Here we split $|||$ into a *left interleaving* operator $|||^l$ and a *right interleaving* operator $|||^r$ so that:

$$F \mathbin{|||} G = (F \mathbin{|||^l} G) \,\Box\, (F \mathbin{|||^r} G)$$

In ACP the parallel operator is split into three parts: a left merge, a right merge (defined in terms of the left merge), and a communication merge; in a subtheory, PA, there is no communication, and the parallel operator, now an interleaving one, is split into left and right parts [5]. The idea of splitting an associative operation into several operations can be found in a much wider context [11] where the split into two or three parts is axiomatised by the respective notions of dendriform dialgebra and trialgebra.

Our left and right interleaving are defined by the following "binary deconstructor" equations:

$$\begin{aligned}
(F \sqcap F') \mathbin{|||^l} G &= (F \mathbin{|||^l} G) \sqcap (F' \mathbin{|||^l} G)\\
\left(\Box_{i=1}^{n} a_i F_i\right) \mathbin{|||^l} G &= \Box_i\, a_i((F_i \mathbin{|||^l} G) \,\Box\, (F_i \mathbin{|||^r} G))\\
G \mathbin{|||^r} (F \sqcap F') &= (G \mathbin{|||^r} F) \sqcap (G \mathbin{|||^r} F')\\
G \mathbin{|||^r} \left(\Box_{i=1}^{n} a_i F_i\right) &= \Box_i\, a_i((G \mathbin{|||^l} F_i) \,\Box\, (G \mathbin{|||^r} F_i))
\end{aligned} \tag{15.11}$$

As may be expected, these equations also have unique solutions, now given by:

$$\begin{aligned}
F \mathbin{|||^l} G &= \{(\varepsilon, W) \mid (\varepsilon, W) \in F\} \cup \{(w, W) \mid (u, W) \in F,\ (v, W) \in G,\ w \in u \,|^l\, v\}\\
F \mathbin{|||^r} G &= \{(\varepsilon, W) \mid (\varepsilon, W) \in G\} \cup \{(w, W) \mid (u, W) \in F,\ (v, W) \in G,\ w \in u \,|^r\, v\}
\end{aligned}$$

where $u \,|^l\, v$ is the set of interleavings of u and v which begin with a letter of u, and $u \,|^r\, v$ is defined analogously. It is interesting to note that:

$$F \mathbin{|||^l} (G \sqcap G') = (F \mathbin{|||^l} G) \sqcap (F \mathbin{|||^l} G')$$

and similarly for $|||^r$.

15.6 Adding divergence

The treatment of CSP presented thus far dealt with finite divergence-free processes only. There are several ways to extend the refusal sets model of Section 15.3 to infinite processes with divergence. The most well-known model is the *failures/*

divergences model of [13], further elaborated in [29]. A characteristic property of this model is that divergence, i.e., an infinite sequence of internal actions, is modelled as *Chaos*, a process that satisfies the equation:

$$Chaos \,\Box\, x = Chaos \sqcap x = Chaos \tag{15.12}$$

So after *Chaos* no further process activity is discernible.

An alternative extension is the *stable failures* model proposed in [6], and also elaborated in [29]. This model equates processes that allow the same *observations*, where actions and deadlock are considered observable, but divergence does not give rise to any observations. A failure pair (w, W) – now allowing W to be infinite – records an observation in which w represents a sequence of actions being observed, and W represents the observation of deadlock under the assumption that the environment in which the observed process is running allows only the (inter)actions in the set W. Such an observation can be made if after engaging in the sequence of visible actions w, the observed process reaches a state in which no further internal actions are possible, nor any actions from the set W. Besides failure pairs, also traces are observable, and thus the observable behaviour of a process is given by a pair (T, F) where T is a set of traces and F is a set of failure pairs. Unlike the model $\mathcal{R}_f$ of Section 15.3, the traces are not determined by the failure pairs. In fact, in a process that can diverge in every state, the set of failure pairs is empty, yet the set of traces conveys important information.

In the remainder of this paper we add a constant Ω to the signature of CSP that is a zero for the semilattice generated by $\sqcap$. This will greatly facilitate the forthcoming development. Intuitively, one may think of Ω as divergence in the stable failures model.

With respect to the equational theory CSP ($\Box$) of Section 15.3 we thus add the constant Ω and the single axiom:

$$x \sqcap \Omega = x \tag{15.13}$$

thereby obtaining the theory CSP ($\Box, \Omega$). We note two useful derived equations:

$$\begin{aligned} x \sqcap (\Omega \,\Box\, y) &= x \sqcap (x \,\Box\, y) \\ (\Omega \,\Box\, x) \sqcap (\Omega \,\Box\, y) &= (\Omega \,\Box\, x) \,\Box\, (\Omega \,\Box\, y) \end{aligned} \tag{15.14}$$

Semantically, a *process* is now given by a pair (T, F), where T is a set of traces and F is a set of failure pairs that satisfy the following conditions:

1. $\varepsilon \in T$
2. $wa \in T \Rightarrow w \in T$
3. $(w, W) \in F \Rightarrow w \in T$
4. $(w, W) \in F \wedge V \subseteq W \Rightarrow (w, V) \in F$
5. $(w, W) \in F \wedge \forall a \in V.\, wa \notin T \Rightarrow (w, W \cup V) \in F$ (where $V \subseteq A$)

The two components of such a pair P are denoted T_P and F_P, respectively, and for $w \in T_P$ we define $\mathrm{fut}_P(w) := \{a \in A \mid wa \in T_P\}$. We can define the CSP operators on processes by setting

$$P \text{ op } Q = (P \text{ op}_{\mathcal{T}} Q, P \text{ op}_{\mathcal{R}} Q)$$

where $\text{op}_{\mathcal{T}}$ is given by:

$$\begin{aligned}
\mathtt{Stop}_{\mathcal{T}} &= \{\varepsilon\} \\
a \rightarrow_{\mathcal{T}} P &= \{\varepsilon\} \cup \{aw \mid w \in T_P\} \\
P \sqcap_{\mathcal{T}} Q &= T_P \cup T_Q \\
P \,\Box_{\mathcal{T}}\, Q &= T_P \cup T_Q \\
f_{\mathcal{T}}(P) &= \{f(w) \mid w \in T_P\} \\
P \backslash_{\mathcal{T}} a &= \{w \backslash a \mid w \in T_P\} \\
P \parallel_{\mathcal{T}} Q &= \{w \mid w \in T_P,\ w \in T_Q\} \\
P \,|||_{\mathcal{T}}\, Q &= \{w \mid u \in T_P,\ v \in T_Q,\ w \in u|v\}
\end{aligned}$$

and $\text{op}_{\mathcal{R}}$ is given as $\text{op}_{\mathcal{R}_f}$ was in Section 15.3, but without the restriction to finite sets W in defining $\mathtt{Stop}_{\mathcal{R}}$. For the new process Ω we set

$$\Omega_{\mathcal{T}} = \{\varepsilon\} \qquad \text{and} \qquad \Omega_{\mathcal{R}} = \emptyset$$

This also makes the collection of processes into a CSP $(\Box, \Omega)$-algebra, $\mathcal{F}$.

A process P is called *finitary* if T_P is finite. The finitary processes evidently form a subalgebra of $\mathcal{F}$; we call it $\mathcal{F}_f$.

Lemma 3. *Let P be a finitary process. Then, for every $w \in T_P$ there is an $n \geq 0$ and $V_1, \ldots, V_n \subseteq \mathrm{fut}_F(w)$ such that $(w, W) \in F_P$ iff $W \cap V_i = \emptyset$ for some $i \in \{1, \ldots, n\}$.*

Proof. Closure conditions 4 and 5 above imply that $(w, W) \in F_P$ if, and only if, $(w, W \cap \mathrm{fut}_P(w)) \in F_P$. Thus we only need to be concerned about pairs (w, W) with $W \subseteq \mathrm{fut}_P(w)$. Now, as $\mathrm{fut}_P(w)$ is finite, for any relevant $(w, W) \in F$, of which there are finitely many, we can take V to be $\mathrm{fut}_P(w) \backslash W$, and we obtain finitely many such sets. □

Note that it may happen that $n = 0$, in contrast with the case of Lemma 1.

Lemma 4. *All finitary processes are definable by closed* CSP $(\Box, \Omega)$ *terms.*

Proof. Let P be a finitary process. We proceed by induction on the length of the longest trace in T_P. By the previous lemma there are sets $V_1, \ldots, V_n$, for some $n \geq 0$, such that $(\varepsilon, W) \in F$ iff $W \cap V_i = \emptyset$ for some $i \in \{1, \ldots, n\}$. Define T_a and F_a, for $a \in T_P$, by:

$$T_a = \{w \mid aw \in T_P\} \qquad F_a = \{(w, W) \mid (aw, W) \in F_P\}$$

Then it is not hard to see that each $P_a := (T_a, F_a)$ is a finitary process, and that

$$P = \left(\bigsqcap_{i} \Box_{a \in V_i} a \to P_a\right) \sqcap \left(\Omega \Box \Box_{a \in T_P} a \to P_a\right)$$

As the longest trace in T_a is strictly shorter than the longest one in T_P, the proof concludes, employing the induction hypothesis. □

Proposition 3. CSP $(\Box, \Omega)$ *is ground equationally complete with respect to both* $\mathcal{F}$ *and* $\mathcal{F}_f$.

Proof. This time we recursively define a normal form as a CSP $(\Box, \Omega)$-term of the form

$$\bigsqcap_{L \in \mathcal{L}} \Box_{a \in L} a \to t_a \qquad \text{or} \qquad \Omega \Box \Box_{a \in K} a \to t_a$$

where $\mathcal{L}$ is a finite non-empty saturated collection of finite sets of actions, K is a finite set of actions, and each term t_a is in normal form. Every term is provably equal in CSP $(\Box, \Omega)$ to a term in normal form; the proof proceeds as for Proposition 1, but now also using the derived equations (15.14). Next, by Lemma 6 below, if two normal forms have the same denotation in $\mathcal{F}$ then they are identical. So the result follows for $\mathcal{F}$, and then for $\mathcal{F}_f$ too, as all closed terms denote finitary processes. □

Theorem 4. *The algebra* $\mathcal{F}_f$ *of finitary processes is the initial* CSP $(\Box, \Omega)$ *algebra.*

Proof. Let the initial such algebra be I. There is a unique homomorphism $h : \mathrm{I} \to \mathcal{F}_f$. By Lemma 4, h is a surjection. By the previous proposition, $\mathcal{F}_f$ is complete for equations between closed terms, and so h is an injection. Hence h is an isomorphism, completing the proof. □

As in Section 15.5, in order to deal with deconstructors, particularly hiding, we replace external choice by deterministic external choice. The availability of Ω permits useful additional such operators. The equational theory CSP$(|, \Omega)$ has as signature the binary operation symbol $\sqcap$, and for any deterministic action sequence $\mathbf{a}$, the n-ary operation symbols $\Box_{\mathbf{a}}$ (as in Section 15.5), as well as the new n-ary operation symbols $\Box_{\mathbf{a}}^{\Omega}$, for $n \geq 0$, which denote a deterministic external choice with Ω as one of the summands. We adopt conventions for $\Box_{\mathbf{a}}^{\Omega}$ analogous to those previously introduced for $\Box_{\mathbf{a}}(t_1, \ldots, t_n)$. We write $\Box_{\mathbf{a}}^{\Omega}(t_1, \ldots, t_n)$ as $\Omega \Box \Box_{i=1}^{n} a_i t_i$. We also write $\Omega \Box (c_1 \to t_1) \Box \Box_{j=2}^{n} c_j t_j$ for $\Omega \Box \Box_{j=1}^{n} c_j t_j$, so that the c_j $(j = 1, n)$ must all be distinct.

The first three groups of axioms of CSP$(|, \Omega)$ are:

- $\sqcap, \Omega$ Is a semilattice with a zero – here Ω is the 0-ary case of $\Box_{\mathbf{a}}^{\Omega}$,
- Both deterministic external choice operators $\Box_{\mathbf{a}}$ and $\Box_{\mathbf{a}}^{\Omega}$ are commutative, as explained in Section 15.5
- Both deterministic external choice operators distribute over internal choice, as explained in Section 15.5,

Given commutativity, we are, as before, justified in writing deterministic external choices $\Box_{a\in I} at_a$ or $\Omega \,\Box\, \Box_{a\in I} at_a$, over finite, possibly empty, sets of actions I, assuming some standard ordering of pairs (a, t_a) without repetitions. Next, using the analogous convention to (15.6) we can then also understand $\Omega \,\Box\, \Box_{j=1}^{n} c_j t_j$, and so also $\Omega \,\Box\, (c_1 \to t_1) \,\Box\, \Box_{j=2}^{n} c_j t_j$, even when the c_j are not all distinct. With these conventions established, we can now state the final group of axioms. These are all variants of Axiom (15.7) of Section 15.5, allowing each of the two deterministic external choices to have an Ω-summand:

$$\left(\Omega \,\Box \Box_{i} a_i x_i\right) \sqcap \left(\Omega \,\Box\, (b_1 \to y_1) \,\Box \Box_{j=2}^{n} b_j y_j\right) \sqsubseteq \Omega \,\Box\, (b_1 \to y_1) \,\Box \Box_{i} a_i x_i$$

$$\left(\Omega \,\Box \Box_{i} a_i x_i\right) \sqcap \left((b_1 \to y_1) \,\Box \Box_{j=2}^{n} b_j y_j\right) \sqsubseteq \Omega \,\Box\, (b_1 \to y_1) \,\Box \Box_{i} a_i x_i$$

$$\left(\Box_{i} a_i x_i\right) \sqcap \left(\Omega \,\Box\, (b_1 \to y_1) \,\Box \Box_{j=2}^{n} b_j y_j\right) \sqsubseteq (b_1 \to y_1) \,\Box \Box_{i} a_i x_i$$

$$\left(\Box_{i} a_i x_i\right) \sqcap \left((b_1 \to y_1) \,\Box \Box_{j=2}^{n} b_j y_j\right) \sqsubseteq (b_1 \to y_1) \,\Box \Box_{i} a_i x_i \qquad (15.15)$$

As in the case of Axiom (15.7), restricting any of these choices to be deterministic results in an axiom of equivalent power. We note two useful derived equations:

$$\Box_{i} a_i x_i \sqcap \left(\Omega \,\Box \Box_{j} b_j y_j\right) = \Box_{i} a_i x_i \sqcap \left(\Box_{i} a_i x_i \,\Box \Box_{j} b_j y_j\right)$$

$$\left(\Omega \,\Box \Box_{i} a_i x_i\right) \sqcap \left(\Omega \,\Box \Box_{j} b_j y_j\right) = \left(\Omega \,\Box \Box_{i} a_i x_i\right) \Box \Box_{j} b_j y_j \qquad (15.16)$$

where two further notational conventions are used: $(\Box_{i=1}^{m} a_i t_i) \,\Box\, (\Box_{j=1}^{n} b_j t'_j)$ stands for $\Box_{k=1}^{m+n} c_k t''_k$ where $c_k = a_k$ and $t''_k = t_k$, for $k = 1, m$, and $c_k = b_{k-m}$, and $t''_k = t'_{k-m}$, for $k = m+1, m+n$; and $(\Omega \,\Box \Box_{i=1}^{m} a_i t_i) \,\Box\, (\Box_{j=1}^{n} b_j t'_j)$ is understood analogously. In fact, the first three axioms of (15.15) are also derivable from (15.16), in the presence of the other axioms, and thus may be replaced by (15.16).

The collection of processes is turned into a CSP$(|, \Omega)$-algebra $\mathcal{F}_d$ as before, writing:

$$P \,\mathrm{op}_{\mathcal{F}_d}\, Q = (P \,\mathrm{op}_{\mathcal{T}_d}\, Q, P \,\mathrm{op}_{\mathcal{R}_d}\, Q)$$

and defining $\mathrm{op}_{\mathcal{T}_d}$ and $\mathrm{op}_{\mathcal{R}_d}$ in the evident way:

$$\begin{aligned}
P \sqcap_{\mathcal{T}_d} Q &= T_P \cup T_Q \\
(\square_{\mathbf{a}})_{\mathcal{T}_d} (P_1, \ldots, P_n) &= \{\varepsilon\} \cup \{a_i w \mid w \in T_{P_i}\} \\
\left(\square^{\Omega}_{\mathbf{a}}\right)_{\mathcal{T}_d} (P_1, \ldots, P_n) &= \{\varepsilon\} \cup \{a_i w \mid w \in T_{P_i}\} \\
\left(\square^{\Omega}_{\mathbf{a}}\right)_{\mathcal{R}_d} (P_1, \ldots, P_n) &= \{(a_i w, W) \mid (w, W) \in F_{P_i}\}
\end{aligned}$$

with $\sqcap_{\mathcal{R}_d}$ and $(\square_{\mathbf{a}})_{\mathcal{R}_d}$ given just as in Section 15.5. Exactly as in Section 15.5, but now using the derived equations (15.16), we obtain:

Theorem 5. *The algebra $\mathcal{F}_d$ is complete for equations between closed* CSP($|, \Omega$) *terms.*

Theorem 6. *The finitary subalgebra $\mathcal{F}_{df}$ of $\mathcal{F}_d$ is the initial* CSP($|, \Omega$) *algebra.*

Turning to the deconstructors, relabelling and concealment can again be treated homomorphically. For relabelling by f one simply adds the equation:

$$h_{Rl}\left(\Omega \square \bigsquare_i a_i F_i\right) = \Omega \square \bigsquare_i f(a_i) h_{Rl}(F_i)$$

to the treatment in Section 15.5, and checks that the implied algebra satisfies the equations. Pleasingly, the treatment of concealment can be simplified in such a way that the deconstructor $\square$ is no longer needed. For every $a \in A$ one defines $h_a : T_{\mathrm{CSP}(|,\Omega)}(\emptyset) \to T_{\mathrm{CSP}(|,\Omega)}(\emptyset)$ homomorphically by:

$$h_a(P \sqcap Q) = h_a(P) \sqcap h_a(Q)$$

$$h_a\left(\bigsquare_{i=1}^{n} a_i P_i\right) = \begin{cases} h_a(P_j) \sqcap (\Omega \square \bigsquare_{i\neq j} a_i h_a(P_i)) & (\text{if } a = a_j, j \in \{1 \ldots n\} \\ \bigsquare_{i=1}^{n} a_i h_a(P_i) & (\text{if } a \neq \text{any } a_i) \end{cases}$$

$$h_a\left(\Omega \square \bigsquare_{i=1}^{n} a_i P_i\right) = \begin{cases} h_a(P_j) \sqcap (\Omega \square \bigsquare_{i\neq j} a_i h_a(P_i)) & (\text{if } a = a_j, j \in \{1 \ldots n\} \\ \Omega \square \bigsquare_{i=1}^{n} a_i h_a(P_i) & (\text{if } a \neq \text{any } a_i) \end{cases}$$

Note the use of the new form of deterministic choice here. One has again to verify that the implicit algebra obeys satisfies the required equations. The treatment of the binary deconstructors $\square$, $||$ and $|||$ is also a trivial adaptation of the treatment in Section 15.5. For $\square$ one adds a further auxiliary operator $\square^{\Omega, a_1 \ldots a_n}$ and the equations:

$$(\Omega \square \bigsquare_i a_i P_i) \square Q = (P_1, \ldots, P_n) \square^{\Omega, a_1 \ldots a_n} Q$$

$$\begin{aligned}
(P_1, \ldots, P_n) \square^{\Omega, a_1 \ldots a_n} (Q \sqcap Q') = &\left((P_1, \ldots, P_n) \square^{\Omega, a_1 \ldots a_n} Q\right) \\
&\sqcap \left((P_1, \ldots, P_n) \square^{\Omega, a_1 \ldots a_n} Q'\right)
\end{aligned}$$

$$(P_1,\ldots,P_n)\,\Box^{\Omega,a_1\ldots a_n}\left(\Box_j b_jQ_j\right) = \left(\Omega\,\Box\,\Box_i a_iP_i\right)\Box\,\Box_j b_jQ_j$$

$$(P_1,\ldots,P_n)\,\Box^{\Omega,a_1\ldots a_n}\left(\Omega\,\Box\,\Box_j b_jQ_j\right) = \left(\Omega\,\Box\,\Box_i a_iP_i\right)\Box\,\Box_j b_jQ_j$$

$$(P_1,\ldots,P_n)\,\Box^{a_1\ldots a_n}\left(\Omega\,\Box\,\Box_j b_jQ_j\right) = \left(\Omega\,\Box\,\Box_i a_iP_i\right)\Box\,\Box_j b_jQ_j$$

For $||$ one adds the auxiliary operator $||^{\Omega,a_1\ldots a_n}$ and the equations:

$$\left(\Omega\,\Box\,\Box_i a_iP_i\right) \,||\, Q = (P_1,\ldots,P_n)\,||^{\Omega,a_1\ldots a_n}\, Q$$

$$(P_1,\ldots,P_n)\,||^{\Omega,a_1\ldots a_n}\,(Q \sqcap Q') = \left((P_1,\ldots,P_n)\,||^{\Omega,a_1\ldots a_n}\, Q\right) \sqcap \left((P_1,\ldots,P_n)\,\Box^{\Omega,a_1\ldots a_n}\, Q'\right)$$

$$(P_1,\ldots,P_n)\,||^{\Omega,a_1\ldots a_n}\left(\Box_j b_jQ_j\right) = \Omega\,\Box\,\Box_{a_i=b_j} a_i\left(P_i \,||\, Q_j\right)$$

$$(P_1,\ldots,P_n)\,||^{\Omega,a_1\ldots a_n}\left(\Omega\,\Box\,\Box_j b_jQ_j\right) = \Omega\,\Box\,\Box_{a_i=b_j} a_i\left(P_i \,||\, Q_j\right)$$

$$(P_1,\ldots,P_n)\,||^{a_1\ldots a_n}\left(\Omega\,\Box\,\Box_j b_jQ_j\right) = \Omega\,\Box\,\Box_{a_i=b_j} a_i\left(P_i \,||\, Q_j\right)$$

Finally, for $|||$ one simply adds extra equations:

$$\left(\Omega\,\Box\,\Box_{i=1}^{n} a_iP_i\right) |||^l\, Q = \Omega\,\Box\,\Box_i a_i\left((P_i \,|||^l\, Q)\,\Box\,(P_i \,|||^r\, Q)\right)$$

$$Q\,|||^r\left(\Omega\,\Box\,\Box_{i=1}^{n} a_iP_i\right) = \Omega\,\Box\,\Box_i a_i\left((Q\,|||^l\, P_i)\,\Box\,(Q\,|||^r\, P_i)\right)$$

15.7 Combining CSP and Functional Programming

To combine CSP with functional programming, specifically the computational λ-calculus, we use the monad $T_{\mathrm{CSP}(|,\Omega)}$ for the denotational semantics. As remarked above, CSP processes then become terms of type `empty`. However, as the constructors are polymorphic, it is natural to go further and look for polymorphic versions of the deconstructors. We therefore add polymorphic constructs to λ_c as follows:

Constructors

$$\frac{M:\sigma \quad N:\sigma}{M \sqcap N:\sigma} \qquad \frac{M:\sigma}{a \to M:\sigma} \qquad \Omega:\sigma$$

Unary Deconstructors

$$\frac{M:\sigma}{f(M):\sigma} \qquad \frac{M:\sigma}{M\backslash a:\sigma}$$

for any relabelling function f, and any $a \in A$. (One should really restrict the allowable relabelling functions in order to keep the syntax finitary.)

Binary Deconstructors

$$\frac{M:\sigma \quad N:\sigma}{M \,\square\, N:\sigma} \qquad \frac{M:\sigma \quad N:\tau}{M \mid\mid N:\sigma \times \tau} \qquad \frac{M:\sigma \quad N:\tau}{M \mid\mid\mid N:\sigma \times \tau}$$

The idea of the two parallel constructs is to evaluate the two terms in parallel and then return the pair of the two values produced. We did not include syntax for the two deterministic choice constructors as they are definable from $a \to -$ and Ω with the aid of the $\square$ deconstructor.

For the denotational semantics, the semantics of types is given as usual using the monad $T_{\mathrm{CSP}(|,\Omega)}$, which we know exists by the general considerations of Section 15.2. These general considerations also yield a semantics for the constructors. For example, for every set X we have the map:

$$\sqcap_X : T_{\mathrm{CSP}(|,\Omega)}(X)^2 \to T_{\mathrm{CSP}(|,\Omega)}(X)$$

which we can use for $X = [\![\sigma]\!]$ to interpret terms $M \sqcap N:\sigma$.

The homomorphic point of view also leads to an interpretation of the unary deconstructors, but using free algebras rather than just the initial one. For example, for relabelling by f we need a function:

$$h_{Rl} : T_{\mathrm{CSP}(|,\Omega)}(X) \to T_{\mathrm{CSP}(|,\Omega)}(X)$$

We obtain this as the unique homomorphism extending the unit $\eta_X{:}X{\to}T_{\mathrm{CSP}(|,\Omega)}(X)$, equipping $T_{\mathrm{CSP}(|,\Omega)}(X)$ with the algebra structure

$$\mathcal{A} = \left(T_{\mathrm{CSP}(|,\Omega)}(X), \sqcap_{\mathcal{A}}, \square_{\mathcal{A}}, \square_{\mathcal{A}}^{\Omega}\right)$$

where, for $x, y \in T_{\mathrm{CSP}(|,\Omega)}(X)$,

$$x \sqcap_{\mathcal{A}} y = x \sqcap_X y$$

$$\left(\Box_{\mathbf{a}}\right)_{\mathcal{A}}(x_1,\ldots,x_n) = \left(\Box_{f(\mathbf{a})}\right)_X (x_1,\ldots,x_n)$$

and

$$\left(\Box_{\mathbf{a}}^{\Omega}\right)_{\mathcal{A}}(x_1,\ldots,x_n) = \left(\Box_{f(\mathbf{a})}^{\Omega}\right)_X (x_1,\ldots,x_n)$$

Concealment $-\backslash a$ can be treated analogously, but now following the treatment in the case of $\mathcal{F}_{df}$, and defining $\mathcal{A}$ by:

$$x \sqcap_{\mathcal{A}} y = x \sqcap_X y$$

for $x, y \in T_{\mathrm{CSP}(|,\Omega)}(X)$,

$$(\Box_{\mathbf{a}})_{\mathcal{A}}(x_1,\ldots,x_n) = \begin{cases} x_j \sqcap (\Omega \,\Box\, \Box_{i\neq j}\, a_i x_i) & (\text{if } a = a_j,\ \text{where } 1 \le j \le n) \\ \Box_{i=1}^{n}\, a_i x_i & (\text{if } a \neq \text{any } a_i) \end{cases}$$

and

$$(\Box_{\mathbf{a}}^{\Omega})_{\mathcal{A}}(x_1,\ldots,x_n) = \begin{cases} x_j \sqcap (\Omega \,\Box\, \Box_{i\neq j}\, a_i x_i) & (\text{if } a = a_j,\ \text{where } 1 \le j \le n) \\ \Omega \,\Box\, \Box_{i=1}^{n}\, a_i x_i & (\text{if } a \neq \text{any } a_i) \end{cases}$$

We here again make use of the deterministic choice operator made available by the presence of Ω.

However, we cannot, of course, carry this on to binary deconstructors as we have no general algebraic treatment of them. We proceed instead by giving a concrete definition of them (and the other constructors and deconstructors). That is, we give an explicit description of the free CSP($|$, Ω)-algebra on a set X and define our operators in terms of that representation.

An X-*trace* is a pair (w, x), where $w \in A^*$ and $x \in X$; it is generally more suggestive to write (w, x) as wx. For any relabelling function f, we set $f(wx) = f(w)x$, and, for any $a \in A$, we set $wx\backslash a = (w\backslash a)x$. An X-*process* is a pair (T, F) with T a set of traces as well as X-traces, and F a set of failure pairs, satisfying the same five conditions as in Section 15.6, together with:

2′. $wx \in T \Rightarrow w \in T$ (for $x \in X$)

The CSP operators are defined on X-processes exactly as before, except that the two parallel operators now have more general types:

$$||_{X,Y}, |||_{X,Y}: T_{\mathrm{CSP}(|,\Omega)}(X) \times T_{\mathrm{CSP}(|,\Omega)}(Y) \to T_{\mathrm{CSP}(|,\Omega)}(X \times Y)$$

We take $\mathrm{fut}_P(w) := \{a \in A \mid wa \in T_P\}$, as before.

$$
\begin{array}{ll}
\Omega_{\mathcal{T}(X)} & = \{\epsilon\} \\
\Omega_{\mathcal{R}(X)} & = \emptyset \\
\mathtt{Stop}_{\mathcal{T}(X)} & = \{\varepsilon\} \\
\mathtt{Stop}_{\mathcal{R}(X)} & = \{(\varepsilon, W) \mid W \subseteq A\} \\
a \rightarrow_{\mathcal{T}(X)} P & = \{\varepsilon\} \cup \{aw \mid w \in T_P\} \\
a \rightarrow_{\mathcal{R}(X)} P & = \{(\varepsilon, W) \mid a \notin W\} \cup \{(aw, W) \mid (w, W) \in F_P\} \\
P \sqcap_{\mathcal{T}(X)} Q & = T_P \cup T_Q \\
P \sqcap_{\mathcal{R}(X)} Q & = F_P \cup F_Q \\
P \,\Box_{\mathcal{T}(X)}\, Q & = T_P \cup T_Q \\
P \,\Box_{\mathcal{R}(X)}\, Q & = \{(\varepsilon, W) \mid (\varepsilon, W) \in F_P \cap F_Q\} \\
 & \quad \cup \{(w, W) \mid w \neq \varepsilon,\ (w, W) \in F_P \cup F_Q\} \\
f_{\mathcal{T}(X)}(P) & = \{f(w) \mid w \in T_P\} \\
f_{\mathcal{R}(X)}(P) & = \{(f(w), W) \mid (w, f^{-1}(W) \cap \mathrm{fut}_P(w)) \in F_P\} \\
P \backslash_{\mathcal{T}(X)} a & = \{w \backslash a \mid w \in T_P\} \\
P \backslash_{\mathcal{R}(X)} a & = \{(w \backslash a, W) \mid (w, W \cup \{a\}) \in F_P\} \\
P \,||_{\mathcal{T}(X,Y)}\, Q & = \{w \mid w \in T_P \cap T_Q \cap A^*\} \cup \{w(x, y) \mid wx \in T_P,\ wy \in T_Q\} \\
P \,||_{\mathcal{R}(X,Y)}\, Q & = \{(w, W \cup V) \mid (w, W) \in F_P,\ (w, V) \in F_Q\} \\
P \,|||_{\mathcal{T}(X,Y)}\, Q & = \{w \mid u \in T_P \cap A^*,\ v \in T_Q \cap A^*,\ w \in u|v\} \\
 & \quad \cup \{w(x, y) \mid ux \in T_P,\ vy \in T_Q,\ w \in u|v\} \\
P \,|||_{\mathcal{R}(X,Y)}\, Q & = \{(w, W) \mid (u, W) \in F_P,\ (v, W) \in F_Q,\ w \in u|v\}
\end{array}
$$

Here, much as before, we write $P \ \mathrm{op}_{\mathcal{F}(X)}\ Q = (P \ \mathrm{op}_{\mathcal{T}(X)}\ Q, P \ \mathrm{op}_{\mathcal{R}(X)}\ Q)$ when defining the CSP operators on X-processes. The X-processes also form the carrier of a CSP$(|, \Omega)$-algebra $\mathcal{F}_d(X)$, with the operators defined as follows:

$$
\begin{array}{ll}
P \sqcap_{\mathcal{T}_d(X)} Q & = T_P \cup T_Q \\
P \sqcap_{\mathcal{R}_d(X)} Q & = F_P \cup F_Q \\
\left(\Box^{\Omega}_{\mathbf{a}}\right)_{\mathcal{T}_d(X)} (P_1, \ldots, P_n) & = \{\varepsilon\} \cup \{a_i w \mid w \in T_{P_i}\} \\
\left(\Box^{\Omega}_{\mathbf{a}}\right)_{\mathcal{R}_d(X)} (P_1, \ldots, P_n) & = \{(a_i w, W) \mid (w, W) \in F_{P_i}\} \\
\left(\Box_{\mathbf{a}}\right)_{\mathcal{T}_d(X)} (P_1, \ldots, P_n) & = \{\varepsilon\} \cup \{a_i w \mid w \in T_{P_i}\} \\
\left(\Box_{\mathbf{a}}\right)_{\mathcal{R}_d(X)} (P_1, \ldots, P_n) & = \{(\varepsilon, W) \mid W \cap \{a_1, \ldots, a_n\} = \emptyset\} \cup \\
 & \qquad \{(a_i w, W) \mid (w, W) \in F_{P_i}\}
\end{array}
$$

The finitary X-processes are those with a finite set of traces and X-traces; they form the carrier of a CSP$(|, \Omega)$-algebra $\mathcal{F}_{df}(X)$.

We now show that $\mathcal{F}_{df}(X)$ is the free CSP$(|, \Omega)$-algebra over X. As is well known, the free algebra of a theory Th over a set X is the same as the initial algebra of the theory Th$^+$ obtained by extending Th with constants $\underline{x}$ for each $x \in X$ but without changing the axioms. The unit map $\eta : X \rightarrow T_{\mathrm{Th}}(X)$ sends $x \in X$ to the denotation of $\underline{x}$ in the initial algebra. We therefore show that $\mathcal{F}_{df}(X)$, extended to a CSP$(|, \Omega)^+$-algebra by taking

$$[\![\underline{x}]\!] = (\{x\}, \emptyset) \qquad (\text{for } x \in X)$$

is the initial CSP$(|, \Omega)^+$-algebra. We begin by looking at definability.

Lemma 5. *The finitary X-processes are those definable by closed* CSP$(|, \Omega)^+$ *terms.*

Proof. The proof goes just as the one for Lemma 4, using that Lemma 3 applies just as well to finitary X-processes, but this time we have

$$P = \bigsqcap_i \bigsqcup_{a \in V_i} a \to P_a \sqcap \left(\Omega \sqcup \bigsqcup_{a \in T_P} a \to P_a\right) \sqcap \bigsqcap_{x \in T_P} \underline{x} \qquad \square$$

Next, we say that a closed CSP$(|, \Omega)^+$-term t is in *normal form* if it is has one of the following two forms:

$$\bigsqcap_{L \in \mathcal{L}} \bigsqcup_{a \in L} at_a \sqcap \bigsqcap_{x \in J} \underline{x} \quad \text{or} \quad \left(\Omega \sqcup \bigsqcup_{a \in K} at_a\right) \sqcap \bigsqcap_{x \in J} \underline{x}$$

where, as appropriate, $\mathcal{L}$ is a finite non-empty saturated collection of finite sets of actions, $J \subseteq_{\text{fin}} X$, $K \subseteq_{\text{fin}} A$, and each term t_a is in normal form.

Lemma 6. *Two normal forms are identical if they have the same denotation in* $\mathcal{F}_{df}(X)$.

Proof. Consider two normal forms with the same denotation in $\mathcal{F}_{df}(X)$, say (T, F). As $(\varepsilon, \emptyset) \in F$ iff F is the denotation of a normal form of the first form (rather than the second), both normal forms must be of the same form. Thus, there are two cases to consider, the first of which concerns two forms:

$$\bigsqcap_{L \in \mathcal{L}} \bigsqcup_{a \in L} at_a \sqcap \bigsqcap_{x \in J} \underline{x} \qquad \bigsqcap_{L' \in \mathcal{L}'} \bigsqcup_{a' \in L'} a't'_{a'} \sqcap \bigsqcap_{x \in J'} \underline{x}$$

We argue by induction on the sum of the sizes of the two normal forms. We evidently have that $J = J'$. Next, if $a \in \bigcup \mathcal{L}$ then $a \in T$ and so $a \in \bigcup \mathcal{L}'$; we therefore have that $\bigcup \mathcal{L} \subseteq \bigcup \mathcal{L}'$. Now, if $L \in \mathcal{L}$, then $(\varepsilon, (\bigcup \mathcal{L}')\backslash L) \in F$; so for some $L' \in \mathcal{L}$ we have $L' \cap ((\bigcup \mathcal{L}')\backslash L) = \emptyset$, and so $L' \subseteq L$. As $\mathcal{L}'$ is saturated, it follows by the previous remark that $L \in \mathcal{L}'$. So we have the inclusion $\mathcal{L} \subseteq \mathcal{L}'$ and then, arguing symmetrically, equality.

Finally, the denotations of t_a and t'_a, for $a \in \bigcup \mathcal{L} = \bigcup \mathcal{L}'$ are the same, as they are determined by T and F, being $\{w \mid aw \in T\}$ and $\{(w, W) \mid (aw, W) \in F\}$, and the argument concludes, using the inductive hypothesis.

The other case concerns normal forms:

$$\left(\Omega \sqcup \bigsqcup_{a \in K} at_a\right) \sqcap \bigsqcap_{x \in J} \underline{x} \qquad \left(\Omega \sqcup \bigsqcup_{a' \in K'} a't'_a\right) \sqcap \bigsqcap_{x \in J'} \underline{x}$$

Much as before we find $J = J'$, $K = K'$, and $t_a = t_a$ for $a \in K$. $\square$

Lemma 7. CSP$(|, \Omega)^+$ *is ground complete with respect to* $\mathcal{F}_{df}(X)$.

Proof. As before, a straightforward induction shows that every term has a normal form, and then completeness follows by Lemma 6. □

Theorem 7. *The algebra* $\mathcal{F}_{df}(X)$ *is the free* CSP$(|, \Omega)$*-algebra over* X.

Proof. It follows from Lemmas 5 and 7 that $\mathcal{F}_{df}(X)^+$ is the initial CSP$(|, \Omega)^+$-algebra. □

As with any finitary equational theory, CSP$(|, \Omega)$ is equationally complete with respect to $\mathcal{F}_{df}(X)$ when X is infinite. It is not difficult to go a little further and show that this also holds when X is only required to be non-empty, and, even, if A is infinite, when it is empty.

Now that we have an explicit representation of the free CSP$(|, \Omega)$-monad in terms of X-processes, we indicate how to use it to give the semantics of the computational λ-calculus. First we need the structure of the monad. As we know from the above, the unit $\eta_X : X \to T_{\mathrm{CSP}(|,\Omega)}(X)$ is the map $x \mapsto (\{x\}, \emptyset)$. Next, we need the homomorphic extension $g^\dagger : \mathcal{F}_{df}(X) \to \mathcal{F}_{df}(Y)$ of a given map $g : X \to \mathcal{F}_{df}(Y)$, i.e., the unique such homomorphism making the following diagram commute:

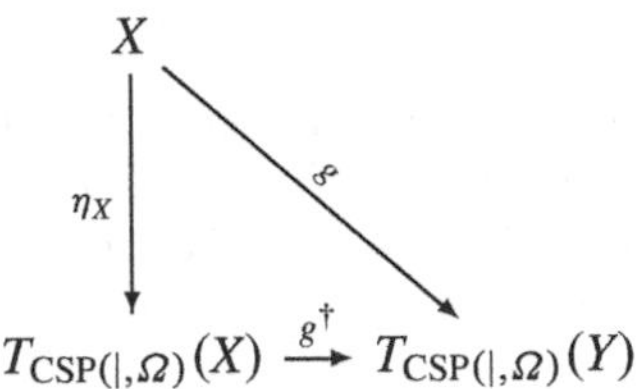

This is given by:

$$\left(g^\dagger(P)\right)_{\mathcal{T}} = \{v \mid v \in T_P \cap A^*\} \cup \{vw \mid vx \in T_P,\ w \in g(x)_{\mathcal{T}}\}$$
$$\left(g^\dagger(P)\right)_{\mathcal{R}} = \{(v, V) \in F_P\} \cup \{(vw, W) \mid vx \in T_P,\ (w, W) \in g(x)_{\mathcal{R}}\}$$

As regards the constructors and deconstructors, we have already given explicit representations of them as functions over (finitary) X-processes. We have also already given homomorphic treatments of the unary deconstructors. We finally give treatments of the binary deconstructors as unique solutions to equations, along similar lines to their treatment in the case of $\mathcal{F}_{df}$. Observe that:

$$(\square_{\mathbf{a}})_X(P_1, \ldots, P_n) = a_1P_1 \,\square_X\, a_2P_2 \,\square_X \ldots \square_X\, a_nP_n$$
$$\left(\square_{\mathbf{a}}^{\Omega}\right)_X(P_1, \ldots, P_n) = \Omega \,\square_X\, a_1P_1 \,\square_X\, a_2P_2 \,\square_X \ldots \square_X\, a_nP_n$$

Using this, one finds that $\Box_X$, $\Box_X^{\Omega,a_1\ldots a_n}$ and $\Box_X^{a_1\ldots a_n}$, the latter defined as in Eq. 15.9 are the unique functions which satisfy the evident analogues of Eq. 15.8 together with, making another use of the form of external choice made available by Ω:

$$\eta(x) \Box P = \eta(x) \sqcap_X (\Omega \Box P)$$

and

$$(P_1, \ldots, P_n) \Box^{a_1\ldots a_n} \eta(x) = \left(\Box_{\mathbf{a}}^{\Omega}\right)_X (P_1, \ldots, P_n) \sqcap_X \eta(x)$$

$$(P_1, \ldots, P_n) \Box^{\Omega,a_1\ldots a_n} \eta(x) = \left(\Box_{\mathbf{a}}^{\Omega}\right)_X (P_1, \ldots, P_n) \sqcap_X \eta(x)$$

As regards concurrency, we define

$$||_{X,Y}: T_{\mathrm{CSP}(|,\Omega)}(X) \times T_{\mathrm{CSP}(|,\Omega)}(Y) \rightarrow T_{\mathrm{CSP}(|,\Omega)}(X \times Y)$$

together with functions

$$||_{X,Y}^{a_1\ldots a_n}: T_{\mathrm{CSP}(|,\Omega)}(X)^n \times T_{\mathrm{CSP}(|,\Omega)}(Y) \rightarrow T_{\mathrm{CSP}(|,\Omega)}(X \times Y)$$

$$||_{X,Y}^{\Omega,a_1\ldots a_n}: T_{\mathrm{CSP}(|,\Omega)}(X)^n \times T_{\mathrm{CSP}(|,\Omega)}(Y) \rightarrow T_{\mathrm{CSP}(|,\Omega)}(X \times Y)$$

$$||_{X,Y}^{x}: T_{\mathrm{CSP}(|,\Omega)}(Y) \rightarrow T_{\mathrm{CSP}(|,\Omega)}(X \times Y)$$

where $a_i \in A$ are all different, and $x \in X$, by the analogues of Eq. 15.10 above, together with:

$$\begin{array}{ll}
\eta(x) \mid\mid Q & = ||^x (Q) \\
\\
||^x (P \sqcap Q) & = ||^x (P) \sqcap ||^x (Q) \\
||^x (\Box_{i=1}^n a_i P_i) & = \Omega \\
||^x (\Omega \Box \Box_{i=1}^n a_i P_i) & = \Omega \\
||^x (\eta(y)) & = \eta((x, y))
\end{array}$$

$$\begin{array}{l}
(P_1, \ldots, P_n) \mid\mid^{a_1\ldots a_n} \eta(x) \quad = \Omega \\
(P_1, \ldots, P_n) \mid\mid^{\Omega,a_1\ldots a_n} \eta(x) = \Omega
\end{array}$$

Much as before, the equations have a unique solution, with the $||$ component being $||_{X,Y}$.

As regards interleaving, we define

$$|||_{X,Y}^{l}, |||_{X,Y}^{r}: T_{\mathrm{CSP}(|,\Omega)}(X) \times T_{\mathrm{CSP}(|,\Omega)}(Y) \rightarrow T_{\mathrm{CSP}(|,\Omega)}(X \times Y)$$

by:

$$P \;|||^{l}_{\mathcal{T}_{df}(X,Y)}\; Q = \{\varepsilon\} \cup \{w \mid u \in T_P \cap A^*,\ v \in T_Q \cap A^*,\ w \in u|^{l}v\} \cup \{w(x,y) \mid ux \in T_P,\ vy \in T_Q,\ w \in u \,|^{l}\, v \vee (u = v = w = \varepsilon)\}$$

$$P \;|||^{l}_{\mathcal{R}_{df}(X,Y)}\; Q = \{(\varepsilon, W) \mid (\varepsilon, W) \in F_P\} \cup \{(w, W) \mid (u, W) \in F_P,\ (v, W) \in F_Q,\ w \in u \,|^{l}\, v\}$$

$$P \;|||^{r}_{X,Y}\; Q = Q \;|||^{l}_{Y,X}\; P$$

One has that:

$$P \;|||_{X,Y}\; Q = P \;|||^{l}_{X,Y}\; Q \;\Box\; P \;|||^{r}_{X,Y}\; Q$$

and that $|||^{l}_{X,Y}, |||^{r}_{X,Y}$ are components of the unique solutions to the analogues of Eq. 15.11 above, together with:

$$\eta(x) \;|||^{l}\; Q = |||^{l,x}\,(Q)$$

$$\begin{aligned}
|||^{l,x}\,(P \sqcap Q) &= |||^{l,x}\,(P) \sqcap |||^{l,x}\,(Q)\\
|||^{l,x}\,(\textstyle\Box_{i=1}^{n} a_i P_i) &= \Omega\\
|||^{l,x}\,(\Omega \,\Box\, \textstyle\Box_{i=1}^{n} a_i P_i) &= \Omega\\
|||^{l,x}\,(\eta(y)) &= \eta(x,y)
\end{aligned}$$

and corresponding equations for $|||^{r}$ and $|||^{r,y}$.

It would be interesting to check more completely which of the usual laws, as found in, e.g., [9, 10, 13], the CSP operators at the level of free CSP($|, \Omega$)-algebras obey. Note that some adjustments need to be made due to varying types. For example, $||$ is commutative, which here means that the following equation holds:

$$T_{\mathrm{CSP}(|,\Omega)}(\gamma_{X,Y})(P \;||_{X,Y}\; Q) = Q \;||_{Y,X}\; P$$

where $\gamma : X \times Y \to Y \times X$ is the commutativity map $(x, y) \mapsto (y, x)$.

15.7.1 Termination

As remarked in the introduction, termination and sequencing are available in a standard way for terms of type `unit`. Syntactically, we regard `skip` as an abbreviation for $*$ and M; N as one for $(\lambda x : \texttt{unit}.N)(M)$ where x does not occur free in N; semantically, we have a corresponding element of, and binary operator over, the free CSP($|, \Omega$)-algebra on the one-point set.

Let us use these ideas to treat CSP extended with termination and sequencing. We work with the finitary $\{\checkmark\}$-processes representation of $T_{\mathrm{CSP}(|,\Omega)}(\{\checkmark\})$. Then, following the above prescription, termination and sequencing are given by:

$$\texttt{SKIP} = \{\checkmark\} \qquad\qquad P;\ Q = (x \in \{\checkmark\} \mapsto Q)^{\dagger}(P)$$

For general reasons, termination and sequencing, so-defined, form a monoid and sequencing commutes with all constructors in its first argument. For example, we have that:

$$\mathop{\Box}_{i=1}^{n} a_i(P_i;\ Q) = \left(\mathop{\Box}_{i=1}^{n} a_i P_i\right);\ Q$$

Composition further commutes with $\sqcap$ in its second argument.

The deconstructors are defined as above except that in the case of the concurrency operators one has to adjust $||_{\{\checkmark\},\{\checkmark\}}$ and $|||_{\{\checkmark\},\{\checkmark\}}$ so that they remain within the world of the $\{\checkmark\}$-processes; this can be done by postcomposing them with the evident bijection between $\{\checkmark\}\times\{\checkmark\}$-processes and $\{\checkmark\}$-processes, and all this restricts to the finitary processes. Alternatively one can directly consider these adjusted operators as deconstructors over the (finitary) $\{\checkmark\}$-processes.

The $\{\checkmark\}$-processes are essentially the elements of the stable failures model of [29]. More precisely, one can define a bijection from Roscoe's model to our $\{\checkmark\}$-processes by setting $\theta(T, F) = (T, F')$ where

$$F' = \{(w, W) \in A^* \times \mathcal{P}(A) \mid (w, W \cup \{\checkmark\}) \in F\}$$

The inverse of θ sends F' to the set:

$$\{(w, W), (w, W \cup \{\checkmark\}) \mid (w, W) \in F'\} \cup$$
$$\{(w, W) \mid w\checkmark \in T \wedge W \subseteq A\} \cup \{(w\checkmark, W) \mid w\checkmark \in T \wedge W \in A \cup \{\checkmark\}\}$$

and is a homomorphism between all our operators, whether constructors, deconstructors, termination, or sequencing (suitably defined), and the corresponding ones defined for Roscoe's model.

15.8 Discussion

We have shown the possibility of a principled combination of CSP and functional programming from the viewpoint of the algebraic theory of effects. The main missing ingredient is an algebraic treatment of binary deconstructors, although we were able to partially circumvent that by giving explicit definitions of them. Also missing are a logic for proving properties of these deconstructors, an operational semantics, and a treatment that includes recursion.

As regards a logic, it may prove possible to adapt the logical ideas of [24, 25] to handle binary deconstructors; the main proof principle would then be that of *computation induction*, that if a proposition holds for all "values" (i.e., elements of a given set X) and if it holds for the applications of each constructor to any given "computations" (i.e., elements of $T(X)$) for which it is assumed to hold, then it holds for all computations. We do not anticipate any difficulty in giving an operational semantics for the above combination of the computational λ-calculus and CSP and proving an adequacy theorem.

To treat recursion algebraically, one passes from equational theories to inequational theories Th (inequations have the form $t \leq u$, for terms t, u in a given signature Σ); inequational theories can include equations, regarding an equation as two evident inequations. There is a natural inequational logic for deducing consequences of the axioms: one simply drops symmetry from the logic for equations [7]. Then Σ-algebras and Th-algebras are taken in the category of ω-cpos and continuous functions, a free algebra monad always exists, just as in the case of sets, and the logic is complete for the class of such algebras. One includes a divergence constant Ω in the signature and the axiom

$$\Omega \leq x$$

so that Th-algebras always have a least element. Recursive definitions are then modelled by least fixed-points in the usual way. See [14,21] for some further explanations.

The three classical powerdomains: convex (aka Plotkin), lower (aka Hoare) and upper (aka Smyth) provide a useful illustration of these ideas [12, 14]. One takes as signature a binary operation symbol $\sqcap$, to retain notational consistency with the present paper (a more neutral symbol, such as $\cup$, is normally used instead), and the constant Ω; one takes the theory to be that $\sqcap$ is a semilattice (meaning, as before, that associativity, commutativity and idempotence hold) and that, as given above, Ω is the least element with respect to the ordering $\leq$. This gives an algebraic account of the convex powerdomain.

If one adds that Ω is the zero of the semilattice (which is equivalent, in the present context, to the inequation $x \leq x \sqcap y$) one obtains instead an algebraic account of the lower powerdomain. One then further has the notationally counterintuitive facts that $x \leq y$ is equivalent to $y \sqsubseteq x$, with $\sqsubseteq$ defined as in Section 15.3, and that $x \sqcap y$ is the supremum of x and y with respect to $\leq$; in models, $\leq$ typically corresponds to subset. It would be more natural in this case to use the dual order to $\sqsubseteq$ and to write $\sqcup$ instead of $\sqcap$, when we would be dealing with a join-semilattice with a least element whose order coincides with $\leq$.

If one adds instead that $x \sqcap y \leq x$, one obtains an algebraic account of the upper powerdomain. One now has that $x \leq y$ is equivalent in this context to $x \sqsubseteq y$, that $x \sqcap y$ is the greatest lower bound of x and y, and that $x \sqcap \Omega = \Omega$ (but this latter fact is not equivalent in inequational logic to $x \sqcap y \leq x$); in models, $\leq$ typically corresponds to superset. The notations $\sqcap$ and $\sqsubseteq$ are therefore more intuitive in the upper case, and there one has a meet-semilattice with a least element whose order coincides with $\leq$.

It will be clear from these considerations that the stable failures model fits into the pattern of the lower powerdomain and that the failures/divergences model fits into the pattern of the upper powerdomain. In the case of the stable failures model it is natural, in the light of the above considerations, to take Th to be CSP($|, \Omega$)

together with the axiom $\Omega \le x$. The X-processes with countably many traces presumably form the free algebra over X, considered as a discrete ω-cpo; one should also characterise more general cases than discrete ω-cpos.

One should also investigate whether a fragment of the failures/divergences model forms the initial model of an appropriate theory, and look at the free models of such a theory. The theory might well be found by analogy with our work on the stable failures model, substituting (15.12) for (15.13) and, perhaps, using the mixed-choice constructor, defined below, to overcome any difficulties with the deconstructors. One would expect the initial model to contain only finitely-generable processes, meaning those which, at any trace, either branch finitely or diverge (and see the discussion in [29]).

Our initial division of our selection of CSP operators into constructors and deconstructors was natural, although it turned out that a somewhat different division, with "restricted" constructors, resulted in what seemed to be a better analysis (we were not able to rule out the possibility that there are alternative, indirect, definitions of the deconstructors with the original choice of constructors). One of these restricted constructors was a deterministic choice operator making use of the divergence constant Ω. There should surely, however, also be a development without divergence that allows the interpretation of the combination of CSP and functional programming.

We were, however, not able to do this using CSP(|): the free algebra does not seem to support a suitable definition of concealment, whether defined directly or via a homomorphism. For example a straightforward extension of the homomorphic treatment of concealment, in the case of the initial algebra (cf. Section 15.5) would give

$$(a.\underline{x} \,\Box\, b.\mathtt{Stop})\backslash a = \underline{x} \sqcap (\underline{x} \,\Box\, b.\mathtt{Stop})$$

However, our approach requires the right-hand side to be equivalent to a term built from constructors only, but no natural candidates came forward – all choices that came to mind lead to unwanted identifications.

We conjecture that, taking instead, as constructor, a *mixed-choice* operator of the form:

$$\Box_{i} \alpha_i.x_i$$

where each α_i is either an action or τ, would lead to a satisfactory theory. This new operator is given by the equation:

$$\Box_{i} \alpha_i.x_i = \bigsqcap_{\alpha_i = \tau} x_i \sqcap \left(\Box_{\alpha_i = \tau} x_i \,\Box\, \Box_{\alpha_i \neq \tau} \alpha_i.x_i \right)$$

and there is a homomorphic relationship with concealment:

$$\left(\Box_{i} \alpha_i.x_i \right) \Big\backslash a = \Box_{i} (\alpha_i \backslash a).(x_i \backslash a)$$

(with the evident understanding of $\alpha_i \backslash a$). Note that in the stable failures model we have the equation:

$$\Box_i \alpha_i.x_i = \bigsqcap_{\alpha_i=\tau} x_i \sqcap \left(\Omega \,\Box \Box_{\alpha_i \neq \tau} \alpha_i.x_i \right)$$

which is presumably why the deterministic choice operator available in the presence of Ω played so central a rôle there.

In a different direction, one might also ask whether there is some problem if we alternatively take an extended set of operators as constructors. For example, why not add relabelling with its equations to the axioms? As the axioms inductively determine relabelling on the finitary refusal sets model, that would still be the initial algebra, and the same holds if we add any of the other operators we have taken as deconstructors.

However, the X-refusal sets would not longer be the free algebra, as there would be extra elements, such as $f(x)$ for $x \in X$, where f is a relabelling function. We would also get some undesired equations holding between terms of the computational λ-calculus. For any n-ary constructor op and evaluation context $E[-]$, one has in the monadic semantics:

$$E[\text{op}(M_1, \ldots, M_n)] = \text{op}(E[M_1], \ldots, E[M_n])$$

So one would have $E[f(M)] = f(E[M])$ if one took relabelling as a constructor, and, as another example, one would have $E[M \parallel N] = E[M] \parallel E[N]$ if one took the concurrency operator as a constructor.

It will be clear to the reader that, in principle, one can investigate other process calculi and their combination with functional programming in a similar way. For example, for Milner's CCS [17] one could take action prefix (with names, conames and τ) together with `NIL` and the sum operator as constructors, and as axioms that we have a semilattice with a zero, for strong bisimulation, together with the usual τ-laws, if we additionally wish to consider weak bisimulation. The deconstructors would be renaming, hiding, and parallel, and all should have suitable polymorphic versions in the functional programming context. Other process calculi such as the π-calculus [30, 33], or even the stochastic π-calculus [16, 26], might be dealt with similarly. In much the same way, one could combine parallelism with a global store with functional programming, following the algebraic account of the resumptions monad [1, 14] where the constructors are the two standard ones for global store [22], a nondeterministic choice operation, and a unary "suspension" operation.

A well-known feature of the monadic approach [14] is that it is often possible to combine different effects in a modular way. For example, the global side-effects monad is $(S \times -)^S$ where S is a suitable set of states. A common combination of it with another monad T is the monad $T(S \times -)^S$. So, taking $T = T_{\mathrm{CSP}(\|)}$, for example, we get a combination of CSP with global side-effects.

As another example, given a monoid M, one has the M-action monad $M \times -$ which supports a unary M-action effect constructor $m.-$, parameterised by elements m of the monoid. One might use this monad to model the passage of time, taking M to be, for example, the monoid of the natural numbers $\mathbb{N}$ under addition. A suitable combination of this monad with ones for CSP may yield helpful analyses of timed CSP [20, 27], with *Wait* n; $-$ given by the $\mathbb{N}$-action effect constructor. We therefore have a very rich space of possible combinations of process calculi, functional programming and other effects, and we hope that some of these prove useful.

Finally, we note that there is no general account of how the equations used in the algebraic theory of effects arise. In such cases as global state, nondeterminism or probability, there are natural axioms and monads already available, and it is encouraging that the two are equivalent [14, 22]. One could investigate using operational methods and behavioural equivalences to determine the equations, and it would be interesting to do so. Another approach is the use of "test algebras" [15, 32]. In the case of process calculi one naturally uses operational methods; however, the resulting axioms may not be very modular, or very natural mathematically, and, all in all, in this respect the situation is not satisfactory.

References

1. Abadi, M., Plotkin, G.D.: A model of cooperative threads. In: Shao, Z., Pierce, B.C. (eds.), Proc. POPL 2009. ACM Press, pp. 29–40 (2009)
2. Abramsky, S., Gabbay, D.M., Maibaum, T.S.E. (eds.), Handbook of Logic in Computer Science (Vol. 1), Background: Mathematical Structures, Oxford University Press (1995)
3. Benton, N., Hughes, J., Moggi, E.: Monads and effects. Proc. APPSEM 2000, LNCS **2395**, pp. 42–122, Springer (2002)
4. Bergstra, J.A., Klop, J.W.: Algebra of communicating processes with abstraction. Theor. Comput. Sci. **37**, pp. 77–121 (1985)
5. Bergstra, J.A., Klop, J.W.: Algebra of communicating processes. In: de Bakker, J.W., Hazewinkel, M., Lenstra, J.K. (eds.), Proc. of the CWI Symp. Math. and Comp. Sci. pp. 89–138, North-Holland (1986)
6. Bergstra, J.A., Klop, J.W., Olderog, E.-R.: Failures without chaos: a new process semantics for fair abstraction. In: Wirsing, M. (ed.), Proc. of the 3rd IFIP WG 2.2 working conference on Formal Description of Programming Concepts. pp. 77–103, North-Holland (1987)
7. Bloom, S.L.: Varieties of ordered algebras. J. Comput. Syst. Sci., **13**(2):200–212 (1976)
8. Borceux, F.: Handbook of Categorical Algebra 2, Encyclopedia of Mathematics and Its Applications **51**. Cambridge University Press (1994)
9. Brookes, S.D., Hoare, C.A.R., Roscoe, A.W.: A theory of communicating sequential processes. J. ACM **31**(3):560–599 (1984)
10. De Nicola, R.: Two complete axiom systems for a theory of communicating sequential processes. Inform. Control **64**, pp. 136–172 (1985)
11. Ebrahimi-Fard, K., Guo, L.: Rota-Baxter algebras and dendriform algebras. J. Pure Appl. Algebra **212**(2):320–33 (2008)
12. Gierz, G., Hofmann, K.H., Keimel, K., Lawson, J.D., Mislove, M., Scott, D.S.: Continuous Lattices and Domains, Encyclopedia of Mathematics and its Applications **93**. Cambridge University Press (2003)
13. Hoare, C.A.R.: Communicating Sequential Processes. Prentice-Hall (1985)

14. Hyland, J.M.E., Plotkin, G.D., Power, A.J.: Combining effects: sum and tensor. In: Artemov, S., Mislove, M. (eds.), Clifford Lectures and the Mathematical Foundations of Programming Semantics. Theor. Comput. Sci. **357**(1–3):70–99 (2006)
15. Keimel, K., Plotkin, G.D.: Predicate transformers for extended probability and non-determinism. Math. Struct. Comput. Sci. **19**(3):501–539. Cambridge University Press (2009)
16. Klin, B., Sassone, V.: Structural operational semantics for stochastic process calculi. In: Amadio, R.M. (ed.), Proc. 11th. FoSSaCS. LNCS **4962**, pp. 428–442, Springer (2008)
17. Milner, A.J.R.G.: A Calculus of Communicating Systems. Springer (1980)
18. Moggi, E.: Computational lambda-calculus and monads. Proc. 3rd. LICS, pp. 14–23, IEEE Press (1989)
19. Moggi, E.: Notions of computation and monads. Inf. Comp. **93**(1):55–92 (1991)
20. Ouaknine, J., Schneider, S.: Timed CSP: a retrospective, Proceedings of the Workshop "Essays on Algebraic Process Calculi" (APC 25), Electr. Notes Theor. Comput. Sci., **162**, pp. 273–276 (2006)
21. Plotkin, G.D.: Some varieties of equational logic. Essays Dedicated to Joseph A. Goguen. In: Futatsugi, K., Jouannaud, J.-P., Meseguer, J. (eds.), LNCS **4060**, pp. 150–156, Springer (2006)
22. Plotkin, G.D., Power, A.J.: Notions of computation determine monads, Proc. 5th. FoSSaCS. LNCS **2303**, pp. 342–356, Springer (2002)
23. Plotkin, G.D., Power, A.J.: Computational effects and operations: an overview. In: Escardó, M., Jung, A. (eds.), Proc. Workshop on Domains VI. Electr. Notes Theor. Comput. Sci. **73**, pp. 149–163, Elsevier (2004)
24. Plotkin, G.D., Pretnar, M.: A logic for algebraic effects. Proc. 23rd. LICS, pp. 118–129, IEEE Press (2008)
25. Plotkin, G.D., Pretnar, M.: Handlers of algebraic effects. Proc. 18th. ESOP, pp. 80–94 (2009)
26. Priami, C.: Stochastic pi-calculus. Comput. J. **38** (7):578–589 (1995)
27. Reed, G.M., Roscoe, A.W.: The timed failures-stability model for CSP. Theor. Comput. Sci. **211**(1–2):85–127 (1999)
28. Roscoe, A.W.: Model-checking CSP. In: Roscoe, A.W. (ed.), A Classical Mind: Essays in Honour of Hoare, C.A.R., pp. 353–337, Prentice-Hall (1994)
29. Roscoe, A.W.: The Theory and Practice of Concurrency. Prentice Hall (1998)
30. Sangiorgi, D., Walker, D.: The π-Calculus: A Theory of Mobile Processes. Cambridge University Press (2003)
31. Scattergood, B.: The Semantics and Implementation of Machine-Readable CSP. D.Phil Thesis, Oxford University (1998)
32. Schröder, M., Simpson, A.: Probabilistic observations and valuations (extended abstract). Electr. Notes Theor. Comput. Sci. **155**, pp. 605–615 (2006)
33. Stark, I.: Free-algebra models for the pi-calculus. Theor. Comput. Sci. **390**(2–3):248–270 (2008)

Appendix: The Computational λ-Calculus

In this appendix, we sketch (a slight variant of) the syntax and semantics of Moggi's computational λ-calculus, or λ_c-calculus [18, 19]. It has types given by:

$$\sigma ::= \mathtt{b} \mid \mathtt{unit} \mid \sigma \times \sigma \mid \mathtt{empty} \mid \sigma \rightarrow \sigma$$

where $\mathtt{b}$ ranges over a given set of base types, e.g., $\mathtt{nat}$; the type construction $T\sigma$ may be defined to be $\mathtt{unit} \rightarrow \sigma$. The terms of the λ_c-calculus are given by:

$$M ::= x \mid g(M) \mid * \mid \mathtt{in}\,M \mid (M,M) \mid \mathtt{fst}\,M \mid \mathtt{snd}\,M \mid \lambda x{:}\sigma.M \mid MM$$

where g ranges over given unary function symbols of given types $\sigma \rightarrow \tau$, such as $0 : \mathtt{unit} \rightarrow \mathtt{nat}$ or $\mathtt{succ} : \mathtt{nat} \rightarrow \mathtt{nat}$, if we want the natural numbers, or $\mathrm{op} : T(\sigma) \times \ldots \times T(\sigma) \rightarrow T(\sigma)$ for some operation symbol from a theory for which T is the free algebra monad. There are standard notions of free and bound variables and of closed terms and substitution; there are also standard typing rules for judgements $\Gamma \vdash M : \sigma$, that the term M has type σ in the context Γ (contexts have the form $\Gamma = x_1 : \sigma_1, \ldots, x_n : \sigma_n$), including:

$$\frac{\Gamma \vdash M : \mathtt{empty}}{\Gamma \vdash \mathtt{in}\, M : \sigma}$$

A λ_c-model (on the category of sets – Moggi worked more generally) consists of a monad T, together with enough information to interpret basic types and the given function symbols. So there is a given set $[\![b]\!]$ to interpret each basic type b, and then every type σ receives an interpretation as a set $[\![\sigma]\!]$; for example $[\![\mathtt{empty}]\!] = \emptyset$. There is also given a map $[\![\sigma]\!] \rightarrow T([\![\tau]\!])$ to interpret every given unary function symbol $g : \sigma \rightarrow \tau$. A term $\Gamma \vdash M : \sigma$ of type σ in context Γ is modelled by a map $[\![M]\!] : [\![\Gamma]\!] \rightarrow T[\![\sigma]\!]$ (where $[\![x_1 : \sigma_1, \ldots, x_n : \sigma_n]\!] = [\![\sigma_1]\!] \times \ldots \times [\![\sigma_n]\!]$). For example, if $\Gamma \vdash \mathtt{in}\, M : \sigma$ then $[\![\mathtt{in}\, M]\!] = 0_{[\![\sigma]\!]} \circ [\![M]\!]$ (where, for any set X, 0_X is the unique map from $\emptyset$ to X).

We define values and evaluation contexts. Values can be thought of as (syntax for) completed computations, and are defined by:

$$V ::= x \mid * \mid (V, V) \mid \mathtt{in}\, V \mid \lambda x{:}\sigma.M$$

together with clauses such as:

$$V ::= 0 \mid \mathtt{succ}\,(V)$$

depending on the choice of basic types and given function symbols. We may then define evaluation contexts by:

$$E ::= [-] \mid \mathtt{in}\, E \mid (E, M) \mid (V, E) \mid EM \mid VE \mid \mathtt{fst}\,(E) \mid \mathtt{snd}\,(E)$$

together with clauses such as:

$$E ::= \mathtt{succ}\,(E)$$

depending on the choice of basic types and given function symbols. We write $E[M]$ for the term obtained by replacing the 'hole' $[-]$ in an evaluation term E by a term M. The computational thought behind evaluation contexts is that in a program of the form $E[M]$, the first computational step arises within M.

Chapter 16
CSP is Expressive Enough for π

A.W. Roscoe

Abstract Recent results show that Hoare's CSP, augmented by one additional operator, can express every operator whose operational semantics are expressible in a new notation and are therefore "CSP-like." In this paper we show that π-calculus fits into this framework and therefore has CSP semantics. Rather than relying on the machinery of the earlier result we develop a much simpler version from scratch that avoids the extra operator and is sufficient for π-calculus: a much generalised *relabelling* operator that is expressed in terms of the others. We present a number of different options for the semantics of fresh names, showing how they give semantics that are largely congruent to each other. Finally, we begin the investigation of how these new semantics might be analysed and exploited.

16.1 Introduction

When I contributed [15] to the volume celebrating Tony's 60th birthday, CSP was just half as old as it is now. I wrote then how remarkable it was that it should have stood the test of so many challenges unimagined by Tony when he created it, and of how frustrating it was to work academically on something that was so "right first time," since one was denied the usual joys of refining and changing it. I have continued to be surprised by its ability to capture new concepts in modelling concurrency and interaction. The present paper recalls recent work quantifying this expressive power and shows that CSP can both represent the π-calculus and provide the vehicle for a wide range of new semantics for that notation.

I can report, however, that my previous frustration has been reduced, since I have finally found an operator to be missing from Tony's original CSP: this will be described below.

A.W. Roscoe (✉)
Oxford University Computing Laboratory, UK
e-mail: Bill.Roscoe@comlab.ox.ac.uk

C.B. Jones et al. (eds.), *Reflections on the Work of C.A.R. Hoare*,
DOI 10.1007/978-1-84882-912-1_16,

When I first described my new expressibility results to Tony, part of his response was *"Which operators of CCS satisfy your definition? Which ones don't? What about π-calculus?"* This paper answers these questions.

While other languages for concurrent systems are often defined in terms of their operational semantics, the CSP approach [6, 16] has always been to regard behavioural models such as *traces* $\mathcal{T}$, *stable failures* $\mathcal{F}$, *failures-divergences* $\mathcal{N}$ and *infinite traces-failures-divergences* $\mathcal{U}$ as equally important means of expression. Thus any operator must make sense over these *behavioural* models in which details of individual linear runs of the processes are recorded by an observer who cannot, of course, see the internal action τ.

Nevertheless CSP has a well-established operational semantics, and congruence with that is perhaps the main criterion for the acceptability of any new model that is proposed.

Operational semantic definitions of languages have the advantage that they are direct, understandable, and of themselves carry no particular obligation to prove congruence results such as those alluded to above. On the other hand definitions in abstract models, intended to capture the extensional meaning of a program in some sense, have the advantage of "cleanliness" and allow us to reason about programs in the more abstract models. The most immediate benefit of CSP models in this respect is that they bring a theory of refinement, which in turn gives refinement checking (with low complexity at the implementation end, as in FDR) as a natural vehicle for specification and verification.

The author has recently [20] defined what it means for an operational semantics to be *CSP-like*, in the sense that it does not require any basic powers beyond what the semantics of the various CSP operators already have. In this paper we will show that the π-calculus (the version presented in [23]) is CSP-like.

The main result of [20] is that every CSP-like operator can be simulated up to strong bisimulation in CSP extended by one more operator. The proof there constructs a very general but complex "machine" for simulating any such operator. In the present paper we will give significantly more straightforward CSP representations (not needing the additional operator) of the constructs we need to give π-calculus a semantics.

In the next section we recall the definitions of a CSP-like operational semantics and the new operator Θ_A needed to complete the general simulation result, as well as summarising the techniques used in that proof. In the following section we will, since it is needed for π-calculus, show how the usual CSP renaming operator can be extended into a much generalised *relabelling* operator that can nevertheless be expressed in terms of standard CSP operators.

There are three significant issues that arise when attempting to give a CSP semantics to π-calculus. The first is the π-calculus containing choices such as $\tau.P + x(y) \cdot Q$ that are resolved by τ; while no CSP operator ever reacts to one of its arguments performing the invisible τ. The second is that the CCS parallel operator used in π-calculus is very different to that in CSP. The third is the requirement that names in π-calculus are generated freshly, without collisions. Since the first two of these arise in CCS, we examine the problem of translating CCS into CSP in Section 16.4. The third problem is handled using generalised relabelling in Section 16.5, where the translation into CSP of π-calculus is presented.

There seems to be quite a bit of choice in how one handles freshness in the CSP model, and we present a number of options that give (at least for the best-known CSP models) the same equivalence between π-calculus terms.

Throughout this paper, when talking primarily about CSP, Σ_0 will denote the alphabet that our underlying language of processes uses to communicate with each other and with the external environment. We will frequently need to extend this alphabet to allow us to build CSP models of operators not directly contained in CSP. This extended alphabet will be termed Σ. We will later define a corresponding alphabet Σ_π for the embedding of π-calculus into CSP.

Our main references for CSP and π-calculus are respectively [16] and [23]. Our notation is drawn largely from these.

16.2 CSP is Very Expressive

Though originally given semantics in behavioural models such as traces $\mathcal{T}$ and failures-divergences $\mathcal{N}$, CSP has long had a congruent operational semantics [2, 4]. By *congruent* here, we mean that the sets of behaviours obtained by observing the LTS created by a process's operational semantics are the same as those calculated in the corresponding behavioural model by a denotational semantics. The operational semantics of CSP and some congruence proofs can be found in [16].

There is a lengthy discussion of what makes an operationally defined operator *CSP-like* in [20]. The first part of the conclusion is that a CSP-like operator has a two-part *arity* (m, I), where m is the finite number of process arguments that are turned **on** at the start of execution, and I indexes a possibly infinite family of arguments that are initially **off**. (Infinite nondeterministic choice and $?x : A \rightarrow P(x)$ for infinite A both have I infinite and $m = 0$. The first action of either of these constructs selects a single one of these **off** operands to turn on, and the rest are discarded.)

When defining a family of operators $\{OP_\lambda \mid \lambda \in \Lambda\}$, the actions of $OP_\lambda(P_1, \ldots, P_{m(\lambda)}, \mathbf{Q})$ are determined by λ and the initial actions of the **on** arguments P_i : they are all the actions deducible under a set of rules determined by λ. There are two sorts of rule:

- A rule *promoting* a τ action for each **on** argument: these take the form:

$$\frac{P_i \xrightarrow{\tau} P_i'}{OP(P_1, \ldots, P_i, \ldots, P_m, \mathbf{Q}) \xrightarrow{\tau} OP(P_1, \ldots, P_i', \ldots, P_m, \mathbf{Q})}$$

  First suggested for CSP in [13], these are termed *patience rules* by van Glabbeek [25] when giving a set of operational rules that respect weak bisimulation.

- An arbitrary collection of rules based on the visible actions of the P_i. Each such rule of OP_λ is represented as a tuple $(\phi, x, \beta, f, \psi, \chi)$ where
  - ϕ is a partial function from $\{1, \ldots, m(\lambda)\}$ to Σ_0 (the alphabet of the underlying processes). Its meaning is that, in order for this transition to fire, each argument P_j such that $j \in dom(\phi)$ must be able to perform the action $\phi(j)$ and become some P'_j. Note that this imposes no condition if $dom(\phi)$ is empty: this corresponds to an action that the operator can perform without reference to an *on* argument, like the initial a in $a \to P$.
  - x is the action in $\Sigma_0 \cup \{\tau\}$ that $OP_\lambda(\mathbf{P}, \mathbf{Q})$ performs as a consequence of the condition expressed in ϕ being satisfied.
  - β is the index of the operator that forms the result state of this action.
  - f is a total function from $\{1, \ldots, k\}$ for some $k = k(\lambda) \geq 0$ to $I(\lambda)$ that represents, in some chosen order, the indexes of the components of $\mathbf{Q}$ (the **off** arguments), that are started up when the rule fires (i.e. become **on**).
  - $\psi : \{1, \ldots, m(\beta)\} \to \{1, \ldots, m(\lambda) + k(\lambda)\}$ is the (total) function that selects each of the resulting state's **on** arguments. It must include the whole of $\{m(\lambda) + 1, \ldots, m(\lambda) + k(\lambda)\}$ in its range.
  - $\chi : I(\beta) \to I(\lambda)$ is the total function that selects the **off** arguments of OP_β.

These rules give us all the information we need to form the state that results after the action it generates once we state the following. Whenever an **on** argument P_i is present in the result state, then it is in its original state if $i \notin dom(\phi)$ and, if $\phi(i) = a$ then P_i is in state P'_i such that $P_i \xrightarrow{a} P'_i$ in the result.

To illustrate this way of representing operators, we will show how some CSP+ operators fit into this framework. None of them, in fact, need to be defined together with any other operator apart from the identity **id** whose arity is $(1, \emptyset)$ and which has the rules $\{(\{(1, a)\}, a, \mathbf{id}, \emptyset, \{(1, 1)\}, \emptyset) \mid a \in \Sigma_0\}$. Here and below we represent the same functions and partial functions as sets of pairs.

- $a \to \cdot$ has arity $(0, \{-1\})$ and the single rule $(\emptyset, a, \mathbf{id}, \{(1, -1)\}, \{(1, 1)\}, \emptyset)$. We have used a negative number to index the **off** argument since it is a convenient way of making sure that they are disjoint from the **on** indices. **id** is (the index of) the identity operator. Thus here $k = 1$ (the number of **off** arguments turned **on**) and the resulting operator **id** has no **off** arguments.
- $\Box$ has arity $(2, \emptyset)$ and, for each $a \in \Sigma_0$, the rules $(\{(1, a)\}, a, \mathbf{id}, \emptyset, \{(1, 1)\}, \emptyset)$ and $(\{(2, a)\}, a, \mathbf{id}, \emptyset, \{(1, 2)\}, \emptyset)$.
- $\setminus X$ has arity $(1, \emptyset)$ and the rules $(\{(1, a)\}, \tau, \setminus X, \emptyset, \{(1, 1)\}, \emptyset)$ for all $a \in X$ and $(\{(1, a)\}, a, \setminus X, \emptyset, \{(1, 1)\}, \emptyset)$ for all $a \in \Sigma_0 - X$.
- $\underset{X}{\|}$ has arity $(2, \emptyset)$ and rules $(\{(1, a), (2, a)\}, a, \underset{X}{\|}, \emptyset, \{(1, 1), (2, 2)\}, \emptyset)$ for all $a \in X$ and both $(\{(1, a)\}, a, \underset{X}{\|}, \emptyset, \{(1, 1), (2, 2)\}, \emptyset)$ and $(\{(2, a)\}, a, \underset{X}{\|}, \emptyset, \{(1, 1), (2, 2)\}, \emptyset)$ for all $a \notin X$.
- $\triangle$ (interrupt) has arity $(2, \emptyset)$ and, for each $a \in \Sigma_0$, the rules $(\{(1, a), a, \triangle, \emptyset, \{(1, 1), (2, 2)\}, \emptyset)$ and $(\{(2, a), a, \mathbf{id}, \emptyset, \{(1, 2)\}, \emptyset)$. This is the interrupt operator.

The reader might like to compare these with the conventional (Structured Operational Semantics, or SOS) descriptions of the operational semantics of CSP given in Chapter 7 of [16]. They express exactly the same semantics when combined with the principle of promoting τs from **on** arguments. In fact, the CSP-like operators are *precisely* those that can be presented in this way. It is, however, possible to describe many operators in the SOS style which cannot be translated into the above form: those that are not CSP-like.

Consider the CSP-like operator $P \Theta_A Q$, which we will read P *throw* Q. It has arity $(1, \{-1\})$ and the rule $(\{(1, a)\}, a, \mathbf{id}, \{(1, -1)\}, \{(1, 1)\}, \emptyset)$ for each $a \in A$ as well as $(\{(1, b)\}, b, \Theta_A, \emptyset, \{(1, 1)\}, \{(-1, -1)\})$ for each $b \in \Sigma_0 - A$.

$P \Theta_A Q$ runs the process P until it communicates an event in A – which you might think of as a set of exceptions – at which point it hands control over directly to Q. It has much in common with the interrupt operator $\triangle$, except that here it is an event of P rather than one of Q that triggers the hand-over to Q: in $P \Theta_A Q$ you could say that P passes the baton over to A, whereas, in $P \triangle Q$, Q can take it at any time by performing a visible event.

In [19], the author showed that Θ_A adds strictly to the expressive power of the CSP language and that $\triangle$ can be expressed in terms of Θ_A and the rest of CSP.

In [20], the author showed that CSP+ (CSP augmented by Θ_A) is capable of simulating any operator with CSP-like operational semantics: for any such operator $OP(P_1, \ldots, P_m, \mathbf{Q})$ we can define a CSP+ context $C_{OP}(P_1, \ldots, P_m, \mathbf{Q})$ that is strongly bisimilar to it. This is done by building a complex "machine" that can interpret any rule of the form outlined above appropriately, and always have the right set of argument processes turned **on** so that the right τs are promoted by CSP.

One of the most important consequences of this result is the following: *every language whose operators are all CSP-like has a denotational semantics in every denotational model of CSP*. Thus, by showing that a language is CSP-like in this way one simultaneously equips it with many different new semantic models with an automatic representation in each.

The established denotational models of CSP take the form of recording one or more sorts of behaviour that an observer might see on a single run of the process: these are *linear* as opposed to *branching* behaviours. In [17, 18], the author defined what a behavioural model of CSP is in the cases of *finite observation* models and *divergence-strict* models. These are congruences that are relational images of two specific models. In the finite observation case this is the model $\mathcal{FL}$ that observes sequences of the form

$$\langle A_0, b_1, A_1, b_2, \ldots, A_{n-1}, b_n, A_n \rangle$$

where the b_i are the visible events performed by the process, and A_i is either the *stable acceptance set* offered by the process in the state from which b_{i+1} occurs, or $\bullet$ meaning that stability was not observed. The final acceptance set can be $\emptyset$, meaning that the process is deadlocked.

In the strict divergence case, two further components are added to get a model $\mathcal{FL}^{\Downarrow\omega}$: infinite sequences of the same sort, and finite sequences with the final A_n replaced by $\Uparrow$, meaning that the process divergences (performs an infinite sequence of τ actions). By *strict divergence* we mean that all extensions of any divergence are also considered to be behaviours of the process: no attempt is made to distinguish two processes on the basis of what they can or cannot do after their first possibility to diverge.

The infinite sequence case is necessary to get a congruence for CSP if *unboundedly nondeterministic* constructs are used. We will find that π-calculus is an exception to this rule.

In the original draft of [20], the π-calculus was used as an example to show how general the concept of a CSP-like operational semantics is. We there demonstrated the existence of a CSP semantics for it as a consequence of the above result. The complexity of our simulation machine means, however, that its translation into CSP+ is scarcely clear, and the fact that Θ_A is not actually required becomes obscured.

The present paper therefore refines these techniques so that the translation into standard CSP, and hence the structure of the resulting semantics in CSP's models, become significantly clearer.

16.3 Generalised Relabelling

The main challenge we will have to meet in giving a CSP semantics to π-calculus is dealing with the concept of fresh names. We will find ourselves needing to change names on-the-fly as a process progresses, in a way that is much more flexible than the usual CSP renaming operator $P[\![R]\!]$. Therefore, in this section, we introduce a *generalised relabelling* operator $P\langle\!\langle G\rangle\!\rangle$ and show that it can be expressed using a combination of standard CSP operators.

CSP has two operators that work by changing the labels on a process's actions: hiding and renaming. The first changes a selection of labels to τ and the second maps each action of a process P to a selection of one or more. In each case the mapping on labels does not change as the process progresses, and no action is blocked from occurring.

We can regard both these operators as instances of *relabelling*: replacing each *visible* action of P with an action (or perhaps a choice of actions). We call this "relabelling" rather than "renaming" because x may be τ and so invisible to the environment.[1] As hiding shows, there is no reason why a visible action should not be replaced by τ. It would, however, not be CSP-like even to let the operator notice τ's performed by P: these must always be promoted *as* τs. In *generalised* relabelling, we will allow two features not seen in either renaming or hiding:

[1] The uses of relabelling we make later only map visible actions to other visible actions.

- We will allow the replacement mapping to vary as the process progresses.
- We will allow the replacement mapping to forbid certain visible actions by P: such actions will map to empty choices of options. So, for example, $P \underset{A}{\|} STOP$ equivalent to the generalised relabelling that maps every event not in A to itself, and has no image for events in A.

The second of these points is clear cut. The first leaves it open as to what can influence the variation of the mapping. It might be the sequence of visible events that P has performed; it might be the sequence of events that these have been mapped to; or it might be nondeterministic. Or, of course, it might be any combination of these. We will initially consider the first of these, which covers the case of the first generalised renaming *HDT* used in this paper.

Suppose G is a relation on Σ_0, Σ_0^* and Σ_0^τ, where $(a, t, x) \in G$ says that whenever process P can perform the event a after trace t, the relabelled process $P\langle\langle G\rangle\rangle$ can perform x. We can give this operator a natural, CSP-like, operational semantics in SOS style as follows:

$$\frac{P \xrightarrow{\tau} P'}{P\langle\langle G\rangle\rangle \xrightarrow{\tau} P'\langle\langle G\rangle\rangle} \qquad \frac{P \xrightarrow{a} P', (a, \langle\rangle, x) \in G}{P\langle\langle G\rangle\rangle \xrightarrow{x} P'\langle\langle G/\langle a\rangle\rangle\rangle}$$

where $G/t = \{(a, s, x) \mid (s, t\hat{\ }s, x) \in G\}$.

In our new style of presenting operational semantics, this translates to $\langle\langle G\rangle\rangle$ having the rule $(\{(1, a)\}, x, \langle\langle G/\langle a\rangle\rangle\rangle, \emptyset, \{(1, 1)\}, \emptyset)$ for each $(a, \langle\rangle, x) \in G$.

Adapting the techniques developed for the most straightforward case of the main theorem of [20], we can re-cast the above operator using two conventional renamings (one one-to-many and one many-to-one), parallel composition with a regulator process, and the hiding of a single event.

We extend the alphabet Σ to include all pairs of the form (a, x) for $a \in \Sigma_0$ and $x \in \Sigma_0 \cup \{\tau\} = \Sigma_0^\tau$ as well as the alphabet Σ_0 of the original processes and the special visible event *tau*, which takes the place of τ in building up the semantics, and will actually become τ via hiding at the outermost level, as we will see below.

We can define two renamings:

$$E = \{(a, (a, x)) \mid a \in \Sigma_0 \wedge x \in \Sigma_0^\tau\} \quad C = \{((a, x), \underline{x}) \mid a \in \Sigma_0 \wedge x \in \Sigma_0^\tau\}$$

where $\underline{a} = a$ for $a \in \Sigma_0$, and $\underline{\tau} = tau$.

Clearly $P[\![E]\!][\![C]\!]$ maps every event of P to all events in $\Sigma_0 \cup \{tau\}$, but we can be a lot more selective by running $P[\![E]\!]$ in parallel with a regulator process. Define

$$Reg(G) = \square\{(a, x) \rightarrow Reg(G/\langle a\rangle) \mid (a, \langle\rangle, x) \in G\}$$

It should be clear that

$$(P[\![E]\!] \underset{\Sigma}{\|} Reg(G))[\![C]\!] \setminus \{tau\} \qquad (*)$$

has precisely the same actions as $P\langle\langle G\rangle\rangle$, and that these two processes are strongly bisimilar on the assumption that the guarded recursion defining $Reg(G)$ does not introduce any τ actions (as discussed in [20], there are two alternative operational semantics for recursion in CSP, one of which introduces a τ for each unfolding and one of which does not).

It is obviously important for practical purposes whether G is, or is not, finitary (respectively finitary relative to P) in the sense that G/s has only finitely many values as s varies (or varies over the traces of P). For we will be able to simulate $Q\langle\langle G\rangle\rangle$ for general Q (or $P\langle\langle G\rangle\rangle$ for specific P) using a finite-state regulator just when these apply.

This implementation illustrates how the concept of one-to-many renaming in CSP, as introduced by Hoare, is enormously powerful in allowing us to express a wide variety of constructs that seem at first sight to be beyond what CSP can express. Even more elaborate one-to-many renamings are used in creating the machine in [20].

As well as conventional renaming and hiding (both history independent in the sense that the relabelling does not depend on what actions have occurred before), the following operations on processes are instances of finitary relabellings:

- Hide every second visible event performed by P.
- Hide all visible events equal to the preceding one.
- Rename all odd-numbered `tock` events to `tick`.
- Prevent all a actions not immediately preceded by member of A.

Rather than deriving the regulator process from G, we can gain maximum freedom in allowing the mapping to vary by instead allowing Reg to be any divergence-free process whose alphabet is $\Sigma_0 \times \Sigma_0^\tau$. The relabelling will be said to be *deterministic* just when Reg is.

We will use this format for presenting most of the relabellings in this paper, even when they could have been given in terms of relations.

16.4 CCS

Since π-calculus is built on top of CCS [9, 10], it is useful to consider that language before proceeding to our ultimate goal.

There is a CCS operator, namely $+$, that stands out as *not* being CSP-like, since this can be resolved by a τ action performed by either of its operands. This is impossible for CSP-like operators since they have to promote τs without changing their own state. Apart from that, the constant *Nil* is equivalent to the CSP *STOP*; the operational semantics of $\alpha.P$ for $\alpha \neq \tau$ are identical to those of CSP prefix or prefix-choice. The semantics of recursion in CCS is essentially[2] identical to the

---

[2] The only difference is that CCS allows this definition to be used unconditionally, even on underdefined terms such as $\mu\, p.p$. The translations from CCS to CSP in this section are therefore restricted to the case where all recursions add at least one initial action.

non-τ version in CSP, and the CCS relabelling operation is a case of CSP renaming. Let us consider the rest of the language: parallel composition $|$, and restriction $\backslash\ \alpha$.

The structure of Σ_0 (as we again call the set of visible action names used in creating processes) with an operator $\overline{\alpha}$ (with $\overline{\overline{\alpha}} = \alpha$ and $\overline{\alpha} \neq \alpha$) causes no difficulties to CSP, although naturally the usual CSP notation does not automatically handle the relationship between α and $\overline{\alpha}$: it has to be programmed explicitly as we do in the CSP model of $|$ below.

The CCS restriction operator has semantics

$$\frac{P \xrightarrow{x} P'}{P \setminus \alpha \xrightarrow{x} P' \setminus \alpha} (x \notin \{\alpha, \overline{\alpha}\})$$

Since α is not τ, this is trivially CSP-like, and indeed is equivalent to the CSP construct $P \underset{\{\alpha,\overline{\alpha}\}}{\|} STOP$ as well as being a generalised relabelling of the sort seen in the last section.

The CCS parallel operator is much more interesting. It has semantics

$$\frac{P \xrightarrow{x} P'}{P \mid Q \xrightarrow{x} P' \mid Q} \qquad \frac{Q \xrightarrow{x} Q'}{P \mid Q \xrightarrow{x} P \mid Q'} \qquad \frac{P \xrightarrow{\alpha} P' \wedge Q \xrightarrow{\overline{\alpha}} Q'}{P \mid Q \xrightarrow{\tau} P' \mid Q'}$$

This is CSP-like, with arity $(2, \emptyset)$ and one set of transition rules for each of these three clauses: the first two have $(\{(1,\alpha)\}, \alpha, |, \emptyset, \{(1,1),(2,2)\}, \emptyset)$ and $(\{(2,\alpha)\}, \alpha, |, \emptyset, \{(1,1),(2,2)\}, \emptyset)$ for all $\alpha \in \Sigma_0$, and the final clause is modelled by $(\{(1,\alpha),(2,\overline{\alpha})\}, \tau, |, \emptyset, \{(1,1),(2,2)\}, \emptyset)$ for all $\alpha \in \Sigma_0$.

Note how similar these are to the rules for $\underset{X}{\|}$ quoted earlier. The main structural difference is that both sorts of rules apply to *all* visible events, rather than being partitioned by X.

The following representation of $|$ in CSP is much simpler than the simulation produced by the [20] machine. Extend Σ_0 by a separate copy $\Sigma_1 = \{\alpha' \mid \alpha \in \Sigma_0\}$. Let *IP* (Identity plus Prime) be the renaming that maps $\alpha \in \Sigma_0$ to both α and α', and let *IDP* (Identity plus Dual Prime) map each such α to α and $\overline{\alpha}'$. Then $P \mid Q$ is equivalent to the CSP construct defined

$$P \mid_{ccs} Q = (IP(P) \underset{\Sigma_1}{\|} IDP(Q)) \setminus \Sigma_1$$

in the sense that the two processes are strongly bisimilar.

We can therefore conclude that, except for $+$, CCS is CSP-like.

It is possible to simulate the whole of CCS in CSP, but in a slightly more complex way that does not imply full compositionality over CSP models or a straightforward theory of refinement. An elementary way of doing this is to replace the event τ by a visible analogue (say *tau* as we have seen elsewhere in this paper), and produce models of CCS operators that model the syntax $\tau.P$ by $tau \rightarrow P$. Finally, at the outermost level (in common with the implementation of generalised relabelling given in the previous section) we would hide *tau*. Thus the model of a closed piece P of CCS syntax would be the CSP term $P' \setminus \{tau\}$, where P' is the syntax of P with all operators replaced by their CSP analogues. In this model the analogue of $+$ would be $\Box$, since *tau* does resolve $\Box$, and the model of parallel would be as above (noting that *tau* is not synchronised) except that the outer hiding $\setminus \Sigma_1$ would be replaced by the renaming that sends all members of Σ_1 to *tau*.

This provides a way of calculating the operational semantics of a CCS term using those of CSP, and also an easy method for using CSP tools such as FDR [15] on such terms.

It is not, in fact, necessary to leave *all* the *tau* actions visible as we build up a term, only those that might resolve a $+$ operator for which our present process becomes (directly or indirectly) an argument. A little structural analysis shows that the only relevant *tau*s are those that are the *first* action that our process performs. It follows that if we apply the following generalised relabelling (standing for "Hide Delayed Taus"), and presented in the relational form discussed earlier, to any term as we build up P', the final result is not affected:

$$\begin{aligned} HDT = {} & \{(a, s, f(s, a)) \mid a \in \Sigma_0 \wedge s \in \Sigma_0^*\} \\ & \text{where } f(tau, s) = \tau \text{ for } s \neq \langle\rangle, f(a, s) = a \text{ otherwise.} \end{aligned}$$

This operator might well be useful if one wants to apply CSP model compressions such as those of FDR [22] in a hierarchical way to CCS constructs, as might the simpler observation that it is always safe to hide any *tau* at a level in the syntax above any $+$.

This translation will allow any finite-state CCS process to be checked on FDR against the types of specification that FDR supports.

An obvious question then arises: can one model CSP in CCS? The immediate answer to this is "no" since CCS cannot model the multi-way synchronisations permitted by CSP: as soon as two events are synchronised in CCS they are hidden. Another consequence of this is that it is seemingly impossible, in CCS, to implement the style of generalised relabelling discussed in the previous section for the same reason: synchronising P and *Reg* would hide the event. Of course there may be further interesting questions to ask here about subsets of CSP or extensions of CCS.

16.5 The π-Calculus

The π-calculus [11, 12, 23] builds on the notation of CCS by adding the concepts of name binding and name passing into the language. Like CCS, it does not need process alphabets to define parallel, and therefore the way it expresses mobility is more implicit than one in which passing a label along a channel explicitly changes the alphabets at the two ends, as seems natural for a direct mobile extension of CSP.

The following syntax for the π-calculus is taken from [23]:

PREFIXES $\pi ::= \bar{x}y \mid x(z) \mid \tau \mid [x = y]\pi$
PROCESSES $P ::= S \mid P|P \mid \nu z\, P \mid !P$
SUMMATIONS $S ::= \mathbf{0} \mid \pi.P \mid S + S'$

Here, $\overline{x}y$ represents the sending of the name y via x (akin to the CSP action $x!y$) and $x(z)$ is a construct binding z that represents the receipt of z over x (akin to $x?z$). Like CCS and unlike CSP it has a construct representing the explicit introduction of τ, and one can guard actions with the assertion that pairs of names are the same.

The process constructs are the same as in CCS except that the infinite replication $!P$ (equivalent to $P \mid !P$) takes the place of recursion and $\nu x\, P$ replaces $P \setminus x$. The effect of having summations in a separate syntactic class is to allow $+$ only to appear in restricted contexts (similar to the "guarded choice" construct introduced as a precursor to $\Box$ in CSP in both of [6, 16]). Some presentations of the π-calculus omit $+$. Others generalise replication to full recursion $\mu\, p.P$, and we shall follow this latter school. We therefore add $\mu\, p.P$ and p to the syntax of PROCESSES, where p represents a process identifier. (We will not, therefore, directly consider $!P$, regarding it as equivalent to $\mu\, p.P \mid \tau.p$.)

The restriction on the use of $+$ imposed by this syntax is crucial in allowing us to give π-calculus semantics in CSP. When giving semantics to summations we will still need to leave τ visible as *tau*; but for the main semantics (of processes) this is not necessary. We will therefore find that this version of π-calculus fits more smoothly and compositionally into the world of CSP than does CCS.

In our treatment of π-calculus we assume unless stated otherwise that the set *Name* is countably infinite with a fixed enumeration $\{n_0, n_1, \ldots\}$. If N is a nonempty subset of names then $\mu(N)$ is the name with least index in N, and when $Name - N$ is nonempty $\gamma(N)$ denotes $\mu(Name - N)$. The visible events communicated by π-calculus processes, and making up Σ_π (which plays the role of Σ_0 for our treatment of π-calculus) are of two forms: $x.y$ represents the input of name y over the channel represented by name x, and $\overline{x}.y$ represents the corresponding output of y over x.

The theory of the π-calculus is complex. This is less because processes can pass names around and use them as channels as it is because of the way new names are "created" fresh and distinct from all others, and may be exported from their original scope.

Our goal is to find a way of dealing with this in CSP in a way that implements the above policy successfully and does not create any artificial distinctions between processes on the basis of exactly which fresh names they extrude.

Example To illustrate the power of the π-calculus, and provide an example for our later semantics, consider the following description of a variable-length buffer. This consists of a chain of processes, which initially consists of the single process $C(in, out, split, export)$, which uses the channels *in* and $\overline{out}$ as the buffer input and output, respectively. Each process additionally has a channel along which it can be told to split in two and one from which the environment can choose to accept outputs in place of them proceeding down the chain. See Fig. 16.1 to see how it might evolve from top to bottom, with the single cell splitting to form two, and then the left-hand one splitting in turn.

$$\begin{aligned} C(i, o, s, e) = {} & i(y).(\overline{o}x.C(i, o, s, e) + \overline{e}x.C(i, o, s, e)) \\ & + s(z).\nu m\, \nu s'\, \overline{z}s'.(C(i, m, s', z) \mid C(m, o, s, e)) \end{aligned}$$

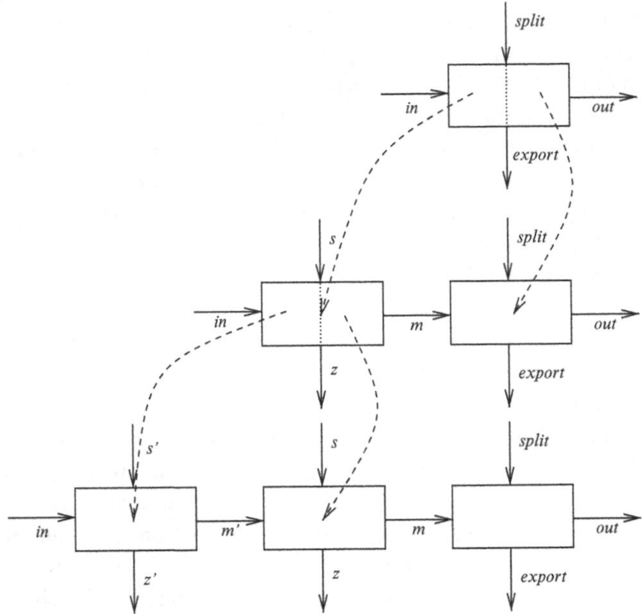

Fig. 16.1 One cell evolving into three

Each command to split (i.e. input on s) inputs a new name z from the environment, and that is used as the external output (e) channel of the new node. A new channel name also has to be extruded to the environment: the one to split the new node. That is the first output along z.

So in the transformation of the top line of the figure to the second, the environment sends z along *split*, and the process replies by sending s back along z. Sending z' along s then causes the second split, with s' being sent back along z'.

This is a somewhat contrived example, designed to use a lot of channel names (input, internal and extruded) to help our later understanding of the semantics of names. The semantics of the π-calculus rely on every name that the process creates being different from each other and from all that the environment has passed to it by that time. No such restriction applies to the environment, though obviously this particular example makes most sense when every name sent by the environment is also fresh.

We now identify two choices that have to be made when constructing our π-calculus semantics.

1. We can ensure that no artificial distinctions arise thanks to the precise choice of names in two ways.

   – The first is to create processes such that, whenever a name is extruded, it is picked nondeterministically from all permitted ones. We will call this the *nondeterministic* approach.

  - The second is to ensure that each fresh name that emerges from a process is completely predictable based on knowledge of the preceding trace. We will implement this by ensuring that the name is always the one with least index that might legitimately appear, and call this the *standardised* approach.

2. One of the trickiest problems in giving the semantics is to ensure that names input by a process from the environment do not get confused with a name that may already exist in the process's scope without having been extruded. It is a basic assumption that these names *are* different, so how do we achieve this?

  - One approach is to allow the environment, at any time, to output any name to the process. The semantics then has to perform an operation related to α-conversion on any fresh and unextruded name it holds that clashes. We will call this the *unified* approach.
  - The opposite of this, which we will call the *bipartite* approach, is to split the fresh name space into two infinite parts and allocate one to the process and the other to the environment. In other words, the process will simply assume at all times that the environment will not output any name to it that is in that part of the process's fresh name space unless that name has previously been extruded by the process.

In this paper we will first consider the unified name space approach, providing an initial translation into CSP followed by constructs that respectively map this into the nondeterministic and standardised approaches. We then summarise the differences in how these steps are taken in the bipartite approach.

We would expect any semantics for π-calculus to have complete symmetry in those names that the environment generates as fresh (though in the unified approach the symmetries will be more complex since they will need to factor in the fact that the names chosen by the environment affect the values of the names chosen subsequently by the process). We would expect any nondeterministic semantics to have complete symmetry in the names chosen by the process.

Think, for a moment, about how these decisions would affect our example. Note that, in it, the creation of names is a *distributed* activity: when we have split the original cell into N pieces, any one of them can input new names from the environment and generate fresh ones without interacting with the others. And yet all of our models except for the *nondeterministic, bipartite* approach seem to rely on there being some sort of instantaneous passing of information between the different cells. In the unified approach one cell has to "know" which names have input by another from the environment so it can avoid generating that name itself. In the standardised approach two cells that are simultaneously able to output channel names to the environment seem to need to know whether the other has done so yet. On the other hand, if (i) the available names for a cell are nondeterministically split into two infinite parts when it splits and (ii) the environment is prevented from creating any of these names, there is no such problem.

Arguably, what the other approaches are doing is placing each process in a framework that forces us to think of processes as sequential, or at least to look at parallel processes through a prism that makes them look sequential. In that sense they are doing no more than what happens when we use an LTS semantics or one based on any of the usual CSP models, for these are all inherently sequential. But this does suggest that an attempt to give a true concurrency semantics might follow the nondeterministic and bipartite approach to names.

16.5.1 Preserving Inequality

The π-calculus is fairly straightforward to translate into our CSP extended by $|_{ccs}$, with the exception of its handling of freshness. We first show how to translate summations. If S is a SUMMATION then $\text{CSP}[S]_+$ will be a CSP term in which τ actions remain visible as *tau*. The corresponding semantics for a PROCESS P is written $\text{CSP}[P]$.

- $\text{CSP}[0]_+ = STOP$
- $\text{CSP}[[x = y]\pi.P]_+ = \text{CSP}[\pi.P]_+ \not< x = y \not> STOP$
- $\text{CSP}[\tau.P]_+ = tau \to \text{CSP}[P]$
- $\text{CSP}[x(y).P]_+ = x?z \to \text{CSP}[P[z/y]]$
- $\text{CSP}[\overline{x}y.P]_+ = \overline{x}.y \to \text{CSP}[P]$
- $\text{CSP}[S + S']_+ = \text{CSP}[S]_+ \,\Box\, \text{CSP}[S']_+$

Here $X \not< b \not> Y$ is Hoare's infix representation conditional choice: it equals X if b it *true* and Y if b is *false*.

We can interpret a summation as a process via hiding, and both process identifiers and recursion translate directly into CSP:

- $\text{CSP}[S] = \text{CSP}[S]_+ \setminus \{tau\}$
- $\text{CSP}[p] = p$
- $\text{CSP}[\mu\, p.P] = \mu\, p.\text{CSP}[P]$

The remaining constructs are parallel $P \mid Q$ and restriction $\nu z P$. These are more difficult because of the way they handle fresh names. The effects we want to achieve are set out below.

- $\nu z P$ creates a fresh name z' for the placeholder z that is used within P. This is different from all other names known to P at the point of creation and all names that P sees subsequently that cannot result from other processes reflecting z' back to P.
- $\nu z P$ may *extrude* this z' from this scope by means of output $\overline{x}z'$ on some other channel (i.e. $x \neq z'$).
- After this extrusion, $\nu z P$ may use the name z' as a channel name, output it again, etc. However, before the extrusion any of P's communications that use it as a channel name are blocked. This, by analogy with CCS restriction $P \setminus \alpha$, explains why this operator is called "restriction." In our example it means that no communication on our internal channels $m, m' \cdots$ are visible on the outside, because these channel names are never extruded.

- In the parallel composition $P \mid Q$, the processes P and Q never extrude the same fresh name.
- Because of the way in which interactions between P and Q are hidden, P may extrude a fresh name z to Q or vice-versa, without the external environment seeing z. This expansion of the scope of z is restricted as above: it may not use the name z in a visible way until z has been extruded *from the parallel composition* via output on a different channel.
- Each fresh name extruded from $P \mid Q$ must be different from all names either P or Q knew originally or subsequently input.

The above must hold for any strategy for assigning and managing the fresh names created within a term P. We use the term "managing" here because there is no sensible way, within the unified approach to name choice, of ensuring that once a fresh value z has been created but not yet extruded, the external environment does not independently invent the same name (we will call this a name collision). If this happened it would cause confusion both in the environment and the process P.

This is why we need to use relabelling. In the instance above, one thing we could do would be to pick a further fresh name z' not known to P, and apply the renaming $[\![^{z,z'}/_{z',z}]\!]$ (transposing the two names) to P from the point where the environment communicates z to it. Thus P will see z as z' (correctly, a value that is fresh to it and distinct from the z it already knows about) and the environment will, if and when P ultimately extrudes z the outside world will see it as z' (correctly, a value it has not seen before). Since neither z nor z' has appeared in the trace before this point, each of these names only has a single role in the whole trace. We will use relabellings such as this to avoid collisions both for $\nu z P$ and $P \mid Q$, the latter because of the scope expansion issues discussed above.

We will introduce a relabelling called $OF(N,K,P)$ ("output first"). Here N is a set of names that the process P might extrude but are not known to the environment. K (disjoint from N) is the set of names initially known to both P and environment: we think of this as their *common knowledge*. $OF(N,K,P)$ introduces a transposition of the above form each time the process inputs from the environment a name that clashes with a member of N. The set N may diminish as the process evolves since some of the names in it may be extruded; and K may increase as P learns more names.

In order to keep track of the transpositions that are introduced as the system evolves, we need to introduce a parameter ξ that is a bijection on *Name*. At any time, ξ will be the the function that maps names as seen on the inside of the relabelling to the corresponding names seen by the environment. While this function will evolve as the system progresses, as soon as a name has been seen in a trace of P its image remains fixed thereafter. It follows that, at the end of a trace, ξ is a permutation on *Name* that translates P's view to the environment's view of every member in the trace. Initially, ξ is the identity function, and remains so on the initial members of K.

The most straightforward way of presenting OF is by defining a Reg_{OF} process that creates the relabelling using the construction $(*)$.

In the following, as with OF, we assume that K and N (the set of potentially fresh names yet to emerge from the process) are disjoint. $Reg_{OF}(K, N, \xi)$ takes the form

$$\Box\{(a,b) \to Reg_{OF}(K',N',\xi') \mid (a,b,K',N',\xi') \in C\}$$

where a is the process P's event, b is the environment's view of the same event, and C is a set of clauses that we will describe below, each representing a different sort of event that the relabelling allows.

We consider the cases of output $\overline{x}.y$ and input $x.y$ events separately, splitting these depending on which of K and N y belongs to. In both cases we restrict x to be K: it is part of the role of OF to prevent P from using names in N before these have been extruded from scope; and if our semantics are sensible P could never use a channel name that is outside $K \cup N$.

We now enumerate the various clauses of Reg_{OF} (K, N, ξ):

- If both the channel and data are part of common knowledge, then an input does not change the parameters:

$$\{(x.y, \xi(x).\xi(y)) \to Reg_{OF}\ (K,N,\xi) \mid x,y \in K\}$$

- If both the channel and data are part of common knowledge, then an output does not change the parameters:

$$\{(\overline{x}.y, \overline{\xi(x)}.\xi(y)) \to Reg_{OF}\ (K,N,\xi) \mid x,y \in K\}$$

- If P outputs a name in N, then this is removed from N and added to K

$$\{(\overline{x}.y, \overline{\xi(x)}.\xi(y)) \to Reg_{OF}\ (K \cup \{x\}, N - \{x\}, \xi) \mid x \in K, y \in N\}$$

- If P inputs a name outside $K \cup N$, then this is equivalent to the environment extruding a name to P, so it is added to the common knowledge:

$$\{(x.y, \xi(x).\xi(y)) \to Reg_{OF}\ (K \cup \{x\}, N, \xi) \mid x \in K, y \notin N \cup K\}$$

- Finally, if P was to input a name y in N, then this is a name collision, since the environment has yet to be told of N by P. However, in the unified approach, there is nothing to stop the environment inventing such a name independently. Therefore, the mapping ξ is changed so that the new name maps outside $K \cup N$ under ξ^{-1}. The simplest way to do this is to transpose x and the name $\gamma(K \cup N)$, which we recall is the one with least index not in this set. We write this transposition (which maps all other names to themselves) as $xp(x, \gamma(K \cup N))$. The clauses of this type are thus

$$\{(x.n, \xi(x).\xi(y)) \to Reg_{OF}(K \cup \{n\}, N, \xi \circ xp(x,n)) \mid x \in K, y \in N\}$$

where $n = \gamma(K \cup N)$.

Notice that all of the above English descriptions are formulated from the point of view of P, with the already established permutation ξ assumed.

It is these transpositions in OF that represent the analogy of α-conversion that we discussed earlier. Both of these things have the role of avoiding clashes between external and bound identifiers. While traditional α-conversion does not change the semantics of a term, our transpositions do, but this is only because "bound" identifiers in π-calculus can, unusually, be seen from the outside.

This relabelling is deterministic since there is only one way $Reg_{OF}\,(K,N,\xi)$ can perform any given action, and clearly it has no τ-generated nondeterminism. Indeed, since there is only one action that $Reg_{OF}\,(K,N,\xi)$ can perform for any given action seen by the environment, $OF(N,K,\cdot)$ could be presented as a relabelling generated by a relation between P's visible actions, the environment's visible actions and the environment's traces. But since it does evolve naturally a step at a time, the above presentation is probably the best.

We are now very close to being able to give a semantics to $\nu z P$, but before we do that we need to establish what the right values are to use for K and N when we come to use OF. We will also need a semantic mechanism to keep the fresh names invented by two parallel processes distinct.

The best way to do these things is to add parameters κ and σ to the semantics so they become $\mathrm{CSP}[S]_{+}\kappa\sigma$ and $\mathrm{CSP}[P]\kappa\sigma$. κ will represent the initial common knowledge of names by P and its environment or context: a finite set of names that includes all free names in P. σ will be an infinite set of names, disjoint from κ, that are available to be used as fresh. So, for example, we will now have $\mathrm{CSP}[P+Q]_{+}\kappa\sigma = \mathrm{CSP}[P]_{+}\kappa\sigma \;\Box\; \mathrm{CSP}[Q]_{+}\kappa\sigma$ and (the only clause given to date with a significant change) $\mathrm{CSP}[x(y).P]_{+}\kappa\sigma = x?y \to \mathrm{CSP}[P]_{+}(\kappa \cup \{y\})(\sigma - \{y\})$.

We can then write

$$\mathrm{CSP}[\nu z P]\kappa\sigma = OF(\{\gamma(\sigma)\},\ \kappa,\ \mathrm{CSP}[P[\gamma(\sigma)/z]](\kappa \cup \{\gamma(\sigma)\})(\sigma - \{\gamma(\sigma)\}))$$

In other words, the name with least index not in κ is chosen to bind to z, and this name is then "protected" by the OF operator, which also prevents it from being used as a channel by P until it has been output.

The interactions between P and Q in $P \mid Q$ are calculated in the same way as in CCS. It follows that the same CSP construction we used in the last section can be used here provided we sort out what happens to the sets of names that P and Q use and generate, and provided we ensure that $P \mid Q$ obeys the rules discussed above for it being an expanded scope for some of these generated names.

The parameter σ gives us the ability to keep the names that P and Q generate distinct from each other. To do this we assume that we have functions Π_i for $i = 1,2,3$ such that, for any infinite set σ of names, $\{\Pi_1(\sigma),\Pi_2(\sigma),\Pi_3(\sigma)\}$ partitions σ into three infinite sets. [One such triple of functions would allocate the names of increasing index in σ to the three sets in a round robin fashion.] In evaluating $\mathrm{CSP}[P \mid Q]\kappa\sigma$ these three sets will respectively represent the sets of fresh names that might be generated by P, by Q, and outside this system.

We can then define $\text{CSP}[P \mid Q]\kappa\sigma$ to be

$$OF(\Pi_1(\sigma) \cup \Pi_2(\sigma),\ \kappa,\ \text{CSP}[P]\kappa(\Pi_1(\sigma)) \mid_{ccs} \text{CSP}[Q]\kappa(\Pi_2(\sigma)))$$

The role of OF here is to protect any fresh names extruded from P or Q into $P \mid Q$ but not yet to the environment. Since it does not know exactly which fresh names have been extruded in this way, it protects the whole of the set $\Pi_1(\sigma) \cup \Pi_2(\sigma)$. Here, of course $\mid_{ccs}$ is the CSP translation given earlier of the CCS operator $\mid$.

Note that as far as P's and Q's choices of names are concerned, we have used what amounts to the bipartite approach by ensuring that they choose from disjoint sets.

16.5.2 Nondeterministic Fresh Names

We might say that the above clauses give a *provisional* semantics, since they suffer from the lack of abstraction discussed above caused by specific choices of fresh names.

In many ways the most elegant approach to this problem is to apply a mapping that in effect maps each assignment of fresh names to a representation of its symmetry class: the processes that might have been obtained under a different strategy for assigning fresh names.

We can attempt to do this by identifying each semantic value $\text{CSP}[P]\kappa\sigma$ with the nondeterministic composition of the set of its values under renamings that change the choices of fresh names it picks from σ. The following operator is perhaps the most natural way to do this.

$$NFN(P,\sigma) = \bigsqcap\{P[\![\xi \cup id_{(Name-\sigma)}]\!] \mid \xi : \sigma \to \sigma, \xi \text{ bijection}\} \quad (\dagger)$$

One can gain much insight into CSP models and the way to use them correctly for π-calculus by analysing whether this approach works or not.

We will now show that there are pairs of processes P and Q that we would like to regard as semantically equivalent for which there is no such ξ with $\text{CSP}[P]\kappa\sigma[\![\xi]\!] = \text{CSP}[Q]\kappa\sigma$.

If we have a process that has two different behaviours on which it extrudes a free name, it should not matter whether these two names are the same or different. Consider, for example, $P = \tau.(\nu z\bar{x}z.0) + \tau.(\nu z\bar{y}z.0)$ (where the above semantics will always output the same fresh name via whichever of $\bar{x}$ and $\bar{y}$ the environment chooses) and $Q = \tau.(\nu z\bar{x}z.0) + \tau.(0 \mid (\nu z\bar{y}z.0))$ (where, depending on Π_2, it may not, and we will assume not). No renaming of the above form can map P to Q. For similar reasons the CSP operational semantics of P and Q with construct (†) applied to them are not bisimilar, since no bijection ξ can map the state P to the state Q.

Thus the *initial* choice of a single permutation does not characterise semantic equivalence in a model where processes are represented as tree structures.

One of the main differences in CSP-style models based on *linear* observations of processes is that they deliberately obscure when choices are made: hence the CSP distributivity law $a \to (R \sqcap S) = (a \to R) \sqcap (a \to S)$, for example. A CSP-style semantics of the processes P and Q above will only let you look at things that occur down a linear observation. However, the structure of P above means that it will not let you examine the consequences of outputting on channels $\overline{x}$ and $\overline{y}$ in the same observation; only in two separate ones. It should not therefore matter, in this style of model, if the choice of a permutation ξ is made initially or in stages as long as every name that actually appears is mapped to the same place as in ξ.

We would expect such a model of $\text{CSP}[P]\kappa\sigma$ still to output the same name along these two channels and $\text{CSP}[Q]\kappa\sigma$ probably to output different ones, so the provisional semantics of P and Q will still be different even if we only record process traces. However, when we look at the effect on their traces of the (†) construct, these two values are mapped to the same value. The point is that any trace of $\text{CSP}[P]\kappa\sigma$ will be the result of some ξ being applied to a trace of $\text{CSP}[Q]\kappa\sigma$, and vice versa. The fact that *different* ξ may be needed for different traces is immaterial: every trace of $\text{CSP}[P]\kappa\sigma$ will be a trace of $NFN(\text{CSP}[Q]\kappa\sigma, \sigma)$ and vice versa.

We can conclude that, at least for the finite traces semantics of CSP, construction (†) gives the provisional CSP semantics the necessary abstraction. There are subtle problems, however, when we come to study types of behaviour that appear in other CSP models. These are, on the one hand, refusal and acceptance sets and, on the other, behaviours recording infinite traces. To avoid this second sort of difficulty, let us assume for the time being that we are interpreting CSP over a model that does not have infinite traces.

Most CSP models have refusal or acceptance sets to enable us to detect things like deadlock. These can lead to undesirable semantic differences between π-calculus terms in two related ways. For example, consider the processes

$$\nu y\overline{x}y.\nu z.\overline{x}z.0 \qquad (\nu y\overline{x}y.0) \mid (\nu z\overline{x}z.0)$$

Each of them simply extrudes two fresh names in succession along $\overline{x}$, and they ought to be regarded as equivalent.

With conventional failures-based models, in which refusal sets are sets of *events*, these two processes are not equivalent under the *NFN* mapping. For the left-hand process will have failures of the form $(\langle\rangle, \Sigma - \{\overline{x}.n\})$, while the largest refusal sets on $\langle\rangle$ of the right-hand process will omit $\overline{x}.n$ and $\overline{x}.m$ for two different names n and m: in effect the parallel structure gives the environment a "choice" of two different names.

A further difficulty arises in more elaborate CSP models such as *refusal testing* where it is possible to see the refusal or acceptance of an event that extrudes a name several steps before it actually appears in the trace. Such a name might or might not get relabelled between these two appearances, which can again lead to undesired inequivalences as well as some confusing-looking observed behaviours.

There is a simple solution to both these problems: in languages such as π-calculus where all communication between processes happens over point-to-point channels, and processes inputting on a channel always do so *non-selectively* – they cannot accept some communications on it but refuse others – we get a better model of refusal and acceptance sets by constructing them solely of channel names, not events. This was recognised for occam in [14].

It will therefore be impossible to tell, in any "channel-based" CSP-style model, between the sequential and parallel processes above that extrude fresh names, to see any fresh name in a recorded behaviour before it is extruded, or indeed to make the same sort of distinctions based on non-fresh names. Thus, for example, $\bar{x}y\,.\,P+\bar{x}z\,.\,Q$ and $\tau\,.\,\bar{x}y\,.\,P+\bar{x}z\,.\,Q$ will be identified as processes (though not as summations) in any such model.

Given any of these channel-based CSP models $\mathcal{M}$ we can therefore give a proper semantics to the π-calculus. The semantics for a summation and a process will be written[3] $\mathcal{M}^1_\sqcap[S]_+\kappa\sigma$ and $\mathcal{M}^1_\sqcap[P]\kappa\sigma$, which are defined to be the respective CSP interpretations over $\mathcal{M}$ of the terms:

$$NFN(\textsc{csp}[S]_+\kappa\sigma,\sigma) \quad \text{and} \quad NFN(\textsc{csp}[P]\kappa\sigma,\sigma)$$

The superscript 1 here means that this is a semantics using a single (unified) name space, and $\sqcap$ means that this is the *nondeterministic* semantics. The alternatives for these are 2 (bipartite) and μ (standardised).

These can readily be turned into denotational semantics. The preliminary semantics $\textsc{csp}[P]\kappa\sigma$ can already be interpreted in this way if we add an extra parameter ρ: an environment that maps process identifiers to functions from common knowledge sets κ and fresh-name sets σ to $\mathcal{M}$.[4] They will thus be written $\mathcal{M}^1_\sqcap[P]\rho\kappa\sigma$. Thus the semantics of a process identifier is given by $\rho(p)\kappa\sigma$. The semantics of each non-recursive operator is then just the interpretation over $\mathcal{M}$ of the CSP syntax into which we have already translated it, applied to sub-terms as appropriate. The semantics of recursion is just the same fixed-point calculation that is appropriate for $\mathcal{M}$: sometimes a refinement-least fixed point, sometimes a subset-least fixed point, and sometimes something more complex as in [17].

The full denotational semantics is then obtained in the same way except that for some syntactic forms (parallel, restriction) it is necessary to apply the operator $NFN(\cdot,\sigma)$ (interpreted as an operator over $\mathcal{M}$) to the result.

[3] It is traditional to write such terms using "semantic brackets," as in $\mathcal{M}[\![\mathcal{P}]\!]$. We do not follow this convention in this paper because the traditional notation is so similar to CSP renaming $P[\![R]\!]$.

[4] These parameters are required because both the common knowledge and availability of fresh names may well have changed at the point of call, and it seems to be correct to evaluate the recursive call in that new world, just as is done by the textual substitution of term rewriting. In the spirit of a pure denotational semantics, fully espousing the traditions of [24], we might well wish to discriminate between *Name* and the identifiers *Ide* that denote them: this would allow definitions of input and restriction without syntactic substitution.

$NFN(\cdot, \sigma)$ was presented above as the nondeterministic choice of a set of renamings. It is easy to reformulate it as a nondeterministic relabelling, if desired.

Since no name other than a member of $fn(P)$ means anything special to a π-calculus term P, we must expect that, for any permutation η of $Name - fn(P)$, the processes P and $P[\![\eta]\!]$ are equivalent. Since *we* give meaning to members of $\kappa - fn(P)$ and σ, we cannot expect that $\mathcal{M}^1_\sqcap[P]\kappa\sigma = \mathcal{M}^1_\sqcap[P]\kappa\sigma[\![\eta]\!]$ in general, but we can expect that

$$\mathcal{M}^1_\sqcap[P]\rho\kappa\sigma = \mathcal{M}^1_\sqcap[P]\rho(\eta^{-1}(\kappa))(\eta^{-1}(\sigma))[\![\eta]\!]$$

The infinite nondeterministic choice used in *NFN* actually goes beyond the CSP syntax that some of the standard models can handle, specifically those which, like the failures-divergences model $\mathcal{N}$, have representations of divergence but not other infinite behaviours such as infinite traces. The reason for this limitation is that when a process has unbounded nondeterminism it is not possible to infer whether $P \setminus X$ can diverge from its finite traces alone. Hiding appears in our CSP translation of π-calculus as part of the definition of $|_{ccs}$. Fortunately, however, the symmetry of π-calculus semantics under permutations on names means that whenever there are arbitrarily long finite traces of terms P and Q that combine under $|$ to give prefixes of a fixed finite trace, then there is also a pair of infinite traces with the same property.[5] It follows that whenever there are arbitrarily long finite traces created by the part of the CSP construction of $|_{csp}$ other than hiding, that the hiding maps to prefixes of a given trace s, then (i) there is an infinite trace of the same process that hides to a prefix of s and (ii) s itself is recorded as a divergence by divergence strictness.

It is therefore not necessary to use CSP models involving infinite traces if one wishes to handle strict divergence accurately in π-calculus. If, however, we want to calculate the infinite traces for other reasons or to handle non-strict divergence using the techniques developed in [17], we need to use a model that represents them explicitly. As we said above, this brings with it the danger of distinguishing

[5] We can deduce this as follows. Consider the operational semantics of P and Q derived from $\text{CSP}[P]\kappa\sigma_P$ and $\text{CSP}[Q]\kappa\sigma_Q$ (without any application of *NFN*, where σ_P and σ_Q are the sets assigned to them by the $\text{CSP}[\cdot]\kappa\sigma$ semantics of $|$). These are finite branching, in the sense that every finite sequence of visible events and τs can only lead to finitely many distinct states. This depends on the fact that no single state of P or Q can have more than a finite number of distinct output $\bar{x}.y$ actions available, for otherwise $|_{ccs}$ might introduce infinite branching on τ.

The existence of arbitrarily long pairs of finite traces of P and Q such that $P \mid Q$, under perhaps different ξs, can give rise to prefixes of a given finite trace s means that $\text{CSP}[P \mid Q]\kappa\sigma$ can itself behave in the same way except that the names of the fresh names extruded might be different. So if we examine that part of the operational semantic tree of $\text{CSP}[P \mid Q]\kappa\sigma$ in which the visible trace is a prefix of s with modifications to the names of extruded fresh names permitted, it is infinite and therefore, by König's lemma, has an infinite path that necessarily ends (as viewed from the outside) in an infinite sequence of τs. It follows that $\text{CSP}[P \mid Q]\sigma\kappa$ has a divergence that is a prefix of s except that the finitely many extruded names might be different. Since there is certainly a permutation η that maps these names to the ones seen in s, it follows that the corresponding exact prefix of s, and hence s itself from divergence strictness, are divergences of $NFN(\text{CSP}[P \mid Q]\kappa\sigma, \sigma)$.

processes that we would naturally hope to be equivalent: consider the following pair of processes:

$$\mu p . \nu z \bar{x} z . p \quad \text{and} \quad \mu p . \nu y \, \nu z \bar{x} z . p$$

These both output an infinite supply of fresh names over channel $\bar{x}$. There is every reason for wanting to identify them, and indeed the terms P and $\nu y P$ when y is not free in P. A little thought, however, will reveal that our CSP[·] semantics will have $\mu p . \nu z \bar{x} z . p$ output all the enumerated fresh names one by one, whereas $\mu p . \nu y \, \nu z \bar{x} z . p$ will only output every other one.

For finite traces, this problem is easily remedied by an appropriate permutation η: any injective finite partial function from a set to itself can be extended to a permutation. This does not work for infinite traces: once we map the single infinite trace of the right-hand process to the single infinite trace of the left-hand one, there is nowhere left to map all the names that the right-hand process has missed out. We must therefore conclude that the semantics we have built to date, if interpreted over a model with infinite traces, makes undesirable distinctions between processes.

We can also conclude that the semantic values it creates are not always *closed*, in the sense that if every prefix of an infinite trace is present, then so is the infinite trace itself. This is not in itself worrying, but it means that the nondeterministic interpretation of π-calculus provides the only example known to the author of a semantics involving hiding in which models like $\mathcal{N}$ work accurately despite the processes not being closed!

An easy, if perhaps extreme, way of solving this problem is to move to having an uncountable set of *Name*; the point being that such a set can never be used up, even in an infinite trace. It is difficult to see how we can otherwise solve it in the nondeterministic spirit of *NFN*, at least in the unified case, when one considers how the environment is also allowed to pick an infinity of fresh names in some infinite traces.

To avoid these difficulties and more complex arguments later in this paper, in this paper's initial treatment of π-calculus via CSP we will only consider CSP models where each recorded behaviour only involves a finite number of names in each trace: ones that are relational images of either $\mathcal{FL}$ (as described earlier) or $\mathcal{FL}^{\Downarrow}$ (with strict divergence but without infinite behaviours), in their channel-based versions where all the acceptance sets consist only of channel names.

The fact that a π-calculus term only "knows" a finite set of names immediately, coupled with the way in which we are using channel-based models, means that all these acceptance sets are themselves finite. It follows that only finitely many members of *Name* appear in any behaviour recorded in $\mathcal{FL}$ or $\mathcal{FL}^{\Downarrow}$. We will use this fact repeatedly. We will refer to these as *finite behaviour models*.

This restriction allows one immediate simplification. The nondeterministic choice in the definition of *NFN* is over an uncountable set of functions. Over a model in which only finitely many names appear in a trace it is equivalent to additionally restrict the set of bijections to those which, except for a finite set of names, are equivalent to the identity. This is now a countable choice.

16.5.3 Standardised Fresh Names

The CSP semantics that emerges from the nondeterministic approach given above has much to recommend it, not least the symmetry. It can, however, be viewed as unnecessarily infinitary, depending as it does on infinite nondeterministic choice.

We can solve this problem by removing from the process all opportunities to choose the fresh names it extrudes. We ensure that each name to appear in this way is always the least allowed: the member of σ with least index that has not already appeared in the trace. We can achieve this with a relabelling $SFN(P, K, S)$ (standardised fresh names) presented in a similar style to OF, namely via its regulator process $Reg_{SFN}(K, S, \xi)$. This is, like Reg_{OF}, formed by composing a sets of clauses with $\Box$. The parameters are similar to those used for Reg_{OF}, except that this time the parameters are based mainly on the external view of the system since it is that which we standardising.

K (initially κ) is the external view of the current common knowledge.
S (initially σ) is the external view of the set of free names that are available to be extruded by the system.
ξ is a partial function, with domain K, that maps the external view of common knowledge to the internal one. Initially this is the identity function on κ.

The clauses forming Reg_{SFN} are:

- If both the channel and data are part of common knowledge, then an input does not change the parameters:

$$\{(\xi(x).\xi(y), x.y) \to Reg_{SFN}(K, N, \xi) \mid x, y \in K\}$$

- If both the channel and data are part of common knowledge, then an output does not change the parameters:

$$\{(\overline{\xi(x)}.\xi(y), \overline{x}.y) \to Reg_{SFN}(K, N, \xi) \mid x, y \in K\}$$

- If P outputs a fresh name x (one not in $range(\xi) = \xi(K)$), then this is seen on the outside as the least index member of S.

$$\{(\overline{\xi(x)}.y, \overline{x}.m) \to Reg_{SFN}(K \cup \{m\}, S - \{m\}, \xi + [m \mapsto y] \mid \\ m = \mu(S), x \in K, y \notin \xi(K)\}$$

- If P inputs a fresh name, then we standardise this so that it is always the one with least index not in K.

$$\{(\xi(x).\gamma(z), x.y) \to Reg_{SFN}(K \cup \{y\}, S - \{y\}, \xi + [y \mapsto \gamma(z)]) \\ \mid z = \xi(K), x \in K, y \notin K\}$$

The way we formulated this last clause means that we have not only standardised the way in which fresh names are extruded from P, but also the names that P inputs as fresh from the environment. The latter is not strictly necessary to achieve the standardised external view of our process, but (i) it has a pleasing symmetry and (ii) it might well make for more efficient automated verification.

As with *NFN*, we can add this new operator to the CSP translation

$$S[P] = (\text{CSP}[P](fn(P))N)\langle\!\langle SFN(fn(P),N)\rangle\!\rangle$$

where $fn(P)$ is the set of free names in P and $N' = Name - fn(P)$. We can also construct a denotational semantics based on any channel-based CSP model if we add an environment of the same form as used in the nondeterministic semantics.

We have the following interesting property of the relabellings used in our two semantics:

Lemma 1. *This result is about CSP processes defined over the alphabet Σ_π which respect the π-calculus discipline that no name not in the initial set K is used as a channel before it is input or output over another channel, and such that the names it thus "creates" through output are confined to the infinite set S disjoint from K.*

For any such process:

(a) For any permutation ξ of names that is the identity on Name−S, $P\langle\!\langle SFN(K,S)\rangle\!\rangle = P[\![\xi]\!]\langle\!\langle SFN(K,S)\rangle\!\rangle$ holds up to strong bisimulation.
(b) The equivalence $P\langle\!\langle SFN(K,S)\rangle\!\rangle) = NFN(P,S)\langle\!\langle SFN(K,S)\rangle\!\rangle$ holds in every finite-behaviour CSP model.

The first part simply says that it does not matter how the fresh names generated by P are permuted if they are to be renamed into standard order. The second part then follows because in any such model the $\langle\!\langle SFN(K,S)\rangle\!\rangle$ operator is distributive over nondeterministic choice.

This lemma implies that the equivalence induced by the nondeterministic semantics is at least as fine as that induced by the standardised one.

If we were to allow CSP models recording behaviours with an infinity of names in individual traces, part (b) of this lemma would not hold in reverse (i.e. with the roles of *NFN* and *SFN* transposed). This is because applying $\langle\!\langle SFN(K,S)\rangle\!\rangle$ to a behaviour b that extrudes an infinity of *Name* from S always maps it to one in which the *whole* of S appears. This means that $\langle\!\langle SFN(K,S)\rangle\!\rangle$ will identify pairs of behaviours that no permutation on S can. This is the same issue we saw when discovering undesirable inequivalences created by the nondeterministic semantics with infinite traces.

If, however, a behaviour b only involves a finite number of names, then the result of applying $\langle\!\langle SFN(K,S)\rangle\!\rangle$ to it is certain to leave an infinite set of names unrecorded in b. As in the earlier example, it is then possible to extend the finite injective mapping from S to itself, created by Reg_{SFN} by the time it has communicated all the names used in b, to a bijection. This proves the following inverse of the lemma above.

Lemma 2. *Under the same conditions as Lemma 1,*

$$NFN(P,S) = NFN(P\langle\!\langle SFN(K,S)\rangle\!\rangle, S)$$

holds in any channel-based, finite-behaviour CSP model.

We can collect these two results into the following theorem:

Theorem 1. *In any such channel-based, finite-behaviour model of CSP the standardised and nondeterministic semantics for π-calculus represent the same equivalence over process terms.*

The author believes that in cases, beyond the scope of this paper, of models including infinite-name behaviours, the standardised semantics will give the correct equivalences. In future discussions in this paper we will concentrate on the standardised form.

The parameters $\kappa \supseteq fn(P)$ and infinite σ disjoint to κ are structurally important to the semantics, but however they are chosen within these constraints they do not change the equivalence induced by the semantics, as is demonstrated by Lemma 4 below. The crucial result needed to establish this is Lemma 3: the role it plays is that it allows us to disentangle the fresh names picked by process and environment.

If b is any finite-name behaviour from a channel-based CSP model, $\mathcal{M}$ let *enames*(b, K) be the (necessarily finite) set of names first *input from* the environment that are not in the common knowledge set K. We then have the following:

Lemma 3. *If P is a π-calculus process with $fn(P) \subseteq \kappa$, and σ (disjoint from κ) is infinite, then*

$$b \in \mathcal{M}^1_\mu[P]\kappa\sigma \Leftrightarrow b \in \mathcal{M}^1_\mu[P]\kappa(\sigma - enames(b, K))$$

Lemma 4. *If P and Q are π-calculus processes with $fn(P) \cup fn(Q) \subseteq \kappa \cap \kappa'$, and σ (disjoint from κ) and σ' (disjoint from κ') are infinite, then over any finite-behaviour channel-based CSP model $\mathcal{M}$ we have*

$$\mathcal{M}^1_\mu[P]\kappa\sigma = \mathcal{M}^1_\mu[Q]\kappa\sigma \Leftrightarrow \mathcal{M}^1_\mu[P]\kappa'\sigma' = \mathcal{M}^1_\mu[Q]\kappa'\sigma'$$

It follows that we can talk about *the* congruence on π-calculus induced by a given CSP model of this type, rather than needing to calculate it relative to a particular κ and σ. In deciding the equivalence of two processes we can compare their semantics with $\kappa = fn(P) \cup fn(Q)$ and $\sigma = Name - \kappa$. The above lemma demonstrates *inter alia* that this is an equivalence relation.

16.5.4 Bipartite Semantics

In the above semantics we ensured that a pair of parallel processes $P \mid Q$ never create names that collide with each other. Our main reason for doing this was to ensure that two fresh names output directly to the environment respectively by P and Q do not collide. It has the side effect, however of meaning that when P inputs a fresh name created by Q or vice versa they never need to call upon the transpositions of OF to avoid collisions.

The only entity that we have not been able to control enough to prevent collisions is the external environment, because we have always allowed it to output *any* name to the process we are observing. It is this that characterises the *unified* approach.

In the *bipartite* approach, the set σ or S of names that the process can choose from is not only infinite, but its complement (the names either initially known or available to be created fresh by the environment) is also infinite. We replace the parameter κ, which we will not need with the bipartite treatment of freshness, with a different set, ζ. This represents the set of names which it is legitimate to receive as inputs over channels. Before the process has started to run ζ is always the complement of σ, but at some points in the semantics it is a proper subset of the complement, the difference being the fresh names that the process has created (and so are no longer in σ) but not yet extruded.

Rather than giving this alternative semantics in detail, we summarise the differences below. The translations of the input and output constructs are now as follows, noting we are defining a second translation $\text{CSP2}[\cdot]$:

$$\begin{aligned}\text{CSP2}[x(y).P]_{+}\zeta\sigma &= x?y : \zeta \to \text{CSP2}[P]_{+}\zeta\sigma \\ \text{CSP2}[\overline{x}y]_{+}\zeta\sigma &= \overline{x}.y \to \text{CSP2}[P]_{+}(\zeta \cup \{y\})\sigma\end{aligned}$$

We get a considerable simplification by being able to drop the most complicated part of the *OF* relabelling. *OF* can in fact be replaced by parallel composition with a process $BOF(\zeta)$ (bipartite output first) that enforces the discipline that no name not in ζ can be used as a channel before being output by the process:

$$\begin{aligned}BOF(Z) = {} & \Box\{x?y : Z \to BOF(Z) \mid x \in Z\} \\ & \Box \\ & \Box\{\overline{x}?y : Name \to BOF(Z \cup \{y\}) \mid x \in Z\}\end{aligned}$$

The translation of $\boldsymbol{\nu} z\, P$ thus becomes

$$\text{CSP2}[\boldsymbol{\nu} z\, P]\zeta\sigma = BOF(\zeta) \underset{\Sigma_\pi}{\parallel} \text{CSP2}[P[\mu(\sigma)/z]]\zeta(\sigma - \{\mu(\sigma)\})$$

There is no need to have the function Π_3 in the semantics of $|$: all we need are functions Π_1' and Π_2' that partition σ into two disjoint infinite sets, with each process having the other's σ incorporated into its ζ, as are any names in $Name-(\zeta \cup \sigma)$ since these have already been declared at the point the parallel composition is started, and we could easily have given the output end of such a channel to P and the input end to Q. $\text{CSP2}[P \mid Q]\zeta\sigma$ is defined to be

$$BOF(\zeta) \underset{\Sigma_\pi}{\parallel} (\text{CSP2}[P]N_1(\Pi_1'(\sigma)) \mid_{ccs} \text{CSP2}[Q]N_2(\Pi_2'(\sigma)))$$

where $N_i = Name - \Pi_i'(\sigma)$.

There is one important respect in which things get more involved. The reasons for needing to use channel-based CSP models are equally valid in this bipartite model, but the use of these models is not quite as easy to justify since processes no longer have the "no selective input" property. Just as with the argument earlier that demonstrated that the $\mathcal{N}$ semantics of divergence is correct despite the fact that processes are not closed, we need to move outside CSP's established "comfort zone." In order for the channel-based models to be valid, we need to ensure that whenever two processes are running in parallel, one inputting and one outputting a value v on a given channel c, if the inputting process is in a state where it can accept any input on c, then it can also accept v, even though there may be values that it does not accept.

This is always true of our CSP models of the π-calculus. This is because the only inputs that $\text{CSP2}[x(y)\cdot P]\zeta\sigma$ cannot make are names that have been reserved for P to generate freshly, or has already generated but not output yet. These are different from (i) the names created by the external environment by the bipartite structure, (ii) names created by other parallel processes, because of the way we use Π_1' and Π_2', and (iii) names previously output by P, by construction.

$\text{CSP2}[P]$ suffers from the same failures of abstraction due to exact choices of fresh names as the unified version $\text{CSP}[P]$. We have the same two choices of how to fix these, using the same operators $NFN(P,\sigma)$ and $\langle\langle SFN(\kappa,\sigma)\rangle\rangle$. The first of these can be used without alteration, as can the second if it is only used at the outside of the semantics. We cannot incorporate this version into a denotational semantics $\mathcal{M}^2_\mu[P]\rho\zeta\sigma$ since it requires the parameter κ. There are two choices: either to incorporate this parameter into the semantics, or to use a modified $SFN'(\sigma)$ that does not standardise how external names appear to the process P, something that is not necessary semantically.

It is interesting to note that one of our four CSP semantics, namely $\mathcal{M}^2_\sqcap[P]\zeta\sigma$, is defined without any use of generalised renaming, though it does use both elaborate renamings and parallel composition with processes that limit traces. This is related to our remark earlier that this semantics is the only where no instantaneous influence between seemingly independent parallel processes is required.

We have already seen that the two unified semantics give the same equivalence, and the equivalence they give is independent of reasonable choices for κ and σ. Simpler arguments of the same type work for the two bipartite semantics. Therefore, we will know that all four agree if we can prove that the two nondeterministic semantics agree.

Theorem 2. *For a finite-behaviour channel-based CSP model $\mathcal{M}$ and π-calculus process P, we have*

(a) $\mathcal{M}^2_\sqcap[P](Name-\sigma)\sigma = \{b \in \mathcal{M}^1_\sqcap[P](fn(P))\sigma \mid enames(b)\cap\sigma = \emptyset\}$ *whenever* $\sigma \cap fn(P) = \emptyset$ *and both* σ *and* $Name-\sigma$ *are infinite.*

(b) $\mathcal{M}^1_\sqcap[P]fn(P)\sigma = \bigsqcap\{\mathcal{M}^2_\sqcap[P](Name-\sigma')\sigma' \mid \sigma' \subseteq \sigma, (Name-\sigma')\ infinite\}$ *for any infinite* σ *disjoint from* $fn(\sigma)$.

- *Consequently, the congruences induced by* $\mathcal{M}^1_\sqcap[\cdot]$ *and* $\mathcal{M}^2_\sqcap[\cdot]$ *are the same.*

Part (a) of this result says that behaviours b of P in a bipartite name space are just those that happen in the unified name space where the environment did not choose to inject any names that it would have been banned from doing so under bipartite rules. The fact that we are in a channel-based model is vital here.

Part (b) essentially observes that for any finite behaviour b of the unified semantics, there is an infinite subset σ' of σ left when we remove *enames*(b), and b will belong to $\mathcal{M}^2_\sqcap[P](Name - \sigma')\sigma'$.

It follows that the choice of which semantics to adopt is largely down to personal taste. For the author, the unified nondeterministic semantics has much to recommend it because it removes the arbitrary choices implicit in the choice of an enumeration for *Name* – the semantic value generated by *NFN* is independent of which enumeration is used in constructing CSP[·] – and a partition of that set into process and environment names. On the other hand it seems likely that the bipartite standardised approach is best suited to most automatic verification methods.

Recall our expandable buffer example, with its four initial names K in the common knowledge of process and environment, and where there are three families of names that get introduced as it proceeds: the z_i introduced by the environment, the s_i extruded by the process, and the m_i used internally by the process but never seen in traces. In the following we will assume that each z_i devised by the environment is fresh.

- In the $\mathcal{M}^1_\sqcap[\cdot]$ semantics, any trace in which all the s_i and z_i are different (and different from K) is allowed.
- In the $\mathcal{M}^1_\mu[\cdot]$ semantics, there are less traces, since each s_i is always the name with least index not seen up to that point.
- With $\mathcal{M}^2_\sqcap[\cdot]$, the s_i and z_i are chosen from two predetermined separate pots.
- And in $\mathcal{M}^2_\mu[\cdot]$, the sequence of s_i is fixed at the outset since they are chosen in order from a pot that is not used for any other purpose.

One of the most interesting things we might observe about this is that nothing in a trace reveals the values or even presence of the m_i to the outside world. In particular the standardised $\mathcal{M}^1_\mu[\cdot]$ semantics seems to use up all the names for the visible names, leaving none for the m_i. Whether or not one regards this as paradoxical depends on one's standpoint: certainly we would not want the abstract semantic value of a process to depend on whether it used a name internally or not.

16.6 Properties and Future Work

We have simultaneously introduced a large number of new semantics for π-calculus, simply because there is one[6] for every channel-based CSP model that does not give a representation to infinite traces. We cannot hope to explore all their properties here. In this section, therefore, we restrict ourselves to establishing a few basic properties and setting out a research programme to explore further possibilities.

[6] We say "one" here, because the four options for presenting it are congruent to each other.

Throughout this section, the $\mathcal{M}$ semantics of a π-calculus process P will be understood to mean the standardised (*SFN*) semantics calculated over the channel-based CSP model $\mathcal{M}$ over a unified name space with parameters $fn(P)$ and $Name - fn(P)$

16.6.1 Refinement and Refinement Checking

The most obvious consequence of having a CSP semantics is that it gives a language a natural notion of refinement. We define refinement, relative to a given model $\mathcal{M}$, by

$$P \sqsubseteq_M Q \equiv \mathcal{M}^1_\mu[P]\kappa\sigma \sqsubseteq \mathcal{M}^1_\mu[Q]\kappa\sigma$$

for any κ containing $fn(P) \cup fn(Q)$, which is the same as the $\mathcal{M}$-equivalence, *as processes*, of P and $\tau.P+\tau.Q$ (simply a translation of the CSP construct $P \sqcap Q$). This equational characterisation means that the definitions of refinement do not depend on which of the four options is chosen.

Our constructions, Lemma 4, and the properties of refinement in CSP imply that $\sqsubseteq_M$ has the compositionality properties one would want, namely

$$P \sqsubseteq_M Q \Rightarrow C[P] \sqsubseteq_M C[Q]$$

for any context C.

As in CSP, one process refines another if its behaviours are a subset of those of the second process. Thus one process trace refines another if all its traces are ones of the second, and so on.

In CSP models that record only finitely observable behaviours (a category that does not include divergence), there is a refinement-maximal process, always equivalent to the simply divergent term $\mu\, p.\tau.p$. There is a refinement-minimal member of the CSP model, but no π-calculus process represents it since the minimal member has the capability of using every name on the first step as an output channel. No π-calculus term can do that. It is possible to construct a minimal process in the traces model subject to knowing the set of names K initially: imagine a system constructed using the replication $!C$ and $!D$ of two sorts of cell. A C is initialised with one name x and can then endlessly either input $x(y)$ or output a fresh name $\overline{x}z$ where z is introduced by νz (and in either case it initialises a further C with name y or z) or initialise a D with value x.

$$C = c(x).\, \mu\, p.\nu z.(x(y).\overline{c}y.p + \overline{x}z.\overline{c}z.p + \overline{d}x.p)$$

D is initialised with two names and then endlessly outputs one over the other.

$$D = d(x).d(y).\, \mu\, p.\overline{x}y.p$$

The process is then defined $\nu c\, \nu d\, !C \mid !D \mid C'[k_1/x] \mid \cdots \mid C'[k_n/x]$ where C' is an initialised copy of C.

The $!C = \mu p.C \mid \tau.p$ construction could not be used in the same way in building refinement-minimal elements of other finite-behaviour models such as stable failures $\mathcal{F}$ because it is never stable itself. It is, nevertheless, possible to adapt the above construction to build a refinement-minimal element for $\mathcal{F}$ for a given initial knowledge K. This is left as an exercise to the ingenious reader!

In FDR, the main mode of verifying processes is to show that they refine other CSP processes representing their specifications. Since our constructions have, in effect, embedded π-calculus within CSP, we have considerable freedom in how to formulate refinement checks using a mixture of the two languages.[7] A reasonably general model is provided by checks of the form

$$\mathit{Spec} \sqsubseteq_M C[\mathit{Imp}]$$

where *Spec* is either a CSP or π-calculus process and C is a possibly null CSP context.

So, for example, deadlock freedom is equivalent to the refinement check

$$\mu p.\tau.p \sqsubseteq_F \mathit{Imp} \setminus \mathit{Events}$$

and we can use the *lazy abstraction* construction from CSP, as in the following *fault tolerance* check from Chapter 12 of [16] that goes a little beyond the model above:

$$\mathit{Imp} \underset{E}{\parallel} \mathit{STOP} \sqsubseteq_F (\mathit{Imp} \underset{E}{\parallel} \mathit{CHAOS}(E)) \setminus E$$

where E is a set of events that trigger erroneous behaviour within *Imp*. This specification says that whatever externally visible behaviour appears with these error events allowed also happens when they are banned.

16.6.2 Prospects for Using FDR

Having formulated specifications as refinement checks, it is interesting to ask whether they can be run on FDR, since this might provide a powerful additional tool to apply to systems designed in π-calculus.

FDR achieves its considerable speed by concentrating on finite-state systems, allowing most checks to be performed in time linear (or sublinear if compressions are used) in the number of states of the implementation. It concentrates on what is the central case of CSP, namely of a number of finite-state processes connected by a static harness built of parallel, hiding and renaming operators.

This is challenged by two aspects of π-calculus. Firstly, π-calculus assumes that every $x(y)$ input communication offers an infinite range of inputs. Secondly,

[7] In such usage it will be necessary to ensure that any CSP used respects the no-selective-input regime required to make channel-based models works.

π-calculus networks are frequently dynamic and potentially unbounded in size, as seen both in our buffer example and in the construction above that built the trace-refinement-minimal process. This takes them outside FDR's "comfort zone" and probably out of its range altogether.

It therefore seems sensible to start by looking at π-calculus networks that create static networks and which generate only finitely new names using $\nu z\, P$ constructs.

We therefore consider networks which take the form

$$\nu x_1\, \nu x_2 \ldots \nu x_n\, (P_1 \mid P_2 \mid \ldots \mid P_m)$$

where the P_i make no use of the operators $\mid$ and νx and are therefore finite-state except for the precise names they contain.

The author conjectures that the majority of trace refinement checks involving such processes can be performed finitely in the following way, thanks to Lazić's theory of data independence in CSP [8].

- Use the bipartite approach to semantics.
- Use a type of $n + k + 2$ names, of which n are tied to the identifiers $x_1, \ldots, x_n$, k are the externally visible names in the system, and the final two are "extras." The reason for there are just two extra names is that every π-calculus term, with the exception of the inequality constraints for fresh names, satisfies the condition **PosConjEqT** from [8], which states that no two members of the data-independent type (here *Name*) are ever compared for equality except in such a way that the consequences of equality are always trace refined by the consequences of inequality. In π-calculus, both (obviously) equality guards $[x = y]$ and communication in $P \mid Q$ represent equality tests of this sort. The first use of any extra name must be as an input along a preexisting channel. Lazić's results show that in similar circumstances, it usually suffices to consider a check in which the data-independent type is of size one or two greater than the number of distinct constant values. This represents a *threshold* value for the refinement check. Thus initially, and until the process has extruded one or more of the names x_i, inputs are restricted to the other $k + 2$ names L.
- Regarding the identifiers x_i as constants, replace the system with $(P_1 \mid \ldots \mid P_m) \underset{\Sigma\pi}{\parallel} BOF(L)$.
- This process may well not be symmetric in the names x_i, but if it is refinement checked against a process that is symmetric in them (for example, by not referring to them at all, as will presumably be the case when the system does not extrude names) it should be equivalent to check that the unsymmetric version refines the specification.

Data independence will, in fact, be applicable to all π-calculus descriptions of systems: it is impossible to create π-calculus processes that are not data independent, at least using the syntax we have adopted for it.

Another class of system that uses an unbounded collection of fresh values has already been widely studied in CSP, namely cryptographic protocols where the values are keys, nonces, etc. (This connection has already been exploited in the Spi Calculus [1].) Several related methods for turning naturally infinite-state refinement checks involving these into finite-state ones have been developed for these protocols [7, 21]. These methods use a combination of recycling values that no longer have any meaning to the system and making room for this by identifying "out of date" values.

It would be interesting to see whether these same techniques can be employed usefully for π-calculus systems that generate an infinite number of fresh names in their lifetimes, but only have a finite number meaningful at any one time.

Using the present version of FDR it is not possible to analyse networks that grow unboundedly. It should, however, be possible to analyse ones that are dynamic but only have a bounded number of active (i.e. nonzero processes in π-calculus terms) at any one time and only have a finite number of patterns that these processes follow. We would need to create a CSP process definition *Flex* that could be initialised to behave like one of these patterns and returns to the state *Flex* once the first pattern has finished. When a process executes a parallel command $P \mid Q$ it would implement one of these (say P) itself and initialise one of the available *Flex*es to behave like Q.

16.6.3 Full Abstraction

All the well-known CSP models are fully abstract with respect to one or more simple tests that can be made of processes in the sense that two processes P and Q are identified in the model if and only if, for all CSP contexts $C[\cdot]$, $C[P]$ passes each of the tests if and only if $C[Q]$ does. (See [16, 18, 19] for information on this.) Thus, for example, the finite traces model $\mathcal{T}$ is fully abstract with respect to the test "P has the trace $\langle a \rangle$" for an arbitrarily chosen visible event a, and the failures divergences model $\mathcal{N}$ is fully abstract with respect to the test "neither deadlocks nor diverges on $\langle \rangle$."

It is clear that, when a given CSP model $\mathcal{M}$ has such a property, then two π-calculus terms P and Q are identified in it if and only if all *CSP* contexts applied to them give the same results for the tests. It is interesting to ask whether the same will hold for *π-calculus* contexts. The author believes that most of these results will indeed carry across in this way, but resolving these questions is beyond the scope of this paper.

16.6.4 Comparison

Equivalences for π-calculus terms have previously been given in terms of bisimulation relations of different sorts. Over other process calculi it is true that bisimulations relations generally give *finer* equivalences than CSP-style models, except that some bisimulations (e.g. weak) do not make the same distinctions based on the potential to diverge that some CSP models do. The author expects that the same will be true for π-calculus.

It seems to the author that the semantics of π-calculus in CSP models have the merit of simplicity, in the sense that each recorded behaviour only gives a single value to each name, whichever of our four options is picked. These models seem no less natural for π-calculus than they do for CSP. Indeed, given that in a unified name space it is inevitable that any branching-lime model for π-calculus there will be recorded behaviours on which the name declared in $\nu z P$ will appear with two different values, the use of linear observations seems *particularly* appropriate here.

While our four different ways of treating the fresh names of π-calculus create different models of a process, they do not change the equivalence induced by the translation. This is in contrast to the usual bisimulation-based equivalences for the languages (early, late, barbed, etc.).

16.7 Conclusions

We have illustrated the enormous expressive power of Hoare's CSP by giving a number of semantics to π-calculus. The author hopes that in addition to providing this demonstration of the power of CSP this paper will also be the key to new understandings and process analysis methods for π-calculus, and that for some audiences it might provide a relatively comprehensible way of explaining the semantics of that notation. In particular, it will be interesting to see if the existence of compositional theories of refinement for π-calculus will have any applications.

In addition to the topics for further work highlighted in the previous section, there is a further open end to be explored, namely the topic of models with infinite traces. Since an infinite trace can contain an infinite number of fresh names, several of the arguments we have used in this paper no longer apply, and it becomes possible for a single trace to contain every single name if there are only finitely many of these.

While this may or may not be apparent to the reader, the author discovered on numerous occasions that the semantic decisions made in the design of π-calculus were absolutely crucial to the creation of a reasonably elegant semantics for it in CSP. A prime example of this is the rule that no fresh name can be used as a channel until it has been passed along another channel is necessary for ensuring that the first time a name appears in a behaviour in a channel-based model is as the "data" field of an actually communicated event. This is key to a number of things working properly in the CSP semantics. Thus, at least to the author, this work demonstrated not only the power of CSP, but also the great elegance of the π-calculus.

Acknowledgements Peter Welch [26] originally persuaded me to look at mobility in CSP. The fact that I managed to create a mobile parallel operator for him was one of the main spurs towards looking for a general expressivity result. My initial work on CCS was inspired by the title of [5]. I had useful conversations with many people about this work, notably Tony Hoare, Michael Goldsmith, Samson Abramsky, Rob van Glabbeek, Gavin Lowe and Michael Mislove. The presentation has benefited greatly from Cliff Jones's advice.

The author's work on this paper was funded by grants from EPSRC and US ONR.

References

1. Abadi, M., Gordon, A.D.: A calculus for cryptographic protocols: the Spi calculus. Proceedings of the 4th ACM conference on Computer and communications security (1997).
2. Brookes, S.D.: A model for Communicating Sequential Processes. Oxford University DPhil thesis (1983).
3. Brookes, S.D., Hoare, C.A.R., Roscoe, A.W.: A theory of communicating Sequential Processes. Appeared as monograph PRG-16, 1981. http://web.comlab.ox.ac.uk/people/Bill.Roscoe/publications/1.pdf and extended in JACM **31**, pp. 560–599 (1984).
4. Brookes, S.D., Roscoe, A.W., Walker, D.J.: An operational semantics for CSP. Oxford University Technical Report (1986).
5. He, J., Hoare, C.A.R.: CCS is a retract of CCS. Unifying Theories of Programming symposium, Springer LNCS 4010 (2006).
6. Hoare, C.A.R.: Communicating Sequential Processes. Prentice Hall (1985).
7. Kleiner, E.: A web services security study using Casper and FDR. Oxford University DPhil thesis (2008).
8. Lazić, R.S.: A semantic study of data-independence with applications to the mechanical verification of concurrent systems. Oxford University D.Phil thesis (1998).
9. Milner, R.: A Calculus of Communicating Systems. LNCS 92 (1980).
10. Milner, R.: Communication and concurrency. Prentice-Hall (1989).
11. Milner, R.: Communicating and mobile systems: the π-calculus. CUP (1999).
12. Milner, R., Parrow, J., Walker, D.: A calculus of mobile systems, Parts I/II, Information and Computation (1992).
13. Roscoe, A.W.: A mathematical theory of Communicating Sequential Processes. Oxford University DPhil thesis (1982).
14. Roscoe, A.W.: Denotational semantics for occam, Proceedings of the 1984 Pittsburgh Seminar on Concurrency, Springer LNCS 197
15. Roscoe, A.W.: Model-checking CSP, in A Classical Mind, essays in honour of C.A.R. Hoare, Prentice-Hall (1994).
16. Roscoe, A.W.: The theory and practice of concurrency. Prentice-Hall (1998).
17. Roscoe, A.W.: Seeing beyond divergence, Communicating Sequential Processes, the first 25 years, Springer LNCS 3525 (2005).
18. Roscoe, A.W.: Revivals, stuckness and the hierarchy of CSP models, JLaP **78**, 3, pp. 163–190 (2009).
19. Roscoe, A.W.: The three platonic models of divergence-strict CSP. Proceedings of ICTAC (2008).
20. Roscoe, A.W.: On the expressiveness of CSP, Submitted for publication.
21. Roscoe, A.W., Broadfoot, P.J.: Proving security protocols with model checkers by data independence techniques. J. Comput. Secur. **7**, pp. 147–190 (1999).
22. Roscoe, A. W., Gardiner, P.H.B., Goldsmith, M.H., Hulance, J.R., Jackson, D.M., Scattergood, J.B.: Hierarchical compression for model-checking CSP, or How to check $10\hat{2}0$ dining philosophers for deadlock. In Proceedings of TACAS 1995 LNCS 1019.
23. Sangiorgi, D., Walker, D.: The π-calculus: A theory of mobile processes. Cambridge University press (2001).
24. Stoy, J.E.: Denotational Semantics: The Scott-Strachey Approach to Programming Language Theory. MIT Press (1977).
25. van Glabbeek, R.J.: On cool congruence formats for weak bisimulation, Proceedings of ICTAC 2005, Springer LNCS 3722.
26. Welch, P.H., Barnes, F.R.M.: A CSP model for mobile processes, Proc CPA 2008, IOS Press (2008).

Chapter 17
The Tokeneer Experiments

Jim Woodcock, Emine Gökçe Aydal, and Rod Chapman

For Tony Hoare, to celebrate his 75th birthday.

Abstract We describe an experiment conducted as part of a pilot project in the Verified Software Initiative (VSI). We begin by recounting the background to the VSI and its six initial pilot projects, and give an update on the current progress of each project. We describe one of these, the Tokeneer ID Station in greater detail. Tokeneer was developed by Praxis High Integrity Systems and SPRE for the US National Security Agency, and it has been acclaimed by the US National Academies as representing best practice in software development. To date, only five errors have been found in Tokeneer, and the entire project archive has been released for experimentation within the VSI. We describe the first experiment using the Tokeneer archive. Our objective is to investigate the dependability claims for Tokeneer as a security-critical system. Our experiment uses a model-based testing technique that exploits formal methods and tools to discover nine anomalous scenarios. We discuss four of these in detail.

17.1 Introduction (by JW)

In 2002, I attended a colloquium in Lisbon to celebrate the UN Software Technology Institute's 10th Anniversary [1]. Tony Hoare gave a talk on the use of assertions in current Microsoft practice, where they instrument programs as software testing

J. Woodcock (✉)
Department of Computer Science, University of York, Heslington,
York YO10 5DD, Great Britain
e-mail: jim@cs.york.ac.uk

E.G. Aydal
Department of Computer Science, University of York
e-mail: aydal@ieee.org

R. Chapman
Altran Praxis Limited, 20 Manvers Street, Bath BA1 1PX, Great Britain
e-mail: rod.chapman@altran-praxis.com

C.B. Jones et al. (eds.), *Reflections on the Work of C.A.R. Hoare*,
DOI 10.1007/978-1-84882-912-1_17,

probes [40]. He went on to describe the greater benefits that would follow from using a tool to check a program's adherence to its assertions: *the Verifying Compiler*. He concluded by saying that building a verifying compiler would be a "splendid opportunity for academic research" and "one of the major challenges of Computing Science in the twenty-first century," likening it to the Human Genome project.

Tony had invited me to lecture at that year's Marktoberdorf Summer School. During one of the excursions, he repeated to me his idea for the verifying compiler as a way of galvanising the computer science community into a productive long-term research programme: a Grand Challenge. This, Tony said, was the dream of Jim King's doctoral thesis [59], a dream abandoned in the 1970s as being well beyond current theorem-proving capabilities. But much progress had been made in the following 30 years, both in hardware capacity and in the software technologies for verification. Tony suggested that the renewed challenge of an automatic verifying compiler could provide a focus for interaction, cross-fertilisation, advancement, and experimental evaluation of all relevant verification technologies. Perhaps by a concerted international effort, we might be able to meet this challenge within 15–25 years. I was now recruited to the cause.

In November that year, there was a UK Grand Challenge Workshop in Edinburgh, where more than 100 proposals were submitted [43]. These proposals were distilled into just seven grand challenges, one of which included the verifying compiler: *GC6—Dependable Systems Evolution*. As its name suggests, this challenge was based on a very broad understanding of software correctness, and tried to include as wide a community of researchers as possible, spanning the range of interests from full functional correctness through to issues of dependability, where formalisation is difficult, if at all possible. Three threads of activity were launched to progress GC6: software verification, dependability, and evolution. Tony Hoare, Cliff Jones, and Brian Randell tried to maintain the breadth of the grand challenge by emphasising the importance of the work on dependability and evolution [44], but proposals like this are shaped by the availability and enthusiasm of the individuals involved, and the only thread that has so far really taken off was the one inspired by Tony's original idea of the verifying compiler. The main activity within this thread has been experimental work on pilot verification projects, as reported in this paper.

The term "verifying compiler" is often misunderstood by researchers, who sometimes hear "verified compiler." It is also often thought of as just a single tool for a single programming language, probably an idealised academic one at that. But this was never Tony's intention. The verifying compiler was a cipher for an integrated set of tools checking correctness, in a very broad sense, of a wide range of programming artefacts. In promoting the grand challenge, Tony talked about things that might have surprised his colleagues only a few years before. He talked not just about full functional correctness, but about checking isolated properties and about the subtler notions of robustness and dependability. He talked about tools that were neither sound nor complete, about inter-operability of tools, and about the practical programming languages used in industry. He even talked about testing.

GC6 has now transformed into an international grand challenge: the Verified Software Initiative, led by Tony Hoare and Jay Misra, and its manifesto [42] represents a consensus position that has emerged from a series of national and international meetings, workshops, and conferences. Overviews of the background and objectives may be found in [52, 77, 78]. Surveys of the state of the art are available [41], covering practice and experience in formal methods [8, 80], automated deduction for verification [68], and software model checking [51].

Interest in the VSI's research agenda has grown from just a few dedicated individuals in 2002 to a distinct community today. There are 55 different international research groups working in the experimental strand alone. Many members of this community are young researchers, making important contributions at early stages of their career. They have their own conference series, Verified Software: Theories, Tools, and Experiments (Zurich 2005 [64], Toronto 2008 [69], and Edinburgh 2010). They have published a series of special journal issues (some are still in press): ACM Computing Surveys, Formal Aspects of Computing [18, 54], Science of Computer Programming [28], Journal of Object Technology, Journal of Universal Computer Science [4], and Software Tools for Technology Transfer. They organise working meetings at leading and specialist conferences: FM Symposium, FLoC, SBMF, ICTAC, ICFEM, ICECCS, and SEFM. They represent six continents: North and South America, Europe, Asia, Australia and Africa.

17.2 The Verified Software Repository

The main focus of the UK's contribution to the VSI is on building a Verified Software Repository [9, 75], which will eventually contain hundreds of programs and components, amounting to several million lines of code. This will be accompanied by full or partial specifications, designs, test cases, assertions, evolution histories, and other formal and informal documentation. Each program will be mechanically checked by at least one tool, although most will be analysed by a series of tools in a comparative study. The Repository's programs are selected by the research community as realistically representing the wide diversity of computer applications, including smartcards, embedded software, device drivers, a standard class library, an embedded operating system, a compiler for a useful language (possibly Java Card), and parts of the verifier itself, a program generator, a communications protocol (possibly TCP/IP), a desk-top application, parts of a web service (perhaps Apache). The main purpose of the Repository is to advance science, but reusable verified components may well be taken up in real-life application domains.

Verification of repository components already includes the wide spectrum of program properties, from avoidance of specific exceptions like buffer overflow, general structural integrity (crash-proofing), continuity of service, security against intrusion, safety, partial functional correctness, and (at the highest level) total functional correctness [45]. The techniques used are similarly wide ranging: from unit testing to partial verification, through bounded model checking to fully formal proof. To understand exactly what has been achieved, each claim for a specific level of correctness is accompanied by a clear informal statement of the assumptions and limitations of the proof, and the contribution that it makes to system dependability. The progress of the project can be measured by the automation involved in reaching each level of verification for each module in the Repository. Since the ultimate goal of the project is scientific, the ultimate aim is for complete automation of every property, higher than the expectations of a normal engineer or customer.

In the remainder of this introductory section, we describe the status of some early pilot projects that are being used to populate the Repository. Mondex is a smartcard for electronic finance. The Verified Filestore is inspired by a real space-flight application. FreeRTOS is a real-time scheduler that is very widely used in embedded systems. The Cardiac Pacemaker is a real system, and is representative of an important class of medical devices. Microsoft's Hypervisor is based on one of their future products. Finally, Tokeneer is a security application involving biometrics. These six pilot projects encompass a wide variety of application areas and each poses some important challenges for verification.

17.2.1 Mondex

The following description is based on [81]. In the early 1990s, the National Westminster Bank and Platform Seven (a UK software house) developed a smartcard-based electronic cash system, Mondex, suitable for low-value cash-like transactions, with no third-party involvement, and no cost per transaction. A discussion of the security requirements can be found in [73, 81]; a description of some wider requirements can be found in [2]. It was crucial that the card was secure, otherwise money could be electronically counterfeited, so Platform Seven decided to certify Mondex to one of the very highest standards available at the time: ITSEC Level E6 [46], which approximates to Common Criteria Level EAL7 [14] (see the discussion in Section 17.3). This mandates stringent requirements on software design, development, testing, and documentation procedures. It also mandates the use of formal methods to specify the high-level abstract security policy model and the lower-level concrete architectural design. It requires a formal proof of correspondence between the two, in order to show that the concrete design obeys the abstract security properties. The evaluation was carried out by the Logica Commercial Licensed Evaluation Facility, with key parts subcontracted to the University of York to ensure independence.

The target platform smartcard had an 8-bit microprocessor, a low clock speed, limited memory (256 bytes of dynamic RAM, and a few kilobytes of slower EEPROM), and no built-in operating system support for tasks such as memory management. Power could be withdrawn at any point during the processing of a transaction. Logica was contracted to deliver the specification and proof using Z [71, 79]. They had little difficulty in formalising the concrete architectural design from the existing semi-formal design documents, but the task of producing an abstract security policy model that both captured the desired security properties (in particular, that "no value is created" and that "all value is accounted for") and provably corresponded to the lower-level specification, was much harder. A very small change in the design would have made the abstraction much easier, but was thought to be too expensive to implement, as the parallel implementation work was already well beyond that point. The 200-page proof was carried out by hand, and revealed a small flaw in one of the minor protocols; this was presented to Platform Seven in the form of a security-compromising scenario. Since this constituted a real security problem, the design was changed to rectify it. The extensive proofs carried out were done manually using some novel techniques [72]. The decision not to use mechanical theorem proving was intended to keep costs under control. Recent work (reported below) has shown that this was overly cautious, and that Moore's Law has swung the balance further in favour of cost-effective mechanical verification.

In 1999, Mondex achieved its ITSEC Level E6 certificate: the very first product ever to do so. As a part of the ITSEC E6 process, the entire Mondex development was additionally subjected to rigorous testing, which was itself evaluated. No errors were found in any part of the system subjected to the use of formal methods.

Mondex was revived in 2006 as a pilot project for the Grand Challenge in Verified Software. The main objective was to test how the state of the art in mechanical verification had moved on in 10 years. Eight groups took up the challenge using the following formal methods (with references to a full discussion of the kinds of analysis that were performed in each case): Alloy [67], ASM [39], Event-B [10], OCL [60], PerfectDeveloper,[1] π-calculus [53], Raise [36], and Z [32]. The cost of mechanising the Z proofs of the original project was 10% of the original development cost, and so did not dominate costs as initially believed. Interestingly, almost all techniques used in the Mondex pilot achieved the same level of automation, producing similar numbers of verification conditions and requiring similar effort (see [54] for a discussion of these similarities).

17.2.2 Verified Filestore

At an early workshop on the Verifying Compiler, Amir Pnueli suggested that we should choose the verification of the Linux kernel as a pilot project. It would be a significant challenge, and would have a lasting impact. Joshi and Holzmann suggested a more modest aim: the verification of the implementation of a subset of the POSIX filestore interface suitable for flash-memory hardware with strict fault-tolerance requirements to be used by forthcoming NASA missions [56]. They required the system would prevent corruption in the presence of unexpected power-loss, and that it would be able to recover from faults specific to flash hardware (e.g., bad blocks, read errors, bit corruption, wear-levelling, etc.) [35] . The POSIX file-system interface [55] was chosen for four reasons: (i) it is a clean, well-defined,

[1] No paper is available on the PerfectDeveloper treatment of Mondex, but see [24] for a general discussion of the PerfectDeveloper tool itself.

and standard interface that has been stable for many years; (ii) the data structures and algorithms required are well understood; (iii) although a small part of an operating system, it is complex enough in terms of reliability guarantees, such as unexpected power-loss, concurrent access, or data corruption; and (iv) modern information technology is massively dependent on reliable and secure information availability. An initial subset of the POSIX standard has been chosen for the pilot project. There is no support for: (i) file permissions; (ii) hard or symbolic-links; or (iii) entities other than files and directories (e.g., pipes and sockets). Adding support for (i) is not difficult and may be done later, whereas support for (ii) and (iii) is more difficult and might be beyond the scope of the challenge. Existing flash-memory file-systems, such as YAFFS2 [50], do not support these features, since they are not usually needed for the functionality of an embedded system.

Freitas and Woodcock have mechanically verified existing Z models of the POSIX API [33] and a higher-level transaction processing API [31, 34]. Freitas has shown how to verify datatypes for the design of operating system kernels [30]. Butterfield, Freitas, and Woodcock have modelled the behaviour of flash memory devices [11–13]. Butler has specified a tree-structured file system in Event-B [26], and has specified some of the details of the flash file system itself [25]. Mühlberg and Lüttgen have used model checking to verify compiled file-system code [65], and Jackson has used Alloy to produce a relational model of aspects of a flash file system [57]. Ferreira and Oliveira have integrated Alloy, VDM++, and HOL into a tool chain to verify parts of the Intel flash file system [29]. Finally, Kim has explored the flash multi-sector read operation using concolic testing [58].

17.2.3 FreeRTOS

Richard Barry (Wittenstein High Integrity Systems) has proposed the correctness of their open-source real-time mini-kernel as a pilot project. It runs on a wide range of different architectures and is used in many commercial embedded systems. There are over 5,000 downloads per month from SourceForge, putting it in the top 250 of SourceForge's 170,000 codes. It is less than 2,500 lines of pointer-rich code, which makes it small, but very interesting. The first challenge is to analyse the program for structural integrity properties, for example, to prove that its elaborate use of pointers is safe. The second challenge is to make a rational reconstruction of the development of the program, starting from an abstract specification, and refining down to working code, with all verification conditions discharged with a high level of automation. These challenges push the current state of the art in both program analysis and refinement of pointer programs.

Déharbe has produced an abstract specification of FreeRTOS [27] and Machado has shown how to generate tests automatically from the code [63]. Craig is working on the formal specification and refinement in Z of more general operating system kernels [22, 23]. Some of his models have been verified by Freitas and Woodcock.

17.2.4 *Cardiac Pacemaker*

Boston Scientific has released into the public domain the system specification for a previous generation pacemaker, and is offering it as a challenge problem. They have released a specification that defines functions and operating characteristics, identifies system environmental performance parameters, and characterises anticipated uses. This challenge has multiple dimensions and levels. Participants may choose to submit a complete version of the pacemaker software, designed to run on specified hardware, they may choose to submit just a formal requirements documents, or anything in between. McMaster University's Software Quality Research Laboratory is putting in place a certification framework to simulate the concept of licensing. This will enable the Challenge community to explore the concept of licensing evidence and the role of standards in the production of such software. Furthermore, it will provide a more objective basis for comparison between putative solutions to the Challenge.

Lawson and his colleagues at McMaster University maintain a web page describing the state of the Pacemaker pilot project [61]. It gives details of the pacemaker hardware reference platform, developed by students at the University of Minnesota, based on an 8-bit PIC18F4520 microcontroller. Macedo, Fitzgerald and Larsen have an incremental development of a distributed real-time model of a cardiac pacing system using VDM [62]. Gomes and Oliveira have specified the Pacemaker in Z, and carried out proofs of consistency of their specification using ProofPowerZ [37].

17.2.5 *Microsoft Hypervisor*

Schulte and Paul initiated work within Microsoft on a hypervisor (a kind of separation kernel), and it has been proposed by Thomas Santen as a challenge project. The European Microsoft Innovation Center is collaborating with German academic partners and the Microsoft Research group for Programming Languages and Methods on the formal verification of the new Microsoft Hypervisor, to be released as part of as new Windows Server. The Hypervisor will allow multiple guest operating systems to run concurrently on a single hardware platform. By proving the mathematical correctness of the Hypervisor, they will control the risks of malicious attack. Cohen has briefly described the Microsoft Hypervisor project [17].

17.3 Pilot project: Tokeneer ID Station

In this section, we describe one of the pilot projects in a lot more detail: the Tokeneer ID Station (TIS), a project conducted by Praxis High Integrity Systems and SPRE for the US National Security Agency. See [15] for an overview of the system, and [6] for an account of how it was engineered. Tony Hoare has already recorded his opinion of the work carried out: "The Tokeneer project is a milestone in the transfer of program verification technology into industrial application" [74]. A report from the US National Academies [48] refers to several Praxis projects as examples of best practice in software engineering, particularly in the areas of formal methods and programming language design and verification.

The Tokeneer project was originally conceived to supply evidence about whether it is economically feasible to develop systems that can be assured to the higher levels of the Common Criteria Security Evaluation, the ISO/IEC 15408 standard for computer security certification [14]. The standard defines seven levels for evaluating information technology security:

- EAL7: formally verified design and tested
- EAL6: semi-formally verified design and tested
- EAL5: semi-formally designed and tested
- EAL4: methodically designed, tested, and reviewed
- EAL3: methodically tested and checked
- EAL2: structurally tested
- EAL1: functionally tested

Barnes et al. report that an evaluation in 1998 to what is now understood as EAL4 cost about US$2.5 million [6].

Numerous smartcard devices have been evaluated at EAL5, as have multilevel secure devices such as the Tenix Interactive Link. XTS-400 (STOP 6) is a general-purpose operating system, which has been evaluated at an augmented EAL5 level. An example of an EAL6 certified system is the Green Hills Software INTEGRITY-178B operating system, the only operating system to achieve EAL6 so far. The Tenix Interactive Link Data Diode Device has been evaluated at EAL7 augmented, the only product to achieve this.

The problem with these higher levels of the Common Criteria is that industry believes that it is simply too expensive to develop systems to this standard. The argument is a familiar one. In 1997, the UK Government Communications Headquarters held a workshop to discuss the view held in industry that it was too expensive to use formal methods to achieve ITSEC Level E6 [76], approximately EAL7. The Mondex project (see Section 17.2) provided evidence to the contrary.

So the objective of the Tokeneer project was to explore the feasibility of developing cost-effective, high-quality, low-defect EAL5 systems, and to provide evidence for both EAL6 and EAL7. It was a rare and valuable opportunity to undertake the controlled measurement of productivity and defect rates. Remarkably, the entire project archive is openly available and may be downloaded from [74].

Praxis have a well-developed software engineering method that addresses not only assurance, but also cost requirements. Their method starts from requirements analysis using their REVEAL technique, continues with specification and development, using formal methods where appropriate, until an implementation is reached in SPARK, a high-level programming language and toolset designed for writing software for high-integrity applications [7]. They have a successful record of using their method to develop commercial applications of formal methods, with costs reportedly lower than traditional manual object-oriented methods.

Tokeneer was the subject of an earlier NSA research project investigating the use of biometrics for physical access control to a secure room containing user workstations (the *enclave*). The Tokeneer ID Station contributed to a further development of the original system. The key idea is that users have smartcard security tokens that must be used both to gain access to the enclave and to use the workstations once the user is inside. There are smartcard and biometric readers outside the enclave; if a user passes their identity tests, then the door opens for entry. Authorisation information is written onto the card for subsequent workstation access. This information describes privileges the user can enjoy for this visit, including times of working, security clearance and user roles.

In what follows, it is important to understand the Tokeneer ID Station security target, in order to answer the question, "Is Tokeneer *really* secure?" The requirements assume that the enclave is situated in a high-security area, and so all the users will have passed a stringent security clearance procedure, either as NSA employees or as accredited visitors. As a consequence, it may be safely assumed that no user will ever attempt a malicious attack on the enclave. Instead, the security measures are intended to prevent accidents: *unintentional, unauthorised access* to the enclave and the data provided by its workstations.

The overall functionality of the Tokeneer ID Station was formalised in a 100-page Z specification. The code was developed in two parts. The core security-related functionality was implemented in SPARK, and amounts to 9,939 lines of code, with 6,036 lines of flow annotations, 1,999 lines of proof annotations, and 8,529 lines of comments. The remainder of the system was not security critical, and so was developed using Ada95, comprising 3,697 lines of code, no flow or poof annotations, and 2,240 lines of comments. The entire development required 260 man-days, provided by three people working part-time over 9 months.

The task set by NSA was to conform to EAL5. The development actually exceeded EAL5 requirements in several areas, including configuration control, fault management, and testing. The main body of the core development work was carried out to EAL5. But the specification, design, implementation and proof of correspondence were conducted to EAL6 and 7. So why would Praxis do more than they were asked to do? Because they were told that, if they could produce evidence at these higher levels within budget, then they should.

The Tokeneer project archive has been downloaded many hundreds of times. Knight [38] has verified Tokeneer properties using the PVS theorem prover [66]. Jackson is working to broaden the range of properties of SPARK programs that are automatically verifiable, thus speeding up verification and supporting use of richer assertions [49]. Work is underway to re-implement Tokeneer using the PerfectDeveloper system (see [24] for details of PerfectDeveloper). Aydal and Woodcock have been analysing the system to search for attacks [3], work reported below.

But how good was the original development of Tokeneer? In fact, only five defects have been found in Tokeneer since it was deployed within NSA in 2004. We describe each of the defects, reflecting on their causes and significance.

17.3.1 Defect 1

This account is based on that in [15, Section 17.3]. When the Tokeneer code was re-analysed in August 2008, in preparation for the public release of the entire archive, the tool that summarised the proof obligations (the POGS tool) revealed a single undischarged verification condition. Further investigation showed this to be in the subprogram `ConfigData.ValidateFile.ReadDuration`. The code in question concerns validation of an integer value that is read from a file, but is expected to be in the range 0–200 s before it is converted into a number of tenths of seconds in the range 0–2000. The offending undischarged VC is essentially:

```
H1:  rawduration__1 >= - 2147483648 .
H2:  rawduration__1 <= 2147483647 .
  ->
C1:  success__1 ->
       rawduration__1 * 10 >= - 2147483648 and
       rawduration__1 * 10 <= 2147483647 .
```

The code is from line `222` of `configdata.adb`:

```
if Success and then
   (RawDuration * 10 <= Integer(DurationT'Last) and
    RawDuration * 10 >= Integer(DurationT'First)) then
```

This VC clearly has a counterexample. For instance, when `RawDuration` $= 10^9$, `H1` and `H2` are true, but `C1` is false. This reflects the possibility of an integer overflow when multiplying by 10 before the range of `RawDuration` is checked. The correction to the code is trivial. If replaced by:

```
if Success and then
   (RawDuration <= Integer(DurationT'Last) / 10 and
    RawDuration >= Integer(DurationT'First) / 10) then
```

then all VCs discharge successfully.

Why was this defect not discovered and reported during the original development? The original project used the SPARK Examiners “`rtc`” switch to generate VCs, which it does for partial correctness and run-time errors, but *omits* those side-conditions relating to Ada’s `Overflow_Check`. Previously, the SPARK toolset was limited in its capability to discharge these VCs, so these were omitted from the original project. Subsequently, the SPARK toolset has become far more capable with regard to overflow conditions, through the use of the compiler-dependent configuration file, and the base-type assertion for integer types. Users can now generate VCs using the “`vcg`” switch, which does include VCs for overflow checks. It is interesting to note that this defect was not discovered by any testing during the original project, or any use or attempt to analyse the system since the initial delivery.

What about the security impact? First, there is a potential denial-of-service attack resulting from this defect: a malicious user holding the "security officer" role can deliberately terminate the TIS core software by supplying a malformed configuration data file, rendering the system unusable. More seriously, the software can be terminated in this fashion with the enclave door open.

17.3.2 Defect 2

The first defect was discovered by Spinellis in October 2008; see his blog [70], where he reports the following. The Tokeneer function `SystemFaultOccurred` is required to return true exactly when a critical system fault has occurred while attempting to maintain the audit log. The code that implements this uses a global variable, `AuditSystemFault`, which is set to true whenever a fault is detected. Spinellis lists all the assignments to `AuditSystemFault` that he found in the code (`OK` is a variable set by various system functions).

```
AuditSystemFault := AuditSystemFault or not OK;
AuditSystemFault := AuditSystemFault or not OK;
AuditSystemFault := AuditSystemFault or not OK;
AuditSystemFault := AuditSystemFault or not OK;
AuditSystemFault := True;
AuditSystemFault := True;
AuditSystemFault := True;
AuditSystemFault := True;
AuditSystemFault := not OK;
AuditSystemFault := AuditSystemFault and not OK;
```

But there is an anomaly in the last assignment, which is used when a log file is deleted. The conjunction used instead of a disjunction has the effect of clearing the `AuditSystemFault` flag if the deletion is successful, and failing to set it if the deletion fails, but no fault was detected before. Spinellis found this bug by inspection in less than an hour of browsing. In fact, it was in the second file he looked at, the first being very short.

17.3.3 Defect 3

The second defect was found by the CodePeer tool on or about 24 August 2009. CodePeer (developed jointly by AdaCore and SofCheck) statically analyses Ada programs for a wide range of flaws, including: pointer misuse, buffer overflows, numeric overflow or wraparound, division by zero, dead code, unused variables, and race conditions. The tool detected the following error.

The procedure KeyStore.DoFind contains the following code sequence:

```
Interface.FindObjectsInit(Template    => Template,
                          ReturnValue => RetValIni);
if RetValIni = Interface.Ok then
   Interface.FindObjects(HandleCount   => HandleCount,
                         ObjectHandles => Handles,
                         ReturnValue   => RetValDo);
  if RetValIni = Interface.Ok then
     Interface.FindObjectsFinal(ReturnValue =>
                                RetValFin);
  end if;
end if;
```

The test in the second conditional statement is wrong: it should be

```
if RetValDo = Interface.Ok then
```

of course. This is almost certainly a cut-and-paste error from the enclosing conditional statements, but why was it not detected during the original verification process? The procedure call above the offending test assigns to RetValDo, but unfortunately, there is a meaningful reference to RetValDo later in the subprogram, so the SPARK flow-analyser fails to spot this as an ineffective assignment, as might have been expected. The offending code also gives rise to several dead paths through the code, since there are paths with traversal condition

```
(RetValIni = Interface.Ok) and
-- then branch of outer if statement
(RetValIni /= Interface.Ok)
-- erroneous else branch of inner if statement
```

But the verification conditions arising from this code are all trivially true, since this procedure has an implicitly true postcondition. Therefore, the SPARK Simplifier does not bother with proof-by-contradiction and so fails to spot the dead paths.

The discovery of this error has led to the development of a new tool, *Zombie-Scope*, to detect dead code. It is similar to the SPARK Simplifier, except that but it looks only for contradictory hypotheses, ignoring the conclusions of all VCs. Any VCs that are found to have contradictory hypotheses are flagged up as indicating dead paths. The security impact of this bug is not known, as it has yet to be analysed closely enough.

17.3.4 Defect 4

The third defect was found using the most recent GNAT compiler, a free, high-quality, complete compiler for Ada95, integrated into the GCC compiler system.

The defect was found in `AuditLog.AddElementToFile. NameOfType`, using the `-gnatwa` flag (all warnings mode). The offending code is:

```
function NameOfType (E : AuditTypes.ElementT )
return ElementTextT
is
  --# hide NameOfType;
  ElementText : ElementTextT := NoElement;
begin
  ElementText(1..
          AuditTypes.ElementT'Image(ElementID)'Last)
    := AuditTypes.ElementT'Image(ElementID);
  return ElementText;
end NameOfType;
```

GNAT reports that the formal parameter `E` is not referenced, which is of course quite right: there is no reference to `E` in the body of that function. The reference to `ElementID`, which is a global variable that is visible from that scope, should be `E` here, so it should read:

```
ElementText(1..
  AuditTypes.ElementT'Image(E)'Last)
    := AuditTypes.ElementT'Image(E);
```

Why was this defect not found before? It would have been difficult to detect the error during development using the tools available at the time. When the code was first written, the much earlier version of GNAT used did not implement this warning. The code in question is not even SPARK, but actually Ada, since it uses a feature that is not part of SPARK (an array-slice in the assignment), and the code has to be hidden from the analyser, which would otherwise reject it. Consequently no flow analysis was conducted at all. The original decision to hide this code was almost certainly a mistake. Bugs like this can creep in without the rigour of the SPARK tools. This bug was also missed in code-review, suggesting that the reviewing of hidden units should have been given more attention. If the code were SPARK, the tools would certainly have spotted it: an unreferenced formal parameter is always reported by the SPARK Examiner.

What is the impact on correctness and security? Curiously, none. There is exactly *one* call to this function, which reads:

```
File.PutString( TheFile => TheFile,
                Text    => NameOfType (ElementID),
                Stop    => 0 );
```

So, in this single call `E` (the formal parameter) is synonymous with `ElementID` (the global variable), so there is no foul. But it is a bug waiting to happen if this code were ever called again with a different parameter, and the developers would fix it given the chance, so it still qualifies as a defect [16].

17.3.5 *Defect 5*

The fourth defect was also found by SofCheck's CodePeer tool, in September 2009, in `TokenReader.Poll.CheckCardState`. CodePeer reports that the final branch of the case statement

```
when Interface.InvalidCardState =>
   MarkTokenBad;
```

is dead—telling us that `CardState` can never have the value

```
InvalidCardState
```

CodePeer (through some surprisingly clever inter-procedural value propagation) is able to determine that the `RawCardState` value returned from

```
TokenReader.Interface.Status
```

is always in the range 1–6, not 0–6. This can be verified by inspection by following the sequence of calls down the call tree into the support software (in `support/tokenapi.adb`). The SPARK tools did not detect this, since the dead-path analysis is *intra*-procedural and based on the contracts of the called units alone.

Is this a bug? Well, not really, but it is an interesting observation that the analysis of the use of subtypes in the code could be improved.

17.4 A Token Experiment

In this section, we report on an experiment that we performed on Tokeneer. Our motivation was to take a system that has been developed using best practice and to see if there is anything more that we can say about it. In particular, since it is a security-critical system, can we break it? One way of proceeding in our experiment would have been to search for undischarged verification conditions and proof obligations, hoping to find that at least one of them would turn out not to be true.

But a second motivation for the experiment was to revisit the original goals of GC6, and to make a small contribution towards understanding not just the functional correctness of Tokeneer *(Does it correctly implement its specification?)*, but to say something about its dependability *(Is it really secure?)*. For this reason, we decided to try to validate the system against its requirements, and in particular, the security requirement of no accidental access to the enclave or to its workstations.

To do this, we used a novel model-based testing technique that exploits formal methods and tools: assertion-guided model-based robustness testing. The main hypothesis of this study was:

> Applying robustness testing in a model-based manner with the use of a separate test model may reveal requirements-related faults that may not necessarily be detected by formal verification techniques.

In addition to this hypothesis, we assumed two test hypotheses that helped us define the test oracle and the test selection algorithm. These hypotheses are valid for very specific kinds of system, and their usefulness must be judged by the quality of the results: have they uncovered any genuine failures? We revisit this point at the end of the paper. We consider first the *Redundant Models Hypothesis*:

> If there are two different specifications of the same System under Test (SuT) that conform to the same set of requirements, then their fault domains must match with respect to some test set T.

By using two models of the same system that are independently produced from the requirements of the SuT, and a test suite generated by using one of these models, we tried to reveal faults within these models by finding inconsistent behaviours in their fault domains. Having one model for code generation and a separate model for test case generation not only introduces the redundancy required for the testing process, but also separates concerns whilst producing these models. Additionally, there may be situations where the design model of the system may not be available due to confidentiality reasons (e.g., in security-critical systems) or the testing of the system may be completely outsourced. For such cases, being able to generate test cases from a separate test model brings flexibility to the testing process.

We used a test selection algorithm based on the satisfaction of assertions characterising the operations of the SuT. In order to make the satisfaction of these assertions more concrete, we introduced the *Alternative Scenarios Hypothesis*:

> For any operation of the SuT, if s satisfies the precondition but t does not, then their corresponding post-states must be different.

This hypothesis is relevant to robust systems, where we want to find situations where the Operation under Test (OuT) has incorrect fault-handling. In general, robustness testing checks that a system can handle unexpected user input or software failures by testing the software outside its expected input range. Thus, by feeding the software with classified unexpected input that fails one precondition at a time, the faults for different situations are uncovered. For the Tokeneer Experiment, a separate test model of the high integrity variant of the Tokeneer was produced in the Alloy modelling language [47]. The test case specifications were produced by falsifying the assertions of the operations modelled in some order. The test case specifications were then fed into Alloy Analyzer, and the test cases generated automatically as counterexamples using SAT-solving technology.

Bearing in mind the high quality of the system under test, including the fact that only five errors have previously been found in Tokeneer since its release, we wish to report a small success in our experiment. We detected nine anomalous behaviours, and we describe four representative scenarios in the rest of this section (see [3] for a more detailed account of how we found the anomalies and for a description of the other scenarios). In Section 17.6, we consider whether these anomalous scenarios really compromise the security of the enclave and its workstations.

17.4.1 Scenario 1

Our first scenario concerns tailgating. The Tokeneer system should be seen as more than the sum of its software and hardware peripherals. It is a *socio-technical* system, and there are interactions between people and their procedures and the hardware and software, and these have to be considered to get a picture of the entire system. We understand that users must undertake not to "tailgate," that is, to follow an authorised user into the enclave without being separately authorised themselves. So we can rule out the possibility of deliberate tailgating, since users agree not to do it, and no one has any malicious intent. But we found a scenario that can be explained by accidental tailgating. Consider the following sequence of events.

1. Miss Moneypenny, an NSA employee, inserts her smartcard into the reader, which checks its validity.
2. She places her thumb on the fingerprint reader, which checks her identity.
3. The system authorises Miss Moneypenny, unlocking the door.
4. Miss Moneypenny enters the enclave, and the door closes behind her.
5. I am a new NSA employee. Since I have not started to work on a project that needs access to the enclave area, my card does not have access to the enclave, but I am not told which areas my card has access to. I assume that my card has access to all areas.
6. I have eyes only for Miss Moneypenny, and as a result I look anxiously at the door to get a glimpse of her.
7. I insert my card into the reader.
8. The screen says

   ```
   ENTRY DENIED
   ```

   but I am not paying attention. There is no provision for audible alarms.
9. I place my thumb on the fingerprint reader, but again I miss the error message.
10. Anyone watching my actions would be satisfied that I appear to be following authorised procedures, and so would have no reason to be suspicious.
11. The door is still unlocked following Miss Moneypenny's entry, and it stays unlocked for a period known as the *latch-unlock duration*. I enter the enclave during this period, and there is no way of detecting my unauthorised entry.

The scenario may be thought rather far-fetched and scarcely credible. It relies on two mistakes: me not noticing either of the error messages. But it does show how I could accidentally gain access to the enclave, even though this appears to be an unlikely occurrence. Perhaps more interestingly, it reveals something about the implementation of the system.

1. Audible alarms could profitably be used to draw attention to the authorisation failures of the card and fingerprint readers.
2. The no-tailgating rule could be enforced with hardware (a physical turnstile or a pair of "airlock" doors), or checked with a video entry-detection system.

3. There is a vulnerability offered by the door being unlocked during the latch-unlock duration. There are two issues here.
   (a) The duration must be long enough to allow Miss Moneypenny to enter, but not so long as to give others the possibility to tailgate; this seems impossible to get right.
   (b) Errors triggered during attempted authorisations do not prematurely end the latch-unlock duration. This is a missed opportunity.

17.4.2 Scenario 2

Suppose now that the security officer decides to shorten the latch-unlock duration, perhaps as a result of discovering my antics in Scenario 1. The security officer needs to update a configuration file on one of the workstations within the enclave, and suppose that he wants to decrease the duration from 30s to 15s.

1. The security officer modifies the configuration file, prepares the configuration data, and writes it to a floppy disk.
2. The security officer successfully authorises his entry and then enters the enclave.
3. He successfully authorises his use of a workstation.
4. He logs in, inserts the floppy disk, and enters the `update` command, but then he sees the following:

   ```
   read/write error
   ```

5. The security officer is uncertain what this means, so he then checks the screen showing the new configuration file. It says very clearly:

   ```
   Latch-Unlock Duration = 15s
   ```

   and he is satisfied that the update really has taken place.
6. Working hours currently stop at 17:00, and entry to the enclave should be forbidden after this time.
7. But I accidentally misread the time, thinking it to be 16:45, when it is really 17:45. This is probably due to my having returned from a foreign trip, and having made a mistake adjusting between time zones.
8. I successfully authorise my entry at 17:45 and enter the enclave.
9. I work until 18:00, 1 h later than permitted.

This scenario is rather puzzling at first sight: how could I have been authorised to enter the enclave in Step 8, clearly outside working hours? To answer this, we need to know a little bit more about how Tokeneer works. There is a default configuration file on the system that is used in case of an update failure. When the system detects a `read/write error` while trying to read the floppy disk or when the file on the floppy disk is incorrectly formatted, it is forced to use this default configuration file. The default file is inaccessible, presumably to prevent accidental interference. It just so happens in our scenario that the default value for the latch-unlock duration is the same as that required by the security officer (15s), and this coincidence persuades him in Step 5 that the update has taken place correctly. But of course, all the other settings now assume their default values. In our scenario, this gives the later working time of 18:00, and so explains my entry in Step 8.

So I have gained accidental entry to the enclave and accidental access to a workstation. Is this an unlikely scenario? It depends on how carefully the configuration data file is prepared and whether or not the floppy disk drive is working properly, and it may well be an ageing device with reliability problems. But if a failure does occur, then it is made worse by a human–computer interface problem: the consequences of the error are not made clear to the security officer.

17.4.3 Scenario 3

The third scenario also concerns configuration data. The system logs information about workstation usage in an audit file, and an alarm is signalled when the file reaches the *minimum log-size* for sounding the alarm.

1. The number of users and tasks increases, with the audit log filling up rapidly.
2. The audit manager visits the enclave several times a day to archive the log.
3. The security officer agrees to raise the threshold to reduce the number of alarms.
4. He copies new configuration data to a floppy disk, authorises his entry and enters the enclave.
5. He logs in to a workstation and updates the system.
6. To check that the update has occurred properly, he logs out, logs back in again and checks the minimum audit-log size. It has the value he requires, so he logs out and leaves the enclave.
7. But the alarm is triggered once more by the old threshold.
8. He discovers later that the update seems to take effect only after the system is rebooted, following a public holiday.

The triggering of the alarm in Step 7 is puzzling. The security officer assured himself in Step 6 that the update had taken place satisfactorily, but later discovers that this doesn't seem to be the case. Again, we need to know more about how Tokeneer works. Although a new file is introduced to the system, and when requested, it can be viewed on the screen, the actual configuration data used for alerting stays the same till the next system start-up. The same thing also happens when a disk is inserted into the system drive for an admin operation. If the disk is not inserted at the start-up time, then the system does not recognise the disk.

This scenario affects the usability of the system, as too many alarms deny proper users the service they require from the system. It is a rather surprising behaviour, and may constitute an accidental denial-of-service attack.

17.4.4 Scenario 4

Our final scenario also concerns configuration files.

1. The security officer wants to change the closing time from 17:00 to 16:00.
2. He prepares a configuration file and writes it to a floppy disk.
3. But he accidentally forgets to erase an old configuration file.
4. He enters the enclave and updates system.
5. I enter the enclave at 16:30, half an hour after the new closing time.

Again the scenario is puzzling, and to explain it we need to know how Tokeneer deals with configuration files. The update function checks the validity of configuration files in the order it finds them on the floppy disk. As there was an older file, this is the one that is used. In our scenario, it was the older file that had a later closing time, creating the problem. Once more, I have gained accidental access to both the enclave and its workstations.

17.5 Analysis

All these stories are revealed by testing 12 operations. The operations realise their intended functionality when all the preconditions are satisfied, at least for one prestate. However, it is only when the test cases exercise system behaviour beyond the anticipated operational envelope that the stories such as the ones given in the previous sections are uncovered. The next section discusses these scenarios in the context of the documentation produced by Praxis-HIS and SPRE during the development of the high-integrity variant of Tokeneer IDS.

To understand the relevance and validity of these stories, we must analyse them with respect to the documentation provided, which explains expected system behaviour and expected security properties. Section 17.5.1 provides information about the security model of the TIS, and evaluates the findings accordingly.

17.5.1 Comparison with Security Model and Requirements

This section compares the scenarios with the system requirements document [19,21] and the security model of the re-developed version of TIS [20]. In [20], the security model of the TIS is identified with the following six security properties.

1. If the latch is unlocked by the TIS, then the TIS must be in possession of either a User Token or an Admin Token. The User Token must have valid ID, Privilege, and I&A Certificates, and either have a valid Authorisation Certificate or have a template that allowed the TIS to successfully validate the user's fingerprint. Or, if the User Token does not meet this, the Admin Token must have a valid Authorisation Certificate, with role of *guard*.

2. If the latch is unlocked automatically by the TIS, then the current time must be *close* to being within the allowed entry period defined for the User requesting access. The term *close* needs to be defined, but is intended to allow a period of grace between checking that access is allowed and actually unlocking the latch. *Automatically* refers to the latch being unlocked by the system in response to a user token insertion, rather than being manually unlocked by the guard.
3. An alarm will be raised whenever the door/latch is *insecure*. *Insecure* is defined to mean the latch is locked, the door is open, and too much time has passed since the last explicit request to lock the latch.
4. No audit data is lost without an audit alarm being raised.
5. The presence of an audit record of one type (e.g. recording the unlocking of the latch) will always be preceded by certain other audit records (e.g., recording the successful checking of certificates, fingerprints, etc.). Such a property would need to be defined in detail, explaining the data relationship rules exactly for each case.
6. The configuration data will be changed, or information written to the floppy, only if there is an administrator logged on to the TIS.

The first and second properties do not prevent the TIS from situations such as the one given in Scenario 1. Here are some of the root causes of these stories:

- None of these properties imposes the condition that the owner of the card shall be the person entering the enclave.
- There is no way of checking whether the person who is authorised outside the enclave actually enters the enclave after removing his/her card from the card reader.
- It is difficult to keep track of users using the enclave without the exit point, which was included in the actual Tokeneer system specification, but excluded in the redeveloped version of TIS.
- No action is taken after an access denial, even if the door is open.

One might argue that some of these statements are not set as the requirements of the high-integrity variant of the TIS, and some of them are even explicitly excluded in the documentation. However, this does not affect the validity of the stories mentioned above. Therefore, if any of them is taken under investigation in the future, one of the root causes listed above must be considered whilst looking for a solution.

Another discussion item relevant to one of the stories is Security Property 6. The property states that the configuration data will be changed by an administrator (more specifically by a Security Officer), and the information (log files) will be written to the floppy by an administrator (more specifically by the Audit Manager). As shown in Scenario 2, in the case of an invalid configuration file, the system replaces the current configuration file with a default one. In other words, if the security officer attempts to update the configuration file with an invalid file by mistake, it is the *system* that updates the file with some default file without the control of the security officer. By taking such an action without the approval of the security officer, the system actually breaks one of the security properties stated earlier. In the Security Properties Document of the TIS [19], it is declared that the proof of this security property is missed, therefore we will not discuss this item any further. However, it is open to discussion whether more attention should be given to the correctness of a file that determines how long the door to a secure enclave can be kept open, the latch of this door can be kept unlocked, the enclave is available to users, etc.

Regarding system faults and the alarms raised, in [5] it is stated that the system faults are warnings, with the exception of critical faults listed as failure to control the latch, failure to monitor the door and failure to write to the Audit Log. It is also mentioned as a requirement that the system shall continue to function following a system fault categorised as a warning, and raise an alarm following a critical fault. During the test case execution process, it was not possible to concretise the test cases that require a critical fault, therefore we are not in a position to state the behaviour of the system under these circumstances. However, there were test cases that required the alarm to be raised due to other causes such as the door being kept open more than allowed or the audit file size exceeding the limit specified in the configuration file. The system continues to perform normally for such cases even though an alarm is raised. Our concern is that the system may behave similarly for the critical faults mentioned above since the only requirement specified following a critical fault is to raise an alarm. The security of the system may not be compromised if the log file is too large, but a failure to control the latch would certainly create a risk, and therefore we believe that the measures taken for the latter case should be more than just raising an alarm.

The next section explains the system-level testing carried out by SPRE Inc previously, and compares the test results of this testing activity with that explained in this report.

17.6 Conclusions

Is Tokeneer really secure? Of course it is! It seems very unlikely that any of the accidents described by our scenarios could really happen and compromise the security of the enclave and its workstations, particularly as an administrator is needed for three of the four scenarios. But these are interesting scenarios nonetheless, and they have been overlooked both by the formal development and by system testing. In fact, the system testing performed by SPRE detected Scenario 2, and the case is closed as solved; however, in our tests, it persisted, using tests generated by a completely different technique.

Additionally, these scenarios may be useful in designing similar systems in the future, as they raise questions about configuration files, audit logs, and alarms that may have been overlooked this time. Perhaps they might be useful if the system were to evolve to include stronger security guarantees, including malicious intent.

The lesson of our experiment is that there is value in diversity: an alternative approach gives us an opportunity to think laterally. De Bono's *lateral thinking* is about judging the correctness of a statement (in this case the correctness of Tokeneer), and seeking errors that contradict that claim of correctness. Even when a considerable amount of effort has been invested in one approach, in this case the application of formal methods, lateral thinking, provided by using a completely different, but principled set of techniques and tools, can still challenge the claim of correctness.

Acknowledgements First, thanks must go to all those involved in the Tokeneer project for releasing into the public domain such a useful project archive. It is incredibly valuable and has done the research community a very great service. The work on Tokeneer reported in this paper was carried out as part of Emine Gökçe Aydal's Ph.D. thesis [3], under the supervision of Jim Woodcock. We also received helpful comments during the development of this work from Andrew Butterfield, Behzad Bordbar, Néstor Cataño, Ana Cavalcanti, John Clarke, John Fitzgerald, Leo Freitas, Rob Hierons, Tony Hoare, Randolph Johnson, Cliff Jones, Bertrand Meyer, Yannick Moy, Marcel Oliveira, Richard Paige, Brian Randell, Shankar and Angela Wallenberg. We presented the results of our experiment to Marie-Claude Gaudel's research group during a sabbatical visit to Université de Paris-Sud, and to audiences in seminars and workshops at the University of Birmingham, Trinity College Dublin, the University of Madeira, Microsoft Research Asia, Microsoft Research Cambridge, the Federal University of Rio Grande do Norte, the University of York and ETH Zurich. We are grateful for all the encouragement we received.

References

1. Aichernig B.K., Maibaum, T.S.E. (eds.): Formal Methods at the Crossroads. From Panacea to Foundational Support, 10th Anniversary Colloquium of UNU/IIST, the International Institute for Software Technology of The United Nations University, Lisbon, Portugal, March 18–20, 2002, Revised Papers, volume 2757 of Lecture Notes in Computer Science. Springer (2003).
2. Aydal, E.G., Paige, R.F., Woodcock, J.: Evaluation of OCL for large-scale modelling: A different view of the Mondex purse. In: Giese, H. (ed.) MoDELS Workshops, volume 5002 of Lecture Notes in Computer Science, pp. 194–205. Springer, Berlin, Heidelberg (2007).
3. Aydal, E.G.: Model-Based Robustness Testing of Black-box Systems. PhD thesis, Department of Computer Science, University of York (November 2009).
4. Banach, R.: Formal Methods: Guest editorial. J. UCS, **13**(5), 593–601 (2007).
5. Barnes, J.: Tokeneer ID Station informed design. Technical Report S.P1229.50.2, Praxis High Integrity Systems. Available from tinyurl.com/tokeneer (2008)
6. Barnes, J., Chapman, R., Johnson, R., Widmaier, J., Cooper, D., Everett, B.: Engineering the Tokeneer enclave protection system. In Proceedings of the 1st International Symposium on Secure Software Engineering, Arlington, VA. IEEE (March 2006).
7. Barnes, J.: High Integrity Ada: The SPARK Approach to Safety and Security. Addison-Wesley, Reading, MA. (2003).
8. Bicarregui, J., Fitzgerald, J.S., Larsen, P.G., Woodcock, J.C.P.: Industrial practice in Formal Methods: A review. In: A. Cavalcanti and D. Dams (eds.) FM, volume 5850 of Lecture Notes in Computer Science, pp. 810–813. Springer (2009).
9. Bicarregui, J., Hoare, C.A.R., Woodcock, J.C.P.: The Verified Software Repository: A step towards the verifying compiler. Formal Asp. Comput. **18**(2), 143–151 (2006).
10. Butler, M., Yadav, D.: An incremental development of the Mondex system in Event-B. Formal Asp. Comput. **20**(1), 61–77 (2008).
11. Butterfield, A., Freitas, L., Woodcock, J.: Mechanising a formal model of flash memory. Sci. Comput. Program. **74**(4), 219–237 (2009).
12. Butterfield, A. O'Cathain, A.: Concurrent models of flash memory device behaviour. In M. Oliveira and J. Woodcock, editors, Brazilian Symposium on Formal Methods (SBMF 2009), 19–21 August 2009, Gramado, Brazil, Lecture Notes in Computer Science, in press. Springer (2009).

13. Butterfield, A., Woodcock. J.: Formalising flash memory: First steps. In 12th International Conference on Engineering of Complex Computer Systems (ICECCS 2007), 10–14 July 2007, Auckland, New Zealand, pp. 251–260. IEEE Computer Society (2007).
14. CCRA.: Common criteria for information technology security evaluation. Part 1: Introduction and general model. Technical Report CCMB-2006-09-001, Version 3.1, Revision 1, Common Criteria Recognition Agreement September (2006).
15. Chapman, R.: Tokeneer ID Station overview and reader's guide. Technical Report S.P1229.81.8, Issue 1.0, Praxis High Integrity Systems. Available from tinyurl.com/tokeneer (2008)
16. Chapman, R.: Private communication. Email, 16 December 2009.
17. Cohen, E.: Validating the Microsoft Hypervisor. In: Misra, JV., Nipkow, T., Sekerinski, E. (eds.) FM 2006: Formal Methods, 14th International Symposium on Formal Methods, Hamilton, Canada, August 21–27, 2006, Proceedings, volume 4085 of Lecture Notes in Computer Science, pp. 81–81. Springer (2006).
18. Cooke, J.: Editorial (VSTTE special issue). Formal Asp. Comput. **19**(2), 137–138 (2007).
19. Cooper, D., Tokeneer ID Station security properties. Technical Report S.P1229.40.4, Praxis High Integrity Systems. Available from tinyurl.com/tokeneer (2008)
20. Cooper, D.: Tokeneer ID Station security target. Technical Report S.P1229.40.1, Praxis High Integrity Systems. Available from tinyurl.com/tokeneer (2008)
21. Cooper, D.: Tokeneer ID Station system requirements specification. Technical Report S.P1229.41.1, Praxis High Integrity Systems. Available from tinyurl.com/tokeneer (2008)
22. Craig, I.D.: Formal Models of Operating System Kernels. Springer (2006).
23. Craig, I.D.: Formal Refinement For Operating System Kernels. Springer (2007).
24. Crocker, D., Carlton, J.: Verification of C programs using automated reasoning. In Fifth IEEE International Conference on Software Engineering and Formal Methods (SEFM 2007), 10–14 September 2007, London, England, UK, pages 7–14. IEEE Computer Society (2007).
25. Damchoom, K., Butler, M.: Applying event and machine decomposition to a flash-based filestore in Event-B. In: Oliveira, M., Woodcock, J. (eds,) Brazilian Symposium on Formal Methods (SBMF 2009), 19–21 August 2009, Gramado, Brazil, Lecture Notes in Computer Science, in press. Springer (2009).
26. Damchoom, K., Butler, MJ., Abrial, J-R.: Modelling and proof of a tree-structured file system in Event-B and Rodin. In Liu, S., Maibaum, T.S.E.. Araki, K. (eds,) Formal Methods and Software Engineering, 10th International Conference on Formal Engineering Methods, ICFEM 2008, Kitakyushu-City, Japan, October 27–31, 2008. Proceedings, volume 5256 of Lecture Notes in Computer Science, 25–44. Springer (2008).
27. Deharbe, D: Modelling FreeRTOS with B. In Oliveira, M., Woodcock, J. (eds,) Brazilian Symposium on Formal Methods (SBMF 2009), 19–21 August 2009, Gramado, Brazil, Lecture Notes in Computer Science, in press. Springer (2009).
28. Dong, J.S., Sun, J.: SCP special issue on the Grand Challenge—Preface. Sci. Comput. Program. **74**(4), 167 (2009).
29. Ferreira, M.A., Oliveira J.N.: Towards tool integration and interoperability in the GC: The Intel flash file store case study. In Marcel Oliveira and Jim Woodcock, editors, Brazilian Symposium on Formal Methods (SBMF 2009), 19–21 August 2009, Gramado, Brazil, Lecture Notes in Computer Science, in press. Springer (2009).
30. Freitas, L.: Mechanising data-types for kernel design in Z. In: Oliveira M., Woodcock, J. (eds,) Brazilian Symposium on Formal Methods (SBMF 2009), 19–21 August 2009, Gramado, Brazil, Lecture Notes in Computer Science, in press. Springer (2009).
31. Freitas, L., Fu, Z., Woodcock, J.: POSIX file store in Z/Eves: an experiment in the Verified Software Repository. In 12th International Conference on Engineering of Complex Computer Systems (ICECCS 2007), 10–14 July 2007, Auckland, New Zealand, 3–14. IEEE Computer Society (2007).
32. Freitas, L., Woodcock, J.: Mechanising Mondex with Z/Eves. Formal Asp. Comput., **20**(1), 117–139 (2008).
33. Freitas, L., Woodcock, J., Fu, Z.: POSIX file store in Z/Eves: An experiment in the Verified Software Repository. Sci. Comput. Program., **74**(4), 238–257 (2009).

34. Freitas, L., Woodcock, J., Zhang, Y.: Verifying the CICS File Control API with Z/Eves: An experiment in the Verified Software Repository. Sci. Comput. Program., **74**(4), 197–218 (2009).
35. Gal, E., Toledo, S.: Algorithms and data structures for flash memories. ACM Comput. Surv., **37**(2), 138–163 (2005).
36. George, C, Haxthausen, A.E.: Specification, proof, and model checking of the Mondex electronic purse using RAISE. Formal Asp. Comput. **20**(1), 101–116 (2008).
37. Gomes, A O Oliveira, M.V.M: Formal specification of a Cardiac Pacing System. In A. Cavalcanti and D. Dams, editors, Formal Methods Symposium (FM 2009), 31 October–6 November 2009, Eindhoven, Lecture Notes in Computer Science, in press. Springer, (2009).
38. Graydon, P.J., Knight, J.C., Strunk, E.A.: Achieving dependable systems by synergistic development of architectures and assurance cases. In R. de Lemos, C. Gacek, and A. B. Romanovsky, editors, WADS, volume 4615 of Lecture Notes in Computer Science, pp. 362–382. Springer (2006).
39. Haneberg, D., Schellhorn, G., Grandy, H., Reif, W.: Verification of Mondex electronic purses with KIV: from transactions to a security protocol. Formal Asp. Comput., **20**(1), 41–59 (2008).
40. Hoare, C.A.R.: Towards the verifying compiler. In Aichernig and Maibaum [1], pp. 151–160 (2003).
41. Hoare C.A.R., Misra, J.: Preface to special issue on software verification. ACM Comput. Surv. **41**(4) (2009).
42. Hoare, C.A.R., Misra, J., Leavens, G T., Shankar, N.: The verified software initiative: a manifesto. ACM Comput. Surv. **41**(4) (2009).
43. Hoare, T., Atkinson, M., Bundy, A., Crowcroft, J., Crowcroft, J., Milner, R., Moore, J., Rodden, T., Thomas, M.: The Grand Challenges Exercise of the UKCRC. report to the UKCRC from the programme committee. tiny.cc/gcreport (29 May 2003).
44. Hoare, T., Jones, C., Randell, B.: Extending the horizons of DSE. In Grand Challenges. UKCRC, 2004. tinyurl.com/ExtendingDSE (2004)
45. Hoare, T., Misra, J.: Verified software: Theories, tools, and experiments: Vision of a Grand Challenge project. In: Meyer, B. and Woodcock, J. (eds,) Verified Software: Theories, Tools, and Experiments. First IFIP TC2/EG2.3 Conference, Zurich, October 2005, volume 4171 of Lecture Notes in Computer Science, pp. 1–18. Springer, Berlin, Heidelberg (2008).
46. ITSEC. Information technology security evaluation criteria (ITSEC): Preliminary harmonised criteria. Technical Report Document COM(90) 314, Version 1.2, Commission of the European Communities June (1991).
47. Jackson, D.: Alloy: A lightweight object modelling notation. ACM Trans. Softw. Eng. Methodol. **11**(2), 256–290 (2002).
48. Jackson, D., Thomas, M., Millett, L.I., (eds.): Software for Dependable Systems: Sufficient Evidence? Committee on Certifiably Dependable Software Systems, National Research Council. The National Academies Press (2007).
49. Jackson, P., Passmore, G.O.: Improved automation for SPARK verification conditions. tiny.cc/jacksonspark (1 August 2009).
50. Jackson, P., Passmore, G.O.: YAFFS (Yet Another Flash File System). www.yaffs.net/ (1 August 2009).
51. Jhala, R., Majumdar, R.: Software model checking. ACM Comput. Surv. **41**(4) (2009).
52. Jones, C.B., O'Hearn, P.W., Woodcock, J.: Verified software: A Grand Challenge. IEEE Computer **39**(4), 93–95 (2006).
53. Jones, C.B., Pierce, K.G.: What can the π-calculus tell us about the Mondex purse system? In 12th International Conference on Engineering of Complex Computer Systems (ICECCS 2007), Auckland, New Zealand, 10–14 July 2007, pages 300–306. IEEE Computer Society (2007).
54. Jones, C.B., Woodcock, J.: Editorial. Formal Asp. Comput. **20**(1), 1–3 (2008).
55. Josey, A.: The Single UNIX Specification Version 3. Open Group, San Francisco, CA (2004.) ISBN: 193162447X.
56. Joshi, R., Holzmann, G.J.: A mini challenge: Build a verifiable filesystem. Formal Asp. Comput. 19(2), 269–272 (2007).

57. Kang, E., Jackson, D.: Formal modeling and analysis of a flash filesystem in Alloy. In E. Börger, M. Butler, J. P. Bowen, and P. Boca, editors, ABZ2008: Abstract State Machines, B and Z, First International Conference, ABZ 2008, London, September 16–18, 2008, volume 5238 of Lecture Notes in Computer Science, pp. 294–308. Springer, Berlin, Heidelberg (2008).
58. Kim, M.: Concolic testing of the multisector read operation for a flash memory. In M. Oliveira and J. Woodcock (eds.) Brazilian Symposium on Formal Methods (SBMF 2009), 19–21 August 2009, Gramado, Brazil, Lecture Notes in Computer Science, in press. Springer (2009).
59. King., J.C.: A Program Verifier. Ph.D. thesis, School of Computer Science, Carnegie Mellon University, (1969).
60. Kuhlmann, M., Gogolla, M.: Modeling and validating Mondex scenarios described in UML and OCL with USE. Formal Asp. Comput. **20**(1), 79–100 (2008).
61. Lawford, M.: Pacemaker Formal Methods Challenge. tiny.cc/pacemaker, 1 (August 2009).
62. Macedo, H.D., Larsen, P.G., Fitzgerald, J.S.: Incremental development of a distributed real-time model of a cardiac pacing system using VDM. In: Cuéllar, J., Maibaum, T. and Sere, K. (eds.) FM 2008: Formal Methods, 15th International Symposium on Formal Methods, Turku, Finland, May 26–30, 2008, Proceedings, volume 5014 of Lecture Notes in Computer Science, pp. 181–197. Springer, (2008).
63. Machado, P.: Automatic test case generation of embedded real-time systems with interruptions for FreeRTOS. In: Oliveira, M. and Woodcock, J. (eds.) Brazilian Symposium on Formal Methods (SBMF 2009), 19–21 August 2009, Gramado, Brazil, Lecture Notes in Computer Science, in press. Springer, (2009).
64. Meyer, B., Woodcock, J., (eds.): Verified Software: Theories, Tools, Experiments, First IFIP TC 2/WG 2.3 Conference, VSTTE 2005, Zurich, Switzerland, October 10–13, 2005, Revised Selected Papers and Discussions, volume 4171 of Lecture Notes in Computer Science. Springer (2008).
65. Mühlberg, J.T., Lüttgen, G.: Verifying compiled file system code. In M. Oliveira and J. Woodcock, editors, Brazilian Symposium on Formal Methods (SBMF 2009), 19–21 August 2009, Gramado, Brazil, Lecture Notes in Computer Science, in press. Springer (2009).
66. Owre, S., Rushby, J.M., Shankar, N.: PVS: A prototype verification system. In CADE-11, 11th International Conference on Automated Deduction, Saratoga Springs, Juny 15–18 1992, volume 607 of Lecture Notes in Computer Science, pages 748–752, Springer, Berlin, Heidelberg (1992).
67. Ramananandro, T.: Mondex, an electronic purse: Specification and refinement checks with the Alloy model-finding method. Formal Asp. Comput. **20**(1), 21–39 (2008).
68. Shankar, N.: Automated deduction for verification. ACM Comput. Surv. **41**(4) (2009).
69. Shankar, N., Woodcock, J., (eds.): Verified Software: Theories, Tools, Experiments, Second International Conference, VSTTE 2008, Toronto, Canada, October 6–9, 2008. Proceedings, volume 5295 of Lecture Notes in Computer Science. Springer (2008).
70. Spinellis, D.: A look at zero-defect code. tinyurl.com/spinellisblog (18 October 2008).
71. Spivey, J.M.: The Z Notation: a Reference Manual. International Series in Computer Science. Prentice Hall (1989).
72. Stepney, S., Cooper, D., Woodcock, J.: More powerful Z data refinement: Pushing the state of the art in industrial refinement. In: Bowen, J. P., Fett, A. and Hinchey, M. G. (eds.) ZUM, volume 1493 of Lecture Notes in Computer Science, pp. 284–307. Springer (1998).
73. Stepney, S., Cooper, D., Woodcock, J.: An electronic purse: Specification, refinement, and proof. Technical Monograph PRG-126, Oxford University Computing Laboratory July (2000).
74. Tokeneer, tinyurl.com/tokeneer (2009).
75. VSR.: Verified Software Repository. vsr.sourceforge.net/fmsurvey.htm (2009).
76. Woodcock, J.: E6: Use of formality, Video Tape G3A, Tape No. 68. Technical report, Government Communications Headquarters, Communications-Electronics Security Group (October 1997).
77. Woodcock, J.: First steps in the Verified Software Grand Challenge. IEEE Computer **39**(10), 57–64 (2006).
78. Woodcock, J., Banach, R.: The Verification Grand Challenge. J. UCS **13**(5), 661–668 (2007).

79. Woodcock, J., Davies, J.: Using Z: Specification, Refinement, and Proof. International Series in Computer Science. Prentice Hall (1996).
80. Woodcock, J., Larsen, P.G., Bicarregui, J., Fitzgerald, J.S.: Formal Methods: Practice and experience. ACM Comput. Surv. **41**(4) (2009).
81. Woodcock, J., Stepney, S., Cooper, D., Clark, J A., Jacob, J.: The certification of the Mondex electronic purse to ITSEC Level E6. Formal Asp. Comput. **20**(1), 5–19 (2008).